WORLD VOYAGE PLANNER

Planning a voyage from anywhere in the
world to anywhere in the world

JIMMY and IVAN CORNELL

**ADLARD
COLES**

LONDON • OXFORD • NEW YORK • NEW DELHI • SYDNEY

Other Cornell titles

World Cruising Routes
1,000 sailing routes in all oceans of the world
paperback: 978-1-4729-4781-9
ePub: 978-1-4729-4780-2

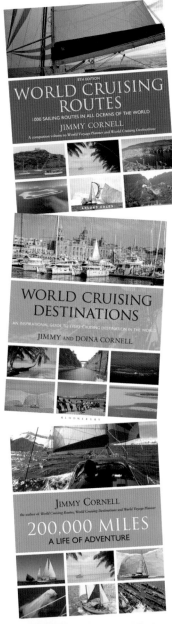

Long established as the bible for long-distance cruisers and a bestseller since its first publication in 1987, *World Cruising Routes* is a comprehensive guide to over 1,000 routes covering all the oceans of the world from the tropical South Seas to the high latitudes of the Arctic and Antarctic. Geared specifically to the needs of cruising sailors, the 8th edition assesses the effects of climate change on voyage planning and provides over 6,000 waypoints to assist navigators in planning individual passages. it is the perfect one-stop reference for planning a voyage anywhere in the world.

World Cruising Destinations
An inspirational guide to every cruising destination in the world
paperback: 978-1-4729-4747-5
ePub: 978-1-4729-4746-8

This fully updated and revised handbook profiles every cruising destination in the world and is a companion volume to *World Cruising Routes*. It contains information on all maritime nations of the world with details of local attractions, formalities, facilities, charter opportunities, websites and cruising guides. Lavishly illustrated throughout, this is not only a must-have reference work for long-distance sailors, but will undoubtedly inspire the adventurous to explore new and challenging destinations.

200,000 Miles
Reflections on three circumnavigations and voyages to Antarctica and the Arctic
paperback: 978-0-9572626-8-3
ePub: 978-1-9997229-8-2

Jimmy Cornell's latest book is based on his extensive knowledge of offshore cruising gained from an experience that stretches over four decades. *200,000 Miles* deals with all essential aspects of offshore voyaging and long-distance cruising. In the last 30 years Jimmy Cornell has organised 29 transatlantic and six round the world rallies. As organiser of these events, he has come into contact with over 15,000 sailors and the experience gained from dealing with so many different boats has been an invaluable source of knowledge of the global cruising scene. While primarily aimed at sailors who are planning a longer voyage, this book will also appeal to tested ocean navigators as well as weekend sailors.

Cornells' Ocean Atlas
Pilot charts for all oceans of the world
paperback: 978-1-9997229-0-6

Jimmy and Ivan Cornell have produced this global atlas of pilot charts aimed at sailors planning offshore voyages. Monthly charts of all oceans of the world show wind speed and direction, current speed and direction, the extent of the Intertropical Convergence Zone, the common tracks of tropical storms, and the mean location of high-pressure cells for each hemisphere. Now in its second edition, it features pilot charts updated with the most recent weather data gathered by meteorological satellites. An indispensable tool for anyone planning an offshore passage and companion to *World Cruising Routes* and *World Voyage Planner*.

There's little debate over the well-established fact that Jimmy Cornell belongs on the very short list of modern sailing's most trusted authorities on long-distance cruising, and with his latest book, *World Voyage Planner*, he has quite literally pulled out all the stops. Lavishly illustrated with maps, pilot charts, tables and photographs, *World Voyage Planner* is nothing less than essential kit for both aspiring blue-water sailors, and those already underway.

Herb McCormick, *Cruising World*

This book is not only a valuable tool for sailors planing a voyage but it should appeal also to those who are still at the dreaming stage, in spirit already roaming the oceans. Cornell weighs up the pros and cons of various routes in every ocean, whether a one-way or round trip. All this in a style that comes obviously from the pen of a professional with great personal experience. This book provides more than just knowhow: it entertains and is pure enjoyment. In one word: it makes you want to go, and this is what makes Jimmy Cornell's book so special.

Uwe Janssen, *Die Yacht*, Germany

World Voyage Planner is a book to pick up for five minutes and put down, reluctantly, two hours later. Clear, organised, authoritative, and considerably wider in scope than the title suggests, there's probably no other sailing author writing today who could have packed so much essential voyaging information into a single volume.

Anne Hammick, Editor *Flying Fish*, Ocean Cruising Club

Jimmy Cornell's remarkable depth of knowledge shines through in this companion to *World Cruising Routes*, *World Cruising Destinations* and *Cornell's Ocean Atlas*. The detailed data for a vast number of voyages is enhanced by gems from many other yachtsmen who have sailed across the world's oceans. Anyone contemplating an ocean passage will learn volumes from this compendium of invaluable information and encourage them to take that first step – planning.

David Glenn, Editor, *Yachting World*

For my generation of cruising sailors Jimmy Cornell has been the leading star for sailors planning ocean voyages anywhere on the globe. In his latest book he tells you when and where you should sail to make your voyage safe and interesting. *World Voyage Planner* helps you plan your voyage, and once you have a plan, Jimmy Cornell will help you with more information and advice with his books *World Cruising Routes, World Cruising Destinations* and the new *Cornell's Ocean Atlas*.

Henrich Nissen-Lie, *Seilas*, Norway

Whether you're planning what author Jimmy Cornell calls a "circular voyage" around the Caribbean, South Pacific or Med, or a "linear" voyage such as an Atlantic crossing or a circumnavigating of the globe, *World Voyage Planner* will serve as your starting point. Planning on cruising off the beaten path? Jimmy's latest book includes the information that you need to plan a voyage to more remote areas of the world as well.

Barbara Theisen, Editor, Seven Seas Cruising Association

As an editor for more than 20 years, I've received thousands of projects and met hundreds of would be circumnavigators all of whom had their own idea of the best round the world cruise but few included a plan B. A mechanical failure, a place you enjoy so much that you stay longer than expected, a geopolitic situation rapidly evolving… Many are the reasons that may modify a round the world voyage. In Jimmy Cornell's book, every route in every ocean and at every season has been taken into account, and hundreds of plans B are extremely well documented. This books is not only a reliable 'spare wheel' that will assist the sailor momentarily parked by the side of the road, but will also help him quit the trade wind highway and discover secondary routes.

Jean-Luc Gourmelen, Voiles & Voiliers, France

To Luc Callebaut, Jackie Lee and their slow-moving *Sloepmouche*

ADLARD COLES
Bloomsbury Publishing Plc
50 Bedford Square, London, WC1B 3DP, UK

BLOOMSBURY, ADLARD COLES and the Adlard Coles logo are trademarks of
Bloomsbury Publishing Plc

First published in Great Britain 2012
This edition published 2018

A catalogue record for this book is available from the British Library

ISBN: PB: 978-1-4729-5473-2; eBook: 978-1-4729-5474-9

2 4 6 8 10 9 7 5 3 1

Typeset in 9/11pt Sabon MT by Margaret Brain
Printed and bound in India by Replika

Bloomsbury Publishing Plc makes every effort to ensure that the papers used in
the manufacture of our books are natural, recyclable products made from wood
grown in well-managed forests. Our manufacturing processes conform to the
environmental regulations of the country of origin.

To find out more about our authors and books visit www.bloomsbury.com and
sign up for our newsletters

FOREWORD

Ever since man first left the safety of land and ventured out to sea, he has always tried to take advantage of existing weather conditions. In ancient times, the Phoenicians had a knack of choosing the right time to sail west across the Mediterranean during spells of easterly winds and return home with favourable westerlies. In the first century CE, the Greek seafarer Hippalus learned the secret of the monsoon winds in the Indian Ocean and in the following centuries, Roman ships sailed from Egypt every July with the SW monsoon to India and Southeast Asia and returned to Egypt with the NE monsoon the following January. *The Periplus Maris Erythreai*, which refers to the Greek name for the Indian Ocean, was a handbook written in the first century CE for the use of merchants and sailors trading between the Mediterranean and Southeast Asia. The instructions concerning prevailing winds, seasons and major ports, were written in a simple language and are as valid today as they were two thousand years ago. Weather-based voyage planning was born.

Throughout maritime history there have been countless examples of planning a voyage around favourable seasons and prevailing wind systems. The Vikings made frequent voyages from Scandinavia to Iceland, Greenland and to what they called Vinland in present North America by sailing west with the favourable winds of high latitudes and returning home with the help of the westerlies that blow further south. Christopher Columbus picked the best route to sail from Europe to the New World with the northeasterly trade winds and returned home the following spring with the prevailing westerlies.

Around the same time as Columbus was lifting the veil on the mysteries of the North Atlantic, Portuguese ships were focusing on the South Atlantic looking for a route around Africa. Soon the Atlantic was teeming with sailing ships searching for new fishing grounds, countries to trade with, and routes that led to lands to be settled.

European explorers were in no way the exception as outstanding ocean voyages were also accomplished around those times in other oceans. Arab traders had identified the regularity of the monsoons of the North Indian Ocean and put the favourable winds to perfect use by sailing from the Persian Gulf area, and later from India, to East Africa with the NE monsoon of winter and returning home with the SW monsoon of summer. Their seaworthy dhows were so well adapted to local conditions that they continued to be used, with hardly any modifications, until recently.

It is now known that further east Chinese navigators had accomplished remarkable lengthy ocean voyages in their distinctive junks that were more than equal in performance to the caravels that spearheaded European exploration from the fifteenth century onwards. Between 1405 and 1433 a large Chinese fleet led by Admiral Zheng He led seven expeditions to what the Chinese called the Western Ocean. Their voyages took them from Brunei in the east as far as Aden in the west, and there is speculation that some of Zheng's ships may have travelled beyond the Cape of Good Hope and into the South Atlantic more than sixty years before Vasco da Gama sailed that same route.

Several centuries earlier, even more valiant mariners achieved the incredible feat of settling the far flung islands of the Pacific Ocean in their double-hulled canoes. It is now believed that this eastward migration originated in Southeast Asia and the remarkable achievements of those Polynesian navigators still fill us with admiration. Not only did they succeed in settling every island group as far as Easter Island, but their canoes reached today's New Zealand, thus completing the vast Polynesian triangle that stretches from Hawaii in the north to Rapa Nui (Easter Island) in the southeast, and Aotearoa, the land of the long white cloud (New Zealand), in the southwest.

The golden era of sailing that followed the voyages of Christopher Columbus, Vasco da Gama, Francis Drake and Ferdinand Magellan, allowed intrepid navigators such as Abel Tasman, Álvaro de Mendaña, James Cook, Willem Barents, Luis Vaez de Torres, Louis Antoine de Bougainville and many others, to gradually fill in the white areas on the world map. The improvements in the art of navigation as well as the quality of the sailing ships led to the oceans of the world being crisscrossed by a spider web of routes. As clippers and square riggers made way for modern ships, the sailing tradition continued to be kept alive by yachts, with outstanding voyages being accomplished by sailors such as Joshua Slocum, Vito Dumas, Francis Chichester, Bernard Moitessier, Ragnar Thorseth, Eric and Susan Hiscock, and countless others. The voyages described in this book have been inspired by the example of all those illustrious pioneers in whose wake we should be proud to follow.

INTRODUCTION

The main objective of this book is to help sailors plan the outline of a voyage in any ocean of the world, with suggestions of alternative routes to certain destinations, recommended times and seasons, attractive places en route and strategically located ports of call to be used in an emergency. *World Voyage Planner* is meant as a companion volume to *World Cruising Routes* and *World Cruising Destinations*, both of which should be consulted for specific information on individual routes and countries.

To facilitate the planning of a voyage in any part of the world, *Cornells' Ocean Atlas*, now in a revised and updated second edition, contains monthly pilot charts based on data gathered by meteorological satellites over the last 25 years. The charts show speed and direction of winds and currents, the extent of the Intertropical Convergence Zones, mean tracks of tropical storms, and the mean location of high pressure cells for each month of the year in every ocean.

In recent years cruising yachts have reached some of the most remote parts of the world from Greenland to the Amazon, and even such challenging destinations, as Antarctica and the Northwest Passage are no longer the preserve of tough explorers. While the main focus of this book is on voyages along the most popular cruising routes, there are also suggested voyages to some less frequented destinations visited by cruising sailors, such as the inland waterways of Europe and North America and some navigable rivers (Danube, Rhone, Amazon, Mississippi).

Linear voyages

The voyages listed are either linear or circular voyages. The former are mainly transocean voyages originating in areas with a concentration of sailing centres in Northern Europe, North America, South America, Australia, New Zealand, Asia and South Africa. Each voyage is identified by a letter (A for Atlantic, P for Pacific and I for Indian) and a number, thus A2 refers to voyages from North America to the Caribbean and Panama. Alternative routes for voyages from the east coast of North America are described separately as A2a Voyages to the Eastern Caribbean, A2b Voyages to the Bahamas, A2c Voyages to the Western Caribbean and A2d Voyages to Panama. Longer transocean voyages, such as a voyage from Panama to Australia, are divided into separate segments with intermediate stops in cruising hubs such as Tahiti and Fiji. When such segments coincide with specific routes

described in *World Cruising Routes*, the relevant routes and their identifying number, as used in the latest edition of that book, are listed at the beginning of each voyage.

Circular voyages

The wise navigator will not only plan a voyage from A to B during the most favourable seasons but should also plan ahead on how to sail back from B to A when the time comes for the return voyage. Such voyages have occurred throughout maritime history and many are well documented as they were often trading voyages. Three thousand years ago the Phoenicians established a widespread commercial empire, each year completing long voyages from their base in present day Lebanon to the furthest corners of the Mediterranean. These voyages took full advantage of prevailing weather conditions and were planned to take place during the most favourable seasons. One of the best examples of trading voyages were those undertaken by Arab traders who sailed their dhows from the Persian Gulf to East Africa every year with the help of the NE monsoon of winter and returned with the SW monsoon of summer. In Papua New Guinea I met the last Motu navigator to sail the traditional Hiri trading route along the coast of Papua New Guinea. Every year large double hulled *lakatoi* canoes sailed west with the SE trade winds carrying a cargo of pottery which was exchanged for sago flour. The return voyage would then be completed after the onset of the NW monsoon.

A well-documented circular voyage is that of Christopher Columbus whose first transatlantic voyage took him from Spain to the Canaries and Bahamas in 1492. The loop was closed on his return voyage the following year by sailing home via the Azores. He repeated that pattern on his three consecutive voyages between Europe and the New World. Hundreds of cruising boats complete a similar North Atlantic circuit every year and the attraction of such circular voyages is that they can be joined at any point just like a merry-go-round. As few cruising voyages are planned to be open-ended, this concept is applied to a number of suggested circular voyages in each ocean.

Each of the suggested circular voyages has four basic objectives: to include a range of attractive cruising destinations and interesting landfalls along the proposed route, to be sailed during the safe seasons, to benefit from favourable conditions throughout its duration, and to bring the boat back to its starting point in the shortest time possible. Every circular voyage is made up of a number of separate segments which usually coincide with a linear voyage. The relevant linear voyages should be referred to for details on passage planning and weather conditions to be expected, while *World Cruising Routes* and *World Cruising Destinations* should be consulted for detailed information on individual routes and landfalls.

Circular voyages are illustrated by flow charts which show the starting point and main intermediate destinations, with the suggested routes outlined in different colours. Alternative routes are shown by dashed lines. The timing of each voyage is planned to take advantage of the most favourable conditions and avoid tropical storm or infavourable seasons. Each voyage is summarized in a table showing the recommended months for each destination, alternative destinations being shown between square brackets.

A round the world voyage is the ultimate circular voyage and the various routes and possible alternatives are also described. Due to prevailing weather patterns, the majority of such voyages proceed from east to west, and

Top: Old pilot chart March
Bottom: New pilot chart March

this is how most are planned, although other alternatives are also outlined.

Pilot charts

Having done all my early sailing at a time when there were no weather forecasts for ocean passages, my offshore tactics had to be based on the actual conditions experienced. Good old habits die hard and even in this age of electronic charts, whether planning a long voyage or a shorter ocean passage, my favourite planning aid continues to be the monthly pilot charts. Their main attraction is that they show average conditions for every month of the year: wind strength and direction, percentage of gale force winds, tropical storms and their tracks, ocean currents, etc. Thus they provide a valuable source of visual information on the kind of conditions that may be expected at a certain time along a certain route. The original pilot charts had been compiled over many years and were based on observations made by ships' captains. Those classic pilot charts present a general image of what can be expected at certain times in any given area of an ocean, but climatic changes, which have occurred in the intervening years, have rendered some of the information shown on those pilot charts to be inaccurate for current users. To present as accurate a picture as possible of the actual conditions which prevail in today's oceans, the charts used in this book are based on the latest weather information as gathered by a network of meteorological satellites. International institutions have been gathering and storing this information and the data presented in this book is a compilation of the satellite data collected in the last twenty-five years.

The example shown here covers an ocean area frequently crossed by sailing boats. A comparison between the old pilot charts and those resulting from the latest observations shows a significant change in the prevailing wind direction west of Panama, especially north of the equator where northeasterly winds are now predominant and require different

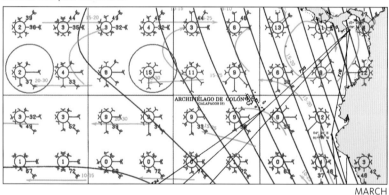

MARCH

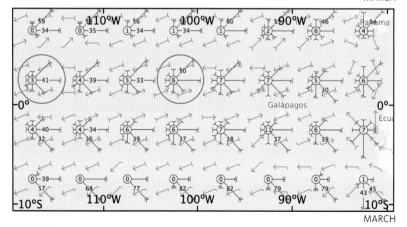

MARCH

tactics for those on a direct passage to the Marquesas.

To help with the planning of a particular passage, the relevant section of a monthly ocean chart is featured alongside the description of each voyage. As it would be impractical to feature such charts for every month of the year, only the months for the recommended time are shown. This normally coincides with the most favourable conditions and is often the time when most passages are undertaken along that route. This is in accordance with the accepted principle that the wise navigator will always try to be in the right place at the right time. Those who wish to plan a voyage at other times of the year may find the relevant information on charts illustrating other voyages, as listed in the index. Detailed global information on wind and current charts for every month and in every ocean can be found in *Cornells' Ocean Atlas*.

Pilot charts are only an indication of the average weather conditions for each month and they may not always reflect the conditions that are encountered. Nevertheless they are most useful for planning purposes, as oceanic weather systems have not changed radically during the period they cover. There is still a regular alternation of monsoons in the North Indian Ocean, prevailing NE winds blow off the coast of Brazil between October and February, the SE trade winds continue to blow consistently in the South Indian Ocean in the austral winter months and westerly winds are still a prevailing phenomenon in higher latitudes.

On each chart, wind roses are located in the centre of 5 degrees squares, each rose showing the distribution of the winds that prevail in that area from eight cardinal points. The arrows fly with the wind and their lengths show

the percentage of the total number of observations in which the wind has blown from that cardinal point. The number of feathers shows the force of the wind, which has been recorded

most frequently from that sector, with each feather being equivalent to one unit of wind force on the Beaufort scale, so that four feathers represent a predominant force 4. In areas with winds blowing mostly from the same direction, the resulting arrow would be too long, in which case the percentage is shown numerically on the shaft. The figure in the centre of the circle gives either the percentage of calms (less than force 2) in blue, or the percentage of storms (greater than force 7) in red, whichever is greater.

Also shown on the charts are ocean currents, the green arrows indicating their prevailing direction while the rate is reflected in the number of feathers, each being equivalent to 0.25 knots. Therefore, an arrow with four feathers indicates a mean rate of 1 knot during the month in question. Variable currents, with no single prevailing direction, are shown as a dotted arrow. The direction and rate of the current have been calculated for each 2.5 degrees area, as it would have been impractical to depict more arrows on such small-scale charts. However, as 2.5 degrees cover a relatively large area, the resulting arrows may be slightly misleading, especially in places where currents flow along a variable axis, such as the Agulhas Current, or meander considerably, as in the case of the Gulf Stream.

Cruising hubs

To help with the planning of a voyage, but also in case of an emergency stop, a number of suggested ports of call are listed at the end of each section. Although described as cruising hubs, some may not merit that description but are listed due to their strategic location in case of an emergency. According to the standard and range of available facilities, every hub is rated by one to five stars, with one star granted for each of such important services: essential repair facilities, haul-out for emergency repairs, safe storage or docking facilities to leave the boat unattended, hospital with emergency services, international airport, good provisioning and fuel. Places are also rated for their safety record, ease of formalities, availability of assistance in an emergency, and similar considerations. Places which do not have some essential services, whose facilities do not meet the expected requirements, or are of a low standard, had their overall rating adjusted accordingly.

What next?

Each section in this book concludes with a brief description of the various alternatives for the continuation of the voyage.

VOYAGE PLANNING SURVEY CONTRIBUTORS 2012

No	Name	Flag	Design	Material	LOA	Year built	Years owned	Total miles sailed	Owner	Circum-navigation
1	Alparena II	Germany	Asmus 52	Aluminium	52	1988	4	60,000	Klaus Girzig	c
2	Archrival	UK	Bowman 40	FRP	40	1989	21	110,000	John Whyte	c
3	Aventura	UK	Van de Stadt	FRP	36	1974	11	54,000	Christopher Soames	c
4	Aventura III	UK	OVNI 43	Aluminium	43	1989	15	70,000	Jimmy & Gwenda Cornell	ccc
5	Berrimilla 2	Australia	Brolga	FRP	33	1977	18	80,000	Alex Whitworth	c
6	Bumfuzzle	USA	Wildcat catamaran	FRP	35	2002	4	35,000	Pat & Ali Schulte	c
7	Cloud Nine	USA	Bowman 57	FRP	57	1975	30	220,000	Roger Swanson	ccc
8	Dreamtime of London	UK	Westerly Ocean	FRP	43	1998	3	30,000	John & Alison Wicks	
9	Equus	USA	Camper & Nicholson	FRP	48	1974	20	40,000	Steve Lochner	
10	Harmonie	USA	Amel Super Maramu	FRP	51	1996	10	65,000	Ann Harsh & Ralph Nehrig	c
11	Hawk	USA	Samoa	Aluminium	47	1998	13	80,000	Beth Leonard & Evans Starzinger	c
12	Hornblower	USA	Morgan 46	FRP	46	1981	9	30,000	Judy & Bob Hall	c
13	Interlude	USA	Deerfoot 74	Aluminium	74	1986	11	60,000	Kurt Braun	c
14	Jennifer	Sweden	Beneteau Oceanis	FRP	50	1988	22	150,000	Lars Hässler	cc
15	Lady E	USA	Baltic 51	FRP	51	1980	21	40,000	Barry Esrig	
16	Leon	France	Jeanneau Sun Odyssey	FRP	42	1991	11	22,000	Patrick Canut	
17	Maupiti	France	Beneteau Oceanis 393	FRP	39	2002	9	20,000	Marc & Corinne Martinez	
18	Nakia	USA	Hans Christian	FRP	33	1982	19	30,000	John Gratton & Linda Hill	
19	New Chance	Puerto Rico	Morgan	FRP	40	1979	8	41,000	Bill Butler	
20	Nine of Cups	USA	Liberty 458	FRP	45	1986	12	63,000	Dave & Marcie Lynn	c
21	Pegasos	Finland	Finnsailer	FRP	34	1982	10	45,000	Antti Louhija	c
22	Poé Maïa	France	Lagoon 380 catamaran	FRP	38	2000	5	10,000	Bruce Andrieux	
23	Que Sera Sera	USA	Hans Christian	FRP	40	1988	23	65,000	Don & Lois Babson	c
24	Sea Gem	USA	Gulfstar 54	FRP	54	1986	25	110,000	Charles & Saundra Gray	c
25	Sea Quest	New Zealand	Colin Childs	Steel	47	1982	18	60,000	Michael & Tere Batham	
26	Second Sally	USA	Peterson	FRP	44	1978	12	40,000	Greg & Marie Rogers	
27	Street Legal	UK	MG RS34	FRP	34	1984	21	100,000	Guy & Annika Oury	c
28	Vellamo	USA	Swan 48	Vinylester	48	1997	13	30,000	Phil Gibbins	
29	Wanderlust	USA	Hunter 49	FRP	49	2007	3	50,000	Mike Harker	c
30	White Princess	Barbados	Renegade 43	Steel	44	2001	10	60,000	Mike Dorsett	c
31	Yamma	UK	Hallberg Rassy	FRP	36	1991	6	40,000	Steve Moss	

No	Name	Flag	Design	Material	LOA	Year built	Years owned	Total miles sailed	Owner	Circum-navigation
	**VOYAGE PLANNING SURVEY CONTRIBUTORS 2012 AND 2018**									
1	Ardent Spirit	USA	Moody 58	FRP	58	1986	30	160,000	Arthur & Germaine Beiser	
2	Aventura II (La Aventura)	Australia	Aventura 40	Steel	40	1989	23	60,000	James & Pattti Hunt	c
3	Aventura IV	UK	Garcia Exploration 45	Aluminium	48	2014	3	200,000	Jimmy & Gwenda Cornell	ccc
4	BeBe	USVI	Amel Super Maramu	FRP	51	2002	11	45,000	Bill & Judy Rouse	c
5	Fuga Dos	Spain	Noray 43	FRP	43	1979	3	300,000	Javier Visiers	ccc
6	Ganesh	USA	Wauquiez Amphitrite	FRP	43	1990	6	180,000	Gary Goodlander	ccc
7	Halekai	USA	Alden 50	FRP	50	1993	25	150,000	Nancy & Burger Zapf	c
8	Igloo	France	OVNI 39	Aluminium	40	1995	23	200,000	Erick & Muriel Bouteleux	c
9	Infini	USA	Westsail 43	FRP	43	1979	20	50,000	Mike & Sue Beilan	
10	Jancris	Italy	Mikado 56	FRP	56	1983	26	120,000	Alfredo & Nicoletta Giacon	c
11	Juggler	UK	Westerly Fulmar 32	FRP	32	1980	2	95,000	John Jameson	c
12	Let's Go!	USA	OVNI 435	Aluminium	44	2003	15	90,000	Jim Patek	c
13	Limerence	USA	Beneteau First 375	FRP	37	1986	25	20,000	Doug & Judy Decker	
14	Mahina Tiare III	Canada	Hallberg Rassy 46	FRP	46	1997	21	365,000	John & Amanda Neal	c
15	New Dawn	Luxemburg	Hallberg Rassy 53	FRP	53	1999	14	110,000	Paul Donnerup	
16	Prophet	USA	Hardin 44	FRP	48	1980	12	205,000	Dale Elsa Norley	
17	Salamander	UK	De Groot	Steel	40	1988	13	35,000	Murray & Caroline Atkinson	c
18	Sänna 2	UK	Bavaria Ocean 50	FRP	49	1999	18	113,000	Dave & Marie Ungless	c
19	Scotia	UK	Bruce Roberts	Steel	42	1997	21	250,000	Hugh & Brenda Fraser	c
20	Sloepmouche	Belgium	Norman Cross trimaran	Plywood	46	1980	23	38,000	Luc Callebaut & Jackie Lee	
21	Soggy Paws	USA	St Francis 44 catamaran	FRP	44	2004	3	80,000	Dave & Sherry McCampbell	c
22	Stampede	USA	Concordia	Kevlar	58	1986	14	60,000	Stu & Julie Conway	c
23	Tenaya	USA	Hallberg Rassy	FRP	40	2006	12	50,000	Jim & Katie Thomsen	c
24	Tulameen II	Canada	Koopmans 39	Aluminium	40	2001	16	72,000	Bill & Frances Stocks	c
25	Tutatis	Brazil	Ronautica	FRP	40	2007	9	30,000	José Prieto	c
26	Vagrant of Clyde	UK	Bowman 40	FRP	40	1989	25	100,000	Bill & Jane McLaren	c
27	Viking Crusader	Norway	Sweden Yachts 40	FRP	40	2009	9	45,000	Ståle & Annelise Larsen	
	**VOYAGE PLANNING SURVEY 2018**									
28	Pearl	UK	Garcia Exploration 45	Aluminium	48	2017	2	470,000	Pete & Tracey Goss	cc
29	Sophie	USA	Lagoon 470 catamaran	FRP	47	2007	11	45,000	Jamie Utzschneider & Jenna Miller	c

PLANNING A VOYAGE

Voyage planning is common sense

SOLAS (International Convention

for the Safety of Life at Sea)

My practical interest in ocean routing was born during our first round the world voyage when I realised, mainly from the books of previous voyagers, just how important it was for the overall safety of a voyage to plan the best route possible. Immediately after our return in 1981 I started working on what was to become *World Cruising Routes*.

For the first years after its publication I felt that *World Cruising Routes* dealt adequately with the subject of voyage planning, but when I started working on the route of the first round the world rally I realised that there was much more to voyage planning than joining up a string of individual routes. Inspired by the success of the ARC (Atlantic Rally for Cruisers), the Europa 92 round the world rally was to be an organised event run along the same principles as the ARC but much more ambitious in scope. Rather than a one-leg transocean event lasting around three weeks, the round the world rally was to last eighteen months along a route of 32,000

miles broken up into 20 individual legs. The limited time allowed for this event, which could easily have lasted three years, was dictated by the time restrictions of most participants, many of whom were still active in their professions and could not allow themselves a longer sabbatical break.

Planning a world event for 36 yachts of various lengths and capabilities, along a route that crossed three oceans and four separate weather systems, called at two dozen countries and transited the Panama and Suez Canals, proved to be quite a challenge that was made more difficult by the self-imposed time frame. With safety being the first priority, I had to narrow down the timing to fit the most favourable conditions by juggling the different sailing seasons and avoiding tropical storm seasons in each of those oceans. Only now, as I am writing these lines, do I realise what a challenging, but deeply satisfying, exercise in voyage planning that first round the world rally had been. The lessons learned from running several such events over the years, combined with the experience gained from my own voyages, has convinced me of the importance of proper voyage planning.

The first round the world rally fleet in Tahiti.

Practical steps from dream to reality

There's magic in water that draws all men away from the land, that leads them over the hills, down creeks and streams and rivers to the sea.

Herman Melville

For most sailors, every voyage starts with a dream, but between the fulfilment of that dream and the reality of the voyage itself lies a period of preparation during which working on a well thought-out plan is of utmost importance.

The initial planning stage should be a period of research and gathering all information that may be relevant to the voyage, such as consulting cruising guides and nautical publications of relevance to the chosen route, reading books, articles or reports written by other sailors who had completed a similar voyage, familiarising yourself with weather conditions and tropical storm seasons by consulting the relevant pilot charts, researching the internet for reports on the countries to be visited and finding out about any specific formalities, permits and official requirements that you should be aware of, and gathering information on any high risk areas that ought to be avoided, be it because of military conflict, political instability, the threat to personal safety or piracy.

This early stage is also the time to make a realistic assessment of the voyage by considering carefully the various things that can go wrong. Queries about such concerns are the most frequently asked questions at my lectures and seminars on long distance voyage planning and preparation. As I am always reluctant to paint too rosy a picture, and thus make it sound easy, my answers occasionally cause disappointment because I believe that it is better to be faced with the true reality at this early stage rather than later on, when a change of plan may be much more difficult to make. I have noticed myself that with age and experience I have become not only more cautious but increasingly prone to ask the 'what if' question whenever faced with an important decision.

From the cases of unhappy or even abandoned voyages that I have encountered over the years, and from my conversations with the owners and crews, I have narrowed down the most common factors that have led to the failure of those voyages. These are the boat itself, the crew, inadequate funds, inability to be self-sufficient, and, finally, the wrong attitude to life at sea and to cruising generally. As these are such important matters for anyone planning a long voyage, while working on the first edition of this book, I decided to conduct a survey among a wide sample of sailors who were undertaking or had completed such a voyage in the recent past. Participants in the survey were told that this poll was being conducted for the benefit of other sailors planning a voyage and were urged to draw on their own experience when commenting on those common causes that can have such a crucial impact on the success or failure of a voyage.

Among the 57 sailors who took part in the original survey, 29 had sailed around the world, several of them more than once; their ages ranged from the late 20s to the early 80s, while their cruising spanned the entire world, from the tropics to Antarctica, the Mediterranean to the Northwest Passage. Their boats were as diverse as their owners, from production boats to state-of-the-art yachts, monohulls and multihulls, a perfect sample of today's cruising scene. This was also reflected in the make-up of the individual crews, with 32 boats being crewed all, or most, of the time by couples. It was a rich fount of knowledge and experience to draw on, which made it possible to deal with all essential aspects of voyage planning from the widest perspective.

When I started work on a revised and updated second edition of this book I realised that most of the findings of that comprehensive survey were still relevant so I decided to contact some of those who had taken part in that survey and ask them for their opinion on the issues they had commented on six years previously. In the meantime several had completed a circumnavigation, and a few were still cruising, either on the same boats or new ones. These experienced sailors have been a valuable source in updating the findings of the original survey.

The boat

I start from the premise that no object created by man is as satisfying to his body and soul as a proper sailing yacht.

Arthur Beiser

What kind of boat to acquire is often a more difficult decision than deciding to do the voyage itself, especially nowadays when there is such a bewildering range of boats available and obtaining unbiased advice is not easy. Over the years I have conducted a number of surveys trying to find out if there was indeed an ideal cruising boat, only to conclude that the ideal cruising boat may be just a chimera, and while a particular boat may be perfect for one sailor or one particular voyage, the same boat might be totally unsuitable for another. Therefore the purpose of the voyage planning survey was not another attempt to discover that elusive ideal boat but to find out from a wide range of cruising sailors the essential features of a boat fit for a world voyage.

This statement, which I made six years ago, may have been true at the time as I was most certainly not planning or even thinking of acquiring another boat. It all changed when I decided to make an attempt at the Northwest Passage, and ended up having a new boat built, which I believe, came closest to my ideal cruising boat. I must also admit that some of the practical suggestions and tips mentioned in that survey sounded so logical and valuable that I incorporated them into the concept of this Aventura.

There is no doubt that the choice of boat can seriously affect the quality and enjoyment of a voyage, and a wrong choice may even lead to the voyage being abandoned. There are many factors that can make a boat unsuitable for a long voyage and the most common is the wrong size, the boat being either too large for it to be handled easily by a shorthanded crew, or too small to be comfortable, having limited storage capacity or not being fast enough on long passages. Comfort is indeed a major aspect and has a bearing not only on the well-being of the crew but on safety itself. Important as size and comfort may be, the most essential consideration when choosing a boat for a long voyage is safety. There are many boats on the market that are perfectly suitable for weekend sailing or short cruises, but which may not be up to the demands of a voyage in tough ocean conditions.

A common reason for some people setting off with what turns out in the long run to be an unsuitable boat is that it was the boat they happened to own at the time and, whether for financial reasons, lack of foresight, or sentimental reasons, they decided that it would do. By the time their mistake became obvious it was too late to put it right and they either chose to carry on regardless, cut short or even abandon the voyage. This may explain the large number of boats for sale in the Caribbean, which is still a better place to take such a painful decision than halfway through a circumnavigation.

As the choice of the right boat is such an important factor, participants in the voyage planning survey were asked to rate their level of satisfaction with their boat as a percentage. They were also asked to point out any design features missing on their boat that would have made a considerable contribution to the quality and enjoyment of their voyage and to name any specific piece of equipment that they would have liked to have had. To complete the section on the choice of boat, they were asked to make a comment or give some useful tip to someone preparing for a long voyage.

One hull good, two hulls better?

To go for one or more hulls is perhaps an even more difficult decision than that of size. Although there are a few cruising trimarans on the market, I still need to be persuaded that trimarans are suitable to be sailed on offshore passages by a small family crew. However things may be changing as a new generation of cruising trimarans may show that their designers have learned from past mistakes and have managed to improve their safety credentials. In the early days there were similar doubts about the suitability of catamarans for offshore sailing, but their design has greatly improved, architects have put a lot of thought into their safety, while builders have done their best to produce strong seaworthy craft. Their ever-increasing popularity among long-distance cruisers is the best proof of that. As they have many advantages over a monohull of the same length, I have an open mind on this subject.

Those who plan to set off in a catamaran on a long voyage must choose their route carefully to minimise the risk of encountering dangerous weather, observe the safe seasons, and always be aware of a catamaran's weak points. Catamarans are much less forgiving than monohulls when weather conditions deteriorate, and whereas a catamaran needs to be helped to overcome extreme conditions, a well-found monohull can be battened down and left to its own devices. It may capsize and lose its mast but it will probably survive upright.

Javier Visiers is a well-known Spanish naval architect, and took many by surprise when he chose a catamaran for the Millennium Odyssey round-the-world rally. Javier did in fact what many other sailors do, and chose what he thought was the most suitable boat for a particular voyage, a pragmatic attitude that I fully share. Other sailors may consider a catamaran, even if with some provisos, as in the case of David Beauchamp. 'I am considering a catamaran for cruising, as a catamaran over 12 metres can be handled by a couple on most occasions with more ease than a monohull. I have spoken to owners of large cats. They are best kept between 30 degrees north and 30 degrees south for safety's sake.'

The number of catamarans on long voyages has been steadily increasing and my global survey was a good opportunity to find out their actual proportion among cruising yachts. Once again, I referred to the detailed statistics obtained from the Azores and found that among the 775 boats that had arrived in Horta (Azores), 103 (13%) were catamarans. That percentage had risen to 17% (185 of 1058) among the Panama Canal transits, with the highest percentage (19%) recorded in Noumea (New Caledonia), with 61 catamarans among a total of 328 boats. The situation in some rallies confirmed this trend, with 17% in the Blue Planet Odyssey, 19% in the World ARC, 14% in the ARC (35 of 259), and 17% among the 209 boats in the Pacific Puddle Jump. The Atlantic Odyssey achieved the highest percentage, with 18 catamarans among the 70 boats (26%) in the 2016 event.

The overall level of satisfaction among the 57 owners was quite high with the majority (46) granting their boats percentages of 90 and above. Ten among them gave the maximum percentage, there were six at 99 percent, and twelve at 95 percent, one of the former explaining that '99 percent is about right as most will agree that 99 percent of boats are 1 foot too short', while among the latter one owner explained that 'it would have cost too much money to get rid of the final 5 percent'. Granting such a rating to your boat is obviously a very subjective assessment but I found it very significant that among such a large sample there was only one owner who was disappointed with his choice, while only six others qualified their level of overall satisfaction by giving ratings between 70 and 85 percent. Several owners pointed out that whereas they found it easy to give an overall rating for their boat, there were specific instances where a lower rating would have been more accurate. Javier Visiers was among them when he said, 'I would give *Antaviana* 100 percent overall, but only 85 percent for the Mediterranean where catamarans are far from perfect.'

The sidebar on this page was contributed by Javier for the first edition so I asked him now if he might have changed his mind. 'Not at all, I sold my 44-foot Sun Odyssey in the USA, and at the moment I own an old 43-foot Noray. I sailed on such a boat in the Parmelia Race in 1979 from Plymouth, England, to Fremantle, Western Australia, to commemorate the voyage of the barque *Parmelia* when she transported the first settlers to Western Australia in 1829.'

The number of catamarans on long voyages has been steadily increasing and the same global survey provided a good opportunity to find out their actual proportion among cruising yachts. Once again, I referred to the detailed statistics obtained from the Azores and found that among the 775 boats that had arrived in Horta, 103 (13%) were catamarans. The situation in some rallies confirmed this trend, with 17% in the Blue Planet Odyssey, 19% in the World ARC, 14% in the ARC, and 17% in the Pacific Puddle Jump. The Atlantic Odyssey achieved the highest percentage, with 18 catamarans among the 70 boats (26%) in the 2016 event.

The optimum size of a cruising boat for a world voyage is such an important factor that it was examined in the original world planning survey. A few owners complained about their boats being smaller than ideal, whereas one skipper was in fact happy with his decision to buy a smaller boat as it allowed him to enter smaller ports and marinas. What some owners found to be a more serious handicap on long voyages than actual size was the lack of storage space, which they blamed on the fact that

Antaviana

Why a catamaran? First of all, I wanted to take Barbara with me, and as she is not a great sailor, I had to make life easy for her, and that meant heeling as little as possible, not having that down-below feeling but a good view of the sea. In a cat that is much better than in a monohull.

A 47 foot cat has the comfort equivalent to a 65 foot monohull and is possibly faster too. But there are other reasons. On a cat you can carry a much bigger dinghy. You have more privacy, as you are in your own hull, and do not hear other people. As you have two identical hulls, you have two of everything, so if there is a problem you can survive until the problem is solved. We did more than 1,000 miles with one engine until Singapore, where we repaired it. We normally use only one engine at a time and the cruising speed is only marginally lower than with both.

A cat has shallow draft, and it is easy to leave it on a beach until the tide changes to do repairs, etc. At anchor you have more comfort. I remember a rolly anchorage where monohulls were heeling badly, and we didn't move. But you have to be very careful with the weight, as catamarans sail well in rough seas but only if they are not overloaded. I remember another catamaran, which was only 38 feet but carried 1 or 2 tonnes more than it was supposed to, and therefore sailed very badly. And yes, at low wind speeds it is difficult to sail upwind, but cruising around the world, who cares?

Now I am back in the Med where cats are not welcome in marinas. So I bought a new boat, a 44 foot Sun Odyssey, with a higher rig, as I enjoy racing and having fun with my friends. But if I do another round the world trip, I will again have a cat.

Javier Visiers

many current boats are built for charter where storage capacity is not a priority.

In the survey on the global movement of cruising yachts conducted in 2016, I attempted to find out more about the actual size of the cruising boats roaming the oceans of the world. Figures obtained from Panama, Tahiti, Bermuda, and Horta, made it possible to calculate their average length, and in order to arrive at a realistic figure, only boats under 60 feet were taken into account as very few of the larger boats would fit the description of a standard cruising boat. Among the 775 boats that passed through Horta, in the Azores, on completion of their passage from the Caribbean, the average length was

The yacht of our dreams

Out of the blackness a breaking crest makes itself known with an alien glow of tumbled phosphorescence as it roars past. This is not what we expected when we set off on the glamour leg of our circumnavigation from Lanzarote to Antigua. Another wave lifts the stern. I can sense the bow is buried deep. It's that pregnant pause when all sorts of forces compete for control of the boat and the outcome is out of your hands. Your fate lies in the past, a designer's pen scratching out a concept, a build team that decided to make something to be proud of. A boat that, when a stranger walks past, their natural inclination is to run their hand along it in appreciation of the curves. All the elements and bits of equipment that make up our new Garcia Exploration 45, just seem to sit together in harmony. There isn't that one angle or bolted bit of equipment that jars. She stops people in their tracks.

The moment is upon us and *Pearl*, seemingly docile, just runs with the wave, straight and true. The B&G autopilot doesn't need to labour as we surf off at 17 knots. I feel safe but not lulled. I have done enough sailing to know these to be dangerous conditions but also revel in the transformation in *Pearl* once the centreboard is up. All lateral resistance moves aft to the rudders and there is no keel to trip us up. As we race down that treacherous liquid slope, a broach couldn't be further from my mind.

Tracey and I spent a long time choosing *Pearl*. She is what we think of as a 'Land Rover of the Sea with BMW interior', a blend of our different expectations. I wanted a robust aluminium hull with watertight bulkheads, twin rudders, a centreboard to reduced draught to open up shallow areas but give directional stability off the wind. Drying out should be easy. She should have lots of storage, a big capacity for fuel and water, be well insulated and no hydraulics. Our new home has to do more than offer utilitarian function. She must be warm, pleasing to the eye below, have a double bed, a good galley and above all she must not be a 'cave' as Tracey describes most boats. Ours must have an all-round view much like a catamaran.

Nothing quite fitted the bill until Yachting World came to the rescue and I saw the Garcia on the front cover. She had something that immediately drew me in. Here was the culmination of Jimmy Cornell's lifetime of long-distance cruising and detailed surveys of other's bluewater lessons. Her DNA was impeccable and she fitted the picture in my mind. It was so exciting. I called Tracey to say that I had stumbled across the yacht of our dreams.

Pete Goss

This is an extract from the April 2018 issue of Yachting World *magazine*

43.8 feet. The average among the 556 arrivals in Tahiti was higher, at 45.2 feet. The Bermuda average for the 560 boats was 46.9 feet, while 45.9 feet was the average for the 617 boats that had transited the Panama Canal. The overall average length for the 2,508 boats under 60 feet that called at the above locations was 45.3 feet. The above results included both monohulls and multihulls.

That average length coincided with that of my own *Aventura IV* and was also confirmed by Pete Goss when he chose the Exploration 45 for a world voyage with his wife Tracey, as described in the above sidebar.

Regardless of actual size, the most common feature that participants in the world planning survey wished they had had was a comfortable, sheltered watch-keeping position. Several mentioned the importance of a protected and ergonomically designed cockpit, if possible with a hard dodger, which would make passages more comfortable in both hot and cold climates. The importance of this feature was stressed by Burger Zapf, 'It is indeed essential, and

every long-term cruiser we know ended up with some kind of cockpit protection.'

Asked to specify any design feature that would have made a considerable contribution to the enjoyment of their voyage, several owners mentioned shallower draft, which would have extended their cruising range. Don Babson fully agreed with the advantages of shallow draft: 'I wish I had a centreboard as I keep running the old girl aground.'

Shallow draft is only one of the advantages of a centreboard, as described in the sidebar on the opposite page. It is also a view shared by Pete Goss.

Other desirable features mentioned by those surveyed were good access to the engine for maintenance, a compact and safe galley, comfortable sea berths, but also provision for a double berth when in port. To this, Arthur Beiser, the author of *The Proper Yacht*, added 'two armchairs in the saloon'. The list was even longer for outside features such as a well-designed stern with dinghy davits, a platform or scoop, with a folding or retractable ladder, for easier access to the dinghy, swimming or landing fish.

According to Mike Dorsett an important feature on a world voyage is 'a larger than standard self-draining gas locker with space for additional tanks when cruising in areas where refilling them can be a problem'.

Suggested improvements at the bows were a retractable bowsprit, quick and easy access to the chain locker, with a vertical drop to avoid the chain getting snagged, serviced by a powerful and reliable windlass. For sail handling a well-thought-out reefing system was considered essential with the lines being led back to the cockpit, ideally to an electric winch.

The three most commonly mentioned pieces of essential equipment were a watermaker, a strong autopilot preferably backed up by a wind-operated selfsteering gear, and an automatic identification system (AIS). As Doug Decker pointed out, 'an AIS transponder provides a high level of safety and communications between ships and small vessels.' The usefulness of AIS was mentioned by several others. Also stressed was the absolute need of a powerful, reliable autopilot, especially on boats sailed by a couple on their own. In such cases a backup autopilot and, if practicable, also a wind operated selfsteering gear.

Other desirable items mentioned were bow thrusters, especially in places such as the Mediterranean and Baltic where manoeuvering in tightly packed marinas can be very difficult, and a cockpit repeater for the chart plotter and, ideally, the radar as well. Several sailors complained about the poor quality of the user's manual provided by some boatyards and the fact that they were not much help when dealing with some essential equipment breakdown, especially in an emergency. It was also pointed out that most production boats were sold without an electric wiring diagram, which can make it very difficult to trace a fault.

As most of those interviewed had spent long periods sailing under trade wind conditions, several mentioned having easily handled downwind sails, such as a cruising chute, asymmetric spinnaker or Parasailor. Patrick Canut, who sailed with two genoas, wished he had had 'two poles while running wing and wing, especially when we had to gybe repeatedly with the wind close to 180°. Although I now believe that a Parasailor would have been a better choice.'

Communication systems were not covered by the survey, although the usefulness of satellite phones was praised. However, as Steve Moss pointed out, 'In spite of satphones, SSB radio is still essential for emails, voice communications with other boats, receiving weather-faxes, etc.'

Centreboard

One of the first questions everyone asks me is how safe it is to sail on a boat without a keel. Having sailed twice across the Drake Passage to Antarctica and back, both times on a centreboard boat, and having experienced on two occasions winds between 50 and 60 knots, this was a perfect opportunity to test the boat's stability under such conditions. On both occasions the boats performed perfectly well and took the high cross-swell in their stride. Both *Aventura III* and *IV* have an integral centreboard, which means that when the board is raised, it is fully retracted into the hull. The ballast is also internal: 3.6 tons on *Aventura III* and 4.5 tons on *Aventura IV*. The ballast to displacement ratio of both is 32, which is similar to that of most modern cruising yachts.

One of the main reasons for choosing a centreboarder is to increase my cruising options, and having a boat whose draft can be reduced instantly is an important advantage. But shallow draft is not only ideal for exploring places which other boats cannot reach, but also a safety factor because it allows you to access a protected spot if needing shelter in an emergency. Also, as most integral centreboard boats have a flat bottom, it means that with the board fully up, the boat can dry out on any beach, tidal bay or estuary.

There is a certain technique in sailing a centreboarder efficiently, not just on the wind but especially off the wind. This is when the centreboard becomes a true asset as it allows you to reduce the wetted surface. Also, the ability to lift the board gradually as the apparent wind goes past 135°, and then continue lifting it up to the point where the board is fully retracted, is a great advantage as the risk of broaching is virtually eliminated. The absence of a keel to act as a pivot in a potential broaching situation means that the boat does not tend to round up when, in a similar situation, a keeled boat would do just that. It is a feature that I have blessed on many occasions, and that has allowed me to continue keeping the spinnaker up longer than I would have done otherwise.

From '200,000 Miles, A Life of Adventure'.

When it came to giving practical advice to would-be voyagers, it was pointed out that many of those with limited experience seem to be unaware of the high demands on electricity of all the equipment installed on cruising boats nowadays. 'Make sure that your electric power demands can be satisfied with the type of electrical storage and generating equipment you have on board and have a diversified portfolio of options – engine, generator, solar, wind,' advised Jim Patek. He also advised 'to decide on what is important and concentrate on making that work well: a powerful reliable engine, strong sails, good quality deck equipment, and backups for what you cannot live without. It is better if you can live with simple good equipment than have too much in the way of fashionable complicated stuff you do not really need.'

One of the main conclusions of the survey was that as many as 90 per cent of owners admitted to having underestimated their electricity consumption. This was usually blamed on autopilots, watermakers, freezers, as well as certain items that normally run on mains power, such as washing machines, microwave ovens, breadmakers, etc. As a result, a high proportion of even relatively smaller boats were equipped with diesel generators. Although the situation seems to be changing as the latest survey highlighted a gradual move away from diesel generators and a definite increase in the use of renewable sources.

Hugh Fraser, who had built his own boat, listed some useful tips which could be easily accommodated on a production boat as well: 'Fit two heavy anchors permanently on the bow, both ready for instant use. For lightning protection a spike on the masthead seems to work, and stow a spare GPS and radio in a tin box or oven in case your boat is hit. For your safety and comfort, make strong stainless steel mosquito screens for the companionway and main hatch, so you can lock yourself in at night and keep cool. Carry a spare computer and a separate hard drive loaded with all your programs.'

The safety aspect, more than any other, should be the overriding factor when choosing a boat for an ocean voyage. This was stressed by several contributors to the survey, although some also highlighted the importance of comfort on a long voyage. Burger Zapf made this very clear. 'Long term cruising is not weekend camping. Look around at your present lifestyle. Try to repeat that on your boat.'

Several people stressed the need to try and keep things simple. Tere Batham, who spent ten years roaming the Pacific, emphasized that 'we do not believe that it is all that sophisticated equipment that really makes the boat. It is good quality winches, anchoring gear and a reliable engine which are paramount as they will give you peace of mind.'

Doug Decker felt that it is very important for a boat to be 'woman friendly'. 'Captains should be reminded that if they want their partners to enjoy cruising, they'd better make it as comfortable as possible. This means comforts like good reading lights, a comfortable bed with proper sheets and pillows, good quality cooking gear, real dishes and glasses (in addition to plastic), an efficient watermaker so one can take showers and wash clothing, and even a vacuum flush toilet that uses fresh water and eliminates that 'boaty' smell of the heads.'

The points made by Doug are of utmost importance when choosing and equipping a boat as illustrated by Javier Visiers' comments. In Javier's case the choice of a catamaran to sail in the Millennium Odyssey round the world rally was quite surprising as he is a well-known Spanish naval architect who designed many successful monohulls. He once held the record for the fastest 24-hour run of 404 miles in one of the earliest Whitbread round the world races, but had different priorities for his latest circumnavigation.

While a boat may be perfect for one sailor, that same boat might be quite unsuitable for another, and no one could have put it better than Alex Whitworth when I asked him about his own wish list and what would have contributed to the quality and enjoyment of his circumnavigation via the Northwest Passage on his 100 percent rated 33 foot *Berrimilla*. 'None. My voyage was sailed on a shoestring: quality and comfort were not a consideration.'

At the other extreme, Kurt Braun, who completed a circumnavigation about the same time on his 74 foot *Interlude* and had also given his boat a 100 percent rating of satisfaction, also answered with 'none' to those same questions. Instead he gave this advice to anyone planning to get a boat and leave on a long voyage: 'Go bareboat chartering and/or passage making on someone else's boat to confirm you will enjoy cruising on your own yacht before making the investment in boat or equipment.'

Among those who seemed to have got closest to their ideal boat were Beth Leonard and Evans Starzinger. 'Because we had done a circumnavigation before we built this boat ourselves, we were able to incorporate everything we really wanted in the design. We had hoped to get it all into 42 feet but ended up at 47 feet. If we could have got everything into 42 feet, we would have preferred it.'

For those who may not be able to buy a new boat, Luc Callebaut pointed out that, 'There are many good quality and reasonably priced used boats on the market. But do get a professional surveyor so you know exactly what you are getting and make sure that other than the buying price, you have money left to cover the refit. The cost of bringing some boats to an acceptable standard might end up being much higher than buying a similar vessel in good condition.'

The findings of this comprehensive survey highlighted many of the essential features that ought to be present on a boat prepared for a world voyage.

The crew

Do your best to find the right crew but expect relationships to change during the voyage.

Paul Donnerup

While many long voyages have been completed success-fully by couples, the same cannot always be said of boats crewed by friends, acquaintances or occasional crew taken on board to supplement the permanent crew. There are many aspects that a skipper should consider when choosing crew for a long voyage or just one ocean passage, such as their experience, physical condition, reliability, as well as compatibility with other crew members and the skipper himself. When the boat is crewed by just two people, the skipper should make sure that in an emergency the other person is able to deal with the essential tasks on board. Many couples sailing on their own have found that on long passages an additional person makes life easier by sharing watches or having an extra hand in an emergency. It may therefore be a good idea to discuss this matter with potential crew well in advance so as to know who may be available if called at short notice.

Health and general fitness should be given a high priority as part of the preparation for a voyage. Whatever the age of the crew, and many long-distance sailors are no longer in their prime, their physical condition should be a major consideration, especially on a long voyage when medical assistance may not be easily available. After a long period of urban, sedentary existence, it is essential to get into good physical shape for the impending voyage. Erick Bouteleux stressed the fact that many people do not realise how important physical fitness can be on a boat. 'You must prepare yourself physically but also mentally for what can be a demanding way of life.'

I regard the subject of crew as one of the most common causes for the failure of some voyages. As I described my own views at length on this subject in my book *200,000 Miles*, I decided to focus here on the opinions, comments and suggestions made by the sailors who contributed to the voyage planning survey.

Over half the boats in the original survey were crewed by couples, who only occasionally took on additional crew, and several stressed that they preferred this arrangement. Bill McLaren, who completed a circumnavigation with his wife Jane, pointed out that 'the advantages of doing long passages as a couple are huge, provided both are fully competent. You only need one decent sea berth; watchkeeping routines are easy and you haven't got the

Dreamtime of London

While fitting out our *Dreamtime of London* for the Millennium Odyssey round the world rally we tried to have backups for most essential systems, especially to have both an autopilot and wind self-steering system. All went well until we left the Galapagos Islands for the 3,000 miles haul to the Marquesas. Problems arose when John was laid low for five days with dysentery until antibiotics overcame the problem. John gradually improved, the trade winds arrived and we were flying along, covering 200 miles a day. Ten days after leaving the Galapagos, the autopilot suddenly ceased to function so that constant hand steering and the use of the windpilot became necessary. The SE winds of 20 to 25 knots with large quartering seas made for an uncomfortable ride at speeds of 8 knots. Twenty-four hours later, at 0400 on John's watch, a huge wave hit the stern and dislodged the windpilot support arm from its mounting bracket. Fortunately John was able to lash the whole structure to the stern rail, quite an exciting undertaking on a wildly rushing boat in the dark. Gradually the winds abated but now someone had to be at the helm every minute and we were getting very tired.

Two days later Alison explained our predicament on the daily radio schedule, and several yachts in the rally res-ponded immediately. The Italian skipper of *Jancris* offered to transfer two crew members from his rather crowded vessel. The Australian *Foxy Lady* arranged to coordinate the agreed rendezvous, while *Jasmin Lee* positioned itself just ahead of us with *Sidereal Times* closely behind, observing this encounter in the middle of the Pacific.

By 2200 hours all our lights converged so we hove to, lowered the dinghy on a long line and prepared for those wonderful young guys from *Jancris*. We hauled Franco and Nico aboard laden with their backpacks, which consisted mostly of packets of pasta and tomato sauce. Apparently they did not expect such stores on a British yacht! They had also come from a dry boat and were delighted to be greeted by an exploding champagne cork! So for the next 1,400 miles we greatly enjoyed and appreciated the company of these two wonderful young men who took their generous stint at the wheel. Ten days later we arrived in Hiva Oa in the Marquesas for an emotional reunion with the other yachts. At the welcoming reception in Tahiti we were given a special prize of two huge blow-up dolls – our new crew.

Alison and John Wicks

responsibility towards other crew.' Nancy Zapf agreed: 'Less is more. The more people in a small place, the more potential for problems. Modern technologies such as autopilot, windvane, GPS, electronic charts, radar and AIS have made it much easier to sail short-handed.' Her views were shared by Dave McCampbell, 'Although for watch standing we would prefer to have at least one extra crew member aboard, the logistics of doing so, and the limited space available, means that just the two of us is a better choice. The extra sleep at night is nice, but having another person to feed and house, and occupying space in the cockpit and down below, isn't quite worth it. And then there's the pressure of meeting the crew's sightseeing and schedule expectations.'

As Tere Batham explained, 'Michael and I only relied upon ourselves for long passages. If we happened to have someone else aboard, we did not expect much of them. We always felt that the two of us could and would always run the boat and that others on board were, in fact, a liability more than a true asset.' Alison Wicks was of the same opinion: 'Very happy with skipper and wife until something goes wrong!' And so it did – see sidebar.

What happened to Alison and John while on a long passage shows why it is so important for the boat to be fully prepared for single-handing in an emergency, although even at normal times one or the other should be able to handle the boat on his or her own. This is also the opinion of Kurt Braun, who sailed the largest boat in the survey. 'We generally find crew to be more hindrance than help. Personality conflicts which would normally not be a problem emerge and are intensified at sea. Our ideal arrangement is double-handing by a couple on a vessel that can be single-handed if necessary, allowing proper watchkeeping underway and the ability to bring the vessel to port in the event of partner injury.'

This is a view that was shared by several couples that updated or confirmed their previous comments in their contributions for this edition. This was also the view of Ståle Larsen: 'I have had experience with non-family sailors pretending to be experienced, but in bad weather they showed to be the opposite. Being on a boat for a long time with non-family sailors can cause stress and irritation. Family members know each other well so stressful situations will normally not cause a serious problem. Best arrangement is sailing with your family.'

Every contributor was therefore asked to state what he or she considered to be the ideal number of crew besides the captain. The answers broadly confirmed the make-up of the sample as 30 stated one extra person to be their ideal, 18 preferred two extra pairs of hands, six would rather have three, one preferred four and one would

go as far as five. Bill Stocks would not commit himself because 'crew number does depend on the size of the boat. For a smaller boat, husband and wife can work very well together; for a larger boat you may need and appreciate a few more hands.' Asked to reconfirm his comments, he replies: 'I would now say that on our 40-foot boat it is easier to equip the boat to allow for two-person handling, than it may be to bring on an extra crew.'

Nancy and Burger Zapf, who completed a circumnavigation on *Halekai*, agreed. 'We sailed without a crew just the two of us. The boat is a confined space and even the best of friends can become a problem over time. The more crew the more problems.'

The participants in the survey were asked to comment on their own experience with crew and the experiences varied wildly, the descriptions ranging from perfect to diabolical. For Phil Gibbins, 'the best crew are friends who do deliveries for a living. No need to watch or tell them anything, which makes passage making enjoyable and stress-free.' Barry Esrig certainly agreed: 'I know of too many disaster passages with personality or inexperience issues. The best arrangement is to have crew that you know personally. You know both their experience and their personality.' Saundra Gray stressed that, 'It is important to have good communications with your crew when planning a voyage and exactly what each person hopes to gain from the experience. If you plan to have guests aboard on a long voyage, be sure you know them well.' Antti Louhija agreed: 'Family members and old friends are best because you know them well enough and they know you. Casual crew members may cause unexpected complications.' John Neal did not entirely agree, 'Family make great crew, but in our case, so do paying sail-training crew.' Few people would know this better than John and Amanda Neal, who have been running their *Mahina Tiare III* for many years as an offshore navigation and sail-training vessel. Fee-paying crews join up for training stages in ocean voyaging and seamanship.

For Doug Decker 'the most important attribute of a crew or guest is congeniality'. Roger Swanson shared that opinion, 'Bring friends along. The camaraderie between crew members has been the most important highlight of my sailing career. It is also a safety factor. One of the greatest dangers on a long passage is fatigue in the event of a long stretch of heavy weather, or possibly an injury or sickness.'

Dale Norley, who is an experienced delivery skipper, feels strongly that 'three people on a long passage is the ideal number. It allows for plenty of rest, while still providing an opportunity to be alone on night watch. Having some time alone is very important when you are at

Sailing happily into old age

Germaine and I have cruised together every summer and some winters since we were married in 1953, more often than not by ourselves after our children grew up. The two of us cruised alone for the last time in 2016 when we were both 85. We sold our 58-ft Moody sloop *Ardent Spirit*, which we had owned for 30 years, the following year because we thought it prudent not to push our good fortune too far. During the sea trial with the prospective buyer, and with Germaine at the helm, *Ardent Spirit* sailed faster and closer to the wind than all the other boats we met, which sealed the purchase.

Ardent Spirit incorporated what we had learned from cruising short-handed in our previous six boats (21 to 70 ft). *Ardent Spirit* was fully equipped when we bought her but later we made many modifications to enable either of us to do almost anything on deck without getting too tired, to be independent of the shore for as long as we wanted, and to be easy for the two of us to dock the boat on our own. These are the most important items of equipment that we ended up with, and should be considered for boats of any size meant to be sailed short-handed:

- Electric jib sheet winches in the cockpit, with a handheld remote control.
- Electric winch at the foot of the mast to be used for the mainsail halyard (assuming the mainsail is not in-mast furling), and also for the reefing lines. Although we didn't have a spinnaker, we used the same winch with the spinnaker halyard to launch and recover the dinghy from its chocks on the forward deck, and for the reefing lines.
- An autopilot that had a ram attached to the rudder quadrant (so it was independent of the steering cables). We also had a spare autopilot that we only used twice in 30 years.
- Two sets of mooring lines, one set light enough to be easily thrown ashore, and a heavy set for long stays or when strong winds were expected.
- A bow-thruster for manoeuvering in port and also to keep the boat headed into the wind when reefing or dropping the mainsail.
- A crane on the radar mast at the stern with a winch to raise and lower the outboard motor between its mount on the aft pulpit and the dinghy tied to the stern.
- Because the 100-lbs. anchor was too heavy for Germaine to lift over the bow-roller for dropping, the roller was moved to the outer end of a robust steel trough pivoted at the bow (using the original shaft of the roller) so that the roller overhung the bow. As the trough tilts, the anchor falls by itself when it is freed from its deck hold-down while the chain was eased out.
- We also found it very useful to have buzzers in each cabin with the switch at the helm so somebody below could be called on deck without leaving the cockpit.

Arthur Beiser, *Ardent Spirit*

---

sea for weeks on end. Too many bodies (along with their personalities) on board make the potential for conflicts or tensions much more likely. Make sure that your crew has the proper attitude for long offshore passages. However, confidence that a crew member will not panic in a crisis and that they are willing to ask if they have a doubt about something they see or hear on watch is paramount to a safe and successful voyage and, in my view, perhaps as important as experience.'

For Dave Ungless 'the biggest problem is crew changes and the need to be at certain pick-up and drop-off ports for deadline schedules such as pre-booked flights. All of our tough sailing experiences due to inclement weather and storms have been the result of crew travel deadlines that had to be met. Without such time schedules we would normally wait for suitable sailing conditions but the pressures of having to arrive at a certain port by a certain date forced us to take abnormal risks.' This was also the firm opinion of Joseph Conrad, well-travelled mariner and successful author. 'More accidents have happened at sea because the captain believed that he needed to be in a certain place by a specific date than any other reason.'

For this reason, Bruce Bandrieux, who sailed his boat from France to Tahiti with casual crew while this survey was in progress, advises that 'in my experience taking on crew can be very successful provided certain rules are followed. Be very precise in what you expect from the people you take on. If you don't want people who smoke, don't take on a smoker even if he promises he won't smoke. If you have to change crew along the way, make sure that the new person is acceptable to the rest of the crew.'

Jim Patek would only take on additional crew at a pinch, 'I prefer one crew member even though it cuts into one's sleep. The best crew member is one's partner. The second best is a friend. Third are your children. There is the parent-child dynamic to manage but this is offset by the reward of the bond that is created and shared forever after. Regarding casual crew, I have had various casual crew in eight years of voyaging. Generally it has worked well but I have had better success when the age difference between the crew and captain has been less than ten years.'

Jim Thomsen is also unsure about taking on crew, 'We tried one long passage with an additional crew member. He was very competent and a long-time friend. Probably the best crew member you could hope for. This allowed a lot more sleep, which was great, but overall we did not enjoy the passage as much as other passages we've done alone. We then decided to make all long passages by ourselves, as we trust each other on watch and Katie is more relaxed without anyone else around.'

Roger Swanson had a different experience, 'I have had over 300 people sail with me during the last 40 years and only three that clearly didn't enjoy the time aboard. It wasn't fun all the time which apparently was what they expected. All three bad experiences were with couples. My advice is: avoid couples that do not have a long history together.'

The participants in the survey also commented on their preferred watch systems. In Murray Atkinson's case, 'when we are three on board, two hour watches with four hours off is a good balance. With only two of us, we have a three hours on, three hours off system when the self-steering is used, but when having to helm manually in bad weather that is reduced to two hours on, two hours off. This worked but was not ideal as there was not enough time off watch for cooking and sleeping as well as all other tasks. I'd like to add that "skipper" is a flexible concept in a husband/wife team with equal experience. Whoever is on watch is in complete charge of the vessel and will only call the other to assist if necessary.'

Jim Thomsen operates a different system, 'Initially we were doing four hour watches. We've changed to six hour watches at night and feel we get plenty of sleep so have no need for additional crew.'

Stu Conway prefers 'three hour daylight watches and two hour night watches. With trade wind passages, even when there is more than just the two of us, we tend to do solo watchkeeping. We all need sleep and those off watch need to be rested and quick to respond if called for help when conditions warrant it.'

José Prieto believes that 'on long passages, the watch time should be optimised when there is a third crew. The skipper should arrange the schedule so that he is available at critical points, such as sail changes, but does not take fixed watches as the others.'

For Arthur Beiser 'one person on watch at a time, with two hours on and six hours off, has worked well. When we crossed the Atlantic the first time, we were seven and there was not enough to do. On the second crossing, we were four and that was a perfect voyage. Now that we sail only shorter distances in the Mediterranean we are often just the two of us and this is also perfect.' When I contacted Arthur for an update for this new edition, he responded that, 'Alas, *Ardent Spirit*, true to her name, had been begging us for the last few years to take her on long cruises as in the past, but at our age (we are both 86) we did not want any longer to face alone the strong storms that were becoming more and more frequent in the Adriatic. So, after 30 years of great pleasure, reluctantly we put *Ardent Spirit* on the market and quickly found a buyer.'

Cruising couples

In December 2017 a yacht ran aground under full sail onto the windward side of Tobago Island in the Caribbean after the skipper had been lost overboard and his wife evacuated at sea. The 44-foot *Vagrant* was being sailed across the Atlantic by the Polish couple Stanislaw Dabrowny, 74, and Elzbieta Dabrowna, 67. They had left the Canary Islands in November and were around 400 miles from Barbados when Stanislaw fell overboard. Apparently he was trying to retrieve the spinnaker at night when he fell or was knocked overboard and was not clipped on nor wearing a life jacket. Unable to handle the boat on her own Elzbieta called their daughter by satellite phone and eventually a rescue operation was put in place and she was taken off the boat. The boat was left adrift still under full sail.

As a result of this tragic accident I decided to ask all those who were sailing as couples if they had made any arrangements to deal with such a situation if the more experienced of them, usually the captain, would be incapacitated.

An interesting finding of a global cruising survey conducted in 2016 was that many more boats on a world voyage were being crewed by couples. Generally, there seems to have been a reduction in the average size of crew on cruising boats. This trend was shown by the figures obtained from the Marquesas, where visiting yachts had an average crew of 2.7, whereas in Cocos Keeling it was 2.6, in St Helena 3.3 and in Vava'u 3.5. At both Cocos Keeling and the Marquesas, well over half the boats were sailed by just couples. An even higher proportion of boats sailed by couples were in the three transatlantic rallies that I organised in 2016. Among the total of 70 boats, 61 were sailed by couples, 40 of them alone, 13 with their children, and 8 also with additional crew.

The majority of participants in the other transatlantic rallies were also sailing couples. As I witnessed a number of problems experienced on such boats, I asked contributors to this latest survey if their boats had been equipped to be easily handled by a small crew. In almost all cases the boats had been thoughtfully prepared and fitted out for this purpose. The most detailed response came from Arthur Beiser and is featured in the sidebar on page 15.

One of the first couples to respond was Patti and James Hunt, who had purchased my second *Aventura* in 1995. 'Since then we have sailed to 73 countries and covered over 45,000 miles. For most of the time we have sailed just the two of us. This was never a problem because *La Aventura* had been purposely conceived and equipped to be sailed short-handed comfortably and efficiently.'

Pete Goss commented that, 'we haven't had to make any special arrangements as the Garcia Exploration 45 has it covered as standard. I think the big thing with sailing two-handed is to be flexible on the watch system so that individual strengths are utilised. We always share sunup, sundown and the main meals. Between that we are pretty relaxed in that as a novice Tracey doesn't like nights so I get a sleep after the evening meal and then cover most of the night and catch up during the day.'

Saundra and Charlie Gray, who had sailed in the Millennium Odyssey round the world rally, pointed out that '*Sea Gem* was set up to be handled by one person but fortunately we did not have to experience that, and the two of us worked very well as a team. Many things can go wrong on a long voyage, and judicious planning is therefore essential. It is also very important to perform regular maintenance, make sure that all systems are in running order, and have backups available. Charlie was so determined to have backups for everything, that I kidded him about where he kept mine.'

Bill Rouse, who had also completed a long world voyage, remarked 'Most of our ten-year world cruise was sailed by just Judy and me. We are very prejudiced in favour of the Amel concept, which is designed for a couple to sail in comfort and security. The concept includes a protected and dry central cockpit with all controls within reach of the helmsperson. It takes no time for the helmsperson to furl the main and genoa, while the two-part pole system is easy enough for almost anyone to rig, including our 12-year old granddaughter.'

In the case of Bill McLaren: '*Vagrant* was set up for short-handed sailing. All work could be done by one person, and whoever was on watch would deal with tacking, reefing or whatever. We had to go to the mast to reef the main, which makes reefing simpler and also means you are used to being on the foredeck. I think this is a good safety feature as the foredeck can be a frightening place if you only go there in an emergency.'

Doug and Judy Decker's *Limerence* was also well prepared, 'we had jib roller furling but did not have mainsail in-mast furling, which we regretted. All lines were brought to an electric winch in the cockpit. For safety reasons, we moved the mainsail traveller from the cockpit to the coachroof forward of the dodger. We had two autopilots, a powerful hydraulic autopilot and a wheel-mounted autopilot as a backup.'

On Burger and Nancy Zapf's *Halekai*, 'all sails were roller furling and could be handled from the cockpit: mainsail, genoa and staysail. However, I wish we also had electric winches, as on a 50-foot boat sails are a lot more to handle than on a 40-footer. For comfort, the cockpit was protected by a hard dodger and roof. We never wore foul weather gear or sea boots in 120,000 blue water miles.'

José Prieto stressed that 'I equipped *Tutatis* to be sailed by one person only and trained Sandra to do all manoeuvres on her own in case of a contingency. At critical moments we were always both in the cockpit. I brought some of my experience as an airline pilot to our trip. Before each passage, I would hold a safety briefing, reminding her what she was expected to do in case of a contingency.'

Bill Stocks was among those who admitted not having made short-handed sailing a priority. 'I would now say that on our 40-foot *Tulameen* it was easier to equip the boat to allow for two-person handling, than having an extra crew. However, we made an effort to avoid becoming too specialised and aimed to make our skills interchangeable, especially in the navigation and radio communication areas. I made up check-lists of everyday procedures and I regarded this as a very good device to improve short-term memory.'

The size of the boat was one of the deciding factors also for Jim and Katie Thomsen. 'One of the reasons we choose the 40-foot Halberg Rassy was its easy handling. From the wheel you can easily reach winches, jib and mainsail sheets. Another decision was to have in-mast furling, something I had never used and was worried about. We went for the electric assisted in-mast furling and it turned out to be the perfect setup and in over 50,000 miles we never had a problem. The great thing about this setup was the ease of reefing with only one of us on watch, as reefing could be done at the push a button. On night watches Katie would reef and unreef whenever the conditions warranted, without needing to wake me.'

Hugh Fraser stressed that 'the safety of Brenda has always been paramount. When I built *Scotia* I drew on my many years of experience sailing in the North Sea; so I fitted 30-inch high lifelines, a deep cockpit, and everything, apart from spinnaker pole and anchors, could be done from the cockpit.'

Ståle and Annelise Larsen have been sailing together for over 30 years, crossing the Atlantic on six separate occasions on their successive *Viking Crusaders*. 'All our boats had been planned and equipped to be sailed short-handed and were very manageable even in bad weather. Annelise does everything on board just like myself, steering, reefing, and navigating. If I were disabled in any way, she would manage to handle the boat herself without any problems.'

Emergency preparations

This was another aspect that was investigated among those long-distance sailors and each was asked about the kind of preparations they had made to deal with an emergency if one or the other might be incapacitated. From their responses it was obvious that all couples had discussed this eventuality and had made proper preparations for it. Jamie Utzschneider, who had just completed a circum-navigation with his wife Jenna and their two children Hazel and Leo on the catamaran *Sophie*, stressed that 'it is essential that both members of a couple should be able to handle the boat on their own in an emergency. Jenna is completely capable of sailing the boat by herself. She knows the boat very well and skippered *Sophie* many times without me on board.' Hugh Fraser started from the premise that each should be able to handle the boat on their own, not just in an emergency, but at all times. 'We retrofitted an in-mast furling mainsail 15 years ago, a good move we never regretted. Brenda can easily reef and never has to go on deck at sea. We also have fuel for 1500 miles at 4 knots. That way she could cope in such a scenario.'

Doug Decker pointed out that 'on *Limerence* we took personal safety very seriously. We wore lifejackets and harnesses at night and were clipped on at all times even in calm weather. We had backup keys for the ignition stored in the nav station. A couple sailing from the ABC Islands to Panama were hit by a wave at night that tore off the hard dodger and threw the captain overboard. The keys were pulled from the ignition. The wife couldn't find backup keys and could not start the engine to attempt to recover her husband. The disabled boat hobbled into the marina in Panama as a sobering lesson to all.'

Mike Beilan commented that 'Sue and I are both capable of handling *Infini* by ourselves. We carried a variety of foresails for all conditions. We used our windvane or autopilot most of the time to escape what I call "the tyranny of steering." We also occasionally practiced man-overboard drills to familiarize ourselves with that procedure.'

James Hunt pointed out that, 'Thankfully Patti knows the boats systems very well and is physically able to sail the boat alone and cope well. We do believe that *La Aventura*'s well-designed layout and systems have helped her to achieve this.'

Bill McLaren admitted that 'Jane was not an expert on the boat systems or navigation, but she knew her way around well enough to get *Vagrant* home without my help. We looked at it a bit like couples that fly light aircraft when the non-pilot learns enough to get the plane back on the ground. Happily we never had to put it to the test!'

Stu Conway also admitted that 'I definitely had much more sailing experience at the outset and when we ventured offshore Julie held the flashlight and passed the tools. But as the voyage progressed, Julie learned how to trim sails, take her turn on watch, manage communications, and take over navigating chores. She challenged my actions and we made decisions together. As experienced by many sailing couples, I began and ended as skipper; Julie began as an apprentice and ended up as the admiral.'

Dave Ungless also admitted 'I always consider myself skipper and the more experienced but even this is a moot point sometimes. For example, making our way north-wards from Hawaii to Victoria, British Columbia, we suffered a knockdown during a particularly nasty storm. I was thrown about the cabin and thought I might have broken my leg. Marie quite calmly ignored my squeals of pain and set about reducing sail herself so that we could run under bare poles; she sorted out our course and the autopilot before attending to me. That's confidence and experience I guess, but we'd never practiced for any of that.'

Dave McCampbell was 'fortunate that Sherry is a computer specialist, expert sailor, navigator, communi-cator and fairly strong for a woman. So I am not too worried about her ability to handle the boat if I am disabled. We do make an effort to both be able to deal with onboard jobs, so if one is disabled, the other can manage.'

When I asked Gary Goodlander that same question his answer was a firm, 'No. Carolyn is with me because she is a wonderful person, not because she is a wonderful sailor. I think it is a mistake to ask your spouse to be able to do everything on the boat. Why? I cannot sew, cook, preserve food, nor make instant friends like her. In many ways she is my superior. We just are who we are and we love each other and that is enough.'

Finances

Make a detailed estimate of anticipated expenses, double it, and then decide if you can stretch your resources to afford it.

Roger Swanson

No voyage should be embarked on without having adequate funds, not just for day-to-day expenses, but also as a reserve for possible emergencies. It is equally important to make suitable arrangements before leaving home so that such funds are easily accessible. The situation is certainly different from 20 or 30 years ago when it was still possible to sail the world on a limited budget. Nowadays, when one has to pay for cruising permits, high marina or port charges, agency fees, expensive fuel, and even for mooring in a previously free anchorage, cruising on a shoestring is, alas, no longer possible. It is therefore advisable to try and set a realistic figure for the possible cost of the voyage before leaving home. Estimating such costs with any degree of accuracy is not easy as a lot depends on how much you have to spend on the boat once underway, and such costs are difficult to estimate as you never know what could break during a long voyage and how much it will cost to put it right. Having a well-prepared boat will certainly keep repair and maintenance costs down, especially as most of the higher costs will have been incurred before the voyage begins. Unexpected costs are obviously impossible to foresee but it would be wise to make allowances for emergencies, as was the case in 2011 when the threat of piracy in the Indian Ocean forced several owners to have their boats shipped from Southeast Asia to the Mediterranean.

Financial matters and the cost of cruising was an important part of the voyage planning survey. Contributors to the survey were asked to state whether their expenses had been as expected, lower or higher, and if higher to name the main cause for that, whether it was due to the cost of living in the countries visited, repair and maintenance costs, docking and marinas fees, or higher cruising costs generally. For simplicity's sake all costs are quoted in US dollars.

Over half (31) regarded their costs to have been as expected, while the rest were evenly split between those who had found them to be lower and those who found them higher than they had made provision for. In most cases the higher than expected expenditure was caused by repair and maintenance and in a few cases by the high cost of marina fees in some parts of the world. This was the point made by Barry Esrig: 'Docking fees have soared in the past few years. Marina fees have gone up and services have become more expensive. Croatia often charges for anchoring, while Turkey now requires an agent to clear in and out.' Jim Thomsen agreed: 'Marinas in the Med are expensive but we wanted to visit many cities in the Western Med so had no choice. Also the US dollar to euro rate was not good.'

Jim Patek made the same comment, 'On my latest voyage I observed right away, and with some sadness, that the day of the shoestring cruiser is gone. Marinas and docking fees are now really high. Many more yachts are cruising now and are creating a supply/demand situation that did not exist on my first voyage. In addition, in some places where we used to anchor, one must now use docking or mooring facilities. So, be realistic about how far you can go on the money you have.'

The financial side of a long voyage can be such an essential factor in the overall success of the voyage that I included this subject in my latest survey and contacted all those contributors who had commented on finances in the initial survey and asked them to confirm that they still have those views or update them if necessary.

The first to respond was Jim Patek. 'I will stick with my comments in general but I would add that it is certainly possible to plan a fulfilling voyage that can take you to places where you will not be required to hire an agent, pay expensive entry fees and be able to anchor at no cost. On my most recent passage from New Zealand to Alaska via Micronesia, Guam and Japan, I encountered no obstacles to cruising at minimal cost and while there are few anchorages per se in Japan, there is always a place to moor in a fishing harbour at no charge.'

Gary Goodlander found on his second circumnavigation 'that our costs were occasionally higher than expected due to a combination of various factors. Clearing in and out costs are now skyrocketing and places which used to want $4 now want $200! I caught up with Gary just as he was leaving on yet another open-ended circumnavigation and his response to my request to add to his previous comments was very clear. 'In fact it is getting worse by the day. What was $200 is now double that! Clearing into the British Virgin Islands used to be a dime; last year I spent hundreds of dollars clearing in on several occasions. It is one thing for an Australian sailor coming to Tonga to fork out over $200–300 for the entire winter season; quite another for me who was in the Cooks last week and will be in Fiji and Vanuatu next month.'

Also preparing for another world voyage was José Prieto. 'For our previous circumnavigation we planned the voyage to be made in 3 years, and had resources for

The cost of major repair work can seriously affect the cruising budget.

a point also made by Dave Lynn who advised anyone planning to leave on a voyage 'to expect maintenance and repair costs to be always higher than allowed for'.

As to day-to-day expenditure, Marc Martinez also found that 'except in the Lesser Antilles, life is not that expensive elsewhere. You can keep costs down by being independent, also, by having a comfortable boat and a watermaker, so there is no need to go into marinas.'

Bill McLaren was pleasantly surprised to discover that 'although we never kept careful accounts, cruising was a lot cheaper than living at home is now! We have seen every-thing from rock-bottom basic budgets to "money no object" cruisers. What makes the biggest difference is the use of marinas, eating out, land travel and how much boat work you do yourself.'

that time. I kept a reserve outside of normal day-to-day expenses, for any eventuality such as health, which in fact we did not have. We spend an average $1500 per month during the trip, including all usual living expenses, maintenance, marinas, etc. We always tried to stay as short as possible in marinas and whenever possible we had meals on board. I did all maintenance work myself.'

Lars Hässler also found costs to be higher than expected: 'They always seem more expensive, especially maintenance and repair. As far as your cruising budget goes, never underestimate costs – calculate high so you can cope with surprises as they always occur.'

Several skippers among those who found the costs of cruising to be as they had expected pointed out that by leaving with a well-prepared boat, with engine, sails and all essential equipment checked and serviced, the day-to-day running of the boat ended up costing little, provided the gear was properly maintained and any running repairs were made by themselves. As Paul Donnerup explained: 'Before setting out I had spent about $85,000 on new equipment and getting the boat in top condition as my plan was to be very well equipped and have many spares on board, so that the running expenses would not be high.' In the meantime Paul had clocked over 75,000 miles and was going through a major refit in Malaysia. 'Costs are much higher than expected, quality and reliability leave much to be desired, but I hope to be soon on my way again and hopefully reach Europe by 2019 bringing this long drawn-out circumnavigation to a happy end.' This is

Kurt Braun found cruising costs as expected for 'the simple reason that the crew still need to eat whether land based or cruising. Grocery or restaurant prices vary but people need to eat everywhere in the world and so we find the food budget while cruising no different than on land.'

Stu Conway also found costs to be as expected, 'Before leaving I spent a reasonable amount replacing and upgrading components. I ordered best quality new sails, I removed finicky bits (air conditioning, washer-dryer), and replaced all electronic equipment with the latest models. I still had lots of repair and maintenance work en route but nothing major. Things like fuel, food, entertainment came in a little higher than anticipated, but we took advantage of many more activities than we ever imagined we would do, we took lots of tours and enjoyed the experience of local cultures. Our circumnavigation was a dream realised.'

This view was shared by Ann Harsh, 'We felt we were on a trip of a lifetime and we did not want to exclude experiences due to money. We did not go overboard on spending and found that many of the most enjoyable experiences cost very little.'

Participants in the survey were asked to make a general comment on their cruising budget and many would agree with Steve Moss when he said 'it's never enough'.

Mike Beilan would hardly disagree. 'What I said six years ago still holds true, although there are so many variables that a specific monthly amount is a difficult to pin down. Besides the usual living expenses we found that

World cruising in style or on a shoestring?

Sooner or later anyone will gasp at the total spent on routine maintenance and we were no exception, although our Amel Super Maramu left on this voyage in perfect condition when she was launched at the factory in France in January 2003. Maintenance on an older boat or different quality construction will likely cost more. Bill does all the work himself but if you have to pay professionals for their labour instead of acting as your own mechanic, refrigeration specialist, electrician, rigger, plumber, computer consultant, etc., the cost goes up.

Another expense is insurance, which we have as our boat is our home and does represent a substantial financial asset. Learning of all the boats lost in the South Pacific in recent years reinforced our decision to continue to carry full insurance on the boat. We do realise that if the boat is damaged, we would be responsible for paying for the environmental damage that might result, especially from diesel carried in the main tank. The cost of that alone is enough to make us realise that, in today's world, boats definitely need to be insured.

We kept accurate records of all our expenditure, which averaged $53,000 per year. This annual average increased dramatically by the unplanned expense of shipping *BeBe* from Southeast Asia to the Mediterranean to avoid piracy attacks.

On completion of our ten-year circumnavigation, Judy and I would like to add to the above that there is a significant difference between world cruising and weekend or charter boat sailing. We realize that most world cruisers begin with no long distance cruising experience. When we started world cruising we had 15 years of sailing experience, had owned two large monohulls, but had never sailed overnight. Our sailing experience had previously been for fun, now our sailboat was to be our home. We believe that many people beginning on a world adventure do not understand this critical difference... and this really impacts expenses. Prior to world cruising all of our sailing had been more like short episodes of vacation time. However, to enjoy an extended time while world cruising, people should attempt to live similar to the way they lived prior to cruising. A simple example is if you showered daily before cruising, you should plan on the availability of water to shower at least daily while cruising, or if you eat a good steak once a week, you should plan to purchase good steaks for once a week. Unfortunately, and usually the man, figures that the couple will change significantly, bathing in saltwater, wearing only a bathing suit, and eating what he catches... or, some degree of that concept. We have seen some real disappointment when the financial cruising plan does not match the lifestyle prior to cruising.

An old adage is that once you have compiled a cruising budget, double it, and that will be about what you will actually spend. We certainly did.

Bill and Judy Rouse, *BeBe*

other costs have become much higher than expected. 'Our health insurance coverage took a big bite of our monthly budget as its cost went up anywhere from 20 to 40% yearly. Boat insurance is also a considerable expense and is geographically limited. At times we put riders on our basic policy to extend our boundaries; all this at extra cost.'

His words reminded me of a comment made by a participant in the Millennium Odyssey round the world rally: 'The cost of cruising? It's something that I've been afraid to really find out.'

Nevertheless, according to Barry Esrig, 'a cruising budget is a great idea, and one should stick to it. To do that one needs to find out in advance the fixed fees (cruising permits, clearance and departure fees, haul-out charges, etc). Make sure that the budget includes an allowance for unexpected expenses, repairs and also the impact of fluctuating exchange rates.'

Alfredo Giacon found that a cruising budget breaks down approximately as 'boat maintenance and repair 40 percent, food 30 percent, telephone and internet 10 percent, marinas only 10 percent as we spend most of the time at anchor'.

Guy Oury pointed out that 'expenditure varies wildly depending on people's expectations and style of cruising. Many seem to find it hard to leave consumerism behind. Also those who rely on others to do repairs and maintenance will need a much higher budget.'

Bill Rouse, who kept an accurate record of all expenses during a ten-year long world voyage reckoned on an average annual budget of about $50,000, and provided an accurate record of their expenditure. Bill's comments are featured in the above sidebar, and a spreadsheet of their annual budget can be downloaded here: cornellsailing. com/downloads.

In the case of Beth Leonard and Evans Starzinger, who could make a compairson between their two circumnavigations, their costs had been higher than expected on the first, while on their second voyage their expenses were as expected. As they pointed out, this was no doubt due to knowing what to allow for but also doing it on a well-prepared boat. Beth Leonard: 'We've interviewed dozens of friends about their budgets. Key factors in falling short: not spending enough on the boat before leaving and then trying to get the boat right in the first year out, currency fluctuations, unexpected emergencies – normally medical.'

In my own case, I also found on my round the world voyage on *Aventura III* that my allowance had been generally right. My annual expenditure was approximately £20,000 ($40,000 at the exchange rate at the time) which included all living and boat expenses, and also regular flights home. Over a period of eight years I left the boat unattended on a dozen occasions in various marinas or boatyards, either to fly home or visit places which I wanted to see but were too far off my route. I found that this way of cruising in stages not only suited my lifestyle but was also a very pleasant way to sail around the world in a relaxed and unrushed fashion.

This manner of cruising in stages has become a common occurrence and several of the sailors interviewed are now doing it, although, as Jim Thomsen discovered, it is a more costly affair as it involves the expense of leaving the boat unattended in a yard or marina, as well as the flights home. 'We didn't consider the price of leaving *Tenaya* in a marina for a month and two airline tickets home from expensive places like Tahiti and New Zealand. But we will continue to return home once a year, as this suits us perfectly. That system worked fine for our ten years of full-time cruising.'

Dave Ungless had a similar experience. 'Logistic travel costs for family crew changes and the need for my wife to return frequently to the UK affects our budget enormously. Boat maintenance is expensive when there is a need to ship out parts urgently and this seems to be experienced by all sailing yachts we've come across. Marinas and their fees can be avoided but boatyards can be expensive. If you set a budget before leaving then it will drive you crazy trying to stick to it. Just double the amount you think you need and you'll be about halfway there. Cost of living expenses are climbing everywhere.'

Contributors to the survey gave a number of helpful tips to those planning a long voyage. Luc Callebaut urged sailors who wish to keep costs down 'to learn how to live locally, barter, reuse, recycle, think outside the box!' Luc and Jackie sent this later addition to their comments. 'Try to develop different sources of income before and during your voyage so your cruising kitty won't dry up suddenly. Ideally have some sort of active source of income that you can do from your boat, such as an internet business, or some kind of seasonal/temporary earning activity.' This is good advice from the expert on 'living locally' as he and Jackie Lee have been roaming the Pacific for many years, earning a living as they go along, from working as divers on pearl farms in the Tuamotus, driving a tourist bus in Tahiti, producing promotional videos in Vanuatu, but also often doing charitable work and helping local communities.

Another long-term cruising couple who took to this way of life wrote, 'We have disposed of our house, most of our possessions and said goodbyes to the family. We'll fly back to see grandkids from time to time but this is a complete life change for us. Our attitude is to roll with the punches, travel when and where the best weather allows and enjoy the world while our health allows it.'

This is also Burger Zapf's advice. 'If you have real estate expect it to increase in value. Expect your boat to lose value! You will not sail forever. If you sold your house and put everything into your boat you might not be able to afford a home later on.'

My own advice on budgets and cruising generally is to allow more than planned and have recourse to funds in a serious emergency. But I also urge you to think carefully before following this last example and making a clean break with shore life. If at all possible you should keep a shore base so if you are forced to change plans, whether for health or financial reasons, you have somewhere to return, especially during a period of economic uncertainty and creeping inflation.

Self-sufficiency

Necessity is the mother of invention. When you're in the middle of nowhere and something breaks, you've got to be resourceful and imaginative enough to make things work.

Dave Lynn

In today's world, when help is usually just a phone call away, the ability to be self-sufficient has been lost by many people – not only the skills required, but even the attitude to try to deal with a problem before calling on outside assistance. This kind of attitude will not do on a boat in the middle of the ocean where you must be able to deal with any emergency yourself. Many are the skills required of the skipper of an offshore boat, such as the ability to repair and improvise, navigate without electronic aids,

The crew of this boat dismasted in mid-Atlantic managed to sail over 1,000 miles with a jury-rig.

be able to dive, give first aid in an emergency, and most certainly have the ability to sail the boat if the engine is out of order. To be able to deal with emergencies, the boat should carry a comprehensive set of tools and essential spares as well as backups for the most important pieces of equipment. There should also be a well-stocked medical chest and at least a rudimentary knowledge of how to deal with a medical emergency.

The subject of self-sufficiency generated a keen response among contributors to the voyage planning survey as many of these experienced world voyagers held strong views on the utmost importance of sailors being self-sufficient. The three main areas that were investigated were tools, spares and the ability to dive and work underwater. Contributors were asked to describe their set of tools, as well as the spares they carried, as comprehensive, adequate or minimal. Well over half (33) described their range of tools as being comprehensive, on 23 boats they were considered adequate and there was only one skipper who described his range of tools as minimal.

Hugh Fraser described his tools as 'truly comprehensive: from a welder to a sewing machine. I have tools to fix just about anything.' So did Gary Goodlander. 'If you are poor, you have to carry a lot of tools. I have tools for woodworking, mechanical and fibreglass repairs. In comparison to that, his spares were described as minimal. 'I used to carry starter motors, alternators and a spare of everything. Now I just carry a head gasket and injectors and fly in the others. It is cheaper because most of the stuff was getting damaged by the dampness.' This is also the

reason why Marc Martinez carries a comprehensive set of tools but 'only essential parts for maintenance as I can order from anywhere online'.

Jim Patek described both his set of tools and spares only as adequate: 'I have had a few mishaps underway such as breaking a spinnaker pole, electrical gremlins affecting charging, instrumentation and refrigeration, a burst hydraulic hose, leaking or failing pumps but nothing that could not be managed with the tools and spares on board.' Jim Patek also suggested 'that it is a good idea to have a "shore crew" who will help you obtain the parts you require should you find yourself with a maintenance issue that goes beyond what you might be able to reasonably carry as a spare. An example, when our freezer failed while sailing to Guam, my brother was able to access technical support for trouble shooting advice, source a replacement unit and have it shipped to Guam so that it was on its way by the time we arrived.'

Patrick Canut had little sympathy for those who are not able to do even simple repairs, 'There is an old French saying that bad workers always blame their tools just as, in my view, a bad sailor always blames his boat.'

Asked to describe their range of spares, 29 skippers considered them to be comprehensive, 23 as adequate and five as minimal. Even among those who described them as adequate, several pointed out that they did carry anything they regarded as essential.

Bill McLaren described his spares as comprehensive but 'you still never have the right bit. It is the First Law of Spares. I think you should carry all consumables you might need (filters, drive belts, pump spares, light bulbs, fuses and the like) as well as essential items like a spare starter motor and alternator. There is no point in carrying spare internal parts for the engine as the chances of you having everything you need to effect a repair are minimal. If you have to ship in something you might as well ship in the lot.'

Marc Martinez advised others to 'carry a good supply of consumables, such as filters, impellers, etc, as they can be very expensive in some places. And keep them in a plastic box with a tight lid to protect them from humidity, which you should do with all your spares.' In my own case, as I had on board a vacuum packer for food, I had all vulnerable spares vacuum packed.

Emergency in the Northwest Passage

After the decision was taken to abandon the attempt of a transit of the Northwest Passage because of the unfavourable ice conditions, we turned around to sail back to Greenland. With gale-force winds forecast for the following day, and being in the typical calm before a storm, we were motoring fast towards the open sea. During Doina's watch I was woken by a loud noise from the engine. I rushed into the cockpit and stopped the engine as it was making a rattling metallic sound. It sounded like we had picked up something on the propeller. I restarted the engine briefly but the noise persisted.

With the engine out of action and an imminent gale upon us, I needed to find out if we had indeed caught something in the propeller. I mounted the GoPro camera with an underwater housing onto the end of an ice pole, lowered it over the side and managed to get a good view of the propeller. A thick black rope was wound around the propeller shaft, with its end trailing behind. I realised that something more serious might have happened, so went to look at the engine and found that the bolts between the propeller shaft and transmission had sheared. To have picked up a rope in those pristine waters, where we had not seen a single fishing boat, was almost impossible to believe. But we had, and it had been strong enough to immobilise the propeller shaft and rip it off its mounts. With much drifting ice as well as large icebergs still about, and the nights getting longer as we moved south, not being able to use the engine for the remaining 1,000 miles to Nuuk would have been a serious handicap.

My mind was soon focused on the imminent gale, so we reefed down and continued sailing until we had consistent winds of over 35 knots. We hove to with three reefs in the mainsail and most of the staysail rolled up. In spite of the large seas, we were quite comfortable and easily rode out the gale. After a dozen hours, the wind started going down and I could work on the engine. Although I had no spare bolts on board, I found some longer bolts and cut them down to size with the electric angle grinder. I retrieved from the bilge the sheared-off bolts, and recuperated their nuts. Hanging upside down over the back of the engine, I managed to pull back the propeller shaft sufficiently to reconnect it to the transmission.

It was now time to deal with the remains of the rope. Although I was able to turn the propeller shaft by hand and it felt as it were free, I dared not start the engine and put it in gear. I donned my dry diving suit and kitted myself out with all the gear needed for a dive in ice-cold water, but decided not to use a tank for a job that may only take a few minutes. Attached to the boat with a safety line, I came close to the trailing rope and managed to cut off some of it, but the violent rolling of the boat, with my head banging against the hull, forced me to give up. But at least I had been able to ascertain that the propeller was indeed free.

Getting out of the water weighed down by 12 kg of lead weights, with the boat bouncing violently in the rough swell, required a superhuman effort. Although I was wearing a dry suit, the hood was not dry and I could feel the cold getting to my head. I knew that I was in a critical situation and, as an experienced diver, was aware that I had to get out of the water quickly because I had only about one minute before serious hypothermia would set in and I may no longer be able to act rationally. It was the sight of Doina standing helplessly above me that gave me the strength to lie on my back and lift my feet one by one out of the water so that she could reach down and pull off my large fins. I then managed to put my foot on the lowest rung of the ladder and was helped up the rest of the way. I dropped exhausted into the cockpit, and Doina later told me that I could hardly speak and sounded incoherent.

When I had recovered, I started the engine and engaged the forward gear, but kept it at slow revs. I checked the propeller with the underwater camera and could see it turning freely, the end of the rope trailing harmlessly behind. After half an hour of motoring, I checked the bolts and they were all tight.

Eight days later we were in Nuuk, where once again I donned my dry suit, but this time also a diving tank. In the calm clear water I reached the propeller, where the black line was still trailing idly in the current. I cut it off with a serrated knife, but could not manage to cut the rest, which was coiled so tightly that it had fused to the propeller-shaft housing. That was a job that had to wait until *Aventura* could be hauled out at a US boatyard, 3,500 miles from where the incident had happened.

From '200,000 miles, A Life of Adventure'

In Dave Ungless' view 'regardless of the tools and spares you carry, there is only so much you can repair yourself. Most sailing yachts we've come across experience the same electronics problems regardless of make or price. Carry spares of anything critical.'

Steve Moss fully agreed as 'the problems that I encountered needed specialist services or equipment. No matter how many spares you have you won't have the one you need.' Nonetheless, Dave Lynn advised others 'to carry spares for anything you can't live or don't want to live without'.

In the case of Mike Beilan, 'as we were planning to go well off the beaten track, we carried fibreglass, epoxy supplies and spares upon spares. At one point we carried 4 spare alternators, admittedly a bit of an exaggeration! However, it is essential to have the right belts, enough oil for several changes, a small hill of filters, an emergency anchor, extra halyards, sail tape, lines of various dimensions and lengths, spare blades for the windvane… the list just goes on and on.'

John Whyte 'started out with more spares than were necessary but gradually as they deteriorated in the harsh environment ended up with those that were truly necessary and useful. I used both the spare starter motor and alternator twice. We had only one serious emergency when we lost steering 120 miles north of New Zealand and had to use the emergency tiller and autopilot to get back to Opua. It needed a bit of ingenuity to set up but it worked.'

When asked to comment on self-sufficiency and the ability to deal with emergency repairs generally, no one would disagree with Hugh Fraser's comment that 'serious cruisers should be able to carry out emergency repairs'. His fellow Scotsman, Bill McLaren, stressed that 'it is one of the most important requirements. It so happens that I am a marine engineer by profession but you do not need specialist skills. You need the confidence to have a go and some basic skills with tools. There is a simple adage that if it is bust, it is of no use to you and you might as well have a go at fixing it.'

Bill McLaren added this comment. 'I still believe strongly in the principle that simplicity trumps most other requirements. If it is not there, it can't break, is a useful adage. Modern electronics are very wonderful but the stress owners suffer to keep it all working and the problems of electrical generation should not be underestimated. For example, Jane and I recently did a delivery of a 48-foot yacht from Helsinki to Denmark. It was a wonderful, exciting and high performance boat, but it had 22 rope clutches around the cockpit, more than ten valves and several pumps involved in getting fuel around the boat and very complex electrical circuits. I spent many hours chasing ground faults (potentially serious with an aluminium hull) and it was more of a struggle than it should have been.'

Marc Martinez agrees and stressed that 'the least one should be able to do is get the engine running again after a fuel blockage, flat batteries, etc, which surprisingly some people are unable to do'. With this in mind, Jim Thomsen suggested that 'it is important to understand how everything operates and also to have good repair manuals'. Erick Bouteleux strongly recommends carrying manufacturers' parts catalogues as 'it is so much more efficient to order a spare by its number than having to describe it'. He also advised to have 'proper 220-volt electric tools to be run off an inverter rather than battery-operated ones which have no power and get quickly discharged'.

Beth Leonard remarked that 'the more remote the area you intend to cruise, the more critical it is that you be self-sufficient. Our ideal was to make the basic boat, hull, mast, steering, as strong as possible and not to have anything on the boat we couldn't fix ourselves unless we have a bulletproof backup for it or we're willing and able to live without it.'

Arthur Beiser made the same point. 'Our first step in being self-sufficient for long periods was to convert two of the original five water tanks on *Ardent Spirit* to fuel tanks. This provided 1,432 litres of diesel fuel, which gave a range under power of over 2,000 nautical miles. Water capacity became 970 litres and we also had a 62 l/hr watermaker. Other changes included an extra large freezer, 18 kg of LPG in four tanks for the galley stove (enough for over four months), and an electric washing machine.'

Bill Stocks believes that 'sailors seem to be much more capable of innovation and problem solving than the general public. It is really necessary for the yacht owner to be able to cope with unexpected problems. If you do not have an innovative mind and are not confident that you can and will solve unexpected problems as they come up, then living on a boat can be hard going. In port, you can hire people to fix broken stuff, but there is no one to help you when you are out there! The trouble is, that depending upon the location, hiring workers to fix broken stuff can be very trying, because of both quality and cost of the repair.'

Paul Donnerup was of exactly the same opinion. 'While in Malaysia I decided to give *New Dawn* a full refit, so I had a new teak deck installed (not happy with the work), new batteries, as well as lots of other job. It's not easy to get quality work done in Malaysia, despite what some people write. They couldn't fix my autopilot and radar, so I had to single-hand to Phuket to have it done. Expensive and frustrating.'

Stu Conway's attitude is that 'if you sail a lot or a little, you have to do your own work. I'm happy not because I think something on my boat won't break but because I know that when it does, I can fix it. Having your equipment regularly serviced by professionals will save a lot of potential anguish. You can also brainstorm with other sailors on radio nets or forums, where there is lots of advice available for the asking.'

Luc Callebaut has that same approach: 'We learn as much as we can from our own experience and that of other cruisers. We always try to fix anything ourselves under the guidance of somebody more experienced if we feel that we might not know enough. When hiring a professional to do a job, we try to quickly judge if that professional knows what he is doing. Never trust local specialists who may not know boats.'

An observation that I made having been in close contact with sailors taking part in recent transatlantic rallies is just how much more they depended on electronic equipment, and the serious problems encountered by the fact that the faulty equipment was often impossible to be repaired with the means available on board or finding a specialist capable of putting it right in some places, even among those regularly visited by cruising boats. This was a point stressed by Dave McCampbell. 'There's one burning issue that comes up all the time when talking with other long distance cruisers, and that is the continual failure of onboard equipment. This seems to be common to all sailboat types regardless of design, price, build or brand. We have had these discussions time and time again with sailors who have been stuck in some remote location making temporary or ad hoc repairs, which seems to have become such a necessary survival skill when long distance sailing, although it usually surpasses the skills needed to sail a boat. Equipment failure is never the talk at boat shows, only when we've grown our grey beards do we accumulate that knowledge.'

The ability to dive and carry out at least some simple jobs underwater, such as clearing a fouled propeller, is rightly considered to be an essential part of self-sufficiency. Yet even in this survey there were two boats on which no one could do a job underwater, not even with a mask and snorkel. On all other boats that took part in the survey there was someone in the crew who could dive. Thirty-five boats had diving equipment on board, with 24 having only tanks while 11 also had a compressor. Among the latter, nine also carried a hookah breathing apparatus as a backup. Among those who had no diving equipment on board was Klaus Girzig, 'That was a big mistake and it was one item I missed during my circumnavigation.'

All of those who had a hookah arrangement found it very useful, as described by Phil Gibbins, 'We did carry tanks initially then switched to a small compressor with 100 feet of hose as I found this arrangement more useful for doing underwater work on the boat.' Beth Leonard agreed: 'We carried a hookah that runs off our batteries and a full drysuit for high-latitude waters.' Doug Decker found this arrangement excellent, 'We carried all scuba gear, two air tanks, and a compressor which was connected to a 60-foot hookah. The compressor could operate off the inverter without shore power, and was very useful in cleaning the hull and doing maintenance jobs underwater.'

To conclude this part of the survey, contributors were asked to give some useful tips to anyone preparing to leave on an ocean voyage. Dave Ungless stressed that 'there is a critical need to be as self-sufficient as possible. If you don't have the skills to deal with emergency repairs then you soon acquire them. On-the-job learning is best achieved by being thrown into the deep end.' Mike Beilan agreed, 'We're always learning, which frequently involves a better approach to problem solving. I've always said we pay for our education, whether in time, money, or both. Emergency repairs should be part of the preparation for voyaging offshore. Tools, manuals and a willingness to tackle projects should be foremost.'

Several skippers highlighted the satisfaction that comes from being able to deal with problems as they occur, and the capability of standing up to the challenges that you may be faced with. John Jameson derives great satisfaction from 'being totally independent for months on end, whether at sea or at anchor in remote locations. For that reason I try to resist the temptation to acquire equipment that requires factory support. I derive deep satisfaction from having dealt with a dismasting in the mid-Atlantic, and major collision damage off the west coast of Madagascar.'

It is a feeling shared by Tere Batham, 'Being prepared and able to tackle your own repairs and maintenance adds a greater, more fulfilling dimension to your cruising experience. Those cruisers who are constantly looking for local fix-it men tend to be very frustrated!'

Phil Gibbins also finds that 'being able to fix most things underway makes the passage enjoyable. After a while, when you realise that problems are not life-threatening, knowing that you can fix most things gives you the drive to explore places most will not venture to and you find these to be the most memorable experiences.'

John Gratton is convinced that 'this is something that the skipper needs to be able to do. We know of people who didn't do any of the work on their boats and as a result didn't know what to do when things went wrong. Being involved in the selection, placement and installation of a piece of equipment gives the skipper the basis for troubleshooting and repairing it later. Don't short yourself on these experiences just because you can afford to have someone else do the work.'

Mike Dorsett also believes that 'there are two ways to run a successful voyage, both of which include good preparation of the yacht. The first is with a large budget when money can then be thrown at problems. This works until you are in the middle of nowhere. The second is full self-sufficiency. Certainly for those of us on a limited budget, a sound knowledge of all the boat's systems is essential.'

This was also the opinion of Dave McCampbell, 'Get your boat basically outfitted and then do some cruising to understand what's really important to you. If you have to hire someone to do something on the boat, make it part of the deal that he teaches you how to repair it yourself next time. We aim to be totally self-sufficient, both in skills, spares and jury-rig-type equipment. This means we lug a lot of stuff around with us, but it also means that we are totally in control of our lives and our cruising. Our friends in remote places often refer to me as their supply clerk.'

This is the reason why Kurt Braun advised that 'if sailing on a vessel with complex mechanical systems in remote areas or countries with difficult customs officials or poor shipping facilities, more spares and on board expertise will be essential'. To which he added: 'Preventative maintenance in proper ports is preferable to emergency repairs in exotic ones.'

As a professional delivery skipper Dale Norley 'must be prepared for anything. I have had to replace halyards, standing rigging, wind instruments, all kinds of engine repairs and jury-rigs for unexpected problems. I recommend everyone to carry assorted rolls of Rescue Tape, which is a self-fusing silicone repair product with infinite uses, as it has replaced many parts and seals along the way for me.'

Doug Decker once got out of trouble with just such a magic emergency material, 'We had an epoxy "liquid steel" tube which came in handy when the engine fresh water pump casing began to leak. We were at anchor in Costa Rica hundreds of miles from any town and while sailing was our preferred choice, there were many reefs and rocks and so we needed to fix the engine, which we did. So do make sure you have on board the complete service manuals for all major systems.'

Alex Whitworth has this advice to would-be voyagers: 'Creative improvisation is the go-to at all times. Know the boat, know what you have aboard and think laterally. There is usually something that can be done. Go through potential disasters in your head in the quiet times as it makes for more fluid thinking in a crisis. I call it catastrophising.'

As a professional airline pilot José Prieto stressed the importance of being prepared for any eventuality. 'For our previous world voyage I opted for a 40-foot sailboat, which I found suitable for a couple to live in, manoeuver safely and efficiently. I equipped it to be totally self-sufficient in terms of energy and potable water: wind generator, solar panels and two watermakers. We had both SSB radio and a satellite phone. We had three independent GPS navigation systems, with antennas and backup charts as well. I had a complete mini-workshop on board, with all essential spares. An important item that was part of my planning for the previous trip and will be also for the next one: first aid. We had a fully equipped pharmacy, and a collection of medical instruments and suture materials. I had paramedic training and I learned how to make sutures. In the dental area, we had a first aid kit and I learned some dental techniques in case of an emergency. It is worth noting that during the trip of almost three years, we did not even have a cold, probably due to the quality of life and little contact with crowds.'

As a former jet pilot and mountaineer Mike Johnson has the same approach, 'We often ponder the risks of a circumnavigation and reported incidents. Certainly the risk levels are changing, but we have always taken the view that the level of risk taken depends on knowledge, preparation and constant review. We use a simple acronym for most of our decision making – DODAR: diagnose the problem; options available; decide on the most appropriate; act upon it; review how it is working. If necessary return to step one. This may sound simplistic but we have seen so many minor situations develop into disasters because people didn't even begin at the first step.'

This is the kind of mental attitude that must be understood and accepted by anyone planning an offshore voyage. Alone on a small boat in the middle of an ocean, far from land and outside help, a skipper has his destiny, and that of his crew, in his own hands. Nothing can describe this condition better than the words of the poet WE Henley.

It matters not how strait the gate,
How charged with punishments the scroll,
I am the master of my fate:
I am the captain of my soul.

The right attitude

If you want to build a ship, don't drum up people to collect wood and don't assign them tasks and work, but rather teach them to long for the endless immensity of the sea.

Antoine de Saint-Exupéry

The choice of a boat that incorporates your main priorities is absolutely crucial for the successful outcome of a voyage but there are other factors which can have a serious effect on its success and they are, as mentioned before, crew, finances and self-sufficiency. There is, however, an even more important factor that can have a bearing on the success of a voyage and that is your attitude to sea and sailing, and to cruising life in general. Setting off on a long voyage and a life on the ocean is a major decision that entails a complete change of both lifestyle and mentality, something that some people may not have considered carefully. Leaving on a voyage in a sailing yacht just because it is a convenient way to see the world is not a good enough reason. I have come across this situation among sailors whom I have met, some of whom were unwilling, or more often unable, to make the transition from a shore-based person to becoming a full-time sailor. This may not be a great problem on a relatively short voyage, such as a return voyage to the Caribbean or Hawaii, but it can have serious consequences for those who leave on a longer voyage of several years. In the final analysis, the ultimate success of a voyage does not depend on the boat, but on you and your attitude.

In my many years of sailing I have met many outstanding people, and invariably what made them stand

Enjoying a fresh breeze with Erick Bouteleux in the Bay of St Tropez.

out was their attitude. What I most admired in them was their profound respect for the sea, and how being on the ocean came to them naturally, undoubtedly because they loved what they were doing. Some I met while cruising, others as participants in the various sailing events which I organised, and over the years several have become close friends. On the eve of my first Atlantic crossing in 1976 I met Erick Bouteleux, also sailing around the world with a young family, and during the next six years our tracks crossed repeatedly, and continue to do so right up to now. During that same voyage I also encountered Albert Fletcher, one of the most skilful sailors I have ever met.

But it was the rallies which gave me the opportunity to know some other remarkable people, one of them in the very first ARC in 1986. Although suffering from multiple sclerosis and confined to a wheelchair, Ernst Torp crossed the Atlantic with a crew of friends and liked the experience so much that he did it again the following year.

Also in Las Palmas I first met Pierre Ribes as he was preparing his 26 foot *Sphinx* for his annual single-handed voyage to West Africa. A serious accident had left him crippled and being no longer able to work he took up sailing. Every year Pierre would load up his boat with medicines, medical equipment and used spectacles collected from French hospitals and take them to Senegal where he distributed them personally to village clinics. Pierre and his faithful *Sphinx* were reported lost at sea in 2005 while on their regular trip to West Africa.

Few sailors would be able to match, nor would they like to imitate, Bill Butler's record: Bill signed up for the America 500 Columbus anniversary rally in 1992, but rather than sail straight from Florida to the start in Spain with his wife Simonne, decided to take the longer westbound route to Europe via the Pacific and Indian Oceans. After their *Siboney* was sunk by pilot whales west of Galapagos, and they were rescued after more than two months adrift in a liferaft, Bill rushed to Miami, bought another boat, named her *New Chance*, crossed the Atlantic to Spain, this time by the shorter route, then sailed in company with another 146 boats the historic route of discovery to America. Forever looking for new challenges, Bill crossed the Atlantic again and also the European continent by taking *New Chance* through the Rhine-Danube waterway system to the Black Sea. Not the man to rest on his laurels, he then circumnavigated the whole of South America 'because I wanted to see Cape Horn with my own eyes before I die' (see page 262).

There are other sailors whose attitude to the sea should be an inspiration and example to anyone who endeavours to follow in their wake. Arthur and Germaine Beiser have been sailing together for over six decades while Saundra

An ice age in old age

Now well past the 65 years mark, many of them spent navigating the oceans (including a family circumnavigation of seven years, sailing to the Antarctic Peninsula, followed by two forays north, first to Spitsbergen, then Greenland), with the arrival of the seventh decade it became obvious that my youth was rapidly being left behind. Was pottering along the coasts of Europe for the rest of my life all that was left to me? Before leaving for the second time for Greenland, on a voyage via the Azores direct from my home port of St Raphael in the south of France, a friend asked me what motivated me to continue to undertake voyages to such unusual destinations.

The answer was not as simple as I first thought, both because of the destination and route chosen and undoubtedly also because of the age of the skipper. I love the sea and long passages and this passion has not diminished with time, yet one more ocean crossing cannot simply be just one more. There is the feeling of anticipation that takes over during the preparatory period, getting the boat ready, preparing yourself mentally for the challenges of those northern seas while trawling through the weather archives to come to grips with what the sea may throw at you. This concentration keeps you busy, takes you over and transports you to a land where dreams fuse with reality. Any error, any omission, will have to be paid for and you can only rely on yourself, being solely responsible for whatever happens and, finally, your own fate.

So much for preparations before leaving. The passage itself will be whatever chance has decided for you, even if modern equipment overflows with weather information. Once you leave, that's it.

To sail to the far north or the far south has no comparison with anything else, and for several reasons. Firstly, it is the light, which gives permanent daytime, secondly it is the ice in all its shapes with this special light cast upon it. The abundance of wildlife is another aspect. Not to speak of the arrival! The voyage is accomplished and you are filled with a feeling of happiness, dream and reality at last combined.

Erick Bouteleux, *Igloo*

and Charlie Gray have spent almost as many years sailing together on their faithful *Sea Gem*. John and Amanda Neal have been running a successful offshore navigation training scheme for over 40 years and have prepared hundreds of sailors to face the challenges of the sea.

It takes a special mindset to embark on a long voyage, requiring qualities such as courage, perseverance, determination and self-confidence. The fact that we live in an age when it is so much easier and safer to sail to the remotest parts of the world has not changed those requirements in any way. What seems to me to have changed is the attitude of the sailors themselves. In recent years I noticed that sailors have become more self-contained but also more self-centred. Maybe this is due to the more individualistic society we live in, maybe because boats and equipment are so much more reliable, and maybe also because nowadays cruising sailors have more money and are financially more independent than in the past.

There have been other changes too, in the attitude of some officials and local people to visiting sailors, especially in some of the more frequented destinations. The safety situation in certain parts of the world is also causing concern, as do the effects of climate change. But there are still plenty of peaceful places to explore, exotic destinations to enjoy, and all that is needed is, in the words of Greg Rogers, a positive attitude. 'Whether it is changing course due to a change in the weather, adapting to the fact that things aren't the way they were stated in a cruising guide, or whether one particular official has a different interpretation of the rules, you will get a lot more out of long-range voyaging if you can roll with the punches and find a way to enjoy things as they actually turn out, rather than bemoan the fact that things did not go as planned.'

In other words, in the final analysis, how satisfying and enjoyable your life on the ocean will be is not determined by how big or small, comfortable or well equipped your boat may be, how much or little money you have, but primarily by your own attitude.

Final preparations

It's all about preparation, especially when things start to get pear-shaped. When that happens, all you have is what you put on the boat and your own ability and knowledge.

Alex Whitworth

The proper planning stage is the second step in setting up a future voyage when, based on the information gathered, the proposed route has been drawn on a small-scale chart. By this time it is helpful to have decided on a tentative departure date so as to be able to adjust the route of the initial stage of the voyage to the weather and other conditions that need to be taken into account for that time of year. The first rule of voyage planning is that you should do everything possible not to be in the wrong place at the wrong time of year. The application of this golden rule starts with choosing the time of departure carefully and considering all possible eventualities. When a realistic date has been chosen, it is always advisable to consult your crew before the final decision is taken, but once that decision has been made, everything possible should be done to stick to it. After the voyage has started, it is only natural that departure dates of subsequent legs can be more flexible, but for psychological reasons the initial start date should be adhered to closely.

Several participants in the voyage planning survey referred to the subject of preparation and while all agreed on the importance of being well prepared, several advised to set a reasonable time limit. As Nancy Zapf stressed, 'Don't overdo the preparations or you'll never leave the dock. It's easy to get up-to-date advice and local knowledge from fellow cruisers and the internet while underway.' John Jameson fully agreed: 'Don't get lost in details, especially towards your desired time of departure. Ask yourself, "Do I really need it?" A lot of things are nice to have, but are not essential, so leave the decision for a later date and go sailing.'

This kind of advice, of not postponing a departure without good reason, or putting off the actual decision to go, was given by such long-term cruisers as Luc Callebaut and Jackie Lee. 'Do not wait too long, as your health and stamina won't be as good anymore! Cruise young and get a desk job when you are older.'

Setting a departure date

The hardest part of any sailing trip is leaving the dock.

Charles Gray

When deciding on a suitable date of departure, local weather conditions should only be part of the equation. Just as important to consider are the conditions that may be encountered en route or those that may be expected at the chosen destination. This is the second rule of voyage planning. The way to apply it is to start working backwards from a chosen destination and a good example is the optimum timeframe for a voyage from Northern Europe to the Eastern Caribbean. The end of the North Atlantic hurricane season in November marks the start of the safe sailing season in the Caribbean, so those planning to sail across the Atlantic from Europe normally plan to get to the Eastern Caribbean by late November or early December. This means leaving the Canary Islands, the most convenient place for the start of an Atlantic crossing, by mid or late November. Timing your arrival in the Canaries for such a departure date makes no sense as no one in his right mind would plan to sail from Northern Europe to the Canaries at that time of year. As the best time to sail south is summer, voyages from Northern Europe are planned to take place between June and early August. This is also the best time to continue to the Canaries even if that means arriving there too early, so some people leave their boat in a marina, fly home and return in time for the Atlantic crossing. The other option is to spend the time between an early arrival and the optimum time for the passage to the Caribbean cruising the islands of the Canarian archipelago.

This example shows why the time of departure on a long voyage has to take into account both the optimum period for its start and also the factors that pertain to intermediate and final destinations. This first stage of a voyage is usually the most critical as the crew may be untried and unfamiliar with offshore conditions, night watches and sailing in waters with heavy shipping. Furthermore the boat itself as well as the equipment may be new or have not been used under strenuous conditions and may not be up to the task.

When faced with a difficult passage, whether at the start of a voyage or later on, it may be a good idea to undertake a virtual voyage along the proposed route by studying the pilot charts for the time of year for your proposed voyage. By seeing the actual data recorded along that route in recent years as shown in *Cornells' Ocean Atlas*, you will be able to envisage what kind of conditions to expect and prepare yourself for them.

The importance of optimum timing in this initial phase of a voyage is shown by the fact that for voyages starting from Northern Europe, or the US East Coast, the very first leg of such voyages is often also the most difficult, whether it entails sailing across the Bay of Biscay en route to the Mediterranean and the Canary Islands, or crossing the Gulf Stream en route to Bermuda, the Bahamas or the Eastern Caribbean. Those two areas are notorious for putting to the test even tried-and-tested vessels and their crews, and for this reason they should not be taken lightly. I was often asked why there was no qualifying offshore passage demanded of boats and crews joining either the ARC or one of the round the world rallies. My reply was simple: Most boats joining the start in Gran Canaria had to sail well over 1,000 miles through an area known for its inclement weather, so if they managed to get to the start of the event the crew had already proven that they were ready for an Atlantic crossing. This was certainly true as, for a variety of reasons, every year a number of boats failed to make the start in Las Palmas, whether the cause was a new untried boat, gear failure, crew problems, or simply because the passage south had started too late in the season and the weather had by then turned against them.

All these tasks that ought to be dealt with during this preparatory stage may sound rather daunting but in reality this can be the most enjoyable part of preparing for a long voyage, when you can daydream of the voyage that lies ahead, and look forward to landfall in a picture-perfect anchorage. You can still put aside the worries about what may happen during the coming night when that blissful situation could be shattered by the anchor dragging in a sudden squall and having to re-anchor in pitch-black darkness while lashed by torrential rain. No wonder some sailors come to regret not having stuck to their daydreaming. Indeed, for those who have any doubts about what they are committing themselves to, it is at this stage of planning that they should ask themselves the hard question: Am I really prepared to undertake this voyage that could affect not only my own life but that of everyone close to me? This is also the time to ask yourself if you are up to it both physically and psychologically. It is infinitely better that these questions are asked before the project acquires its own momentum and can still be abandoned with dignity. These are difficult and painful questions to address but therein lies the most common reason for a curtailed or abandoned voyage.

I must confess that on a few occasions when things were not going well a hint of a doubt had crossed my own mind about the wisdom of what I was doing. But it was always just a passing thought that was quickly extinguished by the memory of the many wonderful moments I had enjoyed. As with almost everything else in life, and certainly an ocean voyage which entails a complete change of lifestyle, there is a price to pay and sacrifices to make. But what I know, both from my own experience and that of my many sailing friends, is that when you look back on a voyage, all you remember are the beautiful moments. Regrets there are none.

Jim Thomsen has this advice to those who may have doubts as to whether the cruising life would actually suit them, 'Leave civilisation only if you enjoy the challenge of figuring out problems and fixing things (not always with the proper parts or tools). And realise that it is like travelling with a house and a car without proper repairmen. It is not an extended vacation but a remarkable adventure. Are you up to it?'

Antti Louhija seems to agree but only to a point. 'Don't be afraid to depart. Soon it might be too late for some reason or other. What you do not know beforehand you will learn soon enough! However, always be prepared to discontinue the voyage if encountering excessive difficulties.'

Having been in close contact with so many sailors who took part in the rallies I organised, when I had to deal with these kinds of questions and help solve their problems, also made me realise just how poorly prepared some people were and, even more important, how little priority many of them had given to adequately planning their voyage. This impression was reinforced in the following years while running the website noonsite.com when I received countless emails on routing, often from sailors who had already embarked on a voyage and were asking for help on how to continue to their intended destination. From their questions, it was quite obvious that they had not done their homework properly as often the route they proposed to sail was unrealistic, as it meant sailing against strong prevailing winds or having to pass through an area where the tropical storm season was already in force. A good example is that of the owner of an 80-foot yacht who wanted to sail from Singapore to Fremantle in Western Australia. In my reply to his email I pointed out that on his proposed schedule, by the time they reached the South Indian Ocean, the trade winds would be blowing at their strongest from the south so they would have to fight against them and, if they were delayed, they would run into the next cyclone season. I suggested that the only reasonable alternative would be to sail a roundabout route via Micronesia, and only cross the equator when they would have a good angle to sail across the SE trade winds in the South Pacific to reach Southeast Australia. Once there, they would have to wait for the favourable time to sail with the easterly winds of summer to Western Australia. He replied that the alternative route I suggested was too long and as he had full confidence in both his boat and crew, he would take the direct route. About two months later I received an email saying that they were back in Singapore after having encountered awful sailing conditions in the South Indian Ocean. With damage to the boat and a near mutinous crew, he decided to turn around. Reluctantly he admitted that I had been right and he was now going to wait for the favourable season to sail the route I had suggested in the first place.

This is just one of many examples that have come to my knowledge of failed attempts to complete a voyage due to bad planning, so the main objective of this book is to help those planning a voyage avoid such an outcome. From contacts with sailors at seminars, and various rallies,

I came to the conclusion that some sailors seem to be unable, or perhaps not interested to construct the outline of a voyage, and then research and gather all the necessary information for its planning. The reasons may be a lack of knowledge of geography, of global weather systems or perhaps just the inability to understand, or appreciate, the importance of being able to draw up a realistic plan to sail from A to B, and later from B to C and so on. This book aims to do just that so that anyone intending to sail from their home base, or, later in their voyage, from wherever they may be to a new destination anywhere in the world, will find here the answer to their query. Rather than describe only the obvious route that links the point of departure to the chosen destination, wherever possible I shall also describe various route options or possible detours and provide sufficient information on each of those options to allow the reader to choose the most suitable or attractive alternative.

As popular cruising grounds such as the Eastern Caribbean, Mediterranean, Baltic and the Bahamas become more crowded and their attraction starts to wane, some sailors, especially those more experienced, are looking for new and challenging destinations. This has led to more people being attracted to high-latitude sailing, whether to Spitsbergen, Greenland, Alaska, Patagonia or Antarctica. Besides voyages to such cold-water destinations, also included in this book are some of the major waterways which can be used to reach a distant destination by a more convenient or interesting route. This is another essential aspect of voyage planning which can be just as important as common sense: a pragmatic attitude. If the season is too far advanced and you are concerned about sailing home from the Mediterranean to Northern Europe around Gibraltar and across the Bay of Biscay, why not drop the mast and take the Rhone-Rhine route to the North Sea? By the same token, many American sailors avoid the tough offshore route to sail south to Florida and use instead the extensive Intracoastal Waterway.

Forward planning

Always have an alternative plan. Allow yourself a way out. Figure out what you're going to do when your plan goes wrong, because some day it will.

WS Kals

FLEXIBILITY
Good voyage planning should also allow for a degree of flexibility once the voyage is underway. I firmly believe in

laying down a thorough plan for a voyage, and preparing well for it, but I also remember a friend once saying that plans are there to be changed, so even the best-laid plans should have some inbuilt flexibility. Such flexibility is most certainly needed to deal with unforeseen circumstances and there are many examples of sailors getting into serious trouble by not avoiding a known risky area simply because a safer alternative route seemed too long or more difficult to sail, or, even worse, when a different course of action was not even considered. This subject will be discussed in more detail on page 39.

Electronic charts are now so widely used that on many boats paper charts are no longer carried, not only because of their cost and the storage space they require but also because they are wrongly regarded as obsolete and unnecessary. While on some commercial and naval ships paper charts for the entire proposed route are still carried as a backup, this is not feasible on a cruising boat, although at least a few general charts should still be carried for use in an emergency. Some chart distributors produce photocopied charts of reduced size at a reasonable price which are perfectly adequate as backups. Also as a matter of precaution the electronic charts should be backed up if possible on a spare computer or hard drive. Furthermore, when planning a voyage, or even just a passage, make sure you have the necessary range of electronic charts to be able to sail an alternative route or make landfall in an unplanned port in an emergency.

Plans need to be changed for a variety of reasons, be it to avoid hazardous areas, accommodate family commitments or explore new countries which had not been included in the original schedule. But the most common reasons for people changing their plans and route are that they hear on the cruising grapevine of an interesting area that should not be missed, to continue sailing in company with new friends, and occasionally just for the pleasure of going where their fancy takes them which, after all, is the main beauty of cruising.

My own voyages are a case in point as they all started with a well-laid plan and route which were then altered repeatedly, often on a whim. The first voyage was meant to last only three years but due to a number of long detours, invariably caused by chance encounters, it stretched to six years and it could easily have lasted longer if the age of our children had not forced us to return home. The second voyage was only meant to limit itself to a half year North Atlantic circuit but ended up as a three-year long circumnavigation when I decided to sail in the first round the world rally myself. The outcome of my third round the world voyage was exactly the opposite as it was planned as a complete circumnavigation which had to be abandoned in the Pacific when other commitments forced me to ship the boat back to the Mediterranean. That voyage was eventually completed seven years later with another circumnavigation which was yet another exercise in utter flexibility. My attempt to transit to Northwest Passage in 2014 followed a similar pattern. Unable to complete the transit from east to west, I decided to improve my chances of a successful transit by sailing south from Greenland to Panama, transiting the canal, and finally succeeded in going through the Northwest Passage from west to east.

My voyages on both *Aventura III* and *Aventura IV* showed the great attraction, if time permits, of breaking up a voyage into separate segments, in other words, of cruising in stages. This allowed me to spend the most favourable seasons exploring a certain area before laying up the boat during the off-season and returning home for shorter or longer periods. Whenever I left *Aventura* unattended I made sure that she was safely laid up, usually ashore, in a secure place and always outside the tropical storm areas. The wide choice of such places throughout the world, combined with the availability of long-distance flights, has added a new and quite different dimension to long-distance cruising. In this kind of cruising in stages, forward planning is even more important than on a continuous voyage when it is easier to improvise or change plans at short notice. Those who have decided on this style of cruising need to plan their forthcoming stop in good time and start making the necessary arrangements to get a place in a marina or boatyard and book flights home well before arrival in the country in which they plan to stop. This kind of logistical work needs to be done by anyone planning to leave the boat unattended and, as the best places often get booked up early, such arrangements must be made well in advance.

It is also part of forward planning to make allowances for other matters that need to be dealt with in advance: visas and cruising permits for certain countries, being near an international airport for crew changes, finding a suitable place with facilities for the regular service of the engine, liferaft, major repair jobs, antifouling the hull, or having a medical check-up of the crew.

Also part of forward planning is putting some thought into your return voyage, not only to ensure favourable seasons and sailing conditions but also to decide on the most suitable route and possible alternatives. A good example is the dilemma faced every year by North American sailors who have reached New Zealand as part of a longer cruise and are faced with the difficult decision of how to return home. For many who were planning to continue around the world via the Red Sea and Mediterranean, the threat of piracy in the Indian

Flexibility

1. Anybody can eat an elephant one bite at a time, i.e. the goal to sail around the world is really a series of small trips that are connected, but not necessarily one entity.

2. We always attempt to take it 'one wave at a time'. There are so many obstacles that prevent most people from attaining their goal that they quit during the process. Don't let the non-issues cloud what you are trying to do. Keep it simple.

3. Avoid the herd mentality and go your own way. A lot of cruisers get caught up in social connections and forget that they are able to make their own decisions. Design your plan for you and you alone.

4. Slow down! I was chastised early on in our cruise by an elderly sailor who told me that I was trying to do too much too fast and that I needed to take more time to enjoy what we were doing. She gave me the best advice I've ever had. Schedules and timetables are OK, however you must be flexible enough to be able to change.

5. Keep in mind that it is your challenge and that the only other people who really understand what you are doing are other cruisers. You will have a totally different concept of how to deal with problems and stress – you will have done it!

Peter and Julie Kranker, *Sojourner*

Ocean had forced them to consider another route. Those who were not attracted by the idea of sailing around the Cape of Good Hope had the choice of sailing home via Tahiti and Hawaii, or via Micronesia, neither of which is a particularly easy route. Others took the option of having their boats shipped by Sevenstar Yacht Transport from Southeast Asia to the Mediterranean. Few could have foreseen such a situation, but it just shows the importance of always having an alternative plan to fall back on.

COMMON SENSE

The safety regulations of the International Convention for the Safety of Life at Sea state unambiguously that 'Voyage planning is common sense'. Indeed, common sense should be an essential ingredient of voyage planning, and of voyaging generally, but if that is the case, why is it that with all the aids to navigation that are currently available, from GPS to chart plotters, radar, AIS, forward-looking sonars, and many others, some cruising boats still get into serious trouble? How can the fact be explained that proportionally just as many yachts get lost nowadays as in the days of astronavigation, inaccurate charts and no access to weather information? An over-reliance on those aids to navigation is certainly one reason some sailors are taking unnecessary risks which sooner or later land them in trouble. Bad timing is another reason, as shown by the cases of boats being caught by a hurricane while cruising during the hurricane season in an area known to be affected by tropical storms, or making a passage in high latitudes at the wrong time of year. Entering an unknown port or anchorage at night or in poor visibility, anchoring on a potential lee shore, and not taking avoiding action in good time when there is a risk of being on a collision course with a ship, were some of the causes of recent incidents that were in almost all cases due to a lack of common sense.

In an ad hoc survey conducted in the Canaries among participants in two recent transatlantic rallies, the majority admitted that they had not used a small-scale paper chart when planning their voyage. After I had unfolded a chart of the North Atlantic and demonstrated the great advantage of having an overview of the route they were going to sail to the Eastern Caribbean, possibly continue to Panama, or of a hypothetical return voyage to Europe, there were few who were not convinced of the essential usefulness of such charts for voyage planning. Both local chandleries ran out of their stock of charts the following day. 'Common sense, dear Watson,' would have exclaimed Sherlock Holmes.

This subject was also examined among the sailors who took part in the latest planning survey, where the results were quite different, as explained by Jim Patek. 'I still prefer to plan a voyage on a small-scale chart so that I can visualise the complete passage (distances, geography, weather regions). For me, visualisation of a complete planned voyage cements that plan in place and insures it will be completed as planned.' Murray Atkinson felt the same. 'We use a paper chart to get a general feel for the passage, and also to identify any potential hazards.'

For Mike Beilan, 'Being old school, we always carried along paper charts and guidebooks of the areas we were going to visit. At one time, we carried over 700 paper charts, but unfortunately many of those charts, both paper and electronic, used such old datum that we always used them with a healthy dose of scepticism and precaution. For overall planning, we felt it was nice to be able to spread out a small-scale chart to roughly plot course, distance, etc.'

James Hunt pointed out that, 'We do all our initial planning using historical information, but actual passages are based on all current weather forecasts from many different sources. We use open CPN on a dedicated laptop for passage planning. We still have some paper charts and sailing directions, which we use for planning. We like to see the whole picture, and still plot a noon position on longer passages – most of the newer sailors consider us dinosaurs!'

Pete Goss, who has sailed over 450,000 miles in all oceans of the world, would hardly qualify as a dinosaur when he declared unequivocally, 'I wouldn't dream of going to sea without paper charts. I use a small-scale chart for all my passage planning and if anyone has doubts about this then read up on *Vesta*'s tragic shipwreck on a reef in the South Indian Ocean while sailing in the Volvo Ocean Race. I also carry charts to cover any potential ports that I can run too on account of weather or repair. In addition I have pilot books to cover any coast I am sailing down. Hitting a rock will always be more expensive than a few charts. If I had a choice it would be paper over electronic; what happens when your electrics go down? As a backup I have a couple of hand-held GPS units stowed in a metal box.'

Dave McCampbell raised the potential inaccuracy of some charts and described their own planning routine. 'We have always felt that having the tools aboard to get good weather data while en route is critical to safety and cruising success. Before we leave, we use planning tools like FastSeas.com. Offshore, we use GRIB files and feed them into a routing module that uses our boat's polars, tweaked for comfort and short-handed sailing, to give us an idea how to get where we want to go without getting bashed to pieces. We don't blindly follow what the routing tool produces, but it does highlight expected wind/weather changes, and you can set parameters like "avoid seas over 10 ft and wind over 25 knots". When the predicted route takes a left turn, you know there's something brewing up to pay attention to. Then we make our own judgements based on all the forecast data we can gather, and our own experience. If the forecast is wildly variable, we look at each other and say, "Not sure what's coming, but something is coming, so let's get ready."'

As a tip to anyone planning to explore truly out of the way places, Dave added these comments. 'We have been up several of New Guinea's river systems and also in some remote Fijian, Indonesian, Micronesian and Philippines locations using Google Earth and SasPlanet charting. That would be impossible using any other charting system. But in order to have this capability aboard, some of the extensive files need to be downloaded prior to getting under way. Those of us out visiting such places would never leave without them.'

Weather and routing

Some people are weather-wise, most are otherwise.

Benjamin Franklin

The availability of forecasts and weather information for cruising boats on ocean passages has had an unprecedented impact on offshore sailing. Forecasts can now be received by a variety of means and there cannot be many cruising boats which have no access to weather information while on passage. The final section of the voyage planning survey dealt with this important subject by investigating the role of weather forecasts and their influence on routing and passage planning generally.

One of the improvements in ocean weather fore-casting is computer-generated gridded binary (GRIB) files, which have now become extremely popular with offshore sailors. Being able to receive such information using GSM, satellite phone, email or HF radio is a great bonus whether on passage or while preparing to leave. For those who are not content with the raw data provided by GRIB files obtained by such means, there are several versions of weather routing software, from some very sophisticated ones aimed at the racing market to simpler products suitable for cruising boats. They are a good aid to route planning but as access to the internet is essential they are normally more useful for forward planning than during an offshore passage. Normally forecasts are downloaded from the internet in the form of GRIB files so that an optimum route can be calculated matching the weather data to the boat's performance. The other solution is to use a provider of enhanced weather data, including GRIB files, by paying a monthly subscription.

While no one denies the usefulness of GRIBs, it must be said that they are only a supplementary source of weather information, and, as the data is solely computer generated, according to meteorologist Lee Chesneau 'GRIBs can often be wrong, especially in unstable and volatile weather patterns'. He points out that 'professional forecasters are well aware of this fact and make important critical adjustments to the forecast process.'

This point was also stressed by meteorologist Bob McDavitt who writes a weekly blog for cruising sailors about conditions in the South Pacific. He warns that 'GRIB files average out the output from global weather models and thus cannot resolve the details of such local phenomena as the South Pacific Convergence Zone and therefore should not be relied on.'

Indeed, several skippers in the survey found GRIBs to be far less reliable than most people believe them to be. According to Gary Goodlander, 'I get the GRIBs and mostly only pay attention to see how often they are wrong.' This was also Mike Beilan's experience, 'The conditions we find on passage have occasionally differed from what we expected from weather forecasts. Frequently micro conditions are impossible to predict accurately.'

Bill Rouse was in that very situation when 'we encountered a low in the Bay of Bengal which had been missed in the forecast. We had 45-knot winds with high seas and had to sail around the outside of the eye of the low. This ordeal turned a 1,000-mile passage into 1,600 miles of tough conditions.'

Mike Dorsett fully agrees with Lee Chesneau about the usefulness of weatherfaxes as it is the human intelligence input which makes them so much more reliable and useful. 'We use weatherfaxes daily. We had a late-season hurricane which formed on our Atlantic crossing. Most of the other boats went through it, but we saw it coming so headed south and missed it. You must be able to

Strong winds in Le Maire Strait.

receive and interpret weatherfaxes, as the usual forecasts are not always available, reliable, or adequately detailed.'

As pointed out by John Whyte, another useful source of weather information on passage is the various maritime radio nets. There are several such radio nets used by cruising sailors throughout the world and their usefulness both for regional weather information and primarily as a safety net and point of contact is invaluable. Stu Conway also found 'SSB weather information well worth listening to when available. In a rally, information from the boats ahead or around you is equally valuable.'

Patrick Canut used an ingenious way to get the latest weather information by having it emailed to him by his wife Marie-France during his passage from France to French Polynesia, 'As I had no access to the internet, she sent me the daily synoptic charts from Meteo France and it worked perfectly.'

To assess the importance they attach to weather information while on passage, and also how it influences their passage planning both before and after departure, participants in the survey were asked how weather forecasts influenced their decision to leave on a passage.

When to leave is always a difficult decision, whether on a long or short passage, and the ready availability of weather information has only made it harder to take that decision. In the past all that a captain had at his disposal was a knowledge of local conditions, any obvious signs of an impending deterioration and, ultimately, his own intuition. All that has now changed through the mass of data available and a skipper has the unenviable task of sifting through all that information to pick the right moment to leave while often also having to contend with pressure from his crew, or the influence of other skippers, who are following the same forecasts and may interpret them differently. No wonder that those with little offshore experience will find such situations confusing and often end up taking the wrong decision, as pointed out by John Whyte, 'When setting out on a long passage I believe strongly that you should seek your own weather information, make your own decision and then go. I have seen so many cruisers stuck in port reading GRIB files, studying weather on the internet, discussing it with other cruisers and looking for the ideal window only to miss them all and then set off at the worst time because they have run out of time. Tonga and Fiji are the worst places for this as people prepare to sail for New Zealand.'

Charles Gray fully agreed, 'We put a great deal of emphasis on planning, and when alone always adhere to good judgement. When cruising with a group, we have occasionally been pressed to leave in less than good conditions.'

Jim Thomsen also preferred to follow his own nose, 'We might have a higher tolerance for weather which other people may wait to pass through. For instance, we had fabulous sailing between the Caribbean islands only to find out later that others were waiting for a "good" weather window. For us 20 to 25 knots on a beam or broad reach was fine. Now we don't talk to other cruisers about weather but rely on our own fact finding.' Dave Ungless also makes the point that when it comes to deciding on a departure day 'we make it a principle not to be tied to a fixed date with guests flying in to join us or having a pre-booked flight home from our next destination'.

In Tere Batham's view 'A weather window is a totally new and man-made concept. But this does not necessarily mean that we wait for perfect weather before setting out.'

In the case of Dale Norley, 'as a delivery skipper I do not always have the luxury of waiting for the optimum window. If I know it is only going to blow 25 knots but from the right direction, and I feel that it is safe, and the vessel and crew are capable of dealing with it, I go for it. Direction is probably the most important factor when it comes to the wind.' This is also Bill McLaren's attitude, 'We normally go when we are ready unless the short-term forecast is totally poisonous. We like to get out of pilotage waters in half-decent conditions and then take whatever comes.'

Most experienced sailors would agree that on long ocean passages in a well-prepared boat if the wind is strong but from a favourable direction it is still preferable to go than wait. Generally speaking, in temperate zones the direction of the wind is more important than its strength whereas in the trade wind zones, where the direction is more constant, the strength of the forecast wind should be the deciding factor. This is particularly the case when there is a forecast of reinforced trade winds, known in Tahiti as *maramu*.

Contributors to the survey were asked how much attention they paid to forecasts before a departure. Hugh Fraser would always consult forecasts before departure in hurricane zones but only occasionally during safe seasons. Alex Whitworth had the same approach but stressed that for him 'the whole shebang depends on leaving at the right time of year for whichever ocean we intend to cross and the need to get away from the shore safely'.

The results of the survey show that the majority of skippers studied the forecasts carefully before leaving and their decisions were quite likely to be influenced by them, but once on passage, while continuing to monitor the weather, the influence of the forecasts was diminished.

John Jameson advised others to 'have enough time and patience to wait for the appropriate conditions. But

Discussing the options ahead.

once underway, it is possible to sail without weather information. However, I enjoy knowing what is going on around me, and routing intelligently. On certain passages I download weatherfaxes every 24 hours.' See page 234.

Antti Louhija also recommends a realistic approach, 'You will, after all, encounter all kinds of weather during ocean passages and must be prepared for it. Waiting for the right windows can mean sitting for a long time in harbours.'

Ann Harsh picked up the habit of following forecasts on a regular basis during her voyage around the world, 'This is the subject in which we gained the biggest increase in our knowledge. We used weatherfaxes constantly.' As part of Ann's voyage took place in high latitudes, this is understandable as in those waters access to weather information can be invaluable. This point was stressed by Beth Leonard when she compared the two circumnavigations she and Evans Starzinger completed under very different circumstances, one in the tropics, the other in high latitudes. While they used weather information very rarely during the former, they depended on it during the latter and used it to best advantage.

As Beth explained, 'On our first circumnavigation in the tropics, we paid attention to our departure window and after that pretty much took what we got. We often did not get forecasts for most of a passage and it didn't really matter. On our second circumnavigation in high latitudes, including 12,000 miles in the Southern Ocean, we downloaded GRIBs daily and when frontal passages were coming through we sometimes downloaded more than once a day. We found we could position ourselves relative to lows coming up behind us and that we could avoid the strongest winds and biggest seas with good weather information. While we would pay attention to weather in the tropics, it would rarely make as big a difference in our passage routing in low latitudes as it does in high latitudes.'

Bill McLaren has a similar approach, 'On our Southern Ocean passage from New Zealand to Chile we used the forecast movement of the low pressure systems to shift our position north or south by perhaps 200 miles in order to stay with the westerlies. We also used weather information to try and find the optimum position for getting through the Intertropical Convergence Zone (ITCZ). Otherwise we just tended to plod on.'

Steve Lochner also found forecasts helpful in high latitudes but of less use elsewhere, 'It all depends on the passage. En route from Japan to Alaska, I would get one or two daily updates and act upon them.' He admitted that, in hindsight, on the passage to Alaska he would have preferred to have subscribed to a better professional route planning service than he had, as a better interpretation of weather conditions by a skilled meteorologist would have been a great help.

Steve was among seven of those surveyed who occasionally used professional shore support and the level of satisfaction was mixed, which I did not find surprising as participants in rallies who paid for such services often complained about the inconsistency of their reliability.

Don Babson had a similar experience, 'On a passage from Florida to the Azores, the router advised us to head southeast. It was a fast point of sail yet after a couple of days the wind began to increase from the north-northeast. Three other boats which had stayed on the rhumb line took long tacks to windward and due to their more northern position ended up with a better sailing angle when the wind moved north and left us far behind.'

In fairness to the routers, it must be said that they usually tend to err on the side of caution with the result that their clients are sometimes asked to wait for a better window and when that does not materialise, they find they have missed a good opportunity which others had taken, so it is only natural for them to be frustrated.

This is a risk that must be accepted by those who decide to let others make such important decisions for them. The main problem is that most forecasts are only good for short-term planning, and are rarely reliable for longer than five days or one week ahead. Therefore making a long-term commitment based on a short term forecast can have serious consequences. Whether the decision on what route to take when setting off on a long passage is taken by you or a professional forecaster, that decision is based on an interpretation of expected weather conditions. If the prospects are good, the normal reaction is to take the shortest route because if conditions change the course can be altered in view of the latest weather data. However, by the time that data becomes available you may have committed yourself to a route where it may be too late to alter course drastically. A good test case is the ARC transatlantic rally as it implies a passage of some 2,700 miles from the Canary Islands to the Caribbean and is sailed every year by over 200 boats. The passage can be sailed along a variety of routes and in the early days of the ARC, when even short-term forecasts were still unreliable and offshore weather information was unavailable, most boats took the traditional route. This entailed sailing first on a southwesterly course until they reached the prevailing trade wind area and only there altering course for their Caribbean destination. This cautious, common sense approach usually worked well as statistically the chances of favourable winds along this route were good and in most years this was born out by the actual conditions encountered. The situation changed when weather information became more easily available and skippers started being influenced in their choice of route, not always with the best results. A good example is that of a recent ARC when predictions favoured a shorter, direct route across the Atlantic, which many boats ended up taking. Between one week and ten days after the start they ran into a system which generated headwinds, and were forced to start tacking. By now most boats, which had taken this shorter route, were too far north to turn south where boats which had taken the classic route were experiencing light easterly winds. Boat for boat the passage times ended up being quite similar, but whereas those who had taken the northern route had a miserable crossing, those who had played it safe had a slow but generally comfortable passage.

This example shows why long-term passage planning should not be allowed to be overly influenced by short- or medium-term forecasts, and why it is still preferable to sail a more conservative route that can easily be modified in view of changing conditions.

Another well-sailed long passage where a similar approach can be applied is the one between the Galapagos and Marquesas. Murray Atkinson explains, 'On passage from the Galapagos to the Marquesas six boats set off at about the same time. Some sailed the rhumb line, others went further south looking for more wind. We ran roughly halfway between the extremes and had a reasonably good passage, the rhumb line boats had to motorsail and the southerly boats got too much wind and some suffered damage.'

Whether those surveyed monitored the weather regularly or only rarely, once on passage less than half (26) were seriously influenced by the forecasts, 16 skippers described themselves as not overly influenced, and 15 as rarely influenced. Lars Hässler was among the latter. 'There is not much choice once at sea, is there? Unless a hurricane is approaching, when I would try to turn around, you are more or less stuck out there.' Alex Whitworth feels the same, 'We are usually stuck with what we get; it's difficult to run away at a walking pace in the Southern Ocean. A good forecast assists with preparation for bad weather but adds to the levels of apprehension. Looking out of the window works just as well.'

In the final part of the survey skippers were asked to comment on the importance of access to weather information on passage generally. Virtually all agreed that it was of great benefit even if this was for a variety of reasons. Most appreciated the ability to get an idea of what to expect, as pointed out by Bill McLaren. 'It is important, but the speed of the normal cruising yacht is too slow to get out of the way of any horror coming your way. Its main benefit is to bring reassurance and give time to prepare for whatever is coming.'

Jim Thomsen shares that view. 'We like to know what is coming our way. We might not be able to do much about it but if something looks ugly we sure will try to avoid the worst of it. We don't have a lot of extra stuff that needs storing in bad weather; our boat is always kept tidy and ready for rough seas.'

Greg Rogers finds 'forecasts on passage very useful as they allow us to fine-tune our intended track. This is important since recent weather patterns do not seem to be reflecting historical trends.' But weather forecasts are useful not only for predicting storms, as pointed out by Dave McCampbell. 'Seeing a calm coming as we approached Pitcairn, we opted to motor for 24 hours to take advantage of the calm weather to stop at Pitcairn. Our friends, being hardy sailors, continued to eke out as much sailing as they could, but missed a whole day at Pitcairn because they wasted it trying to sail at 2 knots.'

Sailing a fast light displacement boat, Kurt Braun needed no convincing: 'The ability to receive weather data without the assistance of land-based communication systems has immensely increased safety at sea especially for faster vessels that depart not on a schedule but on a favourable weather window. Slower traditional vessels are stoutly built for longer passage times and for an era when long-term forecasts did not exist. Faster modern vessels with access to good weather forecasting allow shorter passage times and a lower likelihood of encountering bad weather.'

There are several conclusions that can be drawn from this survey. The first is that in most cases the tendency to consult weather forecasts increased as the voyage progressed and even highly experienced sailors eventually became regular users, even if they were less prone to be influenced by them. It was also interesting to note how many mentioned that they learned meteorology as they went along and then took more and more interest in it. Another observation, quoted by a number of experienced sailors, is the risk of becoming obsessed and having your voyage, and implicitly your cruising life, dictated by weather windows. Just as serious is the risk of allowing yourself to be influenced too much by others. As Gary Goodlander put it in his typically colourful way: 'Don't get rattled by others. Listening to those Nervous Nellies on the radio is useless. Is your mast up and keel down? Fine. It is stupid to attempt to push that storm away with your computer cursor. If you're terribly worried about the weather, you shouldn't be out there.'

Main concerns

There is a general feeling, both among sailors currently cruising and those planning a voyage in the near future, that the world has become a more dangerous place and that roaming the oceans on your own boat is less safe than in the past. The two matters that are causing most concern are personal safety, and the effects of climate change on global weather conditions.

PERSONAL SAFETY

After the general optimism of the 1990s, the first decade of this century gave way to a feeling, both among sailors already cruising and especially those planning a voyage in the near future, that the world had become a more dangerous place and that roaming the oceans on your own boat was less safe than in the past. While personal safety appeared to be the main concern, other areas of concern expressed by sailors planning a long voyage were tropical storm seasons, heavy weather and how to deal with it, and the effects of climate change on global weather conditions.

Personal attacks and acts of piracy involving cruising sailors were the most serious cause of concern probably because violent robberies and piracy attacks involving cruising boats were readily reported in the media, creating the impression that the overall safety situation was far worse than it was in reality. One part of the world that stood out more than any other was the North Indian Ocean, where an unprecedented wave of murderous piracy attacks and abductions involved both commercial vessels and cruising yachts. This was eventually brought to an end by the determined actions of an international coalition of naval forces.

To gauge the reaction of sailors who were already on a world voyage, or preparing to leave on such a voyage, a survey was conducted among a sample of long-distance sailors. Asked how concerned they were about the safety situation and the impact on their current and future plans, the majority responded that they were indeed concerned.

Mark Hoenke was not only very concerned but also profoundly disappointed. 'We want to cruise for fun, meet people, experience other cultures, and see places we only know from photos. The current state of lawlessness and the lack of rule of law in many places greatly affect our voyage planning. We may in fact limit our cruising to much less than we originally thought we would do.' John Whyte shared those feelings. 'I am very concerned as it affects all cruisers and psychologically one would always be nervous about people or boats approaching you. One of the joys of cruising is interaction with local people and this is at risk.'

Bill McLaren, who admitted of being quite concerned, pointed out however that 'it needs to be kept in proportion. There are certain critical areas, which are known and should simply be avoided. In others there is a risk, but it is analogous to that of mugging in a city – manageable with sensible precautions.' Guy Oury agreed. 'After all, we are still more likely to get mugged in our own hometown than hurt while sailing. Sensible precautions are always a good idea, but like in the rest of life, we should not "lock ourselves away in padded cells", otherwise life would not be worth living.'

Jeff Stander also preferred to take a more philosophical approach. 'I think that pirates and robbers, horrible as they are, can be viewed as another risk to assess among the many other risks including falling overboard, sinking, running aground, being rolled over, pitchpoled, etc. It's like trying to decide that you would rather die of cancer or a heart attack.' Jeff also felt that the risk had been exaggerated. 'I not only want to know what happened to one boat, but what did not happen to all the other boats that had a great time in that same area.'

None of those who were already on a world voyage were concerned enough to abandon their voyage but several made alternative plans. Among those who were planning to sail across the North Indian Ocean to the Mediterranean, several decided to take the Cape of Good Hope route instead, a few had their boats shipped to the Mediterranean, from Southeast Asia, and a few preferred to alter their plans. Darrel Smith was among the latter. 'Instead of going around the world we're just going to do a clockwise trip around the Pacific and then continue

Climate change in Antarctica.

eastabout to the Caribbean and finally Europe.' Murray and Caroline Atkinson decided on a similar course of action and 'return to the UK from New Zealand by the tougher route via Panama rather than risk taking the Red Sea route'. In the meantime they have safely completed their circumnavigation and are getting ready to leave on another world voyage.

Jim Patek, who had spent a long time in New Zealand in the past, knew exactly what he wanted. 'I am heading to the South Pacific where I plan to cruise for the remainder of my cruising days.' Also looking into the future, Bill McLaren 'would certainly avoid the North Indian Ocean but I don't think there is anywhere else I would specifically avoid. Being a bit facetious, piracy seems to be a hot weather sport. Stick to high latitudes!'

Beth Leonard agreed that 'the potential risk and the possibility of violence has increased greatly on the Red Sea route and that is reason for concern. Yet the South Africa route is still safe, so there is an alternative.' And she concluded with this advice to anyone planning a voyage. 'The cruising community knows the risk areas. For the moment, most of the world remains safe for cruisers, so it is not hard to avoid the hot spots.'

A good source to assess the latest safety situation is the website noonsite.com, which has been posting reports about incidents involving cruising boats since 2000. Bearing in mind the thousands of yachts that are cruising all over the world, the number of serious incidents involving cruising boats is far lower than comparable crime statistics of similar incidents recorded on land in any country visited by tourists, so while they are certainly worrying, they should be seen in that wider context. This attitude was confirmed by the fact that the overwhelming majority of those surveyed would not allow their plans to be affected by the deterioration in the safety situation and would continue cruising while keeping themselves informed of possible critical areas.

Climate change

The changes that have occurred in global climate in recent years are another cause for concern among sailors, and in spite of arguments to the contrary, this is a phenomenon that can no longer be denied or ignored. Some of the changes are becoming increasingly evident: the Arctic ice cap is melting at an unprecedented rate, the Northwest Passage has been free of ice for several summers, extra-seasonal tropical storms are more common and the tropical storm seasons themselves are less clearly defined and becoming more active. The 2017 North Atlantic hurricane season was one of the most active since records began in 1851 and the prospects for the future do not appear to be any better.

In the original world planning survey, conducted in 2011, more than half of the contributors (31) stated that they were not really concerned about climate change, 15 described themselves as being quite concerned and only ten as very concerned. This was almost the opposite of the concern expressed over piracy and personal safety generally, where nearly half of those interviewed admitted to being very concerned. While all acknowledged the fact that the climate was showing signs of changing, not everyone was prepared to attribute this to human activity. Mark Hoenke was among the skeptics. 'Humans have a pathologic need to blame any change on something or somebody. Change is inevitable. Should we strive to do better, use less? Absolutely. So deal with it and move on.'

Bill McLaren only half agreed. 'While the long-term trends are very concerning, the day-to-day movements of weather systems obey the rules. Any yacht on a long passage always had to be capable of coping with extremes of weather and I see no difference as a result of climate change.'

Beth Leonard, who admitted to being quite concerned, agreed with this attitude. 'We have always made every effort to avoid the tropics during cyclone seasons and passage making in high latitudes during the winter storm season. So, although we are concerned about the issue, it would not change how we deal with weather hazards in general.' However, Beth agreed that hurricane seasons need to be treated with more caution and advised others to avoid being in a tropical area too early or too late in the safe season.

The contributors to the survey were also asked how the current situation would affect their attitude to future voyages and whether they would reconsider their plans and choose a safer route which avoided any critical areas, limit the extent of their voyage to a smaller area, postpone their departure until the situation showed signs of improvement or abandon any plans for a major voyage in the future. Almost all answered that they would choose a safer route but otherwise continue with their plans, although some would restrict their cruising to a smaller area, usually one they knew best. Only a few considered postponing their voyage and putting plans on hold as long as the uncertainty continued.

Scott Trefethen pointed out that 'we lived through six serious hurricanes in the Virgins and were told that in the past they only occurred every 60 years or so. Now it is clear that they may be an annual event. The net effect of this is that we are more motivated to cruise the parts of

We have found both positive and negative results from climate change, but we do not have any profound observations. Ever the optimist, let's start with the positive, as inconsequential as it may seem. The summer of 2017 was our third visit to Svalbard since 2001. We had no idea how much less sea ice to expect north and east of Spitsbergen Island, and could have easily circumnavigated the entire group without concerns of being beset. After our visit when we were headed south to Jan Mayen and Iceland, Amanda said she wished we'd scheduled more time so that we could have explored the east coast. However, the downside was that glaciers we photographed in 2001 and 2006 had receded substantially, and that many of the ice bears were starving with only bird eggs and moss to eat as the ice floes that the seals normally hang out on were far to the north. In overall terms of passage planning, we realize that the hurricane/cyclone seasons can now start earlier and end later, and that frequently the early and late storms can be very destructive, so we are more conservative than before in planning our arrival and departure from areas frequented by tropical storms. We find that we catch far fewer pelagic fish on passage than 10-15 years ago and see only a very few areas in the world including Norway and Alaska where wild fish stocks are intelligently managed and stable, or in some cases growing. In most areas lack of concern and knowledge or commercial pressures have caused fish stocks to plummet. I am no scientist, but I expect that eating wild-caught fish will become a rarity and only for the wealthy before too many decades pass.

John and Amanda Neal, *Mahina Tiare III*

the world where we may do so in relative peace and safety. Our cruising options are being narrowed by geopolitical and geoclimatic changes. One can but look for the silver lining. Perhaps other areas previously less hospitable to us will see climatic changes that prove beneficial to cruisers.'

Mike and Peta Johnson also preferred to look on the positive side. 'Climate change is opening up the Northwest Passage as a route.' A sailor who knew that too well was Roger Swanson as he had made three attempts to transit the Northwest Passage from east to west, with only his third one being successful. Roger stressed that 'If one is going to undertake a major passage, there are always some unavoidable risks. If this uncertainty is not acceptable, then one must severely limit one's sailing plans.'

Several contributors expressed their concern not so much for their own plans but for the world generally. Jon and

Northeast Passage

During summer 2009, the Arctic sea routes have experienced an unprecedented amount of traffic. It was a record year for sailing boats with ten having passed through the Northwest Passage and three through the Northeast Passage. In 2010, the score was seven to two. Less than ten years ago my boat was the first to get through both passages without assistance.

I know the Northeast Passage well since my first transit in 2002 on *Vagabond*. In recent years Russian bureaucracy has become more stringent and specific permissions for each region are indispensable besides the permit for the maritime transit itself. On that first occasion we could move freely on land wherever we stopped. On my transit on *Mango* in 2009 we had less freedom: we often had to stay on board and our visit to the village of Lorino on Chukchi Peninsula was cut short by the arrival of the authorities, despite the enthusiastic reception by the mayor and citizens. At least they waived the compulsory presence of a pilot on board, the authorities having declared me an honorary Russian!

I am currently the only navigator to have transited on board a pleasure craft twice the Northeast Passage (2002 and 2009), and one and a half times the Northwest Passage (2003 and 2010). My experience of these waterways has only increased my curiosity about their future: the melting of the ice cap and the opening of the Arctic to shipping traffic by oil tankers, cruise ships, fishing boats, warships and yachts. Being frequently asked, I am pleased to take part as a consultant in navigation projects in the Russian Arctic, with the intention of ensuring a responsible development of this unique and fragile environment.

Eric Brossier, *Vagabond*

Northwest Passage

At the stroke of noon local time, under blue skies and with the distant glaciers of Bylot Island serving as a striking backdrop, the crew aboard the 64-foot cutter *Ocean Watch* dropped anchor today off the tiny village of Pond Inlet to put the finishing touches on their successful 2009 transit of the Northwest Passage. In so doing, *Ocean Watch* became the first American yacht ever to complete a west to east transit of the elusive northern waterway in a single season, and only the third US boat in history to successfully negotiate the Passage in an eastward direction.

Sailing above the Arctic Circle was everything we'd hoped it would be: challenging, frightening, beautiful, fulfilling. We'd been forced three times to stop and wait for ice leads to open up, constantly wondering if we'd be frozen in for the winter. But our luck always held. We'd been hypnotised and dazzled by the stark landscapes, the whales and polar bears, the never-ending daylight. We'd been humbled by the notion that we were passing through the same historic waters where the heroic Roald Amundsen triumphed and the tragic Franklin expedition came to grief.

But stepping ashore in Pond Inlet was also bittersweet: due to the diminished Arctic ice pack, we were one of many cruising boats that have transited the once impassable Northwest Passage in recent years in record-setting numbers. The Passage remains one of the most remote and difficult voyages on the planet, yet it is also a place that seems forever changed.

Herb McCormick, *Ocean Watch*

Jennifer Glaudemans wrote that 'As citizens of the globe, we are very concerned about the impact of global warming on the seas and coastal areas.' Mike and Sue Beilan also stressed that 'we feel personally responsible for our mini universe, and treat the world's oceans and inhabitants with respect and the knowledge that everything we do has an impact, albeit small from us, but large in aggregate, upon the oceans, atmosphere and environment.'

John Gratton also expressed his concern 'for the planet and the future of the human race. For myself, and as it affects me, I am not overly concerned. I think the situation is longer term than my lifetime.'

Although not concerned on a personal level, Erick

Bouteleux stressed that 'we live in a selfish society, which ignores nature and takes it for granted and as I am part of that society I share the responsibility.'

Bob Bechler, signed off the survey by quoting an old Scottish proverb: 'Be happy while you're living, for you're a long time dead.'

In the seven years that have gone by since that survey was conducted, global weather conditions have produced several instances that should have persuaded most sailors that any doubts about climate change and its consequences can no longer be justified. This question was put to all those who agreed in early 2018 to contribute to the update of the original survey.

Inuit Interlude

Having passed through the Western Arctic and its ice fields much earlier in the season than we had expected, and with the ice situation still unfavorable in the Eastern Arctic, we could slow down and turn the next stage of our voyage into a more leisurely cruise. On arrival at Tuktoyaktuk we tied up to a floating pontoon and walked to the Royal Canadian Mounted Police station to complete entry formalities into Canada. The spread-out settlement of about 900 inhabitants is an important supply centre for Arctic Canada. It also marks the very end of the Trans-Canadian Highway, a route that starts in faraway Newfoundland and crosses the entire continent to reach this remotest of places. Most houses that we passed were pre-fabricated one-family units typical of several urban centers, which had been set up by the Canadian government to provide the native population with medical facilities, schools and airports.

Sailing boats are quite a rarity in the Arctic and we had not seen a single one since we had left Dutch Harbor. We were warmly welcomed wherever we stopped, as the people wanted to know what had brought us to those remote places. While at Tuktoyaktuk, the mayor Darrel Nasogaluake came to greet us and, seeing the Blue Planet Odyssey banner and UNESCO logo on our boom, asked us about the meaning of this event. He then spoke at length about changes in their traditional way of life now greatly influenced by the changing climate.

In spite of the warm welcome at Tuktoyaktuk, it was not what we had expected from a native Inuvialuit settlement, so we took the mayor's advice and made a 200-mile detour to Ulukhaktok, on Victoria Island, having been assured that it was a more traditional settlement.

We dropped anchor close to the settlement in late afternoon and walked ashore but found everything to be closed, as it was Sunday. A local man stopped his quad bike to greet us and introduced himself as Little Jack. He explained that Ulukhaktok had a supermarket, small hotel, a kindergarten for the 12 younger children and a school with one class of 20 pupils between 7 and 12. There were also three churches for the 480 inhabitants: Catholic, Pentecostal and Anglican but that only the latter had a resident priest. We stopped at the church in the hope of meeting him, but the door was locked.

'He's away hunting, like everyone else.' A passing man called over. There were obviously more pressing priorities on a summer Arctic Sunday and religious services could very well wait until winter.

We had been told that Uluhaktok was a settlement where the people lived a more traditional way of life. Nowadays they all had to travel much farther than ever before and the place was so quiet because many families were at summer camps, hunting and fishing for winter supplies. Passing by were three young men who were setting off on their quad bikes to go hunting musk ox. Little Jack commented that climate change was a matter of serious concern and that in recent years they were seeing fish, birds and even bats that they had never seen before. He could have added *Aventura* to that list too as he told us that a sailing boat like ours had not been seen there for more years than the fingers of his hand.

From '200,000 Miles, A Life of Adventure'

The very first response came from Gary Goodlander, a few days before setting off from St John, in the US Virgin Islands, on a new world voyage. 'Yes, the climate is changing. But I am not so much scared of storms as calms; I would hate to be in mid-Pacific for weeks with no wind and a cross-swell. Of course, hurricanes are a problem. The Virgin Islands used to occasionally get a Category 1 hurricane every dozen years... now it is getting destroyed by Category 5 storms within weeks of each other. Twice I have dog-paddled away from floundering vessels, once in Hurricane Hugo with my seven-year old daughter in my arms. No fun!'

The next response came from Dale Norley, who is a professional delivery captain. 'I am much more adamant about having latest weather information available onboard than in the past. Because weather is more severe these days from climate change, I am more likely to consider "ducking in" somewhere than pushing through questionable conditions ahead. As this is not always an option, I am very thorough prior to departure looking far out at wind patterns and possible storms on satellite images to track possible tropical storms and hurricane system. If there is a potential for severe weather looming, I tend to wait longer than in the past knowing the potential severity and unpredictability of what is to come.'

Hugh Fraser shared Dale's views. 'We are concerned about the changing weather patterns and had first hand experience of 'non-normal' weather patterns. But we are still relying on historical data for passage routes and timing, at least in the planning stages. Once under way we alter timing and route according to up-to-date forecasts and any other info we can get. So I guess from now on we can expect to live with the unexpected!'

Alfredo Giacon also believes in a pragmatic approach. 'It is undeniable that the climate is changing, but thanks to modern technologies, the weather forecasts have become more reliable. In some areas of the world the forecasts are valid for several days. This allows us navigators to plan routes and anchorages with greater confidence. Obviously it is always better to stay away from the critical areas during the hurricane season, because as we have seen recently these phenomena have become really violent and gigantic in size. I believe that at this moment in time many novice sailors put too much trust in technology and rely too much on weather forecasts. However, it should not be forgotten that meteorology is not an exact science and the gizmos that we now have on board are very supportive and simplifies our life, but they are not yet able to replace a skipper's perceptions and experience.'

Dave McCampbell agreed. 'More than climate change, experience has taught us that planning a passage around averages never works out well. So, though we use climatology data to plan for the season or month in which we plan to cruise an area or make a passage, we use all the modern tools available to pick the day we leave and the exact route. But the seasons are slowly changing and storm planning is of course still critical, but we now undoubtedly have more accurate weather information to deal with it. Although I am not entirely convinced it's all to do with humankind; the glaciers in Scotland for example were in retreat long before the industrial revolution, and the same for the huge glacier fields we've found for ourselves in Alaska. What is a most definite problem though are the levels of pollution and the amount of human rubbish in the sea… with the terrible affects upon wildlife. It's appalling.'

Jim Patek stressed that 'In passage planning I always take cyclone seasons or winter weather conditions into account. The most problematic was the typhoon belt between the Carolines and Japan, which is unpredictable and even though we picked the "best month" to traverse this area, we were troubled by three typhoons in as many weeks, one before sailing from Pohnpei to Guam, and two while we were in Guam. So, my point is that you can plan by the book, as I have, but that is no guarantee. I have not changed my thinking about voyage planning but climate change has made me even more watchful for anomalous weather patterns in the expectation that they will (not may) occur at some point in a voyage.'

James Hunt stressed that, 'we are very cautious sailors. We have always taken hurricane seasons in the Caribbean seriously. Whilst in the Eastern Caribbean we were up on the hard for two seasons in Trinidad, in the Western Caribbean we were on the hard in Guatemala. Two seasons we avoided the critical area by sailing north up the US east coast.'

Mike Beilan admitted that, 'although very conscious of cyclone seasons, we didn't actually plan our voyage (2007–2017) to make allowances for climate change per se. Often I spent on average of at least 1–2 hours daily on weather and routing, sometimes considerably more. Being amateur radio operators, Sue and I were able to avail ourselves of various sources throughout our voyages, and found this to be of great help. One example that comes to mind were the ham broadcasts during our crossing of the Mozambique Channel; their weather forecasting was spot on in that notoriously difficult patch of ocean.'

In the case of Murray Atkinson, 'For long-term voyage planning the consistency of winds and currents seems to be reduced, but pilot charts are still the best guide. We plan to sail from Panama to the US west coast via Hawaii to take advantage of the favourable winds and currents. They may not happen as hoped, so the journey time may be longer than expected, but we feel it unlikely they will be very significantly different.'

José Prieto would have the same approach. 'No doubt the climate is changing but I think it's still possible to plan voyages with sufficient safety. Today more than ever before, there are new analytical tools, applications for computers, tablets and smart phones, which show good forecasts and meteorological analyses in a clear and efficient way. Communications are better than ever before. The care that I intend to take on my forthcoming world voyage will be to take these climate changes into account, trying to ensure a greater safety margin away from the hurricane seasons, thus avoiding dangerous surprises.'

Paul Donnerup threw the ball back into my own court when he replied. 'Climate change or not, I will continue to follow religiously your own advice: To always try to be in the right place at the best time, and never be in the wrong place at the wrong time.'

Global movement

It's one of the sadder truths about the economic meltdown. As never before, younger sailors are averse to leaving a good job for a family adventure, not knowing if it'll be there when they return. Sailing is becoming an ever-greyer pastime.

Herb McCormick, *Gone to the Sea*

My interest in the global movement of cruising boats goes back to 1987, when I published the results of my first survey on this subject. In the intervening three decades I have conducted every five years a follow-up survey; the latest was done in 2016 and examined the global situation during the previous year. Since the publication of my previous survey on movement and distribution of sailing boats in 2010, the world has been confronted by two major phenomena that have affected offshore cruising both in the short and long term. The political upheavals in the Middle East and North Africa have greatly affected cruising in the Mediterranean as well passages through the North Indian Ocean and Red Sea, but while those effects can be regarded as regional, the consequences of climate change are now affecting the entire world. Global weather conditions in 2015 were also affected by a prolonged El Niño episode that exacerbated the ongoing effects of climate change, most notably in the NW Pacific where at least one typhoon occurred in every month of the year, with a safe sailing season now sadly a thing of the past.

As on previous occasions, in order to construct a realistic image of the global movement of sailing yachts, I contacted officials in the most important hubs in every ocean requesting statistical data on the number of foreign flagged yachts that had passed through those ports in 2015. The resulting global canvas was filled in with figures obtained from the most popular destinations on the world cruising circuit as well as some of the least visited places in the world.

Since my first global survey in 1987, the cruising scene has seen important changes and while this survey has found that in a few places there has been an increase in the number of visiting yachts, the figures from Gran Canaria, Bermuda, Panama, Galapagos, Tahiti, Tonga and Australia seem to indicate that the popularity of long distance voyages may have peaked in 2010. Those numbers may also point to a global trend among potential world voyagers.

There are various reasons for this, but they all seem related to safety concerns. Although climate change has only started to visibly affect offshore weather, most sailors are worried about conditions becoming less predictable, with safe seasons no longer being taken for granted. The world is also regarded as less safe on a personal level, not only in such high risk areas as the North Indian Ocean and Red Sea, Venezuela, Brazil, Honduras, North, East and West Africa, but also in parts of the Eastern Mediterranean and Western Caribbean. The prevailing economic uncertainty may also deter some sailors from setting off on a world voyage not knowing what to expect on their return.

To assess the approximate number of boats that are undertaking a long voyage, I estimate that worldwide there are approximately 8,000 either cruising in a certain area or actually voyaging. About half are in the Atlantic, 1,500 to 2,000 in the Pacific, 1,000 in the Indian Ocean, and 1,000 in the Mediterranean. This estimate is about twenty percent lower than the conclusion I drew in 2000 and 2010, when I reckoned that there were between 10,000 and 12,000 boats roaming the oceans of the world.

Finally, those who are planning a world voyage should take heart from the fact that, in spite of some concerns, such attractive destinations as the Azores, French Polynesia, New Zealand, Tonga, Vanuatu and Indonesia, not to speak of more remote or high-latitude destinations, have not been overrun by visitors and show no signs of that happening soon. A definite result, caused mainly by the above concerns, is a move towards regional cruising with many sailors now preferring to limit their voyages to one area or just one ocean. In line with this trend, for many sailors the aim of completing a circumnavigation seems to have lost its aura and whereas in the past most of those who set off on a world voyage were hoping to eventually sail round the globe, nowadays it is only the most determined who find the motivation to go all the way.

At the start of their world voyage, Pete and Tracey Goss know precisely what they want. 'We are out here to see the world but also to escape the madness of modern life. We want to spend our money on memories not things.'

Read the entire report on the global movement of cruising boats on cornellsailing.com/downloads.

SPITSBERGEN

1990	2000	2010	2015
4	10	55	65

DUTCH HARBOR

2015
23

NORTHWEST PASSAGE

1906	2010	2015
1	6	11

NUUK

2015
32

HORTA

1984	2000	2010	2015
614	1144	1098	1232

MADEIRA

2015
518

BERMUDA

1987	2000	2010	2015
998	1160	905	732

LAS PALMAS

1987	2000	2010	2015
1038	993	1495	903

HAWAII

2000	2010	2015
39	30	30

CUBA

2015
500

BAHAMAS

1966	1977	2000	2010	2015
5144	11295	22444	18467	16000

MINDELO

2010	2015
673	750

PANAMA CANAL

1984	2000	2010	2015
496	790	1177	1079

TRINIDAD

1990	2000	2010	2015
1500	2664	1367	1015

TAHITI

1987	2000	2010	2015
328	442	826	556

GALAPAGOS

1990	2000	2010	2015
90	180	395	280

CABEDELO

2015
81

PITCAIRN

2015
14

COOK IS.

2015
209

ST HELENA

1990	2000	2010	2015
92	184	169	196

EASTER ISLAND

1990	2000	2010	2015
15	22	44	79

PUERTO WILLIAMS

2010	2015
505	283

FALKLANDS

1990	2000	2010	2015
10	22	37	29

USHUAIA

1990	2000	2010	2015
30	105	83	64

ANTARCTICA

1990	2000	2010	2015
8	31	32	18

THE NUMBER OF CRUISING YACHTS THAT VISITED KEY CRUISING DESTINATIONS IN 2015 COMPARED WITH OTHER YEARS

In ports where no data was available, the figures in italics indicate the estimated number of boats that called there during that year.

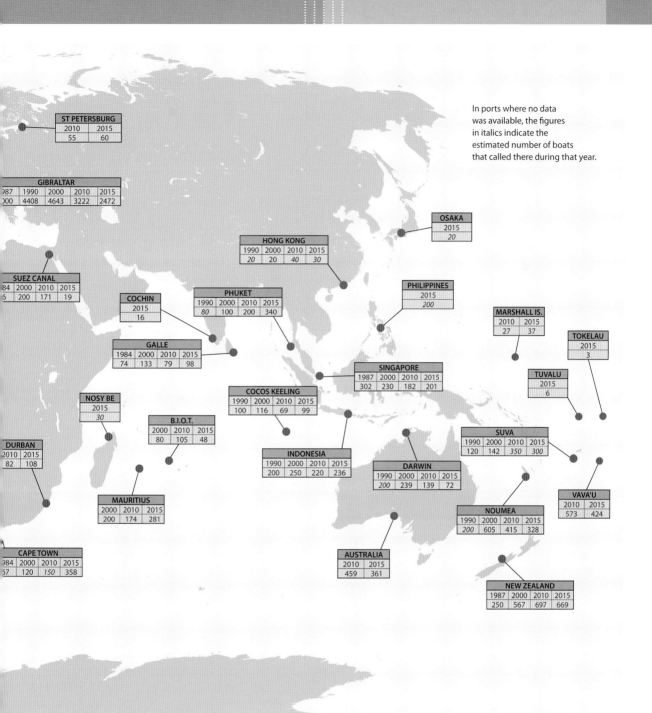

ST PETERSBURG

2010	2015
55	60

GIBRALTAR

987	1990	2000	2010	2015
000	4408	4643	3222	2472

SUEZ CANAL

84	2000	2010	2015
5	200	171	19

OSAKA

2015
20

HONG KONG

1990	2000	2010	2015
20	20	40	30

PHILIPPINES

2015
200

COCHIN

2015
16

PHUKET

1990	2000	2010	2015
80	100	200	340

MARSHALL IS.

2010	2015
27	37

TOKELAU

2015
3

GALLE

1984	2000	2010	2015
74	133	79	98

SINGAPORE

1987	2000	2010	2015
302	230	182	201

TUVALU

2015
6

COCOS KEELING

1990	2000	2010	2015
100	116	69	99

NOSY BE

2015
30

SUVA

1990	2000	2010	2015
120	142	350	300

B.I.O.T.

2000	2010	2015
80	105	48

DURBAN

2010	2015
82	108

INDONESIA

1990	2000	2010	2015
200	250	220	236

DARWIN

1990	2000	2010	2015
200	239	139	72

NOUMEA

1990	2000	2010	2015
200	605	415	328

VAVA'U

2010	2015
573	424

MAURITIUS

2000	2010	2015
200	174	281

CAPE TOWN

984	2000	2010	2015
57	120	150	358

AUSTRALIA

2010	2015
459	361

NEW ZEALAND

1987	2000	2010	2015
250	567	697	669

WORLD WEATHER

How inappropriate to call this planet Earth when it is quite clearly Ocean.

Arthur C Clarke

Ever since man first ventured offshore in a vessel powered by the wind, he has looked for patterns in the wind's behaviour. The fact that there was a regular pattern to the winds was already recognised in ancient times and seasonal sailing routes were a common feature in the ancient world. The importance of defining the prevailing winds in certain areas of the world was recognised by the Portuguese and Spanish navigators during the era of discovery and exploration. This worldwide wind pattern has thus been known for a long time and countless navigators have made use of this knowledge over the centuries.

There are three main factors that influence the formation and direction of the wind: atmospheric pressure, air temperature and the rotation of the earth. The primary cause of wind is a difference of temperature. This in turn leads to a difference in atmospheric pressure mainly because of the tendency of warm air to rise, which is then replaced by cold air drawn from elsewhere. Air also tends to flow from an area of high pressure to one of low pressure. Permanent areas of high pressure are situated between latitudes 20° and 40°, both north and south of the equator. On either side of these cells of high pressure there are areas of low pressure. If it were not for the rotation of the earth, the wind direction would be either north or south, from an area of high pressure to one of low pressure. But because the earth is rotating on its axis in an easterly direction, air which is drawn towards a centre of low pressure is deflected to the right in the northern hemisphere and to the left in the southern one. The result of this movement in the northern hemisphere is the anticlockwise circulation of wind around a low-pressure area and the clockwise rotation around a high-pressure area. The opposite is the case in the southern hemisphere, where the wind circulates in a clockwise direction around a low-pressure area and in an anticlockwise direction around a high-pressure area.

In many areas these systems are distorted by land masses, which are subjected to more pronounced differences of temperature and barometric pressure than the oceans. The wind systems are also affected by the seasons, since the annual movement of the sun causes the areas of high pressure to move towards the poles in the summer. Because of this movement, the wind systems associated with these areas of high pressure, particularly the trade winds, tend to travel a few degrees south or north with the sun.

Trade winds

These steady winds which blow on either side of the equatorial doldrums were so called by the British mariners because of the assistance they gave to the trade of sailing ships. These regular winds are usually NE in the northern hemisphere and SE in the southern hemisphere. They rarely reach gale force and on average blow at force 4–5. The weather associated with the trade winds is usually pleasant, with blue skies and fluffy cumulus clouds. The barometric pressure within the trade wind belt is steady, interrupted only by a pressure wave, which causes a slight rise and fall of the barometer every 12 hours. If the diurnal movement of the barometer ceases, or if it is very pronounced, a tropical disturbance can be expected.

The entire trade wind belt, including the doldrum zone that lies between the two systems, moves north and south during the year. This displacement is influenced by the movement of the sun, although there can be a delay of up to two months between the movement of the sun itself and that of the doldrums.

The Intertropical Convergence Zone

This area of low barometric pressure lying between the trade wind regions of the two hemispheres is known as the Intertropical Convergence Zone (ITCZ), the equatorial trough, or more commonly as the doldrums. The winds in this area are either light or non-existent and the weather is sultry and hot. The only interruptions are occasional squalls and thunderstorms, when rain can be very heavy. The extent of the doldrums varies greatly from year to year and season to season. Although the doldrums have earned their bad reputation because of the frequent calms that could delay ships for days on end, doldrum weather can sometimes be particularly unpleasant, with violent squalls and raging thunderstorms. Weather conditions in the doldrums tend to be worse when the trade winds blow at their strongest.

The location of the ITCZ varies throughout the year. Over land, it moves back and forth across the equator following the sun's zenith point. Over the oceans, where the convergence zone is better defined, the seasonal cycle is more subtle, as the convection is constrained by the distribution of ocean temperatures. The ITCZ moves farther away from the equator during the northern summer than the southern one due to the north-heavy arrangement of the continents.

Variable winds

A zone of light and variable winds extends on the polar sides of the trade winds, corresponding more or less with the high-pressure areas of the two hemispheres, approximately between latitudes 25° and 35°. These zones were given the name of Horse Latitudes, because sailing ships that were becalmed in these areas were sometimes forced to kill the animals on board due to the shortage of drinking water.

Westerly winds

The higher latitudes of both hemispheres have a large proportion of westerly winds, which prevail north and south of latitude 35°. Westerly winds are stronger and more predominant in the southern ocean, where they

The area affected by the Intertropical Convergence Zone which follows the movement of the sun.

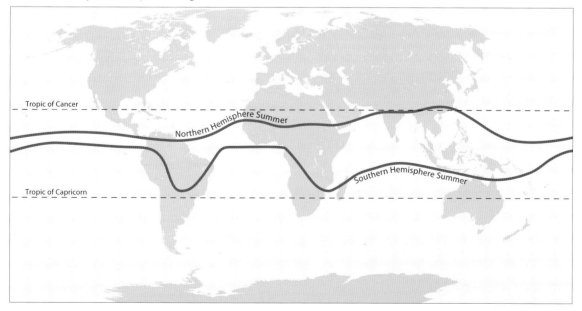

often blow with gale force from the same direction for several days. Because of the more extensive land masses in the northern hemisphere, the westerlies of the northern oceans are lighter and less consistent.

Monsoons

Seasonal winds are experienced in several areas of the world, the name 'monsoon' deriving from the Arabic word meaning 'season'. Such winds blow consistently from one direction for one season and after a short interruption blow with equal consistency from the opposite direction. The most important regions affected by such seasonal winds are the Indian Ocean and West Pacific Ocean.

Depressions

A depression is an area of low barometric pressure which is usually responsible for periods of unsettled weather, although not all depressions are accompanied by strong winds. Depressions occur most frequently in middle and higher latitudes, although the most severe storms encountered at sea are those formed in the low latitudes and are of a revolving nature.

Most depressions move in an easterly direction and the speed at which they move can vary from very little to 40 knots or more. Usually depressions last about four to five days and their movement gradually slows down as they fill and the pressure rises. The strength of the wind generated by a depression is dictated by the closeness of the isobars, which can be seen on a synoptic chart as lines joining areas of equal barometric pressure. The closer the isobars lie together the stronger the wind. The approach of a depression is always indicated by a falling barometer and by a change in the aspect of the sky and cloud formation.

Tropical squalls

This is a common phenomenon encountered in the tropics, especially below latitude 20°. These disturbances travel from east to west at 20–25 knots and are usually perpendicular to the direction of the prevailing wind. They are accompanied by thundery and squally weather. The first indication of an approaching line squall is a heavy band of cumulonimbus cloud to the east. The wind is usually light or calm and the atmosphere oppressive. As the cloud approaches it becomes dark and menacing with occasional thunder and lightning. The bottom of the cloud has the appearance of a straight line but it sometimes changes to an arch as it passes overhead. Suddenly there is a blast of wind from an easterly direction, which on average rises to 25–30 knots, although occasionally it can be much stronger. Shortly after the blast of wind, it starts to rain heavily. Such squalls last on average about half an hour, although sometimes they may last longer. The barometer does not indicate their approach, therefore they can only be detected visually, although they show up on radar. As some of these squalls can be quite violent, it is prudent in squall-prone areas to reduce sail at night, when their approach is more difficult to detect. In the tropical North Atlantic, line squalls occur especially at the beginning and end of the rainy season (May to October). In the South Pacific squalls can occur at all times, although as a rule they are not as violent as in the North Atlantic. Line squalls are less of a problem during the NE monsoon of the North Indian Ocean, but can be violent during the opposite SW monsoon.

Tornadoes

Tornadoes and waterspouts occur in the same areas and during the same season as tropical storms. They usually travel in the same direction as the prevailing wind and their approach can normally be seen, especially as they rarely form at night. The wind generated by a tornado can be extremely violent, but as the actual area covered is very small, the chance of being hit by such a whirlwind at sea is quite remote.

Waterspouts sometimes occur during afternoon thunderstorms near the coast, the ocean side of Chesapeake Bay being particularly vulnerable during the summer months. Tornadoes tend to be much more destructive over land and in spring 2011 several areas in the USA suffered widespread damage and many fatalities.

Tsunamis

These are large waves caused by an earthquake which can occur thousands of miles from the place where the destructive effects of the gigantic wave will be felt. One of the most devastating tsunamis occurred in December 2004 and affected a large area of the Indian Ocean from Thailand to Somalia. Most of the estimated 200,000 fatalities were recorded in Sumatra, Sri Lanka, Phuket and the Nicobar and Andaman Islands, which were closest to the epicentre of the earthquake. Marinas in Malaysia and Thailand suffered badly but boats anchored in deeper water escaped mostly unscathed. A tsunami caused by an earthquake which occurred off the NE coast of Japan on 11 March 2011 caused immense destruction and thousands of fatalities in nearby coastal areas and its effects were felt as far as the coast of Oregon in the USA.

Tropical revolving storms

Tropical revolving storms are the most violent storms that can be encountered at sea and it is both prudent and wise to try and avoid the areas and seasons where such storms occur. The extremely strong winds generated by these storms and the huge seas they raise can easily overwhelm a small boat. Depending on which part of the world they occur in, these storms are known as 'hurricanes', 'cyclones', 'typhoons', or 'willy-willies'. They blow around an area of low pressure, the rotation being anticlockwise in the northern hemisphere and clockwise in the southern hemisphere. The wind does not move around the centre in concentric circles but has a spiral movement, being sucked in towards the core of the storm.

Usually these storms occur on the western sides of the oceans, although they are also found in other parts of the world. They usually form between latitudes 7° and 15° on either side of the equator, but there have been many instances when tropical storms formed closer to the equator. The breeding ground of tropical storms is the ITCZ,

Satellite image showing Hurricane Eugene spinning out of the ITCZ off the Pacific coast of Mexico.

where the two opposing trade wind systems converge. Under certain conditions of barometric pressure, temperature and moisture, the resulting whirlpool of air created at the point of convergence develops into a severe tropical revolving storm. The most dangerous areas affected by such storms are the Western North Atlantic from Grenada to Cape Hatteras, the Western North Pacific from Guam to Japan, the South Pacific from Tonga to the Coral Sea, the north and northwest coasts of Australia, the Western South Indian Ocean, the Arabian Sea and the Bay of Bengal.

As a result of the current climate changes, in some parts of the world tropical storms can occur outside the known dangerous season that usually coincides with the summer months. In the South Pacific Ocean the cyclone season now lasts longer than in the past, while in the North Pacific the force of typhoons seems to be on the increase, with some 'super typhoons' having gusts of close to 200 knots. Because the tropical storm seasons are almost impossible to define accurately, the period indicated at the beginning of each voyage is only approximate. In most oceans tropical storms can occur outside the listed months and therefore this should be borne in mind if a passage is planned at the start or at the end of the accepted tropical storm season.

In addition to their circular motion, tropical revolving storms also have a forward movement. In the northern hemisphere the movement is initially WNW, storms recurving gradually to the N and NE as they reach higher latitudes. In the southern hemisphere the initial movement is WSW, storms recurving to the SE as they approach latitude 20°S. Sometimes a storm does not recurve but continues in a WNW direction in the northern hemisphere, or a WSW direction in the southern hemisphere, until it hits the continental land mass where it gradually breaks up after causing much damage. Occasionally the storm meanders erratically and its direction is impossible to predict with certainty. The speed at which a storm is moving is normally about 10 knots in the early stages and accelerates after recurving.

Tropical storms are most frequent during the late summer and early autumn in both hemispheres. The safe season in the northern hemisphere is from late November to early June, whereas the safe season for the southern hemisphere lasts from June until November. The only tropical area where hurricanes were unknown until recently was the South Atlantic, but Hurricane Catarina, which developed off the coast of Brazil in March 2004, may herald a climate change. In the Western North Pacific no month is considered to be entirely safe, although typhoons are less frequent in winter. In the Coral Sea, extra-seasonal cyclones are not uncommon and have been recorded as late as June and even July. In the North Indian Ocean cyclones do not normally occur in summer, but at the change of the monsoon, either in May to June or in October to November.

The following periods are designated as tropical storm seasons: North Atlantic: June to November; Eastern North Pacific: June to November; Western North Pacific: all year (May to November is the most dangerous period). Bay of Bengal: October to November; Arabian Sea: May to June; South Indian Ocean: November to May; South Pacific: November to May.

Currents of the world

Currents occur at all depths of the oceans, but the only ones of real interest to the small-boat voyager are the surface currents. Because the main cause of surface currents is the direction of the wind, there is a close relationship between their direction and that of the prevailing wind. Constant winds, such as the trade winds, create some of the most constant currents, although these do not always follow exactly the direction of the wind that has generated them. As in the case of the winds, the rotation of the earth has an effect on currents too and therefore in the northern hemisphere currents tend to flow to the right of the direction of the wind, in the southern hemisphere to the left. This is the reason why in the northern hemisphere the currents flow in a clockwise direction, while in the southern hemisphere currents generally tend to follow an anti-clockwise direction.

El Niño and La Niña

This phenomenon occurs along the west coast of South America and is now known to affect weather conditions throughout the world. Its Spanish name derives from the fact that in certain years, around the time of Christmas, the cold north-flowing Humboldt Current was reversed by a warm south-flowing current and, because of the time of year, was named after the Holy Child. El Niño brought havoc to the region every few years but it was not until the widespread devastations caused by it in 1982–1983 and 1997–1998 that the global implications of this natural phenomenon were finally recognised. It is now accepted that El Niño affects weather far beyond the South Pacific.

It is still impossible to predict exactly when a new El Niño will occur, but the 20th century has seen altogether 28 periods, so on average El Niño can be expected to strike every three or four years. Nevertheless, during an El Niño period, sailing during, or close to, the cyclone season should be avoided and, if at all possible, one should attempt to spend the critical period outside the tropical Pacific Ocean. The latest El Niño episode occurred between 2014 and 2016.

When the ocean temperatures revert to a colder period this is now commonly referred to as La Niña. During a period of La Niña, the sea surface temperature across the equatorial Eastern Pacific Ocean can be lower than normal by 3–5°C. During a La Niña episode, the mass of colder water from the Eastern South Pacific is pushed westwards by the easterly winds and accumulates in the northwestern parts of the South Pacific, such as the Coral Sea. The rapid evaporation of the cold water as it collides with the warm air mass can cause widespread climatic disturbances. This happened during the latest La Niña episode, in January 2011, when torrential rains caused disastrous flooding from Queensland to Sri Lanka.

Climate change

Much has been written about this recent phenomenon and few sailors would disagree that global weather conditions seem to be undergoing a radical change. What is quite obvious is that there has been a significant change in weather patterns during the last decade. This has been marked by violent storms in what used to be regarded as the safe season, heavy rainfall and floods in countries where such phenomena were quite unknown, the absence of steady trade winds even on such previously reliable routes as that between the Canaries and the Caribbean, and a visible reduction of both the Antarctic and Arctic ice caps. Although some people still refuse to take notice of what leading meteorologists have been saying for several years, weather patterns are changing and there is no longer any excuse for not taking climate change warnings seriously. This affects sailors on small boats perhaps more than anyone else, so it is worth heeding these warnings and being even more cautious than in the past.

THE ATLANTIC OCEAN

The sea navigated by all the Greeks and the one outside the Pillars called the Atlantis Sea and the Erythraean are one and the same.

Herodotus

The Atlantic Ocean is the second largest of the world's oceans and covers approximately 20 percent of the earth's surface. The earliest known mention of an Atlantis Sea was around 450 BCE in *The Histories of Herodotus*, who in the same quotation referred to the Indian Ocean as the Erythraean Sea. It is believed that both 'Atlantis' and 'Atlantic' are derived from Atlas, one of the titans of Greek mythology. The Greeks believed there was a gigantic river Oceanus which encircled the entire world, part of which included both the Atlantis and Erythraean (Indian) Sea.

Before Europeans discovered other oceans, the term 'ocean' was synonymous with the waters beyond the Strait of Gibraltar, which the Greeks called the Pillars of Heracles (Hercules in Latin), hence the title Admiral of the Ocean Sea that was bestowed on Christopher Columbus after his voyage to the New World in 1492. Columbus was not the first European to discover land on the far side of the Atlantic as he was preceded five centuries earlier by the Norse explorer Leif Erikson who in 1002 or 1003 landed on North America's Atlantic coast while on an expedition from Iceland. The discovery of what the Norse settlers called Vinland is documented in the 13th century Icelandic Sagas and was corroborated by the discovery of an early Norse settlement at L'Anse aux Meadows in Newfoundland.

The first recorded voyage in the Atlantic was made by the Carthagian Hanno in the first half of the sixth century BCE. His fleet passed through the Pillars of Hercules and followed the coast of Africa southwards, founding several colonies as they went along. The voyage continued as far south as modern Gabon, from where they were forced to return as they were running out of provisions. According to the Roman historian Pliny the Elder, Hanno's ships carried on and circumnavigated Africa reaching the borders of Arabia, but this statement is under dispute.

Another remarkable voyage was undertaken by Pytheas of Massilia around 325 BCE. Pytheas described his expedition from Massilia (today's Marseille) to Brittany, Ireland, Britain and Northern Europe in *Peri tou okeanou* (On the Ocean). Only a few excerpts from this work have survived, quoted by later authors, including the Greek historian Strabo. Pytheas was the first person to attribute the tides to being caused by the moon. He also mentioned the midnight sun and introduced the geographical concept of distant Thule, which probably referred to current Norway. This is the earliest record to describe the trade links between southern and northern Europe and shows that there were already regular maritime links between them.

The first Europeans to systematically explore the Atlantic were the Portuguese. Inspired by Prince Henry the Navigator they discovered the island of Madeira in 1419 and the Azores in 1427. They continued exploring the Atlantic coast of Africa and in 1488 Bartolomeu Dias reached the southernmost point of Africa, but it was only in 1498 that Vasco da Gama reached the Indian Ocean by this route. Concerned by the Portuguese successes, and racing to find a trade route to Asia, in 1492 the Spanish monarchs commissioned Christopher Columbus to sail west to reach the Indies. He duly sailed west and did discover land, but it was nowhere near the 'Indies', although until his death that is what he believed he had reached.

England pursued the same aim of reaching Asia by sea and enlisted the services of the Italian navigator Giovanni Caboto (known in English as John Cabot). In 1497 he landed in Newfoundland, thus being the first European to reach that part of North America since the Norse voyages. Cabot was greatly surprised to come across a large number of European fishing boats working the rich fishing grounds of the Grand Banks. It is now believed that the waters off the North American mainland had been visited regularly long before then by Basque, Breton and Norman fishermen who, for commercial reasons, had managed to keep their secret.

Although coastal voyages in small boats had taken place on both sides of the Atlantic since earlier times, it was only by the middle of the 19th century that the first transatlantic voyages were recorded. In 1866, two Americans, JM Hudson and FE Fitch, sailed in 37 days from New York to Margate in England in a 26-foot boat. The first east to west crossing took place four years later in an

Aventura IV on her way to the Northwest Passage.

The first ever couple to complete a transatlantic crossing did so in 1877, also in a 20-foot dory. Thomas and Joanna Crapo took 49 days from New Bedford, Massachusetts to Penzance in England. Originally Thomas had planned to sail alone but his wife insisted on accompanying him. There were many other notable small boat voyages, including that of Joshua Slocum, who in 1895 called at the Azores on the first leg of his world voyage. Slocum went on to complete the first circumnavigation of the globe in a small boat.

During the second half of the 19th century the Atlantic was being crossed regularly by increasingly larger and more luxurious yachts, some of them to take part in regattas in the UK or USA, and this is how the America's Cup came into being. It was only in the early 20th century that yachting became a popular pastime when ordinary people and not just the rich started owning sailing boats. Remarkable round the world voyages successfully completed by people like Sir Francis Chichester or the participants in the first single-handed transatlantic race in 1968 showed what could be achieved in small sailing boats and inspired many others to follow their example. By 1976, when I completed my first transatlantic voyage, hundreds of European and North American boats were sailing every year to and from the Caribbean. The once feared Atlantic was by now jokingly referred to as simply 'the Pond'.

even smaller converted lifeboat of only 20 feet on which the American JC Buckley and Australian Nicholas Primoraz sailed from Cork, Ireland, to Boston, Massachusetts in the USA, an epic voyage that lasted 84 days. The credit for the first solo crossing goes to Alfred Johnson who in 1876 sailed his 20-foot gaff-rigged dory from Gloucester, New Brunswick in Canada to Albertcastle, England.

Even though the North Atlantic is the most researched and monitored body of water in the world, meteorologists have not yet solved all of its mysteries. In spite of the improvements in weather forecasting, violent storms and unsettled weather still sometimes slip by the forecasters, something to bear in mind when putting too much faith in weather forecasts at sea.

WINDS AND CURRENTS

The wild and wasteful ocean.

William Shakespeare

The North Atlantic

THE NORTHEAST TRADE WINDS

The NE trade winds extend in a wide belt north of the equator reaching from the west coast of Africa to the Caribbean Sea. They blow for most of the year on the south side of the anticyclone which is situated in about latitude 30°N, commonly known as the Azores High. The northern limit of the trade winds is around latitude 25°N in winter and 30°N in summer, although the constancy of the trade winds cannot be relied on near their northern limits. The consistency and reliability of the NE trade winds are of particular interest to those who intend to make a transatlantic voyage along the classic route starting in the Canaries. Although the winter months are reputed to have the most consistent winds, there are years in which these winds are found in lower latitudes than normal and it is not unusual for boats to cover almost half the distance to the Caribbean before falling in with steady winds. It is therefore advisable to be certain the trade winds area has been reached before turning west.

The constancy of the trade winds improves during the winter months as does their strength. Although the average strength of these winds is force 3–4, it is not uncommon for them to reach force 6 and even 7 during January to March. The trade winds tend to be lighter and less consistent in summer, which is also the hurricane season. They have more of a northerly component in the eastern part of the ocean and become increasingly easterly in the Caribbean.

Also described as trade winds are the so-called Portuguese trades which blow from between NE and NW off the western coast of the Iberian Peninsula from April to September or October. Another regional variation of the NE trade winds is the harmattan. This is a hot and dry wind, created by the NE trade winds blowing over the deserts of Africa and reaching the sea laden with dust around latitude 20°N. This easterly wind normally occurs between November and February.

Other regional phenomena associated with the area which is normally under the influence of the prevailing NE winds are the strong northerly winds commonly known as 'northers'. During the winter months vast anticyclones develop over the North American continent occasionally

Finally, after a week at sea, the wind settled from behind.

'I think I'll try the twin foresails today,' said Dad. He dropped the mainsail and hoisted the two genoas. Each sail was fixed to a pole that pushed it away from the boat and helped fill it with wind. The sails stretched out either side of the bow like two white wings. An ocean swell lifted *Aventura* up, and then with the wind's help she surfed her way down the other side.

The sky was bright blue with a few puffy clouds passing by.

'Look at those clouds,' said Dad. 'Typical trade wind clouds.'

'Trade winds? Have they come?'

'Maybe... perhaps too soon to tell. But it looks promising.'

'How far have we gone?' we asked yet again and he took his brass dividers and held one of their sharp points against the pencil mark from the day before, moved the other one to today's, and measured off the distance between the two on the scales along the side of the chart.

'Not bad today. 100 miles. We're doing a steady 4 knots.' The following day when we gathered around the chart table he said, 'Look, we have passed the 20° line of longitude.'

'Surprise!' Mum produced two small wrapped presents from behind her back. For lunch Dad made a treat of pancakes drizzled with syrup.

The trades really had come. The winds blew from behind at a steady rate, Dad didn't touch the sails for two weeks and the self-steering did all the work. This was the most pleasant sailing we'd ever known.

Doina Cornell, from *Child of the Sea*

reaching as far as the Gulf of Mexico. A strong northerly flow of cold air develops ahead of this area of high pressure, and becomes a violent norther which is sometimes felt as far away as the Caribbean. The progress of a norther is usually checked by the higher islands of Hispaniola and Cuba, but to the north of these islands it can be particularly dangerous, mainly because of the steep seas which are created when a strong norther blows against the north-flowing Gulf Stream. The approach of a norther is usually heralded by a heavy bank of cloud on the N or NW horizon.

THE INTERTROPICAL CONVERGENCE ZONE

The extent of the trade winds is influenced at all times of the year by the position of the ITCZ or doldrums. The ITCZ stays north of the equator throughout the year, although its position varies greatly, both in accordance with the seasonal movement of the sun and also on a diurnal basis. The width of the doldrums is also variable and averages between 200 and 300 miles, although it tends to be wider near the African coast and narrower near Brazil. The weather inside the doldrum belt is more turbulent in the eastern part of the ocean than in the west, with frequent squalls and thunderstorms occurring.

SOUTHWEST MONSOON

The heat generated by the land mass of Africa during the summer lowers the barometric pressure over that area and causes the ITCZ to be deflected towards the north. The SE trade winds of the South Atlantic are thus drawn across the equator and arrive off the coast of Africa as the SW monsoon. It lasts from June to October between the equator and as far north as latitude 15°N, but in the Gulf of Guinea light SW winds prevail throughout the year.

VARIABLES

A band of variable winds extends across the Atlantic to the north of the NE trade winds. This is the area of high atmospheric pressure which straddles the 30°N parallel, being situated slightly to the north of it in summer and to the south in winter. The winds in the eastern half of this area are usually northerly and can be regarded as an extension of the trade winds. In the western part of the ocean the winds are often very light and long periods of calms are common. This is the area of the Horse Latitudes and the infamous Sargasso Sea where sailing ships used to be becalmed for days on end.

WESTERLIES

Westerly winds predominate in the northern part of the Atlantic Ocean, where the weather is often unsettled, mainly due to the almost continuous passage of depressions that race across the ocean in an easterly direction. The winds in these higher latitudes are less constant in direction than those of the Roaring Forties of the Southern Ocean, although the predominant direction is westerly.

REGIONAL WINDS

A local phenomenon in the Canary Islands is the sudden gusts of wind caused by the high islands. The worst wind acceleration zones are in the channels between the islands and the sudden blasts are called 'mosquitoes' by local sailors as they are only heard when they bite. The wind strength can go up by between 10 and 20 knots and the only warning is a darkening and rippling of the surface of the sea in the direction of the prevailing wind.

TROPICAL SQUALLS

This is a common phenomenon encountered in the tropics, especially below latitude 20°. These disturbances travel from east to west at 20–25 knots and are usually perpendicular to the direction of the prevailing wind. They are accompanied by thundery and squally weather. The first indication of an approaching squall is a heavy band of cumulonimbus to the east. The wind is usually light or calm and the atmosphere oppressive. As the cloud approaches it becomes dark and menacing with occasional thunder and lightning. The bottom of the cloud has the appearance of a straight line hence the common description 'line squall', although it sometimes changes to

an arch as it passes overhead. Its arrival is heralded by a sudden blast of wind from an easterly direction, which on average rises to 25–30 knots, although occasionally it can be stronger. Shortly after the blast of wind, it starts to rain heavily. Such squalls last on average about half an hour, although sometimes they may last longer. The barometer does not indicate their approach, therefore they can only be detected visually, although they show up on radar. As some of these squalls can be quite violent, it is prudent in squall-prone areas to reduce sail at night, when their approach is more difficult to detect.

Hurricanes

A large area of the Western North Atlantic is affected by tropical revolving storms, which can occur theoretically at any time as hurricanes have been recorded over the last few centuries in every month of the year, although very rarely in winter months. The official dates for the hurricane season are from 1 June to 30 November, the highest frequency occurring from August to October, with a lower number occurring in the rest of the season. Both the frequency and intensity of hurricanes vary greatly from year to year, some years being extremely bad with up to a record 15 hurricanes, while other years go by with hardly any being recorded.

Most hurricanes are born in the doldrum area south of the Cape Verde Islands. They usually travel west towards the Caribbean, their tracks moving clockwise around the perimeter of an area of high pressure. The area most affected by hurricanes is the Caribbean Basin, particularly the northern part of the Lesser Antilles, the Virgins, Bahamas, Bermuda, the Gulf of Mexico and Florida. At the beginning and end of the hurricane season, these storms sometimes develop in the Western Caribbean, from where they move in a northerly direction mainly affecting the southern states of the USA. The later months of the season are particularly dangerous for those sailing in the Caribbean, as September and October hurricanes usually develop locally and warnings are shorter. Therefore if one intends to sail in the Caribbean during the hurricane season, especially in the Lesser Antilles, it is safer to plan to do so at the beginning of the hurricane season (June) rather than towards its end (October to early November). The high-frequency months of August and particularly September should be avoided altogether.

The latest tropical storm recorded in the North Atlantic was Hurricane Otto, which formed in the SW Caribbean on 20 November 2016, intensified to a category 3 storm and struck Costa Rica and Nicaragua on 24 November. It was followed in 2017 by a hyperactive Atlantic hurricane season, which started early with Hurricane Arlene on 20 April that passed to the west of the Azores Islands. It was followed by Tropical Storm Bret, which struck the island of Trinidad on 20 June, the first hurricane to directly affect that island since 1933. In early October, Hurricane Nate became to first hurricane to strike Panama. One week later, Hurricane Ophelia became the easternmost major hurricane in the Atlantic basin on record, and later impacted most of Northern Europe as an extra-tropical cyclone.

Currents

The currents of the North Atlantic are part of a vast clockwise-moving system that occupies the entire ocean south of latitude 40°N. The NE trade winds generate the North Equatorial Current, which sets westward from the Cape Verde Islands to the Caribbean. Running to the north of it is the weaker North Subtropical Current. Part of the North Equatorial Current sets into the Caribbean Sea, while another branch flows northward along the Lesser Antilles and is known as the Antilles Current. The mainspring of the North Atlantic circulation is the Gulf Stream, which in spite of its name does not originate in the Gulf of Mexico but is a continuation of the North Equatorial Current. The wide band of warm water sweeps along the eastern side of North America until it meets the cold Labrador Current, which forces it to swing in an easterly direction. From about longitude 45°W the Gulf Stream ceases to be so strong and continues eastwards as the North Atlantic Current although a branch continues to the UK and Norway.

In the eastern part of the ocean the currents are less well defined, the North Atlantic Current fanning out into different directions to form the south-setting Azores Current and further east the Portugal Current. This latter current sets south along the Iberian Peninsula, one branch being deflected through the Strait of Gibraltar into the Mediterranean, while the other sets SW along the African coast to become the Canary Current. Ultimately this current turns west to join the North Equatorial Current, thus completing the clockwise system of the North Atlantic currents.

South of latitude 10°N the pattern of the currents is more complex. Between the two west-setting equatorial currents is the Equatorial Countercurrent. In winter this east-setting countercurrent is most noticeable along latitude 6°N east of about longitude 45°W, but it diminishes in strength towards the South American continent where it disappears altogether. The South Equatorial Current combines in this region with the North Equatorial Current to form a strong west-flowing current which is deflected in a northerly direction along the coast of South America towards the Lesser Antilles.

The South Atlantic

THE SOUTHEAST TRADE WINDS

Because the ITCZ is situated north of the equator throughout the year, it could be said that the South Atlantic Ocean does not have a doldrum zone. The SE trade winds are more constant than their North Atlantic counterpart, the NE trades. They form the equatorial side of the air circulation around the South Atlantic anticyclone, which is situated between latitudes 22° and 25°S and between 30° and 32°S and has a direct bearing on the winds and weather of both the tropical and subtropical South Atlantic. The SE trade winds extend as far as the equator in the southern winter and their northern limit retreats by a few degrees to the south in summer. Their southern limit extends normally to a line joining the Cape of Good Hope to the Brazilian island of Trinidade. Their direction varies from SE or SSE on the eastern side of the ocean to become almost easterly in the western part. The average strength of the SE trades is 15 knots, but they diminish in strength towards the equator.

VARIABLES

A zone of light variable winds extends to the south of the SE trade wind belt and is similar to the Horse Latitudes of the North Atlantic. This region of variable winds coincides with the area of the South Atlantic High. The position of the high is influenced by the seasonal movement of the sun, reaching its southern limit in January and its northern limit in July. To the east of the 0° meridian the winds in those latitudes tend to be mostly southerly and can be regarded as an extension of the SE trade winds. The summer winds in the western half of this region are mostly NE.

WESTERLIES

Winds in the higher latitudes of the South Atlantic are predominantly westerly. This is the region of the Roaring Forties where the continuous passage of depressions from west to east generates winds that are often of gale force. These westerlies are a normal feature of southern waters where they blow unhindered south of the three great capes Horn, Good Hope and Leeuwin.

REGIONAL WINDS

The *pampero* is a burst of cold west or southwest wind resembling a line squall that gets its name from the lowlands (pampas) of Argentina, Uruguay and Southern Brazil and is usually associated with a passing low or cold front. This wind is most common in winter, between May and August, but it can occur also at other times, especially in the River Plate estuary.

TROPICAL STORMS

Until recently tropical storms were unknown in the South Atlantic, but Hurricane Catarina, which developed off the coast of Brazil in March 2004, may be an early indication of the current climate change.

CURRENTS

The currents of the South Atlantic Ocean are part of a well-defined anticlockwise circulation. The South Equatorial Current flows in a broad belt from east to west with its axis roughly along latitude 6°S. The part of this current which is between the equator and latitude 6°S is regarded as one of the most constant currents in the world. The set is always in a westerly direction, usually between WNW and WSW, the average rate being about 1 knot. Further south, to about latitude 20°S, there is the weaker South Subtropical Current also setting to the west. The South Equatorial Current extends across the equator to about latitude 4°N and one branch of it combines with the North Equatorial Current to form a strong current setting towards the Caribbean Sea. The other branch is deflected to the south by the South American land mass and combines with the South Subtropical Current to form the Brazil Current. This current sets strongly south parallel to the coast until it reaches latitude 25°S, where part of it turns east. The remainder carries on as far as latitude 35°S, where it also turns east to join the vast body of water which sets eastward and is generated by the Southern Ocean Current. This broad belt of cold water sets eastward in the southern hemisphere to the south of all continents.

On the African side the main ocean circulation of the South Atlantic is completed by the Benguela Current. This current sets north along the coast of Africa and is a continuation of the Agulhas Current after the latter has passed the Cape of Good Hope. North of latitude 20°S the Benguela Current moves away from the African coast fanning out into the Subtropical and South Equatorial Currents. Near the African coast, however, the set of the current is always northerly and from February to April it reaches as far as the equator.

Replicas of the original vessels leaving Spain during the quincentenary celebrations of 1992.

ATLANTIC OCEAN VOYAGES

Following the light of the sun, we left the Old World.

Christopher Columbus

Whether on a weekend cruise or a long passage, no sailor who has ever experienced the unpredictability and changing moods of the mighty Atlantic would disagree with Shakespeare's description of it as a 'wild and wasteful ocean'. But, true as it may be, it only applies to the higher latitudes, which explains why most voyages planned by North Atlantic sailors aim for warmer waters, whether the Mediterranean, Canaries or Eastern Caribbean for European sailors, or the Bahamas, the Western or Eastern Caribbean for Americans and Canadians. Compared to the thousands of boats that sail every year to the Caribbean, the number of high-latitude voyages is much smaller, although Arctic destinations such as Spitsbergen and Greenland are now visited by increasingly more boats as

sailors are attracted to new and challenging destinations. Even the Northwest Passage is now being successfully tackled by cruising boats as a convenient shortcut between the North Pacific and North Atlantic.

With the same purpose of widening their horizons, more sailors are extending a Caribbean voyage to visit parts of West Africa and Brazil, or sail to more remote South Atlantic destinations. However, whereas the North Atlantic is crisscrossed by a multitude of cruising routes, the same is not the case in the South Atlantic where most voyages follow the well-established routes that lead from South Africa or South America to the Caribbean. But things are changing and, as in the North Atlantic, more boats are being attracted to new destinations, whether in West Africa, Patagonia or Antarctica.

Shakespeare's Atlantic might be wild but it is far from wasteful as dotted about it are some of the most attractive cruising grounds in the world. The voyages described in the following pages include all the current popular destinations in both hemispheres as well as some of the less frequented ones, by outlining the various alternatives on how to sail there, whether by a linear, open-ended or circular route. From the cruising opportunities of the Baltic to the ever-changing scenery of the eastern shore of North America, from the cultural and gastronomic delights of Brittany to the brooding mystery of the Amazon and the exuberance of Brazil's Carnival, the diversity of the countries bordering the Atlantic provides the intrepid voyager an inexhaustible source of cruising opportunities for.

Linear voyages:

Voyages to the Caribbean and Panama

Voyages to the Mediterranean

Voyages to Northern Europe

Voyages to North America

Voyages to South America and Antarctica

Voyages to South Africa

Circular voyages:

Circular voyages from Europe

Circular voyages from the US East Coast

Circular voyages in the South Atlantic

Voyages to the Caribbean and Panama

A1 • **Voyages from Europe**

A2 • **Voyages from North America**

A3 • **Voyages from South America**

A4 • **Voyages from South Africa**

The first small-boat voyages between North America and Europe were undertaken around the middle of the 19th century but it took another hundred years for such voyages to occur on a regular basis. Initially, the destination of choice for European sailors undertaking a longer voyage was the Mediterranean. Also in pursuit of a warm-water winter destination, North American sailors first headed for the Bahamas and only later discovered the attractions of the Virgins and Lesser Antilles. Before long the Eastern Caribbean became the destination for hundreds of boats from both sides of the Atlantic as more and more sailors were undaunted by the long passage. With improved facilities and the opening of charter bases in many locations, the Eastern Caribbean became the Mecca of cruising sailors and its success continues unabated.

Besides the beauty of the islands, the pleasant winter climate and favourable weather conditions, an important reason for this success is that the seasons complement each other perfectly. The best time to be in the Caribbean is from December to May when sailing conditions both in Europe and North America are anything but pleasant, therefore a voyage to the Caribbean can easily be planned to take place at a convenient time, as both the outward and return journeys can be undertaken at the change of seasons. In this way, winter can be spent in a benign tropical climate and summer in the equally pleasant temperate counterpart. With similarly matching seasons and no threat of hurricanes in the South Atlantic, voyages from the southern hemisphere to the Caribbean are equally easy to plan and accomplish.

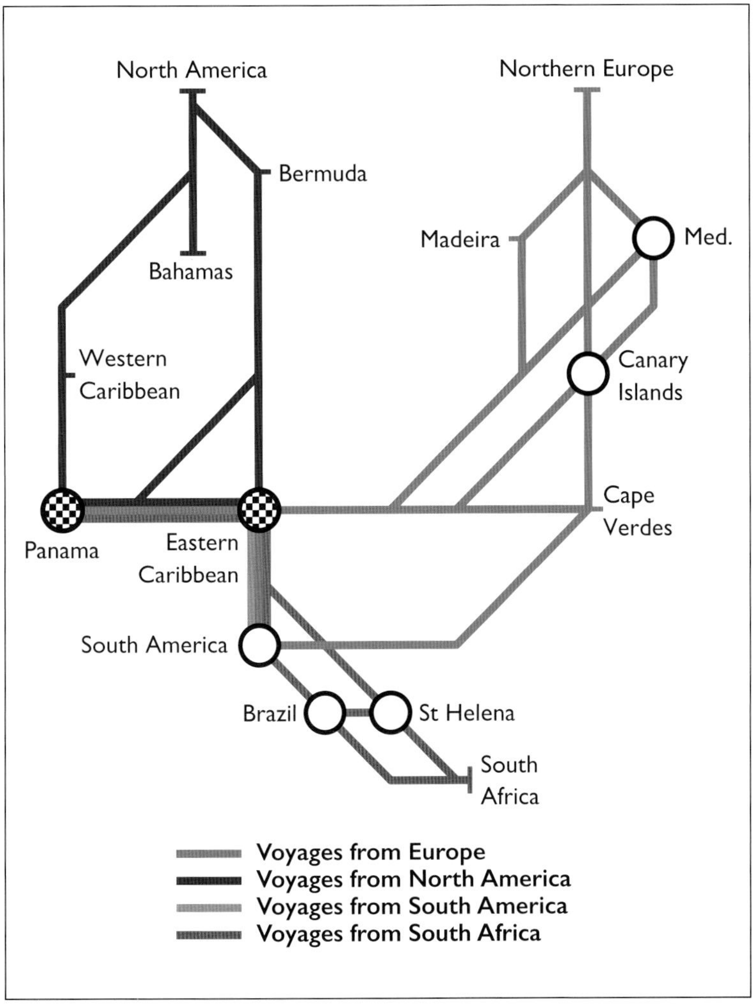

Voyages from Europe
Voyages from North America
Voyages from South America
Voyages from South Africa

For European sailors a voyage to the Caribbean is both a temptation and a challenge, and most hope to realise it at some point in their sailing lives. Whether starting from Northern Europe or the Mediterranean the voyage is relatively easy to plan as the favourable seasons fit perfectly into the overall timing: a summer voyage south from Northern Europe, an autumn arrival in the Canaries, a late autumn departure for the Caribbean, an enjoyable winter sojourn in the Lesser Antilles and Virgin Islands, and a return home the following spring or early summer. This voyage can easily be accomplished in one year. Those who cannot arrange such a long uninterrupted break from their professional lives can divide the voyage into separate segments by doing it in convenient stages: sailing one segment, leaving the boat in a marina, flying home and returning later for the next stage. All this is made possible by the availability of marinas and boatyards as well as a good choice of flights from any of the cruising hubs located at strategic points along the way. This is one of the reasons why the overall voyage has been subdivided into shorter segments and also includes a choice of alternative routes to reach the Caribbean.

A1 • Voyages from Europe

- **A1a** Northern Europe to the Canary Islands
- **A1b** Gibraltar to the Eastern Caribbean
- **A1c** Madeira to the Eastern Caribbean
- **A1d** Canary Islands to the Caribbean direct
- **A1e** Canary Islands to the Caribbean via the Cape Verdes and Brazil
- **A1f** Eastern Caribbean to Panama

A1a Northern Europe to the Canary Islands

Recommended time: June to September

World Cruising Routes:

AN18	Northern Europe to Canary Islands
AN13	Southbound from Northern Europe
AN14	Routes across the Bay of Biscay
AN16	Northern Europe to Mediterranean
AN32	Gibraltar to Canary Islands
AN23	Portugal to Madeira
AN31	Gibraltar to Madeira
AN41	Madeira to Canary Islands
AN19	Northern Europe to Azores
AN136	Azores to Canary Islands

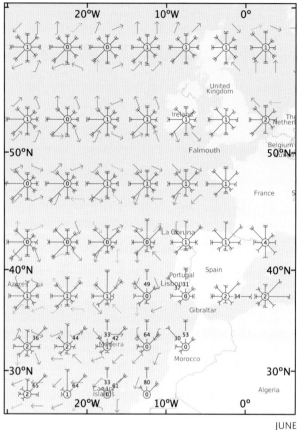

JUNE

JULY

When I planned the structure of this book, I could have started anywhere in the world and only when I put pen to paper, or rather fingers to keyboard, did I realise that my own introduction to offshore sailing happened in these same waters. A passage across the Bay of Biscay is certainly a good introduction to ocean voyaging, even if the experience is not always enjoyable. No one will deny that the Bay of Biscay can be a tricky stretch of water to handle, even by experienced sailors.

Having crossed Biscay on several occasions, I know from personal experience how important it is to not only be well prepared but also to choose a favourable time of departure. This is particularly important for those with limited offshore experience or whose boats are new and untried.

Those for whom the way south leads through the English Channel can wait for a favourable time of departure in one of England's western ports, such as Falmouth. Those leaving from Scandinavia, and who would rather avoid sailing through the busiest part of the North Sea and the crowded English Channel, should

consider the alternative route via the Caledonian Canal and Irish Sea. The detour that this implies is more than made up for by the attractions of this route, which also has the advantage of taking the boat along a more westerly track and thus away from the Bay of Biscay.

Throughout this book I will outline various alternative routes to your chosen destination and this first segment of a voyage to the Caribbean is a good example, as there are several attractive alternatives to reach the Canaries. Those who are in a hurry should sail the direct route to the Canaries, either non-stop or with a slight detour to Madeira. The majority of boats heading south are more likely to make several stops en route, often starting with a short dash across the Bay of Biscay to a port in NW Spain, such as La Coruña or Bayona, then continuing south along the Portuguese coast before either sailing on to the Canaries or turning left for Gibraltar and a longer or shorter foray into the Mediterranean before resuming the voyage south. From either Portugal or Gibraltar, the voyage can continue either directly to the Canaries or be interrupted in Madeira or Morocco, the latter being an

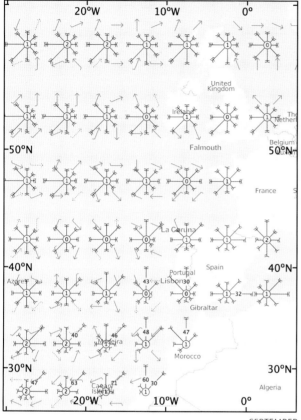

SEPTEMBER

Biscay Ahoy

I have crossed the Bay of Biscay in all of my boats, and every time the experience was marked by a memorable incident. On our first crossing in May 1975, the NE winds gave us a good start and we were sailing fast, *Aventura* coping well with the swell until I decided to put into practice something I had read in a book by a famous sailor about keeping the crew happy. So, when time for lunch came, I trimmed the sails, turned into the wind and hove-to. Suddenly all hell broke loose as the boat was being thrown about by the high swell. Gwenda rushed into the cockpit thinking that we had broken something, while Ivan and Doina were calling for buckets, overcome by the seasickness which they had kept at bay until then. Remembering another bit of wisdom passed down by one of those experienced predecessors, that of trying not to panic even when the odds are against you, I turned the boat onto her old course, set the sails, and never again hove-to for a meal while on an offshore passage.

Aventura II left England on her maiden voyage in March 1988 and the weather in the Bay of Biscay was, as to be expected, rough. In the middle of the dreaded Bay, with the wind increasing, I tried to furl in some mainsail, but however hard I tried, the in-mast furling gear refused to budge. The sail had jammed and the solution was to put a knife to it, something I was not prepared to do. The other alternative was to carry on sailing with a full mainsail and hope for the best. In over 30 knots of wind that was certainly fast and exciting, but we made it safely into Lisbon, where we docked the boat with difficulty with the full mainsail still up.

The crossing on *Aventura III* in 1998 was even more exciting as close to Cape Finisterre we were overtaken in the middle of the night by a large ship which suddenly made a 90 degree turn heading straight for us. Running under full sail and unable to manoeuvre I gybed all standing, started the engine and with full power barely managed to get out of its way as the ship passed a few metres behind us with no one visible on the brightly lit bridge. The only possible explanation was that having reached a waypoint, the autopilot had altered course for the next one.

Jimmy Cornell, *Aventura III*

alternative that is more attractive to boats sailing south from the Mediterranean.

Another alternative route from Northern Europe to the Canaries passes through the Azores, but although the distances involved are not much greater, this route is rarely sailed. The detour is amply justified by the attractions of this archipelago which, surprisingly, does not seem to be regarded as a worthwhile cruising destination in its own right. This is shown by the large numbers of sailors who call there on their way back from the Caribbean and rarely see more than the place where they made landfall.

The voyage from Northern Europe is definitely a summer passage when favourable conditions are normally encountered all the way to the Canaries. From June onwards the proportion of favourable winds gradually increases with northerly winds predominating both across the Bay of Biscay and even more so along the Iberian coast where the Portuguese trades are a constant feature of summer. South of the latitude of Cape St Vincent, the prevailing winds continue to blow from the northerly quarter all the way to the Canaries.

The Canaries are an important cruising hub and an ideal place to prepare for the continuation of the voyage as repair facilities are of a good standard and provisioning can only be described as excellent. There is at least one marina on each island, so that those who arrive too early for the Atlantic crossing can find a suitable place to leave their boats and either return home or spend their time cruising the eight islands of the archipelago. Arriving early is indeed a good tactic as sailing conditions in the Bay of Biscay deteriorate with the approach of autumn and, even south of Gibraltar, by September weather conditions become less favourable.

Although the majority of boats bound for the Caribbean head that way along the traditional trade wind route by starting from one of the Canary Islands, some skippers prefer to buck this trend and start their transatlantic passage from a more northerly port, such as Gibraltar or Madeira.

A1b Gibraltar to the Eastern Caribbean

Recommended time: November

Tropical storms: June to November

World Cruising Routes:

  AN33   Gibraltar to Lesser Antilles

Most of those who that take this option of sailing directly to the Lesser Antilles or Virgin Islands have been delayed in the Mediterranean and may be in a hurry to reach their destination by the quickest way possible. In almost all cases they are either racing boats that have been taking part in one of the late-season regattas in the Mediterranean or charter yachts that are moving their base of operations for the winter season to the Caribbean. Very few cruising boats leave their departure from the Mediterranean so late, and for a very good reason as sailing conditions in the Strait of Gibraltar are often bad at this time of year.

Weather conditions on the direct route to the Carib-

bean in November can be a rather mixed bag, especially in the early stages, as consistent NE winds only become established well to the south of the latitude of the Canaries. Unless you can be sure of having reasonable winds all along the great circle route, the traditional way of taking the longer route by sailing first on a SW course into the trade wind zone area before turning west may still prove to be the best tactic.

A1c Madeira to the Eastern Caribbean

Recommended time: November to February

Tropical storms: June to November

World Cruising Routes:

  AN42   Madeira to Lesser Antilles

With the Canaries, usually being crowded with boats preparing for the Atlantic crossing in November, and services being fully stretched, some sailors prefer to start their passage from Madeira. Although repair facilities and services for yachts are not as comprehensive as in Gran Canaria, Madeira is a good base to prepare for the forthcoming ocean crossing, something that its main port of Funchal has been doing for centuries by victualling ships bound for distant destinations. One mariner who stopped here on several occasions was James Cook and local records show that when the *Endeavour* stopped there in August 1768 she took on 300 gallons of Madeira wine for the exclusive use of the officers and gentlemen on board. The same wine lodge is still in business in Funchal and is well worth a visit as part of the preparations for the forthcoming voyage. As there are no adequate

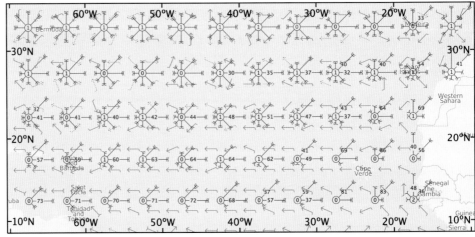

NOVEMBER

docking facilities for visiting yachts in Funchal, one of the marinas, such as Quinta do Lorde, should be used as a base.

Lying that much closer than Gibraltar to the classic transatlantic route, boats leaving from Madeira should apply the same tactics as those setting off from the Canaries by sailing first on a SW course until they have reached the area of prevailing NE winds before setting course for their Caribbean destination.

A1d Canary Islands to the Eastern Caribbean direct

Recommended time: Late November to February

Tropical storms: June to November

World Cruising Routes:

AN51   Canary Islands to Lesser Antilles

While an early arrival in the Canaries is always a good idea, the opposite is true of a landfall in the Caribbean, where the hurricane season is only considered to be over by the middle of November. However, as a consequence of climate change the risk of a late hurricane is now considerably higher, so it is probably not wise to plan to arrive before late November or preferably early December. A longer hurricane season is now an accepted phenomenon in the North Atlantic and should be taken into account when planning a transatlantic voyage. The latest tropical storm recorded in the North Atlantic was Hurricane Otto, which formed in the SW Caribbean on 20 November 2016 and struck Costa Rica and Nicaragua on 24 November. The earliest hurricane in 2017 was Arlene, which struck the island of Trinidad on 20 June.

For many European sailors the voyage to the Eastern Caribbean is their first introduction to trade wind sailing. Before your expectations are raised too high it is important to point out that while NE winds do indeed prevail both in the area of the Canaries and to the south of the islands, strictly speaking these are not the true trade winds, which only blow consistently further south, in the latitude of the Cape Verde Islands. Wind conditions between those two island groups can only be described as light and variable although, depending on the time of year, there can be a higher or lower proportion of NE winds. This is the reason why in the days before long-term forecasts, boats leaving the Canaries were advised not to set a direct course for the Caribbean too soon but to sail a conservative course that passed 200 to 300 miles NW of the Cape Verdes. It is only around that point, where consistent trade winds are usually met, that a course for the chosen destination should be set. Such a conservative approach still has its merits as the shortest route is not necessarily the fastest. Passing that much closer to the Cape Verdes also has the advantage of being able to make an emergency stop there should the need arise, whether to change crew or fill up with fuel if too much was burned in the light winds that can be encountered south of the Canaries.

Once in the trade wind belt, sailing conditions are generally good, with prevailing NE or E winds blowing between 15 and 20 knots, occasionally higher, a quartering swell and favourable current. The North Atlantic trade winds are not as consistent as in other tropical areas of the world and it is quite rare to have an uninterrupted spell of favourable winds all the way across. It is more likely to have the trade winds fail on one or two occasions, although calms rarely last very long. More frustrating are the tropical squalls that can catch out those not yet acquainted with tropical sailing conditions, as a sudden squall can be accompanied both by a stronger wind and a change in its direction. The high number of gear breakages caused by squalls, as reported at the end of transatlantic passages, are a reminder of their potential viciousness.

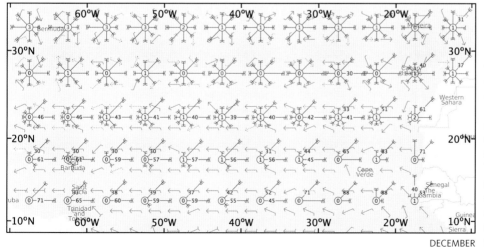

DECEMBER

An African Interlude

We left Dakar at dawn towards Djifère located at the mouth of the Saloum River 60 miles south of Dakar. As we approached the river mouth a large number of grey butterflies landed on the boat, hanging like trembling decorations

from the sails and rigging. The intricate entrance channel must be negotiated at high tide and, for those who have not done it before, preferably with a local pilot. The Saloum Delta extends over a large area and much of it is navigable. We anchored off the village of Djifère, which is entirely dedicated to fishing, the wide continental shelf being very rich in fish. On the beach fronting the village there was a continual ballet of dozens of gaily painted canoes landing passengers and all kinds of colourful fish.

Early the following morning we left for the village of Foundiougne. At dawn the river was calm and quiet and, being wafted along by a favourable current, we could admire the surroundings reeling by in slow motion. Navigation is relatively easy, as the river is wide and deep and the channels are well marked. By late morning we reached Foundiougne, a small town whose riverfront was dotted with baobab and kapok trees. Later, we continued under sail to Mar, a magical trip carried noiselessly downriver by wind and current. Next morning, being Sunday, we decided to take the dinghy ashore to attend mass in the nearby village. The mass was very lively, with beautiful songs and a moving atmosphere. Our last night was spent off Diounar, a small village south of Djifère. We savoured a beautiful sunset as the fiery globe set behind the silhouetted islands dotted about the crescent lagoon that separates us from the ocean that will carry us across to our next destination: the Amazon.

Xavier Duménil, *Yaz*

For boats arriving in the Lesser Antilles from the east, there is a wide choice of landfalls and it is a good idea to choose a suitable landfall that fits your future cruising plans. Barbados is the logical landfall at the end of an Atlantic crossing, as it lies further east than the other islands, and facilities for visiting yachts are slowly improving. St Lucia is a good choice as it lies halfway up the chain of islands, but Rodney Bay Marina can get very crowded during the arrival of the ARC in early December. Martinique, the preferred landfall for French sailors, may be a better option as it has a good range of repair facilities in such places as Le Marin. Antigua is a popular landfall for larger yachts and English Harbour also tends to be crowded in early December. Grenada and Bequia are other possibilities with the advantage that both are close to the Grenadines.

A fact which is worth bearing in mind when drawing up a cruising plan for the Eastern Caribbean is that at the beginning of winter winds tend to be from the NE, becoming increasingly easterly as the winter progresses, veering to SE towards May and the end of the safe season. This means that it makes sense to attempt to cruise the Lesser Antilles from north to south, thus taking advantage of the NE winds of early winter, before reversing the direction of travel in March or April as the direction of the prevailing winds becomes more easterly. This is, in any case, the logical way to go especially for those planning to leave the Caribbean at the end of the safe season, whether to sail back to Europe or North America. This tactic of moving briskly to the northern islands and then cruising south at a more leisurely pace is just as valid for those intending to sail to Trinidad or Grenada to lay up their boats for the summer and the hurricane season. It must be stressed, however, that cruising or leaving the boat in the tropics has become more risky than in the past.

A1e Canary Islands to the Caribbean via the Cape Verdes and Brazil

Recommended time: October to March

Tropical storms: June to November (North Atlantic)

World Cruising Routes:

AN52	Canary Islands to Cape Verde Islands
AN53	Canary Islands to West Africa
AN67	Cape Verde Islands to West Africa
AN64	West Africa to Lesser Antilles
AT11	Canary and Cape Verde Islands to Brazil
AT12	West Africa to Brazil
AT21	Brazil to Lesser Antilles

A quite different way to reach the Caribbean is to sail a roundabout route that calls at the Cape Verde Islands, followed by possible detours to Senegal and Gambia in West Africa, before crossing over to Brazil. This route was first sailed by French sailors, who were attracted to Senegal and its Casamance region, an area of rich wildlife along the river of the same name. The river is navigable for about 80 miles but safety concerns have kept visiting yachts away from this area, with the Saloum River and its extensive delta providing a safer and more convenient substitute. An African experience, very different to that of the more developed coastal area, can be gained by a trip along the neighbouring Gambia River which is navigable for about 160 miles. Safety concerns also affect this area, so the latest situation should be ascertained before planning a visit.

Some boats have ventured further south to neighbouring Guinea-Bissau and Guinea but because of the uncertain political situation in some of the countries that lie further along the Gulf of Guinea few yachts visit

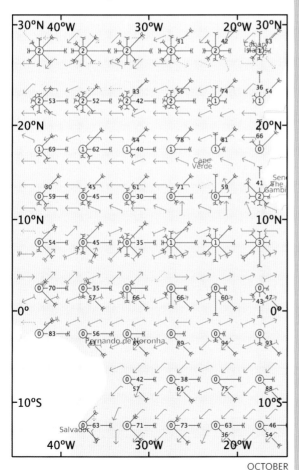

OCTOBER

An Amazon Cruise

After leaving Belém, we roamed the neighbouring *igarapés*, small tributaries that flow into the Amazon, but we were often marooned in our dinghy because as soon as you penetrate a few metres into a creek, you find yourself hemmed in by greenery and immersed in the sounds of the jungle. As the vegetation is dense, it is impossible to go wandering ashore. It is difficult to speak of land, because the banks are flooded at this season and most trees submerged in water.

I never found the long hours spent motoring monotonous as the landscape is flanked by dark green banks of tall trees, remains of the primary forest, occasionally giving way to plantations of palms and secondary forest. The forest is well preserved, but in some places has been decimated by deforestation for logging, farming or cultivation. We passed the time observing the shoreline, lush with vegetation, beautiful trees, toucans, parrots and other colourful birds and, occasionally, neat wooden houses on stilts with small flower gardens.

All the activity is on the main river, where traffic is busy with huge barges that carry dozens of semi-trailers from Santarm, 1000 km to Belém, and on to Manaus over 1500 km further upriver. Occasionally we met large cargo ships loaded with timber and containers as the river is deep a long way inland. The danger is colliding with one of the many floating logs, so one has to be constantly alert. Even worse are the floating islands which crashed into the sides when we were anchored and got entangled in the chain. Their size, length of grass, the strong current and the multitude of insects that accompany them made their removal a complex operation and sometimes the help of a friendly diver was needed.

Outside the few towns, the population is sparse. We always exchanged greetings with the people we met, and children often came out in their dugouts to get a closer look. We never had a sense of insecurity but the reception was rather cool, the children looking disappointed when they didn't get the sweets or T-shirts they asked for.

We were pleasantly surprised by the climate, as we were expecting hot and humid weather. All in all it was interesting to experience this mighty river first hand – but we left with the feeling that to see the real Amazon you had to go much further inland.

Xavier Duménil, *Yaz*

this region. Should the situation become safer and more amenable to tourism generally, this rarely visited corner of Africa may provide some interesting cruising destinations in the future.

Most yachts sailing to the Cape Verdes or West Africa continue to the Caribbean, either direct or via Northern Brazil. The largest country in South America is attracting increasing numbers of cruising boats as there is a plethora of interesting places to visit, attractive anchorages and off-shore islands, and the opportunity to witness the world-famous Carnival. For the more adventurous there is also the thrill of sailing your own boat on the Amazon River. The river is navigable for some 2,000 miles but to get a taste of this mightiest of rivers most sailors are happy to explore only the easier section of the Lower Amazon from Belém as far as Almeirim before turning around and exiting at Afuá.

Weather conditions along this longer route to the Caribbean are mostly favourable, with occasionally lighter winds between the Canaries and Cape Verdes, but consistent northerly winds from there to destinations in West Africa. Direct passages from West Africa to the Caribbean benefit from consistent trade winds as the route stays well to the north of the equator and thus avoids the ITCZ. Closer to the equator conditions are less favourable as the NE winds gradually give way to SE winds as the effects of the ITCZ are increasingly felt.

Boats heading across the equator to more southerly destinations in Brazil will have less favourable conditions at the start of the passage from the Cape Verdes or West Africa, with initially a high proportion of SW winds during the period of the SW monsoon (June to October). The SE trade winds of the South Atlantic start establishing themselves between the equator and 5°S. An interesting and convenient stop on this route is the archipelago of Fernando de Noronha, some of whose islands are a nature reserve. This detour south of the equator is probably more suitable for those on a longer voyage or who are not planning to return from the Caribbean to Europe the same year. This allows them to spend more time in Brazil before continuing to the Eastern Caribbean. Conditions for the passage from Brazil to the Caribbean could not be better, as in March, when most boats make this passage, steady winds and a strong NW setting current make for record-breaking passages, with many cruising boats recording their best ever 24 hour runs.

For boats arriving from the south, Trinidad is a convenient first landfall in the Caribbean, with good facilities but limited cruising opportunities so most sailors that call there rarely linger for long, especially as some may come back towards the end of the safe season to leave their boat at one of the boatyards that have been set up for this very purpose.

A1f   Eastern Caribbean to Panama

Recommended time: December to March

Tropical storms: June to November

World Cruising Routes:

    AN74   Lesser Antilles to Greater Antilles

    AN104   Venezuela and ABC Islands to Colombia and Panama

    AN81   Virgin Islands to Panama

    AN114   Florida and Bahamas to Panama

Having succumbed to the temptations of the Eastern Caribbean many sailors bound for the Pacific often allow too little time for the next stage of their voyage to Panama. As a result they are forced to do it in a hurry with not enough time to stop in at least one of the ABC Islands (Aruba, Bonaire, Curaçao), to acquaint themselves briefly with Colombia by calling at Cartagena, or enjoy the pristine beauty of the San Blas Islands. For those planning to sail to the South Pacific, the timing of the Panama Canal transit is a crucial element in their future cruising schedule. As most people prefer to arrive in French Polynesia at the beginning of the safe season in the tropical South Pacific, the transit of the canal should take place in February to allow for a possible stop in the Galapagos as well as the estimated three weeks for the 3,000 mile passage to the Marquesas. The Marquesas are very rarely visited by tropical storms so most take a calculated risk by arriving

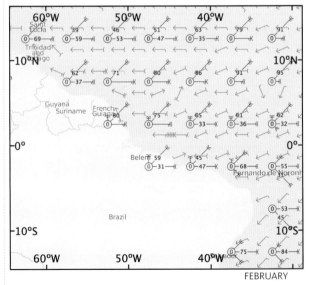

FEBRUARY

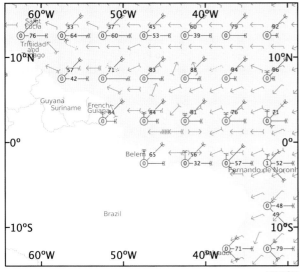

MARCH

there in early April, although officially the South Pacific cyclone season lasts until early May.

Boats bound for the west coast of Central America and Mexico are faced with a similar predicament, although they can leave the Eastern Caribbean somewhat later as they only need to be out of the area affected by North Pacific hurricanes by early June.

As anyone who knows the Caribbean well will readily confirm, this is a vast area with countless cruising opportunities that cannot be properly appreciated unless you have plenty of time to do so. One attractive alternative to reach Panama, which I have chosen on three occasions, is to get there by a roundabout way and sail from the Lesser Antilles in a NW direction by calling at the Virgins, Puerto Rico, Turks & Caicos and Bahamas. From there the course turns south towards the Windward Passage with possible further stops in Cuba and Jamaica before sailing on to Panama. Even more ambitious is to continue further west, visit as much as possible of the Southern USA, then regain the Caribbean Sea through the Yucatán Channel and thence to Panama.

Weather conditions in the Caribbean Sea during the safe season are generally good and direct passages from the Lesser Antilles to Panama benefit from favourable winds at virtually all times. The NE trade winds are at their most consistent in this area and while they do ensure fast passages, occasionally they may be too strong for comfort. At the height of winter, when the trades blow at their strongest, the constant easterly winds pile up the water in the western part of the Caribbean Sea, producing a large swell with rough seas which become

progressively worse further west. The best way to avoid these conditions is to make this passage at the start of the safe season, when the trade winds are not too strong, or towards the end of winter when they start losing their strength.

Passages that keep to the southern part of the Caribbean Sea cross an area which is very rarely affected by hurricanes, but even so, sailing this route between July and October, at the height of the hurricane season, should be avoided. This fact must be borne in mind by those who decide to sail the longer northern route described above, in which case the passage south to Panama will be undertaken probably towards the end of the safe season. This results in a later arrival in Panama and consequently a later arrival in the South Pacific as well.

A2 • Voyages from North America

The beauty of blue-water cruising is not only the satisfaction of sailing to distant destinations but also the freedom to choose the most attractive route to your chosen landfall. One of the aims of this book is not only to recommend the best route but also to outline other options. A voyage from the US East Coast to the Caribbean is a good way to start, by outlining the various ways to sail there as well as describing a few interesting detours.

- **A2a** Voyages to the Eastern Caribbean
- **A2b** Voyages to the Bahamas
- **A2c** Voyages to the Western Caribbean
- **A2d** Voyages to Panama

A2a Voyages to the Eastern Caribbean

Recommended time: Late November, April to May

Tropical storms: June to November

World Cruising Routes:
- **AN145** North America to the Eastern Caribbean
- **AN143** North America to Bermuda
- **AN126** Bermuda to Eastern Caribbean
- **AN127** Bermuda to Western Caribbean
- **AN113** Florida and Bahamas to Eastern Caribbean

If the intention is to sail the offshore route from the US East Coast to the Eastern Caribbean, the timing of this

Caribbean Overview

I sailed into the Caribbean in 1969, arriving in Grenada. The days of the topsail sailing schooners had just passed, but many fishing boats and cargo sloops still operated under sail. When heading up to Carriacou in the early morning, it was always a pleasure to watch a fleet of about 20 little double-ended fishing boats with brown sails darting off to the fishing grounds. There were not many yachts. Grenada had a new marina, home to a fleet of wooden charter yachts, St Vincent had just started one of the first bareboat fleets out of Blue Lagoon, English Harbour was a crewed charter base in Antigua, and that was just about it. There were few facilities anywhere else. In any waterfront bar you could meet someone who had become stuck waiting for something vital to arrive; money, an engine part, a bit of a rig. If you went away on a two week cruise he would still be there when you returned.

Building had not yet had much of an impact on the environment and the anchorages were uncrowded. We would often share the Tobago Cays with maybe four other boats, ten seemed a crowd. The islands were poor, most people lived in small wooden houses without electricity and had to carry water from a village standpipe. The roads were full of potholes, with more goats and sheep than cars.

Today, by comparison, is an age of abundance. The Eastern Caribbean is modern and developed with big supermarkets and shopping malls; the small wooden houses have given way to modern concrete ones, all with full services. Buildings have sprouted replacing vegetation, especially along the shoreline. Many islands have so many cars you can get stuck in traffic jams. We have lots of yachts, and along with these we have expanding marinas and services of all kinds. You can get anything; if it is not immediately available, FedEx or DHL will bring it in a few days. Life is much easier today with many more choices both for visitors and locals. You can have a phone on your yacht and often internet, too. Yachting has contributed to the local economy and helped development, all of which is good. On the other hand, I am happy I experienced those earlier, simpler days. They were not always easy, but my memory has imbued them with a special kind of magic, especially in the Grenadines.

Chris Doyle

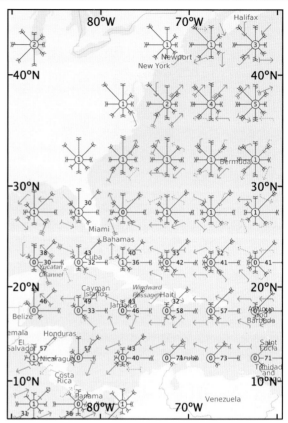

NOVEMBER

voyage is crucial as it needs to balance the risk of a late departure and the possibility of being overtaken by an early winter storm with that of an early arrival in the Caribbean and thus the risk of running into the path of a late hurricane. The most direct route stays well offshore and while a stop in Bermuda might look tempting, this is only justified for boats leaving from ports that are northeast of New York as, for all others, calling at Bermuda implies a shorter or longer detour. Another deterrent is the rather high frequency of gales around Bermuda in November, one more reason why a non-stop passage may be preferable. One possible solution to this dilemma is to sail to Bermuda earlier in the autumn, then wait for a more propitious time to continue the voyage to the Virgins or Lesser Antilles.

Bad weather is not the only hazard on this passage which at some point needs to cross the Gulf Stream, the strong NE flowing current producing rough seas when hit by a strong northerly wind. In late autumn there is a high proportion of N or NW winds in the area of the Gulf Stream, so the wide band of this powerful current should be crossed as quickly as possible, ideally at a right angle, even if this implies a temporary change of course.

A landfall in the Virgins, either US or British, is not only convenient but also logical as the subsequent route can then include all the Lesser Antilles. If the intention is to leave the boat in a safe place, such as Trinidad, during the next hurricane season, a leisurely pace while sailing south is the way to go. However, if at the end of winter the intention is to sail back to the US or Canada, or perhaps to Europe, enough time should be allowed to sail north along the chain of islands towards the end of the safe season. As the trade winds tend to blow from the NE at the start of winter then gradually veer to E and SE as the season progresses, you should benefit from favourable winds on both the way down and back. If, however, the plan is to continue to Panama, then the comments on the passage from the Lesser Antilles to Panama in voyage A1f ought to be read (page 68).

A very different, albeit much longer route to reach the Eastern Caribbean from ports on the US East Coast is to head south, preferably by way of the Intracoastal Waterway, in late autumn but not to arrive in the hurricane-prone area before late October. Once south of Cape Hatteras there is the option of sailing offshore to Puerto Rico or the Virgins, or crossing to the Bahamas and then making your way slowly east in short legs via Turks & Caicos and Puerto Rico. The advantage of the former route is that it is quicker and shorter, but will certainly involve some beating into NE or E winds, something which may suit neither some boats nor their crew.

The other option, of moving east from Florida in shorter island hops, may end up being just as painful but at least it can be stretched over a longer period, thus making it possible to wait for the right conditions before making the next move. This longer detour allows for some interesting cruising to be done along what has been called, no doubt with some justification, 'the thorny path'.

One other alternative has been tried in recent years and follows an intermediate offshore route between those two by heading due east from Florida while staying just north of the Bahamas. As often the only certain way to make good easting is with the help of the engine, the suggested tactic is to wait for a forecast of light winds or calms and then proceed east to about 65°W which is the longitude of the Virgin Islands. That is the point to turn south to find the NE winds that should be blowing in those latitudes in late November or early December when this passage is best undertaken.

A2b Voyages to the Bahamas

Recommended time: November to May (via Florida), November or May (offshore)

Tropical storms: June to November

World Cruising Routes:
> AN146   North America to the Bahamas

The inshore route via the Bahamas, as described above, is usually chosen by boatowners who prefer to make their way south either via the Intracoastal Waterway or by sailing south in short offshore legs, before crossing over to the Bahamas. In the case of those intending to sail to the Outer Bahamas, an offshore passage is both shorter and quicker. The tactics are similar to those outlined in A2a and the passage should be undertaken either at the start of the winter season (November) or at its end (May). Whether setting off from ports north or south of Cape Hatteras, the Gulf Stream should be crossed as quickly as possible before setting course for one of the Outer Bahamas, the island of San Salvador providing one of the easiest landfalls.

A2c Voyages to the Western Caribbean

Recommended time: Late November to December, April to May

Tropical storms: June to November

World Cruising Routes:
> AN148   North America to Western Caribbean
> AN115   Florida and Bahamas to Western Caribbean

The planning and timing of this voyage depend primarily on the point of departure. For boats leaving from anywhere north of Florida the logical route leads offshore via the Outer Bahamas and the Windward Passage before turning west towards the chosen destination. As in the case of voyages to the Bahamas, some may prefer to sail south and reach Florida in shorter stages, in which case the voyage will continue via the Yucatán Channel. This is the shorter route for boats starting from Florida or other southern states and it has the added advantage that it can be done at any time during the safe season. In contrast to that mostly inshore route, the offshore version is much more time-dependent, certainly as far as the Windward Passage, from where there are two choices to reach the western shores of the Caribbean, either by sailing along the southern coast of Cuba, if the intention is to call there, or via Jamaica. In the latter case a good place to interrupt the voyage is at Montego Bay, whose

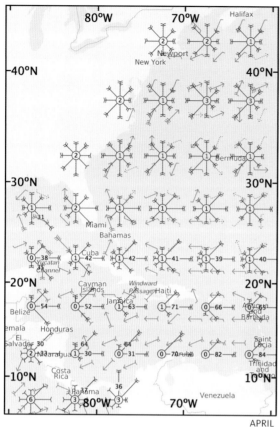

APRIL

A2d Voyages to Panama

Recommended time: Late November to December, April to May

Tropical storms: June to November

World Cruising Routes:

AN147   North America to Panama

AN114   Florida and Bahamas to Panama

AN107   Jamaica to Panama

Few boats leaving from ports on the US East Coast make the passage to Panama non-stop as the Outer Bahamas, which straddle the direct route, make a stop there both logical and convenient. Another reason is that most of those who plan to sail to Panama make their way south sooner and are waiting in Florida or the Bahamas for a suitable time to cross the Caribbean Sea.

For boats leaving from northern ports directly for Panama the best time is either before the start of the hurricane season or after its end. The route passes through the Windward Passage, which may also be taken by those welcoming yacht club has a good range of facilities and an international airport nearby.

Weather conditions at the change of seasons are generally favourable on both the Windward Passage and Yucatán routes. While passing through the latter, in order to avoid the strong NW setting Yucatán Current, southbound boats should favour the Cuban side where there is a slight countercurrent. From there on favourable winds should prevail all the way to your destination.

Cruising opportunities in the Western Caribbean are in rich supply and as these countries attract far fewer visiting yachts than the Eastern Caribbean, you rarely feel crowded, something that is increasingly difficult to say about the Virgins or Lesser Antilles. One other attraction of Mexico, Guatemala, Belize and Honduras is the wealth of things to do and see ashore, foremost among them the magnificent remains of the Maya civilisation.

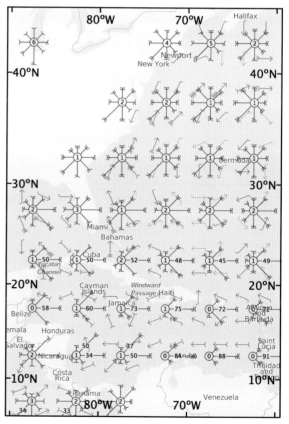

MAY

who are leaving from Florida and prefer to have a better sailing angle for the passage to Panama than the Yucatán Channel. From the Windward Passage, a direct route can be sailed to Cristobal at the entrance to the Panama Canal. Boats that have reached the Caribbean Sea via the Yucatán Channel need to sail a route which passes to the east of all the dangers that litter the western part of the Caribbean Sea before the course is altered for Cristobal. Rather than head straight for that landfall, an attractive, yet only slight detour worth making is to the islands of San Blas, an area of great natural beauty administered as an autonomous region of Panama by the indigenous Kuna people.

A3 • Voyages from South America

- **A3a** Voyages to the Lesser Antilles
- **A3b** Patagonia to the Caribbean

Although sailing, especially racing, has been a popular pastime in Brazil, Argentina and Uruguay for some time, cruising as such has only started to catch on relatively recently. In spite of a beautiful coastline and many opportunities for cruising, much of South America has yet to be discovered by foreign sailors as a destination in its own right. The notable exceptions are at the continent's two extremes: Venezuela in the north and Patagonia in the south.

A3a Voyages to the Lesser Antilles

Recommended time: February to April (from Northern Brazil), March to May (from Southern Brazil and Argentina)

Tropical storms: June to November (Caribbean)

World Cruising Routes:

AS26   Northbound from Argentina

AT21   Brazil to Eastern Caribbean

A northbound voyage that follows the mainland coast closely has plenty of interesting ports of call to choose from as well as attractive cruising areas located at convenient distances. Sooner or later, the majority of foreign boats visiting Brazil will continue their voyage to the Caribbean,

whether they had arrived from Europe or South Africa. Most make landfall at a port in Northern Brazil and, once there, few venture south of Salvador da Bahia. Its famous

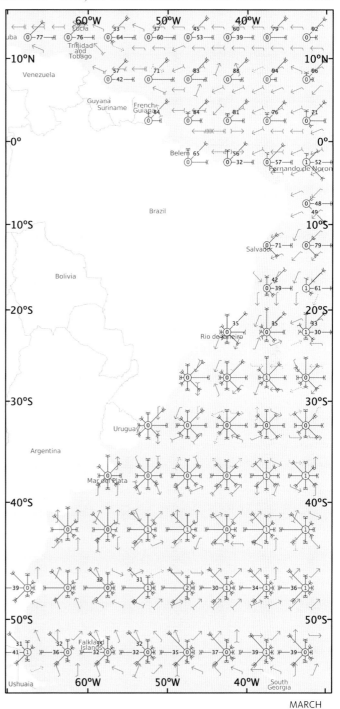

MARCH

street Carnival is a major attraction, although other cities en route to the Caribbean, such as Recife, Fortaleza and Natal, have their own exuberant events to mark the beginning of Lent, preparations for which start as early as December. An interesting, albeit more challenging, detour is a foray into the vast Amazon Delta, parts of which are navigable and easily accessed by a keeled yacht. Although the river is navigable for some 2,000 miles, most boats only go as far as Belém and explore some of the Lower Amazon and its tributaries as far as the port of Almeirim before turning around and exiting at Afuá.

Northbound passages from ports in Southern Brazil have to contend with strong NE winds and a contrary SW setting current between October and February, so ideally such passages should be planned to start after March. For voyages that start from ports in Northern Brazil, weather conditions are generally good and there is no risk of tropical storms south of the equator. The strong NW setting Guyana Current runs about 70 to 100 miles off the Brazilian coast, so a course should be set that is within its axis both to take full advantage of the current and to avoid the discharge from the Amazon River. The winds are normally from E or NE and the doldrums will be encountered close to the equator. The doldrums, with their typically unsettled weather, are limited to a band of 100 to 200 miles width, which is narrowest in the first months of the year.

A3b Patagonia to the Caribbean

Recommended time: March to May

Tropical storms: June to November (North Atlantic)

World Cruising Routes:

| AS25 | Northbound from Patagonia and Falkland Islands |
| AS26 | Northbound from Argentina |

There cannot be many sailors who decide to sail this route entirely offshore but for those who do, Port Stanley in the Falklands makes a good port of call to prepare and provision for the continuation of the voyage. As the Southern Ocean is best left by late February, at the end of the short austral summer, and the latest that the Caribbean should be reached is May, there is plenty of time to enjoy much of South America while moving steadily northward. For those who have less time to play with, there are a number of ports to stop at, whether in an emergency or

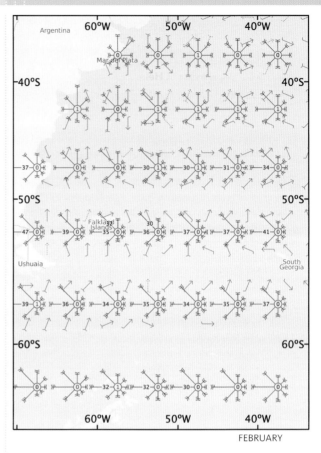

FEBRUARY

just for a break. Among them the Argentine port of Mar del Plata has good repair facilities, as does Punta del Este in Uruguay, while in Brazil, Rio de Janeiro and Salvador da Bahia are two ports which are used to dealing with visiting yachts, both racing and cruising.

The offshore route benefits from mostly favourable winds all the way to about 45°S, but from there on winds from the northerly quarter become increasingly more frequent until the corner is turned at Cape São Roque, when the course becomes NW and the sheets can finally be eased. Therefore, if at all possible, northbound voyages should be planned after February to avoid the northerly winds and south-setting current that is a seasonal feature along the Brazilian coast between October and February. An interesting stop close to the offshore route is the archipelago of Fernando de Noronha off Cape São Roque.

A4 ● Voyages from South Africa

● **A4a** Voyages via St Helena
● **A4b** Voyages via Southern Brazil

There are two very different ways to sail from South Africa to the Caribbean and the majority of sailors prefer the direct trade wind route as it ensures both a fast passage and an arrival in the Eastern Caribbean at the best of times. The other alternative involves a detour to the South American mainland with less favourable sailing conditions but the bonus of visiting several interesting places and cruising areas en route.

A4a Voyages via St Helena

Recommended time: January to March

Tropical storms: June to November (North Atlantic)

World Cruising Routes:

AT25	South Africa and St Helena to Eastern Caribbean
AS11	Northbound from Cape Town
AS13	St Helena to Brazil
AT21	Brazil to Eastern Caribbean

The direct route to the Eastern Caribbean passes so close to St Helena that very few yachts sail by without stopping at this remote British possession where, no doubt due to its isolation, visiting sailors are always assured of a warm welcome. One other landfall, the smaller Ascension Island, is slightly off the direct route, but may also deserve a detour even if the interior is less interesting than that of St Helena. Whether calling at any of these islands, or sailing non-stop, a passage to the Lesser Antilles will benefit from favourable winds on both sides of the equator during the first months of the year, with the doldrums occupying a relatively narrow band close to the point where this route crosses the equator.

Rather than continuing non-stop to the Caribbean, in recent years sailors who call at St Helena ignore the shorter direct route to the Lesser Antilles and prefer to make a detour to Northern Brazil. As most boats leave Cape Town in early January, which is the best time for a northbound passage, the timing is perfect for those who wish to be in Brazil for Carnival. From there, the route north and weather conditions are described in voyage A3a (page 73).

The passage from Cape Town to St Helena can be one of the most pleasant offshore voyages anyone can wish for, with steady SE trade winds, good fishing and hardly any weather concerns, as even tropical squalls are a rare phenomenon while tropical storms are entirely absent.

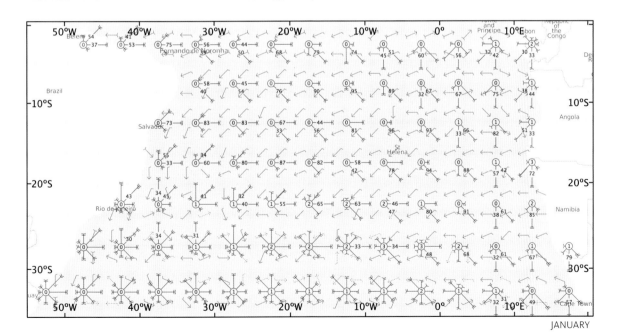

JANUARY

A4b Voyages via Southern Brazil

Recommended time: April to May

Tropical storms: June to November (North Atlantic)

World Cruising Routes:

AS14	Cape Town to Brazil
AS26	Northbound from Argentina
AT21	Brazil to Eastern Caribbean

The distances from Cape Town to the major ports in Brazil are almost the same, with the distance between Cape Town and Recife being only 50 miles longer than the distance from Cape Town to Rio, but weather conditions are anything but similar. Direct passages to ports in Northern Brazil benefit from steady SE trade winds virtually from the start, whereas a passage to Rio de Janeiro may have reasonable winds for the first part, with predominantly southerly winds, but once halfway across the winds can come from any direction, with those from the northern quarter gradually gaining the upper hand as one approaches the continental landmass. It is the same northerly winds, and the south-setting current, which make it difficult to continue the voyage northwards between October and February. The fact that NE winds predominate along most of the Brazilian coast during the entire austral summer, and are strongest between December and February, is something that must be taken into account when planning the next leg of the voyage from Northern Brazil to the Caribbean. This is most important for those who do not want to arrive there too close to the end of the safe season. For details of the continuation of the voyage from Brazil to the Lesser Antilles see A3a.

Cruising hubs

Antigua ****

Regarded as one of the premier yachting centres in the Caribbean and the host of the most popular regatta, the island of Antigua has built up over the years a good range of facilities that can cater for virtually all needs. There are adequate medical facilities. The VC Bird International Airport (ANU) has scheduled flights to the UK, USA, Canada and Germany, Italy and other international destinations.

Barbados **

With the exception of Port St Charles, a marina aimed primarily at superyachts, facilities for cruising boats are limited. Medical facilities are good. Grantley Adams International airport (BGI) has regular flights to the UK, USA, Canada and Panama.

Grenada ****

Over the years Grenada has built up a good network of marinas and yachting facilities. The Maurice Bishop

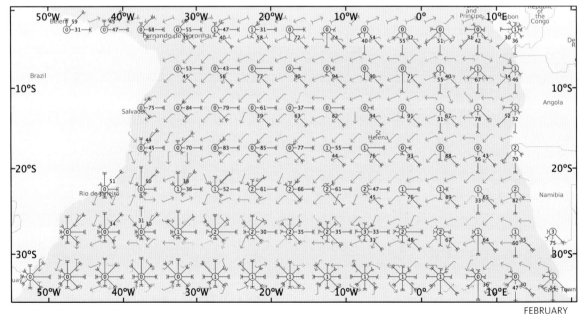

FEBRUARY

International Airport (GND) operates regular flights to the UK, USA, Canada, Germany and Spain. The General Hospital located in the capital St George's has a full range of medical facilities.

Guadeloupe ****

As the destination of several transatlantic races from mainland France, Guadeloupe now has a comprehensive range of services and repair facilities. As in all major French overseas territories, medical facilities are of an excellent standard. Pointe-à-Pitre International Airport (PTP) has regular flights to France, the USA, Canada, Venezuela, French Guiana (Cayenne), the Dominican Republic and Cuba.

Las Palmas *****

This busy port on the island of Gran Canaria has the best repair facilities in the Canaries. Provisioning is very good from several supermarkets and fresh produce markets, and the city has good medical facilities. Gran Canaria International Airport (LPA) has regular flights to several European capitals, also charter flights to other European destinations, and frequent flights to Madrid for onward international connections.

Santa Cruz de Tenerife ****

The capital of the Tenerife is an attractive city with Marina Santa Cruz situated in an ideal location right in the centre of town making it a perfect base for longer stays. Provisioning is excellent with a large fresh produce market within walking distance from the marina. There is a good range of repair services, with haulout facilities at the smaller Marina Tenerife in the northern part of the busy harbour. The University Hospital has a full range of medical facilities. Tenerife has two airports, the smaller (TFN), located close to the capital, operates mostly inter-island flights and to mainland Spain. The larger airport (TFS) is located in the SE of the island and operates international flights to many European and other destinations.

Madeira **

Madeira has a good range of repair facilities concentrated around Marina Quinta do Lorde. The main hospital is in the capital, Funchal. Madeira International Airport (FNC) has regular flights to Lisbon, London, Berlin, Frankfurt, Paris and Amsterdam and charter flights to several more European destinations.

Martinique ****

Yachting facilities are of a good standard and there is also a comprehensive range of marine supplies. Medical facilities are of a high standard. The Aimé Césaire International Airport (FDF) operates regular flights to France, USA, Canada, French Guiana, Dominican Republic and Cuba.

Mindelo **

This commercial port on the Cape Verde island of São Vicente is often used by boats en route to the Caribbean, West Africa and Brazil. It has a good marina and a range of repair facilities. Provisioning is adequate and fuel is available. The Hospital Baptist de Sousa has good medical facilities. The international airport (VXE) operates flights to Lisbon and the Canary Islands. The main international airport (SID) on the island of Sal is served by several European airlines.

Panama **

Yachting services have been expanded with the opening of several new marinas, significantly improving the previously inadequate docking facilities on both the Caribbean and Pacific side. Repair facilities are reasonable and medical facilities are satisfactory. Tocumen International Airport (PTY) operates scheduled flights to the USA, Canada, Germany, Spain, the Netherlands and to all neighbouring countries.

St Helena *

This isolated outpost in the middle of the South Atlantic is a convenient landfall for boats en route to Northern Brazil, the Caribbean and Europe. There are no docking facilities, only an open anchorage, provisioning is reasonably good and fuel is usually available but repair facilities are very basic. There is a general hospital in Jamestown. The new airport (FSX) started operating in 2016 and has now regular flights to South Africa and Ascension Island, as well as some charter flights. The island's other link with the outside world is the supply ship RMS St Helena.

St Lucia ***

Since the annual ARC transatlantic rally made its base in Rodney Bay Marina, yachting facilities have greatly improved but cannot as yet be described as comprehensive. Medical facilities are adequate and there are two international airports. The larger Hewanorra International Airport (UVF) has regular flights to the UK, USA, Canada and Germany. The smaller airport (SLU) at Vigie has mostly inter-island flights to Caribbean destinations including Puerto Rico.

St Martin/Sint Maarten *****

Concentrated on this island, which is half Dutch and half French, are the best yachting services in one place in the

Caribbean. The range of repair facilities is comprehensive with a yard capable of dealing with superyachts, and the chandleries are well stocked with marine supplies. Medical facilities are of a high standard and able to deal with emergencies of any kind. The island has two airports, with the Princess Juliana International Airport (SXM) being on the Dutch side. It operates regular flights to France, the Netherlands, USA, Canada, Brazil, Venezuela and Panama. The smaller Grande Case Airport (SFG), on the French side, only has short-haul flights to other French Caribbean islands.

St Thomas ***

Both yachting services and repair facilities are adequate, and so are the medical facilities. For any major intervention patients may have to be transferred to nearby Puerto Rico. The Cyril E King International Airport (STT) operates flights mostly to Puerto Rico and mainland USA.

Salvador da Bahia ***

Yachting facilities have improved in recent years with a marina located near the city and others within a reasonable distance. There are several haul-out facilities and a reasonable range of repair services. Medical facilities are of a good standard. Salvador International Airport (SSA) operates flights to all major Brazilian destinations as well as to neighbouring countries, North America, Europe and Africa.

Tortola ***

Due to a number of charter operations that are based on the island, repair facilities are good. One major drawback for visiting sailors is that the Terrence B Lettsome Airport (EIS) has no long-distance international flights and all flights must connect through another Caribbean airport such as San Juan, St Thomas, Antigua or Sint Maarten.

Trinidad ***

Due to its position just south of the critical hurricane belt, Trinidad has established itself primarily as a long-term storage location for boats. Repair facilities are adequate and cover a good range. Medical facilities are good. Piarco International Airport (POS) has regular flights to the USA, Canada, UK, Panama and Venezuela.

What next?

The Caribbean hurricane season poses such a real threat that no sailor should ignore it. There are three ways to deal with this annual occurrence: sail home at the end of the safe winter season, leave the boat in a secure place or continue the voyage into the Pacific.

Whether home is in North America or Europe, most sailors choose the first option. North Americans have two main alternatives, either to sail to northern ports on the US East Coast, directly or via Bermuda, or to make their way to Florida and the southern states via Puerto Rico, Turks & Caicos and the Bahamas.

European sailors returning home from the Caribbean may consider a more ambitious alternative by pointing their bows NW instead of NE and visit the USA, a detour which can easily be incorporated into a return voyage to Europe. By leaving the Eastern Caribbean in late spring and moving north with the sun, such a voyage should not be threatened by the coming hurricane season. There are several alternatives to reach the US East Coast, either via the Bahamas to Florida and the southern states, from where the voyage can continue by way of the Intracoastal Waterway, or via Bermuda to more northerly destinations. As you move north, the threat of a hurricane recedes and an eastbound passage across the Atlantic usually benefits from favourable westerly winds and, with a bit of luck, pleasant summer conditions. What's more, the total distance of this more roundabout route from the Caribbean to Europe is only marginally longer than the usual route via the Azores.

One of the highlights of the above route is the thrill of sailing through the very heart of the city of New York and it is there that an even more ambitious alternative might appeal to anyone interested in doing something unusual. The Hudson River, which flows through New York, connects the Atlantic to the Great Lakes, a busy shipping artery that is also used by many cruising boats. Some of them take this route to reach their home ports on the shores of the Great Lakes while others do it as part of the Great Loop. This is a grand tour of the US inland waterways which links the US East Coast to the Great Lakes and continues south via the Illinois and Mississippi rivers to complete the loop in Florida.

Whether sailing to North America or Europe the time most boats leave the Caribbean is between late April and May. Such timing means that the Caribbean is left, and the subsequent voyage undertaken, before the start of the hurricane season. For those who are bound for the Panama Canal and the Pacific the choice of the departure time from the Eastern Caribbean depends primarily on conditions at the point of arrival. Boats bound for the Pacific coast of Central America and Mexico have to contend with the same hurricane season dates when planning the continuation of their voyage as they too have to make sure to be in a safe place after June.

The second alternative, of leaving the boat unattended during the hurricane season, is a solution preferred by those who intend to spend more than one season in the Caribbean. Such a decision needs to be considered carefully in view of the increased threat posed by severe tropical storms as happened during the 2017 hurricane season. Because of the high losses suffered in recent years some insurance companies are now reluctant to ensure boats left unattended during the tropical storm season. Restrictions are also imposed on cruising during the critical period. Whether planning to leave the boat unattended or continue cruising during the hurricane season are matters that need to be raised with your insurance company before such a decision is taken.

For boats bound for the South Pacific the decision is rather more complicated. As the safe sailing season in the South Pacific is well defined, and the weather is usually quite benign in the eastern part of that vast ocean, the time of departure from the Eastern Caribbean is less critical than that of the time of arrival in the tropical South Pacific. The cyclone season in French Polynesia lasts from December until the end of April, but as the Marquesas are

rarely affected by tropical storms many are prepared to take the risk of arriving there earlier. This means transiting the Panama Canal as early as February, a timing which allows for a stop in the Galapagos. The onward 3,000 mile passage from the Galapagos to the Marquesas can be sailed in early March so that the Marquesas are reached in late March or early April. This gives those planning to sail all the way to New Zealand, Australia and the Torres Strait about six months of carefree cruising.

One possible drawback to the above schedule is the need to leave the Eastern Caribbean at the best of times, in late January or February, which, for those who had only arrived one or two months previously, might be too early. The alternative is to remain in the Caribbean until the end of the safe season, then cruise leisurely through those places that are not affected by hurricanes such as the ABC Islands, Colombia and the San Blas Islands. Once in the Pacific, the extra time can be spent exploring some of South America, or leaving the boat in a marina in Ecuador and possibly returning home, before resuming the voyage to the tropical South Pacific the following year.

The capital of Tenerife with Marina Santa Cruz located in the centre of the photograph.

Voyages to the Mediterranean

The dark-blue waters of the Mediterranean Sea have been plied by sailing vessels since the earliest times and many a civilisation has risen and perished on its shores. The people of the Mediterranean have always looked to the sea for inspiration and one never has far to go to get a taste of the fascinating world that has existed for millennia around this sea. The Mediterranean has all the ingredients to make it one of the world's top cruising destinations and the beauty of the surrounding scenery, as well as the wealth of things to see and do ashore, more than make up for the often less than exhilarating sailing

conditions. From the pyramids of Egypt to the Minoan remains on Crete, from the treasures of Asia Minor to the wonders of Ancient Rome, from the Lycian tombs carved into the cliffs of Southern Turkey to the medieval ramparts of Valetta's Grand Harbour and the thrill of sailing your yacht into the heart of Venice, the shores and islands abound in history and many historical sites are close to the sea.

In most parts of the Mediterranean, the sailing season lasts from April until October, but is best enjoyed in late spring and early autumn when the ports are not crowded and the weather is more pleasant than at the height of summer. It is possible to sail in winter but a careful eye has to be kept on the weather as violent storms can occur with little warning. A complete season is the least anyone should plan on spending in the Mediterranean, as distances are deceptive and it is more than 2,000 miles from Gibraltar to the Eastern Mediterranean.

Those with more time on their hands may consider a detour into the Black Sea, an area that has only recently

Gibraltar landfall.

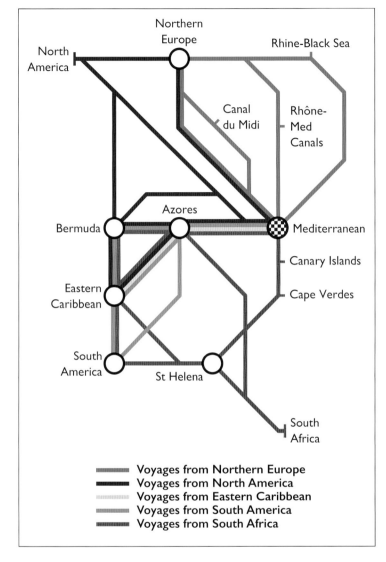

- **Voyages from Northern Europe**
- **Voyages from North America**
- **Voyages from Eastern Caribbean**
- **Voyages from South America**
- **Voyages from South Africa**

A detour into the Red Sea is another possibility to consider as both its northern part and the Gulf of Aqaba are easily accessible from the Western Mediterranean via the Suez Canal. This is a particularly attractive option in winter when weather conditions are more pleasant than in the Mediterranean and there is a wide range of ancient sites to explore and attractive resorts, many with their own marinas, to while the time away until spring.

A5 ● Voyages from Northern Europe

- **A5a** Voyages to Gibraltar
- **A5b** Voyages via the European canal systems

The ocean routes that lead to the Mediterranean have been sailed for centuries and converge in the funnel shaped strait overlooked by the Rock of Gibraltar, or the Pillars of Hercules, or Heracles, as it was known in antiquity.

Sailing to the Mediterranean from Northern Europe is relatively straightforward, but, as it entails a crossing of the Bay of Biscay, passages should be planned for late spring or early summer when favourable conditions are more likely. The alternative is to take the inland route via the extensive European waterway systems and reach the Mediterranean through the French rivers and canals or by the even longer route via the Danube and Black Sea.

A5a Voyages to Gibraltar

Recommended time: June to August

World Cruising Routes:

AN13   Southbound from Northern Europe
AN14   Routes across the Bay of Biscay
AN16   Northern Europe to the Mediterranean

The shortest route to Gibraltar runs across the Bay of Biscay, which can be reached by yachts starting off from

started attracting visiting yachts. With the opening of that area to cruising, foreign yachts are now sailing to the Ukraine, Russia, Georgia, Romania and Bulgaria, each with its own rapidly expanding sailing community. Besides the interest in visiting these formerly closed countries, there are a number of cruising attractions such as the Georgian coast with its dramatic scenery, the Crimean Peninsula with its pleasant subtropical climate, Romania's Danube Delta, one of the most extensive bird sanctuaries in Europe, or the rarely visited coast of Northern Turkey. A cruise to the Black Sea has the added reward of sailing through the Dardanelles, Bosporus and Istanbul, a unique experience which in itself may justify the entire trip.

ports in Northern Europe either through the English Channel or by the more roundabout route via the Caledonian Canal and the Irish Sea. Both have advantages and disadvantages, the former being shorter but entails having to negotiate the busy shipping lanes in the North Sea and English Channel, the latter being longer but more rewarding for the opportunity of exploring some of the cruising attractions of Scotland and Ireland as well as the west coasts of England and Wales. Whichever route is chosen, several tempting landfalls lie in wait along the Atlantic shores of the Iberian Peninsula to weaken anyone's determination to reach the Mediterranean as quickly as possible.

Weather conditions in early summer are usually favourable but even so it pays to wait in a convenient port for the right conditions before setting off across the Bay of Biscay. The prevailing northerly winds that blow along the Portuguese coast in summer normally ensure fast southbound passages but these winds may be lost after Cape St Vincent. Immediately past that prominent lighthouse, which marks the southwesternmost point of Europe, is a small bay sheltered by the Sagres promontory.

High above the anchorage lies the imposing Sagres Castle and it was here that Prince Henry the Navigator founded his School of Navigation whose alumni spearheaded the era of discovery and exploration of the late 15th century. This is just one of several historic places that are worth exploring before reaching Gibraltar. Other interesting detours that can easily be missed are the rivers Guadiana and Guadalquivir, both of which are navigable for some distance. The former forms the border between Portugal and Spain and has several picturesque villages on its shores, whereas the latter leads to the city of Seville and its medieval attractions.

 A5b Voyages via the European canal systems

Recommended time: April to October

Although dealing with such overland routes may seem out of place in a book on the planning of ocean voyages, this can be justified by the fact that every year a considerable number of yachts reach the Mediterranean from the Atlantic by this way. It is indeed a good solution for those who wish to reach the Med early in the season, when a voyage all the way around Gibraltar may not be an attractive proposition. The same is true for voyages in the opposite direction either early or late in the season. There are three basic routes to reach the Mediterranean by way of the European waterway systems: the Canal du Midi route, the Rhône route and the Rhine–Danube–Black Sea route.

The Canal des Deux Mers, which includes the Canal du Midi, is the shortest and perhaps most attractive alternative, but it does not avoid the Bay of Biscay entirely. It also has the disadvantage of being limited to boats that draw less than 1.60m. Aptly called the Canal Between Two Seas, this waterway runs between Royan on France's

Canal du Midi.

Atlantic coast and Sète in the Mediterranean and is made up of several segments: the rivers Gironde and Garonne, the Canal du Garonne, the Canal du Midi and, finally, the Thau Lake. The waterway is 601km long, has 114 locks and the average transit time is two weeks.

The second inland route cuts right across France and exits at Port Saint Louis at the mouth of the Rhône River. It can be used by boats with a maximum draft of 1.80m. There are several French and Belgian ports of access on the North Sea and English Channel and a variety of canals and rivers can be used to reach the River Rhône. The most westerly route starts at Le Havre, where it enters the River Seine, and goes via Paris and the Canal Bourbonnais to reach the Rhône. This is the most popular with yacht owners as it has fewer locks to negotiate than the others. Its total length is 1,330km with 176 locks. The more scenic route uses the Canal de Bourgogne to cut across Burgundy. It has a length of 1,316km with 238 locks. Another route, which also goes via Paris, uses the rivers Marne and Saône to reach the Rhône. It is 1,400km long and has 174 locks.

There is another route which bypasses both Paris and the popular waterways of Burgundy. It is therefore quicker and can be transited in about three weeks. The route starts at Calais and passes through a series of rivers and canals, including the Canal de Bourgogne, to reach the important hub of St Jean de Losne on the Saône River north of the confluence with the Rhône. This route is 1,173km long and has 234 locks.

A more northern route starts at a number of ports on the North Sea and reaches the Mediterranean via the Rhine and Rhône rivers. This route is still used by commercial shipping and is only suitable for faster boats that can cope with the strong currents in the upstream section of the Rhine. For that reason it is used mostly in the opposite direction. There is also the possibility of taking a boat from the Baltic to the Mediterranean by making use of the German waterways to reach the Rhine and thus connect to the Rhône.

An even more ambitious way to reach the Mediterranean from Northern Europe is by way of the Rhine–Main–Danube waterway system. The Europa Canal, which made this possible, was opened in 1992 and connects the Main and Danube rivers across the European watershed. The 3,500km long transcontinental waterway passes through 15 countries and links the North Sea and Atlantic Ocean to the Black Sea providing a navigable artery between the Rhine Delta (at Rotterdam in the Netherlands) and the Danube Delta in Eastern Romania. The final section can be shortened by using the short cut which bypasses the Danube Delta by using the

The Blue Danube

As a boy I dreamed about sailing around the world and during a ten year period, from 1988 to 1998, I finally fulfilled that dream. Back in Stockholm I glanced at a map of continental Europe and realised that there are numerous rivers and canals on which you can sail on your own boat with the mast down. So, for several years I explored the rivers of Europe – the Rhine, Rhône, Oder and Seine – and major cities such as Berlin, Paris, Amsterdam, Lyon and Cologne. However, there was one more river I wanted to conquer: the Danube.

Until recently it had been impossible to reach the Danube from Western Europe and sail all the way to the Black Sea. But all that changed when the Danube and Rhine rivers were finally connected by a canal and the war in former Yugoslavia came to an end. At long last my old dream might come true and so I decided to try it out. The main reason was that, as I am interested in history and travelling, this was a great opportunity to sail through the heart of Central Europe and experience its history from the Middle Ages up to the fall of the Iron Curtain.

We did the trip during two months in 2009, starting from Port Saint Louis where the Rhône flows into the Mediterranean, sailing up the Rhône and through the Rhône–Rhine Canal reaching the Rhine. The Main–Danube Canal finally took us into the Danube itself. From there the long passage wound through cities and farmlands, the beautiful Iron Gates and, at the end of the river, we passed through the incredible Danube Delta into the Black Sea. From there we sailed via Istanbul back into the Med again.

It was an unforgettable journey and another dream fulfilled.

Lars Hässler, *Jennifer*

Danube–Black Sea Canal which exits close to Constantza, Romania's main commercial port.

An even more audacious transcontinental liquid route links the Baltic Sea to the Black Sea by way of the Unified Deep Water Transportation System, a major project of the Soviet era that was opened in 1952 with the completion of the Volga–Don Canal. This was the missing link that brought all the major inland river ports of Russia within reach of the Black, Baltic, Caspian, Azov and White Seas. Although the route is navigable throughout its length, access to foreign vessels, both commercial and pleasure, is currently not allowed. A few yachts have managed to obtain the necessary permission from the Russian authorities to use this waterway and reach the Black Sea by this scenic route which starts at St Petersburg and calls at Moscow and many other historic cities. It is hoped that these restrictions will be lifted as it is indeed a fascinating way to sail through the heart of this interesting country.

The main reason why sailors choose these alternative ways to travel to the Mediterranean is that such inland routes are less dependent on weather and seasons so that the chosen destination can be reached at a pace of your own choosing. Whichever inland route is chosen, the mast must be dropped to be able to pass under low bridges and through tunnels and there are specialised firms providing this service at all points of access.

A6 • Voyages from North America

- **A6a** Direct voyages
- **A6b** Voyages via the Eastern Caribbean
- **A6c** Voyages via Northern Europe

There are three very different ways to reach the Mediterranean from the US East Coast: by a direct transatlantic

passage in late spring or early summer, by sailing to the Eastern Caribbean in November and continuing the voyage the following spring, or by sailing to a destination in Northern Europe, spending the summer there and sailing in the autumn to the Mediterranean. Each alternative has its attractions and many US and Canadian sailors decide to combine a voyage to the Mediterranean with a detour to the Eastern Caribbean as it gives the possibility of spending the winter there and continuing to Gibraltar the following year. The opposite of such a warm-water route is to reach the Mediterranean by sailing first to Northern Europe by making a crossing in higher latitudes and spending the summer exploring some areas of Ireland, Scotland, Scandinavia or perhaps the Baltic before heading south, either on an offshore route or by way of one of the waterways described above.

A6a Direct voyages

Recommended time: May to June
World Cruising Routes:
  AN142 North America to Mediterranean
  AN143 North America to Bermuda
  AN124 Bermuda to Gibraltar

Eastbound voyages across the Atlantic benefit from the best weather conditions in summer but as this is also the

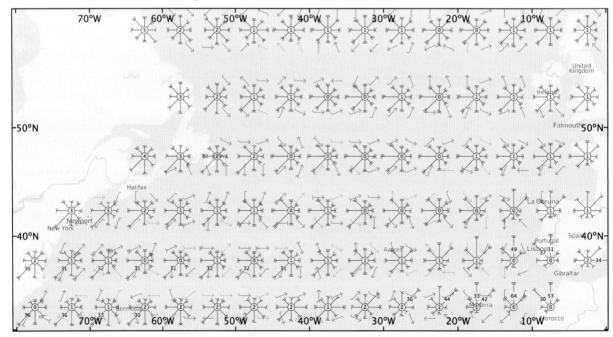

hurricane season, that risk needs to be weighed against the advantage of sailing during the more favourable period. Another factor that may influence the time of departure is the wish to arrive in the Mediterranean early enough in the season to be able to spend the entire summer there. This is the reason why most people plan this voyage for late spring or early summer, just before the start of the hurricane season.

For boats leaving from ports south of Chesapeake Bay the island of Bermuda is close enough to the direct route to justify a stop there, but from more northern ports such a detour makes little sense. By late May or early June, there is a high proportion of southerly winds in the vicinity of Bermuda, so it may be better not to plan a stop there at all. Instead, a route should be plotted that takes advantage of the prevailing westerly winds which blow in higher latitudes and stay with them until the point where the course needs to be altered for Gibraltar. The alternative is to head first for the Azores and visit this offshore Portuguese archipelago which provides a convenient and attractive stopover before tackling the last thousand miles to Gibraltar.

For those who decide to call at Bermuda, the old advice to head NE on leaving the island to reach the area of prevailing westerly winds has been revised in recent years due to the greatly improved access to reliable weather information. The North Atlantic High has a major bearing on the weather conditions to be encountered, so its location will dictate the route to be sailed. Usually by late spring the high is located just west of the Azores with, occasionally, a ridge of high pressure extending towards Bermuda and the American mainland. Therefore boats on an eastbound passage from Bermuda, whether going non stop to Gibraltar or via the Azores, need to stay just north of the high to ensure favourable winds. Having access to information on the extent and location of the high will help choose the optimum course to be sailed to your destination.

A6b Voyages via the Eastern Caribbean

Recommended time: Late November; May–June

Tropical storms: June to November

World Cruising Routes:
AN145 North America to the Eastern Caribbean
AN143 North America to Bermuda
AN126 Bermuda to Eastern Caribbean
AN79 Lesser Antilles to Azores and mainland Europe
AN89 Virgin Islands to Azores and mainland Europe
AN134 Azores to Gibraltar

Rather than spend the winter in some cold place with the boat sitting idle in a marina or boatyard, why not combine a planned voyage to the Mediterranean with a Caribbean sojourn? Those who do not have the time for such an extended voyage but are tempted by the idea of a Caribbean detour should consider breaking up this voyage into separate stages. This can be done by sailing to the Eastern Caribbean in November, planning to leave the boat in a suitable marina, returning for a winter vacation and completing the voyage to the Mediterranean the following spring, including a stop in the Azores. The initial leg to the Eastern Caribbean is described in voyage A2 (page 69) and the subsequent leg to the Azores in A7 (page 86).

A6c Voyages via Northern Europe

Recommended time: June to July

World Cruising Routes:
AN141 North America to Northern Europe
AN16 Northern Europe to Mediterranean

The limited sailing season in Northern Europe makes an early start preferable so as to take maximum advantage of the short northern summer. As sailing conditions in the North Atlantic can still be unpleasant in late May and early June, it is recommended that early passages to Northern Europe do not join the great circle route right at the start but sail along a more southerly track where better conditions should be found. Two other crucial factors that must be borne in mind are the risk of ice and the high incidence of fog that can be encountered in the area SE of Newfoundland, one more good reason to sail the first half of the crossing along a southerly course.

There is a wide choice of European landfalls, with those in Western Ireland and Scotland more suitable for those bound for northern destinations, and continuing to Scandinavia via the scenic Caledonian Canal, while a landfall in Southern Ireland or England will suit those who plan to cross the English Channel to France or Belgium, or the North Sea to the Netherlands.

This is another voyage that lends itself to being completed in separate stages. In such a case, the first segment can be sailed later in summer, when conditions are certainly better and, if the crossing is done in higher latitudes, the risk of hurricanes is no longer an issue. A late arrival in Northern Europe means that the sailing season will be nearing its end so there will not be much time for cruising before laying up the boat in a marina or boatyard, unless the decision is taken to spend the off season on board in an attractive city like Amsterdam, Bruges or London. The

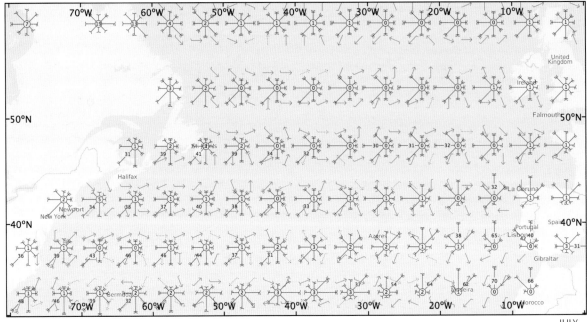

JULY

river Thames is navigable with the mast up as far as Tower Bridge and there are two marinas located close to the city in which to spend the winter months.

After the following summer has been spent cruising in Northern Europe, the continuation of the voyage, as well as the various alternatives to reach the Mediterranean, are described in A5. As mentioned there, an interesting alternative to reach the Mediterranean from Northern Europe is by way of one of the inland waterways routes. Such an alternative not only gives a unique opportunity to see some of mainland Europe from the comfort of your own boat but also makes it possible to spend the entire summer in Northern Europe and only sail south at the end of summer or early autumn when an offshore passage is less attractive.

A7 • Voyages from the Caribbean

Recommended time: May to June

Tropical storms: June to November

World Cruising Routes:

AN78   Lesser Antilles to Bermuda
AN87   Virgin Islands and Puerto Rico to Bermuda
AN125   Bermuda to Azores
AN79   Lesser Antilles to Azores and mainland Europe
AN88   Virgin Islands to Azores and mainland Europe
AN134   Azores to Gibraltar

Every year, as the safe sailing season draws to a close, there is a great exodus of boats from the Eastern Caribbean, with European sailors returning home to complete their Atlantic circle, charter boats sailing to the Mediterranean for the summer season, and North American sailors heading for home or new cruising grounds.

In the early days of Caribbean winter cruising there were very few boats that took the direct route to the Azores as it entailed passing through the often windless Horse Latitudes. In recent years there has been a marked change and the number of boats which sail the direct route now greatly exceeds those that choose to sail via Bermuda. The main reason is that sailors are more willing to use the engine when encountering calms or light winds and also because better access to weather forecasts makes it possible to adjust the route to expected weather conditions. The most difficult part of the passage to the Azores is often the start, especially if it is undertaken too early and the prevailing NE winds that blow in winter in the Eastern Caribbean have not yet veered to E or SE. It therefore pays to wait for a predicted spell of SE winds before setting off. However, waiting beyond the latter part of May is not advisable as by June the new hurricane season is on its way, although early summer hurricanes normally only affect the Western Caribbean.

The pilot chart for June shows that the incidence of calms along the direct route to the Azores is in fact quite low and that the E or SE winds that are normally

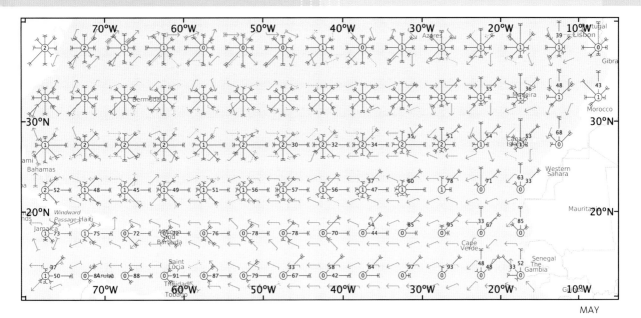

MAY

JUNE

encountered at the start are gradually replaced by SW winds so that an almost direct course can be sailed that takes advantage of those features.

On the continuation of the voyage to the Mediterranean, early summer passages from the Azores to Gibraltar usually encounter variable winds at the beginning which become increasingly northerly closer to the mainland.

A8 • Voyages from South America

Recommended time: January to March (Caribbean route), April to June (Azores route)

Tropical storms: June to November (North Atlantic)

World Cruising Routes:

AT22	Brazil to Azores
AT21	Brazil to Eastern Caribbean
AN79	Lesser Antilles to Azores and mainland Europe
AN134	Azores to Gibraltar

There are two alternatives to sail from South America to the Mediterranean and the choice depends primarily on the place and time of departure. The most commonly used route is the one that follows the contour of the continent to the Lesser Antilles from where it continues to Europe via the Azores. The second alternative is an offshore route which is recommended for direct passages to Northern Europe and uses the Azores as an intermediate landfall before turning east for Gibraltar.

A third possible alternative, via the Cape Verde and Canary Islands, may look feasible as far as the equator,

especially if enough easting has been made while still south of the Line, but north of it NE winds put to serious test any boat that does not sail well to windward. In spite of that, with good planning and ready access to weather information this route to the Mediterranean can also be considered.

For those who are setting off from ports in Northern Brazil, the first alternative is undoubtedly the most attractive and the timing is also the easiest as the most favourable times perfectly complement each other: a February or March passage from Brazil to the Eastern Caribbean, a couple of months cruising the Lesser Antilles, followed by a late May continuation of the voyage to the Mediterranean.

Those leaving from ports in Southern Brazil, Uruguay or Argentina, who intend to sail the Caribbean route, must take into account the NE winds that blow along the Brazilian coast from October to April. This seasonal feature makes northbound passages quite difficult, especially between December and February when those winds are at their strongest. The timing of the arrival in the Caribbean is also important as it should not be left too late so as to be able to pass through the Lesser Antilles and continue the voyage to the Mediterranean, before the start of the hurricane season in June.

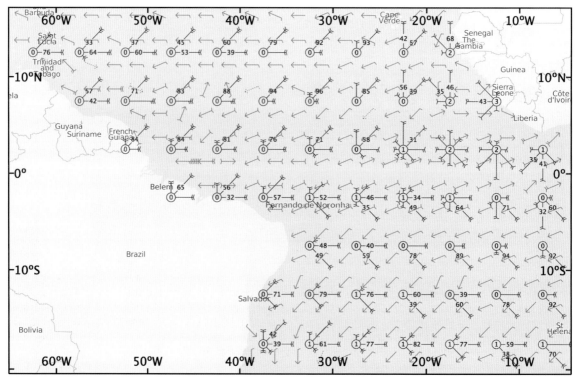

MARCH

Voyages which bypass the Eastern Caribbean and sail directly to the Azores on an easterly route may sail later in the year but still need to avoid the North Atlantic hurricane season. They will encounter more favourable winds off the coast of Brazil as far as the equator but will have to contend with consistent NE winds north of the equator.

A9 • Voyages from South Africa

Recommended time: January to April

Tropical storms: June to November (North Atlantic)

World Cruising Routes:

AT29	South Africa and St Helena to Gibraltar
AT25	South Africa to St Helena and Eastern Caribbean
AN79	Lesser Antilles to Azores and mainland Europe
AT23	South Africa and St Helena to Azores
AN134	Azores to Gibraltar

There are three route options and each has both advantages and disadvantages: the shortest route, via St Helena, the Cape Verdes and Canaries is the most direct but not necessarily the easiest, the Azores route includes the longest offshore segment, whereas the route via Brazil and the Caribbean is the longest but also the easiest.

Boats sailing the first route, and calling at St Helena and Ascension, will have favourable conditions almost all the way to the equator but from there on winds from the northern quarter will be the order of the day as far as Gibraltar. This will entail a fair amount of windward work, and possibly also some motorsailing, so enough fuel should be taken on board as this may not be easily available in St Helena and is even less likely in Ascension. Both between the Cape Verdes and Canaries, and the Canaries and Gibraltar, weather systems approaching from the west in the first months of the year usually generate NW winds that back to W and SW resulting in a brief spate of favourable conditions. Therefore the accepted tactic is to wait in the Canaries for such conditions as they will result in winds from a favourable direction even if they may be on the strong side.

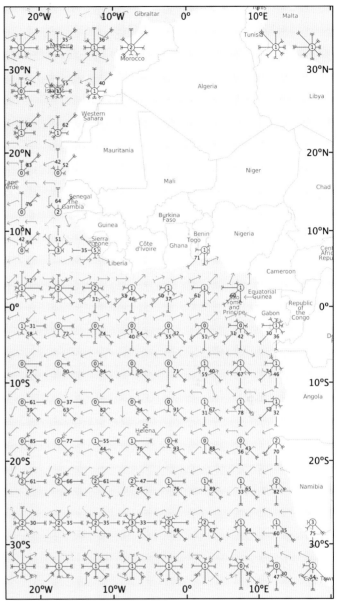

FEBRUARY

The offshore route via the Azores is the least attractive as it is subject to those same NE winds north of the equator as the Cape Verdes route and is also longer. The one advantage of this route is that the winds on the onward passage from the Azores to the Mediterranean are usually favourable.

Unless the decision had been taken already to sail non stop all the way from Cape Town to the Azores, a final choice as to which way to go needs only be made in St Helena as it is there that the three variants diverge. Most boats usually sail the western variant, either non stop to the Lesser Antilles or via Northern Brazil. Such voyages are best done in the first months of the year so as to arrive in the Eastern Caribbean well before the end of the safe season.

Cruising hubs

Gibraltar ***

Once an important yachting centre with the best repair facilities in the Western Mediterranean, in recent years Gibraltar has radically revised its priorities and yachting no longer appears to be among the top ones. Docking facilities have seen an improvement with the opening of a new marina aimed at larger yachts. This may also lead to an improvement in repair facilities which currently can only be described as adequate. Due to its strategic location and VAT-free status within the European Union, Gibraltar continues to be a good place for provisioning and refuelling. Medical facilities are good and there is a well-equipped general hospital. Gibraltar International Airport (GIB) has regular flights to London and other UK destinations, and also to Morocco.

Bermuda****

Bermuda's facilities are split between St George's Harbour and the former Royal Naval Dockyard on Ireland Island, where Dockland Marina is located. Repair facilities are of a good standard. King Edward VII Hospital is located close to the capital Hamilton. Bermuda International Airport (BDA) has regular flights to London and most important US cities.

Horta***

The favourite Azorean landfall for boats arriving from the Caribbean or Bermuda, Horta has greatly improved its facilities to cope with the hundreds of boats which call here on completion of their Atlantic crossing. Repair and haul-out facilities are adequate, and there is a general hospital with good facilities. Horta airport (HOR) has daily flights to Lisbon for onward international connections.

What next?

Regardless of the length of time spent in the Mediterranean, if an Atlantic crossing is planned for the end of the summer season, the Eastern Mediterranean should be left by early August so as to be able to cruise leisurely westward and be on your way to Madeira or the Canaries by late September as autumn weather can be unreliable both in the Western Mediterranean and the Atlantic. Indeed, it is not uncommon for boats to be delayed in Gibraltar by unrelenting westerly winds. For the same reason, a voyage to Northern Europe should also be planned for the summer. Those who are delayed, or prefer an alternative route to reach destinations in Northern Europe, should consider using the waterway systems which connect the Mediterranean to the Atlantic by way of a network of rivers and canals. The Canal des Deux Mers, which incorporates the Canal du Midi, provides a short cut to the Bay of Biscay, whereas the River Rhône and a series of canals provide a link to the North Sea and English Channel. Both these routes have certain draft restrictions.

At the Mediterranean's eastern extremity, the Suez Canal gives access to the Red Sea and North Indian Ocean. Even if a longer voyage along that route is not envisaged, the northern part of the Red Sea and the Gulf of Aqaba are now a popular winter destination for sailors who prefer to spend the cold months in a warmer climate. After a winter spent there a spring return to the Mediterranean opens up a whole new range of cruising opportunities.

Voyages to Northern Europe

A10 • Voyages from North America

A11 • Voyages from the Caribbean

A12 • Voyages from the Mediterranean

A13 • Voyages from West and South Africa

A14 • Voyages from South America

For most North American sailors cruising in Europe means Southern Europe, in other words the Mediterranean, and for non-European sailors generally, the countries of Northern Europe do not rate as enticing cruising destinations, a fact which is borne out by the small number of yachts from further afield that are seen in that part of the world. The challenging sailing conditions of getting there and the relatively short summer season may be used as a passable excuse, but as far as cruising opportunities are concerned there can be few regions in the world that are more attractive or offer a greater variety of beautiful surroundings afloat or ashore. From the picturesque shores of Ireland to the offshore islands of Scotland and the wild beauty of the Norwegian fiords a visiting sailor is spoilt for choice even before reaching the Baltic and its extensive cruising grounds. As more sailors are attracted to sailing to the Arctic, a voyage to Northern Europe can be extended all the way to Spitsbergen, an option described in circular voyage AC14 on page 144.

With so much to see and do a short summer cruise is hardly enough and the way to overcome this is to arrive early, spend an entire season in the area, leave the boat for the winter in a marina or boatyard and resume the voyage the following spring. The alternative is to follow the sun, as many North Europeans do, and sail south at the end of summer to either the Mediterranean or the Canaries.

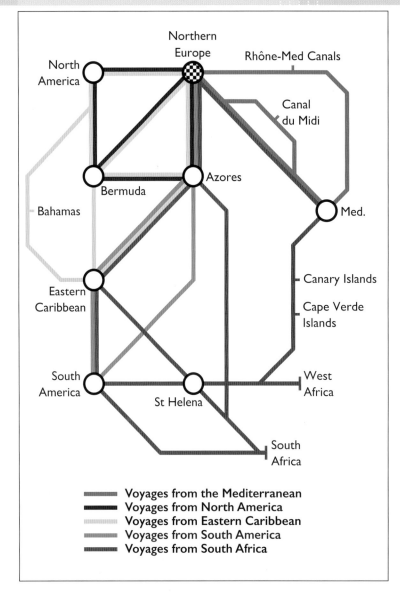

Voyages from the Mediterranean
Voyages from North America
Voyages from Eastern Caribbean
Voyages from South America
Voyages from South Africa

A10 • Voyages from North America

● **A10a** Direct voyages from the US East Coast

● **A10b** Voyages via Bermuda

For boats leaving from the US East Coast, there are three main options for sailing to Northern Europe: a nonstop transatlantic passage, a voyage with an intermediate stop in Bermuda and a high-latitude crossing possibly via Newfoundland. However, there are a number of interesting permutations that are discussed when circular voyages in the North Atlantic are described on page 138.

● **A10a** Direct voyages from the US East Coast

Recommended time: June to July

Tropical storms: June to November

World Cruising Routes:

AN141 North America to Northern Europe

The short sailing season in Northern Europe points to a late spring or early summer departure so as to benefit from the longest time possible once safely across the Pond, although too early a start may be affected by unfavourable conditions for which the North Atlantic is deservedly notorious. One way to avoid some of the worst conditions is to stay well clear of the area to the SE of Newfoundland, which has a high incidence of both fog and ice in late spring and early summer. To stay clear of the area mentioned above, it is recommended that for the initial stages of the passage a course should be sailed that keeps south of the great circle route. The course should be altered for the chosen destination only after the 35°W meridian has been reached. From there, depending on the intended landfall, the route can lead directly to Scotland by staying north of Ireland, or to the south coast of Ireland and then continue north either through St George's Channel and the Irish Sea, or, even further east, through the English Channel and North Sea.

The long offshore passage outlined above may not be to everyone's liking and there is an alternative that can be considered and which, by making several stops en route, shortens the length of the offshore segment from about 3,000 miles to a more acceptable 1,800 miles. Such a voyage can set off from any port in New England before crossing the Gulf of Maine to Nova Scotia. After a possible stop in the French islands of St Pierre and Miquelon the next landfall should be St Johns in Newfoundland. It is only from there that the offshore segment of the voyage is started, with the nearest landfall at Mizen Head, at Ireland's southwesternmost extremity.

A10b Voyages via Bermuda

Recommended time: June

Tropical storms: June to November

World Cruising Routes:
    AN143   North America to Bermuda
    AN123   Bermuda to Northern Europe

For boats setting off from ports south of Chesapeake Bay, breaking the long passage to Northern Europe by a stop in Bermuda is a temptation that is hard to resist, especially early in the season when a more northerly route has certain disadvantages as mentioned earlier. However, voyages that start after the middle of June must take into account the possibility of an early hurricane along such a southerly route and this needs to be borne in mind when planning this passage.

On leaving Bermuda, once meridian 35°W has been reached, a new course can be set along one of three alternative routes. The northernmost route goes north of both Ireland and Scotland and is suitable for boats bound for the west coast of Norway. An intermediate route approaches Ireland from the southwest and then continues through the Irish Sea to Scotland. Boats bound for Southern Scandinavia and the Baltic Sea can use the Caledonian Canal to reach the North Sea. The easternmost route leads to the English Channel and thence to destinations in Western Europe.

Occasionally voyages to Northern Europe that have called at Bermuda also stop at the Azores. While there is little doubt that those islands are an interesting stop, making such a long detour south is not advisable if the aim is to reach Northern Europe as quickly as possible. The tactics for the passage between Bermuda and the Azores are outlined in A6a on page 84.

A High Latitude Summer Cruise

The decision to sail *Let's Go!* from the United States to Europe via the higher latitudes was based on several considerations. Having just completed a circumnavigation along the trade wind route, I was ready for more challenging sailing and longing to experience the solitude that nowadays only remote destinations can provide. Practically, the longest distance between destinations was no more than four days' sail and most of this could be undertaken quite safely in the summer months of July and August.

Our route took us from Maine, along the southern coast of Nova Scotia to Cape Breton Island, up the west coast of Newfoundland to southeast Labrador. From Labrador, we sailed to southwest Greenland making our way through the Prince Christian Sound and from there to Iceland. Next we sailed to the Faroe Islands and our final destination of Shetland.

The *Cruising Guide to Labrador* states '. . . those who travel this coast are primarily on their own: be forewarned and be prepared', so one can imagine the excitement and angst of having selected such a route. Indeed, finding crew was a significant challenge in its own right. Once underway, however, if it was solitude and challenge I was seeking, I was not to be disappointed. Once we left Cape Breton Island we did not see another sailing vessel until we reached Iceland. We were alone in every anchorage with only the sound of the waves and wind, and the occasional barking of an Arctic fox.

While I had read accounts of the fog and ice, I was unprepared for their prevalence. Nevertheless, with vigilance and radar, it was not difficult to avoid icebergs in fog and rain. The pack ice had broken up in early July, a dubious benefit of climate change. Weather forecasts proved unpredictable for more than 24 hours ahead, but we were able to download sufficient weather information to find reasonable weather windows, so that we sailed the entire route in winds that never exceeded 35 knots and seas that never exceeded 3–4 metres. The roughest conditions were in the Gulf of St Lawrence.

The route has a great deal to recommend it: short manageable legs, beautiful destinations, friendly and helpful inhabitants plus the feeling of accomplishment that comes from sailing off the beaten track. The downside was the dreariness of the weather: all that fog and rain! With the ice situation becoming more favourable, I expect Iceland, Greenland and Labrador will become even more popular.

Jim Patek, *Let's Go!*

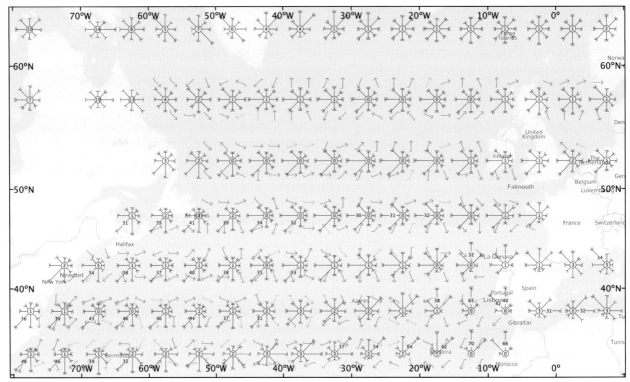

JULY

A11 • Voyages from the Caribbean

Recommended time: May to early June

Tropical storms: June to November

World Cruising Routes:

AN78   Lesser Antilles to Bermuda

AN87   Virgin Islands and Puerto Rico to Bermuda

AN123   Bermuda to Northern Europe

AN125   Bermuda to Azores

AN79   Lesser Antilles to Azores and mainland Europe

AN132   Azores to Northern Europe

The dilemma faced every year by European sailors returning home from the Eastern Caribbean is whether to sail via Bermuda or the Azores, each option having both advantages and disadvantages, the Bermuda route having a better chance of favourable winds but being longer and also colder, while the Azores route can be more comfortable even if it often entails a fair amount of motoring.

There is, however, one further alternative which has many attractions and therefore is well worth considering: to sail to the USA either direct or via Bermuda,

and having cruised along the US East Coast, cross the Atlantic to Northern Europe later in the summer. Besides the opportunity to visit some of the United States, one significant advantage of this route is that by sailing north from the Caribbean in May or early June, you move gradually away from the area affected by hurricanes. While an offshore passage to the US East Coast, nonstop or via Bermuda, is undoubtedly the quickest solution, an even more attractive way is to head northwest from the Virgin Islands towards Florida by calling at Puerto Rico, Turks & Caicos and the Bahamas, the islands spread out along this route providing convenient and interesting stops at every stage. From Florida, the voyage can continue north in short offshore legs or via the Intracoastal Waterway, a system of canals, rivers and lakes which winds it way to Chesapeake Bay. The route then continues through New York City to Long Island Sound and along the shores of New England as far as Nova Scotia and Newfoundland. The transatlantic passage can be embarked on at any chosen point along the way in the knowledge that in these latitudes the prevailing westerly winds will ensure favourable conditions for the crossing to Northern Europe.

Those who would rather take the more commonly sailed route home from the Caribbean, but are unable to

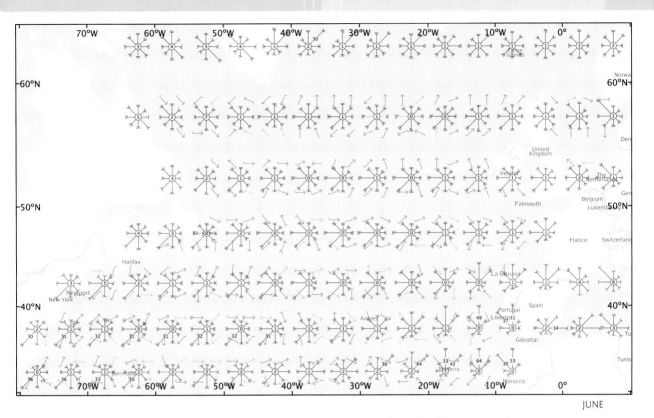

JUNE

choose between the Bermuda or Azores option, should look for inspiration in the current trend. It is interesting that in recent years a much higher percentage of sailors returning to Europe seem to prefer the direct Azores alternative and seem undeterred by the possibility of encountering light winds or occasional calms on this route.

A12 • Voyages from the Mediterranean

Recommended time: late May to mid-August

World Cruising Routes:

　AN34　Gibraltar to Northern Europe

Planning a voyage north from the Mediterranean is not an easy task mainly because of the difficulty of balancing the favourable seasons at the two extremities. Most boats heading north belong to North European sailors returning home at the end of a cruise in the Mediterranean and the time when they would prefer to do this is in summer. While this is certainly the best time to go south, heading in the opposite direction against the strong northerly winds

that blow along the Iberian Peninsula is no easy matter. The way to deal with this is to sail north in June before the Portuguese trades are fully established. However, an early departure from the Mediterranean is not an attractive idea for most people, hence the temptation for those who prefer to spend the summer in the Mediterranean is to try to avoid Gibraltar altogether and get to Northern Europe by way of the canals and rivers that link the Mediterranean to the Bay of Biscay, English Channel or North Sea. The southernmost, and shortest, among them is the waterway known in French as the Canal Entre Deux Mers which is made up of the Canal du Midi, Canal du Garonne and the two rivers Garonne and Gironde, a 600km long inland route that runs from Sète on the French Mediterranean coast to Royan in the Bay of Biscay.

Those who prefer to reach more northerly destinations may find other waterway systems that cross France to be more attractive, as some of them are still used by commercial traffic and thus allow for more draft and air clearance. All northbound routes start off by covering a fair distance going upstream on the River Rhône. At Chalon sur Saône, in the heart of Burgundy, the first of a number of alternate routes branches off in the direction of Paris and Le Havre. Other options open up further

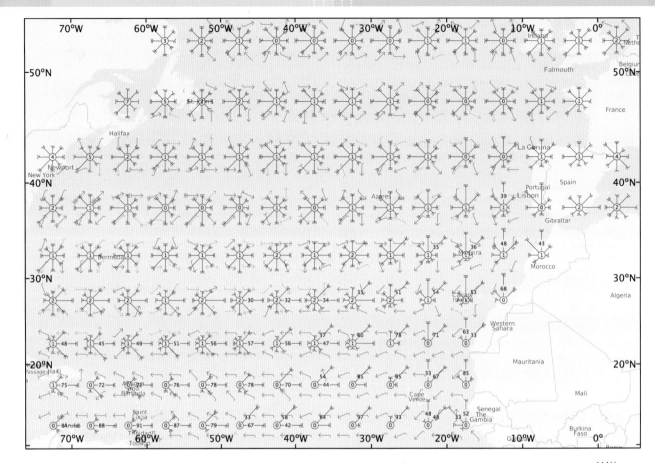

MAY

north to ports on the English Channel, the North Sea and even the Baltic. The various waterways of interest to cruising sailors are described in more detail in voyage A5 on page 82.

A13 • Voyages from West and South Africa

Recommended time: January to May (via Lesser Antilles or Cape Verdes), March to June (via Azores)

Tropical storms: June to November (North Atlantic)

World Cruising Routes:

AT29	South Africa and St Helena to Gibraltar
AT28	South Africa and St Helena to Azores
AN132	Azores to Northern Europe
AT25	South Africa and St Helena to Eastern Caribbean
AS11	Northbound from Cape Town

AS13	St Helena to Brazil
AT21	Brazil to Eastern Caribbean
AN79	Lesser Antilles to Azores and mainland Europe
AN78	Lesser Antilles to Bermuda
AN123	Bermuda to Northern Europe
AN132	Azores to English Channel

There are three route options for reaching destinations in Northern Europe from South Africa: the traditional offshore route via the Azores, the longer but more attractive route via Brazil and the Eastern Caribbean, and the shorter but potentially more difficult route via St Helena, Ascension, the Cape Verdes and Canaries. All these options are feasible whether the voyage originates in South or West Africa.

The voyage via Brazil is the easiest to plan as the favourable seasons in both hemispheres complement each other. This voyage is best done in the first months of the year when sailing conditions in the South Atlantic are most favourable and allows an arrival in the Eastern Caribbean before the end of the safe season. From there, the voyage can be continued in May or June either on a direct route to Northern Europe via Bermuda or by the more roundabout route via the Azores as described in A11.

The other alternatives, either the offshore route via the Azores or the Cape Verde and Canary Islands route, can be sailed later in the year when weather conditions in the South Atlantic are still favourable. Once north of the equator, the time of arrival in the Azores is less crucial as weather conditions in summer are generally good and the winds on the onward passage to destinations in Northern Europe are also better than earlier in the year. This is certainly not the case on the Cape Verde route as arriving in the Canaries after April runs the risk of encountering strong northerly winds on the way north from there. This route is described in A9 (page 89). While this easterly route can be recommended as a perfectly feasible voyage from South Africa to the Mediterranean, for boats bound for destinations in Northern Europe the alternative route via the Azores should be preferred.

A14 • Voyages from South America

Recommended time: April to June (via Azores), January to May (via Lesser Antilles)

Tropical storms: June to November

World Cruising Routes:

AS25	Northbound from Patagonia and Falkland Islands
AS26	Northbound from Argentina
AT22	Brazil to Azores
AT21	Brazil to Eastern Caribbean
AN79	Lesser Antilles to Azores and mainland Europe
AN132	Azores to Northern Europe

South American yachts are rarely seen in Europe and the boats which undertake this voyage usually belong to European sailors on their way home from a voyage to Patagonia or Antarctica, or who are completing a round the world voyage. There are two alternative routes to reach Northern Europe: a direct offshore route via the Azores and the favoured route via the Eastern Caribbean.

Northbound voyages from Patagonia will benefit initially from the prevailing westerly winds which will be gradually replaced by winds from the northerly quarter by the time the River Plate Estuary is reached. Two convenient ports along this route are Port Stanley in the Falklands and Mar del Plata in Argentina.

Voyages which originate from ports in Northern Argentina, Uruguay and Southern Brazil, regardless of whether they are planned to be sailed in longer offshore legs or shorter cruising stages, must take into account the NE winds which blow along the Brazilian coast from October to April. This is particularly important if the intention is to sail the Caribbean route when a late arrival in the Lesser Antilles must be avoided due to the impending hurricane season. The other alternative, of an offshore voyage via the Azores, is not directly affected by the hurricane season in the North Atlantic and therefore can be sailed later. However, although benefitting from more favourable winds off the coast of Brazil, such a direct voyage will have to contend with consistent NE winds north of the equator.

For boats leaving from ports in Northern Brazil, the Caribbean alternative, although longer, is the most attractive. Its timing is probably also easier for planning purposes as the most favourable periods complement each other: a February or March passage from Brazil to the Eastern Caribbean followed by a late May or early June continuation of the voyage to Northern Europe.

Cruising hubs

Port Stanley **
Repair facilities have improved since several charter yachts working in Antarctica use the Falklands as a winter base. The Falkland Islands Company provides a range of repair facilities, including hauling out. Provisioning is good and fuel is available. There is a general hospital with good facilities. International flights from Port Stanley Airport (PSY) are operated by Lan Chile via Punta Arenas to Santiago de Chile for onward connections, and the Royal Air Force, which has regular flights to the UK for military personnel but also takes other passengers.

Mar del Plata ***
Argentina's main yachting centre has a wide range of repair facilities, also fuel and good provisioning. The airport (MDQ) operates frequent flights to Buenos Aires for onward international connections. The private HPC hospital provides general and emergency facilities.

Rio de Janeiro ****
With a large resident yachting community Rio de Janeiro boasts the best facilities in South America. The city also has good medical facilities. Rio International Airport (GIG) has flights to all major capitals in Europe, North

Carlisle Bay in Barbados.

and South America, as well as to many destinations in Brazil itself.

See also Bermuda (page 90), Horta (page 90), Salvador da Bahia (page 78) and Trinidad (page 78).

What next?

For North American sailors the challenge of a return voyage from Northern Europe can be difficult as they are faced with a tough passage against the prevailing westerly winds. One way to avoid that scenario, or at least mitigate it, is to follow the example of the Viking navigators and sail a more northerly route that has a better chance of favourable winds. By making such a sweep to the north, Iceland and possibly also Greenland can be visited before finally turning for home.

Such a return voyage can be undertaken in late summer, towards the end of the sailing season in Northern Europe, when conditions on the west side of the Atlantic are still relatively favourable. A daring extension of such a voyage is to loop even further north all the way to Spitsbergen and turn this voyage into an Arctic circuit as described in voyage AC14 on page 144. The disadvantage of this Arctic detour is that it needs to be sailed in July or early August at the latest, a timing that may not suit some people's plans.

The very opposite of the above suggestion is to choose the more pleasant but considerably longer route that follows the sun south to the Canaries, thence to the Eastern Caribbean and followed by a return home the following spring. This roundabout route completes a warmer circuit of the North Atlantic and is described in detail in voyage AC11 on page 140.

Not all voyages which continue from Northern Europe need to be across an ocean and the alternative is to strike inland and take advantage of the comprehensive European waterways systems to reach the Mediterranean or Black Sea by a variety of highly attractive routes as described on page 82.

For sailors who hail from the South Atlantic a voyage home from Northern Europe is best planned as part of a complete Atlantic Ocean circuit as outlined in voyages AC16 and AC18.

Voyages to North America

A15 • Voyages from Europe
A16 • Voyages from the Caribbean and Panama
A17 • Voyages from South America
A18 • Voyages from South Africa

The eastern seaboard of North America has been blessed with some beautiful cruising areas but very few non-American sailors seem to be aware of this, otherwise many more foreign-flagged boats would be seen in those waters than is the case. The fact that getting there from Europe is quite a challenging undertaking is probably the main reason, but even that obstacle can be overcome by choosing a more benign transatlantic route. Some European sailors forgo the obvious difficulties of an east to west crossing by grafting a North American cruise onto a voyage to the Caribbean. The alternative to sailing the Columbus warm water route to the New World is to reach the American mainland by a more direct but also more challenging high-latitude passage along a route that was sailed by Viking ships over a thousand years ago.

Sailors whose voyages originate in South America are faced with the same dilemma of having to choose between a somewhat shorter offshore route and the mostly coastal alternative that follows the contour of the continent to the Eastern Caribbean. From there the US East Coast is reached either direct or by a detour via the southern states. Similar options are available to voyages from South Africa, of either a long offshore passage or a more leisurely cruise via Brazil and the Eastern Caribbean.

A15 • Voyages from Europe

● **A15a** Voyages from Northern Europe
● **A15b** Voyages from Western Europe
● **A15c** Voyages from the Mediterranean
● **A15d** Voyages via the Canaries and Caribbean
● **A15e** Voyages to the Northwest Passage

There are four alternatives for a voyage from Europe to the east coast of the United States or Canada, and while

the direct way across the Atlantic may be the quickest for certain boats, it is undoubtedly also the most challenging as well as the least comfortable. Sailing against the prevailing westerlies should only be tackled by boats that go well to windward, a prospect which probably has little appeal to most cruising sailors who are likely to prefer one of the southern alternatives.

Those who are undaunted by high latitude sailing should consider a northern route which avoids the worst of those westerlies and which has been sailed for much longer than any other transatlantic route. It is the ancient route sailed by the Vikings.

Most difficulties associated with a cold-water passage, gales and contrary winds can be overcome by considering a third alternative which follows a track just to the south of the zone of prevailing westerlies. This route appeals primarily to boats setting off from the Mediterranean.

The easiest way to reach North America from Europe is by sailing the considerably longer but more pleasant

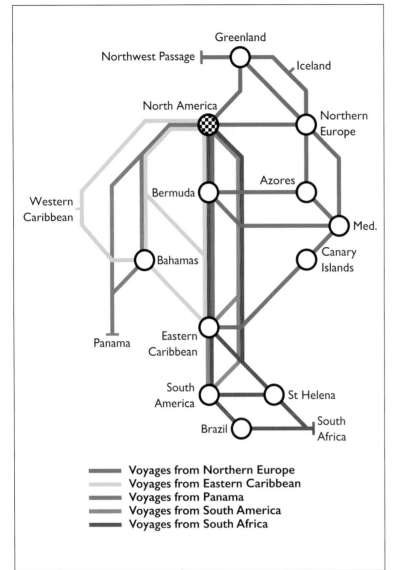

Voyages from Northern Europe
Voyages from Eastern Caribbean
Voyages from Panama
Voyages from South America
Voyages from South Africa

A15a Voyages from Northern Europe

Recommended time: June to July (westbound), August (southbound)

Tropical storms: June to November

World Cruising Routes:

AN164	Norway to Faroes and Iceland
AN155	Scotland to Iceland
AN165	Norway to Greenland
AN156	Ireland to Iceland
AN176	Greenland and Iceland to Spitsbergen
AN177	Southbound from Spitsbergen

Viking ships were crossing the Atlantic regularly long before Christopher Columbus pioneered a warm-water route to America and it is still a mystery how the exploits of the Vikings remained unknown to South European mariners of that age. Those early Viking voyages are documented in the Icelandic Sagas which mention Erik Thorvaldsson, better known as Erik the Red, as the founder of the first Norse settlement in Iceland in the latter part of the tenth century. He is also credited with establishing a settlement on Greenland and it was his son Leif Erikson who is considered to be the first European to reach North America, which he called Vinland. This had been attested by the discovery in 1960 of a Norse settlement at L'Anse aux Meadows in Newfoundland.

Those early Norse navigators noticed that in higher latitudes the prevailing westerly winds are partially replaced in summer by NE winds. This is just as true today, as seen on the July pilot chart which shows a slightly higher proportion of favourable winds for a passage between route via the Canaries and Eastern Caribbean. In many respects, this can be the perfect solution as such a voyage benefits both from good sailing conditions and favourable seasons. A late autumn or early winter passage from the Canaries will bring the boat to the Eastern Caribbean at the start of the safe sailing season which can then be spent cruising the Lesser Antilles and Virgin Islands until May. By leaving the Caribbean at the end of the winter season, the onset of the new hurricane season in June will be of little threat to a boat moving steadily to the north and away from the critical area.

Norway and Iceland. From there, the voyage can turn south towards Newfoundland or, later in summer, it can continue to Southern Greenland by which time that area is normally free of ice. South of 55°N in summer there is a high proportion of SW and S winds which do not bode well for the continuation of the voyage in that direction. The solution to this is to try and sail in short coastal stages from Newfoundland to Nova Scotia and on to Maine by using local conditions to best advantage. A more radical alternative is to sail through the Belle Isle Strait into the Gulf of St Lawrence and reach Lake Ontario by way of

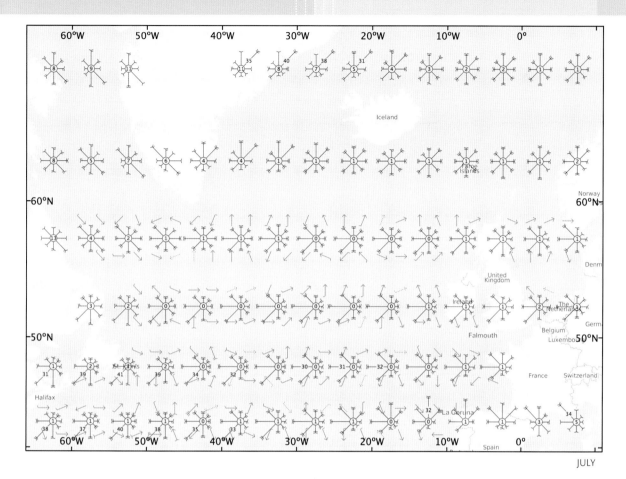

JULY

the St Lawrence River. The Welland Canal links Ontario with Lake Erie which, in its turn, is linked to the Hudson River by the Erie Barge Canal. Thus New York and the US East Coast can be reached by this roundabout but possibly more interesting route.

A15b Voyages from Western Europe

Recommended time: May (southbound), June (westbound)

Tropical storms: June to November

World Cruising Routes:

AN11	Europe to North America (northern routes)
AN12	Europe to North America (southern routes)
AN19	Northern Europe to Azores
AN138	Azores to USA
AN137	Azores to Bermuda
AN121	Bermuda to North America

The pilot charts for the summer months paint a rather grim picture for a direct crossing of the Atlantic with a high proportion of W and SW winds along the entire route. This is the reason why only yachts that are able to sail to windward perform well in the OSTAR race, which runs every four years from Plymouth in the UK to Boston in Massachusetts and is the oldest solo ocean race in the world. Owners of cruising boats are therefore well advised to follow the example of the less competitive participants who prefer to sail a more southerly route which dips outside the area of the prevailing westerlies. This will entail a long detour, possibly as far south as the Azores, and, if you are not bound by racing rules, you might as well call at those attractive islands before resuming your voyage.

The location of the North Atlantic High has a paramount bearing on the winds encountered on the westbound passage. With Bermuda being the next objective and the summer winds having a reasonable proportion of S and SW winds as you move west, at some point it should be possible to sail a NW course. As this passage coincides with the start of the hurricane season, the weather must be monitored closely to avoid running into the path of

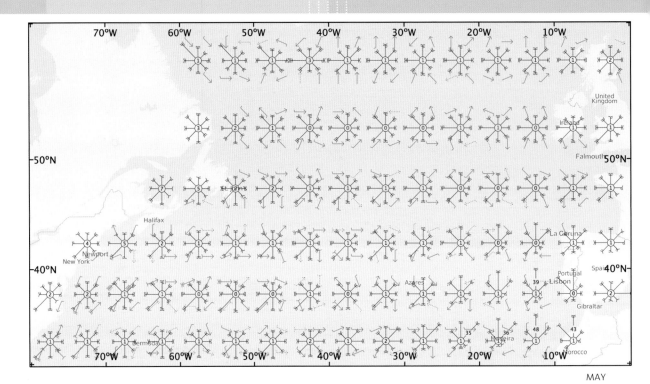

MAY

such storms, some of which have the bad habit of tracking NE into the Atlantic. Whether stopping in Bermuda or continuing nonstop to the mainland, sailing conditions should improve as the percentage of S and SW winds increases as you move west.

A15c Voyages from the Mediterranean

Recommended time: May to June

Tropical storms: June to November

World Cruising Routes:

AN38	Gibraltar to North America
AN36	Gibraltar to Azores
AN138	Azores to North America
AN137	Azores to Bermuda
AN121	Bermuda to North America

The advantage of a direct voyage to North America from Southern Europe or the Mediterranean, as opposed to a departure from a port in Northern Europe, is that the voyage can be undertaken earlier in the season, in May or early June, when weather conditions along this route start to shed their wintery character and there is as yet no risk of a hurricane. Unless this passage is undertaken in late spring, its timing would coincide with the hurricane

season, an important factor that must be taken into account when planning this voyage. This is one reason why some sailors prefer to sail the longer but somewhat less demanding route via the Canaries and Eastern Caribbean, as outlined in the following voyage.

A direct passage across the Atlantic in these lower latitudes looks more daunting than it actually is and, thanks to better weather forecasts, it is being regularly accomplished. The most important factors are patience and access to weather information. The former is needed to wait for the North Atlantic High to be well established, and in a favourable location, as this ensures a spell of NE winds at least for the initial part of the passage. The fact that the North Atlantic Anticyclone is often referred to as the Azores High is explained by its location close to the Azores, usually being to the west of the archipelago in early summer, while later in summer it drifts closer to the European mainland. There are different opinions as to whether it is better to wait for the opportune moment to start the passage in Madeira or one of the islands of the Azores. The former has the advantage that NE winds are a more frequent feature in those latitudes, whereas the latter may ensure a shorter passage.

Whichever point of departure is chosen, it is important to wait until northerly winds are well established. While NE winds would be preferable, a spell of NW

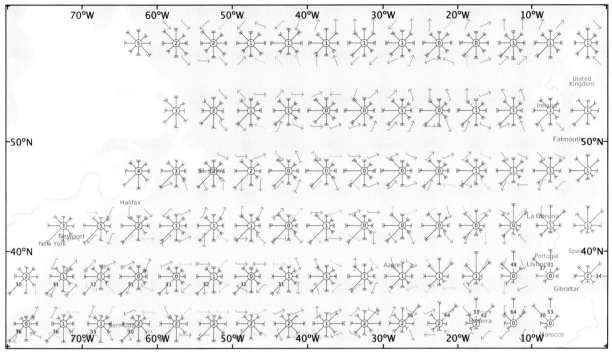

JUNE

winds may entail sailing for a while in a SW direction until the course can be gradually adjusted to pass south of Bermuda. A ridge of high pressure which often extends from the Azores High westwards towards Bermuda and the American mainland helps keep any storm systems or westerly winds well to the north. It is at this stage that the risk of an early hurricane must be kept in mind, especially if the passage is undertaken after the middle of June.

A15d Voyages via the Canaries and Caribbean

Recommended time: June to September (southbound), November to January (westbound), May (northbound)

Tropical storms: June to November

World Cruising Routes:

AN18	Northern Europe to Canary Islands
AN51	Canary Islands to Lesser Antilles
AN77	Lesser Antilles to North America
AN78	Lesser Antilles to Bermuda
AN121	Bermuda to North America

A large proportion of this voyage follows the traditional and well-travelled route from Europe to the Eastern Caribbean. Besides better weather conditions than on any of the other routes to North America, the greatest attraction of this longer voyage is the many cruising opportunities that it offers even before the Canaries are reached. Sailing south from Northern Europe there are so many tempting diversions en route that you can easily take a year to make good a distance that could be sailed offshore in less than a fortnight. To mention only some of the highlights: the Brittany coast of France with its picturesque villages and quaint anchorages, the Galician coast of Spain with its excellent seafood and wines to match, the medieval city of Porto and its even more famous wines, and Portugal's vibrant capital, Lisbon. Lying close to the route to the Canaries is delightful Madeira and its rugged and desolate satellites, aptly called Ilhas Desertas and Ilhas Selvagem (deserted and savage islands).

The segment of the voyage from the Canaries to the Eastern Caribbean is described under voyage A1d (page 65) and the segment onward to North America in A16a (page 105).

A15e Voyages to the Northwest Passage

Recommended time: June to August

World Cruising Routes:

AN157	Ireland and Scotland to Greenland
AN155	Scotland to Iceland

After centuries of failed attempts, the Northwest Passage, which links the Atlantic and Pacific oceans along an intricate route between Baffin Bay in the east and the Bering Sea in the west, is now open to shipping for part of the year. It was only in 2009 that commercial ships were able to transit the passage on a regular basis, as a result of the current climate change. The first navigator to successfully complete the passage was the Norwegian Roald Amundsen who between 1903 and 1906 sailed on the sloop *Gjøa* from Greenland to Alaska.

Several cruising boats have completed the passage successfully in recent years. The time when a transit can be attempted with a good chance of success is in late summer when the ice has receded and there is little risk of having your progress seriously impeded, or even being blocked and thus forced to spend the winter icebound. The latter is nevertheless a possibility and must be taken into account with preparations made for such an eventuality.

As transits from east to west usually start in August, the voyage from Northern Europe to Greenland need not leave too early in the summer. As in June and July the winds on a direct route to Cape Farewell, at the southern extremity of Greenland, have a high proportion of west in them, the tactic used by the Vikings may need to be applied by making a loop to the north to find more favourable winds, which may entail going as far as Iceland. The route around Greenland may have to stay well offshore as in early summer the ice limit extends far to the south of Cape Farewell. The alternative is to use the Prince Christian Sound, just north of Cape Farewell, which is normally free of ice by late summer. The Danish Meteorological Institute collects information regarding ice conditions in the waters around Greenland and distributes this information to ships primarily as ice charts and reports. The Greenland Ice Service can be contacted for information and ice charts by emailing isc@greennet.gl or the latest ice charts can be consulted on the internet at www.dmi.dk/dmi/en/index/gronland/iskort.htm.

Summer winds in the Davis Strait have a slightly higher proportion of S and SE winds and this tendency continues into Baffin Bay and all the way to the entrance into the Northwest Passage. Throughout the Northwest Passage summer winds are rarely strong but there is often fog and, even at the height of summer, there is always some residual ice that may cause damage in a collision. There are several passageways through the Northwest Passage but the southern route that goes through Bellot Strait has been open in recent summers, and although

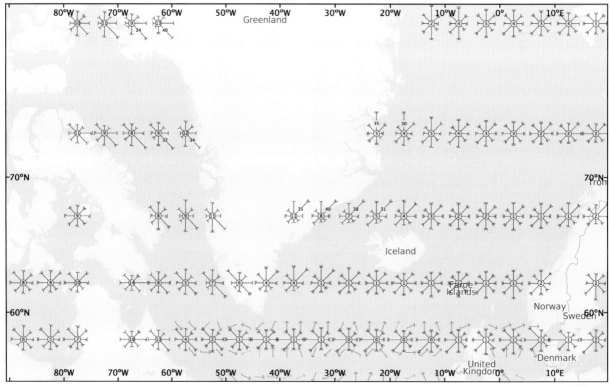

circuitous and occasionally shallow, is the route that is being used by most cruising boats. The route runs from Davis Strait to Lancaster Sound, Bellot Strait, Franklin Strait, Victoria Strait, Coronation Gulf and Amundsen Gulf into the Beaufort Sea and continues via the Chukchi Sea to the Bering Strait.

This useful shortcut to the Pacific Ocean will no doubt be used by increasingly more cruising boats attracted by the challenge more than the actual mileage saved.

A16 ● Voyages from the Caribbean and Panama

● **A16a** Voyages from the Eastern Caribbean
● **A16b** Voyages from the Western Caribbean
● **A16c** Voyage from Panama

With the hurricane season setting some limitations for northbound voyages from the Eastern Caribbean to the US East Coast, the safest time to sail north is at the change of seasons. There is usually more leeway at the end of the safe season, between late April and early June, when this voyage can be undertaken with only a low risk of either a late winter northerly storm or an early hurricane. The autumn window for northbound voyages is less generous as it only lasts from late October to the middle of November. Indeed, the risk of a June hurricane in the Eastern Caribbean is quite low as early in the season hurricanes usually form in the Western Caribbean, whereas the risk of late hurricanes is greater throughout the Caribbean.

A16a Voyages from the Eastern Caribbean

Recommended time: May

Tropical storms: June to November

World Cruising Routes:

AN77	Lesser Antilles to North America
AN86	Virgin Islands to North America
AN78	Lesser Antilles to Bermuda
AN121	Bermuda to North America

Whether the voyage to the mainland is made non stop or via Bermuda, it should benefit from favourable winds for most of the way, with E and NE winds for the first part of the passage followed by mostly S and SW winds. For sailors bound for Florida or southern states, or those who

Northwest Passage tactics

Compared to other high latitude destinations where I had sailed in the past, whether Antarctica, Spitsbergen or Alaska, the challenge posed by the Northwest Passage is entirely different. Whereas in the former places, the success of a voyage depends primarily on the experience of the captain and crew, as well as the suitability of the vessel, in other words, on objective criteria, in the case of the Northwest Passage, there is one major factor that is entirely out of your control: ice.

During the short summer season, the sea ice, which has formed over the long winter, as well as the old ice left from previous winters, melts to a greater or lesser extent. The ice usually retreats from west to east, which means that in most years the central sector of the Northwest Passage is the last to become free of ice. In recent years, the main hurdle to overcome has been Peel Sound, the symbolic gateway to the Northwest Passage for boats coming from the east. This potential chokepoint has been entirely blocked by ice during the last two summers, although some boats have managed to bypass it by using Bellot Strait. Swept by fierce tidal currents and rarely free of ice for more than a few hours, this fortuitous shortcut has been open late in the season in recent years. This was also the case last year when four westbound boats managed to get through and proceed on their way, although none was able to continue into the Pacific. Unfortunately *Aventura* was not among them, as I had decided earlier to abandon my attempt and turn around. The lateness of the season had forced me to realise that even if I could get past that point, we would have to overwinter somewhere in Arctic Canada or Alaska. The prospect of a ten-month long virtual imprisonment was something that I was not prepared to accept.

The decision to turn around was very disappointing, as in spite of having done everything right, being perfectly prepared and having the best boat for the purpose, I only managed to complete half the transit. But what I learned from the example of Roald Amundsen is that challenges are there to be overcome, and that the success of any expedition depends not only on good preparation, and respect for the forces of nature, but also on perseverance.

Rather than hibernate in the Arctic, Aventura turned her bows south towards Newfoundland, continued to the Bahamas, Panama Canal and finally Dutch Harbor, in Western Alaska. By June we were on our way north again.

From '200,000 Miles, A Life of Adventure'

Caicos Revisited

The strong trade winds gave us a fast passage from Puerto Rico to Grand Turk. We made landfall off the northern tip of the island but the large swell made it impossible to anchor anywhere close to the main settlement at Cockburn Town. Over the VHF the harbourmaster directed us to the commercial dock where we were met by customs and immigration. Entry formalities were quick and the customs officer called a taxi to take us on a tour of Cockburn Town, the sleepy capital of this remote British colony. Its main attraction is the small museum, which exhibits items found on a Spanish ship wrecked around 1510 on nearby Molasses Reef. This is the earliest wreck discovered in the New World and the well-preserved objects provide a glimpse into life on board an armed sailing vessel five centuries ago.

Wrecks had been on my mind ever since our arrival, as it was near here that we nearly lost our first *Aventura* in 1977. We had stopped on our way from Puerto Rico to the Bahamas and decided to explore the Ambergris Cays on the edge of Caicos Bank. As we were moving cautiously, slaloming slowly between the coral heads, the sun was briefly obscured by a cloud and suddenly the water ahead turned to quicksilver. Where the coral heads had been clearly visible, everything disappeared behind an opaque silvery curtain. I tried to turn back but we hit something hard and ran aground. I put the engine in full power astern but to no avail. I donned my mask, dived overboard and what struck me was not so much *Aventura*'s keel jammed in a deep cleft on top of the coral but the most amazing underwater scenery. The water was teeming with fish of all sorts, lobsters waving their antennae from their hidey-holes, while brightly coloured fan corals swayed in the current. As to the boat, it was quite clear that we had no chance of getting off on our own. But as Jimmy's luck would have it, we had run aground at low tide and, after a couple of hours of anxious waiting, interrupted by frequent dives to check that the light swell was not causing any damage to the keel, a larger wave took us in her embrace, lifted us gently and deposited us behind the reef.

Jimmy Cornell, *Aventura III*

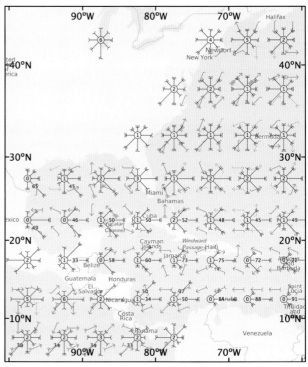

MAY

More northern destinations can be reached either by an offshore route or via the Intracoastal Waterway. From Florida, this system of rivers and canals passes through the states of South Carolina, North Carolina and Virginia before it reaches Chesapeake Bay from where it is just a short offshore leg to New York. Sailing through the very heart of that exciting city is an unforgettable experience. From New York, the inshore route can be resumed to reach ports in New England through Long Island Sound. The other alternative is to continue by way of the Hudson River and the comprehensive system of canals to the Great Lakes and even beyond to the St Lawrence River and Canada.

A16b Voyages from the Western Caribbean

Recommended time: May, early November

Tropical storms: June to November

World Cruising Routes:

AN105   Northbound from Western Caribbean
AN111   Northbound from the Bahamas and Florida
AN112   Florida and Bahamas to Bermuda
AN121   Bermuda to North America

are interested in exploring the US East Coast starting from its southern extremity, there is an alternative way to reach the US mainland from the Eastern Caribbean by sailing the island route via Puerto Rico, Turks & Caicos, the Bahamas and continuing to either Florida or another southern state.

Because of the NE and E winds which prevail in the Caribbean Sea throughout the year, going through the Yucatán Channel is the logical way for a northbound passage from any of the countries on the western shores of the Caribbean. This is quite acceptable to boats bound for Florida or some of the southern states, but to anyone intending to sail further north the route via the Windward Passage and Outer Bahamas would have more appeal, although it is much harder to accomplish. If that prospect is too much of a deterrent, the solution is to go through the Yucatán Channel and continue north along the Florida coast with the help of the Gulf Stream. The rest of the voyage can either continue offshore or via the Intracoastal Waterway which can be accessed from a number of ports south of Cape Hatteras.

Boats that go well to windward can try the Windward Passage alternative, with possible intermediate stops in Jamaica or on Cuba's south coast, but the contrary wind and current may well force a change of plan and a turn for the Yucatán Channel.

The southern segment of this voyage can be sailed at any time during the safe winter months, but the rest of the voyage should be planned for a period when better conditions can be expected north of the Bahamas. This is either in late spring, when the incidence of winter storms has diminished and the hurricane season has not yet started, or in late autumn when the risk of a winter storm is still low.

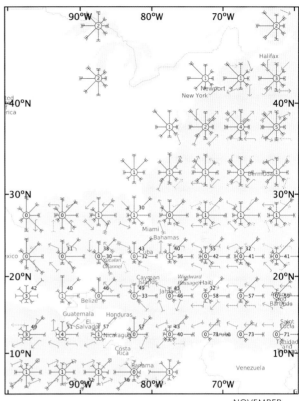

NOVEMBER

A16c Voyage from Panama

Recommended time: May, late November

Tropical storms: June to November

World Cruising Routes:

AN99   Panama to Bermuda and North America
AN111   Northbound from the Bahamas and Florida
AN112   Florida and Bahamas to Bermuda
AN121   Bermuda to North America

Most of what was written for the previous voyage also applies to the timing of this voyage but there is one important difference. As the course from Panama to the Windward Passage is east of north, a boat that sails reasonably well to windward may be able to sail the direct route, although the strong winds and large swell that are a feature of the Western Caribbean Sea may bring about a change of heart. In that case, the course should be altered for the Yucatán Channel, but the route must stay well clear of the reefs, banks and islands that litter this area and pose a serious hazard.

One tried tactic to secure a better sailing angle toward the Windward Passage is to make some easting from Panama by sailing to the San Blas Islands and possibly as far east as Cartagena in Colombia before heading north. The route north of the Windward Passage passes through the Outer Bahamas from where you can continue offshore to your destination, or join the Intracoastal Waterway somewhere along the way.

A17 • Voyages from South America

Recommended time: February to April (from Northern Brazil), March to May (from Argentina and Southern Brazil), May (northbound from Caribbean)

Tropical storms: June to November (North Atlantic)

World Cruising Routes:

AS25   Northbound from Patagonia and Falkland Islands
AS26   Northbound from Argentina
AT21   Brazil to Eastern Caribbean
AN77   Lesser Antilles to North America
AN78   Lesser Antilles to Bermuda
AN121   Bermuda to North America

A direct offshore route that bypasses the Lesser Antilles altogether is the only alternative to the slower but, for a cruising boat, much more attractive route which follows the contour of the South American mainland. Boats setting off from southern ports will probably sail the initial stages of this long voyage by stopping at such conveniently spaced ports of call as the Falklands, Mar del Plata, Punta del Este, Rio de Janeiro and Salvador da Bahia. This route benefits from mostly favourable winds as far north as 35°S but from there on winds from the northerly quarter become increasingly more frequent until the corner is turned at Cape São Roque. Northbound passages from ports in Southern Brazil have to contend with strong NE winds and a contrary SW current between October and February, so ideally passages should be planned to start after March. For voyages that start from ports in Northern Brazil, weather conditions for a passage to the Caribbean are generally good and there is minimal risk of tropical storms south of the equator as there has been only one tropical storm ever recorded in that area, Catarina in March 2004.

The strong NW setting Guyanas Current runs about 70 to 100 miles off the Northern Brazilian coast, so a route should be sailed that is well offshore to take full advantage of the current and also to avoid the vast discharge from the Amazon River which affects a large area. The winds are normally from E or NE and the doldrums will be encountered close to the equator as in the first months of the year the ITCZ extends eastward from the coast of Brazil in the latitude band 10°S to 3°S.

With good timing the Lesser Antilles ought to be reached by March which gives plenty of time to cruise the chain of islands from south to north before continuing the voyage to your North American destination. The time to sail this segment is before the start of the hurricane season in June, so a late May start from the Eastern Caribbean will ensure reasonable weather conditions for this passage that can be sailed nonstop to the US mainland or with a break in Bermuda. Refer to voyage A3b and the pilot charts for the passage to the Caribbean featured on pages 74 and 75.

A18 • Voyages from South Africa

- **A18a** Direct offshore voyages
- **A18b** Voyages via Brazil and the Caribbean

As in the case of voyages from South America, destinations on the East Coast of the United States can either be reached by way of a long offshore passage or by sailing a route that follows the contour of South America and calls at the Lesser Antilles en route to North America.

A18a Direct offshore voyages

Recommended time: March to May

Tropical storms: June to November (North Atlantic)

World Cruising Routes:
  AT25 South Africa and St Helena to Eastern Caribbean

As it is quite unlikely that anyone would plan to sail this long stretch without stopping anywhere, there are two places where you may be tempted to break the long passage, the islands of St Helena and the Brazilian Fernando de Noronha, although the latter is not that close to the direct course. Keeping to windward of the Lesser Antilles, the next possible stop is the island of Bermuda.

A18b Voyages via Brazil and the Caribbean

Recommended time: January to March (to Eastern Caribbean), May (to US East Coast)

Tropical storms: June to November (North Atlantic)

World Cruising Routes:
  AT25   South Africa and St Helena to Eastern Caribbean
  AS11   Northbound from Cape Town
  AT21   Brazil to Eastern Caribbean
  AN77   Lesser Antilles to North America
  AN78   Lesser Antilles to Bermuda
  AN121 Bermuda to North America

There are three options for the South Atlantic segment of this voyage: a route that calls at St Helena before crossing over to Brazil, a direct offshore route to one of the ports in Northern Brazil and, finally, a southern route that reaches the South American mainland in Southern Brazil and continues north along its coast.

On the first two alternatives, passages to St Helena or to ports in Northern Brazil benefit from steady SE trade winds virtually from the start. For those who choose the third alternative, passages from South Africa to ports in Southern Brazil will have mainly southerly winds for the first part, but halfway across, the South Atlantic Convergence Zone needs to be crossed where a noticeable change in the prevailing wind direction occurs. As you approach the mainland, winds from the northern quarter become predominant. These winds, which blow along the Brazilian coast from October to February, must be taken into account as they may delay progress as well as the timing of the next segment from Northern Brazil to the Eastern Caribbean. The latter must be reached by April or early May at the latest to avoid the risk of an early hurricane on the final leg to the US East Coast. It is for this reason that the first two options outlined above make more sense as both allow Northern Brazil to be easily reached in February or March. With such timing both the passage to the Lesser Antilles and the subsequent leg to your North American destination can be completed at the best of times. Refer also to voyages A3a, A3b and A4a, and the accompanying pilot charts on pages 73, 74 and 75.

Cruising hubs

Montego Bay **
Conveniently located at the western end of Jamaica, the Montego Bay Yacht Club provides a good range of repair facilities. Nearby Sangster International Airport (MBJ) is Jamaica's busiest airport with flights to many US destinations, also to several European capitals. Cornwall Regional Hospital in Montego Bay has good medical and emergency facilities.

New York *****
There is a comprehensive range of yachting facilities in and around New York, making this a convenient place for any kind of repairs, as well as crew changes. JFK international airport has flights to all major destinations in the world complemented by Newark airport (EWR) in New Jersey.

Reykjavik ***
As the base for a large fishing fleet, Iceland's capital has a wide range of repair facilities. Keflavik International Airport (KEF) operates flights to several European capitals as well as some major US cities. The National University Hospital in Reykjavik is the country's main hospital with a complete range of facilities.

Nuuk **
As a relatively busy fishing harbour the capital of Greenland has a boatyard with a modest range of repair facilities. Better facilities are at Aasiaat. Provisioning is good and fuel as well as propane are available. Queen Ingrid Hospital acts as the national medical centre, and has a full range of facilities. Nuuk airport (GOH) can only handle smaller airplanes and has connecting fights to the international

Kangerlussuaq airport (SFJ), which operates regular flights to Copenhagen and Reykjavik, as well as to destinations in USA and Canada.

What next?

European visitors to North America will find that thanks to the prevailing westerly winds, a return voyage from the American mainland is much easier to plan and accomplish than the outbound voyage. The one slight impediment that must be taken into account if planning a late summer passage in lower latitudes is the risk of hurricanes, whereas passages along a northern route avoid both this threat and the unfavourable conditions of ice and fog that are a feature of early summer.

Those who do not have time constraints can choose from a wide range of attractive options for the continuation of their voyage from North America. An attractive solution for those who have sailed across the Atlantic from Europe, and who do not intend to return home in the same year, is to spend the summer cruising the US East Coast and, when the days start getting shorter and colder, turn around and head for the tropics, to the Eastern Caribbean, Bahamas or the Western Caribbean. The best time to do this is at the change of seasons, in early November, when the weather has not become too wintery and the safe season is about to start in the tropics. This is also the time to head south if the plan is to continue the voyage to Panama and beyond.

A very different alternative is to leave the boat for the winter in a marina or boatyard and return to Europe the following spring by completing a bigger or smaller North Atlantic loop. This can be done by sailing north via Nova Scotia and Newfoundland and turn east from there, or continue to Greenland and Iceland before heading for home.

Such a northern loop may also appeal to sailors from South America or Africa who can then reach Europe by this roundabout way, and then continue south to the Mediterranean, the Canaries and finally home.

Those who may be tempted by a dose of freshwater cruising can take the inland route which links the Hudson River to the Great Lakes and gives access to a comprehensive network of waterways leading to the vast cruising areas of the Great Lakes themselves, to the St Lawrence River and Canada, and by way of several canals and rivers to the Mississippi and the Gulf of Mexico. The latter section is part of the Great Loop, a popular circular voyage undertaken every year by scores of pleasure boats, both sail and power.

Voyages to South America and Antarctica

From the windswept inlets of Patagonia to the jungles of the Amazon and the palm-fringed beaches of Venezuela, the Atlantic and Caribbean shores of South America are a vast area with infinite cruising opportunities which only started attracting cruising boats from outside the area in recent years. The one exception is Venezuela which, due primarily to its location close to the cruising grounds of the Lesser Antilles, had a brief surge in popularity but a deteriorating safety situation has been keeping most sailors away in recent years. Elsewhere in Atlantic South America, the majority of boats only make brief stops while on their way to somewhere else, usually calling at ports in Northern Brazil en route to the Caribbean. But change is on its way as visiting yachts gradually discover the attractions of other parts of South America. The three main areas are the Amazon Delta in the north, Tierra del Fuego and Patagonia in the far south, and the famous Brazilian Carnival, which can certainly be described as a cruising destination as many sailors make a point of being

in Brazil during that time to enjoy the uniquely exuberant atmosphere that infects the entire populations of such cities as Rio de Janeiro, Salvador and Recife during Carnival time.

Weather conditions in the tropical and subtropical South Atlantic are among the most benign of any ocean and planning a voyage to that area is fairly simple as the favourable seasons on the two sides of the equator complement each other perfectly.

A19 • Voyages from Europe

- **A19a** Voyages via the Canary and Cape Verde Islands
- **A19b** Voyages via the Azores

Whether planning to start from Northern Europe or the Mediterranean, the easiest and most interesting route for a southbound voyage is to call at the Canaries and Cape Verdes before setting course for your chosen destination. Those who are not in too much of a hurry have the opportunity to make a detour from the Cape Verdes to West Africa, whether to nearby Gambia and Senegal, or further south to Guinea and possibly beyond. On the other hand, those who prefer to reach South America from Northern Europe in the shortest time possible may consider the direct offshore route via the Azores.

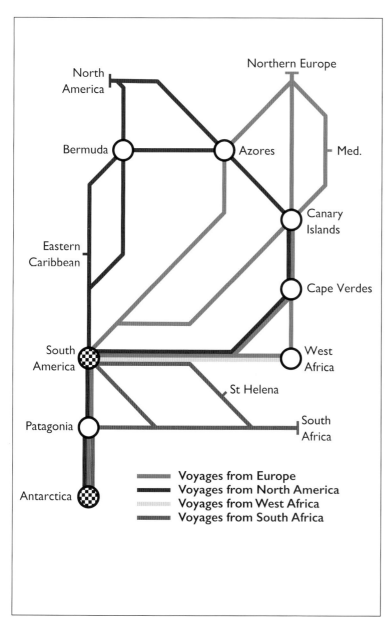

Voyages from Europe
Voyages from North America
Voyages from West Africa
Voyages from South Africa

A19a Voyages via the Canary and Cape Verde Islands

Recommended time: July to September (to Canaries), October to February (South Atlantic)

World Cruising Routes:

AN13 Southbound from Northern Europe

AN18 Northern Europe to Canaries

AN32 Gibraltar to Canary Islands

AN52 Canary Islands to Cape Verde Islands

AT11 Canary and Cape Verde Islands to Brazil

AT12 West Africa to Brazil

The passage south from Northern Europe benefits from the best sailing conditions in summer with a late summer or early autumn arrival in the Canaries allowing plenty of time to prepare for the continuation of the voyage to the South Atlantic. Reasonable weather conditions can be expected

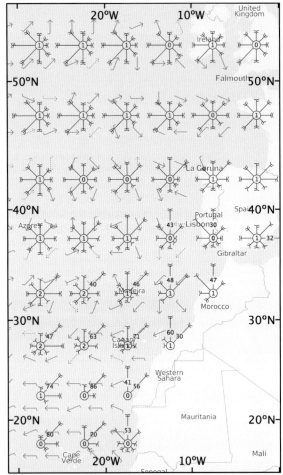

SEPTEMBER

Brazil. A direct passage from the Canaries to Brazil is perfectly feasible, but the route passes so close to the Cape Verdes that a stop there makes sense. South of the equator the predominant direction of the wind is from the southerly quarter and as the worst conditions coincide with the period known as the SW monsoon, between June and August, when winds from that direction prevail, the voyage should be timed so that the equator is crossed later and the South Atlantic is not reached before September or preferably October. During the later months of the year, the winds in the western South Atlantic are predominantly from SE, gradually backing to NE, thus providing good sailing conditions to southern destinations. An October arrival in the South Atlantic also means that Patagonia is reached during the austral summer, which is the best time to cruise the southern extremity of America and sail across the Drake Passage to Antarctica.

A19b Voyages via the Azores

Recommended time: July to August (Eastern North Atlantic), October to February (South Atlantic)

Tropical storms: June to November (North Atlantic)

World Cruising Routes:

AN19	Northern Europe to Azores
AT13	Azores to Brazil
AS23	Southbound from Brazil
AS24	Southbound from Argentina

A direct voyage via the Azores should only be considered by those who are undeterred by long offshore passages, as the distance from the Azores to Rio de Janeiro is nearly 4,000 miles. Weather conditions along this route are generally favourable as far as the equator, with prevailing NE winds during the recommended period. It should be borne in mind that as the voyage south coincides with the height of the hurricane season in the western North Atlantic due allowance should be made for the possibility of running into a brewing storm west of the Cape Verdes. Nor should the arrival in the South Atlantic be timed too early (August), when, as mentioned earlier, there is a high proportion of southerly winds south of the equator. As you move south, those winds are gradually replaced by NE winds, which is the predominant direction between October and February down to about 35°S. From there, winds from the western quarter start taking over, their average strength increasing further south, which is something that should not be much of a surprise for anyone bound for the Southern Ocean.

in October or November for the onward passage into the South Atlantic. For boats bound for ports in Southern Brazil and beyond, the NE winds, which are a constant feature between October and February in the western part of the South Atlantic between latitudes 10°S and 35°S, will ensure fast passages as far south as 35°S. From there on, wind directions are variable and become increasingly westerly further south. Therefore anyone planning to reach Patagonia or sail to Antarctica at the most favourable time, which is the austral summer months of January and February, should plan on a prompt departure from the Canaries in late September or early October so as to have sufficient time to reach Patagonia by January at the latest.

Directions for the initial segment of this voyage are similar to voyage A1e (page 66) which describes the route from the Canaries to the Cape Verdes and

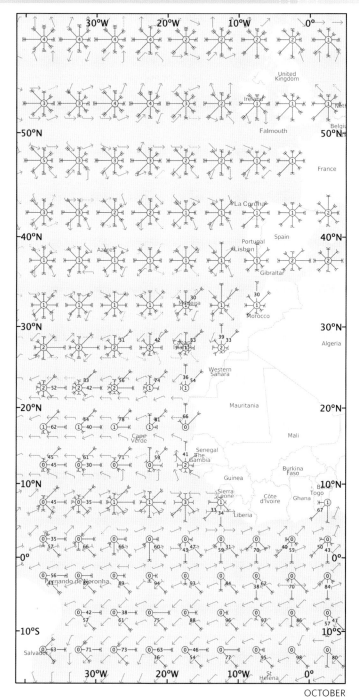

OCTOBER

A20 • Voyages from North America

● **A20a** Direct voyages
● **A20b** Voyages via the Azores, Canary and Cape Verde Islands

So near and yet so far is the best way to describe a voyage to any of the South American countries not bordering on the Caribbean Sea. The direct route, either nonstop or via Bermuda, is feasible, but the offshore segment is so long that it may not appeal to many cruising sailors, especially as there is a more attractive, albeit longer, alternative.

A20a Direct voyages

Recommended time: May to June, November (North Atlantic), September to February (South Atlantic)

Tropical storms: June to November (North Atlantic)

World Cruising Routes:

AN143	North America to Bermuda
AT14	Bermuda and North America to Brazil
AT15	Eastern Caribbean to Brazil

Voyages to nearer destinations in South America, such as Venezuela and Colombia, can be accomplished easily from the US East Coast, sailing either via the Bahamas or from the Eastern Caribbean islands. The latter can also be the starting point for a voyage to Northern Brazil, a challenging proposition, as described in route AT17 in *World Cruising Routes*, which outlines the tactics of dealing with the contrary winds and current on that route.

Direct voyages to more remote destinations in South America need more careful planning if the intention is to get there as quickly as possible. The long voyage can be undertaken nonstop all the way or with an initial stop in Bermuda. The timing of the first part of the voyage is not easy as it has to balance the safe season in the North Atlantic with the most favourable months in the South

Atlantic. The start from the US East Coast is therefore limited to late spring when winter storms no longer pose a serious threat and the hurricane season has not yet started. The other alternative is to start the voyage at the end of the hurricane season and sail on a route that crosses the equator in about longitude 35°W.

The advantage of a November passage is that the percentage of favourable winds in the South Atlantic is higher between October and February. This may be an attractive prospect for those bound for destinations as far south as Northern Argentina, but for those planning to reach the Southern Ocean at the height of the austral summer, such a late departure may result in a late arrival there, a factor which may not suit your plans. Nevertheless, a later summer arrival in Patagonia may be acceptable to those who do not intend to sail to Antarctica but plan to continue west to Chile and the South Pacific, where arriving at any time between February and April is perfect. Bearing in mind all the above factors, the following alternative may prove to be more suitable as it affords more timing flexibility.

A20b Voyages via the Azores, Canary and Cape Verde Islands

Recommended time: May, November (North Atlantic), September to February (South Atlantic)

Tropical storms: June to November (North Atlantic)

World Cruising Routes:

AN144	North America to Azores
AN136	Azores to Canary Islands
AN52	Canary Islands to Cape Verde Islands
AT11	Canary and Cape Verde Islands to Brazil
AT14	Bermuda and North America to Brazil
AT15	Eastern Caribbean to Brazil

Sailing from one half of the American continent to its other half by way of this long detour may not look like the way to go but it certainly makes sense to anyone who is not in a great hurry. Its greatest advantage is that it can be accomplished at the most favourable times by benefitting from favourable weather conditions in both hemispheres. An added bonus is the opportunity to visit some attractive island groups that are fortuitously located along the suggested route, making it possible to break up the longer passages into convenient segments.

A late spring or early summer start from the US East Coast is suggested so that the critical area is passed before the onset of the hurricane season. For boats that leave from ports that are north of Chesapeake Bay, a summer start may be more attractive provided the initial course is set in higher latitudes so as to stay clear of possible hurricanes and take better advantage of the favourable westerly winds. In such a case a nonstop passage to the Azores that bypasses Bermuda is strongly recommended. From the Azores onwards mostly NE winds can be counted on all the way to the equator.

Those who would rather avoid such a long offshore leg, should sail from the Azores to the Canaries and thence to the Cape Verdes, both island groups being good stopover points. This timing also avoids crossing the equator to Brazil during the SW monsoon when winds from that direction as well as the east-setting counterequatorial current make for more difficult sailing conditions in August than later in the year. This is one of the reasons why regardless of the time of the start of this voyage, the South Atlantic should not be reached before September or early October.

South of the Line the proportion of winds from the southerly quarter gradually give way to winds from SE, backing further south to E and NE, thus ensuring generally favourable conditions towards more southern destinations, whether in Brazil or Argentina. This timing is also right for those who are bound for Patagonia and beyond as it allows them to reach the Southern Ocean during the most favourable period at the height of the austral summer.

For those who would rather spend the winter in the Caribbean sunshine in preparation for a voyage to the South Atlantic, the logical alternative is to leave the US East Coast in late autumn, spend the winter in the Eastern Caribbean and join the eastbound migration at the end of the safe season, in May or early June. From the Azores, the voyage then continues to the Canaries, Cape Verdes and on to the South American mainland as described above and in A19a.

The other alternative is to take the shorter, but much more challenging, direct route from the Eastern Caribbean to Northern Brazil (AT17 in *World Cruising Routes*) and continue south by following the contour of the continental landmass. It will be tough going until Cape São Roque has been weathered but from there on winds will become progressively favourable.

A21 • Voyages from West Africa

Recommended time: October to February

World Cruising Routes:

AT12	West Africa to Brazil

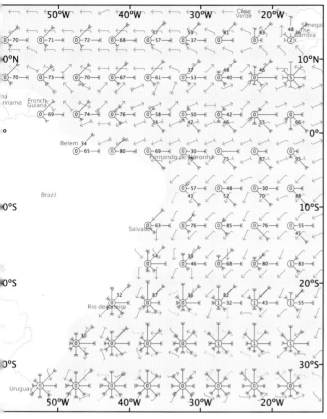

NOVEMBER

A22 • Voyages from South Africa

● **A22a** Voyages via St Helena
● **A22b** Direct voyages from South Africa

The majority of voyages that start from Cape Town are bound for the Caribbean, usually with a stop in St Helena. This is also the route taken by those who intend to see at least some of South America by taking the easy option of a detour from St Helena to Northern Brazil. Those who wish to experience more of South America can sail directly to a port in Southern Brazil and continue north from there, or take the more challenging route to Argentina and head from there for the Southern Ocean.

A22a Voyages via St Helena

Recommended time: January to March
World Cruising Routes:
AS11   Northbound from Cape Town
AS13   St Helena to Brazil

Weather conditions along this route are at their best in the early part of the year and ensure fast passages to ports in Northern Brazil whether sailing nonstop or with a break at St Helena. Besides the opportunity of partaking in the Carnival festivities in a Brazilian setting, there is also the opportunity of making a detour into the Amazon Delta. There are more details about this route, which continues to the Eastern Caribbean, in voyage A4a on page 75.

A22b Direct Voyages from South Africa

Recommended time: December to March
World Cruising Routes:
AS14   Cape Town to Brazil
AS23   Southbound from Brazil
AS24   Southbound from Argentina

The previously outlined voyage to Northern Brazil may have its attractions, especially as it only entails a relatively short detour from the route to the Caribbean, but it misses some of the best of South America and this may explain why the number of yachts taking the southern route from South Africa to Brazil has been increasing. Those who sail

The only West African countries that are visited by a small number of cruising yachts are Senegal and Gambia, although some of the neighbouring countries such as Guinea-Bissau and Guinea have started attracting a few visiting yachts as well. If the safety situation continues to improve in that area, there is little doubt that more sailors will be tempted to explore the shores of the Gulf of Guinea.

Most boats that call at Senegal and Gambia do so as part of a longer voyage from Europe to the Caribbean, which often also includes a detour to Northern Brazil. Voyages bound for the South Atlantic during the recommended time will benefit from favourable NE winds as far as the equator. South of the equator the winds will gradually veer to E and SE, so it may be advisable to keep some easting in hand when crossing the equator so as to have a better sailing angle to reach the area of prevailing NE winds that are a seasonal phenomenon southwards of Cape São Roque. The timing for passages to more southern ports must take into account the season of NE winds that lasts in that area from October to February.

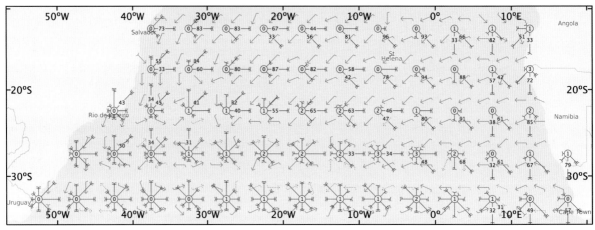

JANUARY

straight across from Cape Town to Rio de Janeiro between December and February will experience for the first half of the passage mostly southerly winds which will be replaced gradually by winds from the northern quarter. The change usually occurs when the South Atlantic Convergence Zone, which lies astride this route, is crossed. Off the Brazilian coast NE winds prevail during those months, something to be borne in mind by those planning to continue north along the coast.

Direct voyages from South Africa to Argentina or Patagonia have a lesser chance of favourable winds and, depending on the time of year, may be accomplished more easily by sailing the shortest route across to the South American mainland making the best of existing conditions. The voyage south is then continued along a route that runs roughly parallel to the Argentine coast where prevailing winds are usually from the western quarter.

A23 • Voyages to Antarctica

Recommended time: December to February

World Cruising Routes:

AS36	Tierra del Fuego to Antarctica
AS33	Falkland Islands to Antarctica
AS37	Antarctica to Tierra del Fuego
AS38	Antarctica to Falkland Islands and South Georgia

The usual departure point for a crossing of the Drake Passage is Puerto Williams, a small Chilean settlement and military base on the southern shore of the Beagle Channel. Formalities need to be completed there by boats bound for the Antarctic Peninsula as this section of

Antarctica is under Chilean jurisdiction. The optimum period for the voyage into the Southern Ocean is during the austral summer and the best timing for the passage to the Antarctic Peninsula is in January or early February when the chances of having favourable conditions for the crossing of the Drake Passage are the best. The ideal time to start the crossing is immediately after the passage of a depression when the winds normally veer from NW to N and briefly to NE before they revert to their prevailing westerly tendency. The Antarctic Convergence Zone is crossed during this passage, an area rich in sea life as countless birds, fish and whales are attracted to these rich feeding grounds caused by an oceanic upwelling. The risk of encountering icebergs during this passage is relatively low in summer, but a good lookout should be kept nonetheless, especially south of the above area.

There is a choice of landfalls along the Antarctic Peninsula and the accepted tactic is to start cruising as far east as possible and continue as far west as time and conditions will permit so as to have a better sailing angle for the return passage to the mainland. The usual tactic is to start at one of the South Shetlands and to leave from the Melchior Islands. A good starting point for a cruise in the sheltered waters off the western side of the Antarctic Peninsula is Deception Island. The best cruising area stretches from there to Marguerite Bay, although the latter can only be reached in those summers when the limit of the pack ice has receded further south.

Deception Island is a partly collapsed crater of a still active volcano, the perfectly sheltered anchorage in Telefon Bay providing a unique opportunity to be moored on top of a live volcano. Steam and hot water bubble up to the surface, warming the water enough for a quick dip. The small island was a major whaling station in the past, its

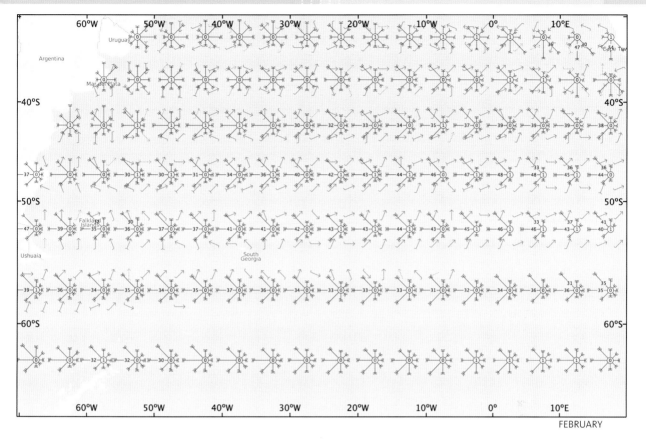

FEBRUARY

decaying installations a grim reminder of their purpose. From there the route leads in a generally SW direction with a good choice of anchorages. The scenery is quite breathtaking and there is lots of wildlife: large penguin colonies, pods of courting humpback whales, and various species of seals, including the enormous elephant seals. There are a number of research stations, some of which welcome visiting sailors.

Weather conditions in summer are quite benign, the days are long and the skies are usually clear. As the temperature rarely falls below freezing and winds are often light, cruising in sheltered waters against a backdrop of stunning scenery is an unforgettable experience. When the time comes to head north, a good departure point is in the area of the Melchior Islands from where the open sea is easily reached. Sailing back to the mainland across the prevailing westerly winds, large swell and east-setting current is never easy. Access to the latest weather information is therefore essential and the optimum time to start the passage is dictated by the expected arrival of an impending depression. Northbound boats normally make landfall close to Horn Island, which has a precarious

anchorage where it is possible to land in settled weather to visit the various monuments erected to the memory of the sailors who over the centuries have passed through, or lost their lives, in these stormy waters.

Those who plan to continue the voyage north into the South Atlantic and do not need to return either to Puerto Williams or Ushuaia should consider sailing directly to the Falklands as the route that passes east of Staten Island benefits from a better sailing angle than the return route from Antarctica to the mainland. Another enticing destination for anyone sailing in those waters is South Georgia. The island is famous for its rich wildlife and early summer is a good time to visit. The best time is the spring breeding season (October to November) but this may be too early to fit into the overall timing of this voyage. But even a later summer arrival should more than justify the detour. It must be noted that visits to both South Georgia and Antarctica can only be done with the special permission of the yacht owner's government, and arrangements to obtain such a permit must be done at least six months before the date of the intended visit.

The Deep South

Beyond 40° S there is no law. Beyond 50° S there is no God.
                                              Old sailor's adage

My fascination with high-latitude sailing began during my Whitbread racing career. Passing by those Southern Ocean islands – mountainous, savage, virtually unknown but to a few, for a professional sailor and amateur mountaineer this was the ultimate draw. It was my first Antarctic 'sailing to climb' expedition in 1988 on *Pelagic* that set the scene for the next 30 years: a mid-life filled with adventure in the deep south where Pelagic Expeditions came to specialise in cold-sailing adventures for yachtsmen but also for climbers, divers, kayakers and film teams.

As the years have gone by, the pressure on these remote locations, like the Antarctic Peninsula, the subantarctic island of South Georgia and other places in the Southern Ocean, has increased to an alarming level, and have led to a tightening of regulations by governments and organisations, such as the Antarctic Treaty Forum, which administer these areas. Gone are the days of ad hoc freedom to roam at will or adventure cruises when no permissions were needed. Also gone is the sense not only of independence and remoteness but also of self-reliance, because access permits, management plans, emergency contingency plans, medical evacuation response and liability insurance coverage are now all mandatory. Recently such requirements have become legally binding. Sailing yachts are still heading south, but also more and more super and mega yachts (unwieldy vessels for any kind of real adventure), aided in the planning by consultancies, piloted and guided by professionals, have now discovered the deep south and this trend is likely to continue.

Gone is the wilderness. The first few of us were lucky enough to experience a sense of freedom, which we look back on fondly and reminisce about continually. The stories are sometimes legend, often myth. We have also been witness to the landscape changing with the climate, which is melancholic to say the least. But rest assured, first-time visitor – the mountains are still feeding the glaciers in abundance, icebergs abound, the weather is there to be fought with and the wildlife is there to be enjoyed. Sailing south will always be worth the extra effort and risk.

Skip Novak, *Pelagic Australis*

Cruising hubs

Ushuaia ★★★

Argentina's southernmost settlement is the starting and finishing point of cruises to Antarctica, and cruising sailors are benefitting from the resulting improvement in facilities with a good range of repair services, provisioning and health care. Ushuaia international airport (USH) has regular flights operated by Aerolineas Argentinas to Buenos Aires for onward connections, Lan Chile to Santiago, and seasonal flights by British, German, and French charter companies.

See also Las Palmas (page 77), Mindelo (page 77), Salvador da Bahia (page 78), Rio de Janeiro (page 97), Mar del Plata (page 97) and Port Stanley (page 97).

What next?

Voyage options from South America are very simple: to go north, south or east. Anyone planning to sail to destinations in the North Atlantic via the Eastern Caribbean must attempt to arrive there before the start of the hurricane season (June to November). Voyages in the opposite direction, towards the southern extremity of the continent, should take place during the summer months, from December to February, and this is also a good time for those planning to cruise the Chilean fjordland. This timing is also perfect for those intending to continue the voyage from Chile towards the tropical South Pacific where the cyclone season ends in early May. By sailing the southern route via Easter Island to Tahiti, French Polynesia will be reached at the optimum time.

Voyages to South Africa are also best undertaken during the summer, those from Patagonia benefitting from the westerly winds of higher latitudes; those from Northern Argentina and Brazil having to count on more of a mixed bag.

Voyages to Antarctica will benefit from most favourable conditions in January and February, both for the crossing of the Drake Passage and for a cruise along the Antarctic Peninsula. That is also the best period for the return voyage to the mainland. Those who plan to continue their voyage into the South Atlantic have the choice of sailing from Antarctica directly to the Falkland Islands. Those who are bound for the Chilean fjordland and beyond will need to call again at Puerto Williams to complete the necessary formalities for the onward voyage through Southern Chile.

Voyages to South Africa

Voyages to South Africa from anywhere in the North Atlantic are a difficult undertaking on account of the contrary winds south of the equator, and even sailing across from South America is not easy, with the notable exception of voyages from Patagonia and Antarctica which benefit from the prevailing westerly winds. Direct voyages to South Africa continue to be the preserve of racing yachts and it is interesting to note that the final result of many round the world races has been decided by the first leg to Cape Town. For cruising sailors planning to sail that way the best solution is to treat the entire exercise as a long cruise and plot a route which takes best advantage of prevailing weather conditions and calls at some interesting destinations along the way.

The pilot charts used to illustrate voyages to South America and Antarctica in the previous section are also relevant for the following voyages.

A24 • Voyages from Europe

- **A24a** Voyages via the Canary and Cape Verde Islands
- **A24b** Voyages via the Azores

There are two basic options for this voyage: a direct route via the Azores, which stays offshore for most of the way and has little appeal to most cruising sailors, and a considerably longer, but both easier and more interesting

route, which calls at the Canary and Cape Verde Islands and also at a number of ports on the South American mainland before crossing over to Cape Town.

● A24a Voyages via the Canary and Cape Verde Islands

Recommended time: July to September (to Canaries), October to February (South Atlantic)

World Cruising Routes:

AN13	Southbound from Northern Europe
AN18	Northern Europe to Canary Islands
AN32	Gibraltar to Canary Islands
AN52	Canary Islands to Cape Verdes
AT11	Canary and Cape Verde Islands to Brazil
AS21	South America to South Africa

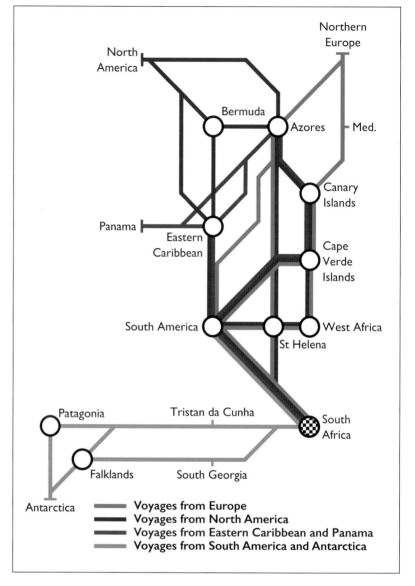

Whether starting from Northern Europe or the Mediterranean, the initial segment of this voyage will end at the Canary Islands, where the port of Las Palmas de Gran Canaria is a perfect place to prepare for the long passages that lie ahead as it has a wide range of repair facilities and excellent provisioning. The voyage to South America can continue from here either directly or via the Cape Verde islands. Early autumn is a good time for the southbound voyage with a suggested stop at the Cape Verde Islands before crossing the equator. A detour to Senegal or Gambia can easily be included at this point, and perhaps continue along the African coast for a while before crossing over to South America. It may be tempting to consider sailing all the way to Cape Town keeping to the east side of the South Atlantic but the prevailing southerly winds that later combine with the north-setting Benguela Current would make this a very hard undertaking. Safety considerations are another reason not to pursue this option as very few of the countries along this route are safe enough to justify such an effort.

Sailing south from the Canaries or Cape Verdes, the winds will be predominantly from E or NE down to about 10°N. The equator should be crossed around longitude 20°W and from that point the winds will gradually back from S to SE. During the later months of the year, which is the best time to undertake this voyage, the winds in the western South Atlantic are predominantly from SE but closer to the mainland the winds gradually turn to NE and provide good sailing conditions to southern destinations. There are many interesting landfalls to choose from along the Brazilian coast, from Salvador da Bahia in the north to

Rio de Janeiro in the south. The point where the ocean will be recrossed depends on the time of year, but unless there is an intention to see more of South America the necessary eastbound passage can be embarked on anywhere south of Rio de Janeiro. Otherwise it may be worth continuing along the coast as far as the River Plate estuary which is virtually on the latitude of Cape Town, although even at that latitude the winds during the crossing may not be entirely favourable. An interesting stop along such a southerly route is the island of Tristan da Cunha.

A24b Voyages via the Azores

Recommended time: August to October (North Atlantic), November to January (South Atlantic)

Tropical storms: June to November (North Atlantic)

World Cruising Routes:

AN19	Northern Europe to Azores
AT13	Azores to Brazil
AS21	South America to South Africa

A direct voyage from the Azores to Cape Town follows a route which stays entirely offshore so adequate preparations should be made for this long offshore passage as no convenient ports of call will be passed anywhere along the way. Weather conditions along this route are generally favourable as far as the equator, with prevailing NE winds during the recommended period. As this voyage coincides with the hurricane season in the North Atlantic the possibility of running into an incipient storm west of the Cape Verdes should be kept in mind. With the prevailing winds south of the equator being from SE, some easting should be kept in hand so that the Line is not crossed further west than longitude 20°W. From there on, the best course that can be sailed will pass to the west of both Ascension and St Helena Island. South of 25°S the winds become more variable in direction, but even so it may be necessary to sail as far south as 32°S before a direct route can be sailed to Cape Town.

A25 • Voyages from North America

● **A25a** Voyages via the Eastern Caribbean
● **A25b** Voyages via the Azores and Canary Islands

A direct voyage from North America to South Africa by a cruising yacht is such a challenging proposition that most American sailors who wish to visit that part of the world seem to prefer to do it at the end of a round the world voyage. Those who are determined to do it sooner have three alternatives: to sail the shortest route south via the Eastern Caribbean, to take the offshore route via the Azores, or to choose the longer but somewhat easier route via the Canary and Cape Verde Islands.

A25a Voyages via the Eastern Caribbean

Recommended time: November (North Atlantic), November to January (South Atlantic)

Tropical storms: June to November (North Atlantic)

World Cruising Routes:

AN145	North America to Eastern Caribbean
AT15	Eastern Caribbean to Brazil
AS21	South America to South Africa

Rather than sail the direct nonstop voyage, as described in *World Cruising Routes*, or the longer route via the Canary Islands, a shorter albeit more challenging option is to sail to South America by way of the Lesser Antilles. The voyage can be undertaken nonstop all the way or with an initial stop in Bermuda. The timing needs to balance the safe season in the North Atlantic with the most favourable period south of the equator. The best time to start from the US East Coast is at the end of the hurricane season by sailing first to the Eastern Caribbean and continue the voyage to South America later, or taking an offshore route that stays east of the Lesser Antilles. The voyage south across the equator to Northern Brazil is the most challenging part of the entire voyage but the advantage of a November start is that the percentage of favourable winds in the South Atlantic is higher between October and February. The continuation of the voyage from Brazil to South Africa is described in A24a.

A25b Voyages via the Azores and Canary Islands

Recommended time: May to June, November (North Atlantic), November to January (South Atlantic)

Tropical storms: June to November (North Atlantic)

World Cruising Routes:

AN144	North America to Azores
AN136	Azores to Canary Islands
AN52	Canary Islands to Cape Verde Islands
AT11	Canary and Cape Verde Islands to Brazil
AS21	South America to South Africa

As both sailing conditions south of the equator and conditions in South Africa are more favourable towards the end of the year, a departure from the US East Coast after the end of the hurricane season is preferable. However, as sailing conditions to the Azores in early winter may be unpleasant, an attractive solution is to sail to Europe in early summer, spend some time in the Azores and Mediterranean, and resume the voyage south in the autumn. The continuation of the voyage from the Canaries to South America and on to Cape Town is outlined in A24a and also in A20b (page 114).

A26 • Voyages from South America

● **A26a** Voyages from Brazil and Northern Argentina
● **A26b** Voyages from Patagonia and Antarctica

There is a marked difference between these two voyage options as those which start from Brazil will encounter mixed sailing conditions, whereas voyages starting from further south will generally benefit from the prevailing westerly winds in those higher latitudes.

● A26a Voyages from Brazil and Northern Argentina

Recommended time: October to January
World Cruising Routes:
     AS21   South America to South Africa

Voyages originating in the northern part of South America will benefit from the prevailing NE winds that blow off the coast of Brazil in the initial part of their passage. The rest of the passage will encounter mixed conditions with the percentage of favourable winds only increasing south of 30°S.

● A26b Voyages from Patagonia and Antarctica

Recommended time: December to February
World Cruising Routes:
     AS35   Patagonia to Falkland Islands
     AS31   Falkland Islands to Tristan da Cunha and Cape Town
     AS37   Antarctica to Tierra del Fuego
     AS38   Antarctica to Falkland Islands and South Georgia
     AS39   Northbound from South Georgia

Voyages from the Western South Atlantic to South Africa are easy to plan on account of the prevailing westerly winds, the only serious limitation being the short season when such voyages should be undertaken. There are four options for voyages starting from Antarctica: a direct passage to Cape Town, a longer passage via South Georgia, the Falkland Islands or Tristan da Cunha, or a return to the South American mainland and continue the voyage to South Africa from there. Sailing conditions during the austral summer are reasonably good.

A27 • Voyages from the Eastern Caribbean and Panama

Recommended time: April to May, November (North Atlantic), November to January (South Atlantic)

Tropical storms: June to November (North Atlantic)

World Cruising Routes:
     AN96   Panama to Lesser Antilles
     AN99   Panama to Bahamas
     AN113   Bahamas to Eastern Caribbean
     AT17   Lesser Antilles to Brazil
     AS21   South America to South Africa
     AN79   Lesser Antilles to Azores
     AN136   Azores to Canary Islands
     AN52   Canary Islands to Cape Verde Islands
     AT15   Cape Verde Islands to Brazil

Similar considerations apply to anyone planning a voyage from the Caribbean to South Africa as to voyages originating in North America. Southbound voyages from the Lesser Antilles have the shorter but more challenging option of a direct voyage to Brazil, or the much longer detour via the Azores and Canary Islands.

Voyages originating in Panama are even harder to accomplish as you are faced either with the difficult task of reaching first the Eastern Caribbean, and sailing to the South Atlantic from there, or taking the longer but somewhat easier route via the Azores and Canary Islands. The other alternative is to sail down the west coast of South America, regain the Atlantic Ocean by way of the Strait of Magellan or Beagle Channel and cross the South Atlantic to Cape Town. This route is described in more detail in voyage PC12 (page 261) which outlines a circumnavigation of South America.

Cruising hubs

▌ Cape Town ★★★★

As South Africa's premier yachting centre, Cape Town has a wide range of repair and service facilities, as well as several yacht clubs where visitors are welcomed. Medical facilities are of a high standard. The international airport (CPT) has direct flights to most major international destinations.

What next?

Unless the aim is to return to South America or the North Atlantic, for anyone arriving in Cape Town from the Atlantic the only logical way to go is east into the Indian Ocean. Rounding the southern tip of Africa is a challenging task but with good timing it can be relatively easy to achieve, especially as there are several ports along the route where shelter can be sought if conditions are not right. With the cyclone season in the South Indian Ocean lasting from late November to May, northbound voyages should not be planned before late May. There are two ways to reach the cruising areas of the Indian Ocean, either by sailing north along the coast of Mozambique to Madagascar or taking an offshore route to the Mascarene Islands. As the safe seasons complement each other on either side of the equator, the voyage can easily be planned to continue into the North Indian Ocean and Southeast Asia during the favourable season there.

Those who wish to continue to Australia will encounter good sailing conditions on the direct route to Western Australia during the austral summer months of January and February. Although this is the cyclone season in the South Indian Ocean, tropical storms do not affect such a high latitude route and they do not pose a serious risk in non-tropical areas of Australia.

Cape Agulhas, the southernmost point of Africa.

CIRCULAR VOYAGES IN THE ATLANTIC OCEAN

*All my life I feel I've been chasing the sun, and at last I feel
I'm going to catch it.*

Christopher Columbus

The wise navigator should not only plan a voyage from A
to B so that it is undertaken during the most favourable
seasons and sailing conditions, but also should plan ahead
on how and when to sail back from B to A when the
time comes for the return voyage. Such circular voyages
have occurred throughout maritime history and some
regular trading voyages are well documented. They were
always planned to take advantage of prevailing weather
conditions and, whenever possible, to be undertaken
during the most favourable seasons.

    With its well-established weather systems, the North
Atlantic lends itself perfectly to circular voyages which,
if planned properly, will benefit from favourable wind
conditions on both outbound and return passages. The
Vikings were almost certainly the first to recognise this
phenomenon and put it to good use as early as the 11th
century by sailing west from Scandinavia along a route
that crossed the Norwegian Sea in high latitudes, where
there was a higher proportion of E and NE winds than
from other directions, and returning home with the
prevailing westerlies of lower latitudes. This is how they
managed to undertake astonishing voyages in their frail
craft, discovering and colonising Iceland in the process
and being the first Europeans to set foot in North America,
which they called Vinland.

    The first fully documented voyage of this nature is
that of Christopher Columbus in 1492–1493 in which a
similar strategy was applied by sailing from Spain to the
Canary Islands and then across the Atlantic with the
prevailing NE trade winds. The following year Columbus
returned home by taking a more northerly route on which
the predominantly westerly winds helped him sail to the
Azores and thence to the European mainland. Almost
more remarkable than the voyage itself is the fact that
Columbus had either known about these wind patterns or
had discovered them by chance, something that has been
puzzling historians ever since. That he had some secret
knowledge may be shown by the fact that, while having his
ships repaired in Las Palmas, Columbus ordered the lateen
rig of his smallest ship to be converted to square sails for
the forthcoming Atlantic voyage as if he knew that from
there on they would encounter following winds.

    Each of the following circular voyages is made up of
separate segments which are described in more detail in
the relevant linear voyage in the previous chapters. They
should be referred to for additional information and also
to consult the accompanying pilot charts.

Cruz Bay on St John, US Virgin Islands.

Circular Voyages from Europe

The Atlantic circuit to the Caribbean and back is now so well established that well over 1,000 boats complete it every year. However, with few exceptions, those who undertake it rarely stray from the usual route and the object of the following circular voyages is to outline some alternatives which may be considered attractive.

AC1 ●	**The Columbus Circuit**
AC2 ●	**The North Equatorial Circuit**
AC3 ●	**The Transequatorial Circuit**
AC4 ●	**The Viking Circuit**
AC5 ●	**The Arctic Circuit**
AC6 ●	**The North Atlantic Circuit**
AC7 ●	**Clockwise Circumnavigation of South America**
AC8 ●	**Clockwise Circumnavigation of North America**
AC9 ●	**Counterclockwise Circumnavigation of North America**

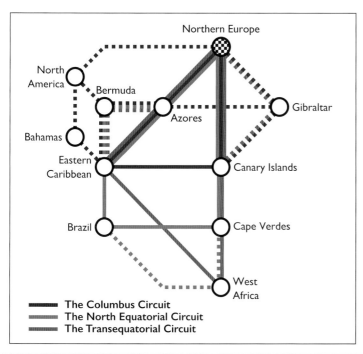

The Columbus Circuit
The North Equatorial Circuit
The Transequatorial Circuit

AC1 ● The Columbus Circuit

Present-day sailors planning to sail a full Atlantic circle cannot do better than follow the Columbus example, as with good timing a transatlantic voyage can benefit from favourable winds most of the way. A late spring or early summer start is recommended for those leaving from Northern Europe so as to cross the Bay of Biscay before the middle of August. This allows some time to be spent cruising the shores of the Iberian Peninsula before heading for the Canary Islands, either direct or via Madeira. As in the case of Columbus the starting point of the Atlantic crossing should be one of the Canary Islands. Unlike Columbus, however, who on his first voyage left La Gomera on 6 September 1492, which then as well as now was at the height of the hurricane season, a later departure for the transatlantic passage is strongly advised. The crossing of the Atlantic can be made in late November or early December so as to arrive in the Caribbean after the end of the hurricane season. The next four or five months can be spent cruising the islands of the Eastern Caribbean, preferably from south to north, so as not to cover the same ground twice.

The return voyage to Europe should start in late April or early May and can be sailed either nonstop to the Azores or with a stopover in Bermuda. The Azores provide a convenient springboard in the mid-Atlantic for a passage home and the completion of the voyage one year after leaving.

The great attraction of such an Atlantic circle for those who cannot take time off in one block is the fact that the voyage can be broken up into several stages. On the first stage the boat is sailed at the beginning of summer from Northern Europe to a southern port close to an international airport where the boat is left in a marina while the crew returns home by air. This initial stage can be extended as far as the Canaries, where there are several marinas and also frequent flights to all parts of Europe. Alternatively, rather than return home, the time until the Atlantic crossing can be spent cruising the attractive Canarian Archipelago.

America 500

I have always been fascinated to follow the routes of history's famous sailors, carried as they were by the wind, at about the same speed – and with the same problems. Thus we were enthusiastic to hear that the America 500 sailing event would cross the Atlantic in 1992 following in Columbus' wake, 500 years after his great exploit. Nina and I decided to sail two-handed in the rally on our small, 34 foot ketch, *Pegasos*.

'Two hours after midnight we saw land at a distance of two leagues. . . We hove to, to await the morning.' This is how Columbus describes the first sight of the New World on 12 October 1492. As we approached San Salvador, we had sailed, just like Columbus, from Palos in Spain and had covered over 4,500 miles.

At 1802 hours a total lunar eclipse began, the night became very dark, and we observed the magnificent celestial show for the next three hours. Just before midnight we saw the flashes of the Dixon Hill lighthouse, and at 0110 we could see the shore with its sandy beaches in the bright light of the full moon, no longer obscured by the earth. *'Tierra! Tierra!'* we cried out. Columbus went ashore at Long Bay and it was here that the Old and the New World met 500 years ago. It is hard to imagine a more historical place for a sailor to anchor.

Different opinions of Columbus exist. His social views, his opinion that foreign people can be subdued without question, are condemnable. But he was a son of his age and his thoughts did not differ from those of his contemporaries. One thing, however, is certain. He was an excellent navigator and knew the sea. He had sailed the Mediterranean from end to end, far south along the African coast and north to the British Isles and beyond. 'Wherever ships have sailed, there I have been.' His instruments for navigation, the quadrant and the astrolabe, were rudimentary and difficult to use on a bouncing deck. His dead reckoning, however, was always unbelievably accurate. He found his way repeatedly across the Atlantic and back, accurately finding his target. In matters of navigation, Columbus was *'sapientisimo y divino'* (wise and divine), as his son Fernando put it.

Following Columbus, the following spring we sailed back to Europe via the Azores to complete the Columbus Circuit.

Antti Louhija, *Pegasos*

Orchilla lighthouse on the island of El Hierro in the Canaries.

The voyage is resumed in the second half of November for the passage to the Eastern Caribbean, which is reached in time for the winter holidays. After a shorter or longer vacation, those who need to return home can do so by leaving the boat in a marina, of which there is a wide choice, as well as frequent flights to Europe from St Lucia, Martinique, Guadeloupe or Antigua, all of which are convenient also for crew changes. Having returned to the Caribbean in late spring, the voyage to the Azores is normally undertaken in May or early June. If necessary, the voyage home can be interrupted in the Azores where, once again, the boat can be left in a marina at either Horta, Terceira or Ponta Delgada, all of which have flights to Lisbon with onward connections to most European capitals. From the Azores, the final stage home can be sailed at any time during the summer. Those who are planning to sail this voyage in stages are advised to make marina reservations well in advance so as to be sure that they have a booked place to leave the boat during their absence.

Those who have the time for a longer version of this voyage ought to consider sailing from the Eastern Caribbean to the Bahamas via Puerto Rico, and Turks &

Caicos, from where they can either continue to Bermuda and take that way home, or extend the loop by sailing up the east coast of the United States and taking their departure for Europe from a more northerly point. The timing of such a detour, whether the shorter or longer version, needs to take into account the forthcoming hurricane season as it affects not just the Bahamas and the southern states but the effects of a tropical storm can be felt as far north as New York. An earlier departure from the Eastern Caribbean is therefore advised so that by June you are clear of the critical area and far enough north along the US East Coast to be out of immediate danger. The voyage can then continue into the summer months with a passage home in higher latitudes and good westerly winds to any destination in Northern Europe.

Route: Northern Europe – [Gibraltar] – Canaries (September to November) – Eastern Caribbean (December to May) – [Bermuda] – Azores (June to July) – [Gibraltar] – Northern Europe

Start: June to August

Return: July to August

Tropical storms: June to November

Total distance: 6,000–8,000 miles

Duration: 11–14 months

AC2 • The North Equatorial Circuit

This is a voyage that may appeal to those who have already sailed the traditional route from Europe to the Caribbean via the Canaries and are looking for an attractive alternative which offers the opportunity to explore some of the more accessible parts of West Africa before crossing the Atlantic to the Caribbean. An even more ambitious version is to cross the equator and visit Northern Brazil en route to the Caribbean (voyage AC3).

Whether this voyage originates in Northern Europe or the Mediterranean, the Canaries should be reached by September or early October so as to have sufficient time for the planned intermediate stops. After many years of being bypassed by the hundreds of boats sailing to the Caribbean, the Cape Verdes are now attracting many more visitors, some making only a brief stop before resuming their passage west, others taking their time to explore the windswept islands of this former Portuguese dependency. The

archipelago abounds in good anchorages, the local people are welcoming and the fishing is excellent. Those who do not intend to go any further south will find steady NE trade winds in these latitudes for the continuation of their voyage to the Caribbean. To be on the safe side, the islands should not be left before the middle of November to avoid the risk of being caught by a late Caribbean hurricane.

The favourable conditions that prevail in this area during the late autumn months make a detour to the African mainland a tempting prospect, with both Senegal and Gambia within easy reach. As in the case of the Cape Verdes, these are underdeveloped countries with no yachting facilities to speak of but good cruising opportunities for the intrepid sailor. The chance to penetrate deep into the interior, whether on the Gambia River or Senegal's Casamance River, both of which are navigable for a considerable distance, is a unique experience well worth pursuing. The area of Casamance in South Senegal has been the scene of unrest in recent years and the River Saloume and its extensive delta, which is a national park, are considered a safe substitute.

One decision that needs to be made early is whether to sail from the Canaries directly to West Africa and call at the Cape Verdes later, or call at those islands first, then sail to West Africa and from there to the Caribbean. Whichever option is chosen, sailing conditions for the passage to the Caribbean, whether in November or later in winter, are usually very good with steady NE and E winds and a favourable current all the way. After a Caribbean sojourn, directions for the return voyage home and the

Fishing boats on the banks of the Saloum River.

completion of this less travelled Atlantic circuit are the same as in voyage AC1.

Route: Northern Europe – [Gibraltar] – Canaries (September to October) – Cape Verdes (October) – [West Africa (November)] – Eastern Caribbean (December to May) – [Bermuda] – Azores (June to July) – Northern Europe

Start: June to August

Return: July to August

Tropical storms: June to November

Total distance: 8,000–8,800 miles

Duration: 11–14 months

AC3 ● The Transequatorial Circuit

This is an ambitious extension of the previous voyage that has the added attraction of visiting the northern part of Brazil and still arriving in the Caribbean during the most favourable season. The timing of the initial segment of the voyage to the Canaries and further south is similar to AC2. In October and November the NE winds will be carried almost all the way to the equator where the doldrums do not present much of a problem as they cover a relatively narrow band. South of the equator winds become S and SE putting boats bound for more southerly destinations in Brazil on a close reach. An interesting stop off Cape São Roque, Brazil's NE extremity, is the Fernando de Noronha Archipelago, a nature reserve where cruising boats are allowed to stop. A number of mainland ports are within easy reach from there: Salvador da Bahia, Recife, Natal, Fortaleza, each being a good place to experience the unmatched Brazilian Carnival. The onward route to the Caribbean passes close to the Amazon Delta with only a relatively short detour needed to explore at least a small part of that great river. The Amazon is navigable for some 2,000 miles but you can get a taste of it by venturing into the Lower Amazon from Belém as far as Almeirim before turning around and exiting at Afuá.

Fernando de Noronha.

Weather conditions for the continuation of the voyage to the Caribbean are very good in the first months of the year, with steady E and NE winds and a strong NW setting current. Directions for the return home from the Caribbean are the same as for voyage AC1.

Route: Northern Europe – [Gibraltar] – Canaries (September to October) – Cape Verdes (October) – [West Africa] – Northern Brazil (November to February) – Eastern Caribbean (February to May) – [Bermuda] – Azores (June to July) – Northern Europe

Start: June to July

Return: July to August

Tropical storms: June to November

Total distance: 10,000–12,000 miles

Duration: 13–15 months

AC4 • The Viking Circuit

The timing of the start of this voyage needs to weigh up the advantage of a higher percentage of favourable winds in late spring or early summer against the risk of more gales in high latitudes at that time of year. Indeed, as summer progresses, the chances of gale force winds diminish but so does the percentage of favourable winds. On the other hand, a later departure means that there is less chance

of encountering ice in the approaches to Greenland or finding that its coasts are still icebound.

Boats setting off from Scandinavia can break the voyage in the Shetlands or the Faroes, whereas boats from Scotland, and certainly those leaving from Ireland, may prefer to sail directly to Iceland. Summer weather in Iceland is fairly pleasant, but conditions in Greenland are harder to predict, although the current change in climate conditions is already resulting in warmer summers. This may tempt the daring to sail deeper into the Labrador Sea and explore parts of Greenland that are rarely visited. Those on a limited time schedule will find that the more accessible SW coast of Greenland provides a good taste of Arctic cruising. After having called at Iceland and possibly also Greenland, a voyage that follows the historic Viking route would turn around in Newfoundland. However, there are many attractive options for the continuation of this voyage: sailing up the St Lawrence River to the Great Lakes, exploring the coastlines of Newfoundland and Nova Scotia, or going as far as the state of Maine and even beyond. Such a detour would be justified as it would gain some useful southing to ensure having good westerly winds on the return passage, although by late summer such winds also prevail in higher latitudes. This circular voyage, loosely based on the ancient Viking routes, offers a wide range of variations, some of which will be explored in the following pages.

Route: Northern Europe – [Scotland] – [Faroes] – Iceland (June to July) – [Greenland] – Newfoundland (August) – [Nova Scotia] – [Maine] – [Ireland] – Scotland (August to September) – Northern Europe

Start: May to June

Return: August to September

Total distance: 4,600–5,400 miles

Duration: 3–5 months

AC5 • The Arctic Circuit

Until not so long ago Norway's Svalbard Archipelago, of which Spitsbergen is the largest island, was rarely visited by yachts, but in recent years their number has increased steadily and now the annual average is around 60 boats, as sailors are attracted to high-latitude cruising in search of more challenging destinations. During its long history Spitsbergen has

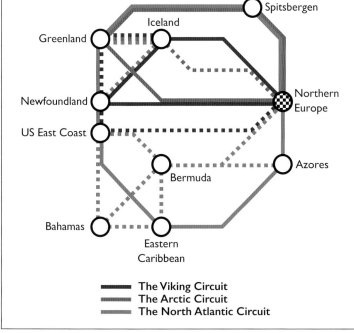

Spitsbergen
Iceland
Greenland
Newfoundland
US East Coast
Bermuda
Azores
Northern Europe
Bahamas
Eastern Caribbean

- The Viking Circuit
- The Arctic Circuit
- The North Atlantic Circuit

Reykjavik.

seen all kinds of visitors: fishermen, hunters, whalers, miners, explorers, and a host of adventurers setting off by sledge, skis, balloon or small aeroplane to reach the North Pole, often with tragic consequences. Even if reaching that elusive destination by yacht is not yet feasible, sailing as far north as 80°N, which is probably about as far north as anyone should wish to go on a cruising boat, is quite easy as the waters in that latitude are clear of ice at the height of summer. The favourite spot to watch your GPS hit the 80 mark is just north of Spitsbergen, close to Moffen, a small barren island a couple of minutes north of 80°N and home to a large walrus colony.

The relatively short Arctic summer season imposes a reasonably early start for this voyage so that Spitsbergen is reached by late June or early July. For this reason, it is probably best to regard the passage north more like a delivery trip and any cruising along the Norwegian coast should be kept to the minimum. In fact, the best strategy

is to sail directly to the Shetland Islands and from there continue non-stop to Spitsbergen. If the temptation to see more of this area is hard to resist, then it is better to limit this voyage to just a return trip to Spitsbergen and enjoy the spectacular western coast of Norway on the way back south. Another solution is to plan on spending the winter in either Lerwick, in the Shetlands, or Bergen, on Norway's west coast, both of which have good facilities for overwintering. This will make it possible to start your voyage north as soon as the weather starts getting better.

A convenient stop en route to Spitsbergen is Bear Island, the southernmost of the Svalbard Archipelago, which is a nature reserve and has a weather station occasionally manned by meteorologists from the mainland. Although all boats are required to call at Longyearbyen on arrival in Spitsbergen, and report to the Governor's office to complete formalities and validate the compulsory cruising permit, an intermediate stop at Hornsund, on the

Hamilton Glacier on Spitsbergen.

SW coast of Spitsbergen, is usually tolerated. There is a research station in this sheltered bay and visiting yachts are welcomed by the resident scientists.

The weather between early July and the middle of August is normally pleasant along the more sheltered western coast of Spitsbergen where most cruising is concentrated. The eastern coast, which is free of ice in late summer in most years, is less frequented and has a richer wildlife. In a good year Spitsbergen can easily be circumnavigated by a well-found yacht.

By early August it is time to set off on the southbound segment of this circular voyage with a passage to Greenland or Iceland. This can be interrupted by a stop at Jan Mayen Island where the Norwegian meteorological office maintains a manned weather station. Landfall in Greenland can be either at Scoresby Sound, and its spectacular fiord scattered with small islands, or Ammassalik, an island on the west side of the Denmark Strait and the most accessible port on Greenland's east coast. Normally in late summer, the entrances of both sounds are free of ice, but this should be ascertained beforehand. The Greenland Ice Service can be contacted for information and ice charts by emailing isc@greennet.gl or the latest ice charts can be

consulted on the internet at www.dmi.dk/en/groenland/hav/ice-charts/.

If the east coast of Greenland is still icebound, it is better to make landfall at Isatfjördjur on Iceland's NW coast and cross over to Greenland when conditions have improved there. Another alternative is to continue south along the coast of Greenland to Ikerasassuaq, the spectacular Prince Christian Sound which provides a narrow passage north of Cape Farewell to Greenland's west coast, most of which is free of ice by mid-summer.

Whether to call first at Iceland or Greenland depends both on the time of year and your next destination. For those planning to return to the west coast of Norway a first stop in Greenland followed by one in Iceland makes more sense. For any other destination Iceland should be visited first as better conditions will be encountered by leaving on the return passage from Southern Greenland, where the percentage of westerly winds is higher than further north. In August, when this passage will most likely be undertaken, the reported percentage of gales is low while air temperatures are not too cold for those latitudes, thus ensuring reasonable conditions for the completion of this challenging voyage.

Route: Northern Europe – [Bear Island] – Spitsbergen (July) – [Jan Mayen] – Greenland (August) – [Iceland] – Scotland – Northern Europe

Start: June

Return: September

Total distance: 3,400–4,000 miles

Duration: 3–4 months

AC6 • The North Atlantic Circuit

If the Vikings had only known what lay to the south of Vinland there is little doubt that they would have extended their voyage to at least as far south as Bermuda. This voyage is therefore a more ambitious variation of AC5 by extending it from one long summer cruise to a full one year voyage. One great advantage of its timing is that by

not having to rush home at the end of summer, a more flexible schedule allows a later start for the initial segment.

This is the most challenging circuit of the North Atlantic but also the most rewarding with rich cruising opportunities at every landfall. The complete itinerary includes some of the most attractive destinations north of the equator. With good planning and, admittedly, a tight schedule, the entire circuit can be completed in a shade over one year. The suggested timing will benefit from the most favourable weather conditions throughout the voyage.

This voyage is aimed at sailors who are taking a year to undertake a return voyage from Northern Europe to the Caribbean but may be looking for a more original way to achieve it. Basically this is a warm-water extension of the Arctic Circuit but, as it also incorporates segments of other voyages described in this chapter, they should be read in conjunction with it. The timing of the voyage to Spitsbergen and on to Greenland is identical to the Arctic Circuit but from there on the timing becomes more flexible,

Lofoten Islands on Norway's west coast.

and the schedule less tight, the only serious concern being the need to avoid the area affected by hurricanes before that season comes to an end in November. This means that the southbound route from Newfoundland can take in some of the most attractive parts of the New England coast.

As the east coast of the United States can be affected by hurricanes as far north as Chesapeake Bay and even New York, a cruise along the New England shores can take place in late summer and early autumn so that the critical area is not reached before late October by which time the chances of a hurricane are lower. An autumn cruise through Long Island Sound to New York and on to Chesapeake Bay provides the opportunity to enjoy the ever changing colours of the forests that line those shores. Depending on how long had been spent to reach that point and if autumn is well advanced, the passage to the Caribbean can start from there and include a possible stop in Bermuda.

The onward voyage to the Caribbean can be undertaken direct or via Bermuda, as described in voyage A2 (page 69). An attractive alternative to the offshore route is to continue south beyond Chesapeake Bay inside the Intracoastal Waterway and reach the Eastern Caribbean by a detour via the Bahamas. Yet another alternative is to complete this sightseeing tour of the USA by carrying on all the way south to Florida, spending the winter in the Bahamas and returning to Europe from there the following spring.

After a winter exploring the Virgins and Lesser Antilles, those who have sailed to the Eastern Caribbean also need to start their voyage home at the end of the safe season. The fastest way to reach Northern Europe is to sail to Bermuda and thence directly to your destination, whereas the longer but more comfortable alternative is to sail home via the Azores. Either route will take you back home by the following summer with the satisfaction of having completed a voyage that combines the achievements of both the Vikings and Columbus, and a lot more beside.

Route: Northern Europe – Spitsbergen (July) – Greenland (August) – [Iceland] – Newfoundland – US East Coast (September to November) – [Bermuda] – Eastern Caribbean (December to May) – [Bermuda] – Azores – Northern Europe

Start: June

Return: July to August

Tropical storms: June to November

Total distance: 9,200–10,000 miles

Duration: 13–15 months

Circumnavigation of South America

This circular voyage appeals particularly to those interested in exploring Southern Chile or Patagonia and can be undertaken in either direction, clockwise or counterclockwise, and can be started from either Europe or the US East Coast. Each alternative has advantages and disadvantages which ought to be considered carefully. The three main disadvantages of a clockwise circumnavigation are firstly that the Chilean fjordland will be sailed from south to north, against the prevailing winds, secondly the tough passage north from Panama across the Caribbean Sea for the return voyage home, and thirdly the fact that the Caribbean will be reached shortly before the start of the hurricane season with any delays prone to cause problems. For boats setting off from the US East Coast, sailing this clockwise route only make sense if it is combined with an initial sojourn in Western Europe or the Mediterranean as it will put the boat in a better position to start the voyage from there. For European sailors a clockwise voyage is easier in its initial stages but more difficult towards its end, whereas a counterclockwise voyage entails some long and tough sailing in the South Pacific to reach Southern Chile from Panama, but is somewhat easier to complete once the South Atlantic is reached.

All these factors make a counterclockwise circumnavigation more attractive for sailors setting off from the US East Coast, such a voyage (AC16) being outlined on page 146. For European sailors the final decision may be dictated by future plans: a clockwise circumnavigation has the flexibility of the route being easily modified if the decision is taken to continue the voyage into the South Pacific – and possibly all around the world – or spend longer in South America so as to then reach the Caribbean at the start of the following safe season and enjoy the freedom of action this entails. Alternatively, if the voyage is to be completed by a return home, then the counterclockwise option would suit Europeans better. For North American west coast sailors considering a clockwise circumnavigation of South America, voyage PC12 on page 261 outlines the suggested route and timing.

AC7 • Clockwise Circumnavigation of South America

The southbound segment of a clockwise voyage to the South Atlantic and Southern Ocean starts with a late summer or early autumn arrival in the Canaries. This suits boats starting off from both Northern Europe and North America. From the Canary Islands reasonable

The Beagle Channel.

weather conditions can be expected in late September or October for the onward passage into the South Atlantic. South of the equator, the NE winds that are a constant feature in the western part of the South Atlantic between October and February will ensure good passage times as far as latitude 35°S. From there on, wind directions are variable and become increasingly westerly. Those who do not plan to sail on to Antarctica can reach the Pacific via the Strait of Magellan or by the longer but more scenic route through the Beagle Channel. Those undaunted by a crossing of the 600 miles wide Drake Passage can keep their bows pointing south towards the Antarctic Peninsula. The optimum period for the voyage into the Southern Ocean is during summer (December to February). Details of this passage and the Antarctic cruise are given in voyage A23 (page 116).

Having returned from Antarctica to the mainland by late February or early March at the latest, the northbound segment of the voyage starts in the Beagle Channel at the southern extremity of the Chilean fjordland. The route north leads through the Chilean fjordland, one of the most spectacular sceneries in the world, past glaciers and waterfalls, precipitous fiords and misty forests, all

seemingly untouched by human hand. The 600-mile stretch from the settlements of Ushuaia and Puerto Williams in the far south to Puerto Eden halfway up the Chilean fjordland is a complete and utter wilderness with not a sign of human habitation. Occasionally, the prevailing NW winds make it hard to tack in the narrow channels and motorsailing is often the only way to make headway. The South Pacific is finally reached through the Canal de Chacao, north of Chiloé Island, a narrow strait that is swept by strong tidal currents. A convenient stop with good facilities along the Chilean coast to prepare for the continuation of the voyage is the town of Valdivia. From there, the alternatives for the continuation of the voyage are an inshore route that follows the continental coastline via Peru and Ecuador all the way to Panama, or an offshore route that swings out to Easter Island and the Galapagos. The inshore route benefits from the north-setting Humboldt Current and light S and SE winds along most of its length. The offshore route will have mostly SE winds from about 35°S to the equator with variable winds between Galapagos and Panama.

Once the Caribbean Sea is reached, ideally before June and the start of the hurricane season, boats that are bound for the US East Coast have the choice of making for either the Yucatán Channel and South Florida or the Windward Passage, the Outer Bahamas and thence home. For boats heading for Europe the Windward Passage route is the better choice as it offers the option of stopping in the Outer Bahamas before continuing to Bermuda and the onward passage home. Those who, having reached the South Pacific, have doubts about the prospect of the long voyage home can do worse than turn their bows west at Easter Island and, en route to Tahiti, call at Pitcairn Island to meet the descendants of some other sailors who once had similar doubts about leaving the South Seas in a hurry.

The total length of this circumnavigation is about 16,800 miles regardless of whether it starts from the US East Coast or Europe. A detour to Antarctica would add approximately 1,800 miles to that total and a similar total distance would be added by a detour to Easter Island and the Galapagos. The voyage can be completed in one year by starting from either the US East Coast or Northern Europe in late spring or early summer and completing it at about the same time. Such timings benefit from favourable seasons throughout the voyage: on the initial segment to the Canaries, on the passage across the South Atlantic, while cruising Patagonia, the Chilean Canals and Antarctica during the austral summer, and by sailing the final leg from Panama home in late spring, just before the start of the Caribbean hurricane season. This is certainly a challenging endeavour but its rewards surpass any difficulties that may be encountered.

Route: US East Coast/Northern Europe – Canaries (September) – Cape Verdes – Brazil (October) – Argentina (November to December) – Falklands (December to January) – [Antarctica] – Beagle Channel (January to February) – Southern Chile (March) – Peru (April) – [Easter Island] – [Galapagos] – Ecuador – Panama (May) – [Bermuda] – US East Coast/Northern Europe

Start: May to June year I

Return: June to July year II

Tropical storms: June to November (North Atlantic)

Total distance: 16,800–20,400 miles

Duration: 13–14 months

Circumnavigation of North America

Whereas a circumnavigation of South America has been possible ever since the Panama Canal became operational, sailing around the northern half of the American continent only became feasible with the opening of the Northwest Passage. Although the first successful transit of that waterway was accomplished by the Norwegian explorer Roald Amundsen a few years before the inauguration of the Panama Canal, it was only in recent years that the Northwest Passage has been transited on a regular basis. Several yachts take that shortcut between the Atlantic and Pacific Oceans every year, and in 2009 the American yacht *Ocean Watch* completed an epic voyage of 27,500 miles by way of the Northwest Passage having successfully sailed around the entire American continent.

That circumnavigation was sailed in a clockwise direction, with a west to east transit of the Northwest Passage, but for voyages starting in the North Atlantic, whether on the US East Coast or Europe, an anticlockwise voyage around North America will generally benefit from more favourable conditions. As a large part of the route is common, it is outlined here for both European and North American sailors. This is also the case for voyages starting from the west coast of North America, as both winds and seasons complement each other better, both in the Atlantic and Pacific sections, as outlined in PC13 on page 264.

AC8 • Clockwise Circumnavigation of North America

As a large part of the route is common, whether a voyage starts in Europe or the east coast of North America, both alternatives are outlined here. The two routes join at the Panama Canal after European sailors have sailed the first segment of their voyage to Panama via the Eastern Caribbean. Boats sailing from the US East Coast also have this option, or may prefer to sail directly to the Panama Canal. The transit into the Pacific Ocean should be planned for March or April so that the passage to Hawaii is sailed before the start of the hurricane season in the Eastern North Pacific.

The offshore route to Hawaii is recommended because of the contrary winds which would be encountered on a route that followed the contour of the continent to Alaska. Although longer, the detour to Hawaii will ensure favourable conditions which would also continue on the subsequent leg to Alaska and the Northwest Passage, as described in voyage P34 (page 228).

An August transit of the Northwest Passage means that the Atlantic will be reached rather late in the season and while ice is rarely a problem in September, strong winds can be expected on the final leg home. Voyages to Northern Europe at least can count on a favourable wind direction. Those bound for the US East Coast may find it hard going against the prevailing SW winds off the coast

Ocean Watch sailing in the Northwest Passage to complete a circumnavigation of the Americas.

of Nova Scotia. One way of dealing with that situation is to take a roundabout way via the St Lawrence River and reach New York via the Erie Canal and Hudson waterway system.

The total distance to be travelled by boats starting from the US East Coast, which have sailed directly to Panama, is approximately 12,000 miles. Voyages originating in Europe will be considerably longer but either route can be sailed in about one year.

Route: Northern Europe/US East Coast – Eastern Caribbean (December to February) – Panama (March to April) – Hawaii (May to June) – Alaska (July) – Northwest Passage (August) – Greenland (September) – Northern Europe/US East Coast

Start: July to August (Northern Europe), November (US East Coast)

Return: September to October

Tropical storms: June to November (North Atlantic and Eastern North Pacific)

Total distance: 12,000–16,200 miles

Duration: 10–11 months

AC9 • Counterclockwise Circumnavigation of North America

Sailing all the way around the northern half of the American continent only became possible with the opening of the Panama Canal in 1914 and the first successful transit of the Northwest Passage by the Norwegian explorer Roald Amundsen between 1903 and 1906. Accompanied by six others on the 47-ton steel sloop vessel *Gjøa*, Amundsen travelled via Baffin Bay, Lancaster and Peel Sounds, James Ross, Simpson and Rae Straits. They spent two winters near King William Island in what is today Gjoa Haven, at Nunavut in Canada.

The possibility of reaching the North Pacific by this more direct route will appeal to sailors on both sides of the Atlantic and, as much of the route is common to all starting points, it is outlined here for both European and North American sailors.

In recent years the Northwest Passage has been mostly free of ice in late summer so a voyage starting from either Europe, the US or Canadian East Coast will benefit generally from favourable summer conditions for the passage to Greenland and the eastern entrance into the Northwest Passage at Lancaster Sound. From this point onwards it is necessary to wait until the ice in the central section of the Northwest Passage has retreated sufficiently to proceed west. As the ice retreats from west to east, this normally happens in late summer, and thus an arrival in the Pacific Ocean by early autumn. High latitude passages in the North Pacific at this time of year can be rough, but conditions improve in lower latitudes for those bound for California or Hawaii. Favourable winds should ensure a fast southbound voyage to California and Mexico, which should not be reached before the end of the hurricane season in November. A transit of the Panama Canal in late November or early December will bring the boat into the Caribbean Sea at the start of the safe winter season. The prevailing NE and E winds will probably make a passage to the Lesser Antilles rather unappealing so the rest of the winter could be spent in the Western Caribbean and Bahamas. The final leg home, whether to Europe, USA or Canada should be sailed in May or June, thus successfully completing this challenging voyage in about one year.

Route: Northern Europe/US/Canada East Coast – Greenland (July) – Northwest Passage (August) – Alaska (September) – [British Columbia] – US West Coast (October) – Mexico (November) – Panama Canal (November – December) – Western Caribbean (December – May) - Bahamas – [Bermuda] – [Azores] – Northern Europe/ US/Canada East Coast

Start: June

Return: June–July

Tropical storms: June to November (Eastern North Pacific and North Atlantic)

Total distance: 11,200–13,400 miles

Duration: 12–13 months

Illustration of Sir John Franklin's Arctic expedition.

Circular Voyages from the US East Coast

Sailors based on the east coast of North America have as wide a choice of circular voyages as those from Europe. The following voyages should satisfy both those interested in some challenging high latitude sailing and those for whom sailing in the tropics is more to their taste. To please both camps, there are also some voyages which combine both cold and warm water cruising.

AC10	●	**The Pinzón Circuit**
AC11	●	**The Mid-Atlantic Circuit**
AC12	●	**The Three Continent Circuit**
AC13	●	**The Maya Circuit**
AC14	●	**The High Latitude Circuit**
AC15	●	**The Sunchasers' Circuit**
AC16	●	**Counterclockwise Circumnavigation of South America**

AC10 ● The Pinzón Circuit

Christopher Columbus got all the credit for putting America on the world map but the unsung heroes of that historic voyage are the Pinzón brothers, two of whom, Martín and Francisco, sailed on *La Pinta* as captain and master, and their younger brother Vicente, the captain of *La Niña*. They were all members of a seafaring family from Palos, in Western Andalusia. Martín Pinzón was an experienced sailor and navigator by the time he met Columbus and lent his full support to the expedition, both with his skills and a substantial financial contribution. It was from the deck of *La Pinta* that Rodrigo de Triana was the first to sight land in the Americas. After the loss of the *Santa María*, Columbus embarked on the home voyage on *La Niña* and Martín Pinzón sailed *La Pinta* on a different course and landed at Bayona, while Columbus made landfall at Lisbon. Without any

knowledge of each other's fate, they both then sailed to their original starting point at Palos, where the two ships arrived on the same day, 15 March 1493. Exhausted, ill with fever and bitterly disappointed at not having gained recognition for his achievement, which he felt he deserved, Martín died a broken man a few days later. Fate had not been fair to him or his brothers, but later historians have tried to put this right by referring to the Pinzón brothers as the co-discoverers of America. Francisco and Vicente took part in several subsequent voyages to the New World and always returned to Europe by the same route, so this circular voyage is named after them.

In 1992, on the occasion of the 500th anniversary of the historic voyage of discovery, over 40 US and Canadian boats sailed east across the Atlantic to join the America 500 rally at its symbolic starting point off Palos, on the River Tinto. This circular voyage is based on the route and timing of America 500 and, as on that occasion, the best time to leave the US East Coast is late spring. A May or early June departure usually avoids a late winter storm and the risk of an early hurricane is also low. The onward route to the Azores normally stays between 38°N and 40°N where steady westerly winds can be expected, while access to long-term forecasts will help in choosing an optimum route. Just as in the case of Columbus' return

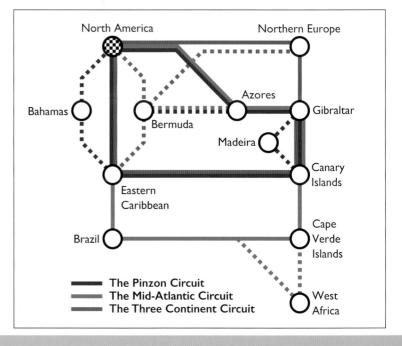

Landfall Bay on San Salvador Island.

voyage in 1493, the Azores provide a convenient landfall, and the attractive port of Horta on the island of Faial is the perfect spot to complete, and celebrate, a successful Atlantic crossing.

From the Azores the voyage continues to the Mediterranean, but before entering that sea at Gibraltar, those who wish to continue in the wake of Columbus should make a short detour to the place from which his three caravels set off in August 1492. The small port of Palos no longer has access to the sea but there is a marina at nearby Mazagón, at the mouth of the River Tinto. The various sites associated with Columbus are all in the immediate vicinity, La Rabida Monastery, where Columbus and his captains had their last briefing, the church of St George, where he and his crews prayed at dawn on the day of departure, and the museum dedicated to the memory and achievements of the Pinzón brothers.

For those who intend to complete an Atlantic circuit in the shortest time possible, an early summer arrival in the Mediterranean allows a few months of cruising before the time comes to head back into the Atlantic and sail to the Canaries. The passage can be interrupted at Porto Santo, the sister island of Madeira, where Columbus lived for several years with his wife Felipa Moniz Perestrelo and where he drew up the plans for the forthcoming voyage. The house where they are believed to have lived is now a museum. There are even more sites from the Columbus era in Gran Canaria and La Gomera, the two islands where he and his ships spent some time before tackling the Atlantic, or the Ocean Sea as it was known then. The last thing to remind us of Columbus, and also the last sight when leaving the Canaries, is Orchilla lighthouse on the island of El Hierro, which marked in those days the end of the known world.

The Atlantic crossing is usually undertaken in late November or early December so as to arrive in the Caribbean after the end of the hurricane season there. After spending the winter cruising those tropical islands, many of them first sighted and named by Columbus on his subsequent voyages, by late spring it is time to head for home. The shorter route leads north either nonstop or via Bermuda, whereas the longer route follows in the Pinzón brothers' wake to the Bahamas. Places with rich historic associations, such as San Juan de Puerto Rico and the Turks & Caicos, where a Spanish wreck from that early period was discovered near Grand Turk and the finds are now displayed in a local museum, make interesting stopover points en route to the Outer Bahamas. There, a symbolic landfall can be made on the island of San Salvador, where the Pinzón brothers dropped anchor on 12 October 1492. See also voyage A16 on page 105.

Route: US East Coast – [Bermuda] – Azores (June) – Mediterranean (July to September) – [Porto Santo] – [Madeira] – Canaries (October to November) – Eastern Caribbean (December to May) – [Bahamas] – [Bermuda] – US East Coast

Start: May to June year I

Finish: June to August year II

Tropical storms: June to November

Total distance: 8,600–10,000 miles

Duration: 12–15 months

AC11 • The Mid-Atlantic Circuit

This voyage is an extension of the Pinzón Circuit and may appeal to those who are interested in exploring both Northern Europe and the Mediterranean. While the timing of this voyage is perfectly feasible for those prepared to stick to a tight schedule, the short North European summer seriously limits the prospects of a longer cruise there unless the intention is to only visit Southern Ireland and some parts of the United Kingdom. As summer starts drawing to a close it is time to start heading south either for a short foray into the Mediterranean or a direct

passage to Madeira and thence to the Canaries, both of which have enough cruising opportunities to while away the time before crossing the Atlantic at the optimum time in late November.

The inclusion of Scandinavia and the Baltic into one summer cruise in Northern Europe is almost impossible unless you are prepared to spend the winter in either Northern Europe or the Mediterranean. This is a solution that is taken by many North American sailors who soon realise that there is simply too much to see and do in Europe to try and squeeze it into one rushed season. Places in which to spend the winter are aplenty and the choice depends on whether you intend to live aboard or leave the boat unattended in a marina or boatyard. Living aboard in a North European port in winter is hardly to everyone's liking, although centrally located marinas in such cities as London, Amsterdam, Oslo, Copenhagen, Stockholm, Lisbon and even Paris offer enough compensation to make up for the cold weather. The Mediterranean is undoubtedly a better bet and, for those who feel the need for some cultural stimulation, cities such as Barcelona, Nice and Palma de Mallorca have much going for them as winter bases. Otherwise there are plenty of marinas in mainland Spain, Italy, Tunisia, Cyprus and Southern Turkey which are used regularly by small communities of cruising sailors. A warmer option is to transit the Suez Canal and spend the cold months in one of the marinas in Southern Egypt and return to the Mediterranean the following spring.

An early start the following spring allows a leisurely cruise through the Mediterranean while making your way progressively west so as to be through the Strait of Gibraltar by summer's end. From there the voyage south can go directly to the Canaries, call at some of the ports on Morocco's Atlantic coast or make a detour to Madeira. From the Canaries, the onward voyage to the Eastern Caribbean is best undertaken in late November or early December. The last segment of the voyage, home from the Caribbean, will be undertaken at the end of the Caribbean winter season, in May or early June as outlined in A16 (page 105).

There are thus four very different ways to undertake this voyage:

Midsummer in the Baltic.

to plan on spending part of the summer in Northern Europe visiting places which are more accessible and then sail to the Canaries with or without stopping in the Mediterranean; to spend part of the summer in Northern Europe, sail to the Mediterranean and spend the winter and following summer there; to spend the winter and second summer in Northern Europe and then continue to the Canaries; and finally, to combine all of the above by spending one winter and summer each in Northern Europe and the Mediterranean.

Route: US East Coast – [Bermuda] – Northern Europe (July to August) – Mediterranean (September) – [Madeira] – Canaries (October to November) – Eastern Caribbean (December to May) – [Bahamas] – [Bermuda] – US East Coast

Start: May to June year I

Finish: June to July year II

Tropical storms: June to November

Total distance: 9,200–10,400 miles

Duration: 13–14 months

AC12 • The Three Continent Circuit

This voyage is also an extended version of the Pinzón Circuit that ventures along a more roundabout way to reach the New World, and if Columbus had decided to sail this route on any of his four voyages, the history of the Americas might have turned out very differently and today's Brazilians may not be speaking Portuguese but Spanish. There are three alternatives for this voyage, the difference being how far south each of them goes before turning around and heading for the Caribbean. This can be at either the Cape Verdes or West Africa, at the end of a short detour to Northern Brazil, or after a longer detour to more southern parts of Brazil. Any of these options can be accommodated within the suggested timing.

A late spring start from the US East Coast dictated by the need to be past Bermuda while the risk of a hurricane is still low will ensure an arrival in the Azores by June thus allowing sufficient time for the next two or three months to be spent in the Mediterranean. This is long enough to go as far east as Croatia, or even Greece, before returning to Gibraltar for the passage to the Canaries. From the

Belém, gateway to the Amazon.

Canaries, the route turns south towards the Cape Verdes. An Atlantic crossing from there in early winter will benefit from more consistent sailing conditions than the longer passage from the Canaries.

Those who are tempted to see more of Brazil and are prepared to cross the equator will find that in December and January they will have E and NE winds almost all the way to the Line and, by crossing it further west, the doldrums will cover only a relatively narrow band before giving way to the SE winds of the South Atlantic. The decision as to how far south to go in Brazil must be taken before the equator is crossed, with a westerly point being suggested if the intention is to make landfall in more northern places in Brazil, while a more easterly crossing would ensure better winds to sail to southern ports.

The Amazon Delta, one of the main reasons why some sailors make this detour, straddles the equator and it necessitates but a short detour to get at least a feel of this mighty river before resuming the voyage to the Caribbean. The alternative is to make landfall perhaps as far south as Salvador da Bahia, which is best visited at Carnival and is renowned for its colourful street shows and processions during that time. Even such a detour still allows sufficient time to visit a few more places while moving gradually north.

Sailing conditions for the continuation of the voyage from Brazil to the Caribbean are invariably good in the first months of the year as described in voyage A3. After a sojourn in the islands of the Eastern Caribbean the final leg home is sailed in May or early June. See also AC10.

Route: US East Coast – [Bermuda] – Azores (June) – [Mediterranean (July to September)} – Canaries (September to October) – Cape Verdes (October) – [Northern Brazil (November to February)] – Eastern Caribbean (March to May) – [Bermuda] – US East Coast

Start: May to June year I

Finish: June to July year II

Tropical storms: June to November

Total distance: 9,600–11,600 miles

Duration: 13–15 months

AC13 • The Maya Circuit

This circular voyage covers a compact area in the Western Caribbean, its offshore segments being shorter and thus easier to plan. It also benefits from favourable conditions throughout the recommended period and can easily be accomplished during one long winter season.

For boats leaving from ports north of Cape Hatteras the start of this voyage needs to fit into a rather narrow window, as ideally it should take place in late autumn, immediately after the end of the hurricane season but before the onset of the winter storms. For this reason, although Chesapeake Bay makes a good starting point, it is probably better to gain some southing in the sheltered waters of the Intracoastal Waterway and only head offshore from one of the ports south of Cape Hatteras. This is the recommended course of action for those who prefer to use the Windward Passage to reach the Caribbean Sea, while others should continue to Florida through the Intracoastal Waterway and sail through the Yucatán Channel to their destination.

The offshore route from the mainland cuts across the Gulf Stream to the Outer Bahamas, where the island of San Salvador makes the perfect

Iceland
Greenland
Spitsbergen
Norway
Newfoundland
North America
Northern Europe
Mexico
Bahamas
Bermuda
Canary Islands
Western Caribbean
Jamaica
Eastern Caribbean

The Maya Circuit
The High-Latitude Circuit
The Sunchasers Circuit

The Maya coast of Yucatán.

landfall as it was here that Christopher Columbus himself made his first landfall in the New World in 1492. Various monuments as well as a large cross mark the spot at Landfall Point, which has been chosen as the symbolic place where that historic event is most likely to have occurred and no self-respecting mariner should leave the island without making a pilgrimage to that very special place.

Long, Acklins and Great Inagua islands can be visited on the way south as they all have good anchorages and lie close to the direct route to the Windward Passage. As winter progresses, the easterly trade winds become firmly established with favourable winds along this entire route. If the plan is to include a cruise along Cuba's south coast, the nearest port of entry is Santiago, otherwise the voyage continues to Jamaica. At the island's western extreme, Montego Bay has a friendly yacht club with its own marina and boatyard. This is a good place to prepare for the next leg of the voyage. A detour to the Caymans can be considered here, or a direct course sailed to the Bay Islands of Honduras where Guanaja is the closest port of entry. The islands of Roatan and Utila, with their many anchorages, can be visited next en route to Guatemala.

Guatemala's prime cruising destination is centered on the Rio Dulce, a picturesque river that empties into the Bay of Amatique. The entrance, close to the town of Livingston, is very shallow with just over 6 feet over the bar at high water. Once past this obstacle, the river deepens and it is easy to navigate the 40 miles to Lake Izabal. There are several marinas on this river where the boat can be left in safety while visiting the Maya sites.

From Guatemala the route turns north towards neighbouring Belize, whose main attraction is its barrier reef with its magnificent underwater scenery and exhilarating sailing in the sheltered waters that lie behind it. The voyage continues in short hops along the Yucatán Peninsula as far north as Isla de Mujeres from where it turns into the Yucatán Channel. From that point, the strong north-setting Gulf Stream will give a welcome boost to a homebound boat along the coast of Florida and beyond. With a new hurricane season knocking on the door, this trip is best completed by late May or early June, the six to eight months that have been allowed for a total distance of just over 3,000 miles giving plenty of time for both cruising and trips ashore.

Route: US East Coast – Bahamas (December) – [Florida – Yucatán Channel] – Windward Passage – [South Cuba] – [Jamaica] – Honduras (January) – Guatemala (February to March) – Belize (March to April) – Mexico (April to May) – US East Coast

Start: November

Finish: June to July

Tropical storms: June to November

Total distance: 2,500–4,000 miles

Duration: 6–8 months

AC14 • The High Latitude Circuit

Sunny weather and balmy winds are almost guaranteed for the best part of the previous voyage, but for hardier sailors the North Atlantic offers a tempting alternative that brings with it the satisfaction of sailing to some areas that are visited by few boats. The object of the exercise is to explore Spitsbergen, Greenland and Iceland during the short Arctic summer.

The most difficult part of the voyage is quite likely to be the very first leg, as an early start from the US East Coast is essential in order to reach Spitsbergen by late June or early July. A late May or early June Atlantic crossing will benefit from favourable, if occasionally strong, westerly winds for probably the entire passage, although you should be prepared for two or three spells of stronger winds as one is overtaken by depressions tracking east.

Having set a course that avoids the area of ice and fog SE of Newfoundland, the rest of the passage should then stay as close as possible to the great circle course. The direct route passes west of Ireland and heads for the north of Scotland possibly continuing nonstop to the Shetland Islands. A slightly longer route goes via the Irish Sea, between Ireland and England, and stays inside the Hebrides to reach the Orkneys and finally the Shetlands. The port of Lerwick in the Shetlands is a good place to provision and prepare the boat for the leg to Spitsbergen, which ideally should be sailed nonstop. The alternative is to make a detour to the Norwegian mainland with a possible landfall in Lofoten Islands. Such a detour could add as much as two weeks or more to the voyage, and would considerably delay the arrival in Spitsbergen.

The direct route from Lerwick to Hornsund, at the southern extremity of Spitsbergen, is 1,100 miles and by early summer the winds will be mostly from NE making this a close-hauled affair. All boats bound for Spitsbergen

Walrus colony on Moffen Island north of Spitsbergen.

need to make their way to the main settlement at Longyearbyen where formalities are completed, although stopping at anchorages en route such as Hornsund is tolerated.

A late June or early July arrival in Spitsbergen will ensure at least one month of cruising, much of it along the island's west coast as far north as the small island of Moffen which lies astride the 80°N parallel, almost a snowball's throw from the North Pole. The west coast of Spitsbergen is usually free of ice by July, and, in a good year, the east coast may be navigable too, which makes a complete circumnavigation of the island possible. This is a very tempting option as there is a lot more wildlife, and plenty of polar bears, in this less visited area than on the west coast. Weather conditions in summer are generally good, with pleasant daytime temperatures and mostly light winds.

By early August the short summer is already showing signs of coming to an end, and so it is time to bid Spitsbergen goodbye and start heading for home. Easterly winds will probably be the order of the day en route to the island of Jan Mayen, conveniently located halfway to Iceland and first visited in the seventh century by the Irish monk Brendan who left the first written record of an Arctic exploration. A good landfall in Iceland is the fishing port of Isafjördur or the capital Reykjavik lying further south. Time will most likely be too short to call at both of these ports, either of which is a good starting point for the passage to neighbouring Greenland. The nearest landfall across Denmark Strait is Ammassalik which is usually free of ice by mid-August. If Ammassalik is blocked by ice, or time is short, an easier alternative is to head straight for the southern tip of Greenland where Prince Christian Sound, north of Cape Farewell, is always accessible by late summer. Daily updates on the ice situation can be obtained by VHF radio from one of the coastal stations, or, further offshore, by SSB radio from Julianehab Radio.

Ice is rarely a problem south of Greenland late in the season and the next leg to Newfoundland should present few problems. From St John's the route continues to Halifax in Nova Scotia, from where it is but a relatively short dash to one of the ports in Maine and eventually home. The alternative to beating into the prevailing SW winds on this last leg is to sail through the Belle Isle Strait into the Gulf of St Lawrence and reach Lake Ontario by way of the St Lawrence River. From there, the Welland Canal leads to Lake Erie, which in turn is linked by the Erie Barge Canal with the Hudson River and New York.

Careful planning and thorough preparation are imperative for this challenging expedition, but with a good boat and experienced crew this voyage can be easily accomplished in four to five months.

Route: US East Coast – [Ireland – Scotland] – Shetlands (June) – Spitsbergen (July to August) – Iceland (August) – [Greenland] – Newfoundland (September) – Nova Scotia – US East Coast

Start: May to June

Finish: September

Total distance: 7,800–8,500 miles

Duration: 4–5 months

AC15 ● The Sunchasers' Circuit

This is a considerably longer but perhaps more attractive version of the previous voyage, which may appeal to North American sailors who would rather chase the sun on their return home than the fog and ice. Instead of taking just one summer season to complete, this extended voyage would take one year or possibly more if a longer detour to the Mediterranean was factored in.

A great attraction of this voyage is that its timing takes advantage of the most favourable seasons throughout its duration by being both in the Arctic and the Caribbean at the best of times. The first segment of the voyage to Spitsbergen is as described in AC13. The voyage south from Spitsbergen follows the coast of Norway up to the point

The fishing port of Câmara do Lobos on Madeira.

where the decision needs to be made whether to continue south across the North Sea to the English Channel, or sail around the west to Scotland and then south through the Irish Sea. If the aim is to reach the Canaries in the shortest time possible, the route that passes between Scotland and Ireland is probably easier, because it avoids the busy shipping lanes in the North Sea and English Channel, and is also more attractive as it can include brief stops in the islands off Scotland's scenic west coast, the little visited Isle of Man and Ireland's east coast. This route also has the advantage of avoiding the Bay of Biscay by passing it well offshore. Time will dictate whether to continue nonstop to the Canaries or stop in Madeira, an interesting and convenient port of call before the Canaries.

The subsequent passage from the Canaries to the Caribbean is best undertaken in late November with an arrival in the Lesser Antilles in early December. After a winter spent there, the loop is closed in June or July with the final leg home and the completion of a challenging and highly satisfying North Atlantic adventure. For more details of the final two segments of this voyage see A1 (page 61) and A16 (page 105), while voyage AC12 (page 141) may offer a tempting alternative to reach the Caribbean by an even longer but more attractive way that would still fit into the overall timing of this voyage.

Route: US East Coast – [Ireland – Scotland] – Shetlands (June) – Spitsbergen (July to August) – Northern Europe (September) – Canaries (October to November) – Eastern Caribbean (December to May) – [Bermuda] – US East Coast

Start: May to June year I

Finish: June to July year II

Tropical storms: June to November

Total distance: 11,400 – 12,000 miles

Duration: 12–13 months

AC16 • Counterclockwise Circumnavigation of South America

Because more favourable weather and wind conditions will be encountered by sailing around South America in a counterclockwise direction, this option is recommended for voyages starting from the US East Coast or one of the Caribbean islands. As described in voyage AC7 (page 133), this voyage can be accomplished also in the opposite direction and although harder, it is better suited for boats starting from Europe. As some European sailors may prefer to sail the version outlined here, the directions for much of the voyage are similar to those aimed at boats setting off from the US East Coast. Whether starting from the US East Coast, or from the Eastern Caribbean by

boats that are already there, both routes converge at the Panama Canal.

The logical route south from the US East Coast to Panama is by way of the Outer Bahamas and the Windward Passage. From there the route leads across the Caribbean Sea to the Panama Canal by keeping well to windward of the various reefs and islets south of Jamaica. If time permits, a detour to the San Blas Islands is well worth the effort, and could easily be accommodated before the Canal transit. Boats leaving from other points will make their way to Panama either by crossing directly from the Eastern Caribbean or by taking the route north of Puerto Rico to the Outer Bahamas and the Windward Passage.

The best time to start this voyage is late spring, just before the start of the hurricane season in the Caribbean (June). This allows enough time to reach Southern Chile at the optimum time (October to January). Such timing will also fit in with a possible voyage to Antarctica where the most favourable months are January and February.

Having reached the Pacific Ocean, there are two main options for the southbound voyage from Panama: a detour via the Galapagos Islands or a track that follows the coast of South America. If the latter option is chosen a good landfall in Ecuador is Puerto Lucia Marina in the resort of La Libertad. This is a convenient place to leave the boat to visit the interior, whether the High Andes or the Ecuadorian region of Amazonia. The route then continues along the coasts of Peru and Chile, with several

Tranquil anchorage in the San Blas Islands.

Navigating the Cockburn Channel in Southern Chile.

ports to stop at for fuel and provisions. Light SE winds, the contrary Humboldt Current and the long distances to be covered will make this a slow journey on which a reliable engine and plenty of fuel will be of utmost importance.

The alternative is to seek better winds offshore, which means covering more miles but being able to sail most of the way compared to the inshore route. One further advantage of such an offshore route is the opportunity to call at two attractive destinations: Galapagos and Easter Island. The winds between Panama and Galapagos are mostly northerly at the start becoming light and variable nearer the islands. On the next leg from Galapagos to Easter Island the prevailing winds will be from the SE, which means that much of this leg will be close on the wind. However, there is a price to be paid for this detour and there is no easy way to sail from Easter Island to mainland Chile. Although it may be possible to motorsail through the South Pacific High, probably the better way is to head south from Easter Island to reach the area of prevailing westerly winds, which will be found somewhere south of latitude 35°S. From there the route heads for the Chilean coast with a landfall at Canal de Chacao, north of Chiloé Island. This narrow body of water is swept by strong tides and leads to Puerto Montt, which is the best place to get provisions and information on Southern Chile.

Once the Gulf of Peñas is reached south of the island of Chiloé, it is possible to sail in sheltered waters all the way to the Beagle Channel and Horn Island at the southern extremity of the continent. This vast area, which stretches for well over 1,000 miles, is a maze of fiords, narrow passages, ancient forests, snow-clad mountains and mighty glaciers. Solitude is absolute.

Weather conditions in Southern Chile in summer (October to December) are generally good and the prevailing winds are from NW. Stronger winds with violent gusts (the infamous williwaws) become more frequent as one moves south so one should be prepared for these sudden blasts both when sailing and at anchor. Puerto Eden, about halfway between Chiloé and the Beagle Channel, is the only place to get fuel or provisions for the southern segment of the Chilean fjordland as it is the last settlement before Ushuaia. Self-sufficiency is therefore an absolute necessity in this part of the world.

This spectacular route reaches its conclusion with the Beagle Channel and a choice of ports: the larger, better endowed Argentine port of Ushuaia, or the remote Chilean military base of Puerto Williams. The former has all essential facilities, including an airport with direct flights to Buenos Aires. Puerto Williams is a favourite port of call for boats heading for either Cape Horn or Antarctica, both of which fall under the jurisdiction of Chile, so formalities to head south must be completed here. Those who have decided to make this the southernmost point of their voyage will continue east via the Beagle Channel past Staten Island before turning north towards the Falkland Islands. Those undaunted by a crossing of the Drake Passage can keep their bows pointing south towards the Antarctic Peninsula. Crossing the 600 miles wide Drake Passage in a well-found boat during the optimum summer time (December to February) should present no great problems. Directions for the passage to Antarctica and suggestions on cruising there are outlined in voyage A23 on page 116.

When it's time to head north from Antarctica, a good departure point is in the area of the Melchior Islands from where the open sea is easily reached. Getting back to Cape Horn against the prevailing westerly winds and east-setting current is not easy, so if you want to visit Horn Island, where it is possible to land, it is better to do this before setting off for Antarctica. Then the return voyage from Antarctica will be much easier as a direct course can be set for the Falklands staying east of both Horn and Staten islands.

Port Stanley is the main settlement of the remote Falklands community and makes a good port of call for boats heading north. The Argentine coast south of Mar del Plata has few attractions and is best passed well to seaward. Mar del Plata itself is a busy seaside resort with several yacht clubs and good facilities. From there, the northbound route continues parallel to the Brazilian coast with plenty of landfall and cruising opportunities.

Going north from the Falklands the prevailing winds will be westerly with a favourable north-setting current. Along the Brazilian coast the prevailing winds up to April are NE and this is something that needs to be taken into account as it may delay the optimum time of arrival in the Caribbean. Once past Cape São Roque wind directions become favourable and there is also a strong northwest-setting current ensuring a fast passage to the Lesser Antilles. As the Eastern Caribbean will be reached near the end of the winter season, there will be little time to linger and a good pace needs to be maintained to embark on the homebound leg to the US East Coast before the onset of the new hurricane season in June.

European boats have the option of sailing the same route to the Eastern Caribbean, and returning home from there via the Azores. Those who prefer to sail a shorter route home from the South Atlantic, and are not deterred by fewer landfall possibilities and some longer offshore segments, can do so by sailing from Argentina to St Helena

and continuing north from there to the Cape Verdes and Canaries. The other alternative is to return to Europe by taking the offshore route from the South Atlantic to the Azores, which entails even fewer potential stopovers than the Cape Verde route. Both alternatives are outlined in voyages A13 and A14 (pages 96 and 97).

The total distance for a voyage from the US East Coast, including the detours to Easter Island and Antarctica, is 16,800 miles, whereas the alternative inshore route is some 3,000 miles shorter. With good planning and careful preparation either option can be accomplished in the 12 to 14 months that should be allowed for the entire voyage.

Voyages starting from Northern Europe are considerably longer, not just in miles but mainly in time, as spending the winter cruising in the Caribbean so as to be in the right place for the transit of the Panama Canal the following year will add one year to the total duration. Those who find this too long should consider doing the voyage in the opposite direction, which would only take about one year to complete even by tacking on a cruise in the Caribbean at its end. The total distance of 17,600 miles is for the inshore route along the west coast of South America and does not include the additional miles of the longer offshore route via Easter Island nor a detour to Antarctica, but both those detours can be covered within the same time frame.

Route 1: US East Coast – Panama (May to June) – Ecuador – [Galapagos – Easter Island] – Chile (September to October) – Beagle Channel (November to December) – [Antarctica (January)] – Brazil (February to March) – Eastern Caribbean (April to May) – US East Coast

Start: May year I

Finish: June to August year II

Tropical storms: June to November (North Atlantic)

Total distance: 13,800–16,800 miles

Duration: 13–15 months

Route 2: Europe – Canaries (October to November) – Eastern Caribbean (December to April) – Panama (May to June) – Ecuador – [Galapagos – Easter Island] – Chile (September to November) – Beagle Channel (December) – [Antarctica (January)] – Falklands (February) – [Brazil – Eastern Caribbean – Azores] – St Helena (March) – Cape Verdes – Canaries (April) – Europe

Start: June to July year I

Finish: May to July year II

Tropical storms: June to November (North Atlantic)

Total distance: 17,600–20,600 miles

Duration: 23–25 months

Circular Voyages from South America and South Africa

Several circular voyages originating in Europe or North America cross the equator into the South Atlantic and may provide a tempting pattern for sailors from that part of the world to follow their example and plan similar voyages in the opposite direction. The following voyages follow the same pattern of combining a route that takes advantage of safe seasons and favourable conditions with interesting destinations and attractive landfalls.

AC17 • The Discovery Circuit

AC18 • The Rainbow Circuit

AC19 • The Explorers' Circuit

AC20 • The South Atlantic Circuit

AC21 • The Southern Ocean Circuit

Salvador de Bahia procession.

AC17 • The Discovery Circuit

This voyage can start at any point on the shores of South America and reach the Eastern Caribbean by following a track which runs roughly parallel to the contour of the mainland. The timing of the voyage is very important if the intention is to benefit from favourable seasons and have sufficient time to call at the most attractive destinations along the route. The first target is to arrive in the Lesser Antilles early in the season so as to have enough time to cruise the islands before continuing the voyage to Europe. Sailors leaving from Argentina or Southern Brazil need to bear this in mind when planning their northbound passage and the contrary winds they may encounter along the Brazilian coast between October and February. Once past Cape São Roque the timing becomes more flexible, as the favourable seasons can be fitted more easily into the overall plan. The eastbound passage from the Caribbean to the Azores is normally undertaken in late May or early June. This timing is ideal also for the continuation of the voyage to the Mediterranean as both the passage to the Azores and the onward passage to Gibraltar will be sailed in the most favourable period. The entire summer can be spent enjoying the attractions of the Mediterranean before the time comes to turn south for the Canaries. An interesting option is to sail from the Azores to Northern Europe. Such a detour could add as much as one year to the overall duration of the voyage if both Northern Europe and the Mediterranean are to be visited unless a minimum of time is spent in those two places.

The return voyage should be planned for late summer, if starting from Northern Europe, or early autumn if leaving from the Mediterranean. The Canary and Cape Verde Islands are convenient staging points for the voyage south which should take place in October or November.

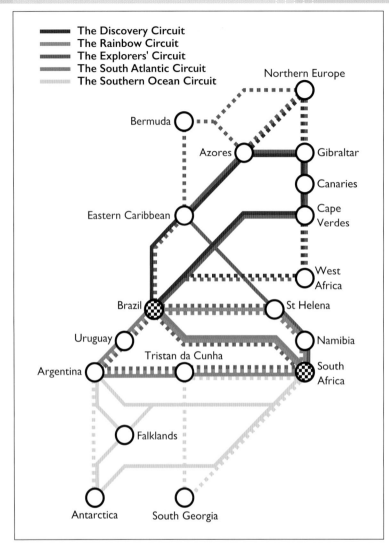

The Discovery Circuit
The Rainbow Circuit
The Explorers' Circuit
The South Atlantic Circuit
The Southern Ocean Circuit

AC18 • The Rainbow Circuit

Both ocean races and cruising rallies that take place in the South Atlantic tend to go from east to west, mainly to take advantage of the high proportion of easterly winds. South American sailors who find this trend frustrating can easily turn the tables by doing this circular voyage whose route is planned in such a way as to limit the impact of unfavourable conditions. The voyage can start from any South American port, but those who set off from more northern places need to make some southing to reach an area where the proportion of easterly winds is no longer predominant. As this means sailing south as far as the River Plate Estuary, it is possible to call at ports in both Uruguay and Northern Argentina before crossing to Cape Town. Places like Punta del Este or Mar del Plata have good facilities and therefore make a good base to prepare for the next leg of the voyage. The passage to Cape Town will follow roughly its own latitude where, in December, the percentage of favourable winds is notably higher than further north. An interesting stop almost straddling that route is remote Tristan da Cunha whose small population always extends a warm welcome to the few sailors who make the effort to pay them a visit.

A detour to West Africa can be included before crossing the equator on the final leg home. Details of this section are described in voyage A19 (page 111).

Route: South America – Eastern Caribbean (January to May) – Azores (June) – [Northern Europe] – Mediterranean (July to September) – Canaries (October) – Cape Verdes (October to November) – [West Africa] – South America

Start: November to February year I

Return: November to February year II

Tropical storms: June to November (Western North Atlantic)

Total distance: 8,800–10,200 miles

Duration: 12–15 months

The return voyage from South Africa will benefit from favourable winds throughout. Rather than take the offshore route from Cape Town, as most boats do, before bidding farewell to the African continent, an interesting detour on the way to St Helena is Namibia. The main ports of Luderitz and Walvis Bay both have yacht clubs where visiting sailors are welcomed. The boat can be left at either club to visit the interior, with Walvis Bay being more convenient for the famous game parks and wildlife reserves. From there, SE trade winds will ensure a fast passage to St Helena.

From St Helena, the prevailing SE winds will provide similarly good conditions for the passage to Brazil where a popular first landfall is the archipelago of Fernando de Noronha. During summer, the NE winds that blow along the Brazilian coast between October and February will speed you along the remaining part of the voyage home.

Route: Brazil – [Uruguay] – [Argentina] – [Tristan da Cunha] – South Africa (December to January) – [Namibia] – St Helena (February) – Brazil

Start: October to December

Return: February to March

Total distance: 7,800–9,200 miles

Duration: 5–6 months

AC19 • The Explorers' Circuit

The Discovery Circuit outlined earlier may appeal also to sailors based in South Africa as the voyage can easily be extended to start and finish in Cape Town. The outward leg calls at St Helena from where it continues either directly to the Eastern Caribbean or via a detour to Northern Brazil. A December or January departure from Cape Town means that the Caribbean will be reached by February or March so there will be enough time to cruise the chain of the Lesser Antilles before sailing to the Azores in May.

Along a route which abounds in tempting detours, one choice to be made is whether to use the foray into the North Atlantic to also visit parts of Northern Europe, a decision that is best made in the Azores. It is also from there that the suggested itinerary heads for Gibraltar and the Mediterranean, an area so rich in attractions that it may take much longer than planned to resume the voyage home and thus complete this giant loop.

The Mediterranean should be left by September for the Canaries and from there to the Cape Verdes. At that point a detour to Senegal or Gambia in West Africa could be considered before crossing the equator to Northern Brazil. Mostly favourable winds will be enjoyed while sailing south along the Brazilian coast, possibly as far as Argentina from where the higher percentage of westerly winds would make for an easier passage to Cape Town than starting from further north.

Route: South Africa – [Namibia] – St Helena (December to January) – [Brazil] – Eastern Caribbean (February to May) – [Bermuda] – Azores (June) – [Northern Europe] – Mediterranean (July to September) – Canaries (October) – Cape Verdes – [West Africa] – Brazil (November to December) – [Uruguay] – [Argentina] – [Tristan da Cunha] – South Africa

Start: December to January year I

Return: January to March year II

Tropical storms: June to November (Western North Pacific)

Total distance: 13,800–17,800 miles

Duration: 13–16 months

The Azores.

AC20 • The South Atlantic Circuit

This shorter version of voyage AC18 can easily be completed in only one season as favourable conditions can be counted on during the recommended time. To make sure of that, the voyage ought to start in December when the SE trade winds will ensure a fast passage to St Helena, unless the decision is made to sail nonstop to the Brazilian mainland. From St Helena, the subsequent passage to Brazil has a wide choice of landfalls, with the offshore archipelago of Fernando de Noronha being a favourite introduction to that multifaceted country. The ensuing cruise down the Brazilian coast will provide countless more opportunities to explore the wealth of both shore attractions and those of the offshore islands.

This southbound segment of the voyage continues to Uruguay and Argentina before heading east for the home run, or it could be combined with voyage AC20 by those who wish to gain the experience of some cold water, high latitude sailing.

Route: South Africa – [St Helena] – Brazil (January to February) – Uruguay (March) – Argentina – [Tristan da Cunha] – South Africa

Start: December

Jamestown, the main settlement on St Helena.

Return: March to April

Total distance: 8000–9000 miles

Duration: 4–5 months

AC21 • The Southern Ocean Circuit

As the best time to visit any destinations in the Southern Ocean is the austral summer months of January and February, ideally this voyage should start in late November or early December to be sure of encountering favourable conditions, especially if the intention is to also sail to Antarctica. The percentage of westerly winds on a passage from Cape Town to South America in early December is quite low provided the course does not stray south of 35°S too soon. This can easily be done if the intention is to stop first in Northern Argentina from where the onward passage can either continue south along the coast, and call at some ports in Southern Argentina, or take the offshore route to the Falklands.

The voyage continues to the Beagle Channel which can be reached by sailing east or west of Staten Island. Having reached Tierra del Fuego, there are three options before returning home: spend some time cruising the area of the Beagle Channel with the possibility of looping around to

exit through the Strait of Magellan, continue west for a foray into the Chilean fjordland, the recommended timing allowing for such a detour, provided it is limited to their southern part, or cross the Drake Passage to Antarctica. The Antarctic detour would add between 1,500 and 1,800 miles to the overall total distance.

The tactics for the passage across the Drake Passage and Antarctic landfall are dictated by the intended return destination. Those who intend to sail back to the mainland at the end of their Antarctic cruise need to take into account the prevailing westerly winds as well as the east-setting current in the Drake Passage if they want to be sure of a reasonable sailing angle on the return leg. With this in mind, by making landfall at a place such as Deception Island, the Antarctic Peninsula can be cruised from NE to SW. The Melchior Islands are the usual departure point for the northbound passage. The task of the return passage is greatly eased if aiming for a landfall east of the South American mainland, such as the Falkland Islands. Those bound for Cape Town may even decide to head straight for

their destination and thus put those consistent westerlies to their best advantage. Those who prefer to call at the Falklands on their return voyage can sail from there either directly to Cape Town or via Tristan da Cunha.

There is one other landfall that may be considered on the return voyage from Antarctica, and that is South Georgia. The island lies almost on the direct course from the Antarctic Peninsula to Cape Town and, due to its rich wildlife, provides an enticing destination for anyone sailing in those waters. A stopover in that remote island would cap this challenging and highly rewarding voyage.

Route: South Africa – Argentina – Falklands (December) – Beagle Channel (January) – [Antarctica January to February] – [Falklands] – [South Georgia] – [Tristan da Cunha] – South Africa

Start: November to December

Return: March to April

Total distance: 8,500–9,300 miles

Duration: 4–6 months

Antarctic anchorage.

THE PACIFIC OCEAN

We are about to stand into an ocean where no ship has ever sailed before. May the ocean be always as calm and benevolent as it is today. In this hope I name it Mar Pacifico.

Ferdinand Magellan, 17 November 1520

The Pacific Ocean is the largest of the earth's oceans. It extends from the Arctic in the north to the Southern Ocean in the south. It covers nearly one-third of the earth's total surface and almost half of its water surface. Important human migrations occurred in the Pacific in prehistoric times, the most remarkable being those of the Polynesians who came from Asia and settled a vast area from Easter Island in the southeast to Hawaii in the north and New Zealand in the southwest.

The Pacific Ocean was sighted by Europeans early in the 16th century, first by the Spanish explorer Vasco Núñez de Balboa who crossed the Isthmus of Panama in 1513 and named it Mar del Sur (South Sea). Its current name was given by the Portuguese explorer Ferdinand Magellan who called it *Mar Pacifico*, meaning 'peaceful sea'.

During the 16th century, Spanish expeditions sailing from Mexico to the Philippines discovered several island groups. They were followed by other explorers searching for the elusive Terra Australis, a vast continent that was believed to balance out the large land masses of the northern hemisphere. Although Captain Cook is credited with having discovered Australia, it was the Dutch navigator Willem Janszoon who is believed to have been the first European to sight Australia in 1606.

A possible explanation for the surprisingly small number of new discoveries is that thanks to the prevailing winds in the Pacific, the ships were sailing most of the time before the wind, thus being able to keep a relatively straight course. Having a field of vision of only a few miles, it is no wonder that so many hundreds of islands were missed. There is unfortunately another explanation and that is the fact that many of those early explorers discovered some islands the hard way when their ships were wrecked on them and, even if there were survivors, news of their discovery often died with them. Some of those mysterious disappearances were only solved in recent years with the discovery of the remains of such tragic events.

The true discoverers of the Pacific were the Polynesians, whose ancestors set off from East Asia in search of new lands to settle. Once they reached the South Pacific about 1,500 years ago, in a remarkably short span of time they discovered and settled nearly 500 islands scattered about that vast ocean. How those Polynesians managed this extraordinary feat of sea voyaging and discovery may be explained by the fact that their large double-hulled canoes were rather poor at sailing to windward, thus being forced to tack continuously against the prevailing winds. Making slow progress by taking long shallow tacks is probably why they rarely missed any land that happened to be in their way. The Polynesian navigators employed various techniques including the use of stars, the flight of birds and the effect of islands on swell patterns. Having discovered and settled O'Tahiti and Te Fenua 'Enata (the Marquesas), the Polynesians then sailed north and discovered Hawaii.

The Hawaiian Archipelago was another one of those islands 'missed' by European explorers until in 1778 Captain Cook finally put them on the world map. This greatest of all Pacific explorers discovered and charted more islands than all the previous European expeditions put together. It is ironic that he paid with his life for his last discovery at the hands of the heirs to those magnificent Polynesian navigators.

In the very year of Cook's death, his contemporary Captain William Bligh achieved, very much against his will, one of the most remarkable small-boat voyages of all times. Having been cast adrift in the ship's 23 foot launch by the *Bounty* mutineers near Tonga, he and a crew of 18 loyal sailors survived a seven week 3,600-mile voyage to reach the island of Timor in today's Indonesia.

An equally impressive achievement is that of Bernard Gilboy who in 1882 made the first attempt to cross the Pacific single-handed. He had a 19 foot double-ended schooner built in San Francisco for a voyage which he expected would last five months. Unfortunately, his stores ran out 164 days after his departure and he was rescued only 160 miles from Australia having sailed 6,500 miles.

There have been many other notable voyages to the idyllic South Seas, some of them by authors whose writings have left a lasting image of the beauty of those islands and their people. One of the earliest was Herman Melville who in 1841 sailed on the whaler *Acushnet* on a

voyage to the South Seas. While in the Marquesas, Melville and a friend jumped ship and spent several months on the island of Nuku Hiva. Melville eventually returned home in 1844, his Pacific adventures resulting in three of his most successful books: *Moby Dick*, *Typee* and *Omoo*.

Probably inspired by Melville, the Scottish writer Robert Louis Stevenson spent several years in the late 1880s sailing on a number of yachts to several island groups in the Central Pacific. He eventually settled in Samoa where he died in 1894. The impressions and experiences of those years are preserved in his collection of letters and the book *In the South Seas*.

Already established as the most successful American writer of his time, in 1906 Jack London had the 45 foot *Snark* specially built for a circumnavigation of the globe on which he set off with his wife Charmian and a small crew. They crossed the Pacific to Australia visiting several island groups on the way but the voyage had to be abandoned for health reasons in Sydney. Jack London chronicled his sailing adventure in *The Cruise of the Snark* and *South Sea Tales*.

The passing of time has not diminished in any way the lasting lure of the South Seas and sailors continue to find its spell irresistible.

WINDS AND CURRENTS

There was a grandeur in everything around which gave a solemnity to the scene. No human being but ourselves for miles; and no sound heard but the pulsations of the great Pacific!

Richard Henry Dana

The North Pacific

THE NORTHEAST TRADE WINDS

These winds blow on the southern side of the area of high pressure, which is normally located around latitude 30°N. The NE trade winds are particularly consistent in both direction and strength over large areas of the North Pacific. Their direction is north and even northwest near the American coast, becoming increasingly easterly in the Western North Pacific. Their strength is about 10 to 15 knots, although they can become fresher at times and at the height of the trade wind season winds of 30 knots are not uncommon. The strongest winds are likely to be encountered in winter, between November and March, but they diminish in strength as one moves south towards the equator.

The entire trade wind belt moves north and south throughout the year in accordance with the declination of the sun. However, their northern and southern limits do not run in a straight line from east to west, but in a curve which reaches its highest point in summer in about latitude 35°N about 200 miles from the American coast, the corresponding southern limit being in latitude 8°N. The northern limit of the trade winds in winter is 29°N, in about longitude 150°W, with the southern limit for the same period being the equator.

INTERTROPICAL CONVERGENCE ZONE

The NE trade winds are bound to the south by the ITCZ, which remains north of the equator throughout the year east of 160°W. To the west of that longitude it moves south of the equator during the northern winter, from about December to April or early May. During the summer in the northern hemisphere, when the SE trade winds are at their strongest in the South Pacific, the ITCZ disappears altogether west of about 160°W, where the two trade wind systems run into each other and the belt of doldrums is virtually non-existent. In the Western North Pacific, the ITCZ is only present during the changeover periods of the monsoons, from mid-April to mid-May and from mid-

September to mid-November. The weather inside the zone is typical doldrums weather, with calms or light winds alternating with squalls, heavy rain and thunderstorms. However, as one moves west, the frequency of calms and light variable winds diminishes and the prevailing winds, even inside the doldrums, are easterlies.

THE NORTHEAST MONSOON

This monsoon affects a large area of the Western North Pacific mainly due to the intense cold of the winter months over the landmass of Asia which creates an area of high pressure over parts of East Asia. The resulting wind circulation around this winter high produces a flow of NE winds which prevail during the winter months in the China Sea and adjacent waters. The NE monsoon of the Western North Pacific is particularly noticeable between latitudes 5°N and 30°N. Its eastern limits are more difficult to define as it merges with the NE trade winds of the North Pacific. At its height, the NE monsoon of the China Sea forms a continuous wind system with the NE trade wind of the North Pacific, so that in December and January there is a belt of strong NE winds right across the ocean from California to China.

The arrival of the NE monsoon depends on latitude and it starts earlier in the north and later in the south. Although it commences around September at its northern limit, the NE monsoon is only fully established by late November and lasts until March. The changeover period to the SW monsoon, in April–May and August–September, is marked by calms and variable winds. The strength of the wind is also influenced by latitude, the monsoon being strongest in the north, where it blows an average 25 knots, decreasing to 15 knots and less among the islands of the Philippines and Northern Indonesia. At the height of winter, in December and January, the monsoon can blow with gale force for many days, the stormiest area being the open waters between the Philippines, Taiwan and Japan.

THE SOUTHWEST MONSOON

A reversal of the NE monsoon occurs during the summer when the heating up of the Asian land mass creates a large area of low pressure over the eastern part of the continent. As a result, the SE trade winds of the Indian and Pacific Oceans are drawn across the equator. Because of the rotation of the earth, the SE winds are deflected to the right becoming the SW monsoon in the western

part of the Pacific Ocean. In the China Sea the winds are predominantly S and SW, whereas towards Japan they are either S or SE. The area affected by the SW monsoon is generally situated west of 140°E and south of 40°N. Steady SW winds are experienced in the China Sea during July, but further north the monsoon is felt less and variable winds become increasingly common. The weather during the SW monsoon is often unsettled and there is a high frequency of squalls, in which the wind reaches gale force.

VARIABLES

The two monsoons and the NE trade winds are replaced on the polar side of the North Pacific High by a belt of variable winds which is relatively narrow and rarely exceeds 300 miles in width. The variable zone is influenced by the position of the high-pressure area, which moves north in summer, when light and variable winds can be expected between latitudes 35°N and 40°N. In winter the high moves south when it stretches from about 25°N to 30°N. The movement of air around the North Pacific High has a direct bearing on the winds of the variable zone. In the eastern half of the ocean, winds tend to be northerly in summer and merge with the NE trades. In the western part of the ocean, the direction of the winds is more southerly so that they form an extension of the SW monsoon.

WESTERLIES

North of about 35°N the zone of variable winds is gradually replaced by an area of prevailing westerlies. These are not as boisterous or consistent as the westerlies of the Southern Ocean and the northern limit of the variables is more difficult to define. Westerly winds are more reliable both in direction and strength during winter when conditions can be rough and stormy while in summer the weather is more benign as fewer depressions race across the North Pacific between Japan and Alaska. The best weather can be expected in July, when light to moderate westerly winds predominate north of latitude 40°N.

REGIONAL WINDS

There are two local winds that occur off Mexico's Pacific coast. The *chubasco* is a violent wind which occurs mostly in summer and early autumn. It affects the entire Pacific coast but is worst in the Sea of Cortez where it can gust to 70 knots. A *chubasco*, which means 'squall' in Spanish, often strikes at night. A similarly dreaded local wind affects the Gulf of Tehuantepec, and is called by sailors the *tehuantepecer*. Such winds can occur throughout the year, with the worst period between December and

February. Winds can reach hurricane force in a relatively short time and with very little warning.

A local wind which occurs off Nicaragua and El Salvador is the *papagayo*, a violent north or northeast wind occurring between October and April with the worst period between the end of November and the end of January. Its effects can be felt as far as 150 miles offshore.

TROPICAL STORMS

There are two areas of the North Pacific Ocean that are subject to tropical revolving storms: the typhoons of East Asia and the hurricanes of the Eastern North Pacific. The region affected by hurricanes lies in the vicinity of the American coast, south of latitude 30°N to about latitude 10°N. This area includes the Pacific coasts of Mexico and Central America and extends as far as longitude 140°W, just west of Hawaii, an aspect that must be borne in mind by those planning to cross this area during the dangerous season. Theoretically the hurricane season lasts from May to November, although most hurricanes have been recorded between June and October, the month with the highest frequency being September. The only four months considered to be safe are January to April, as on a few occasions hurricanes have occurred in December. As a general rule only the earlier hurricanes travel to the western limit, whereas later in the season hurricanes are more likely to stay close to the coast. Therefore if a passage through this area is undertaken towards the end of the hurricane season, it is advisable to move offshore as quickly as possible.

The region affected by typhoons covers a much larger area stretching all the way from Micronesia to Japan. To the east the area is bound by Guam and the Mariana Islands, to the west by the Philippines, Taiwan and the northern part of the South China Sea. The typhoon season is less well defined than the hurricanes of the Eastern North Pacific and no month can be regarded as completely safe. However, most typhoons occur between May and December, and during this period over half the typhoons have been recorded between July and October. September is the most dangerous month, with an annual average of over four typhoons. The period with the least likelihood of typhoons is January to April. As no typhoons have been recorded from December to April in the area between the northern part of the China Sea and the western side of the Sea of Japan, this is considered to be the safest time for passages to and from Japan. In recent years, as a result of climate change, the Philippines and some areas of Micronesia have been affected by typhoons in every month of the year.

More tropical cyclones form in the tropical North Pacific, especially in its western part, than anywhere else in the world. On average, more than 25 tropical storms develop each year and about 18 become fully fledged typhoons. These typhoons are the most intense tropical storms in the world. Each year an average of five typhoons generate maximum winds of over 130 knots. The critical area usually covers more than 600 miles in diameter. Most of the storms form east of the Philippines and move across the Pacific towards the Asian mainland, Japan and China. A few storms form in the South China Sea. There is a noticeable seasonal shift in storm tracks in this region. From July through September, storms move north of the Philippines before they recurve to N and NW. Early and late in the season, typhoons move on a more westerly track through the Philippines before recurving.

CURRENTS

The surface circulation of the North Pacific Ocean resembles a huge merry-go-round in which various currents move in a clockwise direction around a cell located slightly off-centre in the northern hemisphere. The main spring of this circular movement is the North Equatorial Current which flows westward with its axis at about latitude 12°N. To the south of this current is the eastward flowing Equatorial Countercurrent, which has its southern limit between latitudes 2°N and 4°N where it is bound by the South Equatorial Current.

The North Equatorial Current is fed mainly by the California Current and the northern branch of the Equatorial Countercurrent. Further west it is reinforced by the North Pacific Current and further west still it divides in two, the southern branch reversing its direction to become the Equatorial Countercurrent, while the northern branch carries on towards Taiwan and Japan. This is the main source of the Kuroshio Current, a flow of warm water similar to the Gulf Stream of the North Atlantic. The main difference is that the direction of the Kuroshio is seasonal, setting to the NE during the SW monsoon, but reversing its direction in winter, at the height of the NE monsoon.

Along the southern coast of Japan the main direction of the Kuroshio is NE. It subsequently fans out in about latitude 35°N to form the North Pacific Current. Reinforced by the Aleutian Current, this current flows in a broad band across the North Pacific towards North America. East of latitude 160°E this current starts fanning out, part of it turning south, while the main body continues eastwards towards the North American continent where it turns SE and its name is changed to the California Current. It then flows into the North Equatorial Current thus completing the clockwise circulation round the North Pacific basin.

The surface circulation along the Pacific coast of Central America and the Gulf of Panama is more erratic, with pronounced seasonal variations that make predictions impossible. In the Gulf of Panama the movement of water is more complicated, with an inflow of water at both extremes and an outflow in the centre that joins the South Equatorial Current.

TSUNAMIS

Earthquakes that occur under the ocean floor can cause large waves that can affect low-lying countries and islands thousands of miles away. The North Pacific has been devastated by many tsunamis in the past. There have been six destructive tsunamis in Hawaii during the last century: one of the worst occurred in 1960, causing great destruction in Hilo where over 60 people lost their lives. A tsunami caused by an 8.8 magnitude earthquake in Chile on 27 February 2010 affected large areas of the Pacific Ocean and caused serious damage as far as Japan. Boats are normally unaffected by tsunamis at sea or if anchored in deeper water.

On 11 March 2011 an earthquake of magnitude 9, one of the strongest tremors ever recorded, struck NE Japan. The resulting tsunami was also one of the most destructive causing widespread devastation in nearby coastal areas with hundreds of deaths and entire towns being obliterated. Its effects were felt throughout the Pacific with wave damage reported as far as the state of Oregon in the USA.

The South Pacific

THE SOUTHEAST TRADE WINDS

The majority of cruising routes in the South Pacific are dependent on these winds which blow over a large area of this ocean. The SE trade winds blow on the equatorial side of the high-pressure area situated in about 30°S. In the vicinity of South America the trade winds blow from between S and SE, but their direction becomes increasingly easterly in the western part of the ocean. In the vicinity of Australia the winds become SE again, especially during the winter months. During the summer months, from November to April, the trade winds are less steady over large parts of the ocean. West of about 140°W, there are frequently winds from other directions, although the prevailing direction remains between NE and SE.

The average strength of the SE trade wind is 15 knots, although in some areas it can increase to 20 or even 25

knots. The strongest winds are experienced in the Coral Sea, where they reach 30 knots. However, the SE trade winds of the South Pacific are neither as steady nor as constant as the trade winds of other oceans. A continuous belt of SE winds blowing steadily across the entire ocean exists only during the months of June, July and August. During the rest of the year the force and direction of the trade winds is not so constant. In an area that is approximately 600 miles wide and stretches diagonally across the trade wind belt, from the Phoenix Islands through the Tuamotus as far as Easter Island, the direction of the wind often changes to the NE and is succeeded by calms. After a while the winds revert to blowing strongly from the SE and are frequently accompanied by heavy rain squalls.

Reinforced trade winds are a regional phenomenon which often bring stronger than expected winds. It occurs mostly south of 10°S and depends on both the location and intensity of the South Pacific High. Even stronger winds, usually from the south, are generated by the passage of a front. Ahead of such a front, the SE winds get lighter as they back to E and NE. The passage of a front generates SW winds which gradually back to S and SE, often to be followed by a period of reinforced trades.

INTERTROPICAL CONVERGENCE ZONE
The northern limit of the SE trade winds is determined by the position of the ITCZ, which stays north of the equator throughout the year east of 160°W. In the western half of the ocean, it moves to the southern hemisphere from about November to April, reaching furthest south in February, at the height of the southern summer. The movement of the ITCZ is most pronounced in the vicinity of Australia and Papua New Guinea, where the width of the doldrum belt can be greatest. On average it has a width of about 150 miles, but in some places it can be twice as wide, whereas in other areas it can be entirely absent. Weather conditions inside the zone are typical of doldrums everywhere, with calms or light variable winds alternating with rain squalls and thunderstorms.

SOUTH PACIFIC CONVERGENCE ZONE
One special feature of South Pacific weather is the South Pacific Convergence Zone (SPCZ), which occurs during winter and stretches roughly ESE from 5°S, 155°E to 20°S, 150°W, and affects a large area between the Solomon Islands and Tahiti, particularly in the central area between French Polynesia and Tonga. The SPCZ, which must not

be confused with the ITCZ, moves along the above area and affects weather conditions when it is active or when a front passes through it. The winds usually shift rapidly from NE to S and can reach gale force. The location of the SPCZ, and whether it is active or not, is mentioned in some local weather forecasts.

THE NORTHWEST MONSOON

During the summer months, prevailing NW winds blow over the Western South Pacific west of meridian 180°. The NW monsoon normally lasts from December to March, which coincides with the cyclone season. The areas mostly affected by the NW monsoon are the Solomon Islands, Papua New Guinea and Northern Australia. The direction of the wind is mainly N or NE near the equator, becoming NW or even W in more southerly latitudes. The NW monsoon is not consistent in either strength or direction, but at the height of the season, winds from between S and E are quite rare. The strength of the monsoon is light or moderate, although it can reach gale force in squalls, which are quite frequent. The weather is generally cloudy and overcast, with heavy rainfall. Close to the coast the direction of the wind can be greatly affected by local conditions.

VARIABLES

An area of variable winds exists between the southern limit of the SE trade winds and the northern limit of the westerlies. This belt of variable winds extends from 25°S to 40°S during the summer months and from 20°S to 30°S during winter. The belt does not extend across the entire ocean and its position varies from year to year. East of about 85°W, the prevailing winds are S or SE, being an extension of the SE trade winds. The strength and direction of these variable winds can vary considerably, although they tend to become stronger in higher latitudes.

WESTERLIES

The prevailing westerly winds or Roaring Forties predominate south of the South Pacific High, which is situated in about latitude 30°S. In the west, these winds are influenced by the movement of anticyclones tracking east from Australia. The continuous passage of depressions from west to east causes the wind to vary greatly in both direction and strength. The westerlies are most consistent between latitudes 40° and 60°S. Gales are common in winter, although strong winds can be experienced at any time of the year.

REGIONAL WINDS

Williwaws are sudden violent katabatic gusts which descend from a mountainous coast to the sea. They are most common in Southern Chile and the Strait of Magellan.

TROPICAL STORMS

A large area of the South Pacific is affected by cyclones between November and early May. The most affected area is south of about 8° to 10°S and west of 140°W, and covers a wide belt stretching all the way from Tahiti in the east to the Torres Strait in the west. The most dangerous months are January to March, when tropical depressions which develop over the Coral Sea or the Gulf of Carpentaria can turn into a cyclone. The number of tropical storms varies greatly from year to year as do their tracks. In some areas within the cyclone belt, such as Tahiti, cyclones may not occur for many years while in others, such as the Coral Sea, tropical storms have occurred occasionally outside of the accepted cyclone season.

Officially, the tropical storm season in the South Pacific is supposed to last from November to the end of April, but due to the current climate change the cyclone season is now considered to last longer with the critical period defined as from mid-November to the end of May, or even early June in the western part of the ocean. Cyclone activity is also being recorded closer to the equator as in the case of Cyclone Percy which devastated Tokelau in February 2005. For these reasons, the South Pacific tropical storm season mentioned at the beginning of each voyage has been expanded to November to May, even if in some areas this may not be the case.

CURRENTS

The main surface circulation of the South Pacific Ocean is counterclockwise. Around the edges of the South Pacific, the four components of this counterclockwise movement are the west-setting South Equatorial Current, the south-setting East Australia Current, the east-setting Southern Ocean Current, and finally the north-setting Humboldt Current.

The South Equatorial Current has its northern limit from 1°N to 5°N depending both on season and longitude. The South Equatorial Current decreases in strength south of latitude 6°S, although it maintains its westerly direction. Between latitudes 6°S and 20°S, this weaker current is known as the South Subtropical Current.

The Southern Ocean Current sets E or NE in higher latitudes. Most of this current flows into the Atlantic Ocean south of Cape Horn, but one part of it turns north along the west coast of South America to become the Humboldt Current. This cold current flows north towards the equator and eventually feeds into the South Equatorial Current. The flow of the Humboldt Current is sometimes reversed by the Equatorial Countercurrent.

EL NIÑO AND LA NIÑA

For centuries the people of the fishing communities in northern Peru and Ecuador have used the term El Niño to describe an occasional warming of the offshore waters during December. The name was due to this phenomenon usually occurring around Christmas, and was therefore called El Niño or the Holy Child Current. El Niño is now used to describe extensive warming of the ocean surface across the Eastern and Central Equatorial Pacific. When this oceanic region switches to below normal temperatures, it is called La Niña.

In years when it is fully established this warm current can greatly influence weather conditions not just in the Eastern South Pacific, but in the entire Pacific Basin – and indeed throughout the world. After the devastations caused by El Niño in 1982–1983, weather conditions were closely monitored when it occurred again in 1997–1998. As a result, this major natural phenomenon is now much better understood, and some of its effects can be predicted. It is now accepted that El Niño affects weather far beyond the South Pacific. It is still impossible to predict exactly when a new El Niño episode will occur, but the 20th century has seen altogether 28 episodes, so on average El Niño can be expected to strike every three or four years. Nevertheless, in an El Niño period, sailing during, or close

to, the cyclone season should be avoided and, if at all possible, one should attempt to spend the critical period outside the tropical Pacific Ocean. The latest El Niño episode occurred between 2014 and 2016.

When the ocean temperatures revert to a colder period this is now commonly referred to as La Niña. During a period of La Niña, the sea surface temperature across the equatorial Eastern Pacific Ocean can be lower than normal by 3° to 5°C. This colder water usually results in stronger trade winds in the Central South Pacific, larger swell and fewer tropical storms. During a La Niña episode, the mass of colder water from the Eastern South Pacific is pushed westwards by the easterly winds and accumulates in the northwestern part of the South Pacific, such as the Coral Sea. The rapid evaporation of the cold water as it collides with the warm air mass can cause widespread climatic disturbances. This happened during the La Niña episode, in January 2011, when torrential rains caused disastrous flooding from Queensland to Sri Lanka.

TSUNAMIS

Several tsunamis have been recorded in the South Pacific over the years. A tsunami occurred on 29 September 2009 when a powerful 8.1 magnitude earthquake struck in the Central South Pacific causing widespread devastation in Samoa, American Samoa and Tonga, killing 200 people. Its effects were felt thousands of miles away. A powerful tsunami caused by an 8.8 magnitude earthquake in Chile on 27 February 2010 affected large areas of the Pacific Ocean and caused serious damage but no fatalities as far as Japan.

PACIFIC OCEAN VOYAGES

To cross the Pacific Ocean, even under the most favourable circumstances, brings you for many days close to nature, and you realise the vastness of the sea.

Joshua Slocum

A voyage to the islands of the South Seas figures in many sailors' long-term plans, but their remoteness, which is one of their main temptations, keeps them beyond the scope of the average voyage. This is the reason why in spite of the proliferation of yachts worldwide, the number of boats cruising the South Pacific is still relatively small and is not likely to increase much in the foreseeable future. No other part of the world offers so many cruising opportunities or such diverse attractions as the South Pacific, from the spectacular anchorages of the Marquesas to the turquoise lagoons of the Tuamotus, from the giant statues of Easter Island to the traditional villages of Vanuatu, the sheltered waters of Vava'u or the remote island communities of Tokelau and Tuvalu. The vastness of the Pacific Ocean, and the great distances which separate most island groups,

make long passages a normal feature in this part of the world. The islands' isolation and scarcity of facilities require the boat and her crew to be well prepared and self-sufficient.

As in other tropical areas of the world the best weather conditions in the South Pacific are a feature of the winter months (May to October) and for this reason most sailors plan to arrive in the Marquesas in April. Although officially the South Pacific cyclone season lasts from November to May, the Marquesas are very rarely affected by tropical storms, so an April arrival can be considered to be of low risk. The main attraction of such an early arrival, primarily for those on a tight schedule, is a welcome extension of the cruising season. In spite of the huge distance between Panama and the Torres Strait, boats regularly cover the 9,000 miles in one season. This tight timescale is dictated by the fact that one has to be through the Torres Strait by September in order to benefit from favourable conditions in the South Indian Ocean. To do it proper justice the South Pacific deserves more than just one season and those who prefer to stay longer have

the option of either spending the cyclone season in a safe place in the tropics or sailing out of the cyclone belt to New Zealand or Australia. The number of cyclone-proof places in the islands is quite limited and this should be borne in mind if planning to spend the summer in the islands. The locations with reasonable protection in case of a cyclone are Tahiti, Raiatea, Vava'u, Pago Pago, Savusavu, Suva, Vuda Point and Nouméa.

Weather conditions during the safe season are normally good and are dominated by the SE trade winds. Generally, the most reliable winds can be expected at the two extremes of the traditional transpacific route: between the Galapagos and Marquesas, and in the Coral Sea. In between those two areas, it is just a matter of luck, with long spells of steady trade winds in some years, or a mixed bag of short periods of two or three days of steady winds alternating with squally weather, thunderstorms and irregular winds, particularly in El Niño years. The worst area is between French Polynesia and Tonga, where the effects of the South Pacific Convergence Zone (SPCZ) can be most pronounced.

Most boats follow the traditional route that sweeps in an arc from Panama to the Torres Strait. Favourable SE trade winds are the usual feature of this route during the winter months although occasionally the weather conditions can be affected by various factors, such as the El Niño or La Niña phenomena. The latest El Niño episode occurred between 2014 and 2016, and it is now believed that it can occur every three or four years, although of variable intensity. During El Niño, trade winds are lighter and less consistent than normal, there is a higher risk of tropical cyclones and the cyclone season tends to last longer.

When the ocean temperatures in the Eastern South Pacific revert to a colder period this is now referred to as La Niña. During La Niña the trade winds are usually stronger than normal and there is a lower incidence of tropical cyclones. A weak La Niña episode occurred in 2016–17. A constant feature which affects weather conditions throughout the tropical South Pacific is the SPCZ. This moves northeast during El Niño and southwest during La Niña events.

In the North Pacific, the three main weather features that have a major bearing on voyage planning are the NE trade winds, the hurricane season of the Eastern North Pacific and the typhoons of the Western North Pacific. Whereas the hurricanes have a fairly well-defined season between June and November, and affect the coasts of Mexico and parts of Central America, as far west as Hawaii, the typhoon season in the Western North Pacific is less clearly defined. These violent storms affect a large

area from the Philippines to Japan, as well as much of Micronesia, and in some areas can strike at any time of the year. The one redeeming feature of the North Pacific is the NE trade winds, which blow consistently throughout the year in the tropical areas, winds from that direction also being predominant in subtropical areas. In contrast to the South Pacific, where most voyages are undertaken in the tropics during the winter season, North Pacific voyages, most of which take place outside the tropics, are sailed between late spring and early autumn.

The vast Pacific Ocean is a spider's web of sailing routes which makes planning a voyage to any destination a complex task as in almost every case there are several alternatives. To ease the task of navigating the various alternative routes, some of the arterial routes are divided into separate segments, each starting or finishing at one of the important major cruising hubs of Tahiti, Fiji and Hawaii, where most long voyages converge and diverge. Occasionally the alternative routes overlap with a certain segment being common to each, so rather than repeat the same information, there is a reference in the text to the full description of that particular segment.

Several routes fan out from Panama into the Pacific Ocean, the number of cruising boats which turn left towards the South Pacific being roughly equal to those bound for Central and North America. Sailors bound for the South Seas fare somewhat better both for choice of destinations and generally more favourable weather conditions. The situation is very different for American and Canadian sailors heading for home as they are faced by a tough choice: to sail the shorter but tougher route that runs roughly parallel to the mainland coast and is bedevilled by contrary winds and current, or take the offshore route that benefits from more favourable weather conditions, but is much longer and may even entail a detour to Hawaii.

The principal arterial routes in the Pacific are mostly westbound: Panama to the Torres Strait, Panama to Asia via Hawaii, North America to New Zealand and Australia, and North America to Asia. The only eastbound arterial route is from New Zealand and Australia to North America. The two main transpacific routes, the South Pacific route from Panama to Torres, and the North Pacific route to Hawaii and Southeast Asia, are often sailed as part of a round the world voyage. Because of the length of these arterial routes, for both planning and logistical purposes they are broken into separate segments, each starting or finishing in an important cruising hub. Thus the voyage from Panama to the Torres Strait is divided into three segments: Panama to Tahiti, Tahiti to Fiji, and Fiji to the Torres Strait, while the voyage from Panama to

Southeast Asia is made up of two segments, with Hawaii at its centre.

Most Pacific voyages are sailed along one of the above arterial routes, the most travelled being the classic route which stretches from Panama to the Torres Strait and often forms part of a longer, round the world voyage. Affectionately nicknamed by English sailors 'the Milk Run', as it reminded them of the daily milk delivery back home, the name later evolved to a more suitable regional variation as the 'Coconut Milk Run'. This route is joined mainly by boats arriving from the Panama Canal and the Caribbean, or from the Pacific coasts of Central and North America. A second east to west route runs from Panama across the North Pacific to Asia, but is less travelled as sailors continue to be attracted by the more popular South Pacific destinations. There is more traffic on a third arterial route, sailed by North American boats to the South Pacific directly or via Hawaii. Some of those boats return home via a fourth arterial route, from Tahiti to North America, which is joined by boats sailing to the North Pacific from Australia and New Zealand, usually at the end of a South Seas cruise. A transpacific route links South and North America and is sailed by boats which have completed a voyage to Southern Chile, Tierra del Fuego or Antarctica. Finally, a west to east route originating in Asia is sailed by boats on voyages bound for the cruising destinations in the North or South Pacific.

Just as in ancient times all roads were supposed to lead to Rome, so in the South Pacific all sailing routes eventually lead to Tahiti. Lying at the heart of Polynesia, Tahiti has been a favourite landfall for mariners ever since its discovery by the outside world and continues to be the most important cruising hub in the South Pacific. From sailors to painters, musicians to film stars, its temptations have proved irresistible and this fascination with the symbol of the South Seas continues to this day. Most boats arrive there by the route from Panama to the Torres Strait or by boats sailing from the west coast of North America, with a lesser number of boats arriving from New Zealand and Southern Chile.

In Fiji the largest numbers of boats also arrive from the east and it is from Fiji that those who plan to spend another season in the South Pacific leave for New Zealand or Australia, usually returning to the tropics after the end of the cyclone season. From Fiji the main arterial route continues to Vanuatu and thence to Northern Australia. This is the route sailed by boats bound for the Indian Ocean, often as part of a voyage around the world. Those who intend to take the Cape of Good Hope route need to pass through the Torres Strait by early September so as to have enough time to reach South Africa before the start of the South Indian Ocean cyclone season in November. The timing for boats bound for Southeast Asia and the North Indian Ocean is more flexible as the passage through Torres Strait can be delayed until October. A similar flexibility is enjoyed by those intending to sail to Southeast Australia as they only need to be out of the critical area by November, before the start of the cyclone season in the Coral Sea.

There is another way to reach the Indian Ocean which may suit those who plan to explore the islands of Papua New Guinea, which are not affected by tropical cyclones and are safe to visit during the critical period. Having cruised the outer islands of New Guinea, rather than continue via the Torres Strait a route can be sailed in a northwesterly direction towards Southeast Asia. The timing is less season-dependent than the Torres Strait route and the area to be crossed is generally also free of North Pacific typhoons between December and February. Such timing makes it possible to continue along this route into the North Indian Ocean and catch the end of the NE monsoon for the passage to the Red Sea and Mediterranean.

North of the equator, Hawaii plays a similar role as a hub on the east to west arterial route but the greatest share of the traffic is to or from North America by boats on either return voyages from the mainland to Hawaii, or on longer voyages to or from the South Seas. Hawaii is also used as a hub by boats on voyages from Asia to the Pacific.

Linear voyages:

Voyages to Tahiti

Voyages to Fiji

Voyages to New Zealand and Australia

Voyages to Hawaii

Voyages to Panama and Central America

Voyages to North America

Voyages to South America

Voyages to Asia

Circular voyages:

Voyages from the US West Coast

Voyages from Australia and New Zealand

Voyages from Asia

Voyages to Tahiti

P1	Voyages from Panama and Central America
P2	Voyages from Mexico and California
P3	Voyages from US West Coast
P4	Voyages from Hawaii
P5	Voyages from South America
P6	Voyages from Australia and New Zealand
P7	Voyages from East Asia and Japan

As the safe sailing season in the South Pacific is well defined, and the weather is usually fairly benign in the eastern part of this vast ocean, for sailors arriving from the east the most critical decision concerns the time of arrival in the first tropical island group. Most boats transit the Panama Canal before the onset of the hurricane season in the Caribbean (June to November), with the busiest transit period being February and March. This is also the time when boats sailing from Mexico and Central America should start leaving for the South Pacific. Those who plan to sail in one season all the way to Australia or the Torres Strait need to reach the Marquesas not later than April to be able to cover the considerable distances ahead of them in only five months. Those with more time on their hands may decide not to sail the usual route from Galapagos to the Marquesas, but make a detour to Easter Island and arrive in French Polynesia by way of the Gambier Islands.

Tahiti is the most important cruising hub in the South Pacific, where all the voyages outlined in this section converge, thus turning the Pacific into a spider's web with Tahiti at its centre. The majority of boats arrive from the NE, whether from Panama or the west coast of North America. Fewer boats arrive from other points of the compass but this is bound to change as new cruising grounds, whether in Asia or South America, are added to the list of favourite destinations.

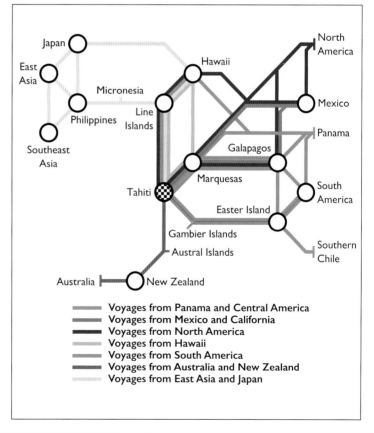

Voyages from Panama and Central America
Voyages from Mexico and California
Voyages from North America
Voyages from Hawaii
Voyages from South America
Voyages from Australia and New Zealand
Voyages from East Asia and Japan

Pacific Odyssey

Our entry into the Pacific was dramatic. Poised high in the Miraflores Lock of the Panama Canal, we caught our first glimpse of that great ocean stretching out to the horizon. Little did we guess that the Pacific would cast such a spell that instead of the planned one year, we would spend three years criss-crossing it.

Sailing in a small boat across the vast ocean, I felt so much closer to the countries and peoples than if I had flown in by air. This is Oceania, whose countries are all islands, traditionally linked by the sea. Often I thought of the Polynesian legends, and when we were at sea for many days, I put myself into the minds of those early navigators in their canoes. I imagined how they must have felt, exactly as we did, when the first coconut palms spiked up on the horizon, or a tiny speck of island emerged where we had expected it to be.

Three weeks out from South America, we felt this way when we sighted Rapa Nui, our first Pacific island, also known as Easter Island. Some islands have no air links and rare sea links, and sailing into such places, where other visitors are few, has a special significance. Since contacts with the outside world are rare the islanders are as interested in us as we are in their way of life, their music and traditions. Being a family has made an enormous difference to our travels. We are a social unit that the Pacific Islanders well understand, for children have a special place in their affections.

Leaving Papua New Guinea, we will be leaving the Pacific and sailing back home via the Indian Ocean and Red Sea. Looking ahead at that troubled part of the world we have many regrets in leaving the Pacific, for above all it has been for us a peaceful ocean, one full of friendly welcoming people. It has left its mark on the children and on us, too. We feel at home sitting cross-legged on a fine mat. We have learnt to enter a house or meeting place from the lagoon side and not from the sea, so as to be regarded as friends, not enemies.

The saddest part of our travels is always the leaving, and nowhere is this experience more poignant than in Polynesia. So often we have taken the lingering scent of the islands back to *Aventura* in our frangipani crowns, but we are incurably superstitious sailors and always throw them into the ocean on leaving, hoping this will bring us back one day.

Gwenda Cornell, from *Pacific Odyssey*

P1 • Voyages from Panama and Central America

- **P1a** Voyages via Galapagos
- **P1b** Direct voyages via the Marquesas
- **P1c** Voyages via Easter Island
- **P1d** Marquesas and Gambiers to Tahiti

There are three major alternatives to reach Tahiti from Panama and Central America, each with its own attractions. Those who prefer to arrive in French Polynesia as quickly as possible should consider sailing nonstop from Panama to the Marquesas. Most sailors, however, stop at Galapagos as the islands lie close to the direct route and this also shortens the considerable length of a direct passage to the Marquesas. A tempting alternative is to sail a more roundabout route that swings south from the Galapagos to call at such rarely visited places as Easter Island and Pitcairn. By this southern route landfall in French Polynesia is made at the Gambier Islands, but, as in the case of arrivals in the Marquesas, those islands should not be reached before April as occasionally cyclones, or at least their effects, have been felt as far east as the Gambiers and even Pitcairn. The Gambiers can also be reached by sailing directly there from the Galapagos Islands, the distance being the same as the Marquesas route, although this long passage can be shortened by stopping at Pitcairn and possibly at some of the uninhabited islands which belong to it.

A more ambitious alternative is to sail south along the mainland coast of South America to Ecuador and Peru, and turn west from there to Easter Island and beyond. The main attraction of this route is the opportunity to visit some of South America. To travel in the interior, the boat can be left at Puerto Lucia Marina at La Libertad in mainland Ecuador, a convenient place from which to visit the High Andes or Amazonia, about one-third of the Amazon Basin being located in Ecuador. In Peru, the port of Callao, close to the capital Lima, can serve as a similar base to leave the boat while touring the Inca remains, Lake Titicaca and even some neighbouring countries.

The one serious objection to these two southern routes is that they miss the Marquesas, the most beautiful of all French Polynesian archipelagos. However, this need not necessarily be the case as from the Gambiers you can sail north to the Marquesas, and visit some of the Outer Tuamotus on the way. Those who prefer to continue from the Gambiers to Tahiti without this additional detour can either sail nonstop or call at some of the Southern Tuamotus that lie close to this route. A challenging detour from the Gambiers is to the Austral Islands, the southernmost and least visited island group in French Polynesia. With good planning any of these objectives can be reached and the additional mileage more than justifies the effort of visiting some of the most remote islands in the South Pacific.

P1a Voyages via Galapagos

Recommended time: March to May

Tropical storms: June to November (North Pacific), November to May (South Pacific)

World Cruising Routes:

PT11	Southbound from Panama and Central America
PS11	Ecuador to Galapagos
PS12	Galapagos to Marquesas
PS22	Marquesas to Tuamotus and Tahiti

As the last lock of the Panama Canal opens and the wide vista of the Pacific stretches before your eyes, the sight of that mighty ocean induces a feeling of awe mingled with the happy anticipation of all those wonderful places that are now finally within reach. The first of the various routes that can be sailed to Tahiti presents itself right at the start when a decision needs to be made whether to sail from Panama directly to the Galapagos, or call first at the mainland to see some of South America before turning your back on it. Such a detour can easily be incorporated in a longer voyage and is well worth considering, as even a relatively short stay in Ecuador makes it possible to visit the Andean Highlands as well as a corner of Amazonia.

Whichever route is taken, the ITCZ needs to be crossed at some point to reach the hoped for balmy trade winds, and during February and March the winds between Panama and Galapagos are quite variable in nature. They usually have a northerly component for the first half of the passage, with an increased proportion of SE and S winds as you get closer to the equator. It is therefore advisable to keep some easting while sailing south so as to have a better angle as you approach the islands.

Those who intend to visit both Galapagos and mainland Ecuador need to decide where to head first; if the plan is to continue west from Galapagos, then the mainland should be visited first. The winds on the direct route to mainland Ecuador are mostly northerly at the beginning becoming increasingly more southerly, but such winds are usually light. Winds between the mainland and Galapagos also have a high percentage of light southerly

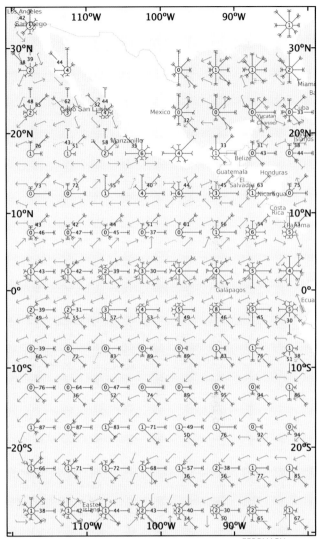

FEBRUARY

winds, usually SW at first becoming SE closer to the islands.

Close to the route from Panama to the Galapagos lies Malpelo Island, which is uninhabited except for a small military post manned by the Colombian Army. Visitors need a written permit from the Colombian Ministry of Ecology to stop as the island is a nature reserve. The island is very popular with divers as it has a very rich underwater fauna with large colonies of various species of sharks. There is no well-protected anchorage in the lee of Malpelo, but mooring close to the rocky shore provides some shelter from wind and swell. Emergency stops are usually tolerated but as the recommended route to the

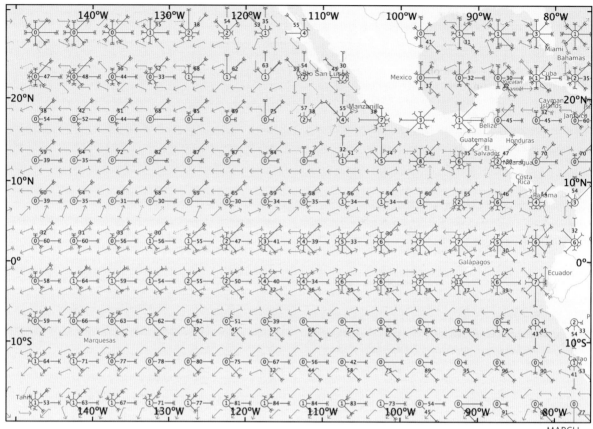

MARCH

Galapagos passes east of the island so as to avoid the calms associated with it, it is better to sail that way unless you are determined to stop at Malpelo.

As one of the most important biological reserves in the world, the Galapagos Islands are a national park and the Ecuadorian authorities are determined to ensure the protection of their unique environment. Every visiting yacht must be in possession of special permit, which must be obtained in advance with the assistance of a local agent. There are certain restrictions on the movement of visiting yachts which must clear into one of the two ports of entry, Baquerizo Moreno on San Cristobal and Puerto Ayora on Santa Cruz Island. Boats are usually allowed to spend several days there and may also stop at Puerto Velasco Ibarra on Floreana and Puerto Villamil on Isabela provided this has been cleared with the authorities on arrival. No other places may be visited on your own boat unless arrangements have been made in advance to obtain an additional cruising permit, which can be a lengthy and costly operation. For those who wish to see more of the Enchanted Islands, and do not have such a permit, the solu-

tion is to leave the boat in one of the two ports of entry and join a local excursion boat to visit the various islands. The abundance of wildlife, ashore, in the air and in the sea, as well as its variety is staggering. Every island has its own resident species, penguins on San Salvador, sea iguanas on Santa Fé, land iguanas on Fernandina, frigate birds on Seymour, sea lions on San Cristobal, giant tortoises on Isabela, white-tipped sharks at Bartolomé, while Española has the largest colony of blue-footed boobies whose gentle dance performed by courting couples is a sight to behold.

A last stop at Puerto Villamil on Isabela, where the local port captain usually tolerates short stays, is a perfect place to prepare for the long passage to the Marquesas. Although the largest island of the archipelago, Isabela is off the beaten track, its wild interior probably not looking very different to what it must have been like when only giant tortoises and pirates roamed these islands.

On the passage to the Marquesas, the prevailing SE trade winds become gradually established as you move west. Even if the winds are favourable on leaving the Galapagos, the usual tactic is not to set a direct course but to follow a slight arc towards your destination by sailing first to the SW to reach the area of more consistent winds before altering course for the Marquesas. Early in the season, in March and even April, the winds may be light for the first third or even half of the passage before steadier winds set in but sailing conditions are invariably pleasant. This is the longest offshore passage that you may ever experience, an uninterrupted 3,000 mile expanse of ocean, with only the wide sky, the sun and the stars for company.

For boats arriving from the east, the nearest island is Fatu Hiva, but as it is not a port of entry a first landfall in French Polynesia should not be planned there but at the small port of Atuona on the island of Hiva Oa. This island's fame is mostly due to being the place where the French painter Paul Gauguin ended his days; the house where he painted many of his most famous canvasses has been restored and now contains reproductions of the works he painted during his troubled sojourn on the island.

P1b Direct voyages via the Marquesas

Recommended time: April to June

Tropical storms: June to November (Eastern North Pacific), November to May (South Pacific)

World Cruising Routes:

PT13	Panama to Marquesas
PT14	California and Mexico to Marquesas

There are various reasons why more and more sailors decide to bypass the Galapagos Islands and sail directly to the Marquesas. For many sailors, the aim is to reach the Marquesas as early as possible so as to be able to enjoy a full season in the tropical South Pacific. A direct voyage should also be the preferred option for those who cannot make an early start and therefore wish to reach the South Pacific without missing too much of the favourable season. This includes those who have arrived through the Panama Canal and prefer to sail nonstop to the Marquesas and bypass the Galapagos, whether to gain time or avoid the lengthy formalities there.

The dilemma faced by anyone planning this nonstop voyage to the Marquesas is whether to sail the initial part of the passage north of the equator, or sail south from Panama, cross the equator and go south of the Galapagos Islands. The pilot charts for February and March show a high percentage of E and NE winds north of the equator and those who are determined not to stop in either mainland South America or Galapagos may prefer to take advantage of these winds and cross the equator further west. Although slightly longer, this northern route may

not be slower as it will avoid the light and variable winds in the area of the Galapagos. Those who prefer to sail the traditional southern route and wish to play it safe will have the option of stopping in the Galapagos in an emergency. Where the equator is crossed by those sailing the northern route will depend on the state of the SE winds south of the Line but normally this should be somewhere between 100°W and 110°W.

Once the Galapagos Islands are passed, there is no other speck of land along this 4,000-mile long passage but there are two interesting stops closer to the start, which are worth mentioning. Close to the northern route is Cocos Island (Isla de Coco), a nature reserve which belongs to Costa Rica. The island is a great favourite among diving enthusiasts who have voted it as among the ten best diving spots in the world due to the breathtaking marine life in the waters surrounding it. The main attractions are the large colonies of hammerhead sharks, manta rays and many pelagic species, which are abundant at this meeting point between deep and shallow waters. Permission to stop must be obtained in advance and there are two good anchorages. Short emergency stops are usually tolerated by the resident wardens. Further to the north is Clipperton Atoll, an uninhabited French possession, which is also renowned for its excellent underwater scenery and wildlife. As this is an out-of-bounds nature reserve vessels are not allowed to anchor nor is anyone permitted to dive or land ashore.

South of the equator, SE trade winds will ensure good sailing conditions for the rest of the passage to the Marquesas. The recommended landfall, and port of entry, is Atuona on the island of Hiva Oa, as it lies to windward of the other islands. The only exception is Fatu Hiva but as it is not an official port of entry stopping there first is not permitted.

P1c Voyages via Easter Island

Recommended time: February to June

Tropical storms: November to May

World Cruising Routes:

PT11	Southbound from Panama and Central America
PT12	California and Mexico to Galapagos
PS13	Galapagos to Easter Island
PS15	South America to Easter Island
PS16	Westbound from Easter Island
PS28	Gambier Islands to Tuamotus and Tahiti

The itinerary of this longer voyage to Tahiti includes some interesting destinations and, although considerably longer, can easily be planned to take advantage of good sailing conditions throughout its duration. One of the

APRIL

attractions of sailing this more roundabout way to Tahiti is that it can be done earlier in the season. As the Eastern South Pacific is not affected by tropical storms, voyages in that part of the world can be undertaken at any time of the year. Thus, boats can sail from Panama or Central America to the Galapagos or mainland Ecuador as early as December or January, and then make their way west to Easter Island and Pitcairn at a leisurely pace so as to arrive in French Polynesia at the start of the safe season.

While the basic route follows the track Panama–Easter Island–Tahiti, there are choices to be made at every intermediate point. The first decision to be made is whether to sail from Panama directly to the Galapagos or via the mainland. It is also at this point that a decision needs to be made whether to then continue from the mainland to Easter Island via the inshore route or sail the offshore route from Galapagos. Those who wish to visit both mainland Ecuador and the Galapagos Islands, and then sail from Galapagos directly to Easter Island, should call at the mainland first. Those who intend to continue south from Ecuador, along the inshore route, should visit Galapagos first and sail from there to the mainland. Weather conditions along the coastal route are benign throughout the year, with light S and SE winds

and a contrary but manageable north-setting Humboldt Current, so you should expect to cover some of this passage under power. Peru's main port, Callao, close to the capital Lima, is a convenient base to explore the interior and take your departure for Easter Island. At the recommended time, the winds on this passage are favourable and blow consistently from E and SE.

Those same winds will provide good sailing conditions for the offshore route from Galapagos to Easter Island, even if some of it may be close-hauled. Calling at that remote Polynesian outpost on your own boat is an unforgettable experience and a suitable introduction to Polynesia. The next port of call, Pitcairn, is lasting proof of the irresistible power of seduction that the South Seas and its people have had on visitors ever since the arrivals of the first outsiders. The most famous victims, the *Bounty* mutineers, chose this tiny island as their secret refuge and the few yachts that call are always welcomed by their descendants who live there.

The closest of French Polynesia's five island groups, the Gambier Islands, are only a short distance from Pitcairn and it is there that the choice must be made as to which of the four route options to Tahiti to take: sail on to the Tuamotus, turn right for the Marquesas, left for the Australs, or carry on nonstop to Tahiti. The Tuamotus are so close to the direct route to Tahiti that stopping at one or two atolls to get at least a feel of the Dangerous Archipelago can easily be done. Similarly, the Tuamotus make an interesting stop for those who choose to take the detour to the Marquesas. The isolated Austral Islands are rarely visited as they lie off the usual sailing routes but their very remoteness is one of their charms.

Whichever route is sailed from Panama, Tahiti, and its capital Papeete, is a perfect place to conclude this first chapter of your South Seas adventure, and prepare for the next stage of your voyage.

P1d Marquesas and Gambiers to Tahiti

Recommended time: April to June

Tropical storms: November to May

World Cruising Routes:

PS22	Marquesas to Tuamotus and Tahiti
PS28	Gambier to Tuamotus and Tahiti
PS29	Australs to Tahiti
PS21	Gambier to Marquesas

Among the various routes that end in Tahiti, the one from the Marquesas is the most travelled as it brings in the bulk of boats bound for the South Seas, whether from Panama and Galapagos, Central and North America, or Hawaii. The winds between April and June are predominantly from E and SE, and weather conditions at that time of year are generally pleasant. The direct route from the Marquesas to Tahiti cuts across the Western Tuamotus and few yachts pass by without stopping at least at one or two of its atolls. The nearest to the route and easiest to access are Ahe, Rangiroa and Manihi, but they are also the most visited. Those who are prepared to get off the beaten track, and explore some of the less frequented atolls,

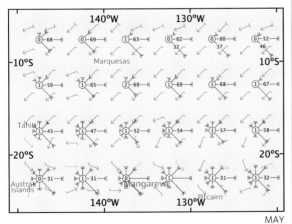

MAY

Tuamotu diving highlights

The Tuamotu atolls offer some truly great diving opportunities. If you carry all the equipment to be self-sufficient, including tanks and compressor, and are an experienced diver, the possibilities are endless as practically every pass into the lagoons offers an exciting dive. Those not so equipped can still enjoy drift-snorkelling the passes. There are dive centres in Rangiroa, Fakarava and other more frequented atolls for divers who don't have their own gear or who prefer the safety and security of an organised operation.

There can be strong currents in and near the passes, which is why you see such great fish action, but which also requires a good dive plan and safety considerations. Always go at incoming tides as the water will be clearer and if there is a problem you will end up inside the lagoon in calmer waters and not out at sea! If you go at slack water (before the incoming tide) you will have little or no current at all.

In most passes there is plenty of coral and fish life to enjoy. Drift-snorkel by hanging onto the sides of the dinghy, ready to drop the anchor if you want to stay in one place. If scuba-diving, make sure you have a surface buoy and someone on watch in the dinghy. If you watch the locals you will see that even with a good current running in the pass you can find calmer areas or even countercurrents in the shallow water on the edges of the pass.

Rangiroa is well worth all the hype and publicity that it receives and Tiputa Pass lives up to its reputation as a world-class dive site. Experienced divers should do the drift-dive in the pass with a local dive operator for more safety and fun. Tiputa Pass can have some wild conditions; strong countercurrents, overfalls, whirlpools. You can expect to see dolphins, manta rays, all types of sharks, Napoleon wrasse, turtles, maybe a marlin or swordfish and tons of fish in a swirling current.

The diving in the south pass of Fakarava Atoll is less hair-raising than Tiputa Pass in Rangi, but is a fun and exciting dive all the same. Expect to see sharks, groupers, maybe a giant moray and plenty of predatory schools of jackfish. The dive centre has some buoyed sites outside the pass to enjoy an underwater vista of coral and reef.

There is also excellent drift-diving and snorkelling at Makemo, Tahanea, Faaite and Raraka. At Anse Amyot on Toau there are two families that have been welcoming yachts for 20 years and will show you the best sites for diving.

Jackie Lee, *Sloepmouche*

should sail a more easterly course from the Marquesas and then make their way towards Tahiti along the chain of atolls. The nearest landfall on such an easterly route from the Marquesas is Tepoto, but as it has only a fair-weather anchorage it is better to continue to Makemo, whose atoll is accessible by two passes. Sailing from there between the parallel strings of atolls, among those with reef passes are Tahanea, Katiu, Kaehi, Fakarava, Apataki and Manihi.

A similar route can also be sailed if coming from the Gambier Islands as the route from there to Tahiti intersects some of the Tuamotu Archipelago. Those who have arrived in the Gambiers from the east and missed the Marquesas can easily make a detour, the SE winds ensuring an easy ride to the Marquesas. Some of the Eastern Tuamotus straddle this direct route, such as the rarely visited Tatakoto and Pukapuka atolls, neither of which have passes into their lagoons, only anchorages in their lee.

Ever since its discovery by the outside world, Tahiti has been a favourite landfall among sailors. Over the years, Tahiti's capital Papeete, once a quiet backwater, has turned into a busy city dominated by noisy traffic that thunders along its attractive waterfront. Only a short walk from there, a glimpse of old Tahiti still survives at the vibrant daily market with its dazzling displays of vivid tropical colours on the fruit and flower stands.

There is much to see and do in Tahiti and the best time to be there is during the annual 'Heiva i Tahiti' festival, which is held from the end of June to the middle of July. This flamboyant occasion provides a unique opportunity to witness the best in traditional dancing and singing as groups of artists congregate here from all the five widely scattered archipelagos of French Polynesia.

Festivities are held at this time in all the Society Islands, from spectacular Moorea to fashionable Bora Bora. The least developed by tourism is Huahine where life moves at a tranquil pace. Huahine has some of the best preserved historic remains in the Society Islands, although the most important *marae* in all Polynesia is the sacred site on neighbouring Raiatea. This is the site of ancient Havaiki, the symbolic centre of the Polynesian triangle whose far-flung corners stretch to Rapa Nui (Easter Island), Hawaii and Aotearoa, the Land of the Long White Cloud (New Zealand). Bora Bora, once described as the most beautiful island in the world, has preserved that beauty but, as a victim of its own success, much of its previous charm has been lost. It is now time to move on in search of some still untainted Polynesian beauties.

P2 • Voyages from Mexico and California

P2a Voyages via Galapagos
P2b Voyages via the Marquesas

There are several factors which can influence the planning of a voyage from the North American mainland to the South Pacific: the point of departure, the optimum time of arrival in the tropics, future cruising plans and, ultimately, the choice of route.

Whereas a direct voyage to French Polynesia undoubtedly appeals to those who are forced to make a late start, those who have less time restraints can plan this voyage differently and may decide to sail the long way via the Galapagos although the lengthy formalities, both in advance and on arrival, could be a strong disincentive to considering a stop there.

An early start for this voyage is advisable if the intention is to arrive in French Polynesia at the start of the safe season. Rather than make an early start from California, a better solution may be to plan on spending the winter in Mexico. The winter can then be spent making your way south along the Mexican and possibly Central American coast before sailing to the Galapagos. This initial phase can even be extended by a detour to the South American mainland before sailing to the Galapagos.

By not being dependent on the Panama Canal to reach the South Pacific, voyages that start from either Mexico or California are easier to plan as the time of departure is only dictated by weather considerations. For most sailors, the aim is to reach the Marquesas as early as possible so as to be able to enjoy a full season in the tropical South Pacific, and this points to a March departure. Weather conditions at this time are usually favourable with NE winds down to the equator followed by a gradual shift to SE. The doldrums cover a relatively narrow band in the area to be crossed, with better conditions for those on a direct passage to the Marquesas than those bound for Galapagos.

As the timing of this voyage is dictated by similar parameters as for boats leaving from the Caribbean, those who intend to arrive in the Marquesas at the start of the safe season will probably reach the Galapagos at their busiest time. This may be one of the reasons why more North American sailors now choose to bypass Galapagos and sail directly to the Marquesas. The fact that a detour to the Galapagos adds nearly 3,000 miles to the overall distance is another reason why voyage P2b may be more attractive, as the distance from San Diego to the Galapagos is over 2,600 miles compared to just 2,900 miles from San Diego to the Marquesas on the direct route.

P2a Voyages via Galapagos

Recommended time: February to May

Tropical storms: June to November (Eastern North Pacific), November to May (South Pacific)

World Cruising Routes:

PT12   California and Mexico to Galapagos

PS12   Galapagos to Marquesas

Weather conditions for a southbound voyage in February and March from both California and Mexico are favourable with NE winds. Later in the year the ITCZ moves northwards and by May can be located at 10°N. The doldrums cover a relatively narrow band in the area to be crossed. South of the ITCZ the winds gradually shift to S and SE. For this reason, some easting should be made while north of the ITCZ so as to have a better sailing angle towards Galapagos, if landfall is to be made there, and even more so if going to the mainland.

Winds between the mainland and the Galapagos have a high percentage of light southerly winds, usually SW at first becoming SE closer to the islands. Such winds will continue on the subsequent passage to the Marquesas and in March and April the prevailing SE trade winds only becoming established as you move west. Often on leaving the Galapagos winds can be variable and almost give the impression of being in the doldrums.

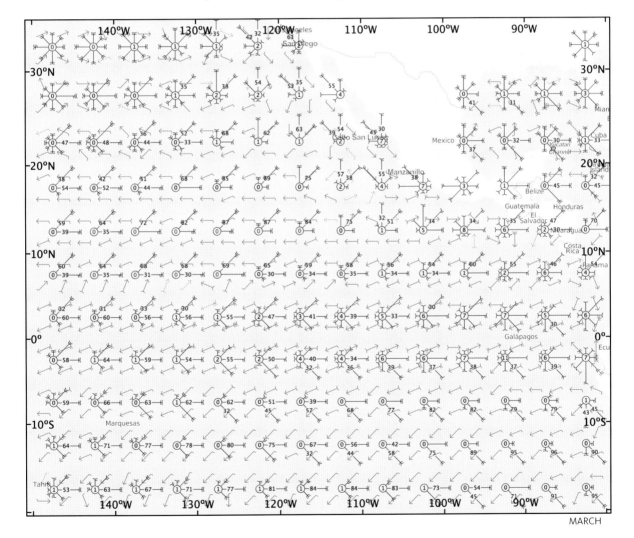

MARCH

For those who prefer to sail to the mainland first, a convenient landfall in Ecuador is Puerto Lucia Marina just north of Salinas, where the boat can be left unattended while visiting the interior. On the subsequent leg from the mainland to the Galapagos, the winds will be generally light, usually from SW at first, becoming SE closer to the islands.

As one of the most important nature reserves in the world, the Ecuadorian authorities have imposed certain restrictions on the movement of visiting yachts which must clear into one of the two ports of entry, Baquerizo Moreno on San Cristobal and Puerto Ayora on Santa Cruz Island. For more details on Galapagos and the subsequent passage to the Marquesas see Voyage P1a.

P2b Voyages via the Marquesas

Recommended time: March to May

Tropical storms: June to November (Eastern North Pacific), November to May (South Pacific)

World Cruising Routes:

PT15	California to Marquesas and Tahiti
PT18	Mexico and Central America to Marquesas
PS22	Marquesas to Tuamotus and Tahiti

Weather conditions for a southbound voyage in February and March from both California and Mexico are favourable with NE winds down to around latitudes 5°N or 7°N which is the northern limit of the ITCZ in March. The situation is similar in April, with consistent NE winds ensuring a thrilling start. The crossing of the doldrums should present no great problem, especially for those prepared to motor through this area as quickly as possible.

An interesting stop for boats leaving from Mexico is the uninhabited Clipperton Atoll lying about 700 miles off the Mexican coast. The lagoon of this tiny territory administered by France is not accessible, but there is a good anchorage in its lee and diving enthusiasts will be rewarded by the opportunity to dive at such an unspoilt and little frequented site.

Once across the equator, SE winds should establish themselves between 3°S and 5°S, from where a direct course can be set for your destination. Although Taiohae on the island of Nuku Hiva has a better anchorage, and better facilities generally, than Atunoa on Hiva Oa, the latter should be preferred as a landfall as it lies to windward of most other Marquesan islands thus making it the logical point to start a cruise among those spectacular islands. The popular island of Fatu Hiva is not a port of entry and therefore a first landfall in French Polynesia should not be planned there.

P3 • Voyages from US West Coast

P3a Voyages via Galapagos
P3b Voyages via the Marquesas

Those who plan a voyage to Tahiti from anywhere north of Southern California have a choice between taking the more commonly sailed route by way of the Marquesas or the less frequented alternative via Hawaii. Each has certain points in its favour, the Marquesas option being more direct and shorter both in miles and time. Breaking up this voyage into separate segments will greatly simplify its planning and also make it more enjoyable. The other option is to sail to Hawaii the previous season which means that the passage can take place at the best of times and the coming winter can be spent enjoying Hawaii's mild winter climate. An alternative is to leave the boat there, return home and resume the voyage the following season. A similar arrangement can be made by those who would rather not make an early start from California but prefer to spend the winter in Mexico.

The decision as to which route to take may also be influenced by the fact that neither the favourable seasons in the two hemispheres nor the optimum passage times can easily be matched to ensure an arrival in the South Pacific at the start of the safe cruising season. This does not apply so much to voyages that start from Southern California, as to those from the Pacific Northwest. In the latter case, an arrival in French Polynesia at the start of the safe sailing season, April in the Marquesas or May in Tahiti, entails a late winter or early spring departure when sailing conditions in the North Pacific can still be rough. If an early arrival in the South Pacific is a high priority, the voyage needs to be planned differently by sailing to Southern California, Mexico or Hawaii during the previous season, and thus be in a better place to embark on the subsequent passage to the South Pacific as soon as conditions are right.

P3a Voyages via Galapagos

Recommended time: February to May

Tropical storms: June to November (Eastern North Pacific), November to May (South Pacific)

World Cruising Routes:

PT12	California and Mexico to Galapagos
PS12	Galapagos to Marquesas

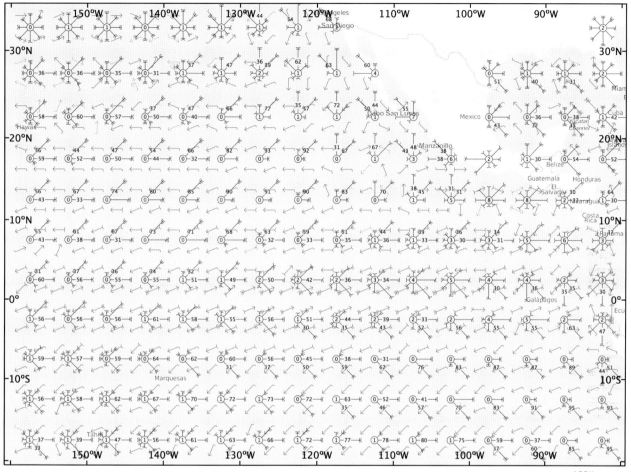

APRIL

An early departure from the Pacific Northwest is essential for those who intend to both visit Galapagos and arrive in French Polynesia not long after the start of the favourable season. Weather conditions for a southbound voyage in early spring can be rough and any improvement can only be expected south of latitude 40°N, or even further south. Later departures can count on better conditions but in either case consistent favourable winds will only be found south of 30°N. From there, NE winds will ensure a fast passage down to the ITCZ, which in late spring is located around latitude 5°–7°N. The doldrums cover a relatively narrow band in the area to be crossed. South of the ITCZ the winds gradually shift to S and SE. For this reason, some easting should be made while north of the ITCZ to ensure a better sailing angle towards the Galapagos or the mainland.

Voyages to the Galapagos from Northern California and the Pacific Northwest may find it difficult to make

the necessary easting to the Galapagos and may therefore find a direct passage to the Marquesas more appealing. This option should be considered, especially by those who are forced to leave later in the season and therefore wish to reach French Polynesia as quickly as possible. Those who do not have such time restraints can plan their voyage differently and may conclude that calling at the Galapagos Islands and possibly the mainland justifies the long detour.

A popular solution among those who have the time is to forgo the problems of an early start as described above and spend the winter in Mexico. In this case the first stage of the voyage can commence with a passage from California to Mexico in early November soon after the end of the hurricane season in the Eastern North Pacific. In November, the winds off the coast of California have a strong northerly component and are favourable for the passage to Mexico. The winter can be spent making your way south along the Mexican and possibly Central American coasts before sailing to the Galapagos or the South American mainland. For more details on the Galapagos and the subsequent passage to the Marquesas see voyage P1a.

P3b Voyages via the Marquesas

Recommended time: March to May

Tropical storms: June to November (Eastern North Pacific), November to May (South Pacific)

World Cruising Routes:

PT17	Pacific Northwest to Marquesas
PT15	California to Marquesas and Tahiti
PT18	Mexico and Central America to Marquesas
PS22	Marquesas to Tuamotus and Tahiti

An early departure from the Pacific Northwest, as dictated by the need to arrive in the Marquesas at the start of the

cruising season, may not be an attractive prospect as winter weather conditions still prevail in those latitudes. Whereas strong N and NW winds predominate in March, there is also a considerable percentage of winds from other directions and this may call for a different approach, as mentioned earlier: either to leave later, and thereby arrive in the Marquesas well into the cruising season, or move south earlier and start the voyage from a more propitious place.

Conditions on a direct passage from the Pacific Northwest to the Marquesas in March only become comfortable south of 30°N from where winds between north and east are a constant feature almost as far as the equator, with SE winds becoming gradually more prevalent further south. The point where the equator should be crossed is a perennial matter of debate but what is agreed is that it must not be further west than 120°W or

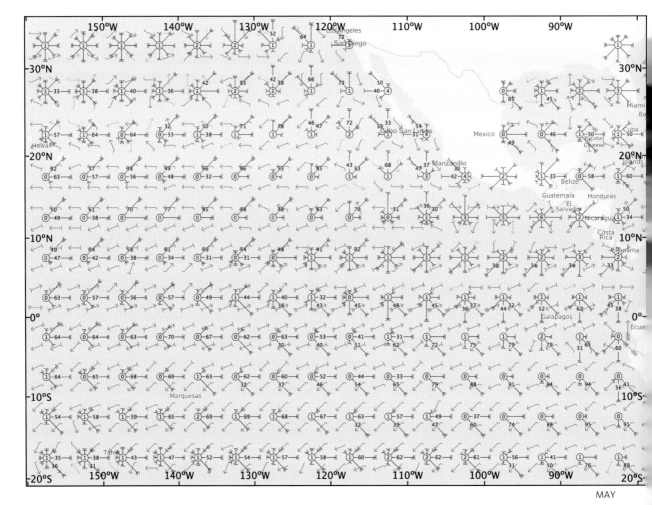

MAY

the SE winds may turn out to be too close for comfort in the approaches to the Marquesas, so it is better to err on the side of caution and switch hemispheres further east. A more easterly crossing point is certainly advisable if the intention is to make landfall at Atuona on the island of Hiva Oa.

Once across the equator, SE winds become fully established between 3°S and 5°S, from where a direct course can be set for your destination. Coming from the northeast, although Taiohae on the island of Nuku Hiva may look more convenient as it is closer, has a better anchorage and also more facilities than Atunoa on Hiva Oa, the latter should be the preferred landfall as it lies to windward of most other Marquesan islands and makes a better place to start a cruise among the islands. One of the most popular anchorages is the sheltered bay at Hanavave on the easternmost island of Fatu Hiva, an amphitheatre of soaring peaks which dwarf the boats moored at their feet. Towering peaks and a wild mountainous interior are the hallmarks of Ua Pou, while at Ua Huka a deep inlet flanked by sheer black walls leads to the main settlement at Vaipape. As the setting of Herman Melville's *Typee*, Nuku Hiva abounds in ancient sites and inspired that gripping adventure story based on the author's stay on the island.

P4 • Voyages from Hawaii

P4a Direct voyages

P4b Voyages via the Line Islands

P4c Voyages via the Marquesas

There are three options for this southbound voyage: to sail nonstop to Tahiti, or to go via either the Marquesas or Line Islands. From Hawaii, NE winds will ensure a fast passage as far as the ITCZ, which is normally located between 4°N and 6°N, immediately to the north of the Line Islands. SE winds are a predominant feature south of the equator and it is therefore advisable to make some easting before that point is reached so as to have a better sailing angle towards Tahiti. As the Line Islands are located almost on the direct course, stopping there can be very tempting even if that might result in a tighter sailing angle on the leg to Tahiti. An alternative, which is gaining popularity with southbound boats, is to sail from Hawaii to the Marquesas rather than directly to Tahiti. Such a detour provides the opportunity to visit those islands as well as the Tuamotus and ensures a better sailing angle for the subsequent passage to Tahiti

P4a Direct voyages

Recommended time: April to May

Tropical storms: June to November (Eastern North Pacific), November to May (South Pacific)

World Cruising Routes:

  PT24 Hawaii to Tahiti and Marquesas

Although this passage can be sailed at any time during the South Pacific winter months, the possibility of a North Pacific hurricane after June means that the safest time to sail south is at the recommended time. This statement needs clarification as an April arrival is only suggested for the Line Islands, Tahiti only being considered to be safe from May onwards.

A direct passage to Tahiti should pass well to the east of the Line Islands, the necessary easting being easily made with the help of the prevailing NE winds which blow consistently south of Hawaii. In April and May, the doldrums will be met around latitude 5°N, from where SE winds will gradually take over, hence the suggestion to gain some ground to the east while north of the ITCZ.

APRIL

P4b Voyages via the Line Islands

Recommended time: April to May

Tropical storms: June to November (Eastern North Pacific), November to May (South Pacific)

World Cruising Routes:
   PN35   Hawaii to Line Islands

Those who prefer to stop at the Line Islands will have steady NE winds as far as the ITCZ, whose northen limit at that time of year is on the latitude of Palmyra Island. These easternmost islands of Micronesia are conveniently placed for a break in the journey and worth the detour even if this may result in a more difficult onward passage to Tahiti. The first possible stop is Palmyra Island, once an important refuelling stop for transpacific flights and now a nature reserve under US jurisdiction with Nature Conservancy scientists usually based there. Permission to visit the atoll must be obtained from the US Fish and Wildlife Service before leaving Hawaii. Since 2009 Palmyra has been part of the Pacific Remote Islands

Marine National Monument, which includes several other uninhabited islands protected for their unique environment.

The other Line Islands are outposts of Kiribati and visiting sailors are warmly welcomed by their isolated communities. Among them, Fanning is the favourite stop as it has a well-protected lagoon accessible through a pass. Christmas Island (now Kiritimati), the main island of the group, was used as a weapons testing ground in the 1950s and, even after all these years, the island is still littered with decaying hardware. The route to Tahiti continues close to the Southern Line Islands of Malden, Vostok, Caroline and Flint. All are uninhabited, with Malden having suffered a similar fate to Christmas, scattered with rusting fuel drums and military vehicles, which nature is slowly reclaiming. Each of them has an anchorage in its lee suitable for a stop in settled weather.

P4c Voyages via the Marquesas

Recommended time: April to May

Tropical storms: June to November (Eastern North Pacific), November to May (South Pacific)

World Cruising Routes:
   PT24   Hawaii to Tahiti and Marquesas
   PS22   Marquesas to Tuamotus and Tahiti

As in the case of direct passages to Tahiti, for boats bound for the Marquesas it is even more important to make enough easting while sailing with the NE winds of the North Pacific to be able to cope later with the consistent SE winds which prevail south of the equator. There are two different approaches to make the necessary easting: one is to sail right from the start as close to the wind as possible and thus be able to cross the equator far enough to the east to ensure a good sailing angle to the Marquesas, the other is to sail as fast as you can go to the northern limit of the ITCZ and make the easting just north of the equator. The latter approach is quite a gamble and should only be done if you are confident that making your easting in that way will not be even more trouble than being hard on the wind. In any case, the equator should not be crossed before meridian 140°W has been reached but, depending on the state of the winds south of the equator and the windward going capabilities of your boat, it may be necessary to continue as far east as 130°W before crossing the Line.

The main island of Nuku Hiva, with its picturesque and well-sheltered bay of Taiohae, is the easiest landfall, but it has the disadvantage that it lies to leeward of all the other Marquesan islands. Rather than beating to windward from Nuku Hiva to visit the rest of the

MAY

Marquesas, it would be much easier to make the necessary easting earlier and attempt to make landfall at Atuona on Hiva Oa, the easternmost port of entry and thus the best start for a Marquesas cruise. Besides their outstanding beauty, each island has something interesting to offer, be it Fatu Hiva's spectacular Hanavave Bay, Ua Pou's wild interior overlooked by its distinctive rocky spires, or Nuku Hiva's ancient sites hidden in the moist and brooding jungle.

The onward voyage to Tahiti can be sailed nonstop, but that is rarely done as the Tuamotus lie invitingly across the direct route. Most atolls have a pass into their lagoons and the easiest accessible ones, and those closest to the direct route to Tahiti, are Manihi, Ahe and Rangiroa. Those who are interested in visiting some of the more remote atolls should sail a more easterly course from the Marquesas and start their Tuamotu cruise closer to the eastern end of the archipelago. The luxury of GPS, radar and forward-looking sonar has greatly minimised the earlier risks, but navigation in that area is still far from easy and demands constant attention. Access to the inner lagoons of some of the atolls can be an exhilarating experience due to the swift currents racing through the narrow passes.

Coming from the Marquesas, Amanu Atoll makes an interesting first landfall as it had the first recorded European visitor: the navigator Pedro Fernández de Quirós who stumbled upon it in 1606 during his search for the mysterious southern continent of Terra Australis. Several 16th century Spanish cannons were found on Amanu in recent years indicating that an earlier Spanish vessel had been wrecked there, possibly the caravel *San Lesmes* which was one of seven ships taking part in the second round the world voyage in 1526. In the intervening years, many other explorers have discovered the Tuamotus this hard way, among them the *Kon-Tiki* raft in which the Norwegian Thor Heyerdahl attempted to prove that South American people could have sailed to Polynesia in pre-Columbian times. *Kon-Tiki* ended her days on the reef of Raroia Atoll in 1947 and in spite of Heyerdahl's theory being shown later to have been mistaken, the story of the international expedition is one of the best adventure stories ever written.

Sailing on towards Tahiti, along the parallel chains of atolls, some of those with passes through their reef are Makemo, Tahanea, Katiu, Kaehi, Fakarava, Apataki and Manihi. Papeete itself, the capital and main port of Tahiti, is also accessible through a reef pass which leads into the sheltered harbour where the visitors' dock fronts the city's main promenade. Modern Papeete may not feel like the dreamy place which seduced countless sailors over the ages, but don't be fooled by first appearances as much of the true Polynesian spirit is still alive and only waiting to be discovered. Never is there a better time for that than during the 'Heiva i Tahiti' festival, an extravagant festival of dance, music and arts held every year from the end of June to the middle of July.

P5 • Voyages from South America

P5a Voyages via Galapagos
P5b Voyages via Easter Island

There are two major routes from South America to Tahiti and the choice depends primarily on the point of departure. For voyages which originate north of Peru the traditional route via Galapagos and the Marquesas is the obvious way to go. For those who are starting off from a more southern place, or who are looking for a more interesting way to reach French Polynesia, the southern route via Easter Island provides a highly attractive alternative by calling not only at that fascinating Polynesian outpost but also at remote Pitcairn Island and the rarely visited Gambier Islands.

Weather conditions along both routes at the recommended times are generally favourable and, as there are no tropical cyclones at Easter Island and the risk is low at both Pitcairn and Gambier, this route can be sailed earlier than the northern alternative thus making it possible to arrive in French Polynesia at the very beginning of the safe season. Although the earliest recommended time for sailing this route is given as March, this applies for the entire area and in fact conditions in January or February would be equally favourable for those who decide to sail both to the Galapagos and Easter Island, provided the time of arrival in French Polynesia coincides with the start of the safe season there.

P5a Voyages via Galapagos

Recommended time: Late March to May

Tropical storms: November to May

World Cruising Routes:

PS11	Ecuador to Galapagos
PS12	Galapagos to Marquesas
PS22	Marquesas to Tuamotus and Tahiti
PS13	Galapagos to Easter and Gambier Islands
PS28	Gambier Islands to Tuamotus and Tahiti

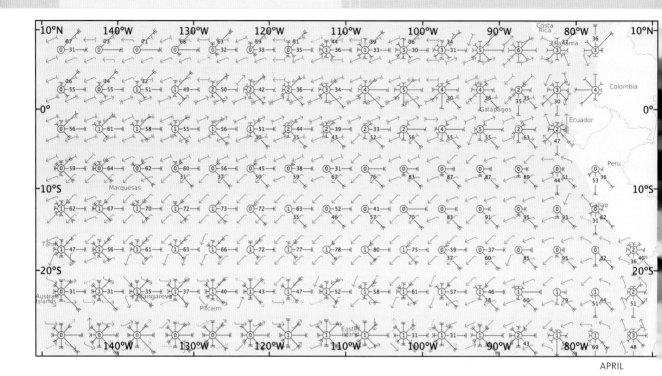

APRIL

The usual route from Galapagos to Tahiti is part of the main arterial route that cuts across the entire South Pacific and is by far the most travelled route south of the equator. (See P1 voyages.) While the Galapagos are a destination that few wish to miss, there are other alternatives continuing from Galapagos that are well worth considering. The simplest alternative, and one which is surprisingly very little sailed, is a direct passage to the Gambier Islands, the small archipelago located on the SE fringe of French Polynesia. Favourable winds prevail in April all the way to the Gambiers and also down to the latitude of Easter Island, so voyages to any of these remote destinations can be confidently planned (see P1c).

The population of the Gambier Islands has shrunk to a few hundred people, most living in the main settlement at Rikitea, on Mangareva. Spending a few days here is a perfect introduction to the way of life of a small Pacific community in the modern age. The onward voyage to Tahiti can be sailed nonstop or some of the Tuamotus can be visited en route (see P1d).

P5b Voyages via Easter Island

Recommended time: February to May

Tropical storms: November to May (Western South Pacific)

World Cruising Routes:

PS14	Ecuador to Peru and Chile
PS15	South America to Easter Island
PS18	Northbound from Chile
PS16	Westbound from Easter Island
PS28	Gambier Islands to Tuamotus and Tahiti

A voyage from the South American mainland to Tahiti along this southern route may be more challenging than its northern equivalent, but it has its rewards. The mystery that surrounds Easter Island and its original inhabitants is a perennial source of wonderment and there are few places in the entire world that can match the excitement of making landfall there on your own boat. Two very different routes lead from the mainland to Easter Island, one sailed by boats coming from the north, whether directly from a continental port or the Galapagos Islands, the other by boats that have been cruising Southern Chile. Those who sail the former have the choice of either reaching Easter Island by an offshore route or taking the inshore route south from Panama and calling at the various countries along that coast, a perfect opportunity to also explore some of their interior.

Weather conditions along the coastal route are benign throughout the year, with light S and SE winds and the north-setting Humboldt Current, so you should expect to cover some of it under power. Peru's main port, Callao, close to the capital Lima, is a convenient base to explore the interior, and the boat can be left at Yacht Club Peruano. This is also a good place to prepare for the passage to Easter Island.

Those who arrive from Southern Chile, can either sail directly to Easter Island or take the longer route by calling at the Juan Fernández Islands. This small archipelago is known mainly for having been the temporary home of a Scottish castaway named Alexander Selkirk, who was the inspiration for Daniel Defoe's novel *Robinson Crusoe*. Both the real and fictional castaway have islands named after them, with the main settlement of a few hundred people living on Robinson Crusoe Island.

Whether stopping at those islands or sailing the shortest route from Chile to Easter Island, some northing needs to be made to reach the area of SE trade winds which, in the austral summer months, extend as far as 30°S and occasionally even farther south. Those same winds will be a constant companion from Easter Island onwards, to Pitcairn, Gambier and all the way to Tahiti.

As one of the most remote and isolated places on the planet, Easter Island is fully exposed to the elements, one of its three alternative anchorages providing adequate protection in all but the worst conditions.

The next port of call, Pitcairn, is a lasting proof of the irresistible power of seduction that the South Seas and its people have exerted on visitors ever since the arrival of the first outsiders. The most famous victims, the *Bounty* mutineers, chose this tiny island as their secret refuge and the few yachts that call are warmly welcomed by the small community made up almost entirely of the direct descendants of the rebellious members of Captain Bligh's crew. Occasionally the Pitcairners ask a visiting yacht to take a few of them to Henderson Island to collect wood for the carvings which they sell to passing ships. It is a good way to help these people and also to visit this uninhabited island. Henderson has been declared a world heritage site due to its unique flora. Also part of the Pitcairn group is the similarly uninhabited Ducie Island, which over the centuries has provided shelter to various shipwrecked crews.

The closest of French Polynesia's five island groups, the Gambier Islands, are only a short distance from Pitcairn. It is in the Gambiers that a decision needs to be made as to which of the four route options to take to

Tahiti: to carry on nonstop to Tahiti, sail through the Tuamotus, turn right for the Marquesas or left for the Australs. The Tuamotus are so close to the direct route to Tahiti that stopping at some of the more accessible atolls of the once feared Dangerous Archipelago can easily be done. Similarly, the Outer Tuamotus make an interesting stop for those who choose to sail from the Gambiers to the Marquesas. The isolated Austral Islands are rarely visited by cruising boats as they lie off the usual sailing routes but their very remoteness is their main attraction.

While weather conditions are on the whole favourable on these long passages, unfortunately the same cannot be said about local conditions and the anchorages at all these islands are precarious and should not be trusted, hence the rule imposed by the port captain at Easter Island that boats must not be left unattended and one crew member should remain on board while the others are visiting ashore. Fortunately all islands have alternative anchorages that offer some protection if you are forced to abandon the main anchorage at Hanga Roa.

P6 • Voyages from Australia and New Zealand

Recommended time: May to July

Tropical storms: November to May

World Cruising Routes:
PS91   New South Wales to New Zealand
PS67   New Zealand to Tahiti

Eastbound voyages from Australia are never easy on account of the prevailing E and SE winds, and, for a cruising boat, sailing all the way to Tahiti along a tropical route is virtually impossible. The only reasonable solution is to plan a voyage along a route in higher latitudes where there is a good chance of encountering favourable winds. For most voyages, and certainly for those starting in New South Wales, this means an intermediate stop in New Zealand. This applies not just to voyages bound for Tahiti but also for nearer destinations, such as Fiji or Tonga. A passage across the Tasman Sea to North Island during the recommended period will probably encounter some mixed conditions but with a higher percentage of southerly winds. This passage can be undertaken at virtually any time of the year as tropical cyclones do not reach that far south, although their effects may be felt. The continuation of the voyage from New Zealand will not fare much better unless the course dips south into the area of prevailing westerly winds.

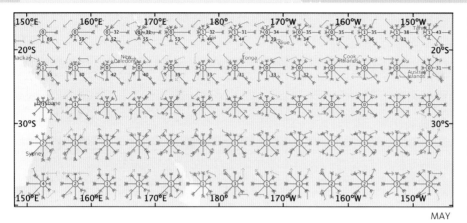

MAY

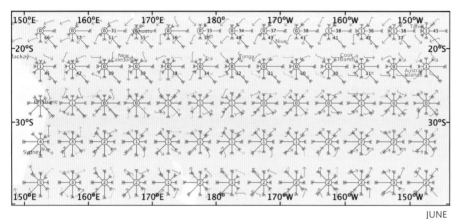

JUNE

at the time and this is certainly one area where access to weather forecasts can make a great difference.

With the cyclone season in the South Pacific only ending in May, the earliest time for this passage is late April or May and as that is the late austral autumn, the possibility of encountering strong or even gale force winds in those latitudes cannot be discounted. In spite of that, the temptation should be resisted to turn north too soon, and ideally the point where this happens should not be before the longitude of your destination has been reached. For voyages bound for Tahiti, that point is usually the Austral Islands as by then enough easting has been made to benefit from a good sailing angle for the final leg to Tahiti. Tubuai makes a good landfall, as it is the main island of the group and has the best amenities.

Voyages between New Zealand and the rest of Polynesia have a long history and even if most of them were only one-way there must have been some in the opposite direction as well. About 800 years ago, the original Polynesian settlers of New Zealand sailed their double-hulled canoes from their ancestral home Havaiki, located in today's Cook or Society Islands. It is believed that they made several return voyages to bring more settlers to their new home which they called Aotearoa, the land of the long white cloud. How the Polynesian navigators managed to sail back to their original home is a mystery, although they may have used the current tactic of making their easting with the help of the predominantly westerly winds of higher latitudes before turning north for their desired destination. This is indeed the accepted way to reach the islands of Eastern Polynesia and therefore the first stage of a voyage to Tahiti should be sailed along the latitude of departure where, between latitudes 35°S and 38°S, there is a good chance of finding westerly winds. How far south you should go in search of those westerlies before straying into the Roaring Forties depends on weather conditions

from a good sailing angle for the final leg to Tahiti. Tubuai makes a good landfall, as it is the main island of the group and has the best amenities.

Those who wish to see more of these remote islands should continue on their easterly heading to Rapa, the southernmost inhabited island of the group, and of French Polynesia generally. Lying on almost the same latitude as Rapa Nui (Great Rapa, now known as Easter Island), with which it shares its Polynesian name, Rapa has its own unsolved mystery, a series of hillside forts whose origin has never been explained. Having made landfall that far south, some of the other Australs can be visited on the way to Tahiti, such as Raivavae, where the damp fern forests and grey skies of Rapa give way to a beautiful lagoon and palm trees. You feel at once that you have arrived in the tropics. From the Australs the prevailing SE trade winds should ensure a fast reach to Tahiti. May is a good time to undertake this voyage as by that time the cyclone season should be over and arriving in Tahiti so early in the safe season ensures up to five months of carefree tropical cruising.

New Zealand to Tahiti

I've made the trip from New Zealand to Tahiti seven times, with landfalls in the Australs at Raivavae, Tubuai and Rurutu, and this first leg has almost always been difficult. The trick is to wait in Auckland until a frontal passage occurs, and head SE down to around 40°S to try and find westerlies. Sometimes the passage has been better, and occasionally worse. It is always our most popular leg, and our crew were ecstatic that it was so rough and difficult.

Well, this year has been different. The weather appeared much too pleasant for the Southern Ocean with spinnaker flying, no foul-weather gear needed on deck and a visit from two swallows so, to make conditions more challenging, the SPCZ has dropped in between us and Rurutu. It's covering a large area and the GRIB files and Commanders' Weather forecasts indicate winds of 25–35 gusts over 40 knots and seas to 16 feet. Fortunately the wind is not directly on our

bow. We've slightly eased sheets and have been consistently averaging 150–170 miles per day even though the seas are rough and confused. For two days as wind speeds built the crew received plenty of mainsail reefing and unreefing experience until stronger winds dictated leaving the third reef in the main and using the furling headsail for further sail reductions. The conditions in the cockpit are OK but every once in a while a real doozy of a wave comes over the top of the dodger to wake up the cockpit watch.

Our landfall in Rurutu really made it worthwhile. The gendarmes had never had a yacht arrive during their one and a half years there and hadn't a clue on how to check us in! There are still places like that left, which I find gratifying to know. If anything, I sense less interest among today's cruisers to visit difficult-to-get-to places.

John Neal, *Mahina Tiare III*

P7 • Voyages from East Asia and Japan

P7a Voyages via Hawaii
P7b Voyages via Micronesia

It has now been established that the Polynesian islands were settled by people who originated in present-day Taiwan and sailed their double-hulled canoes to Samoa, Tahiti and as far away as Easter Island. Those amazing feats of navigation are a source of deserved admiration by anyone following in their wake, and attempting to replicate a voyage to any of those destinations in a modern yacht shows just how skilled and resourceful those ancient mariners must have been.

There are two alternative ways to sail from East Asia to Tahiti, a northern route via Japan, and a southern route via Micronesia. The timing of a voyage along either of these routes points to an April or early May departure which both minimises the risk of encountering a typhoon west of the dateline, and ensures an arrival in Tahiti at the best time to start a cruise in the South Pacific.

P7a Voyages via Hawaii

Recommended time: April to May

Tropical storms: All year (Western North Pacific), June to November (Eastern North Pacific), November to May (South Pacific)

World Cruising Routes:
> PN63   Routes to Japan and Korea
> PN75   Japan to Hawaii
> PT24   Hawaii to Tahiti and Marquesas

Although tropical storms can occur throughout the year in the North Pacific west of 180°, the critical period is between June and October with the highest frequency of storms in August and September. As presumably the aim of this voyage is to reach Tahiti at the beginning of the safe season in the South Pacific (late May, early June), the timing of this voyage can easily be adjusted to coincide with the most favourable periods in both hemispheres. The passage from the mainland to Japan can be planned for the changeover period between the NE monsoon of winter and the SW monsoon of summer.

The onward voyage from Japan can be undertaken by a roundabout route via Hawaii or the more direct route via Micronesia. The main disadvantage of the Hawaii

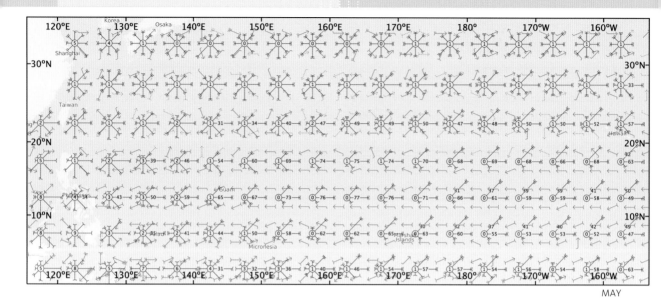

MAY

alternative is the high percentage of E and NE winds at all times of the year, which makes this a rather uncomfortable passage even for a boat that sails well to windward. The possible way to avoid that is to make sufficient easting in high latitudes, where there is a high percentage of westerly winds, until a point is arrived at from where Tahiti can be reached on a better sailing angle. From Hawaii, the rest of the voyage can be accomplished either via the Line or Marquesan islands as described in voyage P4.

A possibly more attractive solution is to forgo Hawaii and turn south from Japan for Micronesia, as outlined in the following voyage. An even more radical alternative is to expand this voyage into a pan-Pacific voyage by staying in high latitudes and sailing to Alaska and the west coast of North America and reach French Polynesia by that roundabout way, a challenging but highly rewarding undertaking which is the object of voyage PC7b (page 254).

⬤ P7b Voyages via Micronesia

Recommended time: April–May

Tropical storms: All year (Western North Pacific), November to May (South Pacific)

World Cruising Routes:

PN62	Routes to the Philippines
PN76	Japan to Eastern Micronesia
PN45	Singapore to North Borneo
PN55	Philippines to Palau
PN81	Eastbound routes
PT24	Hawaii to Tahiti and Marquesas

The difficulties associated with the previous voyage can be partially avoided by heading south from Japan in the hope of finding better conditions in the tropics. The same is also true for voyages originating on the Asian mainland as eastbound voyages from anywhere south of Hong Kong are encumbered at all times by the prevailing NE winds. The alternative in both those cases is a route via Micronesia. Although the prevailing winds throughout Micronesia are also from NE, the light winds just north of the equator combined with an east-setting current would make it possible to achieve the required easting.

Regardless of the point of departure, the main priority is to reach the lower latitudes as soon as possible as it is only there that the necessary easting can be made with any certainty. For voyages originating in East Asia the shortest route leads across the Philippines to Palau and continues in a SE direction. Voyages originating in Southeast Asia and Singapore should take a route that passes north of Borneo and south of the Philippines. From there, the shortest route should be sailed to the Line Islands as that is the nearest point to cross the equator and ensure a good chance of a reasonable sailing angle across the SE trade winds on the subsequent leg to Tahiti. The temptation to cross the equator further west should be resisted at all cost and as much easting as possible should be made while still north of the equator. Those who prefer to visit the Marquesas first should continue east past the Line Islands. While not easy, this can be best achieved just north of the equator, approximately in the latitude of the Line Islands which coincides with the ITCZ at that time of year. The light winds, which are typical of this area, combined with the east-setting counterequatorial current provide the right conditions to gain precious ground in the right direction. At certain times along this route, the use of the engine to make progress may be the only solution, so sufficient fuel should be carried for this eventuality.

On the positive side, this potentially slow passage offers the opportunity to make landfall in a number of places that are off the usual cruising track, such as Palau and several of the more remote Caroline Islands. Other island groups which straddle or are close to this route are Kiribati and the Line Islands. The northernmost Line Island is Palmyra, a nature reserve under US administration, where brief stops are allowed provided permission for this has been requested in advance. The other islands belong to Kiribati and permission to stop at any of them is usually granted on arrival by the local authorities.

From the Northern Line Islands the route to Tahiti passes close to the Southern Line Islands of Malden, Vostok, Caroline and Flint, all of which are uninhabited. Each has an anchorage in its lee suitable for stops in settled weather.

Cruising hubs

Galapagos *
The attractions of this popular landfall do not extend to its facilities for visiting yachts which are barely adequate. The open anchorage at Puerto Ayora, the islands' main centre, is overcrowded with local boats, whereas the anchorage at Baquerizo Moreno is safer and also less crowded. Repair facilities are basic, fuel is usually available and provisioning is reasonable. Medical facilities can also be only described as adequate. There are frequent flights from the two main ports to Guayaquil and Quito with onward connections to neighbouring capitals, as well as destinations in the USA and to a number of European destinations.

Easter Island *
The government workshop can deal with emergency repairs and there are docking facilities offering limited shelter at Hanga Piku. Hanga Roa Hospital is well equipped and can deal with medical emergencies. Lan Chile operates regular flights to Santiago de Chile and Tahiti.

Nuku Hiva *
Taiohae, the main settlement in the Marquesas, has a limited range of repair facilities and a haul-out arrangement that can be used in emergencies. Provisions and fuel are available and medical facilities are good.

There are daily flights to Tahiti's international airport (PPT) with onward connections to Paris, the USA, New Zealand and South America.

Kiritimati *
Facilities in the administrative centre of the Line Islands, formerly known as Christmas Island, are very basic and so is the range of provisions. Fuel is available but only in small quantities. The local airport (CXI) operates flights to Tarawa, the capital of Kiribati, with onward connections to Australia, Fiji and Hawaii.

Tahiti ****
The capital of French Polynesia has greatly improved its yachting facilities, with good repair services and haul-out arrangements. Provisioning is very good, fuel is easily available and the general hospital has the best services of any Pacific island. Papeete international airport (PPT) has flights to the USA, Europe and Australasia provided by Air France and Air New Zealand, and to South America with Lan Chile.

San Diego ****
San Diego has several marinas, a wide range of repair and haulout facilities, as well as good marine supplies. San Diego airport (SAN) has flights to many US destinations, Mexico and also London.

What next?

Tahiti and her islands may be associated in most people's minds with the South Seas but many more of that area's attractions are to be found in the islands that lie farther west. Straddling the arterial route that runs from Tahiti to the Torres Strait are a number of distinct island groups, each of them a cruising destination in its own right. Therefore a painful dilemma faced by anyone setting off from Tahiti is where to call and what to leave out. The choices start right on leaving Bora Bora, where you have the option to either turn left, and visit the Southern Cooks and Southern Tonga, or turn right for the Northern Cooks, Niue, Northern Tonga and Samoa.

For many sailors Tahiti is only an intermediate point on a longer transpacific or round the world voyage, and therefore they may need to plan for a departure from Tahiti in late June or early July so as to have enough time to visit some of those other islands en route.

Northbound voyages are invariably destined for Hawaii and most of those who undertake them are North American sailors on their way home. Later in the season,

Aventura I sailing past Pitcairn.

with the threat of the approaching cyclone season, some boats set off for Hawaii to spend the austral summer there and return to Tahiti the following year in May to resume their cruise. This is a relatively new trend which makes sense for those who do not wish to stay in Tahiti during the cyclone season or rush west to New Zealand or Australia to spend the season there. There are, in fact, several places in French Polynesia where the boat can be left unattended during the cyclone season, both on the island of Tahiti itself, at a boatyard in Raiatea, and also at Apatiki in the Tuamotus.

East and southbound voyages from Tahiti are less common because of the contrary winds but that still does not deter some hardy sailors from undertaking them. Those who plan to sail to Panama have the alternative of sailing to the Marquesas, crossing the equator and making their easting by motorsailing within the doldrums, or heading south via the Australs into the area of prevailing westerly winds and then making their way gradually north to Panama. The same southerly route can be sailed to the the South Atlantic by continuing to Southern Chile or even around Cape Horn. The famous French sailor Bernard Moitessier sailed that very route nonstop from Tahiti to France in 1966. He wrote about his epic voyage in *Cape Horn: The Logical Route*, a description that some cruising sailors may not entirely agree with.

Voyages to Fiji

Fiji is at the crossroads of the South Pacific where all major cruising routes converge, with the majority of boats arriving from the east or south. Fewer boats arrive from other directions, although in recent years some boats have sailed to Fiji directly from Hawaii or Asia in pursuit of less travelled routes and destinations. Because of its strategic location Fiji is also the place where sailors are often forced to make a realistic reassessment of their voyage, their careful timing having been sabotaged by the rich temptations of the South Seas.

P8 • Voyages from Tahiti

Recommended time: June to October

Tropical storms: November to May

World Cruising Routes:

PS31	Society Islands to Cook Islands
PS32	Society Islands to Tonga
PS41	Tonga to Fiji
PS45	Samoa to Fiji

This voyage can be planned for any time during the safe season, its timing depending primarily on your plans after Fiji. An earlier arrival, in July or early August, is advisable if the intention is to continue west towards the Torres Strait into the South Indian Ocean, which should be crossed not later than October. A slightly later arrival is acceptable for a subsequent voyage to Southeast Asia and the North Indian Ocean, with a transit through the Torres

Suwarrow Atoll.

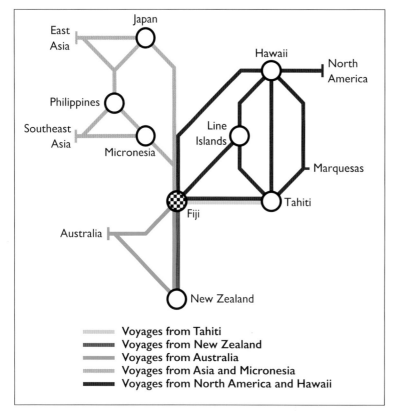

Legend:
- Voyages from Tahiti
- Voyages from New Zealand
- Voyages from Australia
- Voyages from Asia and Micronesia
- Voyages from North America and Hawaii

Strait in late September or early October. Those who plan to spend the cyclone season in the South Pacific, whether outside the tropics or in Fiji itself, can arrive in Fiji as late as October. These suggested arrival times are also valid for arrivals from other points of departure.

Westbound voyages from Tahiti can be undertaken through out the safe season and while sailing conditions are generally favourable, much of the area to be crossed is under the influence of the SPCZ, which is more active during the austral summer although its effects are also noticeable during the winter months. When it is active, the trade winds are interrupted by spells of disturbed and squally weather. During El Niño episodes, the SPCZ is displaced east of its mean position, and during La Niña the SPCZ drifts west, so passages on this route are more affected in El Niño years.

The route from Tahiti is flanked by several attractive island groups and it is not easy to decide which ones to leave out. On leaving Bora Bora, there is a choice of a northern route that touches upon the Northern Cooks and continues to either Northern Tonga or the Samoas, and a southern route that reaches Tonga via the Southern Cooks. An interesting stop shortly after leaving Bora Bora

is Maupiti, a small atoll which is accessible through a pass. The nearest of the Cook Islands is Aitutaki, which also has a pass through its reef leading to a well-protected anchorage. A visit from Aitutaki to the capital Rarotonga entails a rather long detour, which should not be a deterrent if it can be planned for early August when people from all the islands congregate in Rarotonga for 'Te Maeva Nui', a ten-day festival of colourful cultural, dancing and sporting activities celebrating the Cook Islands' declaration of independence in 1965.

From Rarotonga the southern route continues west to Nuku'alofa on Tongatapu, Tonga's capital and main island group, with its gingerbread royal palace and ancient Polynesian remains. This southern route is the shortest way to Fiji but it misses two very special landfalls in the Cooks, the atolls of Palmerston and Suwarrow. Palmerston is home to the descendants of an English sailor, William Marsters, who landed there in 1863 and sired a large family with his three Polynesian wives. About 50 Marsters, all direct descendants of William Marsters' 23 children, still live on Palmerston and encourage sailors to pay them a visit and, if they come from Rarotonga, bring their mail and essential supplies. The lagoon has no pass, only an open anchorage in its lee, but the islanders have laid some moorings for the use of visiting boats.

A long-time favourite among sailors roaming the South Pacific is Suwarrow, an uninhabited atoll where, between 1952 and 1977, New Zealander Tom Neale lived his solitary dream in this idyllic spot. The voluntary castaway's sojourn is described in his book *An Island to Oneself*. The remains of Tom's house survive on Direction Island, where the Cook Islands government has built a clubhouse for the use of visiting sailors and where a caretaker is based during the peak sailing season. Such a welcoming attitude is nowhere more evident than at nearby Niue where permanent moorings have been laid in the lee of the island for visitors who also have access to the island's Wi-Fi network.

Another perennial South Seas favourite among cruising sailors is Vava'u, a reef-enclosed group of islands

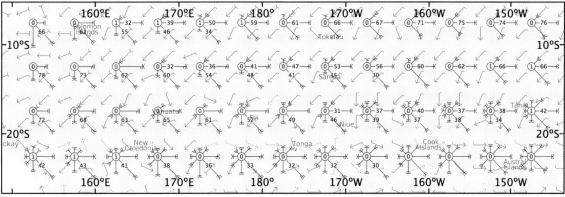

JULY

AUGUST

in Northern Tonga. Its maze of islets and reefs provides one of the best cruising grounds in the South Pacific and also good protection as one of the best hurricane holes in the South Pacific. The main settlement at Neiafu overlooks one of the most beautiful anchorages in the world. The sheltered Port Refuge was the base of the first ever charter operation in the South Pacific and continues to be a popular charter base. The sheltered waters of Vava'u also attract travellers of a different kind as humpback whales gather here in large numbers in winter to breed. They are to be found throughout the islands accompanied by their young and don't seem to mind divers or snorkellers provided they don't get too close.

Sailing west from Tonga, Polynesia gradually gives way to Melanesia, Fiji's eastern islands being the point where those two ethnic entities fuse into each other. Rather than sailing the shortest route from Tonga to Fiji, a detour to the north includes more Polynesian islands: the two Samoasand Wallis. Pago Pago's main attraction is the convenience of stocking up with American goods. Nearby independent Samoa prides itself on the association with

Robert Louis Stevenson whose grave overlooks the main harbour of Apia. The small French administered islands of Wallis and Futuna are the last stops before finally reaching Fiji.

Fiji's most attractive cruising areas are at its two extremes, the Yasawas in the west, and the Lau Group in the east. Some of the island communities which make up the latter still live a traditional way of life, and access to them is strictly controlled to protect them from too much interference from the outside world. Special permission must be obtained from the authorities in Suva to visit any of those islands.

A convenient port of entry into Fiji is Savusavu, on the south coast of Vanua Levu Island. Several operators have laid down moorings in the narrow, well-protected inlet. Occasionally, it has been possible to obtain a permit here to visit some of the closer Lau Islands. Eventually all routes come together at Fiji's capital Suva, the most important cruising hub in the Central South Pacific.

Western Fiji is where much of the tourism is concentrated, as well as several marinas and boatyards that have been built in recent years on the west coast of Viti Levu, Fiji's main island. Close by lie two island groups that are popular with both charter and cruising yachts: the Mamanucas and Yasawas. The latter are a string of largely unspoilt islands with clear waters and scenic anchorages. The most popular of the Mamanucas is Malolo Lailai Island which is home to the Musket Cove Yacht Club, founded by Dick Smith, an Australian sailor who swallowed the anchor here and created one of Fiji's first resorts. His informal yacht club continues to be a place of great affection among cruising sailors and one of the most popular watering holes in the South Pacific.

P9 • Voyages from New Zealand

Recommended time: May to June

Tropical storms: November to May

World Cruising Routes:
PS64   New Zealand to Fiji
PS65   New Zealand to Tonga

Late austral autumn and early winter mark the start of this northbound migration from New Zealand as those who have spent the cyclone season there return to the tropics accompanied by New Zealand sailors setting off on their own voyages. The passage north is best planned for the period between the middle of May and June when

the cyclone season in the tropics has drawn to an end and winter weather has not yet arrived. Weather conditions on leaving New Zealand can be unfavourable so it pays to wait for a decent forecast. However, one should not make the common mistake of waiting until a high is established over North Island and adjacent waters, as the nice weather this high gives Kiwis back home will probably bring light winds to anyone heading north. However, such a high may occasionally generate strong winds of over 30 knots in the so-called 'squash' zone where the high meets the prevailing SE trade winds. The pilot chart for May shows a higher percentage of southerly winds on departure which gradually give way to the prevailing SE winds. Not surprisingly, the June pilot chart shows a higher proportion of strong winds with the approach of winter in the southern hemisphere.

Sailors have long memories and the nightmare of the vicious storm, now known as the Queen's Birthday Storm, which struck a group of boats heading north from New Zealand in June 1994, still reverberates among those preparing for this passage to the tropics. That storm was undoubtedly an exceptional occurrence and while lessons have been learned from it, countless successful passages have been made in the intervening years. In view of the current concern over longer tropical storm seasons, and thus the risk of an early cyclone, passages are best planned for late May and early June. The ideal condition to wait for is a high-pressure system to be established after a low has passed over New Zealand. The leading edge of

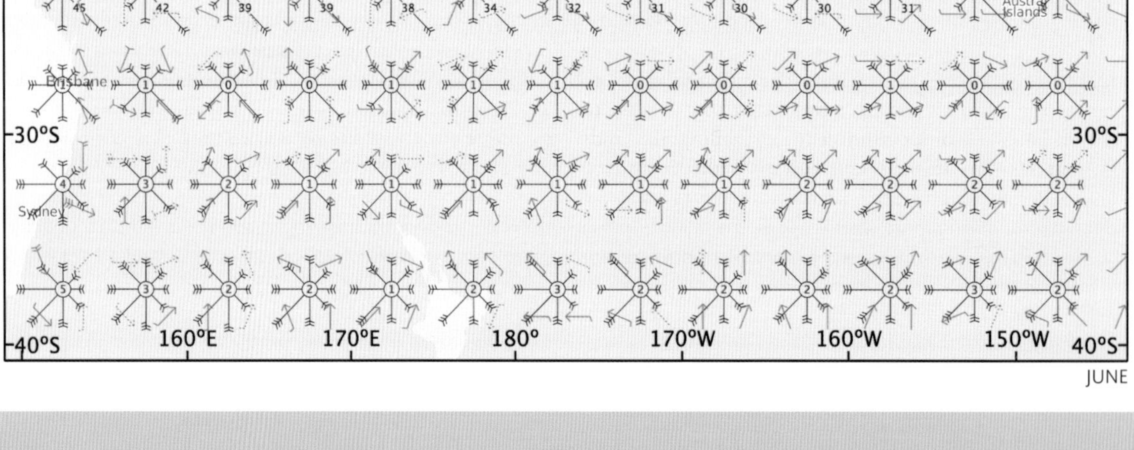

JUNE

the high should ensure favourable southerly winds. Such conditions normally last for a few days before northerly winds take over, so it is imperative to leave as soon as conditions are right.

An early June arrival in Fiji allows some five months of carefree cruising, whether that time is spent in the Central South Pacific or making your way gradually to the northwest into the Coral Sea and beyond.

Rather than sail directly to Fiji, many sailors prefer to sail first to Tonga, the easting thus gained allowing them to see more both of that country and others that they may have missed, or not spent sufficient time in, during the previous season.

There are some interesting stops to consider in settled weather on either of those alternative routes: the South and North Minerva Reefs on the way to Fiji, or the Kermadec Islands en route to Tonga.

P10 ● Voyages from Australia

- **P10a** Direct voyages
- **P10b** Voyages via New Zealand

Australian sailors heading for the tropical South Pacific have a difficult choice to make between a beat against the prevailing E and SE winds, or a long detour via New Zealand.

P10a Direct voyages

Recommended time: May to June

Tropical storms: November to May

World Cruising Routes:
  PS93   New South Wales to Fiji
  PS104   Queensland to Fiji

A reliable long-term forecast is essential to decide whether a direct course for Fiji is a feasible proposition or to take the alternative but longer route that passes close to Norfolk Island in order to meet the prevailing SE winds at a better angle. If the worst comes to the worst, the passage can be interrupted in either Norfolk or New Caledonia to wait for a change in weather that may bring better conditions. For boats setting off from ports north of New South Wales, an intermediate stop in Norfolk

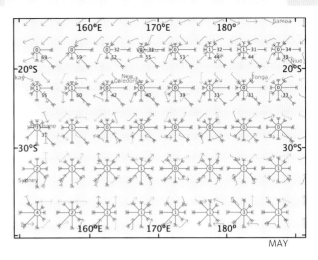

MAY

has a certain attraction as it still keeps open the choice of a direct passage from there to Fiji, or a detour to New Zealand. The one drawback of this tactic is that Norfolk Island has no all-weather anchorage and is therefore not a place to linger for too long. Whichever alternative is chosen, if the prospects still look unfavourable, the ultimate fallback is to make the required easting in higher latitudes.

P10b Voyages via New Zealand

Recommended time: May to June

Tropical storms: November to May

World Cruising Routes:
  PS101   Queensland to New Zealand
  PS91   New South Wales to New Zealand
  PS64   New Zealand to Fiji
  PS65   New Zealand to Tonga

Besides the better chance of having more favourable winds this route also has the advantage that it can be sailed earlier in the season. As this southern route is outside the cyclone area, the passage across the Tasman Sea can be sailed at any time of year. Once in New Zealand, the best time can be picked to sail to the tropics and, by taking the more easterly route to Tonga, both that country and Samoa can be visited before arriving in Fiji.

Those who start on this voyage from ports in Queensland or even Northern New South Wales should consider sailing first a shorter leg south before heading east to New Zealand either nonstop or via Lord Howe Island.

P11 • Voyages from Asia and Micronesia

P11a Voyages via Japan
P11b Voyages via Micronesia

There is a choice of two different ways to reach the Central South Pacific both of which pass through Micronesia. By sailing from the mainland first to Japan, voyages originating from ports in the East China Sea may benefit from a better sailing angle across the NE winds that will be encountered later. Voyages from more southern ports would find it easier to sail through the Philippines before heading for lower latitudes and make their easting there. Voyages starting from Southeast Asia will have the same choice of making their eastbound passage in lower latitudes.

P11a Voyages via Japan

Recommended time: April to May

Tropical storms: All year (North Pacific), November to May (South Pacific)

World Cruising Routes:

PN63	Routes to Japan and Korea
PN76	Japan to Eastern Micronesia
PN81	Eastbound routes
PT27	Kiribati to Tuvalu
PS59	Southbound from Tuvalu

The timing of this voyage needs to take into account the tropical storm seasons on either side of the equator. A late spring start from East Asia or Japan, both of which are prone to typhoons, is therefore advisable as the risk of such a storm in April is quite low. This timing also fits in perfectly with an arrival in the South Pacific in late May or early June, after the end of the cyclone season there.

Southbound passages from Japan in April will experience a high percentage of E and NE winds from about 30°N all the way to Micronesia. An attempt should be made to make some easting on leaving Japan so that the route passes east of the Mariana Islands and prevailing NE winds are met at a better angle. A convenient and interesting stop on this route is the Marshall Islands, from where the route continues south to Kiribati. The location of the Kiribati Islands, which straddle the equator almost due north of Fiji, marks the point where the equator should be crossed. The Kiribati capital, Tarawa, is the recommended landfall as none of the outer islands can be visited without having cleared in there first. Having crossed the equator, some useful easting could be gained by also stopping in Tuvalu before the final leg to Fiji.

P11b Voyages via Micronesia

Recommended time: April to May

Tropical storms: All year (North Pacific), November to May (South Pacific)

World Cruising Routes:

PN62	Routes to the Philippines
PN64	Routes to Micronesia
PN54	Philippines to Guam
PN81	Eastbound Routes
PT27	Kiribati to Tuvalu
PS59	Southbound from Tuvalu

The NE and E winds which prevail north of the equator make eastbound passages from Southeast Asia very difficult to accomplish. The usual tactic is to attempt to make your easting in an area where the predominant winds are lighter, calms are more common and, ideally, there is also a favourable current. Such an area exists just north of the equator, in approximately latitude 5°N, which coincides with the ITCZ. Making progress even there is not easy, but a good dose of perseverance combined with a willingness to motorsail in opportune moments, will eventually yield the desired results. Some of the most remote Caroline Islands are close to this route, their inhabitants extending a warm welcome to the rare visitors. One of the least visited among them is Kapingamarangi whose small population is of Polynesian origin.

As outlined in the previous voyage, the nearest point at which the equator should be crossed, so as to ensure a decent sailing angle across the SE trade winds, is at the Kiribati Islands. From there, the route to Fiji passes close to Tuvalu, where boats are expected to clear first at the capital Funafuti, but short stops in the outer islands are usually tolerated.

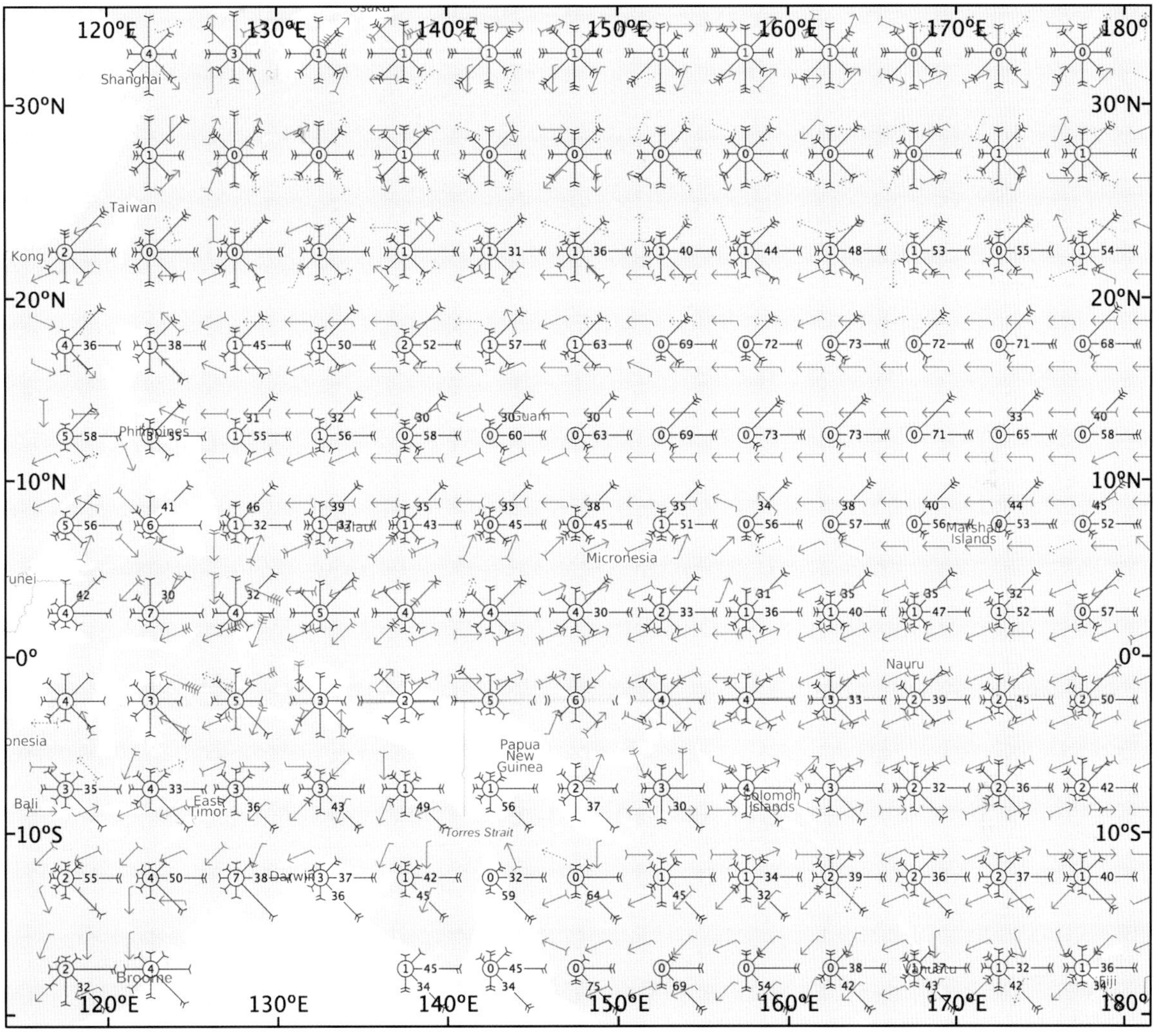

APRIL

P12 • Voyages from North America and Hawaii

Recommended time: April to May

Tropical storms: June to November (Eastern North Pacific), November to May (South Pacific)

World Cruising Routes:

PN11	California to Hawaii
PN16	Pacific Northwest to Hawaii
PN35	Hawaii to Line Islands
PN36	Hawaii to Eastern Micronesia
PT27	Kiribati to Tuvalu
PS59	Southbound from Tuvalu

As mentioned earlier, most South Pacific voyages lead to Tahiti and few sailors are prepared to explore other, perhaps more convenient, routes to reach their further destinations. For North American sailors who may wish to reach New Zealand, Australia or the Torres Strait by a shorter route, a direct voyage from Hawaii to Fiji will have a certain attraction. A voyage along such a route will benefit from favourable winds throughout its length. Strong winds may be experienced in April if an early departure from the mainland is planned so as to reach Fiji some time in late May or early June, at the start of the safe season. If that is not the case, the departure can be postponed until later provided the hurricane season in the Eastern North Pacific is taken into account. From Hawaii

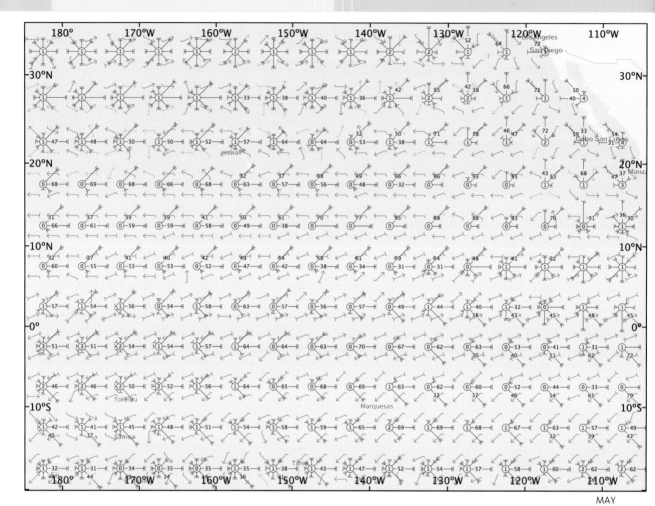

MAY

onwards, there are two alternatives for the continuation of the voyage, a northern route via the Marshall Islands, Kiribati and Tuvalu, or a southern route via the Line Islands, Phoenix, Tokelau and Samoa Islands. On both routes there are several interesting places to visit, among them the rarely visited Phoenix Islands which have been declared a UNESCO World Heritage Site and are currently the largest marine conservation area in the Pacific.

Cruising hubs

Raiatea ***
The main charter base in the Society Islands has built up a good range of repair and haul-out facilities over the years. There is good provisioning and fuel, and medical facilities are also of a good standard. There are frequent flights to Tahiti for onward international connections.

Rarotonga *
The capital of the Cook Islands has been attempting for many years to improve its facilities with only limited success. Docking facilities are still inadequate but there is a haul-out facility and some repair services. Provisioning and medical facilities are of an acceptable standard. Rarotonga airport (RAR) has flights to New Zealand, Tahiti and Australia.

Vava'u **
As the site of the first charter operation in the South Pacific, Vava'u has a good range of repair and haul-out facilities. Provisioning and medical facilities are adequate. Although designated an international airport (VAV) it only operates charter flights to foreign destinations. International flights are handled from the Tongan capital Nuku'alofa, with flights to Fiji, Australia and New Zealand.

Pago Pago *

As an important fishing port, Pago Pago has a good range of repair services, haul-out, but no docking facility for visiting boats. Both provisioning and medical services are of a good standard. The only international flights go to Honolulu for onward connections.

Suva **

Fiji's capital has a good range of facilities for visiting yachts centred on the yacht club and nearby government shipyard. Provisioning is good and so are its medical facilities. Suva's airport only operates international flights to New Zealand and Australia, with more international destinations served by the country's main airport at Nadi, on the west coast.

Lautoka **

Yachting facilities have seen a noticeable improvement on Fiji's west coast, with a good range of repair and haul-out facilities available at Vuda Point Marina. Nearby Nadi airport (NAN) operates flights to Australia, New Zealand, USA, Korea and several Pacific destinations.

See also Tahiti (page 185)

What next?

An early arrival in Fiji gives enough time for those bound for the Indian Ocean to explore the various island groups en route: Vanuatu, the Solomons and Papua New Guinea, or make a foray inside the Great Barrier Reef and take that inshore route to the Torres Strait. It is in Fiji where a major decision must be taken concerning the impending cyclone season: to spend it in a safe place in the tropics, or leave for New Zealand or Australia. Some marinas and boatyards on Viti Levu's west coast have facilities for storing boats during the critical period, and there is also a small basin at Musket Cove. The well-protected anchorage at Savusavu has some cyclone-proof moorings which have performed well in recent years. The Tradewinds anchorage at Suva is used by local boats as a well-protected hurricane hole.

The alternative is to sail south to New Zealand or southwest to subtropical Australia, spend the summer there and enjoy the many cruising opportunities or travel inland. There is a wide choice of marinas and boatyards in both countries, and the range of repair facilities provides a good opportunity to carry out essential maintenance work.

Hanavave anchorage at Fatu Hiva in the Marquesas.

Voyages to New Zealand and Australia

- **P13** • Voyages from Fiji and Tonga
- **P14** • Voyages from North America and Hawaii
- **P15** • Voyages from Asia

Most sailors would agree that the South Pacific deserves more than just one season and for this reason the majority spend at least two winters there, usually by leaving the tropics during the summer cyclone season and sailing south to New Zealand or Australia. Although in recent years a number of sailors have taken advantage of the improved facilities in Fiji to leave their boats there during the summer, the majority still prefer to head out of the tropics. The annual migration starts in October as boats make their way either south to New Zealand or southwest to one of Australia's subtropical ports. One of the advantages of spending the summer season outside the tropics is being able to go to a place with good repair and service facilities. Both countries provide not just a safe place to leave the boat unattended, or spend the summer

New Zealand's Bay of Islands.

visiting their interior, but also the opportunity to have maintenance or refitting work done by skilled workers at one of the many well-endowed boatyards.

P13 • Voyages from Fiji and Tonga

- **P13a**   Fiji and Tonga to New Zealand
- **P13b**   Fiji to Australia and the Torres Strait

An important decision needs to be made in Fiji, especially if the safe season is far advanced; to sail to New Zealand or Australia for the cyclone season, or continue west towards Vanuatu and thence to the Torres Strait and beyond. Besides the annual cyclone season, the only other matter of certainty in the South Pacific is that even the best laid plans often have to be drastically altered, and, due to its location, Fiji is the place where the fate of many a voyage, or at least a new direction, is decided.

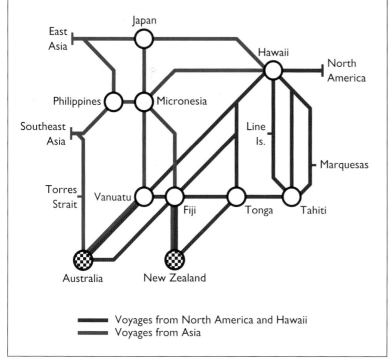

Voyages from North America and Hawaii
Voyages from Asia

passages to New Zealand the winds are mostly from E or SE down to about 28°S or 30°S. From there on, the winds can come from any point of the compass but as the passing of a front or depression usually results in a spell of northwesterlies, it does no harm if some westing is made while under the influence of those southeasterlies.

An interesting stop south of Tonga is at the North and South Minerva reefs, both of which have temporary anchorages and are popular with boats sailing this route. As they lie east of the direct route from Fiji, it may be better to call there on the return voyage. Another possible stop, especially if sailing from Tonga, is at the Kermadec Islands, which belong to New Zealand. Three of the islands, Raoul, Macauley and Curtis, have anchorages but they are only suitable in settled conditions. The islands and surrounding waters are a nature reserve and only brief stops are tolerated. With the exception of Raoul, which has a meteorological station, all of the islands are uninhabited.

Yachting facilities in New Zealand are of a high standard, with most being concentrated in the top half of North Island where both facilities and the weather are generally better than in the rest of the country. There is a

New Zealand continues to be the favourite summer destination and the majority of boats sail there in late October, shortly before the start of the cyclone season. Most of those who sail to New Zealand intend to return to the islands and resume their voyage the following year, and New Zealand is conveniently located for this purpose. Those who intend to spend the cyclone season in Australia continue west from Fiji and sail to a port in New South Wales or Southern Queensland. Both Vanuatu and New Caledonia lie close to this route and provide the opportunity to experience the different cultures of these two Melanesian nations.

P13a Fiji and Tonga to New Zealand

Recommended time: October

Tropical storms: November to May

World Cruising Routes:

PS55   Fiji to New Zealand

PS43   Tonga to New Zealand

Most boats sail this route in the second half of October with the majority of boats leaving from Fiji and fewer from Tonga. On

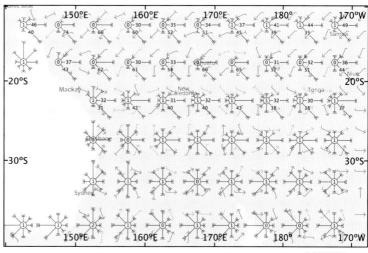

OCTOBER

wide choice of marinas and boatyards, starting with the first port of entry at Opua in the Bay of Islands. Further south, the small town of Whangarei is a favourite among visiting sailors as it has a marina in the centre of town and a full range of specialist workshops and boatyards. Auckland itself has several marinas, such as Westhaven, close to the city centre, while Bayswater, Westpark and Half Moon Bay marinas are located in quieter suburbs. Some are suitable for living on board while others only accept boats which are left unattended.

P13b   Fiji to Australia and the Torres Strait

Recommended time: July to October

Tropical storms: November to May

World Cruising Routes:

PS54	Fiji to New Caledonia
PS73	New Caledonia to New South Wales
PS53	Fiji to Vanuatu
PS77	Vanuatu to Queensland and Torres Strait
PS78	Vanuatu to Solomon Islands
PS81	Solomon Islands to Papua New Guinea
PS85	Papua New Guinea to the Torres Strait

Voyages along this final segment of the main transpacific route can be sailed at any time during the safe season as sailing conditions from May onwards are favourable with consistent SE trade winds west of Fiji. Weather conditions across the Coral Sea are generally favourable with consistent SE trade winds all the way to the Torres Strait. Few plan to make this long voyage without stopping at some of the island groups and while New Caledonia entails a detour, several islands of Vanuatu are within easy reach of the direct route. Calling at the Solomons and Papua New Guinea will need more time which may not be fitted easily into a tight schedule.

Close to the route to the Torres Strait, the island nations of Vanuatu and New Caledonia provide the opportunity to experience, and compare, the very different impact that outside influences have had on their cultures. In the former, a traditional way of life still survives in many islands, while in the latter the French influence has strongly influenced the customs and way of life of the Melanesian population.

New Caledonia is a country of contrasts in many respects, from the pristine beauty of its outer islands to the bleakness of Grande Terre's slopes denuded by mining, the slow pace of life in the remote Kanak villages to Nouméa's unmistakably French atmosphere. After a cruise in the scenic Loyalty Islands or the Île des Pins, described as 'the closest island to paradise', the capital's Port Moselle provides the perfect place from which to enjoy some aspects of the French influence, for the well-being of both crew and boat. There are good yachting services both in and around the marina, as well as several restaurants. Although tropical cyclones occasionally reach this area, the well-sheltered port has not been greatly affected and many French voyagers keep their boats here during the cyclone season.

North of New Caledonia, the islands of Vanuatu stretch out in a long chain, with one of their main attractions the southernmost island of Tanna and its live Yasur volcano. The volcano has been reclaimed by the villagers who live on its slopes and they guide visitors to the rim of the mighty crater. This is probably as close as anyone would wish to get to a live volcano as even from a safe distance the spewing volcano is a sight to behold. Another attraction, which is unique to Vanuatu, is the ancient ceremony held on the island of Pentecost to celebrate the yam harvest. It is held between April and June, when young men put on a death-defying performance by diving from a high tower, their fall being checked at the last moment by lianas tied to their ankles. As the land-divers of Pentecost only perform during a short period each year, being there at the right time will only suit those who can make an early start in the season which may not be easy unless you are prepared to spend longer in that part of the world.

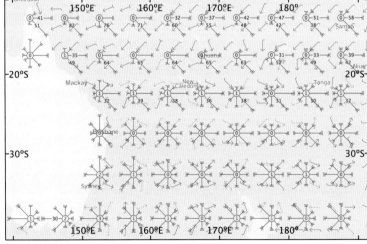

SEPTEMBER

Rather than sail directly to the Torres Strait, an attractive alternative is to divert at some point to Northern Queensland, where Cairns is a convenient port of call with good repair and provisioning facilities. From there, the route stays inside the Great Barrier Reef and enters the Torres Strait from the south, the Indian Ocean finally within reach.

The passage through the Torres Strait used to be dreaded by sailors in pre-GPS days as the main shipping channel winding its way between reefs and small islands was difficult to locate, the situation made worse by swift currents and strong trade winds. All that has now changed thanks to advanced aids to navigation but the intricate tide-swept channels should still be treated with due caution.

P14 ● Voyages from North America and Hawaii

Recommended time: April to May (North Pacific), June to August (South Pacific)

Tropical storms: June to November (Eastern North Pacific), all year (Western North Pacific), November to May (South Pacific)

World Cruising Routes:

PN11	California to Hawaii
PN16	Pacific Northwest to Hawaii
PN36	Hawaii to Eastern Micronesia
PT27	Kiribati to Tuvalu
PS59	Southbound from Tuvalu to Fiji
PN35	Hawaii to Line Islands
PS54	Fiji to New Caledonia
PS55	Fiji to New Zealand
PS73	New Caledonia to New South Wales

There are two basic alternative routes for this long voyage which cuts right across the Pacific Ocean from northeast to southwest. The first is the classic route via Tahiti, which can be reached either directly via the Marquesas or by way of Hawaii. This alternative, and its component segments, are described in voyages P3 (page 174), P4 (page 177) and P8 (page 187). A more direct route P12 also goes via Hawaii but continues from there to Fiji and thence to either New Zealand or Australia.

The main advantages of this direct voyage to the Southwest Pacific are that it can be planned to be sailed at the most favourable times in both the North and South Pacific, and also that it calls at some of the least visited island groups on either side of the equator. The timing of this voyage is dictated by the need to avoid the risk of tropical storms in the North Pacific. Those who wish to reach the Southwest Pacific at the beginning of the safe season (June) need to plan on an early start from the mainland to Hawaii, which should present no problem for those leaving from California, but may mean a rough trip from the Pacific Northwest. The alternative is to sail to Hawaii the previous summer and continue west from there in April, when the risk of typhoons in Western Micronesia is still low. From Hawaii, the suggested route calls first at the Marshall Islands en route to Kiribati. As the Marshalls can be affected occasionally by typhoons, it may be safer to sail directly from Hawaii to Kiribati. From there the route turns south across the equator to Tuvalu and thence Fiji.

A safer and possibly more attractive alternative is to sail from Hawaii to the Line and Phoenix islands, neither of which are affected by tropical storms. The Phoenix Islands are a marine reserve and make an interesting stop, especially for those interested in diving. Tokelau is another rarely visited island group lying close to the route to Tonga and Fiji. Boats bound for Australia can sail west from the Phoenix Islands via Tuvalu to Vanuatu and thence to destinations on the east coast of Australia. Those who wish to reach the South Indian Ocean by the shortest route can reach the Torres Strait via the Solomon Islands.

P15 ● Voyages from Asia

P15a Voyages to Northern Australia and the Torres Strait

P15b Voyages via Micronesia

Voyages from the Asian mainland to the islands of Oceania are encumbered by the prevailing easterly winds that are a constant feature in all areas of the tropical and subtropical Pacific Ocean. Even voyages to close destinations can be challenging and, with the exception of Northern Australia, sailing from mainland Asia to any other part of Australia can be a difficult undertaking. This difficulty is faced both by visitors and Australian sailors returning home from an Asian cruise. There are basically two alternatives; a relatively short hop across the Arafura Sea from Southeast Asia, or a more challenging voyage from mainland China and Japan via Micronesia to destinations on Australia's east coast. Voyages to New Zealand would follow a similar route via Micronesia.

P15a Voyages to Northern Australia and the Torres Strait

Recommended time: May, October

Tropical storms: November to May (South Pacific and South Indian Ocean)

World Cruising Routes:

IT24	Southeast Asia to Torres Strait
IS23	Indonesia to Darwin
IS12	Darwin to the Torres Strait

From Southeast Asia the bulk of Australia looks so near that few of those who intend to sail to destinations on the east coast of Australia imagine just how hard this can be. The exception is voyages to Northern Australia which are easier to undertake during the favourable time. Because of the consistent SE winds in the Coral Sea and the need to avoid the cyclone season, the best time to undertake voyages to more remote destinations is the changeover period to NW monsoons when light, and possibly even favourable, winds can be expected in the Timor and Arafura seas.

The first part of the voyage, across Indonesia, is relatively easy but south of the Indonesian islands sailing conditions during the SE trade winds season can be hard even to such relatively near destinations as Darwin. Voyages bound for the Torres Strait, which continue inside the Barrier Reef to SE Australia, have to contend with both prevailing SE winds and a north-setting current. With enough time, the voyage south can be sailed in short stages as there are plenty of convenient ports along this interesting route.

P15b Voyages via Micronesia

Recommended time: February to April (North Pacific), May to July (South Pacific)

Tropical storms: All year (Western North Pacific), November to May (South Pacific)

World Cruising Routes:

PN44	Singapore to Philippines
PN55	Philippines to Palau
PN77	Japan to Western Micronesia
PT29	Southbound to Melanesia
PS84	Papua New Guinea to Queensland

Whether the point of departure is in Southeast Asia, further north on the Asian mainland coast or Japan, the only feasible way to sail to either SE Australia or New Zealand is to make sufficient easting at least as far as 165°E, before crossing into the South Pacific. The prevailing winds throughout Micronesia are from NE, but approximately 5°N lighter winds and an east-setting current make it possible to gain the required easting.

Boats setting off from Singapore and Southeast Asia should stay just north of Borneo and continue south of the Philippines to reach the suggested lower latitudes, whereas boats leaving from East Asia should attempt to attain those same low latitudes by the shortest route possible. An area where several piracy attacks have occured in recent years and should be avoided is off the NE coast of Borneo and SE Palawan, the entire Sulu archipelago and the SW coast of Mindanao. How long to stay north of the equator depends on the final destination; for ports in Northern Queensland, the equator can be crossed as far west as 155°E, the southbound leg passing through the outer islands of Papua New Guinea

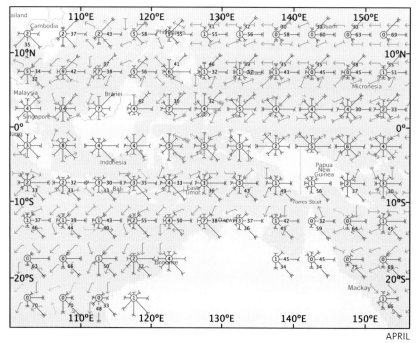

APRIL

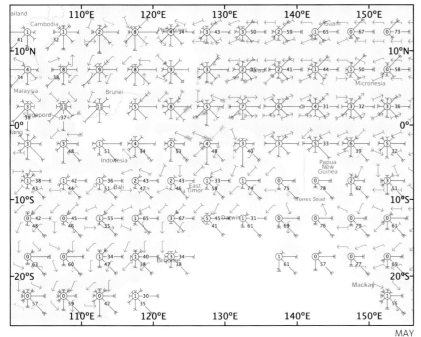

MAY

Auckland *****

New Zealand's main yachting centre has a wide range of repair facilities with several boatyards and marinas. Medical services are of a high standard. Auckland international airport (AKL) is a major hub with flights to destinations in Australasia and North and South America.

Nouméa ****

There is a good range of repair facilities concentrated around Port Moselle Marina. Medical services are of a high standard. The international airport (NOU) has flights to Paris, Auckland, Sydney, Tokyo, Port Vila and some other regional destinations.

Sydney *****

Australia's premier yachting centre has a complete range of repair and service facilities. There are about a dozen marinas within reach of the city, some very close to the centre. The Kingsford Smith International airport (SYD) has flights to all important destinations in the world, to neighbouring islands in the Pacific and Southeast Asia as well as a comprehensive network of internal flights. Medical facilities are of a high standard.

Brisbane ****

In recent years Brisbane has become popular among long distance cruising sailors looking for a safe summer base during the cyclone season. Several marinas are located either along the Brisbane River or within a short distance of the city. Repair, service and medical facilities are of a good standard. Brisbane airport (BNE) has direct flights to all neighbouring countries and via Sydney or Singapore to destinations in USA, Europe and Asia.

Cairns ****

Cairns has a wide range of repair and haul-out facilities and a well-endowed hospital. Cairns airport (CNS) operates flights to a number of cities in Australasia, with connections to further destinations.

Facilities in Vava'u, Pago Pago and Fiji are described on pages 194 and 195.

before reaching the Coral Sea and the point where the route can swing west towards the chosen landfall. More easting needs to be made before the equator is crossed and a new course set for ports in South Queensland and New South Wales.

There is a good choice of interesting and rarely visited places to break those long passages, with some of the Southern Caroline Islands lying close to the suggested track north of the equator, while in the South Pacific, Papua New Guinea and the Solomon Islands provide a variety of landfalls for boats bound for Australia. Those bound for New Zealand may need to carry on as far as Kiribati before turning south, possibly calling at Tuvalu and Fiji on the way to New Zealand.

Cruising hubs

Honolulu *****

The best facilities in Hawaii are concentrated on the island of Oahu where due to Honolulu's large resident yachting community there is a good range of docking and repair facilities. Provisioning and medical facilities are of a good standard. Honolulu international airport (HNL) operates flights to many destinations in North America and Asia, as well as some of the Pacific islands.

What next?

Most cruising boats come to New Zealand or Australia to spend the cyclone season outside the area affected by these storms and as soon as that risk is over, they hasten back to the tropics to resume their voyage. Those who intend to return to the Central Pacific prefer to make New Zealand their summer base, while Australia attracts those who plan to sail the following year inside the Great Barrier Reef to the Torres Strait and Indian Ocean.

The northern migration from New Zealand starts in May with Tonga and Fiji being the most common destinations. A return to Tonga provides the opportunity to explore more of the Central Pacific islands before continuing west into the Coral Sea. The alternative is to sail from New Zealand to New Caledonia and Vanuatu before heading for the Torres Strait either direct or by making a detour to Northern Queensland and continuing the voyage inside the Great Barrier Reef. Fewer boats visit the Solomon Islands and Papua New Guinea nowadays, primarily because of safety concerns.

Those who intend to stay for more seasons in the South Pacific by spending the cyclone season in either New Zealand or Southeast Australia have the advantage of an early start in the new season as some of the most attractive cruising destinations in the South Pacific are located in or around the Coral Sea, something to bear in mind when drawing up the optimum timing and routing of your voyage. An early start from New Zealand will allow more time to be spent en route to the Torres Strait by visiting the Melanesian island groups of Vanuatu, the Solomon Islands and Papua New Guinea. This timing makes it possible to transit the Torres Strait sooner, so that some of the time gained can be spent in Darwin, in Northern Australia, where the boat can be left to visit Australia's interior, and there would still be time to call at some of the islands in the South Indian Ocean on the way to South Africa, or explore some of Indonesia on the way to Singapore and beyond. Darwin is also a good base to prepare for voyages to neighbouring Indonesia.

The other alternative is to sail north inside the Great Barrier Reef, an option which is usually taken by those who have spent the cyclone season in a port in New South Wales or South Queensland, such as Sydney, Brisbane, Mooloolaba or Bundaberg, which are popular summer bases with visiting sailors. As in the case of New Zealand, the range of facilities, both marinas and repair services, is of a good standard, with the added attraction of Australia's vast hinterland to explore.

For some sailors, either from the USA or Canada, who are not attracted by the idea of a complete circumnavigation of the globe to get back home, a return voyage from Australia or New Zealand via Tahiti and Hawaii offers a considerably shorter alternative. The voyage can easily be accomplished in one season. Its hardest part is usually right at the start with a passage in higher latitudes to the Austral Islands and thence to Tahiti. From there the route continues north to Hawaii and thence to the mainland. A more challenging and possibly quicker alternative is to sail north from New Zealand to Fiji and continue across the equator into the area of prevailing westerlies of high latitudes and reach North America by that route, possibly with a detour to Alaska.

Those who prefer to head for more challenging destinations in the South Pacific can sail from New Zealand to the Australs and continue all the way to Southern Chile. From there, they have the choice of turning left and sailing north along the coast of South America to Panama, or turning right and reaching the South Atlantic via the Magellan or Beagle Channel, or even a possible detour to Antarctica.

Voyages to Hawaii

Hawaii is the fulcrum of a complex network of sailing routes and many voyages converge at this important cruising hub. For North American sailors Hawaii is the preferred offshore destination, whether for a two-way voyage which can be accomplished easily in one season, or as an intermediate point on a longer voyage. The main transpacific route from Panama to Asia also passes through Hawaii and while many more boats continue to take the South Pacific route as part of a round the world voyage, there has been an increase in the number of sailors who take the less travelled North Pacific route from Hawaii to Micronesia and beyond.

Waikiki Beach.

P16 • Voyages from Panama and Central America

Recommended time: February to May, November

Tropical storms: June to November

World Cruising Routes:

PN23	Panama, Central America and Mexico to Hawaii
PT12	California and Mexico to Galapagos
PT17	Galapagos to Hawaii

A great circle route of 4,500 miles from Panama to Hawaii makes this one of the longest offshore passages between two points of land anywhere in the world. No wonder that most sailors try to break it into shorter, more manageable segments. The obvious way to achieve this is to sail first to Mexico and only leave for Hawaii from there, thus reducing the offshore leg by some 1,400 miles.

There are two basic alternatives to sail the long passage to Hawaii, whether along the northern, more direct, track or the southern but longer route. The attraction of the northern route is that it gives the opportunity to call at various places in Central America and Mexico before striking offshore, thus also considerably shortening the subsequent passage. The attraction of the southern route is that some of the South American mainland as well as the Galapagos Islands can easily be included in the itinerary without adding too much to its length.

Long as it may be, the idea of a direct voyage from Panama should not be discarded as, with good planning, it can be completed in a reasonable time. In April and May, when most passages along this route are sailed, the area of prevailing NE winds extends almost as far as the equator, so on leaving Panama the aim should be to reach that area as quickly as possible.

Just west of Panama and close to this route is Cocos Island (Isla de Coco), a nature reserve which belongs to Costa Rica. It is one of the most popular offshore diving sites in the Pacific and has been rated among the best diving spots in the world thanks to the breathtaking marine life in the waters surrounding it. Permission to stop must be obtained in

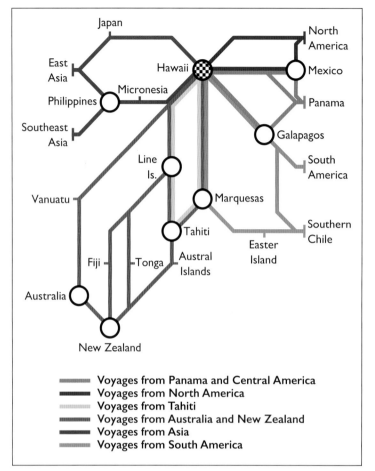

Legend:
- Voyages from Panama and Central America
- Voyages from North America
- Voyages from Tahiti
- Voyages from Australia and New Zealand
- Voyages from Asia
- Voyages from South America

and are patrolled by the Mexican Navy which has a base on the main island of Socorro where visiting boats must call first. The few anchorages provide limited protection.

Because of the difficulty posed by the prevailing N and NE winds for direct passages from Panama to the US West Coast, boats bound for those destinations are usually forced to apply a similar tactic to make the required northing before going offshore and attempting to reach California or the Pacific Northwest that way. If the conditions prove to be too hard to make progress, as is often the case, the roundabout route via Hawaii may be the only answer. Reaching the US West Coast by that route will take much longer but be both more comfortable on the crew and easier on the boat.

Although the Eastern North Pacific is regarded as one of the most active tropical storm areas in the world, with an annual average of 16 tropical storms, of which nine become hurricanes, such storms usually affect only mainland Mexico and the Revillagigedo Islands. The west coast of the USA is very rarely affected with only one fully fledged hurricane having reached California in recorded history. Nevertheless offshore passages to Hawaii can be affected and therefore voyages should not be planned to pass through the critical area during the hurricane season.

P17 • Voyages from North America

Recommended time: April to May

Tropical storms: June to November (Eastern North Pacific)

World Cruising Routes:

PN11   California to Hawaii

PN16   Pacific Northwest to Hawaii

The main factor to take into account when planning a voyage to Hawaii is the prevailing NE winds which can make passages from the mainland such an enjoyable experience but the price for that is a difficult return voyage. The hurricane season, which lasts from June to November, is not such a major concern as in other parts of the world,

advance and there are two good anchorages although short stops have been tolerated by the wardens stationed on the island. Further west, located just above 10°N and therefore close enough to the suggested route to merit a stop, the island of Clipperton could provide another interesting break as it has an anchorage in its lee. The uninhabited island belongs to France and is occasionally visited by French military personnel. As this is an out-of-bounds nature reserve vessels are not allowed to anchor nor is anyone permitted to dive or land ashore.

Few boats sail the direct route as the preferred solution for most is to cruise the west coast of Central America in short hops to Mexico, and only set off for Hawaii from one of the ports north of Acapulco, with Cabo San Lucas on the southern tip of Baja California being a favourite port of departure. Those leaving from mainland Mexico may consider stopping at the Revillagigedo Islands which are a group of four volcanic islands known for their unique ecosystem. The islands are a marine reserve

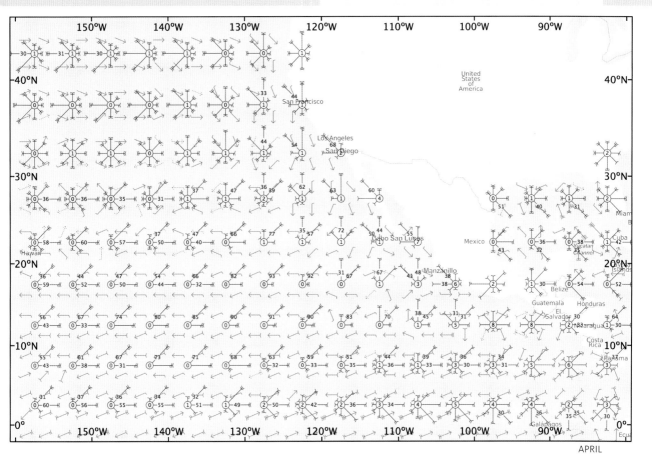

APRIL

and the number of violent tropical storms to reach Hawaii is relatively low.

Summer passages to Hawaii enjoy the most favourable conditions but carry the risk of encountering a hurricane either along the way, on passage from California, or in Hawaii itself. As the likelihood of being caught by a hurricane on a summer voyage from California is quite low, most people seem prepared to take this risk in spite of the fact that both the area between the mainland and Hawaii, and Hawaii itself, can be affected by tropical storms at that time of year. The alternative for those who would rather play it safe is to make this passage before June or after November. Those times, especially the former, are quite feasible along a southern route but may not be attractive for voyages departing from the Pacific Northwest. The recommended times are meant primarily for those for whom the passage to Hawaii is the first leg of a voyage to the South Pacific or Asia.

Deciding on the arrival time in Hawaii is more difficult if the voyage is to continue to Micronesia and

beyond, as the summer months have a high incidence of typhoons in the Western North Pacific. The risk increases as you move west and for this reason voyages that are meant to continue west of the dateline should ideally start from Hawaii in winter as the risk of typhoons is quite low in the first months of the year.

Sailing conditions between the mainland and Hawaii are favourable throughout the year but with considerably stronger winds on late autumn or early winter passages from the Pacific Northwest. Such passages benefit from better winds if the initial part, down to about 40°N, is sailed in a SSW direction before altering course for Hawaii.

Passages from California also need to overcome the often mixed conditions that are experienced on departure, as consistent winds are only found once well out of the influence of land. This fact is well known to participants in the various races between the mainland and Hawaii when occasionally the result is decided not at the finish, but right at the start. Passages starting from South California often fare better by sailing a southern route where there

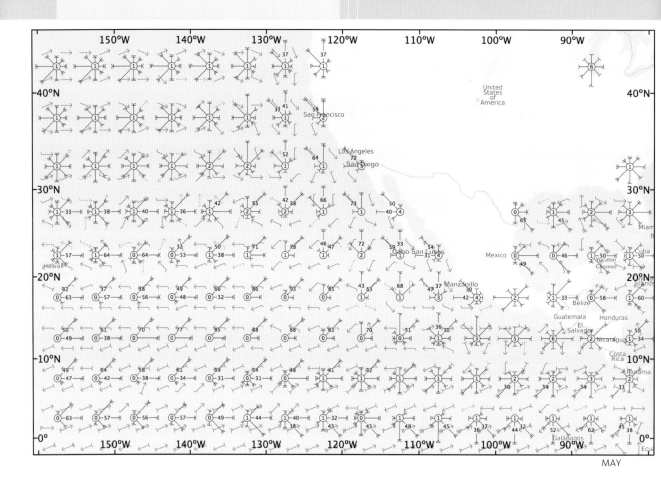

MAY

is a better chance of falling in early with consistent NE winds.

The logical landfall in Hawaii is Big Island as it is nearest to the mainland and also to windward of all other islands, thus making it the perfect start for a Hawaiian cruise. Docking facilities in Big Island are disappointing, especially at the end of a long ocean passage, but they improve as you move west, with those in Honolulu being the best.

P18 • Voyages from Tahiti

P18a   Voyages via the Line Islands
P18b   Voyages via the Marquesas

The SE trade winds ensure good sailing conditions for this voyage as far as the equator from where they are gradually replaced by NE winds. There is a choice of two routes from Tahiti, an eastern route via the Marquesas or a western route via the Line Islands. The former is longer but ensures a better sailing angle north of the equator, whereas the latter is shorter but may end up being harder on the wind north of the Line. There is also the option of a nonstop passage which would follow a route halfway between the other two but is not treated separately as directions are quite similar to those for a voyage via the Marquesas.

The recommended times are at the change of seasons, when favourable conditions prevail in both hemispheres, the earlier time being attractive to those who prefer to reach the North Pacific in May or early June and thus have the entire summer for the continuation of the voyage to the mainland. The later time will suit those who wish to leave the South Pacific at the end of the safe season. However, an October or November departure may be too late to continue the voyage to the mainland, and the alternative is either to spend the winter in Hawaii and

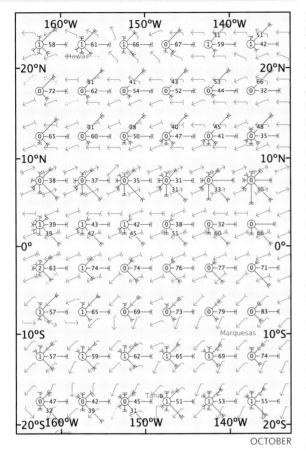

OCTOBER

hence their name, and the direct route from Tahiti to Hawaii, and can make an enticing stop even if that almost certainly makes the final leg to Hawaii hard on the wind. Among the Southern Line Islands the uninhabited islands of Caroline, Flint and Malden lie close to this route and each has an anchorage in their lee where it is quite safe to stop and go ashore if the weather is settled. Caroline achieved short-lived fame by being the first piece of land in the world to enter the new millennium even if it meant moving the international dateline far enough to the east in order to make this possible. The Kiribati government, who administers the Line Islands, including this tiny atoll, even attempted to change its name to Millennium Island but it does not seem to have caught on. What has changed is the time zone for the Line Islands which are now on the same time as the main islands of Kiribati and are thus one day ahead of Tahiti and Hawaii time.

The Northern Line Islands are inhabited, with Christmas (Kiritimati) being the administrative centre of this small archipelago. Among them, Fanning is the favourite with visiting yachts as it has a pass into its protected lagoon and the unmistakable feel of a South Pacific island. The northernmost, Palmyra, is a US territory and a protected nature reserve where stops are only allowed with prior permission. The island's only residents are a few scientists engaged in research and conservation work.

As the Line Islands are almost due south of Hawaii, and the ITCZ is located approximately on the latitude of Palmyra, it may be advisable to gain some easting in this area, before reaching the NE trade winds which prevail all the way to Hawaii.

This voyage to Hawaii is sailed regularly by American and Canadian boats either returning home at the end of a voyage, or who are leaving the South Pacific temporarily to spend the cyclone season in Hawaii and plan to return to Polynesia the following year. It is agreed that this can be a very satisfying voyage, not too demanding from the point of view of sailing, and highly rewarding for the interesting islands that can be visited en route.

resume the voyage the following year, or take a calculated risk by leaving the South Pacific earlier and continuing the voyage to the mainland at a more favourable time even if that means arriving in Hawaii during the North Pacific hurricane season.

P18a Voyages via the Line Islands

Recommended time: May to June, October to November

Tropical storms: November to May (South Pacific), June to November (Eastern North Pacific)

World Cruising Routes:

    PT22   Tahiti to Line Islands and Hawaii

    PN89   Microneisa to Hawaii

The SE trade winds will ensure a fast passage between Tahiti and the equator whether planning to sail nonstop or call at the Line Islands. Where the equator is crossed will decide how close to the wind the onward passage to Hawaii will be. The Line Islands straddle both the equator,

P18b Voyages via the Marquesas

Recommended time: May to June, October to November

Tropical storms: November to May (South Pacific), June to November (Eastern North Pacific)

World Cruising Routes:

    PS23   Tahiti to Tuamotus and Marquesas

    PT21   Marquesas to Hawaii

The recommended route for a direct voyage to Hawaii passes well to the east of the Line Islands so as to have sufficient easting in hand which will ensure a good sailing angle once the area of the NE trade winds is reached. As this track passes close to the west of both the Tuamotus and Marquesas to reach that point, a stop in those islands could be easily included before resuming the northbound voyage. Rangiroa, in the Tuamotus, and Taiohae, on Nuku Hiva, in the Marquesas, are close to this route and as both are also the main islands in their respective island groups, the best facilities are to be found there.

Continuing north from there, the point where the equator is crossed depends on weather conditions and the state of the NE winds north of the equator. While it may not be necessary to go as far east as 140°W, which is the recommended longitude for this passage, that hypothetical point is a useful reference when planning this voyage.

P19 • Voyages from Australia and New Zealand

P19a Voyages via Tahiti

P19b Voyages via Micronesia

There are two radically different routes for voyages from those remote countries to Hawaii; a route via Tahiti, usually sailed by boats which have spent the cyclone season in Australia or New Zealand, and a more direct route via Micronesia.

P19a Voyages via Tahiti

Recommended time: May to June

Tropical storms: November to May (South Pacific), June to November (Eastern North Pacific)

World Cruising Routes:

PS91	New South Wales to New Zealand
PS67	New Zealand to Tahiti
PT22	Tahiti to Line Islands and Hawaii
PS23	Tahiti to Tuamotus and Marquesas
PT21	Marquesas to Hawaii
PN89	Micronesia to Hawaii

The only reasonable way to sail from either Australia or New Zealand to Tahiti is to stay in higher latitudes to take advantage of the prevailing westerly winds. For voyages originating in SE Australia this entails a crossing of the Tasman Sea to New Zealand from where the recommended route continues east between latitudes 35°S and 38°S as far as the Austral Islands. From there the route

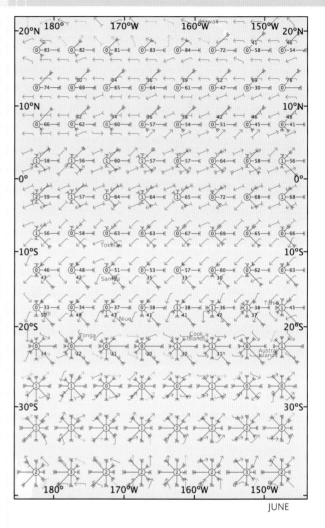

JUNE

turns north as by that stage sufficient easting has been gained to be sure of a good sailing angle across the SE trade winds to Tahiti. See also P6 on page 181.

Those same winds will be encountered all the way from Tahiti to the equator where they will be gradually replaced by NE winds. Those who wish to be sure of a favourable sailing angle on the leg to Hawaii should make the passage from Tahiti further east by staying to windward of the Line Islands. As this track passes close to the west of both the Tuamotus and Marquesas, a stop in those islands could be included. Where the equator is crossed will decide how close to the wind the onward passage to Hawaii will be. The Line Islands straddle both the direct route to Hawaii and the equator, and make an enticing stop even if that almost certainly means the leg to Hawaii will be sailed hard on the wind. The alternative is to sail first from Tahiti to the Marquesas in which case the equator will be crossed much further to the east and the subsequent leg to Hawaii will benefit from a better sailing angle.

P19b Voyages via Micronesia

Recommended time: May to June

Tropical storms: November to May (South Pacific), June to November (Eastern North Pacific). All year (Western North Pacific)

World Cruising Routes:

PS65	New Zealand to Tonga
PS42	Northbound from Tonga
PS46	Northbound from Samoa
PN89	Micronesia to Hawaii

For those who are not attracted by the idea of a high latitude passage to Tahiti, there is an alternative route which has the attraction of being more direct and, for voyages originating in Australia, also considerably shorter than the Tahiti option. The timing of this voyage needs to fit into the narrow window between the end of the cyclone season in the South Pacific and the start of the hurricane season in the Eastern North Pacific. A May departure fits this narrow window perfectly and is also the most favourable time for those who intend to continue from Hawaii to the North American mainland or even Alaska. Similar considerations apply at the end of the safe season in the South Pacific when the aim is to get away before the start of the cyclone season but not to cross the equator before the end of the North Pacific hurricane season.

This is a more complex voyage to plan than the alternatives outlined earlier but its rewards will certainly measure up to whatever challenges it might entail. The voyage is made up of two distinct parts separated by the equator. The first part is by far the easier as its objective is to reach the equator by the quickest way possible, a task much helped by the prevailing SE winds.

A May departure appeals primarily to those who have spent the summer outside the cyclone area. Voyages originating in New Zealand should sail first to Tonga and continue via Samoa in a NE direction with possible stops at Tokelau and Phoenix. Voyages from Australia need to sail a more westerly route which passes through Vanuatu and Tuvalu and thence to either the Phoenix Islands or directly to the equator if the prevailing E winds prove to be too much of a hindrance.

The attraction of sailing this route to the equator is that it passes close to some of the most remote and least visited islands in the world. The Phoenix Islands belong to Kiribati and are made up of eight atolls, all of which are uninhabited except Canton. In 2008 the entire group was declared a protected area, making it the largest marine reserve in the world. From the Phoenix Islands the rest of the voyage can stay offshore all the way to Hawaii or call at the Northern Line Islands. They are also part of Kiribati and four of them support small communities. The one exception is the northernmost island, Palmyra, which is under US administration and is a protected nature reserve.

The NE trade winds which blow north of the equator will turn the final leg into a beat. This may be avoided by making some easting either south of the equator, which may preclude a visit to the Line Islands or, having stopped there, the desired easting can be made just north of the equator. The ITCZ is located approximately on the latitude of Palmyra and the suggested tactic is to make some easting in this area of calms and light winds. The rest of the passage to Hawaii will be dominated by E and NE winds, with easterly winds showing a higher percentage as you move north. For boats coming from the south, Honolulu is the most convenient landfall not just for its location but also its range of facilities.

P20 • Voyages from Asia

P20a Voyages via Japan
P20b Voyages via Micronesia

The Hawaiian Islands form the apex of the vast Polynesian Triangle which stretches all the way to Easter Island and New Zealand. It has now been established that all those islands were settled by the ancestors of today's Polynesians who migrated from present-day Taiwan several thousand years ago. The fact that it took them so long to reach Hawaii and when they did they arrived from the south shows the difficulty faced by eastbound voyages from the Asian mainland. Not much seems to have changed in the intervening millennia and for a sailboat to reach Hawaii is still best done by a roundabout way, either by a northern route via Japan or a southern route via Micronesia.

P20a Voyages via Japan

Recommended time: April to June

Tropical storms: All year (Western North Pacific), June to November (Eastern North Pacific)

World Cruising Routes:

PN63	Routes to Japan and Korea
PN75	Japan to Hawaii

Although typhoons can occur throughout the year in the Western North Pacific, the colder winter months have a much lower incidence. A voyage to Japan before spring may be too early so the recommended time to make this passage is in April when the threat of a typhoon is still low. The passage from the mainland to Japan can be planned for the changeover period between the NE and SW monsoons, although even at that time contrary NE winds are still prevalent.

The onward voyage to Hawaii may be problematic on account of the high percentage of E and NE winds south of 30°N, which could make this a rather uncomfortable passage even for a boat that sails well to windward. One way to avoid that is to continue east along 35°N, or even further north, until sufficient easting has been made to be sure that when the course is finally altered for Hawaii, the NE winds will be met at a better angle. This could mean having to sail east as far as 180° before changing course for Hawaii.

P20b Voyages via Micronesia

Recommended time: February to May

Tropical storms: All year (Western North Pacific), June to November (Eastern North Pacific)

World Cruising Routes:

PN62	Routes to the Philippines
PN44	Singapore to Philippines
PN55	Philippines to Palau
PN77	Japan to Western Micronesia
PN81	Eastbound routes
PN89	Micronesia to Hawaii

A late spring or early summer voyage to Hawaii in high latitudes, when the weather can still be cold, windy and foggy, may not be to everyone's taste in which case the warm-water alternative via Micronesia should be considered. The main disadvantage of the southern alternative is that the necessary easting will have to be made close to the equator to avoid the worst of those NE winds, and may entail much use of the engine. Regardless of whether the voyage originates in mainland Asia or Japan, the first priority is to reach the lower latitudes as soon as possible as it is only there that the necessary easting can be made with any certainty. For voyages originating in East Asia the shortest route leads across the Philippines to Palau and continues in a SE direction. An area where several piracy attacks have occured in recent years and should be avoided is off the NE coast of Borneo and SE Palawan, the entire Sulu archipelago and the SW coast of Mindanao. In both cases, the best tactic is to stay

north of the equator, just below latitude 5°N, so as to take advantage of the lighter winds and east-setting Equatorial Counter Current. At certain times along this route, the use of the engine to make progress will be the only solution so sufficient fuel should be carried for this eventuality.

On the positive side, this potentially slow voyage offers the possibility of a number of attractive Micronesian landfalls that are off the usual cruising track, such as Palau and some of the more remote Caroline Islands.

Straddling this route are the Kiribati Islands with the capital Tarawa just north of the equator. However tempting it may look to strike out directly for Hawaii at this point, the wise navigator will continue east along the same track at least as far as the Line Islands. Lying roughly south of Hawaii they provide a welcome and convenient stop before embarking on the final leg to Hawaii. The ITCZ is located approximately on the latitude of Palmyra and the suggested tactic is to make some easting in this area of calms and light winds so as to be sure of a better sailing angle across the NE winds that will be encountered on the passage to Hawaii.

P21 • Voyages from South America

Recommended time: February to May

Tropical storms: November to May (Western South Pacific), June to November (Eastern North Pacific)

World Cruising Routes:

PS18	Northbound from Chile
PS15	South America to Easter Island
PS16	Westbound from Easter Island
PS21	Gambier Islands to Marquesas
PT21	Marquesas to Hawaii

Depending on the point of departure there are two ways of sailing to Hawaii from South America, a direct route which is suitable for boats setting off from Peru and Ecuador, and a southern route via Easter Island, which appeals mainly to boats leaving from Chile. The northern route is the same as described in voyage P16.

The great attraction of the southern route is that it is made up of several segments, each finishing at interesting islands in the South Pacific: Easter Island, Pitcairn, Gambier, Tuamotu and the Marquesas as well as the possibility of making a detour to such rarely visited islands as Juan Fernández of *Robinson Crusoe* fame.

Although the risk of tropical storms in Eastern French Polynesia is very low, the Gambier Islands should not be reached before April. With the exception of the first

leg, from Chile to Easter Island, when it may be necessary to make some northing to reach the area of consistent SE winds, the rest of the voyage benefits from favourable conditions virtually all the way to Hawaii.

From Easter Island the proposed route heads almost due west to Pitcairn Island whose isolated community extends a warm welcome to visiting sailors. From the Gambier Islands the route swings north to the Marquesas with the possibility of calling at some of the Outer Tuamotus on the way. The spectacular Marquesas, possibly the most beautiful island group in the world, will be a suitable place to bid farewell to the South Pacific while following in the wake of the Polynesian navigators who sailed their sturdy canoes through the same waters to settle a new land which they named after their sacred ancestral home.

Cruising hubs

For details of Easter Island, Tahiti and Honolulu see pages 185 and 201.

What next?

Due to its ideal location and well-defined seasons, planning the next stage of a voyage from Hawaii is relatively easy, even if putting some of those plans into practice is rather more difficult. This is certainly true of voyages to the North American mainland that are at the mercy of the prevailing NE winds and the inescapable need to sail a roundabout way to reach your destination. An attractive alternative is to continue sailing north to Alaska, spend part of the summer there, and then reach your destination with the help of the NW winds of higher latitudes. By contrast, the same NE winds make voyages to other points of the compass an attractive and achievable proposition, be it to the Asian mainland via Japan or the islands of Micronesia to Southeast Asia and beyond. Voyages to destinations south of the equator can also easily be planned to take place during periods with favourable conditions, whether to the Marquesas, Tahiti or even New Zealand and Australia.

Voyages to Panama and Central America

With the exception of voyages from the American continent, both North and South, voyages to Panama from other parts of the world are very difficult to achieve. The main cause is the prevailing winds which make eastbound voyages a very challenging undertaking.

P22 • Voyages from North America

Recommended time: November, April to May

Tropical storms: June to November (Eastern North Pacific and Caribbean)

World Cruising Routes:

    PN12   Southbound from California

    PN22   Mexico and Central America to Panama

The prevailing northerly winds ensure good sailing conditions for southbound voyages from Southern California to Central America throughout the year, whereas those from Canada and the Pacific Northwest are better planned to take place between late spring and early autumn. The main problem is that the summer months coincide with the hurricane season in Mexico and that limits the timing of such voyages to spring and late autumn or early winter.

As the hurricane seasons coincide on both sides of the continent, similar parameters apply to voyages to Panama which are intended to continue to the Caribbean. Although Panama itself is rarely affected by hurricanes, subsequent voyages through the Caribbean Sea should avoid sailing to any of the areas which are affected by hurricanes. The optimum time for passages across the Caribbean Sea is at the change of seasons, in May or in late November, early December, and therefore the timing of voyages from the US West Coast to Panama need to agree with those dates. The alternative is to sail sooner, but still during the safe season, to Mexico or Central America, and continue to Panama at the optimum time to transit the Panama Canal.

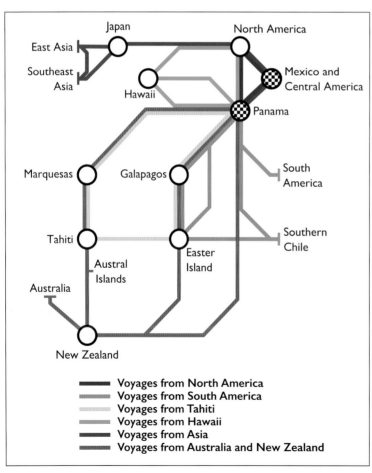

Legend:
- Voyages from North America
- Voyages from South America
- Voyages from Tahiti
- Voyages from Hawaii
- Voyages from Asia
- Voyages from Australia and New Zealand

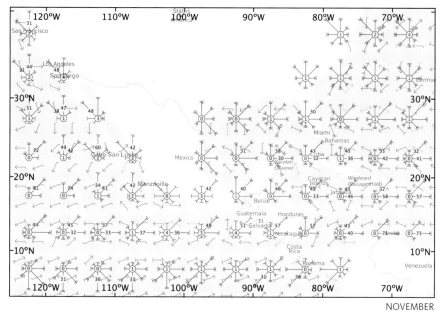

NOVEMBER

P23 ● Voyages from South America

Recommended time: November to May

Tropical storms: June to November (Caribbean)

World Cruising Routes:

PT16   Northbound from Galapagos

PS18   Northbound from Chile

Voyages from South America to Panama can be sailed in principle at any time of year as extreme weather conditions are virtually unknown. The recommended times are meant for voyages which continue into the Caribbean Sea so that the arrival there coincides with the safe season.

There are two route options for voyages which originate in the southern part of the continent. The inshore route follows the contour of the mainland and benefits from mostly light S or SE winds and the favourable north-setting Humboldt Current. Some of the most favourable conditions are at the two extremes of the recommended times, when consistent southerly winds blow along the entire coast of South America.

Those who may not be attracted to what can be a slow and monotonous passage have the option of an offshore route which benefits from better sailing conditions. For voyages originating in Southern Chile such an option can be a mixture of both, by staying inshore as far as the port of Valdivia and then striking offshore to call

The Pacific end of the Panama Canal.

at two rarely visited groups of islands belonging to Chile, both of which lie close to a northbound route: the Juan Fernández Islands and, further north, the Desventuradas Islands. The former are inhabited and are known as the setting of the novel *Robinson Crusoe*, whereas the aptly called Unfortunate Islands are a group of small barren islands with a small detachment of the Chilean Navy stationed on the main island San Felix. A more challenging option is to take a longer detour to Easter Island to visit the most interesting of all Chilean offshore destinations. From there, or any of the other islands, this offshore route continues to another interesting offshore destination, the Galapagos Islands, and thence to Panama.

P24 • Voyages from Tahiti

Recommended time: October

Tropical storms: November to May (Western South Pacific), June to November (Caribbean)

World Cruising Routes:

PT19	Tahiti and Marquesas to Panama
PS25	Tahiti to Austral Islands
PS26	Tahiti to Southern Chile
PS18	Northbound from Chile
PT16	Northbound from Galapagos

A voyage along this rarely sailed route to Panama might appeal to those who wish to reach the Atlantic by the more benign alternative of the Panama Canal rather than by way of the Magellan Strait, Beagle Channel or Cape Horn. This option may also appeal to those who want to avoid the Red Sea or Cape of Good Hope routes for their return to Europe. There are basically two routes to achieve that aim: a direct, but more challenging, route via the Marquesas, or a longer but probably easier route, which makes its easting in higher latitudes, albeit not as far south as the Cape Horn route.

A voyage along the northern route has the best chance of encountering reasonable conditions in October. The route heads northeast from Tahiti, possibly calling at the Marquesas, then continues across the equator into the area of the ITCZ. The necessary easting can be made here by motorsailing in light winds. At that time of year there is also an east-setting current.

The southern route is not much easier as a similar effort needs to be made to find the best winds to make the required easting which can mean having to go as far south as 35°S, if not even further into the area of pre-vailing westerly winds. On leaving Tahiti, the initial route heads in a general SE direction, keeping south of the Tuamotus, but if winds from that direction make it too hard to sail on that heading, it may be easier to turn south and possibly call at the Austral Islands before continuing

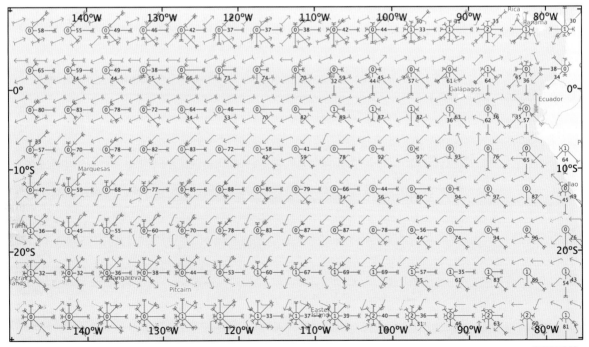

the search for those westerlies. Once they are found, the easterly heading needs to be kept until approximately 105°W is reached. This is where the route turns north into an area where E and SE winds predominate all the way to the equator. Just before that point is reached, the relatively short detour to Easter Island may be considered. Similarly, the passage may also be interrupted at the Galapagos Islands which lie close to the route to Panama, although better sailing conditions may be found nearer to the mainland.

The recommended time coincides with the start of the cyclone season in Tahiti, but as this is also the time when the chances of finding reasonable conditions along either route are at their best, the initial stage of the voyage should be planned to avoid leaving Tahiti too late. This can be accomplished by sailing sooner to either the Marquesas or the Australs, both island groups having a much lower cyclone risk factor than Tahiti itself.

P25 • Voyages from Hawaii

Recommended time: March to May, October (eastbound), May, November (southbound)

Tropical storms: June to November (Eastern North Pacific and Caribbean)

World Cruising Routes:

PN34	Hawaii to Panama, Central America and Mexico
PN33	Hawaii to California
PN12	Southbound from California
PN22	Mexico and Central America to Panama

Voyages from Hawaii to Panama are a challenging proposition, whether they are sailed by the shortest direct route, or the roundabout way via the North American mainland. Because of the prevailing winds, the direct route is mostly to windward but with the right boat, perseverance and

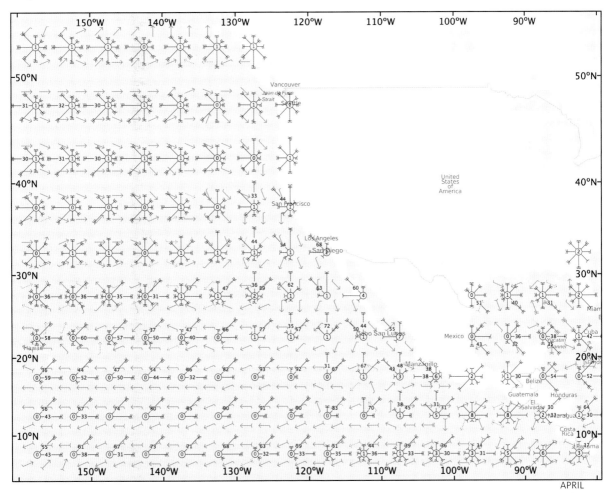

APRIL

the right tactic, it may be possible to achieve. The time to do it is before the start, or after the end, of the hurricane season in both the North Pacific and Caribbean Sea, with either March or April, or November, being the most suitable months. On leaving Hawaii, an effort should be made not to go below 10°N so as to be able to benefit from the fact that east of longitude 120°W the proportion of northerly winds becomes predominant and, with a bit of luck, a direct course can be sailed from there to Panama.

The timing of the route via the mainland also needs to take into account the hurricane seasons, so it is probably easier to plan on doing it in two separate segments. In this case, the leg from Hawaii to the mainland can be undertaken at the most favourable time, which the subsequent leg, from the US West Coast to Panama, to be sailed in November. This timing would avoid the hurricane season in the area of Mexico, and ensure an arrival in the Caribbean during the safe winter season.

P26 • Voyages from Asia

Recommended time: April to July (eastbound), November (southbound)

Tropical storms: All year (Western North Pacific), June to November (Eastern North Pacific and Caribbean)

World Cruising Routes:

PN63	Routes to Japan and Korea
PN75	Japan to Hawaii
PN34	Hawaii to Panama, Central America and Mexico
PN73	Japan to Alaska
PN74	Japan to North America
PN15	Southbound from Pacific Northwest
PN13	Southbound from California

Two radically different solutions present themselves for this potentially arduous voyage. The longer alternative is to sail to North America by way of a high-latitude passage from Japan and continue south to California, Mexico and on to Panama. As such a high-latitude passage is best sailed in summer, the subsequent southbound leg from the US West Coast can only be sailed after the hurricane season in Mexico has come to an end, resulting in a late November or early December arrival in Panama. The other alternative is to sail to Hawaii and from there take the low-latitude route described in voyage P25.

P27 • Voyages from Australia and New Zealand

Recommended time: October to January

Tropical storms: November to May (Western South Pacific), June to November (Caribbean)

World Cruising Routes:

PS91	New South Wales to New Zealand
PS68	New Zealand to Southern Chile
PS67	New Zealand to Tahiti
PT19	Tahiti and Marquesas to Panama
PS25	Tahiti to Austral Islands
PS26	Tahiti to Southern Chile
PS18	Northbound from Chile
PT16	Northbound from Galapagos

An initial voyage in high latitudes seems to be the only suitable way to reach Panama from either Australia or New Zealand. Boats starting from SE Australia should first cross the Tasman Sea to New Zealand and set off from there on the long eastbound trek. The route needs to keep between latitudes 35°S and 40°S where a higher percentage of westerly winds is more likely. The route passes south of all such islands as the Australs, Pitcairn and Easter, but soon after the meridian of the latter has been crossed, the route can turn north and finally point for Panama. The most favourable conditions for this last stage, which can be interrupted in both Easter and the Galapagos Islands, can be expected in December and January, as described in voyage P24, which follows a similar track from Tahiti.

Another alternative route to Panama, also described in voyage P24, goes first to Tahiti from where it follows a more northerly track which uses the Marquesas as an intermediate point. From there, the route crosses the equator to complete the rest of the voyage in an area of light winds where making the required easting may be a less onerous task than along a southern route.

Cruising hubs

Cabo San Lucas **
With four marinas, a boatyard with haul-out and an adequate range of repair facilities, and several supermarkets, Cabo San Lucas is a good place to prepare for an offshore passage. The international airport (SJD) operates flights to several destinations in the USA, as well as Mexico City for onward connections.

To consult other relevant hubs go to: Easter Island (page 185), Galapagos (page 185), Honolulu (page 201), Tahiti (page 185), Panama (page 77).

What next?

The planning of all the above voyages has been based on the assumption that the main purpose of sailing to Panama is to transit the Panama Canal and continue the voyage in the Caribbean Sea. For this reason, it is essential to plan such voyages to avoid the hurricane season which lasts from June to November. The areas which are not affected are the South American countries bordering on the Caribbean Sea (Colombia and Venezuela), as well as the islands in the extreme south (San Blas, Aruba, Bonaire and Curaçao). Besides having to avoid the hurricane season, voyages through the Caribbean Sea have to confront an additional problem, and that is the serious difficulty of sailing from Panama to northern destinations against the strong prevailing winds. One of the toughest challenges is sailing against the prevailing NE winds to the Windward Passage en route to the Bahamas, Bermuda or the USA. Passages to other destinations, such as the Yucatán Channel or the countries of Central America, are somewhat easier to accomplish. The best time to undertake such northbound passages is just before the end of the safe season, in May, when there can be a reasonable percentage of easterly and southeasterly winds in the Caribbean Sea.

Direct passages from Panama to any of the islands in the Eastern Caribbean are practically impossible on account of the prevailing wind direction and while it may be possible to make your easting in short hops along the coasts of Colombia and Venezuela, it would require a great effort to achieve it, with safety considerations also needing to be taken into account. The only realistic solution is to attempt to sail to the Mona Passage or, failing that, to the Windward Passage, and then make your easting along the aptly called 'Thorny Path'.

Parasailor view from top.

Voyages to North America

Voyages to the west coast of North America from virtually any place in the Pacific Ocean are among the most difficult to plan. Whereas in other parts of the world the initial part of a voyage is often the most challenging, for American and Canadian sailors the situation is reversed and while leaving on a voyage can be described as the easy part, returning home is exactly the opposite. The main factor responsible for this situation is the prevailing NE winds which make southbound passages a pleasant experience but can be a nuisance when the time comes to get back home. This is why it is always a good idea when planning any voyage to try and think it through to its end.

The most difficult are return voyages from Mexico, which is a prospect faced every year by many of those who had sailed down that way or by boats returning from the Caribbean and on their way home. Those who have travelled further afield, be it Tahiti, New Zealand, Australia or Southern Chile, will have a relatively easier task by returning home via Hawaii. The following voyages outline some of the alternatives. Also included in this section are voyages from the US West Coast to Alaska and the Pacific Northwest.

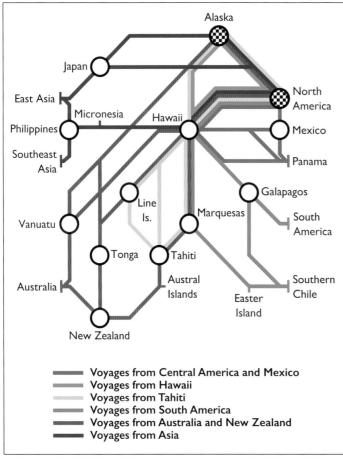

Voyages from Central America and Mexico
Voyages from Hawaii
Voyages from Tahiti
Voyages from South America
Voyages from Australia and New Zealand
Voyages from Asia

P28 • Voyages from Central America and Mexico

P28a   Direct voyages

P28b   Voyages via Hawaii

A voyage to the US West Coast from anywhere between Panama and Baja California is one of the most difficult prospects to be faced by a cruising boat anywhere in the world as the relentless contrary winds make it virtually impossible to sail the shortest route.

There are three solutions to deal with this: take the shortest route along the coast of Baja California, sail offshore in search of better winds, or make a long detour to Hawaii. The first option, aptly called 'the Baja Bash', is undoubtedly the hardest and it entails tacking frequently to make best use of the existing conditions, and possibly stopping at some of the ports along the way to wait for a change in weather. Those taking the offshore route should be prepared to go 200 or even 300

Golden Gate Bridge.

miles out where there is a better chance of finding winds which blow from a more favourable direction and are often also lighter than closer to land. The most radical option is to go all the way to Hawaii and sail home by that much longer roundabout route. The first two options may appeal to those bound for destinations in South California whereas for boats bound for the Pacific Northwest the Hawaii option may prove less daunting. As most of such northbound voyages are planned to take place in May, just before the start of the hurricane season in Mexico, there is enough time for a short stop in Hawaii so that the rest of the voyage can be completed during the summer. Similar considerations also apply for the even more ambitious detour to Alaska and a return home by that longer but more interesting route.

There are two further options that may be considered: to have the boat shipped or trucked. The main advantage of using one of the shipping companies specialised in yacht transport is that the mast need not be taken down. Sevenstar Yacht Transport runs a regular service between Golfito in Costa Rica, Ensenada or La Paz in Mexico, and Victoria in British Columbia. Various trucking companies

operate between Mexico and the west coast of North America. One of the loading ports is San Carlos, located on the eastern shore of the Sea of Cortez where boats are decommissioned and loaded onto low-loader trailers. These solutions are increasingly used by owners who are not keen to fight the elements and prefer to have their boats returned home in this painless way.

P28a Direct voyages

Recommended time: March to May

Tropical storms: June to November

World Cruising Routes:

PN21 Panama and Central America to Mexico

PN24 Panama, Central America and Mexico to California and Pacific Northwest

PN23 Panama, Central America and Mexico to Hawaii

Most voyages in this section take place in May which is the time when boats from the Pacific coast of Mexico, or those that have just transited the Panama Canal from the Caribbean, are trying to get out of the critical area before

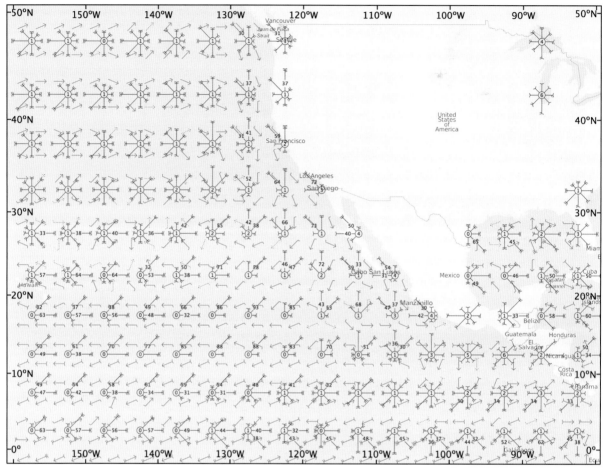

MAY

the start of the hurricane season. As the pilot chart for May makes quite clear, the prospects for a direct offshore passage are limited to boats that go really well to windward, and even they may find it hard going. However, by taking your time to wait for a spell of favourable winds to sail, or light winds to motor, a northbound passage from Baja California can be accomplished. Early in the season it is worth waiting for an approaching low which will generate southerly winds. Those who prefer this option will encounter better conditions by heading immediately offshore where the prevailing northerly winds are gradually replaced by a higher percentage of NE and later NW winds. North of San Francisco the going can be even harder, although the prevailing northwesterly winds are occasionally light enough to make progress with the engine.

Rather than set off immediately on such a long and arduous offshore passage, voyages that start from Panama can be broken up by sailing in shorter legs along the coast of Central America and only go offshore from Northern Mexico. This cruising alternative is more suited to voyages bound for Southern California as continuing in this way to more northern destinations may prove too hard. In that case, there is the alternative to ease the sheets, point the bows towards Hawaii and let those NE winds become your friend by treating you to a most enjoyable passage.

● P28b Voyages via Hawaii

Recommended time: April to May

Tropical storms: June to November

World Cruising Routes:

PN23   Panama, Central America and Mexico to Hawaii

PT12   California, Central America and Mexico to Galapagos

PT17   Galapagos to Hawaii

Reaching the west coast of North America by way of a long detour to Hawaii is a daunting prospect which may look more acceptable if it is treated more like a cruise than a delivery voyage. As outlined above, the long passage from Panama to Hawaii can be considerably shortened if its first part is sailed in short cruising legs along the coasts of Central America and Mexico. This could even include a foray into the Sea of Cortez before heading for Hawaii.

This passage should not be sailed after June when there is a risk of being overtaken by a hurricane. Those who have been delayed may consider taking a southern route from Panama and sailing to the Galapagos, either direct or via the mainland, before setting off on the passage to Hawaii. Although sailing this way from Panama to Hawaii may look like an unjustifiably long detour, it was in fact the route taken in the past by the sailing ships whose masters always preferred the prospect of favourable winds despite the longer distance sailed. This voyage is described in detail in voyage P16 (page 203), while the passage from Hawaii to your final destination is outlined in the next voyage.

P29 ● Voyages from Hawaii

P29a   Direct voyages
P29b   Voyages via Alaska

Because of the prevailing NE winds, eastbound voyages from Hawaii are never easy, the task being further complicated by the location of the North Pacific High. This high-pressure cell is located between latitudes 30°N and 40°W and longitudes 140°W and 150°W, and moves with the seasons, being furthest north in summer, and furthest south in winter. The high is strongest in summer which is the reason for the stronger NE trade winds during that season, and weakest in winter, with the resulting weaker trade winds. The usual tactic on leaving Hawaii is to sail north and adjust the course constantly to take best advantage of the existing winds. This used to be a dreary and frustrating process which nowadays can be significantly ameliorated by having access to weather forecasts thus being able to optimise your route. Even so, it may still be necessary to make a long sweep to the north before gradually turning east.

Some may decide that having gone that far north, the voyage might as well be extended all the way to Alaska, which is an option that is increasingly taken as

more sailors are attracted to high-latitude cruising. The detour can easily be fitted into a summer cruise, especially if it is limited to the more accessible SE Alaska. When the time comes to turn south, the prevailing NW winds will ensure favourable conditions for a passage to the Pacific Northwest, unless the scenic Inside Passage is preferred.

P29a Direct voyages

Recommended time: May to August

Tropical storms: June to November

World Cruising Routes:

PN32	Hawaii to Pacific Northwest
PN33	Hawaii to California
PN15	Southbound from Pacific Northwest

With the NE winds being at their most consistent in summer, a direct voyage to the mainland, especially to California, is well-nigh impossible at that time of year. The main factors that determine the way in which to deal with this situation are your time limitations and the sailing characteristics of your boat. As mentioned earlier, the position of the North Pacific High has a major bearing on the route to be sailed and it is therefore essential to know its location. The usual tactic by those determined to sail rather than motor is to head north keeping to the west of the high until the area of westerly winds is reached, which, in summer, could mean sailing as far north as 35°N or even further. As the high travels with the seasons,

Tactics for a homebound voyage from Hawaii

Leaving Hawaii I took on enough fuel to motor at 7 knots for 72 hours with enough emergency fuel in reserve. I calculated this based on the shape and location of the Pacific High at the time of my departure. Heading due north for the first several days on a nice reach I watched for the wind to begin to lay down. At that point I changed course to NNE so as to intersect the narrow portion of the high. I knew that you had to resist the temptation to head east too soon as there is a risk of being headed on the other side of the high. Once I was about 3 degrees below the top of the centre of the high, I turned due east through the calms as I had enough fuel to make it to the other side and into the trades. From there on we had a great ride all the way to San Diego.

Dale Norley

earlier passages can put this to good advantage when the high is located further south even if the weather is colder and the percentage of strong winds is higher in those latitudes.

Later in summer, the high migrates further north and you could end up in the Aleutian Islands if trying to go over the top of the high, so keeping tabs on the location of the high is of utmost importance.

Those who prefer not to be entirely dependent on the wind and are prepared to use their engine to reach the mainland by the shortest and most efficient route possible should also set off from Hawaii in a roughly northerly direction and attempt to sail, or motorsail, as close as possible to the wind, constantly adjusting the course to the existing wind direction. Another tried tactic is to sail north-northeast on leaving Hawaii and then make use of North Pacific depressions to make as much easting as possible. Usually this takes you into the southern edge of the Pacific High when turning on the engine may no longer be a matter of choice. Out of the high, northerly winds start taking over and make it possible to sail the rest of the passage to the mainland.

P29b   Voyages via Alaska

Recommended time: Mid-June to August

Tropical storms: June to November

World Cruising Routes:

PN31   Hawaii to Alaska

PN14   Southbound from Alaska

Planning a voyage to Alaska is a straightforward affair compared to the complexities involved in sailing from Hawaii to the mainland. The route heads almost due north keeping to the west of the North Pacific High. By early July, which is the best time for this voyage, westerly winds should become the dominant feature from about 40°N onwards and continue right into the Gulf of Alaska. This is a vast cruising area which stretches from the Aleutians in the west to the Alexander Archipelago in the east and would take much more than one season to explore properly. However, with good planning, a cruise that starts at Dutch Harbor, or Kodiak if time is short, can pack most of Alaska's main attractions into one long summer. Those who cannot afford more than a few weeks can compromise by limiting their cruise to around Sitka where, in a relatively small area, are concentrated some of Alaska's most spectacular sites.

When it is time to head south, there is the choice of an offshore route, or the spectacular Inshore Passage which winds its way all the way to Vancouver Island where the ocean can be regained through the Juan de Fuca Strait. From there, the prevailing NW winds, which are a constant feature along the Pacific Northwest coast, will ensure favourable conditions to your destinations.

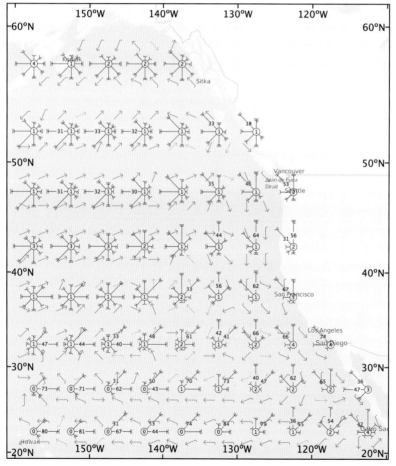

JULY

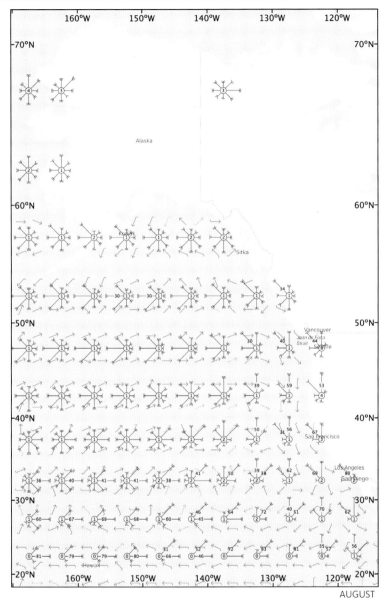

AUGUST

PS23	Tahiti to Tuamotus and Marquesas
PT21	Marquesas to Hawaii
PN32	Hawaii to Pacific Northwest
PN33	Hawaii to California
PN31	Hawaii to Alaska
PN14	Southbound from Alaska

Planning a nonstop voyage from Tahiti along the shortest route to the west coast of North America is an almost futile exercise as weather conditions along such a route are unfavourable at any time of the year. The reasonable solution is to sail there via Hawaii. As outlined in voyage P18 (page 206) there are three alternatives for this passage: to sail it nonstop, via the Marquesas or the Line Islands. The next leg from Hawaii to the mainland can be sailed directly or via a detour to Alaska, both options being described in voyage P29. The recommended times take into account the tropical seasons in both hemispheres.

P31 • Voyages from South America

P31a Voyages via Galapagos
P31b Voyages via Easter Island

The difficulties faced on voyages from Panama to North America also apply to voyages from South America as sailing directly to the west coast of North America from anywhere in the southern half of the continent can be a very difficult task. There are two basic alternatives, each including a long detour to Hawaii. Depending on the point of departure there are two ways of sailing from South America to Hawaii, a direct route via Galapagos, which is suitable for boats setting off from Peru and Ecuador, and a southern route via Easter Island, which applies mainly to voyages originating in Chile.

P30 • Voyages from Tahiti

Recommended time: May to June, October to November

Tropical storms: November to May (South Pacific), June to November (Eastern North Pacific)

World Cruising Routes:

| PT22 | Tahiti to Line Islands and Hawaii |
| PN89 | Micronesia to Hawaii |

● **P31a** Voyages via Galapagos

Recommended time: February to May

Tropical storms: June to November (Eastern North Pacific)

World Cruising Routes:

PS11	Ecuador to Galapagos
PT17	Galapagos to Hawaii
PN32	Hawaii to Pacific Northwest
PN33	Hawaii to California

Although at first sight it may look possible to reach the west coast of the USA by following the contour of the continent to Central America and beyond, in reality such an attempt probably will not get far past Baja California before being forced to head offshore. For this reason, boats leaving from Peru or Ecuador may fare better to sail first to the Galapagos and from there pick up the traditional sailing route to Hawaii. As shown by the pilot chart for May on page 176, sailing a direct course to Hawaii may be feasible by staying with the prevailing SE winds to about 120°W before crossing the ITCZ into the area where the predominantly E and NE winds will ensure good sailing conditions all the way to your destination. Having sailed that far west it may be worth considering stopping in the Marquesas and continue from there as outlined in voyage P18b.

● **P31b** Voyages via Easter Island

Recommended time: February to May

Tropical storms: November to May (South Pacific), June to November (North Pacific)

World Cruising Routes:

PS15	South America to Easter Island
PS16	Westbound from Easter Island
PS21	Gambier Islands to Marquesas
PT21	Marquesas to Hawaii
PN32	Hawaii to Pacific Northwest
PN33	Hawaii to California

The great attraction of this southern route is that it can be divided into separate segments, each finishing at some of the most interesting islands in the South Pacific: Easter Island, Pitcairn, Gambier, the Tuamotus and the Marquesas as well as the possibility of making a detour to such rarely visited islands as Juan Fernández.

This voyage may appeal to North American sailors who have been cruising in Southern Chile and wish to get home in the shortest time possible. The first leg of the voyage, from mainland Chile to Easter Island, can be sailed entirely offshore from Southern Chile, or, if starting from a more northern point, via the Juan Fernández Islands. This small archipelago is mainly known for having been the temporary home of a castaway named Alexander Selkirk, who was the inspiration for the novel *Robinson Crusoe*. Both now have islands named after them, with the main settlement of a few hundred people living on Robinson Crusoe Island.

From Easter Island, the voyage continues to Pitcairn and enters French Polynesia at the Gambier Islands. It is there that a major decision needs to be made whether to continue to the Marquesas, and thence to Hawaii, or make a detour to Tahiti, before resuming the voyage across the equator and on to Hawaii.

Although the risk of tropical storms in Eastern French Polynesia is very low, the Gambier Islands should not be reached before April. With the exception of the first leg, from the mainland to Easter Island, when it may be necessary to make some northing to reach the area of consistent SE winds, the rest of the voyage benefits from favourable conditions all the way to the equator.

From Easter Island the proposed route heads almost due west to Pitcairn Island and on to the Gambier Islands where the route swings north for the Marquesas with the possibility of calling at some of the outer islands of the Tuamotus on the way. The spectacular Marquesas will be a suitable place to bid farewell to the South Pacific.

The route for a direct voyage from the Marquesas to Hawaii passes well to windward of the Line Islands so as to have sufficient easting in hand to ensure a good sailing angle once the area of the NE trade winds is reached. The point where the equator is crossed depends on the state of the NE winds north of the equator, as well as the sailing abilities of the boat. A recommended tactic is to attempt to stay on the longitude of the Marquesas, thus ensuring a good sailing angle north of the equator.

For the continuation of the voyage from Hawaii to the mainland, voyage P29 should be consulted for details. There are two alternatives for the last stage of this voyage: to sail directly to the mainland or to make a detour by continuing to Alaska and reach the final destination by that roundabout, but more rewarding, route. This option may appeal to those who are returning from a cruise in the Chilean fjordland and would like to cap that achievement by sailing to the two extremities of the Pacific Ocean during the same voyage.

P32 • Voyages from Australia and New Zealand

P32a Voyages via Tahiti

P32b Voyages via Hawaii

P32c Direct voyages

Sailing from one end of the Pacific Ocean to the other is not an easy undertaking, primarily because of the easterly winds which prevail along the most direct route in both hemispheres. The solution therefore is to attempt to sail a roundabout route which avoids the worst effects of those contrary winds. There are three very different options to choose from: the commonly sailed route via Tahiti and Hawaii, which is usually sailed by boats which have spent the cyclone season in either New Zealand or Australia, a shorter route which bypasses Tahiti and sails directly to Hawaii, which appeals more to voyages starting in Australia as it is more direct, and, finally, a more challenging route which heads north across the Pacific into the high latitudes to reach North America that way.

P32a Voyages via Tahiti

Recommended time: May, November

Tropical storms: November to May (South Pacific), May to November (Eastern North Pacific)

World Cruising Routes:

PS91	New South Wales to New Zealand
PS67	New Zealand to Tahiti
PT22	Tahiti to Line Islands and Hawaii
PS23	Tahiti to Tuamotus and Marquesas
PT21	Marquesas to Hawaii
PN89	Micronesia to Hawaii
PS66	New Zealand to Cook Islands
PN32	Hawaii to Pacific Northwest
PN33	Hawaii to California
PN81	Eastbound routes
PT23	Cook Island to Hawaii

Eastbound voyages from Australia are never easy on account of the prevailing E and SE winds, and the only reasonable solution is to sail in higher latitudes where there is a much better chance of encountering favourable winds. This is currently the accepted tactic to reach the islands of Eastern Polynesia from either Australia or New Zealand. For voyages originating in SE Australia this

entails a crossing of the Tasman Sea to New Zealand from where the recommended route continues east between latitudes 35°S and 38°S as far as the Austral Islands before it turns north for Tahiti. From there, the prevailing SE trade winds will ensure a fast reach to Tahiti, and similar conditions will continue all the way to the equator. To be sure of a favourable angle across the NE trade winds in the North Pacific, the route should stay east of the Line Islands and the recommended meridian where the equator should be crossed is 140°W.

A quite different alternative is not to sail as far east as Tahiti but to turn north from the high latitude route sooner and head for the Cook Islands instead. A convenient landfall would be Rarotonga, the main island of the group, from where the route continues to the Northern Cooks, with Penrhyn being the best choice of a possible stop as it is the closest to the direct route and has a pass into its lagoon unlike the neighbouring atolls of Manihiki and Rakahanga. From there, the voyage continues towards the equator with a choice of calling at the Northern Line Islands or staying east of them and sailing nonstop to Hawaii.

P32b Voyages via Hawaii

Recommended time: May to June

Tropical storms: November to May (South Pacific), June to November (Eastern North Pacific)

World Cruising Routes:

PS94	New South Wales to Vanuatu
PS103	Queensland to Vanuatu
PT28	Northbound from Melanesia
PS65	New Zealand to Tonga
PS46	Tonga to Samoa
PS42	Northbound from Tonga
PN89	Micronesia to Hawaii
PN32	Hawaii to Pacific Northwest
PN33	Hawaii to California

For those who are not attracted by the idea of a high latitude passage from New Zealand to Tahiti or even the Cook Islands, there is an alternative route which has the attraction of being more direct and, for voyages originating in Australia, also considerably shorter than the Tahiti option.

The timing of this voyage needs to fit into the narrow window between the end of the cyclone season in the South Pacific and the start of the hurricane season in the Eastern North Pacific. Whether the voyage starts in Australia or New Zealand, the aim is to sail the most favourable route across the prevailing SE trade winds so as to cross the equator at the optimum point for the continuation of the voyage to Hawaii. For this reason, sailing the shortest route to that point makes more sense than a detour to Tahiti. For voyages originating in SE Australia the initial route passes through the islands of Vanuatu and continues in a NE direction to Tuvalu and the Phoenix and Line Islands. Those who leave from New Zealand should sail first to Tonga and from there continue via Samoa to the Line Islands.

From the Line Islands, which straddle the equator almost due south of Hawaii, the next leg is likely to be hard on the wind so it may be advisable to make some easting, either by passing the Line Islands altogether and crossing the equator further east, or making the easting approximately on the latitude of Palmyra where the effect of the NE trade winds is not yet felt as this is the area of the ITCZ.

P32c Direct voyages

Recommended time: May to July

Tropical storms: November to May (South Pacific), June to November (Eastern North Pacific)

Those who intend to sail to Alaska or take the high-latitude route to Canada and the US West Coast and are not interested in stopping in Hawaii have the option of sailing a very different route from New Zealand by sailing first to Fiji. From there the voyage continues due north along a route that keeps slightly to the west of the international Date Line by calling at Tuvalu, Kiribati and the Marshall Islands. Being so much further west than Hawaii, the NE winds will be more manageable and make it possible to stay on the starboard tack until the area of prevailing westerlies is reached. Once those higher latitudes are reached, the voyage can continue straight to the Aleutian Islands and hence to Alaska, or turn east for the American mainland.

A May departure from New Zealand would ensure an arrival in Alaska, or the Pacific Northwest, at the beginning of summer. Even the risk of typhoons north of the equator would be minimal as Micronesia would be crossed far enough to the east where their incidence is low. The recommended time takes into account the safe seasons in both hemispheres which are also the most favourable times to make this voyage, whether to Alaska, British Columbia or the Pacific Northwest.

P33 • Voyages from Asia

P33a Voyages from East Asia and Japan
P33b Voyages via Micronesia and Hawaii

A voyage from one rim of the Pacific Ocean to the other is a challenging proposition that can be fraught with many difficulties but can also be rich in rewards. There are two very different ways to bring it about, either by sailing a cold water high-latitude route via Japan, or a warm water route via Micronesia and Hawaii. The northern route has the advantage of a high percentage of favourable winds, the southern route of being able to count on more benign weather.

P33a Voyages from East Asia and Japan

Recommended time: June to August

Tropical storms: All year (Western North Pacific), June to November (Eastern North Pacific)

World Cruising Routes:
PN63	Routes to Japan and Korea
PN73	Japan to Alaska
PN74	Japan to North America
PN14	Southbound from Alaska
PN15	Southbound from Pacific Northwest

There are two alternatives for this high-latitude voyage: direct to Canada or the US West Coast, or via Alaska. An early April or even May start from the mainland, dictated by the need to minimise the risk of being caught by an early typhoon, needs to be balanced against the prospect of leaving on this high-latitude passage when weather conditions in the North Pacific still have a wintery edge to them. A late June departure from Japan may be the best compromise as it means arriving in Alaska in early summer. Fog is a perennial feature in these high latitudes and that, combined with the large number of cargo ships and fishing vessels, calls for constant alertness. North of 40°N, there is a higher percentage of favourable winds and the passage to Alaska should encounter better winds if sailed in higher latitudes.

An interesting detour, which could be easily included on this voyage, is to the Russian port of Petropavlovsk on the Kamchatka Peninsula. The chain of the Aleutian Islands can be followed from there to Dutch Harbor, a good starting point for an Alaskan summer cruise.

Those who are planning to sail directly to the American mainland will also have to stay in higher latitudes to reach

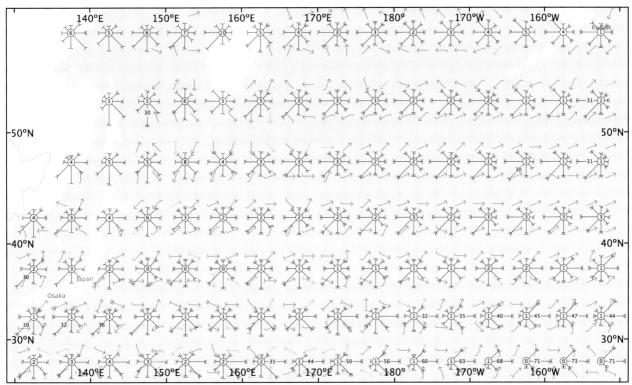

JULY

the area nearer the coast where there is a high proportion of NW and N winds and alter their course only there for the desired destination. This is certainly a passage where access to accurate forecasts can make a big difference in choosing the optimum course.

P33b Voyages via Micronesia and Hawaii

Recommended time: April to August

Tropical storms: All year (Western North Pacific), June to November (Eastern North Pacific)

World Cruising Routes:

PN44	Singapore to Philippines
PN45	Singapore to North Borneo
PN55	Philippines to Palau
PN81	Eastbound routes
PN89	Micronesia to Hawaii
PN32	Hawaii to Pacific Northwest
PN33	Hawaii to California

Those who do not find a high-latitude voyage to their taste may consider this alternative which may look like following a more benign route, at least as far as Hawaii, but poses its own problems. The downside of this route is

that in order to avoid fighting against the prevailing NE trade winds, a route needs to be sailed which stays close north of the equator where the necessary easting will be made in an area of light winds and favourable current. At certain times along this route, the use of the engine to make progress will be the only solution.

Regardless of where the voyage originates, the first priority is to reach the lower latitudes as soon as possible as it is only there that the necessary easting can be made with any certainty. For voyages originating in East Asia the shortest route leads across the Philippines to Palau and continues in a southeasterly direction. Voyages originating in Southeast Asia and Singapore can sail a route that passes north of Borneo and south of the Philippines. In both cases, the best tactic is to stay north of the equator, in about latitude 5°N, so as to take advantage of the lighter winds and east-setting Equatorial Countercurrent. An area where several piracy attacks have occured in recent years and should be avoided is off the NE coast of Borneo and SE Palawan, the entire Sulu archipelago and the SW coast of Mindanao.

On the positive side, this potentially slow voyage offers the possibility of a number of attractive landfalls in several places that are normally off the usual cruising

Singapore to Alaska

Looking for a way to return home from Singapore to North America we finally decided that the only logical way to sail was via Japan. We left Singapore on 21 April and worked our way east and north along the coast of Borneo and the east side of Palawan Island. We departed Subic for Japan in early June, taking the Bashi Channel through the Luzon Strait where we were chased by a forecast typhoon which never caught us.

We arrived at Ishigaki in Japan, 16 June. Here is where I really fell behind schedule as it took much longer to work our way up the chain of Japanese islands than anticipated, due both to our enjoyment of the various landfalls and waiting for weather windows.

Finally we left Yokohama for Alaska the first week in August. We tried to follow the Japanese Current as long as possible to get away from 'typhoon alley'. This took us more easterly than the rhumb line route. We encountered a number of calms, as well as a lot of lows, coming across from Siberia. Eventually we turned north and arrived at Adak in the Aleutian Islands after a 22-day passage.

I would recommend an earlier departure date as we were running from developing lows much of the time. Fortunately we did not encounter a typhoon per se. I think we made an error in trying to follow the Japanese Current and not taking the more direct route. Again, an earlier departure from Japan would probably mean a lower risk of typhoons, and time to go more to the north, perhaps even stop in Petropavlovsk.

We used a weather router, and although he seemed well intentioned, things did not work out very well. I am confident that the passage from Japan to Alaska would have been much faster and more comfortable if I'd had better access to weather information and, ideally, a competent weather router.

After having been chased into the Aleutian Island chain by the first winter storm, we found Alaska so unique that we decided to spend at least one additional sailing season there. This is our second summer of cruising in Alaska, which is quite an exceptional territory with wonderful people.

Steve Lochner, *Equus*

track, such as Palau and several of the more remote Caroline Islands. Two other island groups which straddle this route are Kiribati and the Line Islands. Once the latter have been passed, the route needs to swing north towards Hawaii. The continuation of the voyage from there to the mainland is described in P29.

P34 • Voyages to Alaska and the Northwest Passage

P34a Voyages from the US West Coast to Alaska

P34b Voyages to the Northwest Passage

In recent years, Alaska has become a popular summer destination for sailors not just from British Columbia and the Pacific Northwest but also from more distant places. There are three alternative ways to sail to Alaska from the US West Coast: two offshore routes, either direct or via Hawaii, and an inshore route which goes through the Inside Passage to Southeast Alaska.

P34a Voyages from the US West Coast to Alaska

Recommended time: June to August

World Cruising Routes:

PN13	Northbound from California
PN11	California to Hawaii
PN16	Pacific Northwest to Hawaii
PN31	Hawaii to Alaska

Direct passages from the US West Coast are initially encumbered by the N and NW winds which are a constant feature at least as far as 45°N. Sailing in short hops along the coast is not much easier as conditions early in the season can change quickly and many ports have dangerous bars. As the summer season in Alaska is relatively short, those who wish to enjoy an entire season there should treat this as a two season voyage by moving as far north along the coast as possible in the first summer, leaving the boat in a suitable place in the area of Seattle or Vancouver, and resuming the voyage the following year by taking the Inside Passage in May or June. The other solution is to sail to Hawaii, leave the boat there for the winter, and sail from there to Alaska the following season.

Alaska covers a vast cruising area which stretches from the Aleutians in the west to the Alexander Archipelago in the east and would take much more than one season to explore properly. With good planning, a cruise that starts at Dutch Harbor, or if time is short, at Kodiak, can include most of Alaska's main attractions into one long summer. Those who cannot afford more than a few weeks can limit their cruise to the area around Sitka where, in a relatively small area, some of Alaska's most spectacular sites are concentrated.

An Arctic maiden voyage

Gjoa Haven is the one place that no Arctic sailor would miss as it was in this Nettilik settlement that Roald Amundsen spend the first two winters of his voyage. The relationship between the Kabluna (foreigners) and Nettiliks was very amicable and locals still speak about Amundsen's stay as if it happened ten, not 110 years ago.

Our enjoyable stopover in Gjoa Haven had to be cut short when the ice charts forecast an imminent improvement in the conditions ahead of us. With more than 300 miles to the point that would give us access to the Atlantic, we set off immediately. This last section of the Northwest Passage proved to be the most difficult of the entire voyage, as we had to contend with both strong contrary winds, and having our route blocked by several areas of large ice concentration. With the prospect of achieving our aim of completing a transit of the Northwest Passage almost within reach, we spared no effort to make good progress and carried on valiantly towards Bellot Strait and Peel Sound, the last obstacles on our way.

We timed our arrival at Bellot Strait carefully as the 17 miles-long strait is renowned for its fierce tidal currents and can only be negotiated on a favourable tide. Halfway through the strait we passed Zenith Point that marks the northern extremity of continental America. Having sailed my former *Aventura* past Cape Horn, at the continent's southern extremity, I now had reached its northernmost point. As we approached the eastern entrance of the strait, the current peaked at over 8 knots, and we completed the transit of the entire strait in only 90 minutes... and exactly one month to the day since we had left Dutch Harbor.

The euphoria of our achievement was soon dampened by the prospect of the remaining 1200-mile-long passage to Nuuk. As I knew from the previous year, we could expect both strong winds and flat calms in the area ahead of us. In due course we had both. We finally reached the open sea and caught the south-setting West Greenland current that gave us a boost but also brought with it a procession of icebergs that it had picked up from calving glaciers along the way. And then the fog descended, visibility dropped to a boat's length, and we had to be on high alert to avoid running into one of those glistening behemoths, floating silently by.

Later that day we crossed the Arctic Circle and, in the view of those who only consider a successful transit of the Northwest Passage by having crossed this symbolic gateway both on the way north and south, we had achieved our aim. Since we had passed the latter point 34 days earlier, we have sailed 3728 miles. While working out that total, I also noticed that Aventura had clocked 20,000 miles since she had left Cherbourg in late May 2014. What is remarkable is that we completed the transit with no breakages or any serious technical problems, and arrived in Nuuk with all systems in perfect working order. If this challenging passage still counts as *Aventura IV*'s maiden voyage, this has been a very long honeymoon indeed.

From '200,000 Miles, A Life of Adventure'

P34b Voyages to the Northwest Passage

Recommended time: June to September

World Cruising Routes:

PN13	Northbound from California
PN31	Hawaii to Alaska
PN73	Japan to Alaska
PN19	Eastbound through the Northwest Passage

A good base to prepare for the expedition through the Northwest Passage is Dutch Harbor on Unalaska Island. From there the route to the Northwest Passage leads north through the Bering Sea to the strait of the same name to enter the Chukchi Sea. The Arctic Circle is crossed on the way to the town of Barrow, close to the northernmost tip of Alaska, which is a last place for provisions and emergency repairs before crossing the Bering Sea to access the Northwest Passage. There are several different routes through the Canadian Arctic Archipelago, including the McClure Strait, Dease Strait and the Prince of Wales Strait, some of which are only navigable by smaller vessels.

The first vessel to transit the passage from west to east was the Canadian ship *St Roch* in 1942 under Captain Henry Larsen. This was only the second successful attempt to conquer this challenging waterway, the first having been that of the Norwegian Roald Amundsen who completed a westbound voyage on the sailing vessel *Gjøa* between 1903 and 1906. In recent years the Northwest Passage has been open every summer and several small boats have succeeded in sailing it in both directions.

A transit starting from the Pacific may be easier to accomplish as in most years the western approaches to the Northwest Passage become free of ice by late July or early August, making it possible to follow the retreating ice eastwards.

Cruising hubs

◉ Dutch Harbor **

As a major base for fishing vessels operating in the Bering Sea, Dutch Harbor has a good range of repair and service facilities. Provisioning is also very good. Medical services are provided by Iliuliuk Family & Health Services, which operates the local clinic for residents of Unalaska and the fishing fleet. Unalaska airport (DUT) has regular flights to some mainland destinations, as well as to Anchorage for onward connections.

◉ Sitka **

Docking as well as repair and haul-out facilities are of a good standard. Sitka airport (SIT) operates a few local flights and summer flights to Seattle.

◉ Kodiak **

As a busy fishing harbour, Kodiak has a wide range of repair and haul-out facilities, as well as good medical services. Kodiak airport (ADQ) operates flights to Anchorage for onward connections as well as several Alaskan destinations.

◉ Vancouver ****

Docking, repair and haul-out facilities are of a high standard, and so are its medical services. Vancouver international airport (YVR) has flights to major airports in Canada and the USA, Europe, Asia and New Zealand.

Other cruising hubs relevant to voyages in this section are: Honolulu (page 201), Cabo San Lucas (page 216), Galapagos and Tahiti (page 185).

What next?

As pointed out at the beginning of this section, voyages departing from the west coast of North America are much easier to plan than inbound voyages. The prevailing northerly winds provide perfect conditions for southbound voyages to Mexico and Central America. Such voyages usually leave from California in November, after the end of the hurricane season. This is also the time to leave for those who are bound for the Panama Canal and the Caribbean. Voyages to the South Pacific need to start later so as to avoid arriving in French Polynesia before the cyclone season has come to an end there in May.

Voyages to Hawaii benefit from favourable winds throughout the year but summer passages need to take into account the risk of hurricanes. Those who have a taste for high-latitude sailing, or who are looking for a truly challenging route to the Atlantic and Europe, could head north to Alaska and the Northwest Passage. For those for whom Alaska is a turning point, when it is time to head south at the end of summer, there is the choice of an offshore route, or the spectacular Inshore Passage which winds its way all the way to Vancouver Island where the ocean can be regained through the Juan de Fuca Strait. From there, the prevailing NW winds, which are a constant feature along the Pacific Northwest coast, will ensure favourable conditions to your destination.

Voyages to South America

In spite of the large number of yachts which arrive in the Pacific Ocean through the Panama Canal every year, plus the considerable number of North American boats that head south for the winter, only very few seem to be interested in exploring the west coast of South America by sailing further south than Ecuador or the Galapagos Islands. The main attraction in the southern half of the continent is the Chilean fjordland and the majority of those who cruise there arrive from the east by way of the Magellan Strait or Beagle Channel. Arrivals from other directions are quite rare due to the prevailing winds which blow in the tropical areas of the Pacific Ocean and make eastbound voyages a difficult and frustrating task. The exception is high-latitude passages which take advantage of the prevailing westerlies and enable a few brave souls to take on that challenge to reach Southern Chile from as far away as Tahiti, New Zealand and even Australia.

P35 • Voyages from Central America and Mexico

Recommended time: September to December

Tropical storms: June to November (Eastern North Pacific)

World Cruising Routes:

PT11	Southbound from Panama	
PT12	Central America and Mexico to Galapagos	
PS14	Ecuador and Galapagos to Peru and Chile	
PS11	Ecuador to Galapagos	
PT19	Central America to Easter Island	
PS13	Galapagos to Easter Island and Gambiers	
PS17	Easter Island to Chile	

The prevailing southerly winds which blow along the South American coastline down to about 40°S, combined with the north-setting Humboldt Current, make southbound voyages from Panama and Central America a lengthy and frustrating undertaking. Closer destinations, such as Galapagos and mainland Ecuador, are more easily reached as those persistent southerly winds only become a permanent feature south of their latitude. The opposite is

Romance Glacier in Southern Chile.

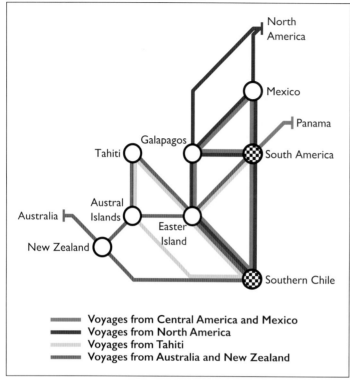

Voyages from Central America and Mexico
Voyages from North America
Voyages from Tahiti
Voyages from Australia and New Zealand

summer, between November and March. Those who plan to continue to Tierra del Fuego, and possibly also Antarctica, need to be in Southern Chile by October or November if they wish to keep the best months, from December to February, for the rest of their austral voyage.

The pilot chart shows persistent southerly winds to 40°S and their impact on a southbound voyage, is quite clear. This is the reason why few sailors taking the inshore route venture further south than Callao. Those who are bound for Southern Chile are better advised to sail an offshore route and make the best use of the existing winds. The alternative is to head for Easter Island, and sail the entire distance offshore. With the die thus cast, you must then be prepared to make a sweep to the south from Easter Island and reach your destination with help from the westerlies of higher latitudes. Such a detour may look daunting but the effort will be certainly repaid by the opportunity to visit that remote Polynesian outpost and one of the most fascinating places in the world.

Sailing south from Easter Island it is only around 35°S that the winds become favourable from where it becomes possible to shape a course for the mainland. The approach to the Chilean fjordland is through the Chacao Channel which leads to Puerto Montt and is the usual place to prepare for the forthcoming cruise. South from there opens up one of the most spectacular cruising grounds in the world, a vast area of steep-sided fjords, rocky islands, narrow inlets and mighty glaciers that stretches all the way to Cape Horn.

true in the case of northbound voyages, a prospect to be enjoyed by those who may be on their way home from the Southern Ocean.

As the entire area south of Panama is not affected by tropical storms, voyages to the Galapagos and the mainland can be planned for any time of the year. This also applies to voyages from Central American places that are not affected by the North Pacific hurricane season. The Galapagos Islands have two distinct seasons, the colder, so-called dry season, between June and December, and the warm season from December to May. During the latter season the weather is more tropical, with rain and cloudy skies, and the birds are very active, whereas the skies are clearer during the cold period, when it is the turn of the land animals to be more active. The best time to visit is in April and May, or between September and November, when the number of tourists is at its lowest.

As extremes of weather are unknown in this part of the world, the timing of a voyage should be decided by other factors, such as the best time to arrive at your destination. If that destination is in the tropical South Pacific, where the safe season starts in May, an arrival in South America in February would be about right. However, if your destination is Southern Chile, the timing would be quite different as the best time there is during the austral

P36 • Voyages from North America

Recommended time: September to December (southbound voyages)

Tropical storms: June to November (Eastern North Pacific)

World Cruising Routes:

PT12 California and Mexico to Galapagos
PT11 Southbound from Panama and Central America
PS14 Ecuador to Peru and Chile
PS11 Ecuador to Galapagos
PS13 Galapagos to Easter Island and Gambier Islands
PS17 Easter Island to Southern Chile

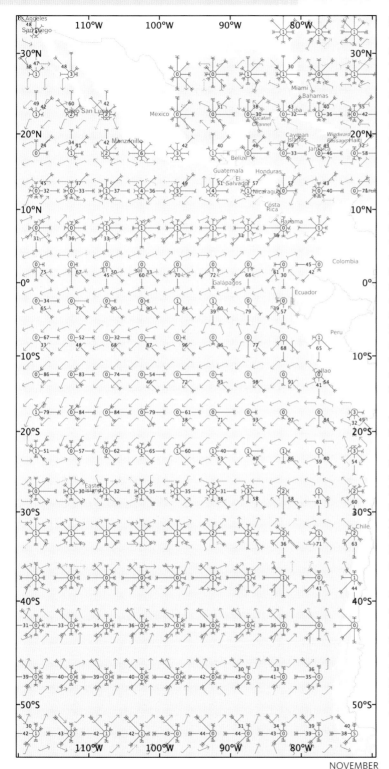

NOVEMBER

Sailing between the two halves of the American continent has very few alternatives to choose from. Southbound voyages usually follow the contour of the continental land mass, its proximity making it easy to sail south by coastal cruising. The timing of the voyage depends entirely on the optimum time of arrival at the final destination. Those who intend to spend longer in South America, and wish to be in Southern Chile during the austral summer, ought to plan on arriving there by November or December. This could mean sailing south from the US West Coast during the hurricane season in Mexico, so ideally that segment of the voyage should be sailed either before or after the hurricane season so as to be outside of the critical area for the start of the South American part of the voyage. Similar considerations apply to voyages that will continue from South America towards the tropical South Pacific with an arrival there not earlier than April in the Marquesas, or May in Tahiti.

Regardless of the point of departure, an important decision that needs to be made is whether to sail to the Galapagos first, and continue the voyage to the mainland from there, or head for the mainland first. The advantage of the latter is that the timing of the voyage south is more flexible and a convenient place can be found in Ecuador as a base to explore some of the interior, or to leave the boat unattended until the time comes to resume the voyage.

There are basically three alternatives for a South American cruise: to concentrate on the mainland and follow an inshore route, to visit only part of the mainland, such as Ecuador, before sailing an offshore route to the south of the continent, possibly by calling at Easter Island, or a mixture of the two by switching between the inshore and offshore options.

Southern Ocean passage

Jane and I chose to take *Vagrant* south and we sailed from New Zealand bound for Southern Chile in January, the height of summer. The plan was to be far enough south to get the westerly winds, but not far enough to meet ice or the gales of high latitudes. The route takes you close to the point on earth farthest from land. There are few places where you are more alone and far from help. It is not for the faint hearted, and you must have confidence in your ship and crew.

This is one of the classic sailing ship routes and in earlier years we might have seen a great wool clipper from Australia or a Nantucket whaler heading home with a hold full of valuable oil. As it happened we saw no other ships and our only companions were the pelagic seabirds.

Both the beginning and end of our journey were at about 40°S but the great circle route would have taken us down to about 55°S, which at this time of year is right in the path of the endless parade of low-pressure systems marching eastwards. If we were some single-handed racer of the lunatic fringe, we would have been down there revelling in the storms and piling on more sail to ride the lows. But we are rather more conservative and fancied neither the storms nor the risk of meeting ice, or indeed the possibility of being run down by a 30 metre racing trimaran doing 25 knots with its solo skipper asleep below!

So we stayed between 42°S and 45°S and sought to position ourselves just far enough south to get the westerlies but no further. Generally we had quartering winds in the 20–25 knots range and a number of gales with the wind above 35 knots, but we only had one severe gale with sustained winds of 45–50 knots and gusts to perhaps 55 or 60 knots. *Vagrant* performed beautifully towing a parachute drogue to hold her stern up to the sea and we never had any doubt of her care for us. As always you learn from the experience, we realised that we should have had some more sail up as we were actually going too slowly, which allowed some of the breaking seas astern to come on board.

Bill McLaren, *Vagrant of Clyde*

P37 • Voyages from Tahiti

Recommended time: October

Tropical storms: November to May

World Cruising Routes:

PS25	Tahiti to Austral Islands
PS26	Tahiti to Southern Chile
PS17	Easter Island to Southern Chile

There are two radically different approaches to this challenging voyage: to take the classic sailing route with the prevailing westerlies of the Roaring Forties, or sail a more conservative route by staying just south of the area of prevailing SE trade winds and hope for the best. The southern route has undoubtedly the best chance of favourable winds, although in summer it may be necessary to go even further south than 40°S to be sure of getting the best of those prevailing westerlies. The northern route may be able to stay between 30°S and 35°S, and while the direction of the winds in November can be from virtually any point of the compass, the percentage of winds from a favourable direction is higher.

An attraction of the northern route is that it does not require a long detour to visit some of the islands that are passed, such as the Australs, whose main island of Tubuai has a limited range of facilities. The suggested route is outside the area affected by cyclones which only reaches as far east as Pitcairn Island. Easter Island is another worthwhile stop to relieve not only the monotony of a long passage, but to visit one of the most interesting islands in the world. The recommended landfall for voyages bound for the Chilean fjordland is the Chacao Channel, whereas Cape Pilar marks the entrance into the Magellan Strait for those bound for the South Atlantic.

P38 • Voyages from Australia and New Zealand

Recommended time: October to December

Tropical storms: November to May

World Cruising Routes:

PS91	New South Wales to New Zealand
PS67	New Zealand to Tahiti
PS25	Tahiti to Austral Islands
PS26	Tahiti to Southern Chile
PS17	Easter Island to Southern Chile
PS68	New Zealand to Southern Chile

Those who plan to sail this long stretch to South America have the same two options as voyages originating in Tahiti, a high-latitude route in the Roaring Forties, or a compromise route which keeps just south of the belt of prevailing SE trade winds and also the area affected by tropical storms. As the southern route has a better chance of favourable winds most of those who make this passage prefer to sail that way. At least, if they tire of the boisterous conditions they have to endure, they have the option of going north and stopping at one of the islands en route.

Cruising hubs

Puerto Montt *

As the main support centre for cruises in Southern Chile, Puerto Montt has an adequate range of repair and haul-out facilities, most of which are concentrated at Marina del Sur. Puerto Montt Hospital has both general and emergency services. Most flights from El Tepual airport (PMC) are to the capital Santiago de Chile for onward international connections.

For details of Tahiti, Easter Island and Ushuaia see pages 118 and 185.

What next?

Most voyages to South America continue from there in a westerly direction towards the tropical South Pacific by the classic route from Galapagos to the Marquesas and beyond. An alternative way to reach French Polynesia is to sail a southerly route via Easter Island, Pitcairn and the Gambier Islands. This is also the route taken by boats which have cruised Southern Chile, although rather than point west some would turn south to cruise the islands of Tierra del Fuego, or even cross the Drake Passage to Antarctica. The alternative is to head east via the Magellan Strait or Beagle Channel and continue their voyage into the South Atlantic.

For those who prefer to stay in the Pacific, northbound voyages from South America are quite straightforward as far as Mexico but continuing from there to the US West Coast is more difficult on account of the prevailing winds. The preferred solution for those who are not prepared to fight those winds is to make a detour to Hawaii and reach North America by that roundabout way. The advantage of this latter option is that the voyage to Hawaii can be easily planned to benefit from favourable conditions whether it starts in Southern Chile, Peru, Ecuador or Panama.

Voyages to Asia

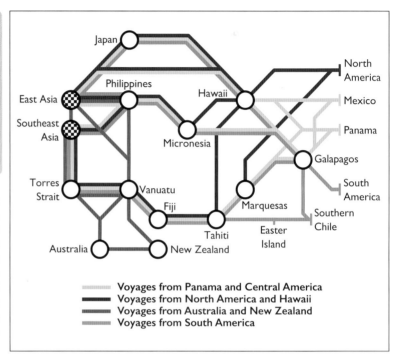

Voyages from Panama and Central America
Voyages from North America and Hawaii
Voyages from Australia and New Zealand
Voyages from South America

Compared to the transpacific route from Panama to Asia via the South Pacific, which is sailed every year by hundreds of cruising boats, the more direct route to Asia via Hawaii and Micronesia is considerably less travelled. One of the reasons is the risk posed by tropical storms in the Western North Pacific and this fact must be taken into account when planning a voyage to Asia from anywhere in the Pacific.

P39 ● Voyages from Panama and Central America

P39a Voyages via Tahiti
P39b Voyages via Micronesia

The lasting lure of the South Seas continues to persuade most sailors to sail the roundabout route to Southeast Asia via Tahiti and the Torres Strait rather than what appears to be the more logical route via Micronesia. For voyages bound for Asia, this shorter and more convenient route should be the preferred alternative as the attractions of some of the Micronesian islands are often on a par with those of the South Pacific.

P39a Voyages via Tahiti

Recommended time: March to September (South Pacific), October to February (Southeast Asia)

Tropical storms: November to May (South Pacific)

World Cruising Routes:

PT11	Southbound from Panama and Central America
PT12	California and Mexico to Galapagos
PS12	Galapagos to Marquesas
PS22	Marquesas to Tuamotus and Tahiti
PS32	Society Islands to Tonga
PS41	Tonga to Fiji
PS53	Fiji to Vanuatu
PS77	Vanuatu to Queensland and Torres Strait
IS13	Westbound from Torres Strait
IT11	Bali to Singapore

The classic route from Panama to the Torres Strait, and thence via Indonesia to Southeast Asia, stretches right across the South Pacific. In spite of its considerable length of close to 9,000 miles, with good timing it can be sailed in one long season. In order to do that, the arrival in Tahiti must coincide with the start of the safe season, which is May. Such tight timing must be observed throughout the South Pacific so that the Torres Strait is transited before the end of September or early October. In spite of its tightness, this schedule still allows time to call at the most interesting places en route, and can even incorporate a detour from Vanuatu to Northern Queensland so that a stretch of the Great Barrier Reef can be enjoyed before bidding goodbye to the Pacific. Once the Indian Ocean is reached, the voyage continues to Indonesia and Singapore.

Weather conditions in the South Pacific during the recommended time coincide with the winter trade wind season and are generally favourable. Similar conditions will continue in the Indian Ocean. Light winds, with a high proportion of southerly winds, will be encountered on the final leg to Singapore. Individual segments of this long voyage, and possible alternative routes, are described in detail in voyages P1 (page 167), P8 (page 187), P13 (page 196) and I1 (page 274).

P39b Voyages via Micronesia

Recommended time: December to May

Tropical storms: June to November (Eastern North Pacific), all year (Western North Pacific)

World Cruising Routes:

PN25	Panama, Central America and Mexico to Micronesia
PN23	Panama, Central America and Mexico to Hawaii
PT11	Southbound from Panama and Central America
PT18	Galapagos to Micronesia
PN82	Westbound routes
PT17	Galapagos to Hawaii
PN37	Hawaii to Japan
PN71	Japan to China and Hong Kong
PN88	Palau to Philippines
PN52	Philippines to China and Hong Kong
PN51	Philippines to Singapore

Destinations in Asia can be reached by two different routes from Panama, the shorter route via Micronesia, or the longer route via Hawaii which is of interest to boats bound for Japan and Northern China. Both Micronesia and Hawaii can be reached by a northern, more direct, route or a southern route that dips close to the Galapagos. The attraction of the northern route is that it gives the opportunity to call at various places in Central America and Mexico before striking offshore, thus considerably reducing the length of the subsequent passage. The attraction of the southern route is that some of the South American mainland as well as the Galapagos Islands can easily be included in the itinerary without adding too much to its length. Voyages via Micronesia should be planned for the early months of the year when the risk of typhoons is lowest, whereas those via Hawaii have more flexibility. These options are described in more detail in voyage P16 (page 203).

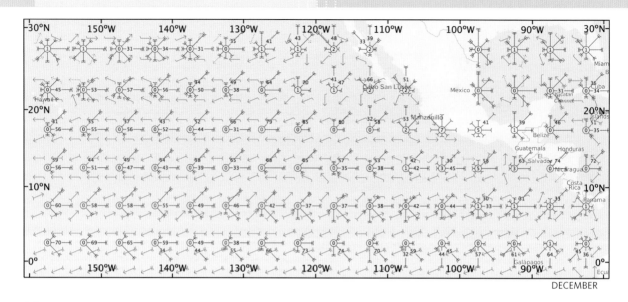

DECEMBER

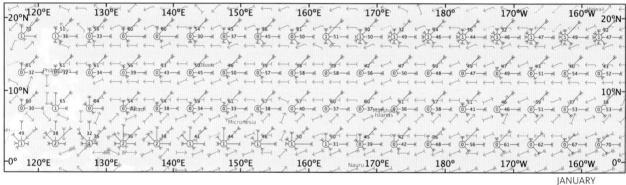

JANUARY

P40 • Voyages from North America and Hawaii

P40a Voyages via Hawaii
P40b Voyages via Tahiti

The two main alternatives for voyages between North America and the Asian mainland are similar to those for voyages from Panama, a shorter direct route that keeps to the North Pacific, and a much longer route via the South Pacific.

P40a Voyages via Hawaii

Recommended time: January to April

Tropical storms: June to November (Eastern North Pacific), all year (Western North Pacific)

World Cruising Routes:

PN11	California to Hawaii
PN16	Pacific Northwest to Hawaii
PN37	Hawaii to Japan
PN71	Japan to China and Hong Kong
PN36	Hawaii to Eastern Micronesia
PN82	Westbound routes
PN85	Guam to Japan
PN84	Guam to Philippines
PN52	Philippines to China and Hong Kong
PN51	Philippines to Singapore

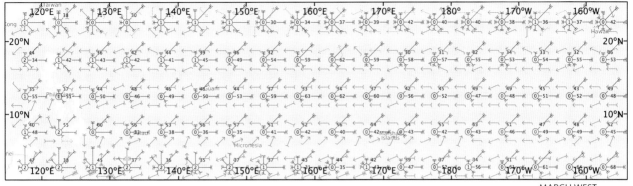

MARCH WEST

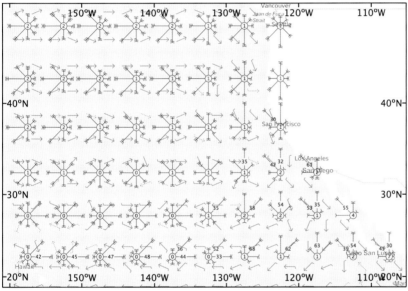

MARCH EAST

will benefit from good winds all the way, with possible stops in Guam and Okinawa.

Voyages to Japan will fare worst during the winter months when NE winds are only predominant to approximately 25°N, north of which there is an increasingly higher percentage of NW winds. For this reason, direct winter passages from Hawaii should be avoided and as much as possible should be sailed within the trade wind band, sailing as far as Guam or even Okinawa before turning north for Japan. From Guam, the northbound route passes through the Mariana Islands and if any stops are envisaged, permission must be obtained from North Mariana's representative in Guam. From Okinawa the route follows the chain of the Ryukyu Islands, one of Japan's most beautiful and less developed areas, the subtropical mountainous islands being covered in dense jungles and surrounded by coral reefs. The islands owe their verdant nature to the high rainfall, often caused by passing typhoons, which pose a real threat in summer. That is one of the main reasons to plan the voyage from Hawaii to Japan for the early part of the year when the risk of typhoons is lowest.

The planning of this voyage is dictated primarily by the optimum time of arrival at your chosen destination, which is the period when the risk of typhoons in East Asia is lowest. Although tropical storms can occur in East Asia at any time, the risk factor during the first months of the year is acceptably low and a calculated risk can be taken provided the weather is carefully monitored so as to be able to take the necessary avoiding action should that need arise. The NE trade winds are consistent during the early months of the year with favourable conditions in most of the area west of Hawaii.

There are two alternative routes from Hawaii, a northern route to either Japan or directly to the mainland, and a southern route to Micronesia and the Philippines. Voyages to mainland destinations, such as Hong Kong,

The situation is much easier on the southern route which benefits from favourable winds almost down to the equator making it easy to stop at any of the island groups en route. From the Marshall to the Caroline Islands and on to Palau and the Philippines, there is a wide variety of interesting destinations along this southern track. The chain of tropical islands that straddles this route provides excellent cruising opportunities, with many of its remote islands being rarely visited by outsiders. The Marshall Islands are the nearest group to Hawaii and there is a visible American influence due to a formerly large US military presence, which has shrunk considerably in recent years. But even here, outside the main settlements, life moves at a slow unhurried pace. The feeling that the modern world has barely affected the life of the small isolated communities is even more apparent in the outer islands of Kiribati and Micronesia where, in some of the more remote islands, a traditional way of life is still strictly adhered to. The southern route leads to Palau and its renowned diving sites before continuing via the Philippines either to North Borneo and on to Singapore, or to destinations in East Asia. Reaching those destinations by way of this warm-water route is probably a more attractive proposition than by a passage in higher latitudes. An area where several piracy attacks have occurred in recent years and should be avoided is off the NE coast of Borneo and SE Palwan, the entire Sulu archipelago and the SW coast of Mindanao.

P40b Voyages via Tahiti

Recommended time: March to June (to Tahiti), June to October (Tahiti to Torres Strait)

Tropical storms: June to November (Eastern North Pacific), November to May (South Pacific)

World Cruising Routes:

PT14	California and Mexico to Marquesas
PT15	Pacific Northwest to Marquesas
PS22	Marquesas to Tuamotus and Tahiti
PN11	California to Hawaii
PN16	Pacific Northwest to Hawaii
PT24	Hawaii to Tahiti and Marquesas
PS31	Society Islands to Cook Islands
PS32	Society Islands to Tonga
PS41	Tonga to Fiji
PS53	Fiji to Vanuatu
PS77	Vanuatu to Queensland and Torres Strait
IS13	Westbound from Torres Strait
IT11	Bali to Singapore

This considerably longer way to reach Asia will only appeal to those who want to cruise the South Pacific and are not deterred by how long it may take to reach their final destination. There are two alternatives to reach Tahiti from the west coast of North America, a direct route via the Marquesas or a longer route via Hawaii. The Hawaii route is usually used by boats which have sailed from the

mainland the previous year so as to be able to head for the South Pacific as soon as it is safe to do so. In practice this means an arrival in the Marquesas in April and in Tahiti in May or June. This segment coincides with Voyage P3 (page 174), which should be consulted for details.

From Tahiti, the voyage heads west calling at the Cook, Tonga, Samoa Islands and Fiji before continuing through the Coral Sea to the Torres Strait. These segments are described in voyages P8 (page 187) and P13 (page 196), while the final leg from Torres to Singapore is outlined in voyage I1 (page 274).

P41 • Voyages from New Zealand and Australia

P41a Voyages to Southeast Asia

P41b Voyages to East Asia

Most voyages to Southeast Asia, and especially those destined for Western Malaysia and Thailand, take the shorter route which leads through the Torres Strait. Destinations in East Asia can be best reached by sailing north through the Coral Sea and continuing across the equator either to the mainland or to the Philippines and Japan.

P41a Voyages to Southeast Asia

Recommended time: September to November

Tropical storms: November to May (South Pacific and South Indian Ocean)

World Cruising Routes:

PS62	New Zealand to Queensland
PS63	New Zealand to New Caledonia
PS75	New Caledonia to Vanuatu
PS77	Vanuatu to Queensland and Torres Strait
IS11	Torres Strait to Darwin
IS14	Northbound from Darwin
IT11	Bali to Singapore
PS81	Solomon Islands to Papua New Guinea
PT28	Northbound from Melanesia
PN51	Philippines to Singapore

The timing of a voyage from either New Zealand or Australia to Southeast Asia is a relatively simple matter as it can easily be planned to coincide with the safe seasons on both sides of the equator. Although the departure from the South Pacific can be delayed until near the end of the safe season, most people prefer to do it sooner so as to be in Singapore by late October or early November, which means a transit through the Torres Strait in late September or early October. According to the pilot charts favourable winds can be expected during September and October, with consistent SE winds in the Coral Sea, and lighter S or SE winds in the Arafura and Timor Seas.

Voyages originating in New Zealand have a choice of routes across the Coral Sea, either by sailing a direct route and calling at the various island groups, or diverting at some point for the Australian mainland and continuing the voyage inside the Great Barrier Reef. Cairns, in Northern Queensland, is a popular port of call among those who have sailed the offshore route but want to experience some of Australia, as well as to get a taste of the Great Barrier Reef, before leaving the South Pacific.

Boats leaving from Southeast Australia have a similar choice of sailing an offshore route and calling at some of the islands in the Coral Sea, or taking the route inside the Great Barrier Reef. Once through the Torres Strait, most boats call at Darwin, in Northern Australia, a favourite port of call on the world cruising circuit. Provisioning

and repair facilities are of a good standard and Darwin is also a convenient place to leave the boat unattended while visiting some of Australia's interior.

Those who are on a tight schedule may prefer to sail nonstop from the Torres Strait to Indonesia. The nearest port of entry is Kupang. In 2016 the Indonesian authorities decided to ease formalities for sailors intending to cruise the islands of this vast archipelago by abolishing the requirement for a cruising permit obtained in advance. Some formalities still have to be completed at the first port of entry but the situation is much more amenable than in the past.

There is an alternative route which bypasses the Torres Strait and reaches Southeast Asia by sailing north from Vanuatu to Papua New Guinea. North of the equator the route can call at Palau, the Philippines and North Borneo on the way to Singapore. An area where several piracy attacks have occured in recent years and should be avoided is off the NE coast of Borneo and SE Palawan, the entire Sulu archipelago and the SW coast of Mindanao.

OCTOBER

P41b Voyages to East Asia

Recommended time: September to October (South Pacific), December to February (North Pacific)

Tropical storms: All year (Western North Pacific), November to May (South Pacific and South Indian Ocean)

World Cruising Routes:

PS63	New Zealand to New Caledonia
PS75	New Caledonia to Vanuatu
PS94	New South Wales to Vanuatu
PS106	North Queensland to Papua New Guinea
PS78	Vanuatu to Solomon Islands
PS81	Solomon Islands to Papua New Guinea
PT28	Northbound from Melanesia
PN85	Guam to Japan
PN52	Philippines to China and Hong Kong
PN51	Philippines to Singapore

Voyages to East Asia need careful planning to avoid arriving in the North Pacific at the wrong time. As the tropical storm seasons complement each other across the equator, the most propitious time for a northbound voyage is during the northern winter, when the incidence of typhoons is at its lowest level. Such timing allows a voyage starting from New Zealand or Australia to sail north through the Coral Sea, calling at various islands, just before the end of the safe season in the South Pacific. The route continues through the outer islands of New Guinea, an area which is not affected by tropical storms. An arrival north of the equator early in the new year means that the voyage to destinations on the Asian mainland or Japan takes place during the relatively safe time of the year. Voyages to destinations in low latitudes, such as Palau, North Borneo or Singapore, are not normally affected by tropical storms.

P42 • Voyages from South America

P42a Voyages via Micronesia

P42b Voyages via Tahiti

In spite of the vast distance that separates them, voyages between these two extremities of the Pacific Ocean are relatively easy to plan as, with good timing, favourable conditions can be counted on throughout their considerable length. There are two very different alternatives, a northern route via Micronesia, which may appeal to sailors bound for East Asia, and a southern route via Tahiti, which may be more interesting to those bound for Southeast Asia.

P42a Voyages via Micronesia

Recommended time: October to November (to Micronesia), December to January (North Pacific)

Tropical storms: November to May (South Pacific), June to November (Eastern North Pacific), all year (Western North Pacific)

World Cruising Routes:

PS11	Ecuador to Galapagos
PT18	Galapagos to Micronesia
PS12	Galapagos to Marquesas
PN82	Westbound routes
PT17	Galapagos to Hawaii
PN37	Hawaii to Japan

This voyage linking the South American and Asian mainland appeals to sailors on a round the world voyage who have transited the Panama

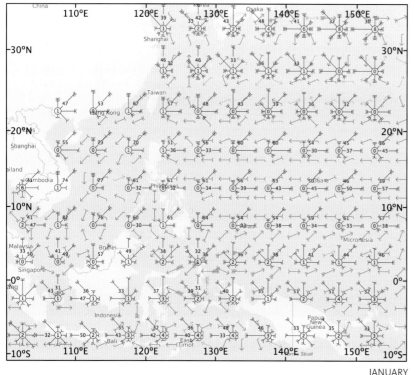

JANUARY

Canal and wish to see some of the best that the South Pacific and North Pacific have to offer. Having explored some of the inland attractions of Ecuador, that country's offshore archipelago makes a perfect first stage on this voyage of exploration. From there, a direct offshore route can be sailed to the Line Islands in Eastern Micronesia, unless a detour to the Marquesas, and the opportunity to visit those spectacular islands, proves more tempting. Although the Marquesas are very rarely affected by tropical storms, this is a risk that needs to be taken into account if contemplating calling there during the critical period, whereas the direct route to the North Pacific would encounter favourable conditions throughout its length.

The chain of Micronesian islands provides excellent cruising opportunities, with many of its remote islands being rarely visited by outsiders. The westbound route then leads to Palau before continuing via the Philippines either to North Borneo and on to Singapore, or to destinations in East Asia. An area that should be avoided along this route is off the NE coast of Borneo and SE Palawan, the entire Sulu archipelago and the SW coast of Mindanao, as several piracy attacks have occurred in recent years.

The timing of this voyage is dictated primarily by having to decide on the safest time of arrival at the final destination, as this needs to coincide with the time of year when the risk of typhoons in East Asia is still low. Although tropical storms can occur in East Asia at any time, the risk factor during the first months of the year is acceptably low enough to justify taking a calculated risk, provided the weather is carefully monitored so as to be able to take the necessary avoiding action.

Boats bound for Japan may prefer to take a more northerly route by sailing from Galapagos or the Marquesas directly to Hawaii and continue from there to either Japan or the Asian mainland although the Micronesian route may be more appealing for an early winter passage.

P42b Voyages via Tahiti

Recommended time: March to June (to Tahiti), June to October (Tahiti to Torres Strait), September to October (Torres to Southeast Asia)

Tropical storms: November to May

World Cruising Routes:

PS19	Northbound from Chile
PS15	South America to Easter Island
PS16	Westbound from Easter Island
PS11	Ecuador to Galapagos

PS12	Galapagos to Marquesas
PS22	Marquesas to Tuamotus and Tahiti
PS28	Gambier Islands to Tuamotus and Tahiti
PS32	Society Islands to Tonga
PS41	Tonga to Fiji
PS53	Fiji to Vanuatu
PS77	Vanuatu to Queensland and Torres Strait
IS11	Torres Strait to Darwin
IS14	Northbound from Darwin
IT11	Bali to Singapore

This voyage, which provides the opportunity to experience some of the best of the South Pacific, allows even more permutations than the previous voyage. The first choice to be made is at the very start as, depending on the point of departure, it offers the choice of either sailing to Tahiti via Galapagos and the Marquesas, or by way of Easter Island, Pitcairn and the Gambiers. The former would appeal to boats that have reached the Pacific by way of the Panama Canal, the latter to those who may have been cruising Southern Chile. One further early alternative presents itself in the Marquesas to those who may prefer to forgo the rest of the South Pacific and switch to the northern hemisphere by sailing to either Micronesia or Hawaii and continuing along one of the routes described earlier. Westbound voyages from Tahiti have a variety of alternative routes to reach the Torres Strait, from where the usual route to Southeast Asia calls at Bali before crossing the Indonesian archipelago to Singapore.

As much of this voyage coincides with the safe season in the South Pacific, its timing can be more flexible as there are only two critical factors that need to be observed: not to arrive in Tahiti before May and to avoid arriving in the South Indian Ocean after the end of October, which is the start of the NW monsoon west of the Torres Strait, with the cyclone season also due soon.

Cruising hubs

Guam ***

Due to a resident sailing and fishing community, there are good repair and haul-out facilities, and also a typhoon shelter. Medical services are of a good standard. Guam international airport (GUM) has flights to mainland USA, Hawaii, several Asian cities, Australia and some Pacific countries.

Dutch Harbor visitors dock.

Okinawa *

Yachting facilities in Naha are basic but the American Seaman's Club can help with emergency repairs. Okinawa airport (OKA) operates flights to mainland Japan, East Asia and the USA.

Hong Kong ****

With several yacht clubs and an active sailing community, facilities in Hong Kong are of a high standard. The international airport (HKG) has frequent flights to all major destinations in the world.

Manila ***

Yachting facilities are concentrated around the Manila Yacht Club, which has a good range of repair services, docking facilities for visitors and is a typhoon shelter. Manila International airport (MNL) operates flights to all major Australasian destinations, USA and Europe. The Philippine General Hospital is operated by the University of Manila and has a wide range of facilities catering for both public and private patients.

See also Honolulu (page 201), Tahiti (page 185) and Darwin (page 289).

What next?

Having arrived in Asia from the east the logical way would seem to be to continue west and visit some of the countries in Southeast Asia before crossing the North Indian Ocean to the Red Sea and Mediterranean, or swing south to join the South Indian route which calls at the various island groups en route to the Cape of Good Hope and the South Atlantic.

Those who are reluctant to leave the Pacific have the option of turning south from Micronesia and visiting some of the countries in the Coral Sea, including Australia, and then continuing west through the Torres Strait, or completing the loop by sailing to New Zealand and returning to the tropics from there. For those who are on a world voyage and prefer to return home to either North America or Europe by an eastbound route from Asia, the only reasonable alternative is a passage through high latitudes, either in the North or South Pacific. Some of the circular voyages originating in East Asia outline some interesting route suggestions that may fit your long-term cruising plans, such as the challenging loop which can be achieved by sailing north to Japan and returning to the North American mainland by a high-latitude route, or making an even bolder detour to Alaska.

CIRCULAR VOYAGES IN THE PACIFIC OCEAN

Many world cruisers become caught in the South Pacific gyre for many years. And why not, as these are the finest islands anchored in any ocean.

Tom Walker

The greatest disadvantage of the Pacific Ocean from a cruising point of view is that it does not lend itself to a logical circumnavigation, a fact recognised as early as the 16th century by the Spanish navigators. Faced by the difficulty posed by an eastbound passage against the prevailing winds to their point of departure, they were often forced to continue all the way around the world. Today's voyagers are faced with the same dilemma, but at least the improved windward-going capability of their craft and better weather information make it easier to find a solution. In some cases this points to a circular voyage.

These circular voyages should be regarded as a merry-go-round which can be joined, or left, at any point. For example, voyage PC1 can be used by voyagers starting in Australia or New Zealand as a template for a circular voyage to the west coast of North America, whereas voyage PC7 can be joined by sailors starting off from any of the countries on the Pacific rim.

PC1	•	The Polynesian Circuit
PC2	•	The Intermediate Polynesian Circuit
PC3	•	The Short Polynesian Circuit
PC4	•	The Tropical Circuit
PC5	•	The North Pacific Circuit
PC6	•	The Pacific Circuit
PC7	•	The Grand Pacific Circuit
PC8	•	The Southern Cross Circuit
PC9	•	The Hibiscus Circuit
PC10	•	The Southeast Asia Circuit
PC11	•	The Australasia Circuit
PC12	•	Counterclockwise Circumnavigation of South America
PC13	•	Counterclockwise Circumnavigation of North America

PC1 • The Polynesian Circuit

This is the most popular circular voyage in the Pacific and for good reason as its itinerary includes some of the most attractive cruising destinations in the world and, with good planning, it can be accomplished in about 18 months during favourable seasons throughout its duration. For those who do not have the time to complete the entire circuit, or who are looking for a different route for the return voyage to the North American mainland, there are shorter variations to choose from.

Voyagers starting from the Pacific Northwest need to plan on an early departure when sailing conditions in the North Pacific can still be rough. Those who wish to arrive in the South Pacific at the start of the safe cruising season, April in the Marquesas or May in Tahiti, might have to sail to Southern California or Mexico during the previous season, and thus be able to make an early start for the South Pacific the following year. Most sailors aim to be in the Marquesas as early as possible after the end of the cyclone season so as to be able to enjoy a full cruising season in the tropical South Pacific.

Weather conditions for a passage to the Marquesas in March are generally favourable, but those who intend to sail first to the Galapagos need to make an earlier start, in late January or February, so as to be sure of arriving in the Marquesas by early April. The next leg to Tahiti can be sailed nonstop, but as the direct route passes close to the Tuamotus, calling at some of the more accessible atolls can easily be included. As the Tuamotus are the first of several potential detours, it would be advisable to have a rough cruising plan for the season ahead. For those who plan to leave the tropics during summer, the one fixed deadline is the passage to New Zealand, which should be sailed before the onset of the South Pacific cyclone season. In view of current climate changes that date has been brought forward to mid-November, so the passage from Fiji to New Zealand should be planned for October.

One other date, albeit less critical, is that of the annual Heiva festival, a celebration of dance, music, arts and sport activities, which is held in Tahiti and the Society Islands between the middle of June and the middle of July. A similar, but less ambitious, festival is held in early August in Rarotonga, in the Cook Islands. West of the Cook Islands, there is a wide choice of tempting landfalls making the task of deciding what to leave out a hard choice. The various alternatives are described in voyage P8 (page 187).

Weather conditions in the Central South Pacific during the recommended period are generally favourable, with long spells of steady trade winds, occasionally interrupted by two or three days of irregular winds, squally weather and thunderstorms. The culprit is the South Pacific Tropical Convergence Zone, a regional phenomenon whose effects can vary from year to year.

New Zealand is a perfect place to spend the off season as it has good marinas, excellent repair facilities and countless attractions, some of which are probably best visited on four wheels. The best yachting facilities are concentrated in the top half of North Island where there is a wide choice of marinas and boatyards, starting with the popular first landfall at Opua in the Bay of Islands. Further south, the small town of Whangarei is a favourite among visiting sailors as

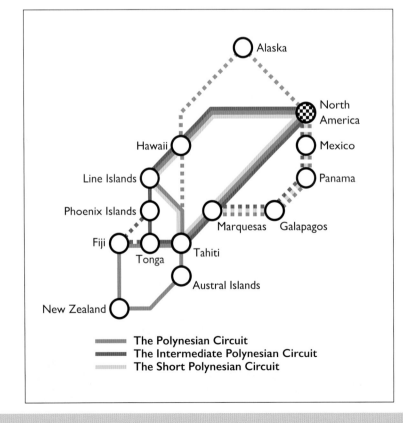

The Polynesian Circuit
The Intermediate Polynesian Circuit
The Short Polynesian Circuit

it has a marina in the centre of town. Auckland itself has several marinas, such as Westhaven, close to the centre, while Bayswater, Westpark and Half Moon Bay marinas are located in the suburbs.

The start of the return voyage to Tahiti is best made at the end of the cyclone season, in May or early June, before the onset of the southern winter. If a prompt departure is made from New Zealand, there is sufficient time to reach the west coast of North America via Hawaii by late summer or early autumn. The eastbound route from New Zealand must stay within the band of westerly winds but still far enough north to avoid straying into the Roaring Forties. Between latitudes 35°S and 38°S there is a good chance of finding a reasonable percentage of westerly winds to make the required easting as far as the Austral Islands, which lie almost due south of Tahiti. From there, the prevailing SE trade winds should ensure a fast reach to Tahiti. Those who have passed through here quickly on their onward voyage will now have a second chance to see more of Tahiti but should not linger too long if they intend to reach North America before winter.

The SE winds will continue from Tahiti to the equator, with several uninhabited islands close to the route, such as Caroline, Flint and Malden, each having a fair-weather anchorage in their lee. The Northern Line Islands are inhabited, with Christmas Island being the administrative centre of this small group belonging to Kiribati. Among them, Fanning is the favourite with visiting yachts as it has a pass into its protected lagoon. The northernmost island, Palmyra, is US territory and a protected nature reserve, the only residents being a few scientists engaged in research work.

Those who wish to be sure of a better sailing angle on the subsequent leg to Hawaii may decide to make the passage from Tahiti further east by staying to windward of the Line Islands. As this track passes close to the west of both the Tuamotus and Marquesas, a stop in those islands can easily be included.

The onward voyage from Hawaii to the mainland is greatly affected by the position of the North Pacific High. The accepted tactic is to sail north keeping to the west of the high until the area of prevailing westerly winds is reached, when the course can be altered for the mainland. Alternatively, from Hawaii the voyage can continue north towards Alaska, although such a detour, however attractive, will add several thousand miles to an already rather arduous schedule.

Route: California – [Mexico] – [Galapagos] – Marquesas (April) – Tahiti (June) – Tonga (July to August) – Fiji (September to October) – New Zealand (November to April) – Australs – Tahiti (May to June) – [Line Islands] – Hawaii (July) – [Alaska (July to August)] – US West Coast

Start: February to March year I

Return: August to September year II

Tropical storms: June to November (Eastern North Pacific), November to May (South Pacific)

Total distance: 14,000–17,000 miles

Duration: 17–19 months

PC2 • The Intermediate Polynesian Circuit

This shorter circular voyage has the great advantage that it can be done in one long season. The initial stages are the same as the full circuit but, depending on time considerations, the return voyage can be started at any point west of Tahiti. If the intention is to get back to the mainland before the autumn, the voyage from the South Pacific to Hawaii must start no later than early August. This means that if the Marquesas have been reached by early April and less time is spent in French Polynesia it will be possible to visit several islands as far as Tonga before turning north for the equator and Hawaii. There are two different options for this northbound voyage: a relaxed cruise with stops at various island groups which lie close to this route: Tokelau, Phoenix and the Northern Line Islands, or a nonstop passage to the equator, with an attempt to make sufficient easting so as to cross the equator to windward of the Line Islands and thus ensure

Tahiti welcome.

Neiafu in Tonga's Vava'u Archipelago.

a better sailing angle towards Hawaii. It must be stressed that Hawaii can be affected by tropical storms during the North Pacific hurricane season, which lasts from June until November, so this fact must be borne in mind if an arrival in Hawaii during that period is envisaged, even if the risk factor is not very high.

A safer solution would be to spend the entire safe season in the South Pacific by sailing as far as Fiji, or possibly even Vanuatu, and embarking on the passage to Hawaii as late as October. This timing would avoid both the coming South Pacific cyclone season and the North Pacific hurricane season which should have come to an end before the equator is crossed en route to Hawaii. Such a late arrival in Hawaii means that the winter has to be spent there which will be a great advantage the following year when the homebound voyage can be sailed during the most favourable season, and even a detour to Alaska could easily be accommodated.

Route: California – [Mexico] – [Galapagos] – Marquesas (April) – Tahiti (June) – Cook Islands (July), Tonga (August) – [Fiji (September)] – Tokelau – Phoenix Islands (October) – [Line Islands] – Hawaii (November) – US West Coast

Start: February to March year I

Return: June to August year II

Tropical storms: June to November (Eastern North Pacific), November to May (South Pacific)

Total distance: 10,500–13,000 miles

Duration: 15–18 months

PC3 • The Short Polynesian Circuit

This shorter circuit, that takes advantage of prevailing conditions and favourable seasons, can be accomplished in one year. Those who wish to arrive in French Polynesia at the start of the safe season should start from Southern California as early in the season as possible. Later departures are quite acceptable but they will limit the time in French Polynesia. The alternative is to sail to Baja California in late autumn, spend the winter on the west coast of Mexico or Central America and head for the South Pacific the following year when the cyclone season has come to an end there. A one-year voyage only allows a few months to be spent in French Polynesia before turning around in July or early August and heading across the equator for Hawaii. Favourable winds should be carried all the way to the Line Islands. North of the equator, the rest of the passage to Hawaii will most probably be hard on the wind, so it may be advisable to make some easting while on the latitude of the Line Islands. Although a late summer/early autumn arrival in Hawaii may run the risk of being caught by a tropical storm, hurricanes are relatively rare in that area. The onward passage from Hawaii to the mainland is usually affected by the light winds and calms associated with the Pacific High. The tactic is to either stay west of the high and reach the coast by a roundabout route that takes advantage of the westerly winds of high latitudes, or take a more direct route and motor across the southern edge of the high.

Landfall at Ua Pou in the Marquesas.

Route: California – [Mexico] – [Galapagos] – Marquesas (April to May) – Tahiti (June to July) – [Line Islands] – Hawaii (August) – US West Coast

Start: February to April

Return: September to October

Tropical storms: June to November (Eastern North Pacific), November to May (South Pacific)

Total distance: 9,000–12,000 miles

Duration: 7–9 months

PC4 • The Tropical Circuit

This voyage follows the same route and directions as the Polynesian Circuit as far as Fiji from where a different return voyage home is taken. While the majority of boats continue to sail the established route from New Zealand to Tahiti via the Austral Islands, other alternatives for a return to the American mainland have been tried out in recent years. Among them is an eastbound voyage via Micronesia to Hawaii, which is the suggested return route for this circular voyage.

From Fiji the voyage continues into the Coral Sea. With the safe season in the South Pacific coming to an end in early November, by late October the northern islands of Vanuatu should be left for the outer islands of Papua New Guinea as that area is not affected by tropical cyclones. How long to spend in the island groups south of the equator depends on the time available but at some point the equator needs to be crossed to commence the eastbound segment of this voyage along a route that passes south of Micronesia. The prevailing NE winds of the North Pacific are a dominant feature as far south as the equator. The accepted tactic is to make your easting just a few degrees north of the equator where the winds are light and progress can be made with help from the engine and the east-setting current. This is a route that appeals to sailors who are prepared to put their engine to considerable use. The upside of this route is the opportunity to call at some of the remote islands of Micronesia, and witness a way of life which has disappeared in other parts of the world.

Straddling this route is the main group of the Kiribati Islands with the capital Tarawa just north of the equator. From there the route continues to the Line Islands which lie roughly south of Hawaii. They provide a

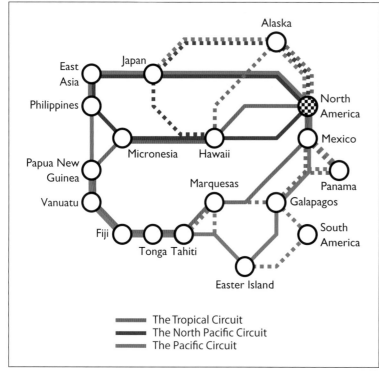

welcome and convenient stop before embarking on the final leg to Hawaii. The passage to Hawaii and the onward voyage to the US West Coast are described in voyage P32b on page 225.

Route: US West Coast – Mexico (February) – [Galapagos] – Marquesas (April) – Tahiti (May to June) – Tonga (July) – Fiji (August to September) – Vanuatu (October) – Papua New Guinea (November to December) – Micronesia (January to February) – Kiribati – [Line Islands] – Hawaii (April to May) – [Alaska (July)] – US West Coast

Start: November year I

Return: June to August year II

Tropical storms: June to November (North Pacific), November to May (South Pacific)

Total distance: 14,000–17,000 miles

Duration: 18–20 months

Taiohae Bay on the Marquesan island of Nuku Hiva.

PC5 • The North Pacific Circuit

This circumnavigation of the North Pacific can be accomplished in about one year and, with careful planning, will benefit from mostly favourable conditions throughout its duration. Depending on the point of departure, different criteria apply for the timing of this voyage. For voyages starting from the Pacific Northwest the best time for a passage to Hawaii would be during summer but there is a risk of hurricanes in the area of Hawaii at that time. Those who prefer to play it entirely safe could sail first south to California and embark on the crossing to Hawaii in late October or early November, when the hurricane season has come to an end.

The next tropical storm season to bear in mind is the one that affects the Western North Pacific, which, in principle spans the entire year, with the winter months being regarded as very low risk. The nearest island groups to Hawaii, Marshall and Kiribati, are rarely affected by such storms and therefore they should be visited in December or January so that other parts of Micronesia are also seen during the safe period.

There are two alternatives for the continuation of this voyage: a shorter version that swings north from Micronesia to Japan, and a longer version which continues to the Philippines and thence to the Asian mainland. Those who prefer to sail the shorter version will either branch off at Guam and reach Japan via the Northern Marianas, or continue to Okinawa and follow from there the chain of the Ryukyu Islands to Japan.

Voyages which continue to the Asian mainland need to loop back towards Japan by June in time for the high-latitude segment which can be sailed either directly to the North American mainland or with a detour to the Aleutian Islands and Alaska.

The one disadvantage of this voyage is that it may be difficult to complete during the safe seasons, and the risk of tropical storms, although remote, must be taken into account both in Micronesia and, especially, Japan.

As in the case of other circular voyages, this North Pacific circuit can be joined at various points, whether in Hawaii, East Asia or Japan, and completed within a similar time frame.

Route: Pacific Northwest – [Southern California (October to November)] – Hawaii (November to December) – Marshall Islands (December) – Kiribati (January) – Micronesia (February) – [Japan] – Philippines (March) – East Asia (April to May) – Japan (June to July) – [Alaska (July to August)] – US West Coast

Start: June to July year I

Return: August to September year II

Tropical storms: June to November (Eastern North Pacific), all year (Western North Pacific)

Total distance: 12,000–15,000 miles

Duration: 13–15 months

PC6 • The Pacific Circuit

This circular voyage, which includes several of the most attractive cruising destinations in both the South and North Pacific, can be completed in approximately 18 months. As in previous examples of voyages starting from the US West Coast, the advantage of an early start for the initial passage to the tropics makes it advisable to move south to Southern California, or preferably Mexico, before the end of the year. This voyage may also appeal to sailors arriving from the Caribbean who may not be interested in a complete circumnavigation of the globe and who may find this two-year Pacific circuit more to their liking.

In the first months of the year southbound voyages from Mexico or Southern California benefit from generally favourable conditions to the Galapagos. From there, the voyage can continue on a direct offshore route to Easter Island, unless an inshore route is preferred as it gives the opportunity to visit Ecuador and Peru before turning west. This is the first of several optional detours along this route, especially in the next segment, from Easter Island to Tahiti, as outlined in voyage P5b on page 180. The islands of French Polynesia are reached at the start of

the safe season with the prospect of nearly six months of carefree South Seas cruising.

From Tahiti the voyage continues along the classic trade wind route all the way to Vanuatu where two very different alternatives beckon: to spend the rest of the safe season visiting the island groups dotted about the Coral Sea, or to sail to Australia and continue the voyage inside the Great Barrier Reef. Whichever option is chosen, the Coral Sea must be left by late October before the start of the cyclone season. As the islands of Papua New Guinea are not affected by cyclones, some time can be spent there before crossing the equator in January or February when the risk of typhoons in the Western North Pacific is still very low.

The early months of the year can be spent slowly cruising north, either from Northern Borneo to Vietnam and China, or to Palau, the Philippines and that way to Hong Kong and the Asian mainland. Those who prefer to bypass the mainland can sail via Okinawa to Japan.

The onward eastbound passage from Japan should not be embarked on too early as weather conditions in those high latitudes only start improving with the arrival of summer. The voyage to the American mainland can be completed nonstop, unless a detour to Alaska, and a summer cruise there, can be fitted into this rich programme.

Route: US West Coast – Mexico (January) – Galapagos (February) – [South America] – Easter Island (March to April) – Pitcairn – Gambier Islands (April) – [Marquesas] – Tuamotus – Tahiti (June) – Tonga (July) – Fiji (August) – Vanuatu (September) – [Australia (October)] – Papua New Guinea (November to December) – Philippines (January to February) – [East Asia (March to April)] – Japan (May to June) – [Alaska (July to August)] – US West Coast

Start: November year I

Return: August to September year II

Tropical storms: June to November (Eastern North Pacific), November to May (South Pacific), all year (Western North Pacific)

Total distance: 19,500–22,000 miles

Duration: 20–22 months

PC7 • The Grand Pacific Circuit

PC7a A Grand Pacific Circuit from North America

PC7b A Grand Pacific Circuit from Asia

PC7c A Grand Pacific Circuit from Australia

PC7d A Grand Pacific Circuit from New Zealand

In spite of an even more ambitious programme than the previous voyage, this truly grand circuit of the Pacific Ocean can be completed within a similar time frame of approximately two years by taking advantage of the most favourable seasons throughout its duration. As such a Pacific merry-go-round can be joined at any point along the way, separate descriptions are given for voyages starting from the west coast of North America, East Asia, Australia or New Zealand.

There are three points where longer or shorter detours can be considered. The first entails a detour to Alaska, the second is the possibility of shortening the overall length of the voyage by sailing directly from California or Mexico to French Polynesia via the Marquesas rather than Easter Island, and the third is to take a similar decision by sailing only as far as the Galapagos and from there to the Marquesas and Tahiti.

PC7a A Grand Pacific Circuit from North America

As far as Fiji, the timing and overall routing suggestions are the same as for voyage PC6. Rather than continue westwards from Fiji, this voyage turns south for New Zealand to spend the cyclone season there. The voyage is resumed with a return to the tropics at the start of the following safe season. Once in the Coral Sea, the voyage can either continue via the various island groups directly to the Torres Strait, or turn west from either New Caledonia or Vanuatu for Australia and reach the Torres Strait by sailing inside the Great Barrier Reef.

The port of Darwin in Northern Australia is a popular first stop in the Indian Ocean as a good base to visit some of Australia's interior and prepare the boat for the continuation of the voyage. As Indonesia is not affected by tropical cyclones, those islands can be reached by late October or early November. The vast archipelago can be crossed along two very different routes: a western route that leads from Bali to Singapore, or an eastern route that stays east of Borneo, although the security situation should be ascertained before sailing this route, which passes through an area, where piracy incidents have been reported in the past.

For those who have chosen the longer version, from Singapore the voyage continues along the coast of Western Malaysia to Phuket in Thailand before turning around to catch the end of the low-risk months in the Western North Pacific. From North Borneo the route turns north with Japan being reached either directly or via the Asian mainland. An early spring arrival in Japan will make it possible to sample at least some of its cruising highlights before setting off on the long high-latitude passage home. One final detour, which could easily be fitted into the overall programme, as it only necessitates a relatively

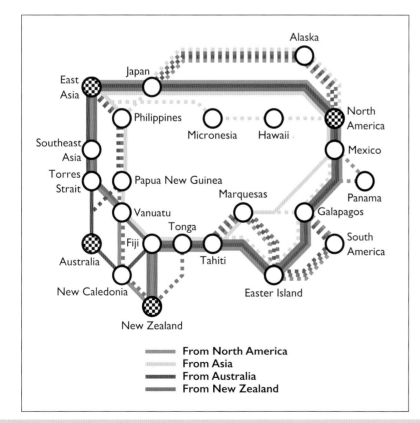

From North America
From Asia
From Australia
From New Zealand

Hangaroa anchorage at Easter Island.

Tropical storms: June to November (Eastern North Pacific), November to May (South Pacific), all year (Western North Pacific)

Total distance: 23,000–25,000 miles

Duration: 22–24 months

PC7b A Grand Pacific Circuit from Asia

A reasonably early start needs to be made for the passage from East Asia to Japan before embarking on the high-latitude voyage to North America. The fact that the timing of this voyage has allowed for a two or three months' stay on the US West Coast means that a detour to Alaska can be easily incorporated into the overall programme. If that option is taken, at the end of summer the route from Alaska can take the scenic Inside Passage to British Columbia and the Pacific Northwest.

The winter can be spent either in Southern California or Mexico, so that a prompt start can be made the following year, especially if the intention is to sail first to the Galapagos and include a possible detour to the South American mainland. A later start can be made from California or Mexico if sailing directly to the Marquesas which need only be reached by April.

A more ambitious option is to continue from the Galapagos to Easter Island and arrive in Tahiti by that route. Whichever alternative is chosen, French Polynesia will be reached at the start of the safe season so that the next five months can be spent leisurely visiting the various island groups of Polynesia and Melanesia as far as Papua New Guinea. The northern hemisphere is regained early in the new year so that this loop of the Pacific Ocean can be closed in less than two years after it had started.

This itinerary can be extended by making a detour via the Torres Strait and Indonesia to Southeast Asia and completing the loop that way. Such a detour would not affect the overall timing as a passage through the Torres Strait in September would make it possible to complete the voyage in the first months of the following year.

The route can be shortened by sailing from the US West Coast to Hawaii at the end of summer. The voyage can then be completed by continuing west from Hawaii

short swing to the north, is a summer cruise in Alaska. However, those who may wish to turn this voyage into a truly grand tour of the Pacific could extend that detour by calling first at Petropavlovsk, the Russian port on the Kamchatka Peninsula, on the western shores of the Bering Sea, and continue from there to Alaska along the Aleutian chain. Whether any of these tempting detours are made or not, this ambitious and challenging voyage has all the ingredients of a once in a lifetime experience.

Route: US West Coast – Mexico (January) – Galapagos (February) – [South America] – Easter Island (March) – Pitcairn – Gambier Islands (April) – [Marquesas] – Tuamotus – Tahiti (June) – Cook Islands (July) – Tonga (August) – Fiji (September to October) – New Zealand (November to May) – New Caledonia (June) – Vanuatu (July) – [East Australia] – Torres Strait (September) – Darwin – Indonesia (October to November) – [Singapore (November to December)] – [Western Malaysia – Phuket (December to January)] – Borneo (December to February) – East Asia (March to April) – Japan (May to June) – [Alaska (July)] – British Columbia – US West Coast

Start: November year I

Return: August to October year III

Alaska's Glacier Bay.

to destinations on the Asian mainland during the same winter season. Boats bound for Japan may have to wait in either Hawaii or Micronesia to complete the final leg home the following spring.

Route: East Asia – Japan (June to July) – [Alaska (July to August)] – North America (September – October) – [Hawaii – Micronesia] – Mexico (November to February) – [Galapagos] – [Easter Island] – Marquesas (April to May) – Tahiti (June) – Fiji (August) – Vanuatu – [Torres Strait (September)] – Darwin – Indonesia (October to November) – [Singapore (November to December)] – [Western Malaysia – Phuket (December to January)] – [Borneo (December to February)] – Papua New Guinea (November to December) – Philippines (January) – [Japan] – East Asia

Start: April to June year I

Return: February to April year III

Tropical storms: All year (Western North Pacific), June to November (Eastern North Pacific), November to May (South Pacific)

Total distance: 19,600–23,200 miles   **Duration:** 21–24 months

PC7c A Grand Pacific Circuit from Australia

There are two quite different ways to start this grand Pacific loop from Australia, both of which fit into the overall timeframe of this ambitious voyage. As outlined in voyage PC7a, the longer option is to make a detour via the Torres Strait to Southeast Asia and sail as far as Phuket before turning around to reach the North Pacific

via North Borneo. The more direct route to East Asia goes north through the Coral Sea via Papua New Guinea and, having crossed the equator, can continue to the Asian mainland via Palau and the Philippines, or go directly to Japan. Both versions can be tailored to take place during the safe winter season when the threat of typhoons in the North Pacific is lower. From Japan, the route and timing are the same as for voyage PC7a to the US West Coast and then PC6 for the return to Fiji.

Route: East Australia – Torres Strait (September) – Darwin – Indonesia (October to November) – [Singapore (November to December] – [Western Malaysia – Phuket (December to January)] – Borneo (December to February) – [Papua New Guinea (November to January)] – East Asia (March to April) – Japan (May to June) – [Alaska (July)] – British Columbia – US West Coast (August to October) – Mexico (November to January) – Galapagos (February) – [South America] – Easter Island (March) – Pitcairn – Gambier Islands (April) – [Marquesas] – Tuamotus – Tahiti (June) – Cook Islands (July) – Tonga (August) – Fiji (September) – New Caledonia (October) – Southeast Australia

Start: August to September year I

Return: September to October year III

Tropical storms: November to May (South Pacific), all year (Western North Pacific), June to November (Eastern North Pacific)

Total distance: 23,000–25,000 miles

Duration: 22–24 months

The north coast of Borneo.

PC7d A Grand Pacific Circuit from New Zealand

The initial stage of this voyage can follow three very different routes. The first option is to start with a passage to either Tonga or Fiji, continue west into the Coral Sea and reach the Torres Strait either direct or via the east coast of Australia and the Great Barrier Reef. The second option is a passage across the Tasman Sea to Australia followed by a cruise inside the Great Barrier Reef. The third option is a mixture of the other two by sailing directly to New Caledonia and either continuing on an offshore route to the Torres Strait, or sailing north via Vanuatu, the Solomons and Papua New Guinea to reach Asia by this shorter route which bypasses Southeast Asia altogether. The rest of the circuit follows the same route as the previous P7 voyages.

Route: New Zealand – [Tonga] – Fiji – [Southeast Australia] – [Torres Strait (September)] – Darwin – Indonesia (October to November) – [Singapore (November to December] – [Western Malaysia – Phuket (December to January)] – Borneo (December to February) – [Papua New Guinea (November to January)] – East Asia (March to April) – Japan (May to June) – [Alaska (July)] – British Columbia – US West Coast (August to October) – Mexico (November to January) – Galapagos (February) – [South America] – Easter Island (March) – Pitcairn – Gambier Islands (April) – [Marquesas] – Tuamotus – Tahiti (June) – Cook Islands (July) – Tonga (August) – Fiji (September to October) – New Zealand

Start: May to July year I

Return: September to October year III

Tropical storms: November to May (South Pacific), all year (Western North Pacific), June to November (Eastern North Pacific)

Total distance: 23,000–25,000 miles

Duration: 26–29 months

Moorea.

PC8 • The Southern Cross Circuit

This circuit includes much of the best that the South Pacific has to offer and can be completed in one long season. Voyages originating in Australia will start with a passage across the Tasman Sea to New Zealand. The route from New Zealand to Tahiti needs to stay in high latitudes where there is a better chance of encountering favourable winds for the passage to the Austral Islands where the route turns north for Tahiti. The remote Australs are the least visited of all French Polynesian islands and sailing by without stopping would be a mistake. An arrival in Tahiti at the start of the safe season in June ensures five months of carefree cruising among the various island groups flanking the route to Fiji: the Cooks, Tonga, Samoa as well as Wallis and Futuna.

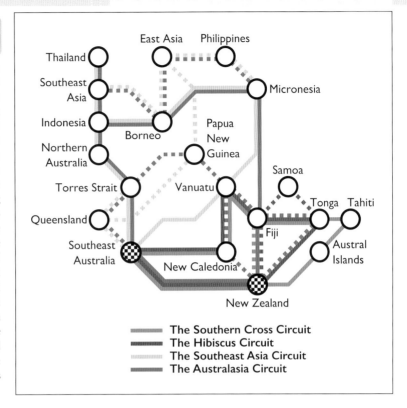

The Southern Cross Circuit
The Hibiscus Circuit
The Southeast Asia Circuit
The Australasia Circuit

Beachcomber anchorage in Tahiti.

Boats intending to return to New Zealand can sail south from Fiji unless the decision is taken to stay with those bound for Australia by continuing to Vanuatu and New Caledonia and sail home from there.

Route: Southeast Australia – New Zealand (May to June) – Australs – Tahiti (June) – Cook Islands (July) – Tonga (August) – Fiji (September) – [New Zealand (October)] – Vanuatu – New Caledonia (October) – Southeast Australia

Start: February to May

Return: October to November

Tropical storms: November to May

Total distance: 5,800–6,600 miles

Duration: 7–9 months

PC9 • The Hibiscus Circuit

This compact version of the Southern Cross Circuit may appeal to Australian or New Zealand sailors who would rather avoid the tough passage to Tahiti by focusing on the tropical islands that are nearer to home. It may also appeal to sailors who have spent the cyclone season in either Australia or New Zealand and wish to return to the tropics for another season.

From New Zealand, the passage to the tropics can head straight north to Fiji, although by sailing first to Tonga, a number of attractive islands, such as the two Samoas, Wallis and Futuna, can be visited on the way to Fiji. The rest of the voyage is as PC8.

The small marina at Malolo Lailai Island on Fiji's west coast.

Route: Southeast Australia – New Zealand (May to June) – Tonga (June to July) – [Samoa] – [Wallis] – Fiji (September) – [New Zealand (October)] – Vanuatu – New Caledonia (October) – Southeast Australia

Start: March to May

Return: October to November

Tropical storms: November to May

Total distance: 4,300–5,000 miles

Duration: 6–8 months

PC10 • The Southeast Asia Circuit

In recent years this voyage has become quite popular among Australian as well as New Zealand sailors who, mainly because of safety considerations, no longer seem to be tempted by the idea of a voyage around the globe when some of the best cruising grounds in the world happen to be right on their doorstep.

For voyages originating in SE Australia there are two alternatives for reaching the Torres Strait, by an inshore route inside the Great Barrier Reef or an offshore route via the islands dotted about the Coral Sea. Whichever route is sailed, the Indian Ocean should be reached by early October so as to be out of the critical area before November and the start of the cyclone season in the South Pacific and Northern Australia. With Darwin being close to the route to Indonesia, most boats make a stop there before resuming their voyage. After the Indonesian

Indonesia's Banda Islands.

authorities decided in 2016 to abolish the formerly compulsory cruising permit, cruising this interesting country has become much simpler.

With good planning, and an earlier passage through the Torres Strait, a detour to Western Malaysia and Thailand can be accommodated within the suggested timeframe. Another possible detour, to Vietnam, Southern China and even Hong Kong, can also be accomplished during the northern winter months when the risk of typhoons is at its lowest.

Whether either of these detours is embarked upon, or the return voyage starts in Singapore or Northern Borneo, boats bound for Southeast Australia need to make sufficient easting north of the equator to be sure of having a decent sailing angle across the SE winds of the South Pacific. The usual tactic is to stay just north of the equator, within the doldrum belt, where light variable winds, an east-setting current and the use of the engine should make it possible to gain the desired easting. An interesting place to stop on this slow passage is the remote Micronesian island of Kapingamarangi. From there, it may be necessary to go as far east as 165˚E before crossing the equator.

South of the equator are some equally rarely visited islands, such as Nukumanu and Ontong Java, which belong to the Solomon Islands. The route south continues via the outer islands of the Solomons towards Vanuatu before finally turning west for the Australian mainland. Boats bound for North Queensland will have an easier task as they can cross the equator sooner, head for the outer islands of Papua New Guinea and turn for home as soon as they have passed the eastern extremity of Papua.

Route: Southeast Australia – Torres Strait (August to September) – Darwin (October) – Indonesia (October to November) – [Singapore] – [Western Malaysia – Thailand (December to January)] – Borneo (November to February) – [Vietnam] – [East Asia (February to March)] – [Papua New Guinea (March to April) – North Queensland (May)] – Micronesia (March to April) – Vanuatu (June) – Southeast Australia

Start: June to August year I

Return: June to July year II

Tropical storms: November to May (South Pacific and South Indian Ocean), all year (Western North Pacific)

Total distance: 6,800–11,500 miles

Duration: 10–13 months

Port Refuge in Vava'u.

PC11 • The Australasia Circuit

There are two basic alternatives for the start of this voyage from New Zealand: to sail first to New South Wales, which can be done at any time as the south of the Tasman Sea is not affected by cyclones, or delay the start until the return of the safe season in the tropics. In the former case, the voyage can be continued either inside the Great Barrier Reef or by way of the islands in the Coral Sea. In the latter case, the initial destination can be anywhere from Tonga to New Caledonia and, with an entire safe season before you, there are plenty of choices on how to spend that time. The three most obvious choices are to spend longer cruising the Central South Pacific between Tonga and Vanuatu, to sail directly from New Zealand to New Caledonia and cruise the islands of the Coral Sea as far as Papua New Guinea before heading for the Torres Strait, or to transit the Torres Strait earlier and cruise the Indonesian Archipelago until it is time to return home.

There is one further option, which I took on my last circumnavigation by making an early departure from New Zealand with the sole aim of being in Vanuatu for the Nagol land-diving ritual which takes place on the island

of Pentecost between the end of April and early June. Such an early arrival in the Coral Sea meant that after having witnessed that unique event there was still sufficient time for a leisurely cruise among the northern islands of Vanuatu and the Louisiade Archipelago of Papua New Guinea before sailing through the Torres Strait. It needs to be stressed that a May arrival in the Coral Sea was admittedly too early but such a calculated risk was only taken in the knowledge that in case of an early cyclone we would have been able to seek shelter either in Nouméa (New Caledonia), Port Vila or one of the nearest ports on the Australian coast.

The continuation of the voyage after the transit of the Torres Strait is the same as outlined in the previous voyage PC10. The main difference concerns the final leg home as sailing from Southeast Asia to New Zealand is even more difficult than sailing to Australia as you have to sail further east before the equator is crossed. Doing this just north of the equator, as described earlier, is the only feasible solution if the aim is to reach New Zealand during the same safe season. Arduous as it undoubtedly is, the dreariness of this long passage can be attenuated by the opportunity to visit some truly isolated communities in Southern Micronesia. To be sure of a decent wind angle later on, the route needs to stay north of the equator as far as Kiribati, whose islands will make an interesting stop, as will those of Tuvalu. From there the southbound route continues to Fiji and thence to New Zealand.

Route: New Zealand – [SE Australia] – [Tonga – Fiji (June to July)] – Vanuatu – [North Queensland] – [Papua New Guinea (August)] – Torres Strait (September to October) – Darwin (October) – Indonesia (October to November) – [Singapore] – [Western Malaysia – Thailand (December to January)] – Borneo (November to February) – [East Asia (January to March)] – Micronesia (March to April) – Kiribati (June) – Tuvalu (July) – Fiji (August to September) – New Zealand

Start: May to June year I

Return: September to October July II

Tropical storms: November to May (South Pacific and South Indian Ocean), all year (Western North Pacific)

Total distance: 12,500–16,000 miles

Duration: 15–17 months

PC12 • Counterclockwise Circumnavigation of South America

Because more favourable weather and wind conditions will be encountered by sailing around South America in a counterclockwise direction, this alternative may be preferable to voyage AC9 described on page 136.

The suggested departure point is Panama where the voyage can be joined by boats arriving from the Caribbean, but for boats starting from the US West Coast, Mexico or Central America, the Galapagos Islands or mainland Ecuador are a more convenient point to join. The timing of this voyage is dictated by the need to reach Southern Chile at the optimum time (October to December). This means that the voyage to the Galapagos must take place before June and the start of the hurricane season in the Eastern North Pacific. This timing should suit both voyages starting from the US West Coast and those arriving from the Caribbean at the end of the safe cruising season there.

There are two alternatives for the onward route from Galapagos

or mainland Ecuador: an offshore route to Easter Island and that way to Southern Chile, or an inshore route that follows the contour of the mainland to Peru and Chile. There is also an intermediate option that combines those two alternatives: to sail from Galapagos to Ecuador, follow the mainland coast as far as Peru, and go offshore from there to Easter Island.

The offshore alternative will entail covering many more miles but being able to sail most of the way compared to the inshore route. The price to be paid for the detour to Easter Island is that there is no easy way to sail directly from there to mainland Chile. Although it may be possible to motor through the South Pacific high, probably the better way is to head south into the area of prevailing westerly winds and reach the Chilean coast with a landfall at the Canal de Chacao, north of Chiloé Island. Past the Gulf of Peñas it is possible to sail inshore and in sheltered waters all the way to the Beagle Channel at the southern extremity of the continent. This vast area, which stretches for over 1,000 miles, is a maze of fjords, narrow passages, ancient forests, snow-clad mountains and mighty glaciers.

Weather conditions in the austral late spring and early summer (October to January) are generally good and the prevailing winds are from the northwest, hence the earlier recommendation to cruise this area from north to south. Stronger winds with violent gusts (the infamous williwaws) become more frequent as you move

A colony of king penguins in the Falkland Islands.

south so you should be prepared for these sudden blasts both when sailing and at anchor. Puerto Eden, about halfway between Chiloé and Cape Horn, is the only place to get fuel or provisions along this route, so self-sufficiency is an absolute necessity in this part of the world.

Those who have reached the southernmost point of their voyage here can continue east via the Beagle Channel and then turn north towards the Falkland Islands. Those undaunted by a crossing of the Drake Passage can keep their bows pointing south towards the Antarctic

Peninsula. A good starting point for a cruise inside the sheltered waters off the western side of the Antarctic Peninsula is Deception Island. From there the route leads in a generally SW direction with a choice of good anchorages. The scenery is quite spectacular and there is lots of wildlife: large penguin colonies, pods of courting humpback whales, and various species of seals, including the enormous elephant seals. Weather conditions in the optimum summer months are quite benign, and the temperatures rarely fall much below freezing.

Circumnavigating South America

Our sail plan was from Puerto Rico to the Panama Canal, down the west coast of South America to the Chilean Canals, through the Beagle Channel, around Cape Horn, north along the east coast of South America and back to San Juan.

Panama Canal, 8 August

Fully loaded with water and fuel, we headed towards the legendary Southern Ocean. Out of curiosity, I punched into the GPS the latitude and longitude of our destination, Cape Horn. We had 5,349 miles to go.

Callao, Peru, 3 September

In dense fog, followed by a legion of seals, dolphins and dozens of squawking gulls, we make our approach into the busy harbour of Callao.

Arica, Chile, 18 September

On Chile's National Independence Day we enter Arica. Since it never rains, wheat is stored in huge mounds in the open, no doubt the reason most birds in the area appeared so incredibly fat.

Robinson Crusoe Island, 30 January

The shadow of Alexander Selkirk still hangs over this small island where no more than 200 people now reside. Since their principal resource is lobsters, we ordered one each for supper. When the bill for $120 arrived we concluded their second resource was robbery.

Southern Chile, 26 February

Fjords, glaciers and icebergs met us every few miles as we entered the southern fjords, the high peaks of the snow-covered Andes serving as a backdrop. Cascades, often a dozen

side by side, form intricate patterns as they drop 2,000 feet into the sea below.

Cape Horn, 4 March

Midnight, 10 miles to go. The wind began to build as squalls passed through. First 35, then 45, later a sustained 60, with gusts of 70 knots. We tacked south, around the outside to get closer to Horn Island. Monster waves forced us to turn north. Twenty minutes later, with better light, I decided to give it another try. Waves engulfed New Chance anew. We held course, but made no progress as each wave attempted to swallow us. There was no way to proceed without endangering all. With regret, I ordered the boat about. Landing at Cape Horn would have to wait.

Comodoro Rivadavia, Patagonia, 4 March

We headed north past the whale sanctuary of Península Valdés where two baby killer whales followed us for miles, perhaps thinking we were Mom.

San Juan, Puerto Rico, 1 July

Words can scarcely describe the 13,774 miles logged by New Chance as she sailed from the tropics to the Antarctic. Air and water temperatures ranged from 3°C to 33°C. One day in Magellan we experienced snow, hail, bright sunshine, then rain. The barometer swung from a high of 1026 to a low of 983 millibars and we never figured out which provided better sailing. We got whacked by gales with both high and low barometers. Less than one year after our departure, New Chance once again passed under the parapets of El Morro de San Juan. Mission accomplished!

Bill Butler, New Chance

Getting back to Cape Horn against the prevailing westerly winds and east-setting current is not easy, so if one wants to visit Horn Island, where it is possible to land, it is better to do it on the way out. In this case the return voyage from Antarctica will be much easier as a direct course can be set for the Falkland Islands. From there, the northbound route continues parallel to the Argentinian and Brazilian coast with plenty of landfall and cruising opportunities. Going north from the Falklands the prevailing winds are westerly with a favourable north-setting current. Along the Brazilian coast the prevailing winds up to April are NE, so this section should not be attempted too early in the year. Once the equator is reached the winds become easterly and there is also a strong northwest-setting current ensuring a fast passage to the Lesser Antilles. As the Eastern Caribbean will be reached near the end of the safe season, there will be little time to linger and a good pace needs to be maintained to embark on the homebound leg before the onset of the hurricane season in June.

For sailors who hail from the west coast of North America the next leg will lead across the Caribbean Sea to the Panama Canal. The challenging return voyage from Panama to the US West Coast, and the alternatives available, are described in voyage P28 (page 218). Those who wish to reach California before the start of the hurricane season off the coast of Mexico need to keep up a sustained rhythm and transit the Panama Canal by April. Such a tight schedule means missing out much of South America as well as the Eastern Caribbean. The way to overcome this is to accept a later arrival in the Caribbean, spend the hurricane season in a place like Trinidad, and resume the voyage in November, or transit the Panama Canal in May or June, spend the hurricane season south of the critical area and complete the voyage home after November.

A sheltered bay in the Sea of Cortez.

The total distance, including the detours to Easter Island and Antarctica, is 19,800 miles and is based on a direct voyage from Panama to the US West Coast, but a detour via Hawaii will make it much longer, both in miles and time. With good planning and careful preparation the shorter version can be accomplished in the 16 months that have been allowed. Another six months, or possibly more, should be added if the decision is made to only return home after the Caribbean or Mexican hurricane seasons.

Route: [US West Coast] – Mexico (March to April) – [Galapagos (June)] – Ecuador – Peru (July to August) – [Easter Island (September)] – Southern Chile (October to November) – Beagle Channel (December) – [Antarctica (January)] – Falkland Islands – Argentina (March) – Brazil – Caribbean (April) – Panama (May) – US West Coast

Start: March year I

Return: June to July year II

Tropical storms: June to November (Eastern North Pacific and North Atlantic)

Total distance: 18,000–19,800 miles

Duration: 16–26 months

PC13 • Counterclockwise Circumnavigation of North America

The opening of the Northwest Passage to shipping, with cargo ships, cruise liners and sailing yachts now using this shortcut regularly, is creating new cruising opportunities. In recent years there has been an increasing interest in high-latitude cruising so a circumnavigation of North America, which is now finally possible, will no doubt appeal to some intrepid sailors. This circuit can be sailed in both directions but for voyages starting on the west coast of North America, a counterclockwise circumnavigation will benefit from better conditions along most of its length.

The initial passage to Panama needs to take place early in the season so as to take advantage of a full favourable season in the North Atlantic. Sailors starting from British Columbia and the Pacific Northwest may decide to move south to California or Mexico sooner so as to be able to start on the southbound voyage to Panama by February or March. The transit of the Panama Canal ought to take place in April or May so that the US East Coast is reached at the beginning of summer. The passage north from Panama can follow two routes: via the Windward Passage and Outer Bahamas, or the Yucatán Channel and Florida. The former is more direct but also more difficult on account of the prevailing NE winds in the Caribbean Sea, while the latter may be slower but perhaps less challenging.

With the entire summer at your disposal to sail to the Northwest Passage there will be plenty of time to make your way north along the coast of New England, Nova Scotia and Newfoundland all the way to Greenland. As westbound transits through the Northwest Passage are best undertaken in late summer, ice should present no real problem while sailing in Greenland waters. The same is also the case inside the Northwest Passage itself where ice has normally receded by August. There are several routes through the Northwest Passage, and the southern route that goes through Peel Sound is usually used by cruising boats.

Having reached the Beaufort Sea, the route continues through the Bering Strait along the west coast of Alaska to Dutch Harbor or Kodiak. From there, the Gulf of Alaska is crossed to reach destinations on the mainland by way of the Inside Passage, or by a direct passage to your home port and the successful completion of this challenging voyage.

A clockwise circumnavigation of North America is described in AC8 on page 135, but the main disadvantage for sailors from the US West Coast of covering the route in that sense is the difficulty of sailing the final leg from Panama home as it may entail a long detour to Hawaii.

Route: US West Coast – Mexico (March to April) – Panama (May) – [Bahamas] – US East Coast (June to July) – Newfoundland – Greenland – Northwest Passage (August) – Alaska (September) – [British Columbia] – US West Coast

Start: February to April

Return: October

Tropical storms: June to November (Eastern North Pacific and North Atlantic)

Total distance: 10,900–12,400 miles

Duration: 7–9 months

THE INDIAN OCEAN

We have traversed more than 30,000 miles of immense water spaces and have beheld in the ocean huge waves like mountains rising in the sky, and we have set eyes on barbarian regions far away hidden in a blue transparency of light vapours, while our sails, loftily unfurled like clouds day and night, continued their course as rapidly as a star. . .

Zheng He, 1432

The Indian Ocean is the third largest of the world's oceans, covering approximately 20 per cent of the water on the earth's surface. The Ancient Greeks called it *Erythra Thalassa*, the Eritrean Sea, which literally means 'red sea', a name found on several old charts. The Chinese called it the Western Ocean, the current term Indian Ocean becoming established during the age of European discovery and exploration.

There have been voyages on this large body of water since the earliest times. It is known that maritime trade between Mesopotamia and the Indus Valley was conducted 3,000 years ago and it is believed that the Phoenicians may have traded in that area around the same time.

Some of the earliest Egyptian records state in approximately 1470 BCE that some ships sailed to Punt, thought to be present-day Somalia. The reliefs of Hatshepsut's voyage to Punt, displayed at her temple at Deir el Bahary, on the Upper Nile, depict seagoing vessels carrying the expeditionary force returning from Punt. This has given rise to the suggestion that a navigable link existed at that time between the Red Sea and the Nile. During the initial feasibility studies conducted in the 19th century for the Suez Canal, French cartographers discovered the remnants of an ancient canal running along Lake Timsah to the Bitter Lakes. Traces of a second canal running to the Nile were also discovered and they were dated to the period of the Punt expedition.

One of the most remarkable ancient documents is the *Periplus of the Erythraean Sea*, written in Alexandria in the first century CE. The manuscript gives details of several trading ports in the Red Sea, but also describes the coast of East Africa, which was referred to as Azania, and even the coasts of India as far as the Ganges River. The manuscript also describes the voyage of a Greek mariner named Hippalus from the Red Sea to India in the first century BCE. As the Romans expanded their empire during the first and second centuries CE, intensive trade relations developed between Roman Egypt and the Tamil kingdoms in Southern India, and several Roman coins from that period have been discovered in India. Trade across the ocean continued throughout the Middle Ages with the establishment of seasonal trading routes between India, the Persian Gulf and East Africa.

Chinese records show that from 1405 to 1433 during the Ming Dynasty Admiral Zheng He led large fleets on several voyages to the Western Ocean and reached the coast of East Africa, and there is even speculation that Zheng He's ships sailed into the Atlantic Ocean.

In 1497, the Portuguese navigator Vasco da Gama rounded the Cape of Good Hope and became the first European to sail to India. It was this voyage, and the knowledge of a passage around Africa, that inspired Magellan's round the world voyage. Those early voyages brought about a rapid expansion of trade between Europe and Asia spearheaded by Portuguese, Dutch and British merchantmen. During the 19th century, the Indian Ocean was plied by some of the most magnificent sailing ships ever built – the famous China tea clippers. These fast ships were ideally suited to carry low-volume, high-profit goods, such as tea, opium, spices, passengers and mail. Competition among the clippers was public and fierce, with their times recorded in the newspapers.

When fully rigged they could maintain average speeds over 16 knots. Given their speed and manoeuvrability, clippers were frequently armed and were also used for piracy, privateering and smuggling, as well as in the fight against such activities. The heyday of the clipper era was marked by the Great Tea Race of 1866, a competition between the fastest clippers of the China tea trade to bring the season's first crop of tea to London. Among the main competitors were *Fiery Cross*, *Ariel*, *Taeping* and *Serica*. The ships left China on 29 May 1866, each laden with approximately 500 tonnes of tea. The race took over three months, crossing the South China Sea, passing through the Sunda Strait, across the Indian Ocean, around the Cape of Good Hope and on to the English Channel. On 6 September, the three leaders docked in London within a short time of each other having taken 102 days to sail three-quarters of the way around the globe. The *Taeping* won with a mere 20 minutes lead over *Ariel*, with *Serica* third. *Fiery Cross* had the best 24 hour run of all the competitors when she sailed 318 miles averaging 13.7 knots. The best surviving example of those swift tea clippers is the *Cutty Sark*, preserved in dry dock at Greenwich, in London.

Unfortunately the clippers' glory was short-lived as only three year later, in 1869, the opening of the Suez Canal signalled the end of the age of these wonderful sailing ships as the new link to Europe consolidated the dominance of steamships. However, sailing ships engaged in trading continued to ply the Indian Ocean as they had been doing since time immemorial. For hundreds of years trading boats sailed the seasonal monsoon winds, eastward to India between July and September, and westward from India to Arabia and East Africa between December and February. The largest of these dhows were capable of carrying loads of 1,000 tonnes. They plied their trade until late in the 20th century.

An unfortunate by-product of trade in any ocean was piracy, and the Indian Ocean has had its fair share of it. During the 16th and 17th centuries there were frequent European piracy attacks against Indian vessels, especially those en route to Mecca. Later, Indian pirates attacked British shipping and demanded that ships of the East India Company pay taxes if sailing through their waters. Madagascar was a favourite base and Saint-Marie Island, on its east coast, was a popular base for pirates throughout the 17th and 18th centuries. The south coast of the Persian Gulf became known as the Pirate Coast as raiders based there harassed foreign shipping.

In more recent times, the two main areas where acts of piracy have been reported are the Malacca Straits and Gulf of Aden, especially in the vicinity of the island of Socotra off the Horn of Africa. Socotra has been a refuge for pirates for centuries and their activities were already highlighted by famous travel writers such as the Venetian adventurer Marco Polo and Ibn Battuta, a famous 14th century Arab traveller.

Cruising sailors have always been aware of this menace, and yachts on passage to or from the Red Sea sail through the Gulf of Aden as quickly as possible and keep well clear of Socotra and the Somali coast. Even so, during the 20th century there were several incidents involving attacks on yachts by Yemeni pirates. The situation showed a relative improvement after the end of the civil war in Yemen, only to flare up as a consequence of a similar conflict in neighbouring Somalia. The prolonged Somali civil war resulted in the disintegration of the Somali state in the early 21st century and a total collapse of law and order. One of the direct consequences of this was that the failed state could no longer protect its coastal waters and other nations took advantage of this. A United Nations report suggests that piracy off the coast of Somalia was initially caused by the dumping of toxic waste in Somali waters by foreign vessels and illegal fishing which have severely affected the ability of locals to earn a living and forced many to turn to piracy instead. According to the UN report and other sources, the actions of the pirates in the early days were to protect their fishing grounds and exact compensation for the abuse of their marine resources. Once those early vigilantes realised the enormous potential of this new activity, those acts of retribution took on a very different turn, but there is no denying the initial responsibility of the outside world in the resulting state of affairs.

The long history of piracy may be one of the reasons why small-boat voyages were never such an important feature in the Indian Ocean as in the Atlantic or Pacific oceans, although sailing yachts have been plying its waters regularly for many years, usually as part of a longer, round the world voyage. Starting in the early years of this century increasing numbers of sailors decided to forego the northern route and instead reach the Atlantic Ocean by the Cape of Good Hope route. Although by 2018 the threat poised by Somali pirates had been virtually brought under control, the political uncertainty in the countries bordering the Red Sea continues to keep cruising boats away from that area.

One of the most famous small-boat voyages of all times was also completed in the Indian Ocean. In 1789 Captain Bligh and 18 loyal seamen were cast off near Tahiti by the *Bounty* mutineers in the ship's 23 foot launch. With food and water for only a few days, a sextant, pocket watch, but no charts or compass, they managed to sail all the way to Timor in the Dutch East Indies, their epic 3,618 mile voyage lasting 47 days.

WINDS AND CURRENTS

The winds and weather of the entire Indian Ocean are dominated by the monsoons, which although affecting primarily the northern half of the ocean, also have a bearing on the weather pattern of the tropical South Indian Ocean. The NE monsoon prevails when the sun has a southern declination and the SW monsoon when the sun's declination is north.

North Indian Ocean

THE NORTHEAST MONSOON
A predominantly NE wind blows during the winter months in the North Indian Ocean, Bay of Bengal and the Arabian Sea. The wind is very steady and constant over most parts of the North Indian Ocean, blowing with an average 10–15 knots, its strength diminishing towards the equator. On rare occasions the monsoon can reach gale force, but for most of the time sailing conditions can be described as near perfect as possible. There are two areas in which the monsoon is less reliable and the winds more variable. In the Arabian Sea, north of latitude 20°N, the weather pattern is sometimes affected by the passage of depressions to the north of the area. The other area lies SE of Sri Lanka, between latitude 5°N and the equator, where winds are less constant in strength and direction, the normal direction of the wind being northerly. Further east, in the Malacca Strait, the monsoon is also less pronounced than elsewhere.

The NE monsoon lasts from November to March, beginning earlier in the northern part of the region where it is well established by the middle of November. Towards the equator it does not arrive in full strength until December. The winter monsoon is preceded and followed by a transitional period as it is replaced by the SW monsoon and vice versa. This transitional period coincides with the movement across the region of the Intertropical Convergence Zone (ITCZ) which separates the air masses of the northern and southern hemispheres. The ITCZ is most active in April to May and October to November, which are also the months when most cyclonic storms occur over the North Indian Ocean. During this transitional period the weather is often squally and the winds can reach gale force in these squalls. Otherwise this period can be compared to the doldrums of other oceans, with light winds and calms, which are gradually replaced by the coming monsoon. This doldrum belt is not so distinctly defined as in the Atlantic and Pacific Oceans.

THE SOUTHWEST MONSOON
The heating of the Asian landmass during the summer months creates a large area of low pressure over the NW part of the Indian subcontinent. This causes the SE trade wind of the South Indian Ocean to be drawn across the equator where it joins the general movement of air that flows in a counterclockwise direction around the area of low pressure lying over India. This is the SW monsoon which is felt from June to September in the same areas as its NE counterpart. The SW monsoon is a consistent wind blowing at an average 20 knots for long periods and frequently reaching gale force. An area lying about 200 miles to the east of Socotra Island is reputed to be the windiest spot in the Indian Ocean with a frequency of gales in July higher than that of Cape Horn in summer! The winds diminish gradually in strength during August, and by September both the strength of the wind and its direction become less constant. In October and November, the winds are often light until the arrival of the NE monsoon. The weather during the SW monsoon is overcast and often unsettled with heavy rainfall.

TROPICAL STORMS
Tropical storms or cyclones occur in the Arabian Sea and the Bay of Bengal. The two periods of the year when their frequency reaches a maximum coincide with the transitional period between the two monsoons. The first period of cyclonic activity is at the beginning of the SW monsoon from late May to the middle of June. The second period coincides with the onset of the NE monsoon and lasts from the end of October to the second half of November. Most of these storms form in the vicinity of the ITCZ when it is situated between latitudes 5°N and 15°N.

In the Arabian Sea, the cyclone season is from May to the middle of June and from September to November. In the Bay of Bengal, the cyclone season lasts from March to May, and from September to December. Most of the storms that occur in May and June are bred in the Arabian Sea from where they move either in a NW and W direction, or in a northerly direction recurving towards the NE and the coast. Some of the cyclones that form in the Bay of Bengal in October and November move westward across South India into the Arabian Sea. Both in the Arabian Sea and Bay of Bengal, October has the highest frequency of cyclones. Their frequency decreases in November and they are rare in December and January, none having been recorded in February and March. After the middle of April the likelihood of a cyclone begins to increase.

The most powerful cyclone ever recorded in the Arabian Sea was Cyclone Gonu which occurred on 1 June 2007. It caused many fatalities and widespread damage in Oman and the United Arab Emirates. The worst ever tropical storm recorded in the Bay of Bengal was Cyclone Sidr which formed on 12 November 2007. The worst damage was caused in Bangladesh where over 3,000 people lost their lives.

LOCAL STORMS

A violent storm that affects the Strait of Malacca is known as a 'sumatra' and is named after the island that generates these storms. The warning is very short compared to other depression-like weather phenomena, and many mariners have been caught out by it. Approximately one hour before it arrives, a very distinctive low dark cumulonimbus cloud can be seen over the western horizon. It is followed by strong gusts of westerly winds of 30 to 40 knots, which eventually die out about two hours later. There is a heavy downpour as well as vivid lightning towards the closing stages of the storm.

CURRENTS

Due to the monsoons, the currents of the North Indian Ocean follow a seasonal pattern and reverse their direction under their influence. The Northeast Monsoon Current occurs during the NE monsoon and reaches its peak in February. It is located between the equator and latitude 6°N and has a westward set. Its counterpart is the Southwest Monsoon Current which occurs from May to September and is considered to be a continuation of the Somali Current. This current can attain very high rates, especially off the coast of Somalia and in the vicinity of Socotra, where some of the strongest sets in the world have been recorded, with rates of up to 7 knots. Although the initial set is NE, the current becomes east in the open waters of the Arabian Sea until it reaches the landmass of India and turns SE.

At the time of the NE monsoon, the Somali Current flows SW along the African coast as far as the equator where it meets the north-flowing East Africa Current. In December and January, the current turns east and becomes the Equatorial Countercurrent. The Equatorial Countercurrent is the only current of the North Indian Ocean which does not reverse its direction as a result of the monsoons. However, its strength is reinforced during the transitional periods between the two monsoons. It sets east throughout the year and lies to the north of the west-setting Equatorial Current. The Equatorial Countercurrent reaches its southern limit in February, at the height of the NE monsoon, when it sometimes flows very close to the Northeast Monsoon Current. This means that by moving slightly to the north or south, it is possible to shift from a west-setting to an east-setting current. The southern limit of this current is always south of the equator, regardless of season.

TSUNAMIS

Earthquakes that occur under the ocean floor can cause large waves that can affect low-lying countries and islands thousands of miles away. In the Indian Ocean, the most devastating tsunami occurred in December 2004 and affected a large area from Thailand to Somalia. Most of the estimated 200,000 fatalities were recorded in Sumatra, Sri Lanka and the Nicobar and Andaman islands, which were closest to the epicentre of the earthquake. Marinas in Malaysia and Thailand suffered badly, but boats anchored in deeper water escaped mostly unscathed.

South Indian Ocean

The weather in the tropical zone of the South Indian Ocean is greatly influenced by the advance of the NE monsoon south of the equator during the northern winter and its corresponding retreat during summer. Outside of the tropics the weather follows a normal pattern.

THE SOUTHEAST TRADE WINDS

These winds blow on the equatorial side of the counterclockwise circulation of air that exists around the area of high pressure situated in about latitude 30°S. Compared to the other oceans, the South Indian High rarely consists of a single cell and often contains a succession of east-moving anticyclonic systems. The trade winds blow on their north side and form a wide belt that stretches across the ocean from Western Australia to Madagascar and the coast of Africa. Between July and September this belt spreads over a very large area and becomes continuous with the SE trade winds of the South Pacific. The entire belt moves north and south throughout the year, its northern limit varying from latitude 2°S in August to latitude 12°S in January. The fluctuation of the southern limit is less pronounced, from 24°S in August to 30°S in January. The average strength of these trade winds is between 10 and

15 knots in summer and 15–20 knots in winter. Over the central region, the wind blows steadily from SE or ESE, especially from May to September when the SW monsoon is in force north of the equator.

THE NORTHWEST MONSOON

From November to March, when the ITCZ is situated south of the equator, the NE monsoon of the North Indian Ocean is drawn into the southern hemisphere. Because of the rotation of the earth it is deflected to the left and becomes a NW wind in the northern part of the South Indian Ocean. Winds are generally light and vary considerably both in direction and strength during this period. The weather is often squally and unsettled.

MONSOONS OF THE INDONESIAN ARCHIPELAGO

The weather pattern of the Indonesian Archipelago is more seasonal than that of the adjacent areas, which are dominated by the two monsoons. The SE monsoon generally lasts from April to September and is replaced by a NW monsoon from October to March. Though neither of them is very strong, the SE monsoon is the more consistent both in strength and direction, particularly during July and August when it becomes continuous with the SE trade winds of the South Pacific and Indian oceans. During the NW monsoon, the direction of the winds is predominantly NW, although their strength and consistency is less pronounced among the southern islands. South of latitude 4°S the weather is often squally alternating with calms, variable winds and rain.

VARIABLES

On the polar side of the SE trade wind belt there is an area of light variable winds which coincides with the high-pressure region. The axis of this high is situated in about latitude 30°S in winter, moving further south towards latitude 35°S during the summer. The weather varies greatly within this zone, which has similar characteristics to the Horse Latitudes of the Atlantic Ocean.

WESTERLIES

Westerly winds prevail on the polar side of the South Indian Ocean high-pressure region. The continuous passage of depressions from west to east causes the wind to vary considerably in direction and strength. Particularly in the higher latitudes of the Roaring Forties and further south, the frequency of gales is high, the weather cold and the seas rough.

TROPICAL STORMS

The cyclone season of the South Indian Ocean lasts from November to May, although December to April are considered to be the dangerous months, as cyclones occur only rarely in November and May. In Mauritius, which on average is visited by one cyclone per year between late November and late March, the months with the highest frequency are January and February. The most recent cyclone recorded during what is still described as the safe season was Cyclone Phoebe which developed north of Cocos Keeling in August 2004.

The willy-willies that affect the coasts of Western and Northwestern Australia occur mostly between December and April. They can extend as far as the Timor Sea and Arafura Sea, the latter being also subject to South Pacific cyclones that occasionally hit Northern Australia.

CURRENTS

The main surface circulation of the South Indian Ocean is counterclockwise but because of the monsoons of the North Indian Ocean there is only one Equatorial Current. The west-setting Equatorial Current always flows south of the equator, its northern limit varying between latitudes 6°S and 10°S depending on longitude and season. The limit is nearer the equator during the SW monsoon of the North Indian Ocean. On the western side of the ocean, the northern part of the current flows past Madagascar until it reaches the coast of Africa. The current splits in two, one branch following the coast in a northerly direction, the other setting south into the Mozambique Channel. This becomes the Mozambique Current which further south alters its name to that of the Agulhas Current.

The Agulhas Current contains not just the waters of the Mozambique Current but also those of the southern branch of the Equatorial Current. The two currents meet off the coast of Africa in about latitude 28°S from where the combined current sets strongly SW before it passes into the South Atlantic. One part of the Agulhas Current branches off to the SE where it joins the Southern Ocean Current. The south side of the main circulation of the South Indian Ocean is formed by this current which sets in an E and NE direction. The eastern side of this counterclockwise movement is formed by the West Australian Current, which sets in a NW direction along the west coast of Australia. Eventually it turns into the Equatorial Current, thus completing this giant cycle.

Winds and Currents in the Red Sea

The distinctive long shape of the Red Sea, bordered by low arid coasts with high mountains rising some 20 miles inland, dictates in some measure the direction of winds, which tend to blow parallel to these coasts, either from a NW or SE direction. These winds differ significantly in the southern and northern areas of the Red Sea, and in the south show a seasonal variation due to the movement of the convergence zone between the wind systems of the northern and southern hemispheres. Generally it can be assumed that in the northern half of the Red Sea the predominant winds are northerly, and mostly southerly winds in its southern part.

Although the Red Sea is well to the north of the equator, the ITCZ moves into this area and reaches its farthest northern position in July, around 12°N. At this time of year the ITCZ marks the boundary between the SW monsoon of the Indian Ocean and the prevailing NW winds of the Northern Red Sea. During these summer months NW winds often blow down the entire length of the Red Sea, merging into the SW monsoon of the Gulf of Aden.

In winter the ITCZ lies well to the south of this region, but there is another unrelated convergence zone which lies around 18°N from October to May and marks the boundary between the SE winds in the southern part of the Red Sea and the NW winds of the northern section. This convergence zone is usually marked by cloudy skies in contrast to the ubiquitous sunshine prevailing in the region as a whole. This convergence zone is associated with rain and drizzle.

SE winds predominate from October to January in all areas south of the convergence zone. From January to May the SE winds predominate in the most southerly areas and in the Strait of Bab el Mandeb. These winds are strongest from November to February, averaging around 20 knots, but gale force winds of 30 knots and over occur fairly frequently. September and May are transitional months with lighter winds. In the Strait of Bab el Mandeb a funnelling effect increases wind speeds at all times of the year, but especially in the winter months of November to March, when winds blow frequently at 25 knots or more.

In the northern part of the Red Sea from around 20°N, winds from the N to NW predominate in all months of the year, being stronger in winter than in summer. However,

in the most northerly part, the Gulf of Suez, wind speeds are more frequently over 20 knots from April to October with the highest frequency of gale force winds during this time. Wind conditions vary greatly over the Red Sea but, in spite of occasional calms, most of the time the winds are moderate to strong. In the middle section of the Red Sea, light to moderate winds are quite common, but at the two extremes calms and light winds are rare and short-lived, and are usually followed by a period of strong winds. No tropical storms have been recorded in any part of the Red Sea. There are, however, two strong winds occurring in this region. The *haboob* is akin to a short squall accompanied by strong winds from south or west of over 35 knots which occurs off the coast of Sudan, raising lots of sand and dust. These winds occur particularly in the Port Sudan area and are most common between July and September. The other wind is the *khamsin*, a strong dry S to SE wind, which blows off the land and causes sandstorms. It occurs most commonly between February and May.

Both these winds reduce visibility considerably, especially near the coast. On the other hand, due to the special refraction conditions prevailing in the Red Sea, the coast, islands and prominent landmarks are often visible for much greater distances than normal, sometimes as far as 100 miles away. A brilliant luminescence some-times occurs in the Red Sea making the water appear shallower. With the presence of unlit reefs extending far offshore in several places, these conditions may explain why so many yachts used to come to grief in this region in the past. Satellite navigation has improved safety considerably, but navigation should still be treated with due caution as some charts do not agree with satellite observations and the positions of many dangers are only approximate.

The Red Sea area is a hot arid region with a low rainfall. The average temperature is very high, around 30°C, but often reaches over 40°C in daytime and even temperatures exceeding 50°C are not uncommon. Temperatures are lowest in winter in the more northerly part, dropping to 18°C in the Gulf of Suez on a winter night. This contrasts with the southern areas of the Red Sea, where in August the temperature is over 40°C by day and does not drop below 32°C even at night.

Currents

The overall direction of the currents in the Red Sea is influenced by the monsoons in the Indian Ocean. From November until April, during the NE monsoon, water is pushed into the Red Sea and there is a predominantly north to northwest-setting current along the axis of the Red Sea. From May until October, when the SW monsoon prevails over the Indian Ocean, water is drawn out of the Red Sea and a south to southeast-setting current prevails. Due to the narrowness and shape of the Red Sea, there is a great variability in the direction of the currents, with lateral currents flowing in and out from the main stream, particularly near islands and reefs. These cross-currents occur in all months and are very variable. The strongest current is experienced in the Strait of Bab el Mandeb, reaching 2 knots during the NE monsoon. There is little or no current in the transitional months between monsoons, in April and May, or in October.

INDIAN OCEAN VOYAGES

In spite of the wide variety of attractive destinations, many of them on a par with the best of the other two great oceans, the Indian Ocean still feels like the Cinderella of the cruising world. One reason is the distance from most of the major sailing centres, and the implicit difficulty of being able to plan a voyage to that part of the world within a reasonable time frame; the other was the occasional menace of piracy which deterred most sailors from even contemplating such a voyage. However valid those reasons may have been, intrepid sailors were undeterred by them and the number of cruising boats plying the waters of the Indian Ocean has been steadily increasing.

There are four main points of access into the Indian Ocean: the Torres and Bab el Mandeb Straits, and the Cape of Good Hope. The movement of sailing vessels is predominantly from east to west being dictated, as in the other oceans, by the prevailing trade winds. The main sailing route passes through the Torres Strait before it divides into a southern branch, which continues across the South Indian Ocean to South Africa, and a northern branch to Southeast Asia and thence to the Red Sea and Mediterranean. For many years, the latter was the preferred westbound route as it provided a shorter route to Europe and weather conditions were on the whole more favourable. The large

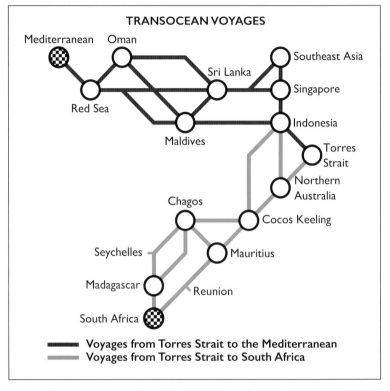

TRANSOCEAN VOYAGES

Mediterranean
Oman
Southeast Asia
Singapore
Sri Lanka
Red Sea
Indonesia
Maldives
Torres Strait
Northern Australia
Chagos
Cocos Keeling
Seychelles
Mauritius
Madagascar
Reunion
South Africa

▬▬▬ **Voyages from Torres Strait to the Mediterranean**
▬▬▬ **Voyages from Torres Strait to South Africa**

number of attacks by Somali pirates on both commercial ships and cruising yachts at the beginning of this century has caused great concern among sailors planning to cross the North Indian Ocean on their way to the Red Sea. As a result, the route around South Africa has become the preferred option of reaching the Atlantic Ocean. Although the risk of piracy has decreased, mainly due to the firm response of a coalition of naval forces, the political uncertainty in some of the countries bordering the Gulf of Aden and Red Sea continues to deter most sailors from using the Red Sea route. A few, who are determined to reach the Mediterranean that way, seem prepared to take the risk and sail that route, whereas others are having their yachts shipped from SE Asia to the Mediterranean by a specialised company such as Sevenstar.

Bearing in mind the above facts, taking the southern route is both the safer and more attractive solution especially if this decision is taken earlier, ideally while still in the South Pacific. As the cyclone season in the South Indian Ocean lasts from November to mid-May, enough time must be allowed so as to sail through that ocean at the optimum time. This means passing through the Torres Strait not later than August or early September so that South Africa is reached by late October. The most direct route leads via Darwin in Northern Australia to Cocos Keeling, Mauritius, Reunion and on to Richards Bay or Durban in South Africa. A longer alternative leads around the top of Madagascar and reaches South Africa by way of the Mozambique Channel. Weather conditions in the South Indian Ocean during the favourable winter season (June to October) are generally good, even if the SE trade winds are often quite strong, with a swell to match.

Those who have doubts about taking the North Indian Ocean route and decide to go for the South African alternative, need to switch hemispheres as well as seasons. The main difficulty in planning a voyage from SE Asia to the South Indian Ocean is to plan a departure during the favourable NE Monsoon but avoid arriving in the South Indian Ocean before the end of the cyclone season there. The logical solution it to leave SE Asia before the end of the NE Monsoon (March) to avoid contrary SW winds along the route, and spend the intermediate period until the start of the safe season in the South Indian Ocean, possibly in Western Sumatra, an area that is not affected by tropical storms. Such a schedule would result in an arrival in the tropical South Indian Ocean once the safe season is established. Such a timing will ensure at least five months of carefree cruising, with plenty of time to visit Chagos, the Seychelles, Madagascar and other islands on the way to South Africa.

The very south of the African continent is not affected by tropical storms but there are local weather considerations to be borne in mind as sailing in that area needs both careful timing and a dose of good luck. The main culprit is the Agulhas Current which runs parallel to the South African coast and can produce large waves when hit by a southerly gale. Generated by depressions sweeping up from the direction of the Southern Ocean, these lows are carefully tracked by local meteorologists and forecasts normally give enough warning to be able to take avoiding action.

Eastbound voyages in both hemispheres are difficult at all times. In the North Indian Ocean, the favourable times would seem to be the SW monsoon, which lasts from June to September, but as it coincides with the tropical storm season in the Arabian Sea and Bay of Bengal, the timing of such a voyage can be quite difficult. The transitional period between the monsoons is therefore regarded as the safest time, but even then the weather should be monitored carefully.

Voyages originating in South Africa are faced by similar considerations but as they are usually bound for northern destinations, passages during the transitional period between the safe and cyclone seasons have a better chance of encountering winds from a favourable direction.

I1	•	Torres Strait to Indonesia
I2	•	Bali to Southeast Asia
I3	•	Southeast Asia to Mediterranean
I4	•	Torres Strait to South Africa
I5	•	Southeast Asia to South Africa
I6	•	Eastbound voyages from the Red Sea
I7	•	Southbound voyages from the Red Sea
I8	•	Northbound voyages from South Africa

The Indian Ocean is traversed by two major routes both of which form part of a longer, round the world route, and are joined by boats arriving from either the South or North Pacific. The North Indian Ocean is crossed from Southeast Asia by a route which leads through the Red Sea to the Suez Canal, while the South Indian Ocean route starts at the Torres Strait and continues to South Africa. As the boats joining them often switch hemispheres, and may sail only part of either of those transocean routes, each of them is divided into separate segments. As Bali is the hub in which most long voyages converge and diverge, the Torres Strait to Bali section, which is common to both of those routes, is dealt with separately (I1). From Bali, the northern route is made up of two segments: Bali to Southeast Asia (I2), and Southeast Asia to the Suez Canal (I3) whereas the southern route comprises one long section from the Torres Strait to South Africa (I4). Voyage I5 from Southeast Asia to South Africa outlines a north to south route which can be sailed by those who decide to forgo the Red Sea alternative in favour of a voyage around South Africa.

Eastbound voyages in both hemispheres are not as common, as both weather systems and seasons ensure more favourable conditions for voyages in the opposite direction. Voyage I6 outlines an eastbound voyage from the Suez Canal to either Southeast Asia or destinations in the South Indian Ocean.

I1 • Torres Strait to Indonesia

Recommended time: July to October

Tropical storms: November to May (South Pacific and South Indian Ocean)

World Cruising Routes:

IS13	Westbound from Torres Strait
IS11	Torres Strait to Darwin
IS14	Northbound from Darwin

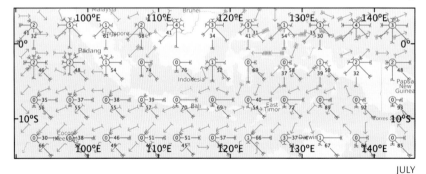

JULY

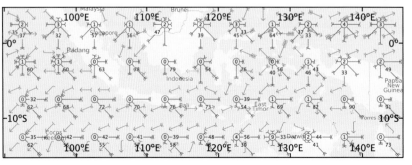

AUGUST

The timing of this voyage depends entirely on the subsequent plans for the Indian Ocean. Those who intend to continue from Bali to Singapore can delay their departure from the South Pacific until near the end of the safe season and transit the Torres Strait as late as October. However, most people prefer to do it sooner so as to be in Singapore by late October or early November, which means passing through the Torres Strait in late September or early October. Consistent SE winds can be expected in the Coral Sea during September and October, and lighter S and SE winds in the Arafura and Timor seas.

The common destination after the Torres Strait is Darwin in Northern Australia, although if time is short, the leg from Torres to Bali can be sailed nonstop. Darwin is an excellent place for either a short or longer stop as it has a wide range of repair services, an active yacht club where visiting sailors are welcome to use its facilities, and Cullen Bay Marina where boats can be left unattended while exploring the interior. For those who have not been able to see more of Australia, Darwin is a convenient place from where to strike inland, whether by rental car, plane or train.

In September and October the winds on the passage to Indonesia are mostly from the SE, becoming more consistent and also stronger as the voyage progresses. An interesting stop about halfway between Darwin and Bali is Ashmore Reef, a nature reserve, where cruising boats can pick up a mooring inside the lagoon which provides good shelter but can be uncomfortable at high tide. Australian customs officers are permanently stationed there and will come out to the boat to complete formalities.

In spite of its important role as a major cruising hub, Bali's facilities are very limited and the marina in Benoa can hardly cope with the large number of yachts that congregate there at the height of the season. In spite of its shortcomings, due to its rich historic background and convenient location, Bali is still an interesting place to visit. The formerly compulsory Indonesian cruising permit is no longer required, and visiting yachts can complete formalities

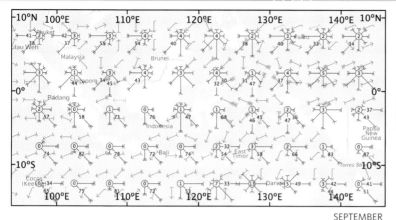

SEPTEMBER

OCTOBER

or Ambon, if coming from the Torres Strait, Manado if arriving from the North Pacific, or Biak from Northern Papua New Guinea.

12 • Indonesia to Southeast Asia

Recommended time: July to October

Tropical storms: March to May, September to December (Bay of Bengal)

World Cruising Routes:

IT11	Bali to Singapore
IN11	Singapore to Western Malaysia
IN12	Western Malaysia to Thailand

The direct route to Singapore is sailed mostly by those undertaking a longer voyage and wishing to reach Southeast Asia in the shortest time possible to be able to spend some time cruising the stretch between Singapore and Phuket before continuing to new destinations. The route cuts across the western part of the Indonesian Archipelago and can easily be sailed in one go, as in October, when most boats undertake this voyage, the winds are mostly favourable.

without an agent. Initial formalities for a simplified cruising permit can be completed online and these are finalised at the first official port of entry. All intended ports of call must be listed on the itinerary, as yachts may not deviate from the ports listed. Restricted areas are East Timor and Papua. AIS (transmit and receive) is mandatory for all foreign yachts cruising in Indonesian waters and the MMSI number associated with the unit must be added to complete the registration forms.

Whether as part of a rally or on your own, exploring more of Indonesia, rather than just rushing through it, is something that is worth considering as the vast archipelago provides a wide range of rewarding cruising opportunities. Sailing conditions among the widely scattered islands are mostly benign and many of the remote communities, which can only be visited by boat, still lead a traditional way of life. Because of their remoteness from any of the more developed centres, the islands of the eastern part of the archipelago are the most interesting, and can be incorporated easily in a cruise starting from one of the easternmost ports of entry such as Kupang, Banda Neira

Singapore provides a welcome respite after the long stretch from Darwin, or even further, with several marinas and yachting facilities of a high standard. The northbound voyage can continue in shorter or longer legs along the Malaysian coast. An interesting landfall is the ancient city of Malacca, an important maritime base throughout its history. The next convenient stop is Port Klang, a busy commercial port and site of the Royal Selangor Yacht Club which provides a convenient base from which to explore the capital Kuala Lumpur. The club organises the annual Raja Muda Regatta, whose mixed fleet of racing and cruising boats makes its way north in late November to join in the end of year sailing events in Langkawi and Phuket. Located in one of Asia's most attractive cruising grounds both Langkawi and Phuket have developed into thriving sailing centres with marinas and a good range of repair facilities. Phuket is used as a base by a number of charter and diving boats which are allowed to operate in the expansive Mergui Archipelago in neighbouring Myanmar (Burma). Access by private yachts to Myanmar is not permitted, but if the situation changes, this would open up a large area with interesting cruising opportunities.

13 • Southeast Asia to Mediterranean

Recommended time: January to March

Tropical storms: May to June, September to November (Arabian Sea), March to May, September to December (Bay of Bengal)

World Cruising Routes:

IN13	Western Malaysia to Sri Lanka
IN14	Thailand to Sri Lanka
IN21	Sri Lanka to Red Sea
IN24	Sri Lanka to Maldives
IN26	Maldives to India
IN27	Maldives to Oman
IN31	India to Red Sea
IN32	Oman to Red Sea
RN1	Gulf of Aden to Port Sudan
RN5	Port Sudan to Southern Egypt

The best time to cross the Indian Ocean is in January or February when the NE monsoon is most consistent and the weather is fair. This timing also fits in with a transit of the Red Sea in March, when conditions there are also favourable, and ensures an arrival in the Mediterranean at the start of the sailing season. The westbound migration starts early in the new year with Phuket and Langkawi being the favourite departure points. Lying close to the route to Sri Lanka are the Nicobar Islands which belong to India as do the Andaman Islands, lying further north. Access to both island groups is only allowed with special permission from the Indian authorities, who are concerned about protecting the traditional way of life of these isolated communities from outside interference. An Indian visa must be obtained in advance and, on arrival, the immigration officer in Port Blair will issue a Restricted Area Permit which limits the boat's movements to Little Andaman and islands adjacent to South and Middle Andaman. A special permit is needed to visit restricted areas.

With the return of the security situation in Sri Lanka to normal, the port of Galle has regained its popularity among cruising boats. Although there have been some improvements in its facilities, these can still only be described as adequate, but at least Galle provides a convenient base from which to explore the interior of this interesting island.

On leaving Galle there are three alternatives for the continuation of the voyage: to sail directly to the Red Sea, to call at the Maldives on the way, or to turn north around the tip of India to Cochin. For those who wish to visit both India and the Maldives, calling at Cochin first makes more sense as sailing back from the Maldives against the prevailing NE winds could prove to be a hard task. As in the case of Galle, facilities in Cochin are fairly basic. The Malabar Yacht Club has some moorings for visitors and

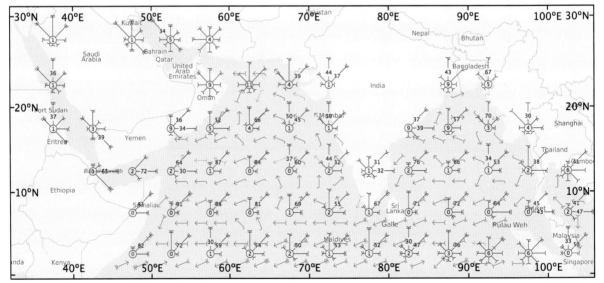

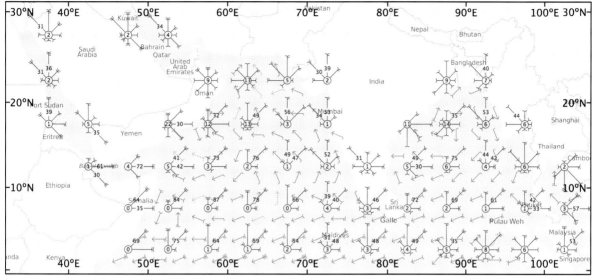

FEBRUARY

can be used as a base for visiting some of India's interior. As a cruising destination, India attracts very few boats, mainly because of the complex formalities and the general absence of yachting facilities. Cruising India's west coast may be a tempting detour for a boat bound for the Red Sea and there are adequate facilities at Goa and Mumbai, both of which have active yacht clubs where the rare visitors are always assured of a warm welcome. The Royal Bombay Yacht Club was founded in 1846 and is India's oldest and most active sailing centre.

The Maldives capital Malé lies close to the route to the Red Sea and makes a convenient port of call, but, just as in Cochin, facilities for visiting yachts are rudimentary. Unfortunately the Maldives, just like Sri Lanka, India and other countries which have a developed tourism industry, have neglected to develop an adequate yachting infrastructure in spite of the potential. As cruising among the Maldivian islands is not encouraged by the authorities, most boats only use the Maldives as an intermediate stop by calling either at Malé itself or, more often, at the

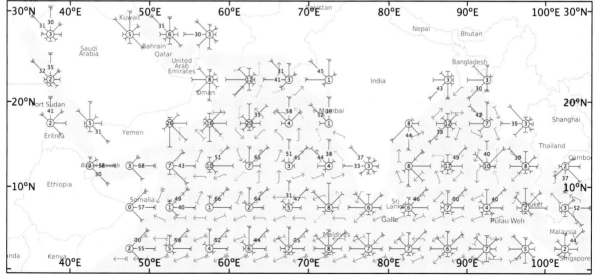

MARCH

northernmost atoll of Uligamu, which is conveniently close to the main route and formalities for a short stop are simple.

As the direct route to the Red Sea passes close to the Horn of Africa and the adjacent Somali coast, many boats now sail along a route which swings north to Oman so as to approach the critical area from that direction and cross the Gulf of Aden as quickly as possible. The Omani Port Salalah, close to the border with Yemen, is a convenient place to prepare for the onward passage to the Red Sea and it also acts as a meeting point for those who wish to join a convoy and sail through the Gulf of Aden in the company of other boats. Such convoys normally keep close to the Maritime Security Patrol Area which is a narrow, internationally recommended transit corridor between Somalia and Yemen. This corridor was established to protect humanitarian aid and reduce the disruption caused by piracy to the shipping routes.

There are only two possible places to stop before tackling the challenges of the Red Sea, and neither could be described as an ideal port of call; the Yemeni port of Aden is unsuitable for cruising boats, Djibouti is the better choice and the latest safety situation should be checked. The former French colony is used as a base by some of the patrolling coalition vessels, and while facilities for visiting yachts are limited, they are still the best in the area.

The favourable NE winds, which normally ensure a fast passage across the Gulf of Aden, turn to southerlies at Bab el Mandeb and continue to blow mainly from that direction about as far as the halfway mark of the remaining distance. The switch to northerlies in the upper half of the Red Sea can be quite sudden but as they are rarely stronger than 20 knots in early spring, they should be able to be dealt with. The usual tactic is to sail in short tacks by taking best advantage of the diurnal changes in wind direction. Boats that go well to windward may be able to do it under sail, others may find it is necessary to resort to motorsailing.

Very few boats sail the entire passage non stop and generally the western side of the Red Sea is preferred as there is a better choice of ports of call. The political uncertainty in the countries bordering the Red Sea when this book went to press (2018) means that some of the ports used by cruising yachts in the past, such as Massawa in Eritrea, Hodeidah in Yemen or Port Sudan, may not be safe to visit, while the Saudi port of Jeddah should only be considered in a serious emergency.

The situation in Southern Egypt has improved with the opening of several marinas, where the boat can be left unattended while visiting the interior, whether Luxor or Aswan. Rather than sailing directly to the Suez Canal, an interesting detour can be made into the Gulf of Aqaba where cruising boats can visit Sharm el Sheikh and Taba Heights on the Egyptian side of the Sinai Peninsula, Tala Bay in Jordan and Eilat in Israel.

This long voyage ends in Port Suez where visiting boats normally dock at the Suez Yacht Club while completing formalities for the transit of the Suez Canal.

14 • Torres Strait to South Africa

Recommended time: June to October

Tropical storms: November to May

World Cruising Routes:

IS13	Westbound from Torres Strait
IS21	Westbound from Bali
IS31	Christmas Island to Cocos Keeling
IS34	Cocos Keeling to Mauritius
IS33	Cocos Keeling to Chagos
IS36	Chagos to Mauritius
IS37	Chagos to Madagascar
IS49	Madagascar to Southern Africa
IS51	Mauritius to Reunion
IS57	Mauritius and Reunion to South Africa
IS62	Durban to Cape Town

This voyage can be undertaken at any time during the safe winter season as consistent SE trade winds are the predominant feature during that period. Often boats arrive from the South Pacific late in the season and transit the Torres Strait as late as September. They must then keep up a sustained pace throughout the South Indian Ocean if the intention is to reach South Africa before the start of the cyclone season. This time constraint leaves little time to properly enjoy the various places, be it Darwin, Bali or any of the islands en route. Those who have spent the South Pacific cyclone season in either New Zealand or Australia could start this voyage that much earlier with an arrival in the Coral Sea in June. Once there, they could visit some of the island groups, or sail inside the Great Barrier Reef, so as to be through the Torres Strait by July and thus be able to give the islands of the South Indian Ocean the time and attention they deserve.

The initial stage of the voyage, from the Torres Strait to Bali, can be sailed either nonstop or via Darwin, as outlined in voyage I1. The onward route from Bali passes two islands administered by Australia: Christmas and Cocos Keeling. The latter is a long-time favourite among sailors and few boats pass by without stopping. Direction Island, near the pass into South

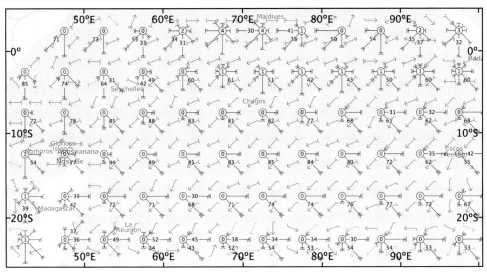

AUGUST

Keeling Atoll, has been turned into a base for visiting sailors and there are rarely less than half a dozen boats in the well-protected anchorage.

From Cocos Keeling there are two alternatives for the continuation of the voyage. The prospect of a possibly tough leg from Chagos to Mauritius has resulted in boats crossing the South Indian Ocean either along the traditional route from Cocos to Mauritius, Reunion and on to South Africa, thus forsaking a stop in Chagos altogether, or a northern route from Cocos to Chagos that continues to Madagascar and, via the Mozambique Channel, to South Africa. The former is the quicker and more straightforward route, whereas the latter is more

attractive as it offers several alternatives, including a possible detour to the Seychelles.

A compromise solution is to take a chance by combining those two options, sailing from Cocos to Chagos and from there to Mauritius. The decision is not easy as occasionally the passage from Chagos to Mauritius can be quite tough, especially later in the season when there is more south in the trade winds. The winter trade winds in the South Indian Ocean are usually more potent than elsewhere and the strong winds, combined with a big swell rolling up from the Southern Ocean, often result in hard sailing conditions. Nowhere is this more evident than in the proximity of Madagascar, with particularly rough

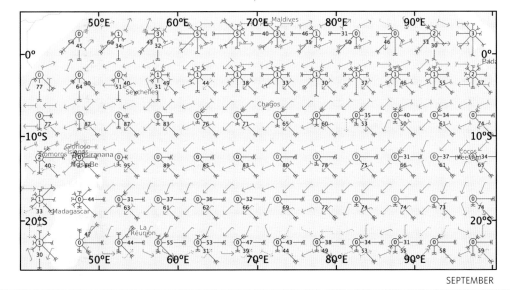

SEPTEMBER

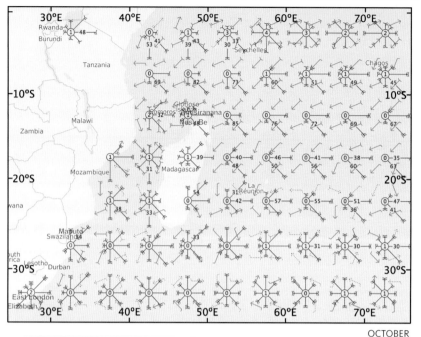

OCTOBER

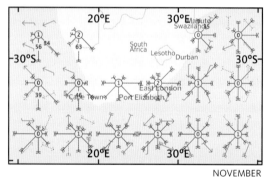

NOVEMBER

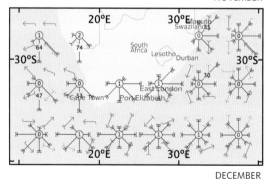

DECEMBER

not so simple at its northern end if it involves boats trying to make landfall at a port in that part of the island, such as Antsiranana. For this reason, those who wish to sail to North Madagascar may fare better by either sailing first to Mauritius and then to Chagos, if the intention is to visit both, or directly from Cocos Keeling to Chagos, and from there directly to Madagascar.

Lying off the usual sailing routes, Chagos and Madagascar, as well as the Seychelles, are not easily included in a voyage constrained by time limitations, but sailing to one or all of them will justify any effort that may be needed to visit them. As part of the British Indian Ocean Territory, restrictions on yachts calling at the Chagos Archipelago have been tightened but permission to make a brief stop while on a long passage may still be obtained if arrangements are made well in advance. The neighbouring Seychelles are another tempting destination, especially the uninhabited islands that lie south of the main group, halfway to Madagascar. As to Madagascar itself, the once rarely visited island is now a popular cruising destination, with its main attraction being the scenic area around Nosy Be. Along the busier arterial route, the more developed islands of Mauritius and Reunion have other attractions to offer the visitor: better facilities, modern communications and, thanks to their French heritage, some culinary delights that are generally absent elsewhere.

By October the trade winds blow strongly throughout the South Indian Ocean and ensure exhilarating sailing conditions all the way to South Africa for boats on a direct offshore passage. Those who decide to make a detour to the cruising area on the northwest coast of Madagascar will continue south from there through the Mozambique Channel. Winds in its northern half are not so boisterous and, closer to the African coast, there is also a favourable current. The alternative is to continue sailing in short hops along the west coast of Madagascar which has many attractive anchorages, but the diurnal shift between land and sea breezes, which can be quite sudden at times, should be borne in mind when choosing an anchorage. Strong winds caused by fronts approaching from the south will also cause rough seas as they strike the south-flowing current in the Mozambique Channel.

seas and violent winds at the two extremes of this large island. At its southern end, those unpleasant conditions can generally be avoided by boats on a passage to South Africa by giving the island a wide berth. The situation is

The long coast of Mozambique has great potential as a cruising destination, foremost being the Quirimbas and Bazaruto archipelagos, both of which are nature and marine reserves. Although the movement of visiting yachts continues to be restricted, the situation is gradually improving as the authorities get used to dealing with cruising yachts.

As the nearest port of entry into South Africa, Richards Bay is a more convenient landfall than busy Durban further down the coast. However, Durban and its welcoming yacht club, is a better place to prepare for the passage around the bottom of Africa. A combination of the swift south-setting Agulhas Current and a strong contrary wind, generated by a passing low, can result in rough conditions. This is a challenging passage at the best of times but with patience and good planning it is not too difficult to accomplish. Weather forecasts are quite reliable, so if favourable conditions are predicted, the boat should be ready to leave at short notice. The worst part is at the very beginning as there is absolutely no shelter for the first 240 miles from Durban to East London along the aptly called Wild Coast. From there on, Port Elizabeth, Knysna and Mossel Bay provide reasonable shelter if the need arises to break the passage. Cape Agulhas, the southernmost point of the African continent, is passed along the way and later also the Cape of Good Hope. Originally known as the Cape of Storms it was on the suggestion of King João II that it was renamed the Cape of Good Hope to lift the spirits of the weary Portuguese sailors returning home from the Indian Ocean. It is a feeling fully shared by modern sailors following in their wake.

15 ● Southeast Asia to South Africa

Recommended time: March to April (North Indian Ocean), June to October (South Indian Ocean)

Tropical storms: March to May, September to December (Bay of Bengal), November to May (South Indian Ocean)

World Cruising Routes:

IN14	Thailand to Sri Lanka
IN24	Sri Lanka to Maldives
IT22	Southbound from Maldives
IT23	Southbound from Sri Lanka
IT25	Sri Lanka to Mauritius
IS36	Chagos to Mauritius
IS51	Mauritius to Reunion
IS35	Chagos to Seychelles
IS47	Seychelles to Madagascar
IS48	Madagascar to Southern Africa
IS53	Reunion to South Africa
IS63	Durban to Cape Town

There are four alternatives for this voyage: an eastern route from Singapore that reaches the South Indian Ocean via Indonesia and the Sunda Strait, an intermediate route that passes west of Sumatra, a central route via Sri Lanka, Chagos and Mauritius, and a western route via the Seychelles, Madagascar and the Mozambique Channel. Every one of these routes has its attraction. The intermediate route provides the opportunity to visit the west coast of Sumatra and then call at the various island groups in the South Indian Ocean; the central route is the shortest and easiest to accomplish, whereas the western

Around the bottom of Africa

Sailing around the bottom of Africa is very much like a game of snakes and ladders as you depend entirely on the weather dice. The one redeeming factor is that while the weather can indeed be bad, it is fairly predictable. On a synoptic chart, the lows and accompanying fronts marching up from the southwest look like beads on a string and as they get closer, the wind swings into the SW and the barometer starts to rise. Once the front has passed, the wind backs to SE and continues slowly to NE. When the barometer starts falling again, it means that the next front is on its way, so it's time to look for shelter. The gap between lows can be anything from three to five days.

As soon as the weather looked right we left East London and made a beeline for the axis of the Agulhas Current. The strongest rate is along the 200 metres line, which we found about 15 miles offshore. Soon we had the thrill of having 3 knots in our favour but the excitement was short-lived as during the night the wind started to shift into the SW, foretelling a blow from that direction. The thing to do in such a situation is to move as quickly as possible inshore, into shallow water, to be out of the current before the winds get too strong as even winds of 25 knots against that swift current can create hellish conditions with huge breaking waves.

Once in shallow waters we spent the rest of the night taking short tacks and making painfully slow progress. On the next forecast, the weather looked relatively settled for the next three days so I decided to push on rather than stop at one of those tempting places along the way: Port Elizabeth, Knysna or Mossel Bay. As it got light we could just make out in the distance the low outline of Cape Agulhas, the southernmost point of Africa. It took us all day to reach the more famous Cape of Good Hope, once called the Cape of Storms. True to form, by nightfall the wind came up stronger and was soon blowing at over 30 knots. It was also bitterly cold with a true whiff of the Antarctic in it but as we got closer to Cape Town the wind eased. Just before dawn we entered the huge harbour and tied up at the Royal Cape Yacht Club.

Jimmy Cornell, *Aventura III*

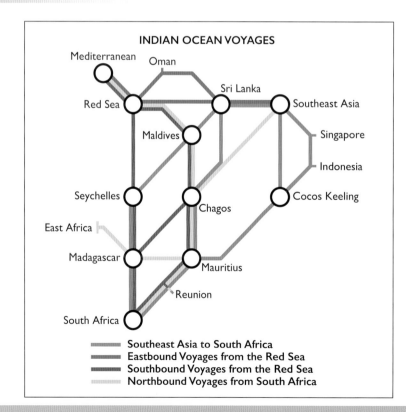

route is more challenging but is possibly also the most interesting from the cruising point of view.

The planning of a voyage along any of these routes has the difficult task of getting the timing right in the two hemispheres, especially if the intention is to reach South Africa at the most favourable time for the continuation of the voyage into the South Atlantic. The best time for a voyage across the North Indian Ocean to the equator is during the NE monsoon, between November and April, but as this is also the cyclone season in the South Indian Ocean, the equator should be crossed either before or after that risk has passed. As the Bay of Bengal is prone to cyclone activity between March and May, with May being the most active month, a passage should be sailed in March or early April, while the risk of cyclones in the Bay of Bengal is still low.

The central route can easily be planned to fit in with the best seasons

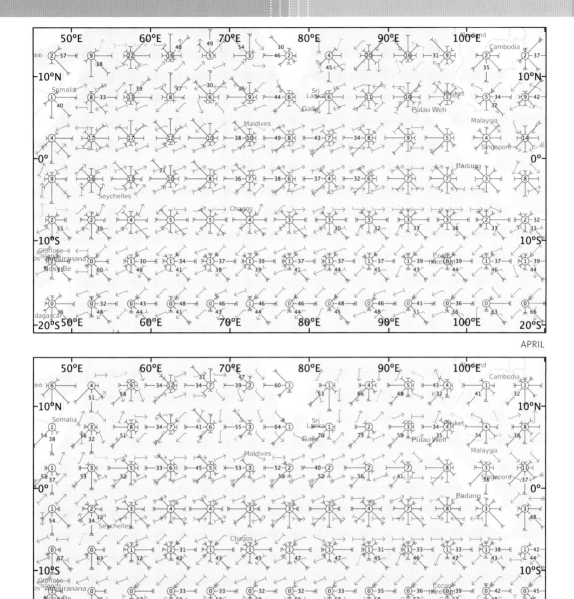

APRIL

MAY

on both sides of the equator. A start in March, just before the end of the NE monsoon, has the benefit of favourable winds for much of the passage, which can be interrupted in Sri Lanka and also in the Southern Maldives so that the equator is only crossed when cyclones no longer pose a threat south of the Line. Chagos would make a convenient landfall during the transitional period, as the archipelago is very rarely affected by cyclones, or, from the Maldives, the voyage could continue directly to the Seychelles. A May arrival in either Chagos or the Seychelles, immediately after the end of the cyclone season, opens up the prospect of an entire safe season which can be spent enjoying the

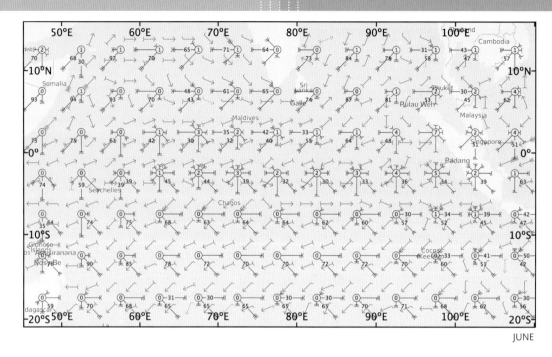

JUNE

various attractions in the South Indian Ocean. Finally, the route which passes west of Sumatra is also best sailed at that time and provides the opportunity to visit this little-known corner of Indonesia. The chain of islands running parallel to the main island is home to some isolated communities while on Sumatra itself the main town of Padang is a good place to get provisions or fuel.

Once in the South Indian Ocean, there are two very different alternatives for the continuation of the voyage to South Africa: to sail east or west of Madagascar. The eastern alternative is more attractive for voyages starting from Chagos as Mauritius, Reunion and some ports on the east coast of Madagascar can be visited en route to South Africa. The western version appeals to those starting from Chagos or the Seychelles and planning to sail south through the Mozambique Channel. Two interesting cruising areas along this route are the western coast of Madagascar and the eastern coast of Mozambique. With late October being the optimum arrival time in South Africa, there should be sufficient time to combine the best of those two alternatives by sailing south from the Maldives to Chagos, thence to the Seychelles and via Madagascar and the Mozambique Channel to South Africa.

16 • Eastbound voyages from the Red Sea

Recommended time: February to March (southbound), April to mid-May, August to September (eastbound)

Tropical storms: May to June, September to November (Arabian Sea), March to May, September to December (Bay of Bengal)

World Cruising Routes:

RS1	Suez to Port Sudan
RS2	Port Sudan to Gulf of Aden
IN33	Red Sea to Sri Lanka
IN36	Red Sea to Oman and India
IN34	Oman to Sri Lanka
IN25	Sri Lanka to Southeast Asia

A voyage from the Mediterranean to Southeast Asia is a difficult task at any time of the year, being hard to accomplish against the NE trade winds of winter, and almost as difficult during the SW monsoon of summer when winds blow from the right direction but there is the risk of cyclones in the North Indian Ocean. Contrary to the Atlantic and Pacific Oceans, where tropical storms normally occur during the summer season, with the highest incidents during the hottest months, in the North Indian Ocean there is a less easily defined pattern. Cyclones affect both the Arabian Sea and the Bay of Bengal. In the Arabian Sea, cyclones do not form in January, February and March and are rare in April, and between July and September. The months when they occur are May and June, and between October and December. In the Bay of Bengal, cyclones are very rare between January and March, but can occur in April and May. During the SW monsoon, between June and September, such storms usually form in the central or northern parts of the Bay of Bengal, while between October and December they form further south.

This complex pattern points to two periods when eastbound voyages run the least risk of cyclones, and can also count on relatively favourable winds: between April and the middle of May, when both areas are normally cyclone-free, and between August and September, when the risk is confined to the Bay of Bengal. Planning the voyage during the latter period will benefit from favourable northerly winds throughout the Red Sea in August and September, and the risk of cyclones in the Arabian Sea in those months is very low, although the risk increases considerably in October both there and in the Bay of Bengal.

A voyage during the earlier period would be easier to plan as a spring passage would benefit from pleasant

Eastabout

After having circumnavigated the globe the normal way, east to west, and sailed many years in the Mediterranean and European waterways, it was time for another extended cruise. This time I wanted to visit countries I had not been to, the Arabian Peninsula, India, China, Japan and Alaska.

Instead of having to cross two oceans, the Atlantic and Pacific, I choose the 'wrong' way, sailing west to east via the Suez Canal, Red Sea and Indian Ocean to Southeast Asia. Not many cruisers chose this route, believing they have to fight headwinds all the way. By choosing the SW monsoon that should not be the case.

Heading south in the Red Sea and continuing east in the Indian Ocean there is the pirate problem. So I took the chance and by sailing close to the Yemeni and Omani coasts I hoped to keep out of the most dangerous area.

Our biggest discomforts on a summer passage in the Red Sea were the heat, humidity, sandstorms, little or no wind and never clear skies. We drank copiously but never had to urinate, we sweated away the liquid. The sand came into the boat, our clothes and bed sheets.

The wind was a disappointment. We did a lot of motoring in the Red Sea and Indian Ocean. I had planned to enter the Gulf of Aden when the SW monsoon would still be strong in August as pirate activity is low when the wind blows hard. Much to our surprise, there was little wind but large swells, which made motoring very rolly.

From Sri Lanka to Thailand we crossed during the transition period between the monsoons. I had hoped to get 50/50 wind from SW and NE but got mostly headwinds, sometimes gale force with rain and thunder, making the trip rather hard and uncomfortable. By then, the NE monsoon had already arrived in force.

All in all, it was a tiring trip but there were many highlights. We visited several interesting places such as Eritrea with its capital Asmara, Yemen with its capital Sanaa, which was the highlight of the entire trip, Oman, Dubai and India. The distance we sailed from Marmaris in Turkey to Langkawi in Malaysia was about 10,000 miles. Perhaps if we had sailed one month earlier, the winds might have been more favourable.

Lars Hässler, *Jennifer*

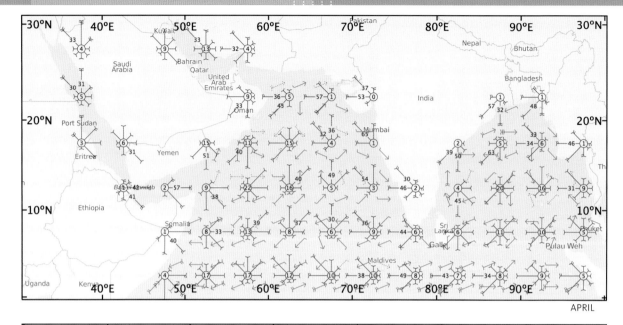

APRIL

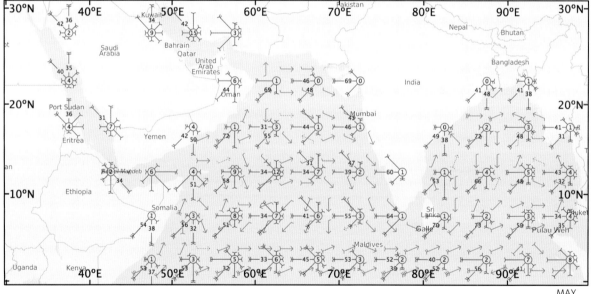

MAY

weather and favourable winds in much of the Red Sea, with no risk of cyclones in the Arabian Sea before the middle of May. Cyclone Gonu, one of the worst tropical storms recorded in the Arabian Sea, occurred at the beginning of June 2007, so passages across the Arabian Sea after the middle of May ought to be avoided. However, as May and June are regarded as a high-risk period in the Bay of Bengal, passages through that area during the critical period should be avoided. The main problem of

this timing is the fact that such an early passage across the Arabian Sea would lead to an arrival in the Bay of Bengal at a time when cyclones start posing a real risk.

For planning purposes this voyage is divided into three segments, with each of the passages through the Red Sea, Arabian Sea and Bay of Bengal being considered separately. The Red Sea passage presents no real problems during spring, nor does a crossing of the Arabian Sea in early May. However, a June arrival in the Bay of

Bengal is not considered a good time, nor would such an early arrival in Southeast Asia, at the height of the SW monsoon, fit most people's plans. A possible solution is to take a calculated risk and, rather than cross the Arabian Sea directly to Sri Lanka, take advantage of the available time to make a detour to the north to Oman, and call at Muscat, Dubai and Abu Dhabi, which are rarely visited by cruising boats. From there, the voyage can continue to India and follow its western shore by calling at Mumbai, Goa, Mangalore, Calicut and Cochin, all of which have yacht clubs where a foreign cruising boat is such a rarity that its crew is assured of a warm welcome.

Sailing this challenging but also more rewarding route should bring the boat to Sri Lanka by September which is a reasonable month to cross the Bay of Bengal as the cyclones that may occur normally form in its central part and move rapidly to the north. An autumn arrival in Southeast Asia allows for the coming winter season to be spent either in Western Malaysia or Thailand, or continuing east from Singapore into the Western North Pacific where the first months of the year provide the most favourable sailing conditions.

would be the choice of those who intend to sail quickly to South Africa before the onset of the cyclone season.

The timing of a late May or June arrival south of the equator needs to follow the same criteria as those outlined in voyage I6. An early spring passage through the Red Sea will benefit from favourable conditions as far as the Gulf of Aden where, due to the risk of piracy, matters become more complicated as the commonly sailed routes to the South Indian Ocean pass through the most dangerous area. To minimise this risk, the safe alternative is to stay in the North Indian Ocean as far as the Maldives, and once there, turn south to cross the equator and make landfall at Chagos. Sailing this route not only avoids the critical area east of Somalia but also gives the opportunity of a more interesting itinerary in the South Indian Ocean.

A later departure is also feasible although southbound passages in the Red Sea in summer can be quite unpleasant because of the very high temperatures. Once the Gulf of Aden is reached, the same considerations apply as those outlined above. As long as piracy continues to be a threat in the western part of the North Indian Ocean, an easterly course across the Gulf of Aden should be maintained

17 • Southbound voyages from the Red Sea

Recommended time: February to March, July (southbound), April to mid-May, August (eastbound), June to October (southbound)

Tropical storms: May to June, September to November (Arabian Sea), March to May, September to December (Bay of Bengal), November to May (South Indian Ocean)

World Cruising Routes:

RS1	Suez to Port Sudan
RS2	Port Sudan to Gulf of Aden
IT21	Southbound from Red Sea
IN35	Red Sea to Maldives
IT22	Southbound from the Maldives

The timing of a voyage from the Mediterranean to the South Indian Ocean is determined by the choice of two different arrival times south of the equator, either at the start of the safe sailing season, in late May or June, or just before the end of it, in August or September. The former would be of interest to those who intend to spend the safe winter season cruising the islands of the South Indian Ocean, while the latter

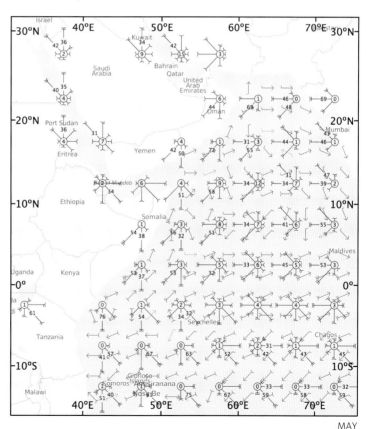

MAY

until it is deemed safe to turn south and cross the equator. In August and September, when this passage is likely to be sailed, there is no risk of cyclones in the Arabian Sea and the SW monsoon ensures consistent westerly winds north of the equator. The choice of the subsequent route to South Africa depends on the available time to call at the various islands en route, and this should also decide how far east the equator is crossed so as to ensure a good sailing angle once the area of the SE trade winds is reached. The various alternatives are outlined in voyage I4 (page 199).

18 • Northbound voyages from South Africa

Recommended time: June

Tropical storms: November to May (South Indian Ocean), May to June, September to November (Arabian Sea), March to May, September to December (Bay of Bengal)

World Cruising Routes:

IS65	Northbound from South Africa
IT15	Chagos to Southeast Asia
IT14	Chagos to Maldives and Sri Lanka
IN25	Sri Lanka to Southeast Asia
IN28	Maldives to Red Sea
RN1	Bab el Mandeb to Port Sudan
RN4	Port Sudan to Southern Egypt

Northbound voyages from South Africa can only count on a reasonable percentage of favourable winds once

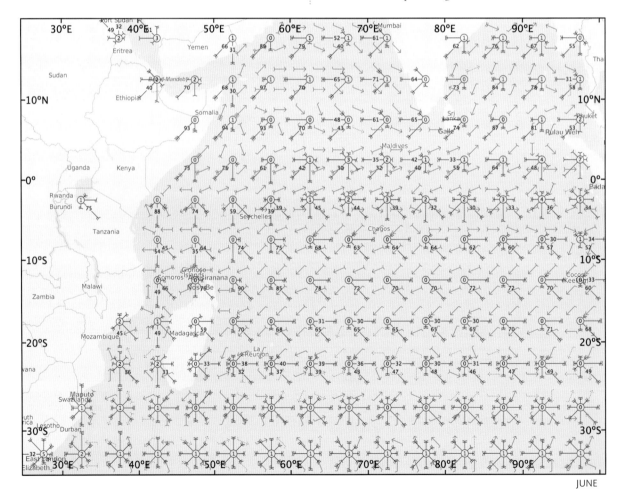

latitude 25°S has been reached, from where the prevailing SE winds become the prominent feature. The islands of Reunion and Mauritius are two convenient landfalls from where boats bound for the North Indian Ocean have the choice of sailing to Chagos, if bound for Southeast Asia, to the Seychelles if bound for the Red Sea, or to Northern Madagascar if bound for that island or destinations in East Africa. These voyages can start at any time during the safe sailing season, but better conditions can be expected in late May or June, before the SE trade winds become too strong.

The timing of the continuation of the voyage depends on the final destination. Voyages to Southeast Asia should plan to cross the Bay of Bengal on the tails of the SW monsoon in September, which will determine the place and time when the equator is crossed and also if the Maldives and Sri Lanka are visited en route or the entire passage to Southeast Asia is sailed nonstop. Although cyclones may occur in the Bay of Bengal in September, the risk on a passage to Southeast Asia is considered to be low. Those on voyages to the Red Sea have more time to play with as their best bet is to wait and make their passage when the NE monsoon is well established and the risk of cyclones in the Arabian Sea has also passed. This allows more time for cruising, as long as the equator is crossed before the start of the cyclone season in the South Indian Ocean.

Cruising hubs

Darwin ***
A major transit port for boats heading into the Indian Ocean and an important fishing harbour, Darwin's yachting facilities cover a wide range of services. The international airport (DRW) has flights to all major Australian destinations, as well as to Singapore and other Asian cities for onward international connections.

Bali *
In spite of its popularity among cruising sailors, Bali's services are limited and only basic repairs can be undertaken at Benoa marina. Good provisioning and fuel are available. Due to Bali's important tourism industry, the airport (DPS) operates flights to many international destinations, including Amsterdam, Sydney and Hong Kong.

Singapore *****
One of the busiest commercial ports in the world, the cruising community is also well served by Singapore's range of repair services, marinas and marine supplies.

Changi airport (SIN) has flights to all major international destinations.

Phuket ***
As one of Asia's favourite cruising destinations, Phuket's yachting facilities cover an adequate range and there are several marinas. There are flights to several international destinations from Phuket airport (HKT).

Langkawi***
Repair and docking facilities have steadily improved in recent years with several marinas, workshops and boatyards offering a good range of services. Spare parts and equipment are easily imported due to Langkawi's duty-free status. Langkawi airport (LGK) operates short-haul flights to neighbouring countries and flights to Kuala Lumpur or Singapore for onward connections.

Durban ****
Durban's Point Yacht Club operates its own marina and boat yard. A comprehensive range of repair and service facilities is available locally. Medical facilities are of a high standard. Durban airport (DUR) operates flights to some neighbouring countries and via Cape Town or Johannesburg for onward international connections.

Port Louis **
The capital of Mauritius provides a limited range of repair facilities. Provisioning is good and so are medical services. Caudan Marina is centrally located and there is a new marina in the north of the island. The international airport (SSR) operates direct flights to London, Paris, Frankfurt, Sydney, Johannesburg, Singapore, Hong Kong and other destinations.

Reunion ***
There are good yachting facilities with two marinas and a good range of repair services. Provisioning is good and medical facilities are of a high standard. The international airport (RUN) operates flights to neighbouring countries and direct flights to Paris.

Salalah **
Port Salalah has good repair, haul-out and medical facilities. Fuel and provisions are available. Salalah airport (SLL) operates flights to Muscat, Dubai and Riyadh for onward international connections.

Djibouti *
Djibouti's yachting repair facilities are basic, but fuel and provisions are readily available. Peltier General Hospital

Chagos.

has good facilities. Djibouti airport (JIB) has flights to various destinations in the Middle East and also direct flights to Paris with Air France.

Port Sudan *

Port Sudan has a limited range of repair services, mostly on engines, and a rudimentary haul-out slipway. Fuel is available but provisioning is basic and so are the medical facilities. Sudan Airways operates flights from a new airport (PZU) to Khartoum and Cairo for onward connections.

What next?

Voyages to the Mediterranean normally transit the Suez Canal in March or April, which fits in perfectly with the start of the sailing season. Those who arrive earlier in Egypt can spend some time in Southern Egypt at one of the marinas near Hurghada to avoid arriving in the Mediterranean before spring. Such an arrival means that even those who plan to continue the voyage into the Atlantic will have five or six months to enjoy many of the delights that the Mediterranean has to offer. If planning to sail to Northern Europe, the voyage north from Gibraltar should not be left later than August. Those planning to sail to the Canaries can delay their departure from the Mediterranean until September.

Those who have sailed the Cape of Good Hope route can resume their voyage in December or January when sailing conditions in the South Atlantic are at their best. The majority of voyages are bound for the Caribbean with an intermediate stop at the island of St Helena followed in most cases by a detour to Northern Brazil. Such timing allows for a March arrival in the Caribbean so that the next two or three months can be spent cruising the Lesser Antilles before the time comes to move on before the start of the hurricane season in June.

Voyages from South Africa can reach the Mediterranean or Northern Europe by a shorter route by sailing from St Helena to the Cape Verdes, Canaries and thence to their final destination.

CIRCULAR VOYAGES IN THE INDIAN OCEAN

Due to its regular alternation between seasonal winds, the Indian Ocean has been the scene of some of the earliest recorded circular voyages. The best known among them are the voyages between the Persian Gulf and East Africa undertaken by dhows using the two monsoons for their annual trading voyage, sailing west with the NE monsoon of winter and returning with the SW monsoon of summer. The word 'monsoon' is derived from the Arabic word *mausim* which means 'season' but also, by implication, a seasonal change in wind direction.

Modern sailors are using these seasonal winds to good advantage but almost exclusively in a unidirectional sense, to sail from Southeast Asia to the Red Sea and Mediterranean during the NE monsoon. There are, however, a number of circular voyages which can benefit from this regional feature, both in terms of wind direction and favourable seasons.

IC1	•	The Tropical Circuit
IC2	•	The Short Tropical Circuit
IC3	•	The South Indian Circuit
IC4	•	The Austral Circuit
IC5	•	The Two Oceans Circuit

IC1 • The Tropical Circuit

This is a voyage normally undertaken by sailors based in Southeast Asia who are not interested in expanding their cruising range beyond the Indian Ocean and wish to explore some of the best cruising destinations in their region. The voyage can easily be accomplished in six months by taking advantage of favourable conditions throughout its length.

The timing of this voyage needs to take into account two crucial factors: an arrival in the South Indian Ocean after the end of the cyclone season and a return passage across the Bay of Bengal during a cyclone-free period and before the onset of the NE monsoon. Voyages originating in Western Malaysia or Thailand can start at any time during the NE monsoon, their departure being dictated by the intended time of arrival south of the equator. There are three alternatives: an eastern route from Singapore via the Indonesian Archipelago to the Sunda Strait, an intermediate route that follows Sumatra's west coast and a western route that goes to Chagos and Mauritius, either directly or via the Maldives.

The main attraction of the first alternative is that places in North Borneo or Western Indonesia can be cruised during the favourable season on the way south, while the second alternative offers the opportunity to explore the rarely visited islands off the west coast of Sumatra. Both of these routes pass through Cocos Keeling, a long term favourite among cruising sailors where the local authorities have done everything possible to make visitors feel welcome. This is no longer the case at the next destination, Chagos, which can only be visited with a special permit issued by the British authorities who administer this territory. Those who are not in possession of the permit, or who prefer to bypass Chagos, can sail

The Seychelles.

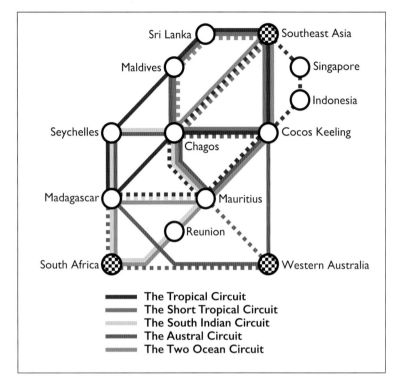

Key:
- The Tropical Circuit
- The Short Tropical Circuit
- The South Indian Circuit
- The Austral Circuit
- The Two Ocean Circuit

IC2 • The Short Tropical Circuit

Those who prefer to make a shorter foray into the South Indian Ocean, or who cannot make an early start from Thailand or Malaysia, can shorten considerably the previous itinerary by sailing directly to either Cocos or Chagos. As Cocos Keeling can be affected by tropical cyclones, the arrival there should not be timed before May. As the start should take place while the NE monsoon is still active, the available time can be spent visiting the west coast of Sumatra and offlying islands so as to arrive in Cocos after the end of the cyclone season.

Any islands that have been missed on the outbound passage, such as the Maldives and Sri Lanka, can be visited on the return voyage. The final leg across the Bay of Bengal should be timed for September when the risk of cyclones in that area is negligible.

Route: Southeast Asia – Cocos Keeling (May to June) – Chagos (July) – [Maldives (August)] – [Sri Lanka] – Southeast Asia

Start: March to April

Return: September

Tropical storms: March to May, September to December (Bay of Bengal), November to May (South Indian Ocean)

Total distance: 5,200–7,600 miles

Duration: 5–6 months

directly to Mauritius and from there to Madagascar. A more direct and somewhat easier route goes directly from Chagos to Madagascar without calling at Mauritius. The main cruising area of Madagascar is on its northwest coast from where the Seychelles can easily be reached when the time comes for the return voyage across the equator. Favourable winds can be expected to continue north of the equator during the recommended time when the SW monsoon is still in full force. The passage can be interrupted in the Maldives and Sri Lanka, both of which lie close to the route across the Bay of Bengal to Southeast Asia. This passage is best timed for September when there is no risk of cyclones in the southern part of the Bay of Bengal.

Route: Southeast Asia – Singapore – Indonesia (March to April) – Cocos Keeling (May) – [Chagos] – Mauritius (June) – [Madagascar (July)] – Seychelles – Maldives (August) – [Sri Lanka] – Southeast Asia

Start: January to April

Return: September

Tropical storms: March to May, September to December (Bay of Bengal), November to May (South Indian Ocean)

Total distance: 7,700–9,200 miles

Duration: 6–8 months

IC3 • The South Indian Circuit

This voyage originating in South Africa can easily be accomplished in one season. In late May or early June, at the beginning of the safe season, better conditions will be encountered by sailing west of Madagascar through the Mozambique Channel, but taking this option would almost certainly forgo a visit to Reunion or Mauritius. However, this route may appeal to those who would be happy to limit their cruise to just Madagascar and the Seychelles and leave the Mascarene Islands for another occasion or possibly for the return voyage.

Caudan marina in Mauritius.

Those who prefer to sail the full circuit should take the route to the east of Madagascar to Reunion and Mauritius en route to Chagos and the Seychelles before turning south for Madagascar and its cruising area based around Nosy Be. Sailing from Mauritius to Chagos may be too much of a detour so a direct passage to the Seychelles may be preferable. From Madagascar, the voyage continues south through the Mozambique Channel either directly to Richards Bay or Durban, or by calling at some of the bays and islands along Mozambique's coast, an area which is opening up to foreign visiting yachts.

Route: South Africa – [Madagascar] – Reunion – Mauritius (June) – [Chagos (July)] – [Seychelles] – Madagascar (August to September) – [Mozambique] – South Africa

Start: May

Return: October

Tropical storms: November to May (South Indian Ocean)

Total distance: 3,800–5,600 miles

Duration: 5–6 months

IC4 • The Austral Circuit

Sailors based in Western Australia have a limited range of cruising opportunities and this voyage offers them the opportunity to visit some of the best cruising destinations in the South Indian Ocean during one season.

Leaving from a place like Fremantle, at the start of the safe season favourable winds will be encountered from about 30°S. North of that latitude, the prevailing SE winds are a dominant feature throughout the South Indian Ocean. The Australian outpost of Cocos Keeling makes an ideal first landfall from where the route turns west towards Rodrigues and Mauritius unless Chagos is visited first. This is indeed a difficult decision as calling at Mauritius first would mean sailing almost back and close on the wind to Chagos, whereas going to Chagos first may result in a similarly close-hauled subsequent passage to Mauritius. The way this dilemma could be solved is by prioritising those three destinations, Chagos, Mauritius and the Seychelles, and possibly deciding which one to leave out. Those who are determined to visit both Chagos and the Seychelles may prefer to sail from Cocos to Chagos and continue to the Seychelles without making a detour to Mauritius. Those who are not keen on calling at Chagos

Anchorage near Phuket.

hemispheres. This voyage may be of interest to sailors from South Africa who are interested in exploring the west coast of Malaysia and Thailand, and taking part in some of the sailing events being held there every year during the winter period.

The timing as far as Chagos is similar to the one outlined in the South Indian Circuit, with the crossing of the equator being timed to coincide with the end of the SW monsoon in the North Indian Ocean. The changeover period to the NE monsoon, with its pleasantly cool winter weather, is the best time to visit places like Penang, Langkawi and Phuket, and explore the cruising areas extending north towards Myanmar. There are many interesting cruising options for the return voyage which can include a detour from Singapore to Borneo to be followed by an Indonesian cruise. The alternative is to sail along the west coast of Sumatra switching between the mainland and offshore islands. This is one of the least visited parts of Indonesia with excellent diving, surfing and fishing all along the 70 islands of the Mentawai Archipelago that runs parallel to Sumatra.

Cocos Keeling is a convenient stop in the South Indian Ocean if the intention is to continue along a southern route to South Africa via Mauritius and Reunion, otherwise it would make more sense to sail to Chagos and from there to Madagascar either directly or via the Seychelles. From Madagascar the route south follows the island's west coast but as there is a higher percentage of contrary southerly winds close to Madagascar, better winds may be found by sailing closer to the African mainland with the possibility of stopping at some of the places along the coast of Mozambique.

should sail to Mauritius, thence the Seychelles and, finally, those who are prepared to forgo the Seychelles should sail to Chagos, Mauritius and directly from there to Madagascar.

The voyage from Madagascar continues south through the Mozambique Channel with the possibility of visiting some of Mozambique en route to either Richards Bay or Durban, if the intention is to also see some of South Africa. As the return voyage home can only count on reasonable winds in higher latitudes, either from one of those South African ports or directly from Madagascar, the best course should be sailed to 35°S, or possibly a little further south, where the prevailing westerly winds should ensure favourable winds for the rest of the passage.

Route: Western Australia – [Cocos Keeling] – Mauritius (July) – [Chagos] – [Seychelles] – Madagascar (September) – [South Africa] – Western Australia

Start: June

Return: October to November

Tropical storms: November to May (South Indian Ocean)

Total distance: 9,200–10,900 miles

Duration: 5–6 months

IC5 • The Two Oceans Circuit

This is an extension of the South Indian Circuit whose timing fits in easily within the favourable seasons in both

---

Route: South Africa – Mauritius – Chagos (July) – [Maldives (August)] – [Sri Lanka] – Southeast Asia (September to February) – Singapore (March) – Indonesia (April to May) – Cocos Keeling (June) – Mauritius (July) – Reunion – [Madagascar (August to September)] – [Mozambique] – South Africa

Start: May year I

Return: October year II

Tropical storms: November to May (South Indian Ocean), March to May, September to December (Bay of Bengal)

Total distance: 11,400–13,600 miles

Duration: 16–18 months

THE MEDITERRANEAN SEA

The capricious Mediterranean where the clouds advance like rutting elephants, enormous and full of rain, they come forward as kings among tumultuous armies, their flags are the lightning, thunder is their drum. . .

Gulshan Rai

The Mediterranean Sea covers an approximate area of 2.5 million km² (965,000 square miles). Its name derives from the Latin word *mediterraneus*, meaning 'in the middle of earth' or 'between lands'. The Mediterranean Sea has been known by various names throughout human history. In the Bible it was referred to as the Great Sea, the Greeks called it *Mesogeios*, which also means 'between lands', while the Romans called it *Mare Nostrum*, 'Our Sea'.

From ancient times, the Mediterranean has been an important seaway for trade and travel, and facilitated cultural exchange between the various peoples whose civilisations flourished on its shores – Egyptian, Phoenician, Greek, Roman, Arab and many others. Seafaring played a major part in the development of those societies and some remarkable feats of seamanship and navigation were achieved by the early mariners who hailed from these shores. The most daring and enterprising mariners of antiquity were the Phoenicians who lived on the eastern shores of the Mediterranean in the area now occupied by Lebanon and Northern Israel. They were remarkable seafarers trading far and wide across the Mediterranean and gradually establishing settlements along its coasts and islands. The earliest record of one of those outstanding

voyages is the *Massaliot Periplus* from the sixth century BCE which describes the sea routes used by traders from Phoenicia. It also gives an account of a voyage from the Greek colony of Massilia (Marseille) along the Western Mediterranean, from Cadiz in Spain to Brittany, Ireland and Britain. The *Periplus* – the word means 'sailing around' – is the earliest document to describe the trade links between northern and southern Europe, and that such a manual existed indicates the importance of those regular trading voyages.

The Greek historian Herodotus, who lived in the fifth century BCE, wrote in *The Histories* that 'The Phoenicians sailed from the Arabian Gulf (Red Sea) into the Southern Ocean (Indian Ocean) . . . and after two full years rounded the Pillars of Heracles (Strait of Gibraltar) in the course of the third, and returned to Egypt.' This sounds like a complete circumnavigation of Africa, which would have been an astonishing achievement for that age, but cannot be accepted as fact as there is no other record of it. To test the feasibility of such a voyage, the British sailor Philip Beale had a boat built based on a traditional Phoenician design. The square-rigged *Phoenicia* took nearly three years to circumnavigate Africa and returned to her starting point in Syria in October 2010.

The seafaring tradition of the Phoenicians was continued by the Greeks with a remarkable voyage being accomplished by Pytheas of Massilia around 325 BCE. In his book *On the Ocean (Peri tou okeanou)*, which has not survived, but has been quoted by several ancient writers, Pytheas described his expedition from the Mediterranean to Northern Europe. Pytheas was the first person to attribute the tides to being caused by the moon. He also mentioned the midnight sun and introduced the geographical concept of distant Thule, which probably referred to current Norway.

The Arab conquests towards the end of the first millennium were accompanied by an expansion of sea traffic throughout the Mediterranean, Arab ships plying their trade as far as the Black Sea and the Eastern Atlantic, with a documented voyage by an Arab ship to Denmark in 844. The Arabs developed the science of navigation and most texts as well as charts were translated into Latin. The first use in the Mediterranean of the compass, a Chinese invention, was mentioned in 1240.

During medieval times the importance of sea traffic in the Mediterranean continued to increase with the expansion of various sea powers: Venetian, Genoese, Spanish, Ottoman and many others up to the current time. Many famous seafarers learned their trade in the Mediterranean only to gain fame elsewhere, men like Cristoforo Colombo, Amerigo Vespucci, Jacques Cartier, Giovanni Caboto, Vicente Pinzón and Giovanni da Verazzano. With such an old seafaring tradition it was only normal for sailing to become a favourite pastime in the Mediterranean, which is now the most popular cruising area in the world, the Mare Nostrum of the Romans now belonging to everyone.

Phoenicia on her African circumnavigation.

WINDS AND CURRENTS

The Mediterranean climate is generally pleasant, marked by long hot summers and mild winters. Most gales and rain occur in winter months, few storms interrupting the long summer. Local conditions vary considerably, stronger winds and squalls often resulting from local phenomena and not due to the overall weather pattern. Tropical storms do not affect this region.

The Mediterranean can be divided into two halves, Western and Eastern, corresponding to the two deeper basins which are separated by a ridge, running through Italy, Sicily, and Malta to the African coast. In the summer the Western Mediterranean comes under the influence of the Atlantic high-pressure area centred near the Azores, while the Eastern Mediterranean is influenced by the low-pressure area east of the Mediterranean, which is an extension of the Indian Ocean monsoon. As a rule weather systems move across the Mediterranean from west to east and this is particularly true of depressions in the winter months. The commonest winds over the entire area are from the northerly sector, more from the NW in the western basin, N in the Aegean and NE in the eastern part. Well chronicled down the centuries are the various regional winds, which are a notable feature of Mediterranean weather.

Close to the coast the weather is greatly affected by the height of the land and other topographical features. Local conditions vary enormously, any prevailing wind usually being lighter near the coast, while land and sea breezes have a strong effect. The land and sea breezes are particularly noticeable in summer months and reach 20 to 30 knots in some places. The direction of the wind changes not only with the time of day, but also with the orientation of the coast. A reversal in the direction of the wind usually occurs between early morning and late afternoon. Local squalls are more frequent where the coast is mountainous and the wind is frequently accelerated down valleys or between islands. These effects are particularly true for high islands and should be borne in mind when anchoring in the lee of such valleys, particularly in Greece in the *meltemi* season.

THE MISTRAL

Magistralis meaning 'masterful' was the name originally given to the cold dry NW wind which holds masterly sway over the Western Mediterranean in both frequency and strength. Now corrupted to *mistral* or *maestral*, these NW winds are formed when cold air flowing down over France is blocked by the heights of the Alps and is diverted to pour into the Mediterranean via the Rhône valley. In summer, the mistral is often strengthened by the area of low pressure which forms over North Africa. The mistral blows strongly in the Gulf of Lion and the Gulf of Genoa, while the Rhône delta area and Marseille receive the full force of the mistral on almost 100 days a year. Blowing on average at 20 knots, the mistral is frequently stronger and can reach 50–60 knots. The mistral often reaches the Balearics and Sardinia and occasionally can be felt as far as Malta and North Africa. The French Riviera east of St. Raphaël is sheltered by the mountains behind the coast and the mistral is felt less there.

The mistral blows at intervals throughout the year, although it is commonest in winter, normally lasting from three to six days, and is typified by clear skies. Along the Spanish coast this NW wind is called the *tramontana*, being strong, dry and very cold in winter.

VENDAVALES

These are strong SW winds which blow between North Africa and the Spanish coast, especially in the late autumn and early spring. These winds, which do not last long, can reach gale force and are associated with depressions moving across Spain and Southern France. The *vendavales* are associated with squalls and thunderstorms, but are less strong near the African coast and the NE coast of Spain. They are much stronger when funnelled through the Strait of Gibraltar. When they hit the west coast of Sardinia and the Gulf of Genoa, these strong SW winds are called *libeccio* in Italian.

SIROCCO

In general usage, this name is used to describe any winds from the south bringing hot air off the continent of Africa. Due to depressions moving east across the Sahara Desert, the sirocco blows off the north coast of Africa very hot and dry, often laden with sand and dust, thus reducing visibility. As these winds pass across the sea, they pick up some moisture, and so in Spain, Malta, Sicily, Sardinia and Southern Italy the sirocco arrives at a lower temperature and with a higher humidity than off the African coast. Rain falling through the dust carried by these winds can sometimes be red or brown.

A similar wind blows off the Arabian Peninsula to affect Israel, Lebanon, Cyprus, Crete and other southern islands in the Eastern Mediterranean, particularly in the transitional periods between seasons, from April to June and September to October. In Egypt the sirocco is called the *khamsin*, which means '50' in Arabic, because it occurs most frequently in the 50 days following the Coptic Easter. It usually blows at gale force for about one day and is most common from February to April. In May and June the *khamsin* is less frequent but can last longer.

LEVANTE

These NE winds blow near the Spanish coast, reaching gale force in spring (February to May) and autumn (October to December). In summer months from June to September, the *levante* is shorter and has less strength. The *levante* is formed when a depression is situated between the Balearics and North Africa, usually when there is a high-pressure area over the European landmass to the north.

The *levante* is most common along the central Spanish coast and can continue into the Strait of Gibraltar, where it is funnelled to become easterly and is known as *levanter*. The *levante* brings lower temperatures and rain, which is often heavy near the coast, while the long fetch produces heavy seas.

GREGALE

These strong winds, also from the NE, are felt in the Central Mediterranean, on the coasts of Sicily and Malta and especially in the Ionian Sea. They flow out of high pressure areas situated over the Balkans and are common in the winter months, especially in February. These winds usually blow at gale force, are cold and produce a heavy swell. The NE coast of Malta is particularly vulnerable as the main harbours are open to the NE. It was a *gregale* that wrecked St Paul on the Maltese coast in the first century CE.

MELTEMI

This wind is more commonly known by its Turkish name meltemi than as the etesian wind, which is taken from the Greek word meaning 'annual'. These regular winds blow steadily over the eastern basin of the Mediterranean all summer, commencing in May or early June and continuing until September or even October. The meltemi is at its strongest and steadiest in July and August. Even when the meltemi is not blowing, or while it is being established in the earlier months, it is rare to get winds from any other direction during this time. Periods of calm can often occur at the beginning of the season. The meltemi has many similarities with a monsoon and can be regarded as an extension of the Indian monsoon caused by the low pressure area east of the Mediterranean.

The meltemi blows from the north in the central Aegean, tending to be more NE in the northern Aegean and NW in the southern areas, extending across the whole eastern basin, although it peters out before reaching the southern shores of the Mediterranean. The meltemi is a fresh wind, on average 15–20 knots, and is associated with fine clear weather. Often it reaches up to 30 knots, especially in the afternoons, and occasionally it reaches 40 knots. It is less strong in the most northerly areas and strongest in the S and SW Aegean. The meltemi tends to decrease at night.

Western Mediterranean

The summers are fine with few storms. Gale force winds do occur, but these are often generated by local depressions over a limited area. Because of this they are difficult to predict and give little warning of their onset, as an impending gale is rarely preceded by a meaningful change in barometric pressure. Strong winds such as the sirocco, *vendavales*, or *levante* are more common in the transitional months of spring and autumn. The mistral can blow in summer but is much less frequent than at other times of the year. The commonest wind over this area is from the NW, except in the most southerly areas near the African coast, where winds from the E and NE are more frequent. There can be calm periods for several days at a time. There is little rain over this area in summer, except for occasional thunderstorms near some of the coasts.

In winter winds are much more variable and gales more frequent. Depressions from the Atlantic track in from the west, either across France or Spain or through the Strait of Gibraltar. Also some local depressions form in the Gulf of Lion or the Gulf of Genoa and track to the south, bringing strong winds and squally weather. The mistral gales are more frequent in winter months and NW winds predominate over this area. *Vendavales* and *libeccio* blow especially in late autumn and early spring. In spite of the increased frequency of gales in winter, there are also some quiet periods. Winter temperatures are mild, there are frequent sunny days and most rain falls as showers.

Eastern Mediterranean

The summers are dominated by the seasonal winds from the northern quarter, which blow strongly but are associated with clear skies and fine weather. Rainfall is scant and almost non-existent on the southern shores. The climate of the eastern basin is a little more continental than the western or central areas, which means fewer fronts, less rain and a lower humidity. It is noted for long hot summers and short winters. Most of the rain falls in winter.

In winter, depressions track in an easterly direction either SE towards Cyprus or NE towards the Black Sea. Although small in size, these depressions can be very violent as they develop rapidly and with little warning. Some violent storms in this area are dangerous as they are local in character, arriving quickly out of a clear sky. Although winds from the northerly sector are commonest in winter too, winds from other directions do occur and there are strong gale force winds particularly from the south. Both S and N winds are more prolonged than E or W winds. November to February are the worst months with cold dry N to NE gales and warm moist SE to SW gales. When a depression passes there can be a change from S to N within a few hours. At the transitional period between seasons, such as in April and May, calms can occur for several days.

coast. In the eastern basin, the east-setting current turns north along the coast of Israel and Lebanon, west along the Turkish coast, and completes the circle along the northern coast of Crete. A branch makes a counterclockwise circulation of the Aegean Sea, being joined in its southward movement by water flowing out of the Black Sea and into the Mediterranean via the Bosporus and Dardanelles. Another branch makes a counterclockwise circulation of the Adriatic.

With the exception of the steady current along the North African coast, the actual currents are very variable and are affected considerably both by the direction and force of the wind and local conditions. For example, when the meltemi is blowing, a south to southwest-setting current predominates in the Central and Western Aegean. The strongest currents are experienced in the Strait of Gibraltar, the Bosporus and Dardanelles. Other straits, such as the Strait of Messina, are strongly affected by tidal currents.

Ionian Sea encounter.

Currents

The Mediterranean loses more water by evaporation than it receives from rivers emptying into it, so there is a general inflow of water from the Atlantic Ocean at all times of the year. This east-setting current is strongest through the Strait of Gibraltar and along the North African coast, where it averages around 2 knots. After passing through the channel between Sicily and Tunisia it gradually loses its strength as it flows eastward. There is a weaker counterclockwise circulation in both of the two basins of the Mediterranean joined by an east-setting current in the Malta Channel between the two areas. In the western basin this current flows north up the west coast of Italy. It turns west along the south coast of France and continues south down the Spanish

MEDITERRANEAN VOYAGES

Malta's capital Valletta.

From the ancient mariners to present-day sailors the lure of the Mediterranean has remained undiminished and, as I was told by an old sailor during my first cruise there, 'you can only blame yourself if you leave disappointed'.

From afar the Mediterranean looks like a large lake surrounded by ancient ports, modern marinas, attractive anchorages and scores of islands dotted about it, in other words an ideal cruising ground. The problem is that this lake is 2,000 miles long and, as everyone soon finds out, the major difficulty is not where to go but what to leave out. Fortunately for voyage-planning purposes, this task is greatly eased as there are only two arterial routes which traverse this landbound sea. The northern route runs from Gibraltar to Greece from where it continues to the Dardanelles and Bosporus by boats bound for the Black Sea. Boats arriving from the Red Sea bound for the Atlantic normally sail a southern route to Gibraltar.

With the majority of Mediterranean cruises consisting of a succession of short legs, forward planning is quite important as there are many local or regional factors which need to be taken into account when drawing up the outline of a longer or shorter Mediterranean sojourn.

APRIL

The sailing season lasts from late April to October, with the peak summer season being between early July and the middle of August. As most ports and marinas get very crowded during that period, you should try to avoid the most popular areas such as the French Riviera, Corsica, Northern Sardinia, the Balearics, Croatia and the Central Aegean during this time. As places in the Western and Central Mediterranean have been getting increasingly more crowded, cruising boats have migrated east, mostly to Turkey and its south coast, now a popular destination which may soon share the fate of similar victims of their own success.

As far as weather is concerned, in some parts of the Mediterranean summer winds can be light, often diurnal, and calms are frequent. The notable exception is the Aegean Sea where strong northerly winds are a feature of the summer months so it is a good tactic to plan an Aegean cruise by making your way north in late spring and then sailing south with favourable winds. Also a summer feature are the frequent, and often violent, thunderstorms in the Adriatic Sea which can affect cruises in Croatia, another area which is best visited in late spring or early autumn when ports and anchorages are less crowded.

The winter season lasts from late October to April when the weather can be changeable, with occasional storms. Between November and March there can be rather cold nights, but frequent sunny days. The relatively benign Mediterranean winters attract many sailors to spend the off season in one of the many marinas, the southern and eastern shores being generally warmer and having a better winter climate. To be certain of getting a place in a preferred marina or boatyard, it is advisable to book a place as early as possible as many places have limited space for visitors, whether afloat or ashore. As countries belonging to the European Union have restrictions on the time a non-EU vessel can spend in their waters, it is essential to make sure that the maximum period is not exceeded. The maximum 18 months stay in the European Union applied to non-EU boats is forcing the owners of such boats to spend some time in a non-EU country, such as Turkey, Tunisia or Egypt, before returning to the EU to start the clock again.

Although the Mediterranean climate makes it possible to live on board and even sail for much of the year, for the more adventuresome there is the alternative of heading south at the end of the summer season. From the Western Mediterranean the obvious destinations are the Canaries and Madeira, while the Northern Red Sea beckons to those in the Eastern Mediterranean.

Yachting facilities are well developed in most parts of the Mediterranean and even countries with no yachting tradition, such as Tunisia or Turkey, have developed excellent facilities in recent years and there are now marinas and boatyards with good repair facilities spread all over the Mediterranean.

MAY

One-season voyages

Port d'Andratx in Mallorca.

Eastbound

Arriving in the Mediterranean from the Atlantic, whether from Northern Europe, the Caribbean or the USA, those who intend to spend only one long summer in the Mediterranean before returning home or continuing the voyage to the Canaries need to be back in the Atlantic by late September. As most such boats only arrive in June or early July, the available time is so short that basically there are only two realistic options: to limit yourself to a shorter cruise in the Western Mediterranean, or to proceed as quickly as possible to the Eastern Mediterranean and attempt to see as much as possible by maintaining a sustained rhythm throughout.

Those who are attracted to the shorter alternative should not expect to get further east than Sicily or Malta, and could start their Mediterranean sojourn by cruising leisurely along the south coast of Spain as far as Alicante, Valencia or even Barcelona, before crossing over to the Balearics. Those islands are always busy but the north

JUNE

coast of Ibiza, the east coast of Mallorca and most of Menorca can be relatively uncrowded even at the height of summer. The same cannot be said of Corsica and the north and east of Sardinia, both of which attract large numbers of yachts from the mainland during the entire summer holiday period. As time might be too short to also visit Sicily or Malta, Tunisia's convenient location makes it possible to visit at least its north coast before heading west for Gibraltar. As there are few suitable ports of call along the North African coast, those who are not tempted to sail nonstop to Gibraltar will have a choice of several attractive ports along the south coast of Spain. Because of the possibility of long spells of strong westerly winds during early autumn in the Strait of Gibraltar, it is preferable to pass through the strait as soon as possible because once this hurdle is past the planning of the next leg is much easier. Once past Gibraltar and with time in hand it is possible to spend some time exploring the Algarve coast of Portugal or make a detour up one of the two navigable rivers in the area: the Guayaquil leading to Seville, or the Guadiana which winds its way in a tranquil rural setting and forms the border between Portugal and Spain.

The initial route of the longer alternative passes through the same areas as far as the north of Sicily and the Messina Strait from where it either heads north for the Adriatic or east for the Aegean. It is at this point that a decision needs to be made whether to visit Croatia or Greece as including both in a one-season cruise may prove to be too much. With Croatia being very crowded at the height of summer, the better solution is to make for the Corinth Canal and enter the Aegean by that short cut thus being upwind of most islands in the Southern Aegean. The return route passes south of the Peloponnese with first Malta and then Tunisia making perfect ports of call on the way to Gibraltar.

Westbound

The task of forward planning is much easier if arriving from the Red Sea as it normally means a spring arrival and therefore an entire season to explore the very best of the Mediterranean while moving west at a steady pace. There are various route options from Port Said, whether to sail east to Israel or Lebanon, north to Cyprus and Turkey or northwest to Greece. Whichever route is chosen, those who wish to see more of the Greek islands should attempt to reach their northernmost point in the Aegean by late May or early June so as to ensure that the strong northerly winds of summer will be at their back. Whether a detour into the Adriatic is feasible, or even justified, during a one-season cruise is hard to say, but probably the best way to sail west from the Aegean is to sail past the three fingers of the Peloponnese, calling at one of the many attractive places in the area, before heading for Malta. The alternative is to visit first the north coast of Crete before sailing to Malta and thence to Tunisia, the Balearics and, finally, Gibraltar. This is the kind of itinerary which the old Med hand mentioned earlier, whom I met all those years ago, might hopefully approve of, although he would more likely point out that the Mediterranean deserves more than just one season of any sailor's life.

JULY

Two-season voyages

The Turkish port of Bodrum.

Eastbound

With two full sailing seasons at your disposal, the first decision should concern the place where the winter will be spent as that will determine both the route and timing of the first season. There are many places to winter in, some more suitable if the boat is left unattended while others are more attractive if living on board. Ideally if the boat is to be left unattended it should be stored ashore and there are several yards offering this service in Croatia, Greece and Southern Turkey. The choices are more limited if planning to remain on board and in that case the first priority is to find a sheltered marina or port in an area where winters are mild, which could be Crete, Southern Turkey, Cyprus, or even one of the Egyptian marinas in the Red Sea. All these places would suit those who have reached the eastern extremity of their planned two-season cruise in the Mediterranean and intend to sail west the following spring. Otherwise there are many more choices to overwinter, be it in Malta, Southern Italy, the French Riviera, the Balearics or mainland Spain.

Even with more available time, an early arrival in Gibraltar is still prefer-able as there is then sufficient time to cruise eastwards at a relaxed pace. An early arrival also means that normally busy places such as the Balearics, the South of France or Corsica can be visited before the floodgates open. From Gibraltar the route follows the Spanish coast and, if the intention is to continue to France, Barcelona should not be missed as it is one of the most attractive and interesting cities in Spain. A detour to the Balearics can be considered before calling at the Catalan capital from where the French coast can be explored in short hops before sailing to Corsica. Some of the Italian islands in the Tyrrhenian Sea, besides Sardinia, such as the Pontine, Napolitan or Aeolian Islands, can be visited en route to the Messina Strait.

AUGUST

SEPTEMBER

A detour into the Adriatic Sea with stops in Albania, Montenegro and Croatia may coincide with the holiday season but this is in fact the best time to visit Venice, the pearl of the Adriatic, and its extensive lagoon, as most locals, and their boats, are away and finding a place in a marina is not a problem at the height of summer. As suggested earlier, the most convenient way to reach the Aegean is via the Corinth Canal. By now, with autumn approaching, the northerly winds of summer should be on their wane in the Aegean making this the perfect time to enjoy the Cyclades and Dodecanese. By late September or early October it is time to bring the year's cruise to an end, and come to rest in one of the marinas popular with other birds of passage. If the season is not too far advanced and the crew is still willing, the southern coast of Turkey and adjacent lands are best explored during this quiet period as in this far corner of the Mediterranean cruising can be extended until November, provided an eye is kept on the weather.

Just as winter comes late in this part of the Mediterranean, so spring arrives early and by late March or early April you can be on the move again, preferably still in this more sheltered area than in the Aegean where it only starts getting warmer in early May. For those who wish to explore the Black Sea, this is the time to head north through the Dardanelles and savour the thrill of sailing through the heart of Istanbul, an unforgettable experience worth the long detour with the added bonus of visiting some of the countries beyond the Bosporus.

Those who decide to forgo the Black Sea can spend the time enjoying more of the Aegean and, in case the Adriatic was bypassed the previous year, this missed opportunity can

be put right now. Similarly, if Corsica and the French Riviera were missed on the way out, the route can be easily adjusted to sail that way and continue via the Balearics and the Spanish mainland to Gibraltar.

Westbound

Arriving in the Eastern Mediterranean from the Red Sea in early spring is a great advantage when planning a two-season cruise as it allows much greater flexibility, with a choice of spending the first season exploring Turkey, Greece possibly the Adriatic, and spending the winter in Corfu, Crete or Malta, so that the following season is spent in the Western Mediterranean. The alternative is to sail north through the Aegean to the Dardanelles, Istanbul and the Black Sea. Depending on the extent of your Black Sea cruise, this detour would still allow you to be back in the Northern Aegean by the middle of summer with enough of the season left to explore the Greek islands at the best time of times. The coming winter could then be spent in Southwest Turkey or Crete before the voyage is resumed the following season with a foray into the Adriatic which is best visited in early summer when weather conditions are at their best. Sailing south from Croatia, Montenegro, Albania, Corfu and the Ionian Islands provides an interesting interlude on the way to either Malta and Tunisia, or the Messina Strait. There are several options to sail to Gibraltar from there, either directly via Sicily, Southern Sardinia and the Balearics or a more roundabout route that passes through the Strait of Bonifacio and provides the opportunity to see some of Northern Sardinia, Corsica and possibly the French Riviera.

OCTOBER

Cruising hubs

There are good quality repair services available all over the Mediterranean. Docking facilities are also of a good standard, even if marinas are usually crowded. Advance bookings are therefore advisable especially for longer stays. This also applies to those planning to leave their boats in a marina or boatyard between seasons. The following places are listed due to their strategic location.

Palma de Mallorca *****

This busy port has several marinas catering for all sizes, including superyachts. The comprehensive range of yachting facilities is of a high standard, as are local medical services. The international airport (PMI) has flights to most European destinations with connections to transcontinental flights in Madrid.

Malta ****

Malta's traditional role as a sailing hub is due to its convenient location at the centre of the Mediterranean. The island has a good range of repair and docking facilities with several marinas spread out around the capital Valletta. Malta airport (MLA) has flights to several European capitals, as well as to North Africa and the Middle East.

Athens ****

Yachting facilities are spread out over a large area around the Greek capital, from the commercial port of Piraeus to Lavrion. The range of services is comprehensive but it may take time to find the right workshop. There are several marinas and boatyards, all with good facilities. Athens airport (ATH) has regular flights to most European capitals, Africa and the Middle East. It also serves a wide network of flights to local destinations.

Bodrum ***

Turkey's popularity as a cruising destination has resulted in a marked improvement in the quality and range of yachting facilities. Repair facilities are of a good standard with several boatyards as well as three marinas. Milas-Bodrum airport (BJV) operates mostly charter or seasonal flights to many European destinations, or to Istanbul by Turkish Airlines for onward connections. There is a fast ferry service to the neighbouring Greek island of Cos.

What next?

Voyages leaving the Mediterranean into the Atlantic have three main choices: to turn left and head for the Canaries, either nonstop or via either Morocco or Madeira, to sail to the Azores, or turn right, cruise along the Iberian coast or sail offshore to Northern Europe. Voyages to the Canaries can be undertaken as late as September or even early October. As many of those sailing to the Azores may have as their final destination the US East Coast, the Mediterranean must be left much sooner, in May or June, so as to avoid the hurricane season in the Western Atlantic. Voyages to Northern Europe have practically the entire summer at their disposal and those who may be delayed, or wish to spend the longest time possible in the Mediterranean, should consider reaching their destination by way of the Rhône and the various waterway systems leading from it.

Voyages into the Red Sea can be limited to its northern part, which can provide a pleasant destination for the winter months, or continue into the Indian Ocean and beyond.

ROUND THE WORLD VOYAGES

If one does not know to which port one is sailing, no wind is favourable.

Lucius Annaeus Seneca

The first circumnavigation of the world has been attributed, wrongly, to the Portuguese Ferdinand Magellan (Fernão de Magalhães) who in 1519 had set off to sail around the world while in the service of the Spanish crown. He discovered and sailed through the Strait of Magellan and reached the Philippines in 1521, where he was killed. The command of *Victoria*, the only surviving ship of the expedition, was taken over in the Molucca Islands, in present-day Indonesia, by the Basque navigator Juan Sebastián Elcano. Sailing with 17 survivors of the original 240 men who had embarked on the expedition, as well as four Timorese men, Elcano sailed around the Cape of Good Hope and reached Spain on 6 September 1522, thus completing a 43,000 mile voyage that had started in 1519. Elcano was awarded a coat of arms by Charles I of Spain, featuring a globe with the motto *Primus circumdedisti me* meaning, in Latin, 'you went around me first'.

A second Spanish expedition, under the command of García Jofre de Loaísa, left Spain in 1525 but it fared even worse as none of the seven ships survived and eventually only a few men returned home on a Portuguese ship.

The second ship to circumnavigate the globe, between 1577 and 1580, was the *Golden Hind* of Francis Drake. He left England with five ships and a total crew of 164 men and reached the Pacific via the Magellan Strait, which they found with the help of a Portuguese navigator, Nuna da Silva, who had been kidnapped during an earlier attack on two Portuguese carracks. Drake had in fact discovered the passage south of Cape Horn,

which now bears his name, but decided to use the other route to reach the Pacific. By now the *Golden Hind* was on her own as the other ships had lost contact. Drake made his way up the west coast of America, plundering Spanish ports, as far as Vancouver, with the intention of returning home via the Northwest Passage. Defeated by bad weather, they turned west reaching the Cape of Good Hope via Micronesia and the Spice Islands. Drake arrived back in England in September 1580 with only 57 men of the original complement, but with a rich cargo of spices and a hoard of looted Spanish treasure.

In the 17th century, with the age of discovery and exploration in full flow, voyages around the world became commonplace. By the 19th century pleasure yachts were undertaking increasingly daring voyages, but it is not known which yacht was the first to sail around the world. What is beyond doubt is that the first single-handed circumnavigation was completed by Joshua Slocum between 1895 and 1898 on the 37 foot sloop *Spray*.

The second man to circumnavigate the world on his own was Harry Pidgeon, who, from 1921 to 1925, and 1932 to 1937, completed two single-handed voyages on his

self-built 34 foot yawl *Islander* and became the first person to circumnavigate solo twice.

A remarkable circumnavigation was completed by the Argentinian Vito Dumas on *Legh II* between 1942 and 1943. During his voyage he only made three landfalls, at the Cape of Good Hope, Wellington and Valparaíso, and was the first man to complete a single-handed circumnavigation of the Southern Ocean, including the first single-handed passage of all three great capes.

In 1967 Francis Chichester sailed *Gipsy Moth IV* around the world with only one stop, at Sydney. Shortly after Chichester had completed his voyage, the *Sunday Times* newspaper offered the Golden Globe trophy and the considerable prize of £5,000 (approximately £100,000 at today's value) for the first person to sail around the globe without stopping anywhere. Seven boats started the race but by the end there were only two serious contenders, Robin Knox-Johnston on the 32 foot *Suhaili*, and Bernard Moitessier on his 42 foot *Joshua*. As *Suhaili* passed Cape Horn and headed for home, *Joshua* was slowly catching up. Alas, the French sailor-philosopher decided that there were better things in life than fame and riches and, in a true gesture of the Sixties, abandoned the race, continued sailing east and ended up in Tahiti. Meanwhile Robin Knox-Johnston stayed the course, claimed victory, and is now regarded as the first man to complete a solo non-stop circumnavigation of the globe. Although he abandoned the race, Moitessier still circumnavigated the world, crossing his track off South Africa, and then sailing almost two-thirds of the way round a second time. There is some dispute as to who should have claimed the honour of being the first person to sail non-stop around the world as he had actually crossed his outward track first.

In 1971 the Scotsman Chay Blyth became the first person to sail non-stop westabout around the world on the 59 foot *British Steel*. The first woman to achieve the goal of sailing single-handed around the globe was the Polish sailor Krystyna Chojnowska-Liskiewicz, who between 1976 and 1978 sailed the 32 foot *Mazurek* around the world by way of the Panama Canal and the Cape of Good Hope. Shortly afterwards, Naomi James completed her own single-handed circumnavigation by sailing south of the three great capes, Horn, Good Hope and Leeuwin. Both women completed their circumnavigation by making stops en route. Finally, in 1988, the Australian Kay Cottee became the first woman to complete a non-stop single-handed circumnavigation on *Blackmore's First Lady*.

One of the most assiduous yet little-known sailors is the Englishman David Scott Cowper who completed in quick succession two solo circumnavigations, sailing in 1980 around the world from west to east and two years later from east to west, thus becoming the first person to sail around the world in both directions. Two years later he sailed westwards round the globe via the Panama Canal in a converted wooden lifeboat, becoming the first person to circumnavigate solo in a motorboat. In 1986 he set off again and four years later completed the first single-handed circumnavigation of the world by way of the Northwest Passage. In 2009 this indefatigable sailor set off on his sixth voyage around the world, which he completed in 2011.

Among the sailors who had taken part in the first single-handed transatlantic race in 1960 was the Australian David Lewis. In 1964 he left on a world voyage with his wife and two small daughters on the 40 foot catamaran *Rehu Moana*. They circumnavigated by way of the Strait of Magellan and the Cape of Good Hope, this being the world's first circumnavigation by a multihull. David Lewis became known for bringing to the world's attention the traditional Polynesian navigation methods.

Some of the most remarkable voyages were undertaken by Irving and Exy Johnson who, between 1934 and 1958, completed seven circumnavigations, three of them on the 96 foot schooner *Yankee*, the next four on a similarly named 63 foot brigantine. On all these voyages they were accompanied by amateur crews who were undergoing sail training and offshore navigation courses.

Following the success of those early single-handed races, the first round the world race by crewed yachts took place in 1973–1974. The first edition of the Whitbread Round the World Race was won by the Mexican yacht *Sayula II*, a surprising victory as the Swan 65, a luxurious cruising yacht, beat several racing yachts thus showing that occasionally comfort and style matter more on a long voyage than sheer brawn.

In the intervening years, racing yachts have become increasingly more sophisticated and crewed by professional sailors. Their speeds have reached unimaginable levels, with the fastest nonstop circumnavigation record by a crewed yacht being reduced to 40 days, and a single-handed circumnavigation of the globe to 42 days. There is little doubt that these records will soon be beaten as their life expectancy is usually about one year.

The first round the world event for cruising boats was held in 1991–1992 and its organisers, World Cruising Club, have been running similar events ever since.

My own sailing dreams were profoundly influenced by those early races and, by a coincidence undoubtedly arranged by fate, *Sayula II* stopped in the Royal Albert Dock in 1974, where I was fitting out my own *Aventura*, on her way to the prize-giving ceremony in London.

RW1 • Round the world voyages from Europe

RW2 • Round the world voyages from the east coast of North America

RW3 • Round the world voyages from the west coast of North America

RW4 • Round the world voyages from Australia and New Zealand

RW5 • Round the world voyages from Asia

RW6 • Round the world voyages from the east coast of South America

RW7 • Round the world voyages from the west coast of South America

RW8 • Eastabout round the world voyages

A large proportion of the voyages described in this book are in the tropics, which is where world voyagers spend much of their time. However, many tropical areas are only safe for six or seven months of the year, the remaining months being liable to tropical storms. In the following pages I shall outline some examples of typical world voyages that can be done with maximum safety. The majority of these round the world voyages are from east to west so as to take advantage of the prevailing wind systems and to sail as much as possible under trade wind conditions. Because much of the time will be spent in the tropics, the suggested timings will avoid sailing through those areas during the tropical storm seasons.

The number of cruising boats trying to accomplish a circumnavigation against the prevailing winds is very small, but in case anyone is interested in an eastabout circumnavigation of the world, there is also a description of such voyages. Similarly, only a small number of round the world voyages take the North Pacific route, but that option is also described. Most other voyages pass through the South Pacific, which continues to be the main attraction for virtually any sailor setting off on a cruise around the world.

Positions of cruising boats reported across the world over one year.

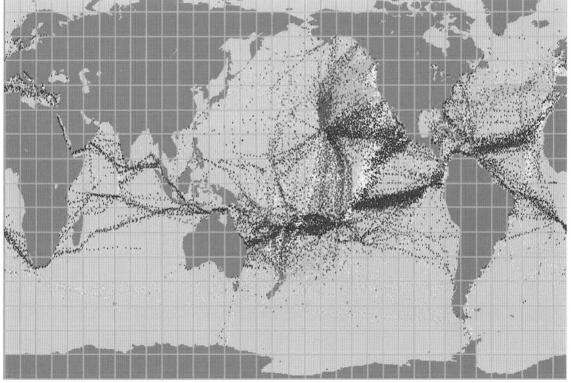

Boat headings:
■ Northern quadrant   ■ Eastern quardrant   ■ Southern quadrant   ■ Western quadrant

Round the world voyages in high latitudes are almost exclusively the preserve of ocean races. Complete high-latitude circumnavigations are rarely accomplished by cruising boats and there are few cruising sailors who can boast having sailed south of those three symbolic capes, Horn, Leeuwin and Good Hope. Only the latter is passed regularly by cruising boats as the vast majority of circumnavigations are accomplished by way of the Panama Canal. However, nowadays more cruising boats are making high-latitude passages to remote Arctic or Antarctic destinations and for this reason a third round the world option is outlined which may suit those who prefer to forgo the Panama Canal to reach the South Pacific by way of the Beagle Channel and Southern Chile.

Regardless of whether the point of departure on a round the world voyage is from Europe, either side of North or South America, Australia, New Zealand or Asia, the majority of cruising boats on a world voyage sail along two basic routes:

1. A route via the Panama Canal, South Pacific, North Indian Ocean, Red Sea, Suez Canal, Mediterranean, North Atlantic and Eastern Caribbean.
2. A route via the Panama Canal, South Pacific, South Indian Ocean, Cape of Good Hope, South Atlantic and Eastern Caribbean.

Both routes have advantages and disadvantages. The former is easier to plan to take advantage of favourable seasons, enjoys better weather conditions, the offshore passages are generally shorter and there are more convenient stopover places. Safety concerns have deterred most sailors on a world voyage to sail this route in recent years.

The Cape of Good Hope route enjoys less favourable weather conditions, needs more careful planning to benefit from favourable seasons and winds, the offshore legs are longer and sailing conditions are also more challenging. The worst among those is the Agulhas Current off the South African coast which makes sailing around the bottom of Africa a difficult undertaking, but with good planning even that problem can be overcome.

Round the world voyages are akin to a huge merry-go-round which can be joined, or left, at any point. The two main round the world routes are made up of a number of separate segments which are common to circumnavigations starting from anywhere on the globe. In almost every instance there are different ways to sail those major routes and the alternatives are outlined briefly here.

Canary Islands to the Eastern Caribbean
Most passages from the Canaries are sailed nonstop to the Lesser Antilles (voyage A1d on page 65) but there is also a longer and more interesting route via the Cape Verde Islands, West Africa and even Brazil (voyage A1e on page 66).

Eastern Caribbean to Panama
Rather than sail the direct route across the Caribbean Sea, an alternative route follows the chain of islands north of Puerto Rico and Hispaniola to the Bahamas and regains the Caribbean Sea by way of the Windward Passage. This route can be extended even further to Florida and the Yucatán Channel. Both alternatives are described in voyage A1f (page 68).

Panama to Tahiti
From Panama this commonly sailed route continues to the Marquesas (voyage P1 on page 166). A different way to reach French Polynesia is to sail a southern route which calls at Easter and Pitcairn island (voyage P1c on page 169).

Tahiti to Torres Strait
The main detour from the direct route across the South Pacific (voyages P8 on page 187 and P13b on page 198) is taken by those who leave the tropics to spend the cyclone season in New Zealand or Australia. This opens up new possibilities of reaching Southeast Asia (voyages P39a and P39b on page 237).

Torres Strait to South Africa
The direct route across the South Indian Ocean (voyage I4 on page 278) can be greatly enhanced for those who wish to see more of Southeast Asia by making a detour as described in voyages P39a (page 237) and I5 (page 281).

South Africa to the Eastern Caribbean
The alternative to the direct voyage A4a (page 75) is a detour from South Africa to Argentina and Southern Brazil as outlined in voyage A4b (page 76).

Panama to Southeast Asia
The shortest route goes by way of the islands of Micronesia which can be reached directly or via Hawaii (voyage P39 page 237). Those who would rather see some of the islands of the South Pacific as opposed to sailing the direct route via Hawaii, as outlined in voyages P16 (page 203) and P39b (page 237), should consider the longer but potentially more interesting alternative via Tahiti (voyage P39b on page 237). A third alternative is a combination of the above two by sailing from Panama to Micronesia, either directly or via the Marquesas.

Southeast Asia to the Suez Canal

An alternative to the direct route, as outlined in voyage I3 (page 276), is to continue west from the Torres Strait to Chagos and continue either to the Maldives or Seychelles before regaining the North Indian Ocean (voyages I1, I2 and I3 on pages 274, 275, 276).

Suez Canal to Gibraltar

The Mediterranean is the sea of alternatives where any permutation is possible.

Gibraltar to Canary Islands

Southbound boats from Gibraltar can sail a variety of routes to the Canaries whether nonstop, via Madeira or Morocco (voyage A1b on page 64).

Gibraltar to US East Coast

Voyages from Southern Europe to North America have the choice of a direct route, as outlined in voyage A15c (page 102), or the alternative via the Caribbean (voyages A1d, A1e on pages 65, 66 and A16a on page 105).

Details of planning passages along these arterial routes are to be found in the description of individual voyages in the ocean sections of this book, while individual routes are dealt with in *World Cruising Routes*.

RW1 • Round the world voyages from Europe

Two-year circumnavigations

The shortest time in which a round the world voyage can be accomplished in a cruising boat is probably two years. By precise timing, careful choice of routes and favourable seasons, participants in the various round the world rallies that I once organised completed a circumnavigation in just under two years. Some people might regard this as being too fast and they are probably right. However, those rallies were organised events and the sailors taking part in them wanted above all to realise their dream of completing a round the world voyage and therefore were prepared to move at a relatively fast pace. Nevertheless, for anyone short of time, the following timing is perfectly feasible as it follows the safe seasons around the world by always trying to be in the right place at the right time.

For voyages whose point of departure is Northern Europe, the recommended time for leaving is during summer when optimum conditions can be expected in the North Sea, English Channel, and across the Bay of Biscay. Departures from Mediterranean ports and Gibraltar can be left as late as October. By then anyone planning to cross the Atlantic should be on their way to the Canaries, whether sailing direct or via Madeira.

It is in the Canaries that the Patagonian route splits from the Panama Canal route. As there is no risk of hurricanes on this route, the southbound voyage can start in September with a first stop in the Cape Verde Islands en route to Brazil. Although calling first at a place in northern Brazil is feasible, it may be wiser to head directly to Rio de Janeiro so as to ensure that the arrival in Patagonia coincides with the favourable summer months. From Rio, the route follows the contour of the mainland with possible stops in Uruguay and Argentina before heading offshore for the Falklands unless the decision is taken to head directly for the Magellan Strait. With the islands of Tierra del Fuego providing a tempting alternative, the longer route to the Beagle Channel ought to be considered as it also offers the possibility of a detour to Antarctica. Whether this option is taken or not, the South Pacific will be reached at some point via Southern Chile. Easter Island, Pitcairn, the Gambiers and Tuamotus are some of the enticing stops on the way to Tahiti where the route which had reached the Pacific via the Panama Canal is rejoined for the remainder of the voyage.

The earliest time for an Atlantic crossing from the Canaries along the NE trade wind route is after the middle of November, as such a departure ensures that landfall is made in one of the Caribbean islands in early December at the beginning of the safe winter season. However, the chances of finding better winds are higher later in winter and some of the fastest passages have been recorded between January and March. After about two months in the Eastern Caribbean, the Panama Canal should be transited in February or early March. This timing allows for a stop in the Galapagos and an arrival in the Marquesas at the start of the safe season, in early April. The Tuamotus can be visited en route to Tahiti and the Society Islands should be left in early June so as to arrive in Fiji by July. As these are the months when the SE trades are at their most constant, these long passages can usually be made at good speeds. Passages from Fiji onwards should

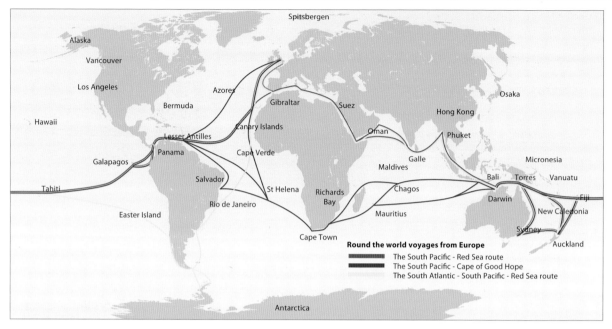

Round the world voyages from Europe
- The South Pacific - Red Sea route
- The South Pacific - Cape of Good Hope
- The South Atlantic - South Pacific - Red Sea route

be timed to pass through the Torres Strait before the end of August or early in September if taking the Cape of Good Hope route.

The passage across the South Indian Ocean will have to be made in a similar rhythm, with long periods at sea and little time to spend in the islands en route. The start of the cyclone season in November indicates a departure from Mauritius or Reunion for the passage to South Africa not later than the end of October. The next leg to Cape Town is best made between November and January, when conditions around the tip of Africa are considered to be the most favourable.

Those planning to take the northern route to the Mediterranean have the advantage that the passage across the North Indian Ocean can be done in January or February, which allows longer time to be spent earlier in the Pacific. This means that the Torres Strait need only be passed in September or even October so that there is enough time to stop in Darwin, and possibly use it as a base to see some of Australia's interior, and later also Indonesia en route to Singapore.

The end of the year will be celebrated somewhere in Western Malaysia or Thailand, preparing for a winter crossing of the North Indian Ocean, when the NE monsoon provides excellent sailing conditions in the first months of the year. The subsequent passage through the Red Sea and the transiting of the Suez Canal in March or April will allow the boat to complete its circumnavigation in less than two years after leaving Europe.

Voyages returning to Europe via the Cape of Good Hope have three choices for a return home: the shortest route, via St Helena, the Cape Verde and Canary Islands, an intermediate route directly via the Azores, and a longer route via Brazil, the Eastern Caribbean and thence to the Azores. On all these routes, Northern Europe could be reached in June or July, exactly two years after the start of the voyage.

Sailors who would rather sail around the world without passing through man-made canals should continue south from the Canary Islands towards the South Atlantic and reach the Pacific by way of the Magellan Strait or Beagle Channel. The route can call at the Cape Verde Islands before crossing the equator to Brazil and continuing to Argentina following the contour of the mainland. The Magellan Strait provides a shorter access to the Chilean Canals although most cruising boats take the longer but more attractive route via the Beagle Channel. Having sailed that far south, a detour to Antarctica may prove to be too tempting to ignore. From Southern Chile the route turns west towards Easter Island and French Polynesia where it joins the more commonly sailed route that reaches the South Pacific by way of the Panama Canal. The rest of the voyage to Europe can be sailed along the North Indian Ocean and the Suez Canal route, or the historic route via the Cape of Good Hope.

As most sailors soon find out, there are so many temptations on the way that often voyages end up stretching into three or even four years. My first circumnavigation took all of six years, so it is rather ironic that the first round the world rally that I organised in 1991 circled the globe in less than one-third of that time. I sailed in that rally myself, and in spite of the sustained pace, I had to admit that being able to accomplish a circumnavigation in such a short time has certain advantages for those who either do not have the time for longer trips or do not wish to be away from home for too long. However, the main purpose of the hypothetical voyages outlined here is to show how it is possible to plan a two-year circumnavigation so as to be always in the right place at the right time.

Round the world via South Pacific, Torres Strait and Cape of Good Hope

Route: Northern Europe – Canaries (September to November) – Caribbean (December to January) – Panama (February) – [Galapagos (March)] – Marquesas (April) – Tuamotus – Tahiti (June) – Tonga – Fiji (July) – Vanuatu – Torres Strait (August) – Darwin – [Bali (September)] – Mauritius (October) – South Africa – (November to January) – [Brazil (February)] – Eastern Caribbean (March to May) – [Cape Verdes (March) – Canaries (April)] – [Azores (May to June)] – Northern Europe

Start: July year I

Return: June to August year III

Tropical storms: June to November (North Atlantic), November to May (South Pacific), November to May (South Indian Ocean)

Total distance: 28,000–31,000 miles

Duration: 23–25 months

Round the world via South Pacific, North Indian Ocean and Mediterranean

Route: Northern Europe – Canaries (September to November) – Caribbean (December to January) –Panama (February) – [Galapagos (March)] – Marquesas – [Tuamotus] – Tahiti (June) –Tonga – Fiji (July to August) – Vanuatu – Torres Strait (September) – Indonesia (October) – Singapore – Thailand (November to January) – Sri Lanka (January to February) – Red Sea (March to April) – Mediterranean (April to May) Northern Europe (August)

Start: July year I

Return: May to August year III

Tropical storms: June to November (North Atlantic), November to May (South Pacific), March to June, September to December (North Indian Ocean)

Total distance: 22,000–26,000 miles

Duration: 22–24 months

Round the world via South Atlantic, South Pacific and Cape of Good Hope

Route: Northern Europe – Canaries (September) – Cape Verdes – Brazil (October) – Argentina (November to December) – [Falklands (December to January)] – Beagle Channel (January to February) – [Antarctica] – Chile (March) – Easter Island – Pitcairn – Gambiers – [Marquesas] – Tahiti (June) – Fiji (July) – Torres Strait (September) – Darwin – [Bali] – Mauritius (October) – South Africa (November to January) – [Brazil (February)] – Eastern Caribbean (March to May)] – [Cape Verdes (March) – Canaries (April)] – [Azores (May to June)] – Northern Europe

Start: June to July year I

Return: June to August year III

Tropical storms: June to November (North Atlantic), November to May (South Pacific and South Indian Ocean)

Total distance: 26,200–29,400 miles

Duration: 24–26 months

Round the world via the South Atlantic, South Pacific and Mediterranean

Route: Northern Europe – Canaries (September) – Cape Verdes – Brazil (October) – Argentina (November to December) – [Falklands (December to January)] – Beagle Channel (January) – [Antarctica] – Chile (March) – Easter Island – Pitcairn – Gambiers – [Marquesas] – Tahiti (June) – Fiji (August) – Vanuatu – Torres Strait (September) – [Darwin] – Indonesia (October) – Singapore (November) – Thailand (December to January) – Sri Lanka (January to February) – [Maldives – India] – [Oman] – Red Sea (March to April) – Mediterranean (May to August) – Northern Europe

Start: June to July year I

Return: August to September year III

Tropical storms: June to November (North Atlantic), Niovember to May (South Pacific)

Total distance: 24,300–25,500 miles

Duration: 25–27 months

Three-year circumnavigations

A two-year circumnavigation as outlined will be much more enjoyable if there is more time available. Although the additional distance covered during a three year long circumnavigation only amounts to about 4,000 miles, the extra year allows more time to be spent in most of the places mentioned earlier, and others to be visited too.

The first part of the voyage will be similar to that described in the previous example. A little more time can be spent in the Caribbean, but the Panama Canal should be transited in February or early March so as to arrive in the Marquesas before the end of April. The following two months can be spent in French Polynesia, allowing you to be in Tahiti for the annual Heiva festivities. Leaving the Society Islands before the end of July makes it possible to spend some time in all the island groups en route to Fiji. Because of the approaching cyclone season, a decision must be made whether to spend the summer in Vava'u, Fiji or American Samoa, all of which have places where it may be possible to spend the cyclone season. Although some people decide to remain in the tropics for the summer, or leave their boats unattended, the majority make their way to New Zealand, which is outside the cyclone belt.

The passage from Fiji to New Zealand is normally undertaken in late October. Most boats spend the entire cyclone season in New Zealand and leave for the Torres Strait and Indian Ocean in May or June. Such a departure allows them to visit some of the island groups bordering on the Coral Sea before reaching the Indian Ocean. Another alternative is to sail across the Tasman Sea from New Zealand to Australia in February or March and, at the end of the cyclone season, sail along the east coast of Australia inside the Great Barrier Reef towards the Torres Strait. Such an early arrival in the Indian Ocean allows more time to be spent at various places along the route, whether in Northern Australia or Indonesia.

The usual route in the South Indian Ocean calls at Cocos and Mauritius but with more time in hand it is possible to sail a more northerly route by stopping at Chagos and possibly the Seychelles before turning south for Madagascar. From Mauritius or Reunion the usual route to South Africa stays east of Madagascar, whereas those who have sailed to the west coast of Madagascar continue the voyage to South Africa through the Mozambique Channel.

The rest of the voyage from South Africa onwards can include a detour to Brazil en route to the Caribbean, but those who wish to reach the Mediterranean as quickly as possible may consider the more direct route which avoids the detour to the Caribbean or the Azores. This route goes via St Helena and Ascension to the Cape Verde Islands and thence to the Canaries.

A return to Northern Europe by way of the North Indian Ocean has the advantage of not only being shorter but also allowing more time to be spent in the South Pacific as the Torres Strait need only be transited by late September or early October. With more time in hand, a stop at either Cairns in North Queensland, or Darwin in Northern Australia, provides the opportunity to see some of Australia en route to Indonesia. Alternatively the extra time can be spent cruising Indonesia before sailing on to Singapore.

There is, however, an interesting alternative to the usual route via the Torres Strait which will fit into the overall timing. Having visited some of the islands in the Coral Sea, this route continues north to the outer islands of Papua New Guinea and reaches Southeast Asia by way of North Borneo. This route is not affected by tropical storms on either side of the equator and rejoins the Torres route in Singapore.

Western Malaysia and Thailand can be visited before the North Indian Ocean is crossed during the NE monsoon of winter. Before embarking on the passage to the Red Sea, there are several interesting places to be visited en route, such as Sri Lanka, the Maldives and Southern India as well as Oman.

A spring arrival in the Mediterranean opens up an entire season of leisurely cruising while making your way west before sailing to Northern Europe to complete this circumnavigation in the three years allowed for it.

The alternative route which reaches the South Pacific via the Beagle Channel or Magellan Strait also suits this three year schedule, and will profit from having more time to spend in either Southeast Asia or the islands in the South Indian Ocean.

● Round the world via the South Pacific, New Zealand, Torres Strait and Cape of Good Hope

Route: Northern Europe – Canaries (September to November) – Caribbean (December to January) – Panama (February) – [Galapagos (March)] – Marquesas (April) – Tuamotus – Tahiti (June) – Cook Islands (July) – Tonga (August) – Fiji (September to October) – New Zealand (November to April) – [SE Australia (February to April)] – New Caledonia (May) – Vanuatu (June) – [Papua New Guinea – North Queensland (July)] – Torres Strait (August) – Darwin – [Bali] – Mauritius (September to October) – [Chagos (September) – Madagascar (October)] – South Africa (November to January) – [Brazil (February)] – Eastern Caribbean (March to May) – [Cape Verdes (March) – Canaries (April)] – [Azores (May to June)] – Northern Europe

Start: June to July year I

Return: June to August year IV

Tropical storms: June to November (North Atlantic), November to May (South Pacific and South Indian Ocean)

Total distance: 32,000–36,000 miles

Duration: 35–38 months

Round the world via the South Pacific, New Zealand, Southeast Asia and Mediterranean

Route: Northern Europe – Canaries (September to November) – Caribbean (December to January) – Panama (February) – [Galapagos] – Marquesas (April) –Tuamotus – Tahiti (June) – Cook Islands (July) – Tonga (August) – Fiji (September to October) – New Zealand (November to April) – [SE Australia (February to April)] – New Caledonia (May to June) – Vanuatu (July) – [Papua New Guinea – North Borneo (October to November)] – Torres Strait (September) – [Darwin] – Bali (October) – Singapore – Thailand (December to January) – Sri Lanka (January to February) – [India] - [Maldives] – [Oman] – Red Sea (March to April) – Mediterranean (May to August) – Northern Europe

Start: July year I

Return: July to September year IV

Tropical storms: June to November (North Atlantic), November to May (South Pacific), March to June, September to December (North Indian Ocean)

Total distance: 25,000–29,000 miles

Duration: 36–38 months

Round the world via the South Atlantic, South Pacific, New Zealand and Mediterranean

Route: Northern Europe – Canaries (September) – Cape Verdes – Brazil (October) – Argentina (November to December) – Falklands – Beagle Channel (January to February) – [Antarctica] – Southern Chile (March) – Easter Island – Pitcairn – Gambiers – [Marquesas] – Tahiti (June to July) – Tonga (August) – Fiji (September to October) – New Zealand (November to April) – [SE Australia (February to April)] – New Caledonia (May) – Vanuatu (June) – Torres Strait (August to September) – [Darwin] – Bali (October) – Singapore – Thailand

(December to January) – Sri Lanka (January to February) – [India] – [Maldives] – [Oman] – Red Sea (March to April) – Mediterranean (May to August) – Northern Europe

Start: June to July year I

Return: July to September year III

Tropical storms: July to November (North Atlantic), November to May (South Pacific)

Total distance: 26,800–28,200 miles

Duration: 37–39 months

Round the world via the South Atlantic, South Pacific, New Zealand and Cape of Good Hope

Route: Northern Europe – Canaries (September) – Cape Verdes – Brazil (October) – Argentina (November to December) – [Falklands (December to January)] – Beagle Channel (January) – [Antarctica] – Southern Chile (March) – Easter Island – Pitcairn – Gambiers – [Marquesas] – Tahiti (June) – Tonga (August) – Fiji (September to October) – New Zealand (November to April) – [SE Australia (February to April)] – New Caledonia (May) – Vanuatu (June) – Torres Strait (August) – Darwin – [Bali] – Mauritius (September to October) – [Chagos (September) – Madagascar (October)] – South Africa (November to January) – [Brazil (February)] – Eastern Caribbean (March to May)] – [Cape Verdes (March) – Canaries (April)] – [Azores (May to June)] – Northern Europe

Start: June to July year I

Return: June to July year IV

Tropical storms: June to November (North Atlantic), November to May (South Pacific and South Indian Ocean)

Total distance: 29,200–30,600 miles

Duration: 35–38 months

RW2 • Round the world voyages from the east coast of North America

Two-year circumnavigations

The timing of the start of voyages originating on the east coast of North America depends on whether the initial leg will be sailed directly to Panama or the Eastern Caribbean. In either case, the voyage can be planned so that the South Pacific, and French Polynesia in particular, is reached at the beginning of the safe season there. In both cases the voyage should start in November, after the end of the hurricane season in the Caribbean. Those who

wish to spend the initial part of their voyage cruising the islands of the Eastern Caribbean will need to be on their way to Panama by February so as to be sure of arriving in the Marquesas by early April. Those who decide to sail directly to Panama in November will have the advantage of a more relaxed programme and be able to visit places en route at a leisurely pace, be it the Bahamas, Cuba or San Blas Islands, or mainland Ecuador if the Panama Canal is transited early. It is worth pointing out that those who intend to return home by the South African route will

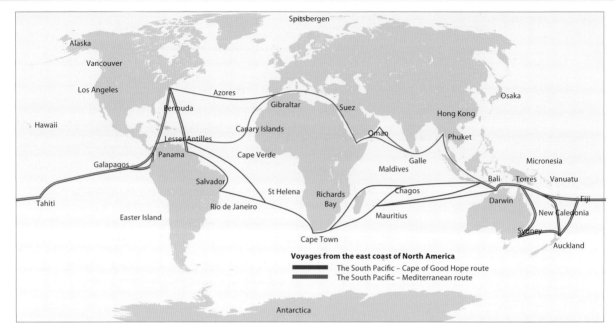

Voyages from the east coast of North America
▬▬▬ The South Pacific – Cape of Good Hope route
▬▬▬ The South Pacific – Mediterranean route

have the opportunity to spend some time in the Eastern Caribbean on their return voyage, so they may prefer to sail directly to Panama. The advantage of an earlier arrival in the Pacific is that the Galapagos can be visited in January or February and take the Easter Island route from there to French Polynesia.

For those who prefer to sail the classic route to the Marquesas, the time to aim to arrive at the Galapagos Islands is late February or early March. This is a busy time as it is also the arrival time of later starters from the Eastern Caribbean. Everyone's ideal timing is to arrive in the Marquesas by early April at the start of the six months-long safe season which normally allows most boats to cruise the entire South Pacific to the Torres Strait before the start of the cyclone season, in November. While perfectly feasible, this tight schedule can only be achieved by keeping to a fairly sustained rhythm, otherwise it might be better to consider the three-year option.

Those who would rather stick to the tighter schedule need to be in Tahiti by May and leave the Society Islands not later than June. The Cook Islands and Tonga can be visited before arriving in Fiji by July. Vanuatu and the Coral Sea must be reached by early August so as to pass through the Torres Strait before the end of August or early September if the intention is to continue the voyage through the South Indian Ocean. Those who intend to switch hemispheres will be able to sail at a more relaxed pace, as described later.

The South Indian Ocean will be crossed in a similar rhythm, with long periods at sea and not much time to spend in the islands en route. The islands of Cocos Keeling, Mauritius and Reunion lie close to the direct route and stops there are easily included. The start of the cyclone season in November indicates a departure for the passage to South Africa not later than the end of October. The tip of Africa should be weathered in December or January when conditions in those waters are the most favourable. From South Africa boats normally sail to Brazil, usually via St Helena, and thence to the Lesser Antilles. An arrival in the Eastern Caribbean in the spring would enable a return to the point of departure less than two years after having left home.

A return to America via the North Indian Ocean, the Red Sea and Mediterranean will certainly make the voyage considerably longer. It is an alternative favoured by sailors who wish to avoid sailing around the Cape of Good Hope. The fact that Southeast Asia need only be reached by the end of the year means that the pace in the South Pacific can be slower and the Torres Strait only transited by late September or early October. A stop at either Cairns in North Queensland or Darwin in Northern Australia provides the opportunity to see some of Australia en route to Indonesia, where Bali is the preferred port of call for those who cannot spend more time in this interesting country.

After Singapore, some of Western Malaysia and Thailand can be visited before the North Indian Ocean is crossed during the NE monsoon of winter. The Red

Sea is transited in March and the Mediterranean is reached by April. It is highly doubtful that anyone would speed through the Mediterranean to complete this voyage the same year, but it can be done. On leaving the Mediterranean, you can sail home directly, or via the Azores and possibly Bermuda, which is best done early in the summer, before the start of the hurricane season.

The alternatives for this fast circumnavigation are summarised below, with a slower paced version being dealt with next.

Round the world via the South Pacific, South Indian Ocean and Cape of Good Hope

Route: US East Coast – [Eastern Caribbean] – Panama (December to February) – [Ecuador] – Galapagos – [Easter Island] - Marquesas (April) – Tuamotus – Tahiti (May to June) – Tonga – Fiji (July) – Vanuatu (August) – Torres Strait – Darwin – [Bali (September)] – Mauritius (October) – South Africa (November to January) – St Helena – [Brazil (February)] – Eastern Caribbean (March to May) – US East Coast

Start: November year I

Return: June year III

Tropical storms: June to November (North Atlantic), November to May (South Pacific and South Indian Ocean)

Total distance: 27,000–29,000 miles

Duration: 20–21 months

Round the world via the South Pacific, North Indian Ocean and Mediterranean

Route: US East Coast – [Eastern Caribbean] – Panama (February) – [Ecuador] – Galapagos – Marquesas (April) –Tuamotus – Tahiti (May to June) – Tonga (July) – Fiji (August) – Vanuatu – Torres Strait – (September to October) – Darwin – Indonesia (October to November) – Singapore – Thailand (December to January) – Sri Lanka (January to February) – Red Sea (March to April) – Mediterranean (April to September) – [Azores] – [Canaries (October to November) – Eastern Caribbean (December to May)] – [Bermuda (June)] – US East Coast

Start: November year I

Return: June year III [June year IV]

Tropical storms: June to November (North Atlantic), November to May (South Pacific), March to June, September to December (North Indian Ocean)

Total distance: 29,000–31,000 miles

Duration: 20–21 months

Three-year circumnavigations

The sustained rhythm described in the previous voyages can be made more relaxed by spending the South Pacific cyclone season in New Zealand or Australia. In that case, more time can be spent in French Polynesia, the Cook Islands, Samoa and Tonga, before the tropics are left for New Zealand in late October. Fiji can be visited either before New Zealand or after. If Fiji is visited the first time around, the following year, when the voyage is resumed from New Zealand, a detour can be made to New South Wales and the Torres Strait is then reached by staying inside the Great Barrier Reef. The other alternative is to sail from New Zealand to New Caledonia and continue to Vanuatu and possibly Papua New Guinea, or to North Queensland and finally the Torres Strait.

Another alternative taken by those who prefer to spend the cyclone season in Australia is to continue west from Fiji and sail via Vanuatu or New Caledonia to their chosen port in subtropical Australia. The following year they can continue to the Torres Strait either by an inshore route inside the Great Barrier Reef, or by an offshore route that calls at various islands in the Coral Sea.

In either of those cases, an earlier arrival in the South Indian Ocean allows you to call not only at the places that are close to the direct route to South Africa, such as Darwin in Northern Australia, Bali in Indonesia and Cocos Keeling, but also to make a detour from Mauritius to Madagascar. Alternatively, a more northerly route can be sailed to Chagos and possibly the Seychelles before turning south for Madagascar. From Mauritius, the passage to South Africa follows a route that stays east of Madagascar, whereas those who make the detour to the west coast of Madagascar continue the voyage to South Africa through the Mozambique Channel. The rest of the voyage through the South Atlantic to the Eastern Caribbean and home is similar to the shorter versions described before.

Voyages bound for the Mediterranean can also follow the schedule described earlier, but as they have more flexibility, two alternatives should be considered. The first is in the Coral Sea, where instead of sailing to Southeast Asia via the Torres Strait and Indonesia, you can take a less travelled but possibly more interesting route that heads north via the outer islands of Papua New Guinea and reaches Singapore along the north coast of Borneo. This detour can easily fit into the suggested timing so that the North Indian Ocean is still crossed early in the new year.

The second alternative concerns the time spent in the Mediterranean. Those who wish to keep to the original schedule by arriving home the same year will need to move through the Mediterranean swiftly so as to cross the

Atlantic before June and the start of the hurricane season. Those who feel that the Mediterranean deserves more time can spend the spring and summer in the Mediterranean, and then sail the longer route via the Canaries to the Eastern Caribbean. This would mean spending the winter in the Caribbean and only getting home by June the following year.

● Round the world via the South Pacific, New Zealand, Torres Strait and Cape of Good Hope

Route: US East Coast – [Eastern Caribbean] – Panama (December to February) – [Ecuador] – Galapagos – [Easter Island] - Marquesas (April) – Tuamotus – Tahiti (June) – Cook Islands (July) – Tonga (August) – Fiji (September to October) – New Zealand (November to April) – [SE Australia (February to April)] – New Caledonia (May to June) – Vanuatu – [Papua New Guinea – North Queensland (July)] – Torres Strait (August) – Darwin – [Bali] – Mauritius (September to October) – [Chagos (September) – Madagascar (October)] – South Africa (November to January) – St Helena– [Brazil (February)] – Eastern Caribbean (March to May) – US East Coast

Start: November year I

Return: June to July year IV

Tropical storms: June to November (North Atlantic), November to May (South Pacific and South Indian Ocean)

Total distance: 24,000–26,000 miles

Duration: 32–33 months

● Round the world via the South Pacific, New Zealand, North Indian Ocean and Mediterranean

Route: US East Coast – [Eastern Caribbean] – Panama (December to February) – Galapagos – [Easter Island] - Marquesas (April) – Tuamotus – Tahiti (June) – Cook Islands (July) – Tonga (August) – Fiji (September to October) – New Zealand (November to April) – [SE Australia (February to April)] – New Caledonia (May to June) – Vanuatu – [Papua New Guinea – North Borneo (November to December)] – North Queensland (August)] – Torres Strait (September) – [Darwin] – Bali (October) – Singapore – Thailand (December) – Sri Lanka (January to February) – [India] – [Maldives] – [Oman] – Red Sea (March to April) – Mediterranean (May to September) – [Azores] – [Canaries (October to November) – Eastern Caribbean (December to May) – [Bermuda (June)] – US East Coast

Start: November year I

Return: June year IV or year V

Tropical storms: June to November (North Atlantic), November to May (South Pacific), March to June, September to December (North Indian Ocean)

Total distance: 30,000–34,000 miles

Duration: 32–44 months

RW3 • Round the world voyages from the west coast of North America

Two-year circumnavigations

There are two very different alternatives for the initial stage of this voyage: a direct route that reaches the South Pacific via the Marquesas, and a longer route that goes via Hawaii. A voyage along the former route needs to start in February or March if the intention is to arrive in French Polynesia at the start of the safe season. In order to be able to do this, voyages which originate north of California may need to move south in late autumn so as to be in a place such as Mexico to leave for the Marquesas at the optimum time. A similar argument can also be made for a voyage to French Polynesia via Hawaii as it would be more convenient if winter had been spent there so that the passage south can be started in late March or early April.

There is one more important matter to be considered before one of these two alternatives is chosen, and that is the voyage home after the transit of the Panama Canal at the end of the proposed circumnavigation. Because of the difficulty of sailing from Panama to the US West Coast it would make more sense to sail to the Marquesas on the outbound voyage and plan to return home via Hawaii.

Whether French Polynesia is reached directly or via the Galapagos, the best time to arrive in the Marquesas is early April. This means that the entire safe season can be spent visiting the various island groups which straddle the route that cuts across the South Pacific to the Torres Strait. One major decision that needs to be taken when planning this voyage is whether to compress the entire South Pacific cruise into one season, which would mean having to transit

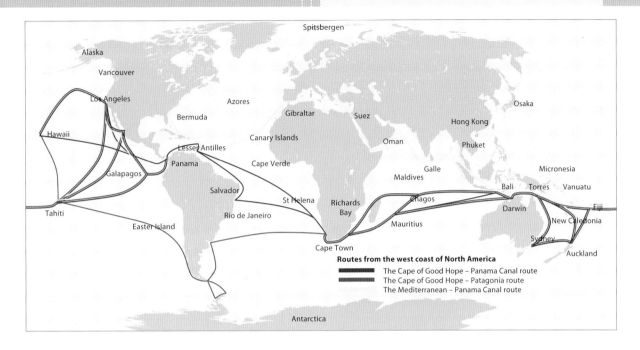

Routes from the west coast of North America

- The Cape of Good Hope – Panama Canal route
- The Cape of Good Hope – Patagonia route
- The Mediterranean – Panama Canal route

the Torres Strait by September, or to spend the cyclone season in New Zealand, and thus be able to spend more time exploring the islands between Tahiti and Fiji which turns the voyage into a three-year circumnavigation.

Those who intend to complete this voyage in the shortest time possible will only have about four months to cover the considerable distance between Tahiti and the Torres Strait. The South Indian Ocean will need to be crossed before the end of October so as to arrive in South Africa before the start of the cyclone season in the South Indian Ocean. A departure from Cape Town early in the new year will result in an arrival in the Eastern Caribbean in late January or early February and in Panama by March or early April. Once through the Panama Canal the choice is between a dash along the coast of Central America and Mexico followed by the aptly called 'bash' to the US West Coast, or a long detour to Hawaii.

With careful planning and by forgoing the option of spending the cyclone season in New Zealand, a circumnavigation via the Cape of Good Hope can be completed in less than two years.

A circumnavigation via the North Indian Ocean and Mediterranean will take longer but can still be completed in less than three years. As the passage across the North Indian Ocean can be done as late as February or March, this allows for a more relaxed pace in the South Pacific with a later arrival at the Torres Strait, if the route via Northern Australia and Indonesia to Southeast Asia is

chosen. The alternative is to sail north of the Coral Sea via the outer islands of Papua New Guinea and reach Singapore via North Borneo. Whichever of those options is chosen, the passage from Southeast Asia to the Red Sea will be sailed in the first months of the year and can include a number of interesting ports of call in Sri Lanka, the Maldives, South India or Oman.

One of the main attractions of this route is the opportunity to spend some time in the Mediterranean. Arriving there through the Suez Canal in April you will have about five months to sail to Gibraltar. From there, the passage to the Canaries can be done in late September and the subsequent crossing of the Atlantic will take place in late November. The Eastern Caribbean only needs to be left for Panama in late March or early April which would still make it possible to embark on the subsequent passage home, either on a direct route or via Hawaii, before the start of the hurricane season in the Eastern North Pacific. On leaving Panama, those who have decided to take the Hawaii option have three alternatives: a nonstop passage, sail to Mexico and start their offshore passage from there, or sail via the Galapagos and thence to Hawaii. The latter option may be of interest to those who had missed the Galapagos on the way out and the total distance will not be much different to the other alternatives.

The difficulties associated with a passage from Panama to the US West Coast, which may entail a long detour to Hawaii, can be avoided by sailing a very different route that bypasses the Caribbean altogether and may appeal to those planning to sail the Cape of Good Hope route. As far as South Africa the route is unchanged but from Cape Town it continues to Argentina. From there it turns south with two options on reaching the Pacific Ocean, via the Magellan Strait or Beagle Channel. The latter option may be more attractive as it can also include a detour to Antarctica. Whichever option is chosen, Southern Chile will be explored next before striking across the South Pacific to Easter and Pitcairn Island. French Polynesia is entered at the Gambier Islands from where the route turns north for the Marquesas and Hawaii. This entire segment will be sailed during the favourable seasons in both the South Atlantic and South Pacific and the suggested timing also allows for Hawaii to be reached just before the hurricane season. The final leg will be sailed during summer bringing the boat home in just under two years since leaving.

Round the world via the South Pacific, Torres Strait, Cape of Good Hope and Panama

Route: US West Coast – [Mexico (February)] – [Galapagos (March)] – Marquesas (April) – Tahiti (May to June) – Tonga – Fiji (July) – Vanuatu (August) – Torres Strait (September) – Darwin – [Bali] – Mauritius (October) – South Africa (November to January) – St Helena –[Brazil (February)] – Eastern Caribbean (March) – Panama (April) – [Galapagos]– [Hawaii] – US West Coast

Start: November year I

Return: June to August year III

Tropical storms: June to November (North Atlantic), May to November (Eastern North Pacific), November to May (South Pacific and South Indian Ocean)

Total distance: 27,000–29,000 miles

Duration: 20–22 months

Round the world via the South Pacific, South Indian Ocean, Cape of Good Hope, Patagonia and Hawaii

Route: US West Coast – [Mexico (February)] – [Galapagos (March)] – Marquesas (April) – Tahiti (May to June) – Tonga – Fiji (July) – Vanuatu (August) – Torres Strait (September) – Darwin – [Bali] – Mauritius (October) – South Africa (November) – Argentina – [Falkland Islands (December)] – Beagle Channel (January) – [Antarctica] – Chile (March) – Easter Island – Marquesas (May) – Hawaii (June) – US West Coast

Start: November year I

Return: July to September year III

Tropical storms: November to May (South Pacific, South Indian Ocean), May to November (Eastern North Pacific)

Total distance: 27,000–29,800 miles

Duration: 20–22 months

Round the world via the South Pacific, North Indian Ocean, Mediterranean and Panama

Route: US West Coast – [Mexico (February)] – [Galapagos] – Marquesas (April) – Tahiti (May to June) – Tonga (July) – Fiji (August) – Vanuatu – Torres Strait (September to October) – [Darwin] – Indonesia (October to November) – Singapore – Thailand (December to January) – Sri Lanka (January to February) – [India] – [Maldives] – [Oman] – Red Sea (March) – Mediterranean (April to September) – Canaries (October to November) – Eastern Caribbean (December to February) – Panama (March) – [Hawaii] – US West Coast

Start: November year I

Return: June to August year III

Tropical storms: June to November (North Atlantic), November to May (South Pacific and South Indian Ocean), North Indian Ocean (March to June, September to December)

Total distance: 29,000–31,000 miles

Duration: 32–34 months

Three-year circumnavigations

Few will disagree that the South Pacific deserves more than one rushed season and for that reason the decision to spend the cyclone season either in the tropics, or preferably in either New Zealand or Southeast Australia, will make it possible to spend more time savouring the attractions of the South Seas. The time gained will have little effect on a voyage bound for the Mediterranean but for voyages sailing the Cape of Good Hope route the pace will be much more relaxed, making the passage through both the Coral Sea and the South Indian Ocean more enjoyable.

Most boats which spend the cyclone season in New Zealand remain there the entire summer and leave for the Torres Strait and Indian Ocean in May, visiting some of the island groups such as New Caledonia, Vanuatu or Papua New Guinea before reaching the Indian Ocean. An alternative is to continue north of the equator and call at Palau, the Philippines and North Borneo on the way to Singapore. An area that should be avoided along this route is off the NE coast of Borneo and SE Palawan, the entire Sulu archipelago and the SW coast of Mindanao, as several piracy attacks have occurred in recent years.

The alternative is to swing north to Vietnam and possibly Cambodia as this area is not threatened by typhoons in the first months of the year. Some of the other countries in Southeast Asia can then be visited as far as Western Thailand before turning around for the South Indian Ocean. Another possibility is to spend less time in New Zealand and sail across the Tasman Sea to Australia in February or March and, at the end of the cyclone season, continue inside the Great Barrier Reef to the Torres Strait. An early arrival in the Indian Ocean will make it possible to see some of Northern Australia as well as Indonesia. From Bali, there is a choice of three routes across the South Indian Ocean: a northerly route which calls at Cocos Keeling, Chagos and possibly the Seychelles before turning south for Madagascar, an intermediate route that goes from Cocos Keeling to Mauritius via Chagos, and a southerly route that calls at Cocos Keeling, Mauritius and Reunion. The two routes which call at Mauritius normally continue east of Madagascar to South Africa, whereas those who have sailed the northern route continue to the west coast of Madagascar and reach South Africa through the Mozambique Channel. The continuation of the voyage from South Africa to the Eastern Caribbean and Panama is the same as for the shorter version of this voyage.

Having spent the summer out of the tropics in either New Zealand or Southeast Australia, those planning to return via the Suez Canal will be able to do much more during the following safe season by either spending longer in the islands of the Western South Pacific, cruising the Indonesian Archipelago or exploring parts of Southeast Asia.

Similarly, the Patagonia route, as outlined earlier, will be greatly enhanced by an additional year spent in the South Pacific and, if time permits, the inclusion of some of the countries of Southeast Asia will make the voyage even more complete even if it would stretch the circumnavigation to four years.

Round the world via the North Pacific, South Pacific, Torres Strait, Cape of Good Hope and Panama

Route: US West Coast – [Mexico (February)] – [Galapagos] – Marquesas (April) – Tuamotus – Tahiti (June) – Cook Islands (July) – Tonga (August) – Fiji (September to October) – New Zealand (November to April) – [SE Australia (February to April)] – New Caledonia (May to June) – Vanuatu – Torres Strait (July to August) – Darwin – [Bali] – Mauritius (September to October) – [Chagos (September) – Madagascar (October)] – South Africa (November to January) – St Helena – [Brazil (February)] – Eastern Caribbean (March) – Panama (April) – [Hawaii] – US West Coast

Start: November year I

Return: June to August year IV

Tropical storms: November to May (South Pacific and South Indian Ocean), June to November (North Atlantic), May to November (Eastern North Pacific)

Total distance: 24,000–26,000 miles

Duration: 32–34 months

Round the world via the South Pacific, Torres Strait, Cape of Good Hope, Patagonia and Hawaii

Route: US West Coast – [Mexico (February)] – [Galapagos (March)] – Marquesas (April) – Tahiti (May to June) – Cook Islands (July) – Tonga (August) – Fiji (September to October) – New Zealand (November to April) – [SE Australia (February to April)] – New Caledonia (May to June) – Vanuatu – Torres Strait (July to August) – Darwin – [Bali] – Mauritius (September) – [Chagos (September) – Madagascar (October)] – South Africa (November) – [Argentina – Falkland Islands (December)] – Beagle Channel (January) – [Antarctica] – Chile (March) – Easter Island – Marquesas (May) – [Hawaii (June)] – US West Coast

Start: November year I

Return: July to September year IV

Tropical storms: November to May (South Pacific and South Indian Ocean), May to November (Eastern North Pacific)

Total distance: 29,600–32,400 miles

Duration: 32–34 months

Round the world via the South Pacific, North Indian Ocean, Mediterranean and Panama

Route: US West Coast – [Mexico (February)] – [Galapagos] – Marquesas (April) – Tahiti (May to June) – Tonga (September) – Fiji (October) – New Zealand (November to April) – [New Caledonia – Vanuatu (June)] – [Australia (March to July)] – Torres Strait (August to September) – [Darwin] - Indonesia (October) – Singapore – Thailand (December) – Sri Lanka (January) – [India] – [Maldives] – [Oman] – Red Sea (March to April) – Mediterranean (May to September) – Canaries (October to November) – Caribbean (December to March) – Panama (April) – [Hawaii] – US West Coast

Start: November year I

Return: June to August year IV

Tropical storms: November to May (South Pacific), March to June, September to December (North Indian Ocean), June to November (North Atlantic), May to November (Eastern North Pacific)

Total distance: 33,000–36,000 miles

Duration: 42–44 months

RW4 • Round the world voyages from Australia and New Zealand

There are several ways to sail around the world from Australia and New Zealand with the most commonly sailed being a northern route via the Mediterranean and a southern route via the Cape of Good Hope. Both routes return to the Pacific Ocean by way of the Panama Canal and usually follow the classic route to Tahiti and beyond. As long as there is a risk of piracy in the North Indian Ocean, the Cape of Good Hope route is considered safer. Its main disadvantage is that it bypasses Europe altogether, although those who are keen to visit the Mediterranean can still do this by sailing the South Africa route, but rather than continue from there to the Caribbean, could take the direct route to Gibraltar via the Cape Verde and Canary Islands, and rejoining their westbound voyage later in the Eastern Caribbean.

There are several alternatives that may be considered, such as the option of sailing from South Africa to Argentina, or possibly directly to the Falkland Islands, and continuing into the South Pacific either via the Magellan Strait or the Beagle Channel. The latter opens up the possibility of a detour to Antarctica before sailing to Southern Chile and reaching French Polynesia via Easter Island. If this option is considered, the voyage through the South Indian Ocean may need to be completed earlier

so as to leave Cape Town before the end of the year and arrive in Patagonia during the favourable summer season. The rest of the voyage all the way from Southern Chile to New Zealand or Australia can be completed during the safe season in the South Pacific.

Circumnavigations from Australia

The following tables summarise the three voyage options outlined above on the premise that each will start from SE Australia. While this undoubtedly suits voyages departing from New South Wales, Queensland and the Northern Territory, sailors setting off from Victoria, South or Western Australia may decide to reach the South Indian Ocean by a shorter and more direct westbound route. Sailing across the Great Australian Bight and around Cape Leeuwin may prove to be a daunting task but once that point has been passed, the winds will be increasingly favourable whether sailing northwest for Cocos Keeling, Chagos or Mauritius, if bound for the Cape of Good Hope route, or north for Southeast Asia and the Mediterranean route. The timing of the start for either route can be planned for any time between June and August, which will allow enough time

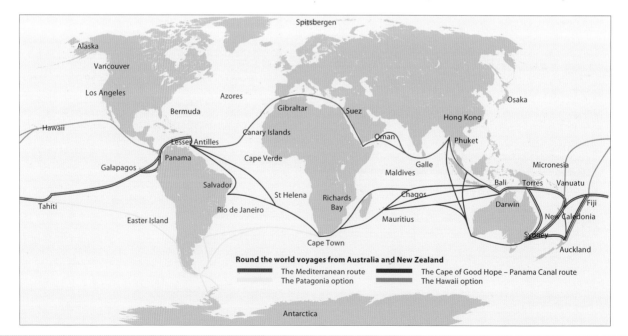

Round the world voyages from Australia and New Zealand

The Mediterranean route
The Patagonia option

The Cape of Good Hope – Panama Canal route
The Hawaii option

to explore the islands in the South Indian Ocean before sailing to South Africa. Voyages bound for Southeast Asia, which can be reached either via the Sunda Strait or by a route which keeps west of Sumatra, have even more flexibility as long as the South Indian Ocean is left before the start of the cyclone season.

● Round the world via the Torres Strait, North Indian Ocean, Mediterranean and Panama

Route: Southeast Australia – [New Caledonia – Vanuatu] – Torres Strait (July to September) – Darwin – Indonesia (August to September) – Singapore (October) – Thailand (December) – Sri Lanka (January to February) – Red Sea (March) – Mediterranean (April to September) – Canaries (October to November) – Eastern Caribbean (December to January) – Panama (February) – [Galapagos (March)] – Marquesas (April) – Tuamotus – Tahiti (June) – Tonga (July) – Fiji (August) – [Vanuatu (September) – New Caledonia] – Australia

Start: May to August year I

Return: October year III

Tropical storms: November to May (South Pacific), March to June, September to December (North Indian Ocean), June to November (North Atlantic), May to November (Eastern North Pacific)

Total distance: 23,900-26,000 miles

Duration: 26–30 months

● Round the world via the Torres Strait, Cape of Good Hope and Panama

Route: Southeast Australia – North Queensland – [New Caledonia – Vanuatu] – Torres Strait (July to August) – Darwin – [Bali] – Christmas Island – Cocos Keeling – [Chagos] – [Madagascar] – Mauritius (September to October) – South Africa (November to December) – St Helena – [Brazil (January)] – Eastern Caribbean (February) – Panama (March) – [Galapagos] – Marquesas (April) – Tuamotus – Tahiti (June) – Tonga (July) – Fiji (August) – [Vanuatu – New Caledonia (September)] – Southeast Australia

Start: June to August year I

Return: October year III

Tropical storms: November to May (South Pacific and South Indian Ocean), June to November (North Atlantic)

Total distance: 22,800–24,600 miles

Duration: 27–29 months

PATAGONIA OPTION

Route: South Africa (November) – [Argentina] – Falklands (December) – Beagle Channel (January) – [Antarctica] – Southern Chile (March) – Easter Island (April) – Gambier Islands – [Marquesas] – Tahiti (June)

HAWAII OPTION

Route: Panama (January) – [Mexico] – Hawaii (March) – [Marshalls–Kiribati] – Vanuatu (May–June)

Circumnavigations from New Zealand

The timing of the start of round the world voyages from New Zealand can be very flexible as long as the tropics are not reached before the end of the cyclone season. There are several alternatives for the initial stage, which can start earlier with a first leg to Australia, or later with a passage to anywhere from Tonga to New Caledonia. Depending on which option is chosen, the Torres Strait can be reached by a route which stays inside the Great Barrier Reef or via the island groups of the Coral Sea. There is also the further option of reaching Southeast Asia along a route which bypasses the Torres Strait and reaches Singapore via Papua New Guinea and North Borneo. This option is only logical for voyages that are bound later for the Mediterranean. An even more radical option for voyages starting from South and Western Australia is outlined on page 322 and may appeal to those who wish to reach the Indian Ocean by this less travelled route.

● Round the world via the Torres Strait, North Indian Ocean, Mediterranean and Panama

Route: New Zealand – [Australia (June to August)] – New Caledonia – Vanuatu – Torres Strait (July to August) – [Darwin] – Indonesia (August to October) – Singapore (November) – Thailand (December) – Sri Lanka (January to February) – Red Sea (March) – Mediterranean (April to September) – Canaries (October to November) – Eastern Caribbean (December to January) – Panama (February) – [Galapagos (March)] – Marquesas (April) – Tahiti (June) – Tonga (July) – Fiji (August to September) – New Zealand

Start: February to June year I

Return: October year III

Tropical storms: June to November (North Atlantic), November to May (South Pacific), March to June, September to December (North Indian Ocean)

Total distance: 25,200–26,800 miles

Duration: 29–30 months

Round the world via the Torres Strait, Cape of Good Hope and Panama

Route: New Zealand – [Southeast Australia] – New Caledonia – Vanuatu – Torres Strait (July to August) – Darwin – [Bali] – Christmas Island – Cocos Keeling – [Chagos] – [Madagascar] – Mauritius (September to October) – South Africa (November to December) – St Helena (January) – [Brazil] – Eastern Caribbean (February) – Panama (March) – [Galapagos] – Marquesas (April) – Tuamotus – Tahiti (June) – Tonga (July) – Fiji (September to October) – New Zealand

Start: February to June year I

Return: October year III

Tropical storms: June to November (North Atlantic), November to May (South Pacific and South Indian Ocean)

Total distance: 23,900-24,800 miles

Duration: 28–30 months

HAWAII OPTION

Route: Panama (March) – [Mexico] – Hawaii (May) – [Line Islands– Phoenix] – Fiji (July)

RW5 • Round the world voyages from Asia

Asian sailors have the same choice of two basic trade wind routes for a circumnavigation of the globe as those setting off from other parts of the world: a northern route via the Mediterranean and a southern route via the Cape of Good Hope, both reaching the Pacific Ocean by way of the Panama Canal. The advantage for voyages originating in Asia is that the points where those arterial routes can be joined are very close: Bali for the South Africa route and any port between Singapore and Phuket for the Mediterranean route. The problem posed by the uncertain safety situation in the Middle East and Red Sea will limit that choice to the Cape of Good Hope route.

Those who choose the northern route need to be

ready for a departure across the North Indian Ocean in the early months of the year, when the NE monsoon provides favourable winds all the way to the Red Sea. Most sailors plan to arrive in the Mediterranean by March or April at the start of the summer season. As the next transocean leg of this voyage, from the Canary Islands to the Caribbean, is best sailed in late November, the intervening time can be spent enjoying the many attractions of the Mediterranean. A North Atlantic passage will bring the boat to the Eastern Caribbean at the start of the safe winter season.

For boats sailing from East Asia, the route to the South Indian Ocean can pass through the Indonesian archipelago, while boats leaving from Western Malaysia

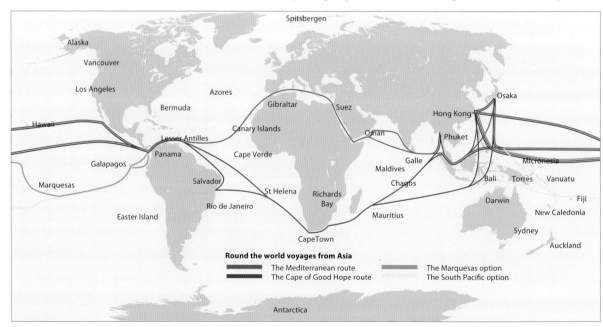

Round the world voyages from Asia
- The Mediterranean route
- The Cape of Good Hope route
- The Marquesas option
- The South Pacific option

or Thailand can sail west of Sumatra to Cocos Keeling and on to Mauritius, or via the Maldives to Chagos and Mauritius. The route around the Cape of Good Hope passes to the east of Madagascar with an optimum arrival time in South Africa by late October. A departure from South Africa early in the new year will result in an arrival in the Eastern Caribbean in late January or early February.

In the Eastern Caribbean the two round the world routes join up and continue together to Panama. The timing of the Panama Canal transit is dictated by the subsequent plans: if the intention is to sail home as quickly as possible, an arrival in East Asia when the risk of typhoons is still low (March) means that the long passage from Panama to either Micronesia or Hawaii should take place in January or early February. This means that the Panama Canal must be transited in January and therefore the Eastern Caribbean must be left at the very beginning of the new year. Such tight timing for the transit of the Panama Canal will affect primarily those who arrive in the Caribbean from South Africa and who need to leave Cape Town promptly.

As such a sustained pace may not be to most sailors' liking, it is at this stage that a decision needs to be taken regarding the plans after Panama, for which there are three basic alternatives. The first alternative is to accept the idea of a speedy voyage home, spend the minimum time in the Eastern Caribbean, sail from Panama directly to Micronesia and thereby arrive in home waters during a relatively safe period. The second alternative will appeal to sailors heading for Japan or China as the suggested route goes via Hawaii, either direct or by way of Mexico. This route can be sailed later so that the onward passage from Hawaii can be sailed in late spring or early summer. The third alternative is considerably more attractive as it entails sailing from Panama to the Galapagos and continuing along the classic South Pacific route visiting the various islands all the way from the Marquesas to Vanuatu. By this route the Coral Sea will be reached by October and from there boats bound for Southeast Asia can sail home via the Torres Strait and Indonesia. Boats bound for East Asia can sail north via the outer islands of Papua New Guinea and continue across the equator to their home destinations.

The route alternatives are summarised below, the options for the segment from Panama to Asia being interchangeable.

Round the world via the North Indian Ocean, Mediterranean, Panama and Hawaii

Route: East Asia – Singapore (December) – [Phuket (January)] – North Indian Ocean (February to March) – Red Sea (March) – Mediterranean (April to September) – Canary Islands (October to November) – Eastern Caribbean (December) – Panama (February) – Mexico (March) – Hawaii (April–May) – Japan (June) – East Asia

Start: December to February year I

Return: June to July year III

Tropical storms: All year (Western North Pacific), March to June, September to December (North Indian Ocean), June to November (North Atlantic), May to November (Eastern North Pacific)

Total distance: 22,400–23,600 miles

Duration: 18–20 months

Round the world via the South Indian Ocean, Cape of Good Hope, Panama and South Pacific

Route: East Asia – South Indian Ocean (June to October) – South Africa (November to January) – St Helena – [Brazil] – Eastern Caribbean (February) – Panama (March) – [Galapagos] – Marquesas (April) – Tuamotus – Tahiti (June) – Tonga (July) – Fiji (July to August) – Vanuatu (September to October) – [Torres Strait – Southeast Asia] – Papua New Guinea (November to December) – East Asia

Start: February to April year I

Return: December to February year III

Tropical storms: June to November (North Atlantic), November to May (South Pacific and South Indian Ocean)

Total distance: 23,600–25,400 miles

Duration: 22–24 months

RW6 • Round the world voyages from the east coast of South America

There are several ways to sail around the world from the east coast of South America and the first decision that needs to be taken is whether to reach the Pacific Ocean by way of the Caribbean and Panama Canal or Patagonia. The Caribbean alternative is more attractive for voyages starting from Brazil, whereas the Patagonian alternative may suit those leaving from Southern Brazil, Uruguay or Argentina. Whichever one of those routes is chosen, they will join in Tahiti and continue together as far as the Torres Strait where they split into a northern route, which reaches the Atlantic via the North Indian Ocean and Mediterranean, and a southern route that crosses the South Indian Ocean to the Cape of Good Hope. Voyages via Panama are probably the easiest to accomplish as they take advantage of the most favourable weather conditions and include some of the most attractive destinations in the world.

Whether the voyage originates in Argentina, Uruguay or Brazil, the first segment leads to the Eastern Caribbean and, via the Panama Canal, to the South Pacific. The route continues via the islands of Polynesia and Melanesia to the Torres Strait, where the two routes split, one route reaching the South Atlantic via the Cape of Good Hope, the other going to Southeast Asia and then crossing the

North Indian Ocean to the Mediterranean. The timing for a voyage on either of these routes in the shortest time possible is outlined below. However, the voyage will be extended by one year if the South Pacific cyclone season is spent in New Zealand or Southeast Australia. Spending that extra time in the South Pacific means that from Fiji onwards the pace will become more relaxed and there will be time to see more of the countries bordering the Coral Sea and in Southeast Asia, and, for boats on the Cape of Good Hope route, to explore more of the South Indian Ocean.

Voyages along the cold water route need to time their start so as to arrive in Patagonia during the favourable summer months. Voyages which start from Brazil will follow the contour of the mainland with possible stops in Uruguay and Argentina before continuing to the Magellan Strait. With the islands of Tierra del Fuego providing a tempting alternative, the longer route to the Beagle Channel ought to be considered as it also offers the possibility of a detour to Antarctica. Whether this option is taken or not, the South Pacific will be reached via Southern Chile. Easter Island, Pitcairn, the Gambiers and Tuamotus are some of the enticing stops on the way to Tahiti where the route which had reached the Pacific

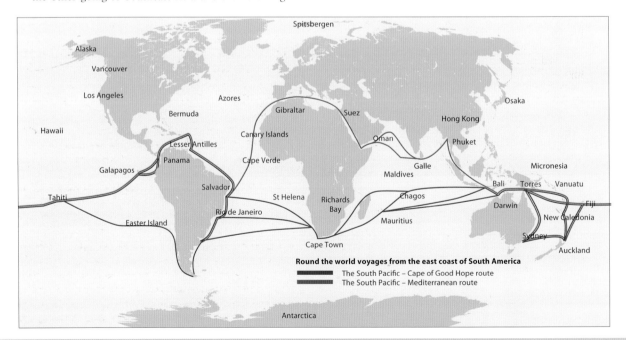

Round the world voyages from the east coast of South America
▬▬▬ The South Pacific – Cape of Good Hope route
▬▬▬ The South Pacific – Mediterranean route

via the Panama Canal is rejoined for the remainder of the voyage to the Torres Strait. From there the rest of the voyage home will be sailed along the same route as outlined for the other alternatives.

Round the world via Panama, South Pacific, Torres Strait and Cape of Good Hope

Route: Brazil – Eastern Caribbean (December to January) – Panama (February) – [Galapagos (March)] – Marquesas (April) – Tahiti (May–June) – Tonga – Fiji (July) – Vanuatu – Torres Strait (August to September) – Darwin – [Bali] – Mauritius (October) – [Chagos – Madagascar] – South Africa (November to January) – [Argentina] – [St Helena] – Brazil

Start: October to November year I

Return: December to February year III

Tropical storms: June to November (North Atlantic), November to May (South Pacific and South Indian Ocean)

Total distance: 21,800–23,200 miles

Duration: 14–17 months

EXTENDED VERSION

Route: Brazil – Eastern Caribbean (December to February) – Panama (March) – Galapagos – Marquesas (April) – Tahiti (June) – Cook Islands (July) – Tonga (August) – Fiji (September to October) – New Zealand (November to May) – [SE Australia (March to July)] – New Caledonia (May to June) – Vanuatu (July) – Torres Strait (August) – Darwin – [Bali] – Mauritius (September to October) – [Chagos (September) – Madagascar (October)] – South Africa (November to January) – [Argentina] – [St Helena] – Brazil

Start: October to November year I

Return: December to March year IV

Tropical storms: June to November (North Atlantic), November to May (South Pacific and South Indian Ocean)

Total distance: 23,200–24,600 miles

Duration: 25–29 months

Round the world via Panama, the South Pacific, Torres Strait and Mediterranean

Route: Brazil – Eastern Caribbean (December to January) – Panama (February) – [Galapagos] – Marquesas (April) – Tuamotus – Tahiti (May to June) – Tonga (July) – Fiji (August) – Vanuatu – Torres Strait (September to October) – [Darwin] – Indonesia (October to November) – Singapore – Thailand (December to January) – Sri Lanka (January to February) – [India] – [Maldives] – [Oman] – Red Sea (March) – Mediterranean (April to August) – Canaries (September) – Cape Verdes – Brazil

Start: November to January year I

Return: October–December year III

Tropical storms: June to November (North Atlantic), November to May (South Pacific), March to June, September to December (North Indian Ocean)

Total distance: 24,300–25,500 miles

Duration: 20–23 months

EXTENDED VERSION

Route: Brazil – Eastern Caribbean (December to February) – Panama (February to March) – [Galapagos] – Marquesas (April) – Tuamotus – Tahiti (June) – Cooks (July) – Tonga (August) – Fiji (September to October) – New Zealand (November to May) – [SE Australia (March to June)] – [New Caledonia] – Vanuatu (June) – Torres Strait (July to August) – [Darwin] – Indonesia (September to October) – Singapore (November) – Thailand (December) – Sri Lanka (January to February) – [India] – [Maldives] – [Oman] – Red Sea (March) – Mediterranean (April to August) – Canaries (September) – Cape Verdes – Brazil

Start: October to November year I

Return: October to December year III

Tropical storms: June to November (North Atlantic), November to May (South Pacific), March to June, September to December (North Indian Ocean)

Total distance: 26,500–27,700

Duration: 23–25 months

PATAGONIA OPTION

Route: Brazil (September to October) – [Uruguay] – Argentina (November to December) – [Magellan Strait] – [Falkland Islands (December to January)] – Beagle Channel (January) – [Antarctica] – Southern Chile (March) – Easter Island – Pitcairn – Gambiers – [Marquesas] – Tahiti (June)

RW7 • Round the world voyages from the west coast of South America

There are three basic routes for a circumnavigation of the globe for those leaving from the west coast of South America, and all three start with a cruise through the islands of the South Pacific. There are two alternatives for the initial part of the voyage, a northern route that reaches French Polynesia via the Galapagos and Marquesas, and a southern route which gets there by way of Easter Island and the Gambier Islands. From Tahiti the route continues west calling at the various island groups as far as the Coral Sea. Having passed through the Torres Strait, the routes diverge, one route heading for the Mediterranean via Southeast Asia, the North Indian Ocean and Red Sea, the other crossing the South Indian Ocean to South Africa.

From South Africa there are two very different alternatives for sailing home, either by way of the Panama Canal or via Patagonia. The route which goes to Panama will suit those whose home port is in the northern part of South America, such as Colombia, Ecuador and possibly Peru, whereas the southern route may be preferred by sailors from Chile. This route heads west from Cape Town to Argentina and reaches the South Pacific via the Magellan Strait or Beagle Channel. The northern route heads for the Caribbean, where it merges with the Mediterranean route before continuing to the Panama Canal and home.

The three alternatives are outlined below and show the shortest time in which those voyages can be completed. Those who wish to cruise the South Pacific at a slower pace, and spend the cyclone season in New Zealand or Australia, will need to add one year to the overall timing.

Round the world via the South Pacific, Torres Strait, Cape of Good Hope and Patagonia

Route: South America West Coast – [Galapagos] – [Easter Island – Gambiers (April)] – Marquesas – Tahiti (May to June) – Tonga – Fiji (July) – Vanuatu – Torres Strait (August) – Darwin – [Bali] – [Chagos – Madagascar] – Mauritius (October) – South Africa (November to December) – Argentina – [Magellan Strait] – Beagle Channel (January to February) – [Antarctica] – Southern Chile (March to May)

Start: January to February year I

Return: March to May year II

Tropical storms: November to May (South Pacific and South Indian Ocean)

Total distance: 23,500–24,800 miles

Duration: 14–17 months

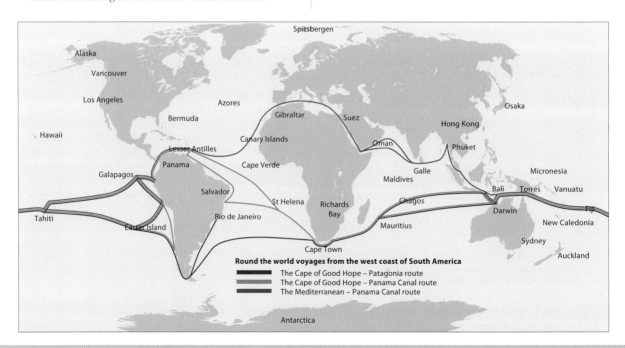

Round the world voyages from the west coast of South America

▬▬▬ The Cape of Good Hope – Patagonia route
▬▬▬ The Cape of Good Hope – Panama Canal route
▬▬▬ The Mediterranean – Panama Canal route

Round the world via the South Pacific, Torres Strait, Cape of Good Hope and Panama

Route: South America West Coast – [Galapagos] – [Easter Island – Gambiers (April)] – Marquesas – Tahiti (May) – Tonga (June) – Fiji (July) – Vanuatu – Torres Strait (August) – Darwin – [Bali] – Mauritius (October) – South Africa (November to December) – StHelena – [Brazil (February)] – Eastern Caribbean (March to April) – Panama (May) – Ecuador (June)

Start: January to February year I

Return: June year II

Tropical storms: November to May (South Pacific and South Indian Ocean), June to November (North Atlantic)

Total distance: 22,200–23,600 miles

Duration: 16–18 months

Round the world via the South Pacific, Torres Strait, Mediterranean and Panama

Route: South America West Coast – [Galapagos] – [Easter Island – Gambiers (April)] – Marquesas – Tahiti (May to June) – Tonga (July) – Fiji (August) – Vanuatu – Torres Strait (September to October) – [Darwin] – Indonesia (October to November) – Singapore – Thailand (December to January) – Sri Lanka (January to February) – [India] – [Maldives] – [Oman] – Red Sea (March) – Mediterranean (April to September) – Canaries (October to November) – Eastern Caribbean (December to April) – Panama (May) – Ecuador

Start: January to February year I

Return: June year II

Tropical storms: November to May (South Pacific and South Indian Ocean), March to June, September to December (North Indian Ocean), June to November (North Atlantic)

Total distance: 22,500–24,600 miles

Duration: 16–18 months

RW8 • Eastabout round the world voyages

The round the world voyages described so far are undertaken from east to west. The main reason for this is the prevailing easterly winds which blow in lower latitudes on either side of the equator. Going around the world against the prevailing systems is certainly harder but it can be done by choosing carefully the right seasons and a route which takes advantage of favourable winds and weather conditions.

As the southern hemisphere in all oceans is dominated by consistent easterly trade winds, an eastbound voyage that keeps to the northern hemisphere is easier to achieve. The routes outlined here summarise the best way to sail around the world from east to west and still see much of it besides water. Whether starting from a port on the US East Coast or from Europe, the first part of the voyage will need to pass through the Mediterranean and Red Sea. As the favourable SW monsoon in the North Indian Ocean coincides with summer, the passage through the Red Sea will be more comfortable if it is done in late spring, so as to avoid the scorching temperatures for which summers in the Red Sea are renowned. By early April the NE monsoon is coming to an end in the North Indian Ocean and eastbound voyages have a fair chance of reasonable winds. In the North Indian Ocean cyclones occur during the pre-monsoon periods, and in the Arabian Sea the worst time is in May and June, so late March or early April is a good time to attempt an eastbound passage

across the western part of the North Indian Ocean. Arriving in Southeast Asia during the SW monsoon is not the best time and it is also too early to continue the voyage into the North Pacific, where the typhoon season is at its peak. The best solution is to stop in a convenient place such as Phuket or Langkawi and resume the voyage later in the year.

The other alternative is to transit the Suez Canal at the end of summer with the aim of crossing the North Indian Ocean in late August or early September just before the end of the SW monsoon. By October the risk of cyclones in the Bay of Bengal is on the increase so the passage east of Sri Lanka should not be delayed beyond September. An October arrival in Southeast Asia fits in perfectly with the timing of the next segment of the voyage as the North Pacific will be reached at the most favourable time. As North Borneo is not affected by tropical storms, it will make a good base to prepare for the North Pacific phase of the voyage.

With the risk of typhoons being lowest in the first months of the year, this is the time to move north, but as this is also the period of the NE monsoon, it may be advisable to wait until its strength has diminished and spring is on its way in northern waters. By March the conditions are as close to optimum as possible so you can either sail to the Asian mainland, calling at ports in South China or Hong Kong, and then cross over to Japan unless an Eastern

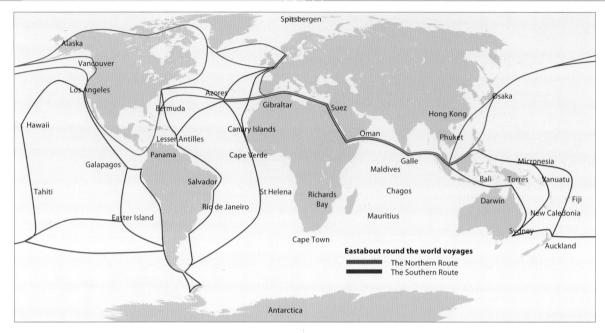

route via the Philippines and Okinawa is preferred. As the subsequent passage to the American mainland is strictly for the summer months, Japan is the ideal place to spend the intervening time as there is plenty to see.

The high latitude passage to the American mainland, either direct or via Alaska, can take place in late June or early July, when sailing conditions in those high-latitudes are as good as they will ever get. A direct passage to the mainland is undoubtedly the easiest way to go but a detour to Alaska is so easy to incorporate in the overall plans that it should be considered. If the decision is taken to make a detour to Alaska, the chain of the Aleutian Islands should be followed to Dutch Harbor or Kodiak. Before doing that, however, it may be worth making a detour to Petropavlovsk, a Russian port on the Kamchatka Peninsula, which would add a special touch to the voyage as sailing yachts are rarely seen in that remote part of the world.

The rest of the summer can be spent cruising Alaska from west to east, then sailing south in late August to British Columbia and the Pacific Northwest. Before leaving Alaska and those northern waters, there is now the opportunity of continuing this voyage through the Northwest Passage and reaching the North Atlantic by this once unforgiving waterway. Late summer and early autumn is the time to do it as the Northwest Passage is normally free of ice, thus holding out a tempting prospect to sailors from Europe or the US East Coast to complete their circumnavigation of the globe along this quite unusual route.

Those who would prefer to sail a more conventional route will benefit from generally favourable conditions while they make their way south towards Mexico which should not be reached before November. It is there that Canadian or American sailors can join this eastbound circumnavigation. After November, when the hurricane season has come to an end in the Eastern North Pacific, the voyage continues from California via Mexico to Panama. With the hurricane season in the Caribbean also having ended, the Panama Canal can be transited at any time during winter. Once in the Caribbean Sea, this voyage is once again faced with the challenge of those prevailing easterly winds, which, so far, it has managed to avoid wherever possible. Hard as it may be, the only solution is to turn north from Panama and head for the Windward Passage or, if that proves to be impossible, head for the Yucatán Channel west of Cuba. For sailors from the US East Coast the voyage has now come close to its end and they have plenty of choices for the final leg home. European and other sailors may attempt to reach the Eastern Caribbean by island-hopping from the Bahamas to Puerto Rico and the Virgins, but if this is too much of a challenge, the rest of the safe season is better spent in the Western Caribbean. In May they can resume the voyage east by sailing to Bermuda and thence to Northern Europe, whereas those bound for the Mediterranean will sail via the Azores to Gibraltar. With that passage safely behind them, European sailors will have completed their circum-navigation, while those who have joined along the way will be able to spend some time in the Mediterranean before continuing the voyage to Southeast Asia and beyond.

Although the Panama Canal route is both shorter and more convenient, those who will have enjoyed the Arctic scenery in Alaska may be tempted to reach the Atlantic by a more attractive, albeit also more challenging, route via the Magellan Strait or Beagle Channel. However, this option will add one year to the overall duration of the voyage. With an optimum arrival time in Southern Chile in September or October, the winter can be spent in Mexico or Central America before resuming the voyage with a passage to the Galapagos in April or May. From the Galapagos, Southern Chile can be reached either by following the contour of the South American mainland or by making a detour to Easter Island. After a cruise through the Chilean Archipelago, the South Atlantic can be reached through either the Magellan Strait or the Beagle Channel. Summer in Patagonia is also the optimum time for a crossing of the Drake Passage to Antarctica which is yet another temptation along this rarely sailed round the world route.

From Patagonia the route heads for the Falkland Islands before turning north towards Brazil. Boats bound for the Mediterranean can sail from the South Atlantic on an easterly route that leads to St Helena, the Cape Verde and Canary Islands, and thence to Gibraltar. Others may prefer to sail a westerly route that leads via Brazil to the Eastern Caribbean. From there, the voyage continues to the US East Coast, or across the Atlantic to the Azores and Europe.

A southern route to the Atlantic can also be sailed by those who may prefer to make their easting in the South Pacific rather than the North Pacific. This third alternative for an eastabout circumnavigation follows the same route and timing as far as Southeast Asia but switches hemisphere by heading SE via Indonesia and the Torres Strait into the South Pacific. This southern alternative, which then continues south inside the Great Barrier Reef before sailing from Australia to New Zealand, is probably preferable to a northern route via Micronesia. In the former case the easting in the South Pacific is made by sailing a high latitude route from New Zealand to Chile, either direct or via such islands as the Australs or Easter Island. The Micronesian route reaches New Zealand by a longer and more roundabout route via Kiribati and Fiji, both alternatives proving the well known fact that making easting in the Pacific is a tough job in either hemisphere.

Circumnavigation via the Mediterranean, Southeast Asia, North Pacific and Northwest Passage or Panama

Route: US East Coast – [Northern Europe (May to July)] – Mediterranean (June to August) – Suez Canal (March, July) – Red Sea (April, July) – North Indian Ocean (April, August to September) – Southeast Asia (September to November) – North Borneo (December) – [East Asia (January to March)] – Japan (March to June) – [Alaska (July to August)] – [Northwest Passage – Northern Europe (August to September)] – US West Coast (September to November) – Mexico – Panama Canal (December to February) – Western Caribbean (March to April) – Bermuda (May) – [US East Coast] – [Azores (June)] – [Northern Europe]

Start: May to June year I

Return: June to July year III

Tropical storms: March to June, September to December (North Indian Ocean), all year (Western North Pacific), May to November (Eastern North Pacific), June to November (North Atlantic)

Mileage: 24,600–26,000 miles

Duration: 24–26 months

Circumnavigation via the Mediterranean, Southeast Asia, North Pacific and Northwest Passage or Southern Chile

Route: US East Coast – [Northern Europe (May to July)] – Mediterranean (June to August) – Suez Canal (March, July) – Red Sea (April, July) – North Indian Ocean (April, August to September) – Southeast Asia (September to November) – North Borneo (December) – [East Asia (January to March)] – Japan (March to June) – [Alaska (July to August)] – [Northwest Passage – Northern Europe (August to September)] – US West Coast (September to November) – Mexico – Galapagos (June) – Ecuador – [Peru (August)] – [Easter Island] – Southern Chile (September – November) – Beagle Channel (December to January) – [Antarctica] – Falkland Islands – Argentina (March) – [St Helena – Cape Verde – Canaries – Gibraltar] – Brazil – Caribbean (April to May) – [Bermuda] – [US East Coast (June to July)] – Azores (June) – Northern Europe (June to July) – Gibraltar (June to July) – [Northern Europe]

Start: May to June year I

Return: June to July year IV

Tropical storms: March to June, September to December (North Indian Ocean), all year (Western North Pacific), May to November (Eastern North Pacific), June to November (North Atlantic)

Mileage: 32,000–33,400 miles

Duration: 36–38 months

Circumnavigation via the Mediterranean, Southeast Asia, South Pacific and Southern Chile

Route: US East Coast – [Northern Europe (May to July)] – Mediterranean (June to August) – Suez Canal (March, July) – Red Sea (April, July) – North Indian Ocean (April, August to September) – Southeast Asia (September to November) – Indonesia – Torres Strait – East Australia – New Zealand – [Australs, Easter Island] – Southern Chile (September – November) – Beagle Channel (December to January) – [Antarctica] – Falkland Islands – Argentina (March) – [St Helena – Cape Verde – Canaries – Gibraltar] – Brazil – Caribbean (April to May) – [Bermuda] – [US East Coast (June to July)] – Azores (June) – Northern Europe (June to July) – Gibraltar (June to July) – [Northern Europe]

Start: May to June year I

Return: June to July year IV

Tropical storms: March to June, September to December (North Indian Ocean), November to May (South Pacific), June to November (North Atlantic)

Mileage: 28,800–31,200 miles

Duration: 36–38 months

Millennium Odyssey boats at Easter Island.

ACKNOWLEDGEMENTS

In all my projects I have been fortunate in being able to draw on the knowledge and experience of my friends, and this book is no exception. Over the years I have made many good friends among participants in the various rallies, which I have organised and I want to thank those who contributed to this book or responded to the voyage planning survey. Among them are former participants in the ARC Ståle and Annelise Larsen, while Bill Butler, Charles and Saundra Gray, Don and Lois Babson sailed in America 500, the Columbus anniversary rally held in 1992, and later also joined the Millennium Odyssey. That round the rally also counted among its participants Javier and Barbara Visiers, Alison and John Wicks, Klaus Girzig, Ann Harsh and Ralph Nehrig, Judy and Bob Hall, Alfredo and Nicoletta Giacon, Stu and Julie Conway.

I want to thank those who agreed to write on specific subjects, their contribution being displayed as a sidebar alongside the main text, among them Javier Visiers, Bill and Judy Rouse, Erick Bouteleux, Arthur Beiser, Bill Butler, Chris Doyle, Xavier Dumenil, Pete Goss, Lars Hässler, Jackie Lee, Steve Lochner, Antti Louhija, Peter and Julie Kranker, Bill McLaren, Amanda and John Neal, Dale Norley, Jim Patek, John and Alison Wicks.

From the two extremes of the planet, Skip Novak in Antarctica and Eric Brossier in the Arctic, sent me their comments on sailing in those waters, as did Herb McCormick who had just completed a circumnavigation of the Americas by way of the Northwest Passage. Two other conquerors of that challenging route, Roger Swanson and Alex Whitworth, also contributed to this book. High latitude sailing is the preserve of such outstanding sailors as Beth Leonard and Evans Starzinger, Bill and Jane McLaren, Steve Lochner and Lars Hässler, and I am very grateful for their contribution.

I owe a debt of gratitude to the many experienced sailors who took part in the original voyage planning survey and wish to thank all those who contributed to the first edition of this book. As the findings of that first voyage planning survey are still so relevant, several of those who had contributed to the original survey were contacted with a request to update their comments. All responded and, as the majority are still sailing, their considerable offshore experience has added a most valuable dimension to this book. My heartfelt thanks to Murray and Caroline Atkinson, Mike and Sue Beilan, Arthur Beiser, Erick Bouteleux, Luc Callebaut and Jackie Lee, Stu and Julie Conway, Doug and Judy Decker, Paul Donnerup, Hugh and Brenda Fraser, Alfredo Giacon, Gary Goodlander, Pete and Tracey Goss, Charles and Saundra Gray, James and Patti Hunt, John Jameson, Ståle and Annelise Larsen, Dave and Sherry McCampbell, Bill and Jane McLaren, John and Amanda Neal, Dale Norley, Jim Patek, José Prieto, Bill and Judy Rouse, Bill and Frances Stocks, Jim and Katie Thomsen, Dave and Marie Ungless, Jamie Utzschneider and Jenna Miller, Javier Visiers, Burger and Nancy Zapf.

As with all my projects, I have been very fortunate in being able to rely on the support and practical help of my wife Gwenda, who thoroughly checked the entire text and made many valuable suggestions. As a result, this ended up a much better book.

Our son Ivan, who had made a crucial contribution to the first edition, has now made the logical step of becoming a co-author. As a computer scientist, Ivan took on the huge task of writing a complex program to extricate the relevant data on winds and ocean currents from the vast amount of satellite observations carried out over the last 25 years. His invaluable contribution to this book cannot be stressed enough and I am very happy not only that the pilot charts used in this book are as up to date as they possibly could be, but also that Ivan's work forms the basis of Cornells' Ocean Atlas, a unique compilation of pilot charts for the entire world.

Finally, I wish to thank my publisher, Janet Murphy, my editor Jonathan Eyers and designer Margaret Brain, for bringing this complex project to a successful completion.

PHOTO CREDITS

Most of the photographs in this book are from Jimmy Cornell's collection. We wish to thank the following contributors for kindly allowing us to use these photographs: David Thoreson of the yacht *Ocean Watch* (page 136), Lars Hässler (140), Patrick Hebel (141 and 149), and Mike Harris of YOTREPS for the use of the diagram on page 309. The image of *Phoenicia* on page 296 is courtesy of www.phoenicia.org and the satellite image on page 51 is courtesy of NASA-Goddard Space Flight Center, NOAA GOES project.

The following photographs were obtained from online agencies: BigStockPhoto.com on pages: 91, 99, 110, 124, 128, 130, 132, 155, 219, 245, 258, 259, 270, 291, 294, 304 and front cover (anchorage with leaning palm tree).

Due credit is owed to the individual photographers of Shutterstock.com: Ron Lander (page 119), Antonio Abrignani (137), Tiago Jorge da Silva Estima (151), Dmitri Ogleznev (196), redswept (236), Hiroshi Sato (251), azaphoto (256), wandee007 (265), Pozzo di Borgo Thomas (281), and Daleen Loest (284).

CRUISING GUIDES

Mediterranean, Adriatic, Ionian, Aegean and Black Sea

777 Harbours and Anchorages – Croatia, Slovenia, Montenegro and Albania, Anna and Rod Bailey, Sailing Books Ltd
Adriatic Pilot, T and D Thompson, Imray
A Yachting Pilot for Crete, Tony and Tessa Cross, RCC
A Yachting Pilot for Southern Cyprus, Rick Munden, free download at http://cruisingtips.net/pdf/Cyprus_Pilot.pdf
Black Sea, The, David Read Barker and Lisa Borre, RCC Imray
Corsica and North Sardinia, J Marchment, Imray
Cruising Bulgaria and Romania, Nicky Allardice, Imray
Dove Navigare, Incontri Nautici
East Aegean, Rod Heikell, Imray
Greek Waters Pilot, Rod and Lucinda Heikell, Imray
Harbour Guide Croatia, Montenegro and Slovenia, E Glaumann, J Hermansson and P Hotvedt, Imray
Ionian, Rod and Lucinda Heikell, Imray
Islas Baleares, G Hutt, RCC Imray
Italian Waters Pilot, Rod and Lucinda Heikell, Imray
Mediterranean Almanac, ed Rod Heikell, Imray
Mediterranean Cruising, The Adlard Coles Book of, Rod Heikell, Adlard Coles Nautical
Mediterranean Cruising Handbook, Rod Heikell, Imray
Mediterranean France and Corsica Pilot, Rod and Lucinda Heikell, Imray
Mediterranean Spain, Costas del Sol and Blanca, John Marchment, RCC Imray
Mediterranean Spain, Costas del Azahar, Dorada and Brava, John Marchment, RCC Imray
North Africa, G Hutt, RCC Imray
Straits Sailing Handbook, Colin Thomas, Hercules Sailing
Turkey Cruising Companion, Emma Watson, Fernhurst Books
Turkish Waters and Cyprus Pilot, Rod and Lucinda Heikell, Imray
West Aegean, Rod and Lucinda Heikell, Imray

West Aegean Cruising Companion, Robert Buttress, Fernhurst Books

Eastern North Atlantic and Baltic Sea

Arholma-Landsort and Gotland (Stockholm Archipelago) English edn, Lars Hassler and Lars Granath, Nautiska Förlaget
Atlantic Crossing Guide, Jane Russell, RCC
Atlantic France, North Biscay to the Spanish border, Jeremy Parkinson, RCC
Atlantic Islands, A Hammick & H Keatinge, Imray
Atlantic Pilot Atlas, James Clarke, Adlard Coles Nautical
Atlantic Spain and Portugal, Martin Walker and A Hammick, Imray
Baltic Sea, The, RCC Pilotage Foundation, Imray
Bristol Channel and Severn Cruising Guide, P Cumberlidge, Imray
Canary Islands Cruising Guide, Oliver Solanas Heinrichs & Mike Westin, Imray
CCC Cruising Scotland, Mike Balmforth and Edward Mason, Clyde Cruising Club, Imray, updates at www.clyde.org
CCC Sailing Directions and Anchorages, five volumes covering Scotland, Hebrides, Orkney and Shetland Islands, Clyde Cruising Club, Imray, updates at www.clyde.org
Channel Islands, Cherbourg Peninsula & North Brittany, P Carnegie, RCC Imray
Crossing the Thames Estuary, Roger Gaspar, Imray
Cruising Almanac, Cruising Association, Imray
Cruising Anglesey and Adjoining Waters, From Liverpool to Aberdovey, Ralph Morris, Imray
Cruising Cork and Kerry, Graham Swanson, Imray
Cruising Galicia, Carlos Rojas and Robert Bailey
Cruising Guide to Baltic Russia, Vladimir Ivankiv, Graham and Fay Cattell, Cruising Association
Cruising Guide to West Africa, Steven Jones, RCC Imray
Cruising Guide to the Netherlands, Brian Navin, Imray

Cruising Guide to Germany and Denmark, Brian Navin, Imray
Cruising Guide to Poland, Nicholas Hill, Cruising Association
Cruising Guide to Sweden, Cruising Association
Cruising in Norway, Howard Steen, Cruising Association
Cruising Ireland Companion Guide, Mike Balmforth and Norman Kean, Irish Cruising Club Publications
Cruising the Canals and Rivers of Europe, Tom Sommers, EuroCanals Cruising Guides, www.eurocanals.com
Cruising French Waterways, Hugh McKnight, Adlard Coles Nautical
Cruising the Wild Atlantic Way, Daria and Alex Blackwell, White Seahorse Publishing
Den Norske Los, Norwegian Pilot Guide Sailing Directions, Norwegian Hydrographic Service, 7 volumes, free downloads at www.kartverket.no
East Coast Pilot, C Jarmin et al, Imray
East and North Coasts of Ireland Sailing Directions, Irish Cruising Club, Imray
Estonian Cruising Guide, Hillar Kukk and Jaano Martin Ots, Estonian Small Harbour Development Center
European Waterways, The, A User's Guide, Marian Martin, Adlard Coles Nautical
Guest Harbours Finland: Käyntisatamat Besökshamnar Suomen Rannikot, Suomen Vierassatamat, www.satamaopas.fi
Harbours of the Baltic States, Cruising and Harbour guide to Lithuania, Latvia and Estonia, Sue Sutherland, Cruising Association
Hidden Harbours of Southwest Britain, Dag Pike, Imray
Hidden Harbours of Wales, Dag Pike, Imray
Hidden Harbours of the Northwest, Dag Pike, Imray
Hidden Harbours of Southwest Scotland, Dag Pike, Imray
Inland Waterways of France, David Edwards-May, Imray
Inland Waterways of Belgium, Jacqueline Jones, Imray
Inland Waterways of the Netherlands, Louise Busby and David Broad, Imray, www.inlandwaterwaysofthenetherlands.com
Isles of Scilly, Mike Lewin-Harris, RCC Imray

Irish Sea Pilot, David Rainsbury, Imray

Labrador and Greenland, Notes on, A Hill, RCC weblink

Landsort-Skanor, English edn includes Åland, Gota Canal and Bornholm Is, Catharina Soderbergh, Nautiska Förlaget

Lundy and Irish Sea Pilot, David Taylor, Imray

North Brittany and Channel Islands Cruising Companion, Peter Cumberlidge, Fernhurst Books

North Sea Passage Pilot, Brian Navin, Imray

Norway, Judy Lomax, RCC Imray

Norwegian Cruising Guide, including Spitsbergen and SW Sweden, P Nickel and J Harries, e-book

Norwegian Cruising Guide: Norway, Svalbard and the west coast of Sweden, www.norwegiancruisingguide.com

Practical Boat Owner's Sailing Around the UK and Ireland, Roger Oliver, Adlard Coles Nautical

Sail to Svalbard, Jon Amtrup, Laeremiddelforlaget

Saimaa Canal Pleasure Craft Guide, Finnish Transport Agency, available at www.liikennevirasto.fi

Secret Anchorages of Brittany, Peter Cumberlidge, Imray

Shell Channel Pilot, Tom Cunliffe, Imray

Shetland Islands Pilot, Gordon Buchanon, Imray

Skanör-Strömstad, Nautiska Förlaget

Solent Cruising Companion, The, Derek Azlett, Fernhurst Books

South Biscay, Steve Pickard, RCC Imray

Southern Ireland Cruising Companion, Robert Wilcox, Fernhurst Books

South and West Coast of Ireland Sailing Directions, Irish Cruising Club

Southern Ireland Cruising Companion, Robert Wilcox, Fernhurst Books

South West Spain and Portugal Cruising Companion, Detlef Jens, Fernhurst Books

Through the French Canals, David Jefferson, Adlard Coles Nautical

Tidal Havens of the Wash and Humber, Henry Irving, Imray

UK and Ireland Circumnavigator's Guide, Sam Steele, Adlard Coles Nautical

Victor Weger Yacht Routing Guide to NW Passage, RCC

Wateralmanac, ANWB

West Country, The, Bill of Portland to the Isles of Scilly, Carlos Rojas & Susan Kemp-Wheeler, Imray

West Country Cruising Companion, Mark Fishwick, Fernhurst Books

Yachting Monthly's Channel Havens, The Secret Inlets and Secluded Anchorages of the Channel, Ken Endean, Adlard Coles Nautical

Western North Atlantic and Caribbean

Abaco, Ports of Call, Tom Henschel, Cruising Guide Publications

Arctic and Northern Waters including Faroe, Iceland and Greenland, Andrew Wilkes, RCC

Atlantic Coast and ICW Planning and Facilities Guide, Chesapeake Bay Magazine

Bahamas Waterway Guide, The, Waterway Guide Publications

Beautiful Bonaire, Sail Adventures, www.sailadventures.nl

Chesapeake Bay Ports of Call and Anchorages, Cruising Guide Publications

Colombia to Rio Dulce, Frank Virgintino

A Complete Cruising Guide to the Down East Circle Route, Cheryl Barr, Yacht Pilot Publishing

A Cruising Guide to the Lesser Antilles, Volume I: The Virgin Islands, Frank Virgintino

A Cruising Guide to the Lesser Antilles, Volume II: The Leeward Islands, Frank Virgintino

A Cruising Guide to the Lesser Antilles, Volume III: The Windward Islands, Frank Virgintino

A Cruising Guide to the Northwest Caribbean, Stephen Pavlidis, Seaworthy Publications

A Thinking Man's Guide To Voyaging South: The Many Facets of Caribbean Cruising, Frank Virgintino, Kindle ebook only

Cayman Islands Cruising Guide, Frank Virgintino

Chesapeake Bay to Florida, Embassy Cruising Guide

Cruising Guide to Abaco, Steve, Jon and Jeff Dodge, Cruising Guide Publications

Cruising Guide to the ABC Islands, Frank Virgintino

Cruising Guide to Belize and Mexico's Caribbean Coast, Freya Rauscher, Cruising Guide Publications

Cruising Guide to Bermuda, Sail Adventures, www.sailadventures.nl

Cruising Guide to Cuba, Frank Virgintino

Cruising Guide to Cuba Vol I and II, Capt. Cheryl Barr, Yacht Pilot Publishing, www.cruisingincuba.com

Cruising Guide to the Florida Keys, Frank Papy

Cruising Guide to Labrador, Cruising Club of America

Cruising Guide to New Jersey Waters, Donald Launer, Rutgers University Press

Cruising Guide to Newfoundland, Cruising Club of America

Cruising Guide to the Northern Leeward Islands, Chris Doyle, Cruising Guide Publications

Cruising Guide to the Nova Scotia Coast, Cruising Club of America

Cruising Guide to Puerto Rico, Stephen Pavlidis, Seaworthy Publications

Cruising Guide to the Southern Leeward Islands, Chris Doyle, Cruising Guide Publications

Cruising Guide to the Gulf of St Lawrence, Cruising Club of America

Cruising Guide to Trinidad, and Tobago, Barbados and Guyana, Chris Doyle, Cruising Guide Publications

Cruising Guide to Venezuela and Bonaire, Chris Doyle and Jeff Fisher, Cruising Guide Publications

Cruising Guide to the Virgin Islands, Stephen Pavlidis, Cruising Guide Publications

Cruising Guide to the Windward Islands, Stephen Pavlidis, Seaworthy Publications

Cruising the Chesapeake, William Shellenburger, International Marine

Cruising Ports: The Central American Route, Capt. Pat Rains, Fine Edge Publications

East Coast of Florida Ports of Call, Tom Henshel, Cruising Guide Publications

Explore Central America Part I, Guatemala, El Salvador, Honduras, Nicaragua, www.svsarana.com

Explore the Virgin Islands, Harry S Pariser, Fine Edge Publications

Exuma Guide, Stephen Pavlidis, Seaworthy Publications

Florida Cruising Guide, Embassy Cruising Guide

Gentleman's Guide to Passages South, Bruce van Sant, Cruising Guide Publications

Georgia Coast, Tom and Nancy Zydler, Seaworthy Publications

Grenada to the Virgin Islands, Jacques
  Patuelli, Imray
Guatemala – A Cruisers' Guide to Rio Dulce,
  Lilia Hartmann and Roberto Trapani,
  Imray
Guide to Cruising Chesapeake Bay,
  Chesapeake Bay Magazine
Haiti Cruising Guide, Frank Virgintino
Leeward Anchorages, Chris Doyle, Cruising
  Guide Publications
Leeward Islands, The, Stephen Pavlidis,
  Seaworthy Publications
Long Island Sound to Cape May, Embassy
  Cruising Guide
New England Coast, Embassy Cruising
  Guide
*Northwest Caribbean: Jamaica, Cayman
  Is, Honduras, Bay Is, Guatemala and Rio
  Dulce*, Seaworthy Publications
Northern Bahamas, The, Stephen Pavlidis,
  Seaworthy Publications
Panama Cruising Guide, Eric Bauhaus,
  Cruising Guide Publications
Panama Guide, The, Nancy Schwalbe Zydler
  and Tom Zydler, Seaworthy Publications
Puerto Rico Cruising Guide, Frank Virgintino
Sailors Guide to the Windward Islands, Chris
  Doyle, Cruising Guide Publications
Southern Bahamas, The, Stephen Pavlidis,
  Seaworthy Publications
Southwest Florida Ports Of Call, Thomas A
  Henschel, Cruising Guide Publications
Street's Guide to the Cape Verde Islands, Don
  Street, Seaworthy Publications
*Turks and Caicos and the Dominican Republic
  Guide*, Stephen Pavlidis, Seaworthy
  Publications
Virgin Anchorages, Cruising Guide
  Publications
Waterway Guide Atlantic ICW, Waterway
  Guide Publications, www.waterwayguide.
  com
Waterway Guide Cuba, Waterway Guide
  Publications
Windward Anchorages, Chris Doyle, Cruising
  Guide Publications
Yachtsman's Guide to the Bahamas, Tropical
  Island Publishers, http://yachtsmansguide.
  com
Yachtsman's Guide to the Virgin Islands,
  Tropical Island Publishers, http://
  yachtsmansguide.com

South Atlantic and Southern Ocean

Antarctica Cruising Guide, P Carey and C
  Franklin
Argentina, Andy O'Grady, Ulla Norlander &
  Pete Hill, C Bibby, RCC
Brazil Cruising Guide, Michel Balette, Imray
Cape To Caribbean Cruising Notes, Tony
  Herrick, www.cruisingconnections.co.za
*Cape Horn and Antarctic Waters including
  Chile, the Beagle Channel, Falkland Islands
  and the Antarctic Peninsula*, Paul Heiney,
  RCC
*A Cruising Guide to French Guiana, Suriname
  and Guyana*, Martin Dixon-Tyrer, RCC
Cruising the Coast of Brazil, Marçal Ceccon,
  Moana Livros
Cruising Guide to the Coast of Brazil Part 1,
  2 and 3, Pete Hill, RCC
Cruising Guide to West Africa, Steven Jones,
  RCC Imray
Cruising Guide to South Orkney, P and A
  Hill, RCC Pilotage Foundation
Falkland Islands Shores and Supplement, P
  and A Hill, Imray
Havens and Anchorages, Tom Morgan,
  Onboard Publications
High Latitude Sailing, Jon Amtrup and Bob
  Shepton, Kindle e-book only
*Islands and Atolls in the Mozambique
  Channel*, Tony Herrick, www.
  cruisingconnections.co.za
*Pleasant Suriname (a Cruising Guide to
  Dutch Guyana)* by John Hoedemakers &
  Jolanda Geerdink, Sail Adventures, www.
  sailadventures.nl
South Africa Nautical Almanac, Tom
  Morgan, Imray
South Atlantic Circuit, Tom Morgan, RCC
*South Atlantic Islands, Gough Island, Tristan
  da Cunha, St Helena, Ascension Island*,
  Pete Hill, RCC
South Georgia, A O'Grady, RCC Pilotage
  Foundation
South Shetland Islands and Antarctic, P Hill,
  RCC Pilotage Foundation
*Southern Africa Cruising Notes – East
  To West*, Tony Herrick, www.
  cruisingconnections.co.za
Southern Ocean Cruising, Sally and Jerome
  Poncet
Southwest Africa, Pete Hill, RCC
Welcome to Durban, A Sailor's Guide, Tony
  Herrick, www.cruisingconnections.co.za

North Pacific

*Aleutian Islands and the Alaska Peninsula to
  Vancouver Island*, Martin Walker, RCC
*Anchorages and Marine Parks: The Guide
  to Popular Pacific Northwest Anchorages*,
  Peter Vassilopoulos, Fine Edge
  Publications
Best Anchorages of the Inside Passage, Anne
  Vipond and William Kelly, Fine Edge
  Publications
Costa Rica, Charlie's Charts
*Cruising Guide to Central and Southern
  California*, Brian Fagan, International
  Marine
*Cruising Guide to Puget Sound and San Juan
  Is*, Migael Scherer, International Marine
Cruising Guide to San Francisco Bay, C and
  B Mehaffy, Paradise Cay
*Cruising Guides to the Salish Sea, Gulf
  Islands, Puget Sound, San Juan Islands
  and Desolation Sound*, Jim Burgoyne and
  Lynne Picard, http://salishseapilot.com
*Docks and Destinations, The Complete
  Guide to Pacific Northwest Marinas*,
  Peter Vassilopoulos, Fine Edge
  Publications
Dreamspeaker Cruising Guides, series, A and
  L Yeardon-Jones, Fine Edge Publications
Ecuador Cruising Guide, www.svsarana.com
Exploring Alaska and British Columbia,
  Stephen E Hilson, Fine Edge Publications
*Explore Central America Part II, Costa Rica,
  Ecuador and Panama*, www.svsarana.com
*Exploring the north coast of British
  Columbia*, D and R Douglass, Fine Edge
  Publications
*Exploring the Pacific Coast, San Diego to
  Seattle*, D and R Douglass, Fine Edge
  Publications
Exploring the San Juan and Gulf Is, D and R
  Douglass, Fine Edge Publications
*Exploring the south coast of British
  Columbia*, D and R Douglass, Fine Edge
  Publications
Exploring Southeast Alaska, D and R
  Douglass, Fine Edge Publications
Exploring Vancouver Island's West Coast, D
  and R Douglass, Fine Edge Publications
Hawaiian Islands, Charlie's Charts
Mexico Boating Guide, Pat Rains, Fine Edge
  Publications
North to Alaska, Charlie's Charts
Cruising Pacific Colombia, www.svsarana.
  com

Pacific Mexico: A Cruiser's Guidebook, Shawn Breeding & Heather Bansmer, Blue Latitude Press

Panama Cruising Guide, Eric Bauhaus, Cruising Guide Publications

Sea of Cortez, Shawn Breeding and Heather Bansmer, Blue Latitude Press

Southern California Channel Islands, F Hawkings, RCC

Southern California, Charlie's Charts

US Pacific Coast, Charlie's Charts

Waggoner Cruising Guide, Mark Bunzel, Fine Edge Publications

Western Coast of Mexico and Baja, Charlie's Charts

South Pacific

Polynesia, Charlie's Charts

Chile, A O'Grady, Imray

Coastal Cruising Handbook, Royal Arakana Yacht Club

Coastal Cruising Companion: Australia's East Coast from Hobart to Bundaberg, Marilyn Graham, Coastal Cruising Australia

Cruising Guide to the Kingdom of Tonga, Ken Hellewell, Imray

Cruising in the Louisiades, Papua New Guinea, Phil & Kristina Challands

Cruising the Coral Coast, Alan Lucas, Alan Lucas Cruising Guides

Cruising the New South Wales Coast, Alan Lucas, Alan Lucas Cruising Guides

Cruising Southern Tasmania, Cruising Yacht Club of Tasmania

Hauraki Gulf, David Thatcher, Captain Teach Press

Landfalls of Paradise, Earl Hinz and J Howard, University of Hawaii Press

Micronesia Cruising Notes, Phil Cregeen, Captain Teach Press

Nautical Rocket Guide to New Caledonia, ebook, Island Cruising

New Zealand Cruising Guide Central Area, K W J Murray & R Von Kohorn, Steven William Publications

New Zealand's Hauraki Gulf including the Mercury Islands, Mercury Bay and Great Barrier Island, David Thatcher, Captain Teach Press

New Zealand's Northland Coast: Whangarei to Cape Reinga and Three Kings Islands, David Thatcher, Captain Teach Press

Northern Territory Coast Cruising Guide, John Knight, Diane Andrews Publishing

Pacific Crossing Guide, Kitty Van Hagen, Adlard Coles Nautical

Patagonia and Tierra del Fuego Nautical Guide, M Rolfo and G Ardrizzi, Editrice Incontri Nautici, www.capehorn-pilot.com

Rob's Passage Planner: For East Coast Australia, Lizard Island to Hobart, Rob Starkey

Rocket Cruising Guide of Vanuatu (CD)

Sail Fiji, Island Cruising Regattas

Sail Tonga, Island Cruising Regattas

Solomon Islands Cruising Guide, Dirk Sieling and Brian Hepburn

South Australia's Waters – an Atlas and Guide, Boating Industry Association of SA

South Pacific Anchorages, Warwick Clay, Imray

Tasmanian Anchorage Guide, Royal Yacht Club of Tasmania

Torres Strait Passage Guide, Ken Hellewell, Cevennes Productions

Vanuatu Cruising Guide, Island Cruising e-book

Western Australian Cruising Guide, West Coast from Darwin to Eucla & the Christmas and Cocos Islands, Fremantle Sailing Club

Whitsunday Islands, The: 100 Magic Miles, David Colfelt, Windward Publications

Yellow Flag Stopover Handbook, New Caledonia, www.nouville-plaisance.nc

Yellow Flag Guide to French Polynesia, Stopover Handbook in French Polynesia (Carnet d'escale en Polynesie francaise) www.portdepapeete.pf

Southeast Asia, Indian Ocean and Red Sea

British Indian Ocean Territory, Tom Partridge, RCC

Cruising South East Indonesia plus the West Coast of Australia: A Guide to Anchorages, W R Burbridge

Cruising Guide to Indonesia, Andy Scott, https://cruisingguideindonesia.com

Cruising Guide to Southeast Asia, Volume II, Stephen Davies and Elaine Morgan, Imray

East Africa Pilot, Delwyn McPhun, Imray

Indian Ocean Cruising Guide, Rod Heikell, RCC Imray

Maldives Cruising Guide, Max Molteni, Edizioni il Frangente

Maldives, Sailing through Paradise, Sail Adventures, www.sailadventures.nl

Red Sea Pilot, Elaine Morgan and Stephen Davis, Imray

Sail Malaysia Guide, http://sailmalaysia.net

Sail Thailand, Artasia Press

Southeast Asia Pilot, Andy Dowden and Bill O'Leary, Image Asia

General Books

French for Cruisers, Kathy Parsons, Aventuras Publishing Company

Spanish for Cruisers, Kathy Parsons, Aventuras Publishing Company

World Cruising Routes, Jimmy Cornell, Adlard Coles Nautical

World Cruising Destinations, Jimmy and Doina Cornell, Adlard Coles Nautical

Cornells' Ocean Atlas, Jimmy and Ivan Cornell, Cornell Sailing Publications

Cruising Guide Online Updates

RCC Pilotage Foundation, www.rccpf.org.uk/Updates-and-Supplements

Imray, www.imray.com

Chris Doyle's Caribbean Cruising Guides, http://doyleguides.info

Cruising Guides App, www.cruisingguides.com

Captains Mate, Cruising Association, www.theca.org.uk

Fernhurst Books, http://fernhurstbooks.com/cruising-companion-updates

Cruising Club of America, : https://cruisingclub.org/cruising-guides-canadian-maritimes and www.pilot-press.com

Free cruising guides, free downloads available at http://freecruisingguides.com

Alan Lucas Guides, www.alanlucascruisingguides.com

INDEX OF CRUISING HUBS

INDEX OF VOYAGES